Constitutional Democracy

Westview Replica Editions

The concept of Westview Replica Editions is a response to the continuing crisis in academic and informational publishing. Library budgets for books have been severely curtailed. Ever larger portions of general library budgets are being diverted from the purchase of books and used for data banks, computers, micromedia, and other methods of information retrieval. Interlibrary loan structures further reduce the edition sizes required to satisfy the needs of the scholarly community. Economic pressures on the university presses and the few private scholarly publishing companies have severely limited the capacity of the industry to properly serve the academic and research communities. As a result, many manuscripts dealing with important subjects, often representing the highest level of scholarship, are no longer economically viable publishing projects—or, if accepted for publication, are typically subjected to lead times ranging from one to three years.

Westview Replica Editions are our practical solution to the problem. We accept a manuscript in camera-ready form, typed according to our specifications, and move it immediately into the production process. As always, the selection criteria include the importance of the subject, the work's contribution to scholarship, and its insight, originality of thought and excellence of exposition. The responsibility for editing and proofreading lies with the author or sponsoring institution. We prepare chapter headings and display pages, file for copyright, and obtain Library of Congress Cataloging in Publication Data. A detailed manual contains simple instructions for preparing the final typescript, and our editorial staff is always available to answer questions.

The end result is a book printed on acid-free paper and bound in sturdy library-quality soft covers. We manufacture these books ourselves using equipment that does not require a lengthy make-ready process and that allows us to publish first editions of 300 to 600 copies and to reprint even smaller quantities as needed. Thus, we can produce Replica Editions quickly and can keep even very specialized books in print as long as there is a demand for them.

About the Book and Editor

Constitutional Democracy:
Essays in Comparative Politics
edited by Fred Eidlin

A frequent criticism of contemporary political science is that empirical research too seldom is combined with in-depth inquiry into the philosophical, historical, and legal foundations of the societies it seeks to understand. Others suggest that political scientists specializing in U.S. government too rarely collaborate with those who study other countries.

The contributions in this volume belie these claims. The authors, all colleagues, students, and friends of Henry W. Ehrmann, represent the U.S., France, Germany, and Canada, the four countries in which Dr. Ehrmann has lived. The essays reflect the breadth and scope of Ehrmann's work as a teacher, scholar, and political activist. The contributions to this volume cover a broad range of topics, among them political theory and methodology of comparative politics and the interrelationships of economic, social, historical, and political developments, and include theoretically oriented studies of such problems as interest group politics, political culture, and parties. Integrating constitutional law and political philosophy with comparative sociological and historical research and theory, Henry Ehrmann's approach to teaching and research sets an excellent example for the contemporary study of political science.

Dr. Eidlin, associate professor of political studies at the University of Guelph, is the author of *The Logic of "Normalization": The Soviet Intervention in Czechoslovakia of 21 August 1968 and the Czechoslovak Response.*

Henry W. Ehrmann

Constitutional Democracy

Essays in Comparative Politics

edited by Fred Eidlin

A Festschrift in honor of
Henry W. Ehrmann

Westview Press / Boulder, Colorado

A Westview Replica Edition

Published in 1983 in the United States of America by
Westview Press, Inc.
5500 Central Avenue
Boulder, Colorado 80301
Frederick A. Praeger, President and Publisher

Library of Congress Catalog Card Number: 83-50066
ISBN 0-86531-948-0

Printed and bound in the United States of America.

10 9 8 7 6 5 4 3 2

Contents

PREFACE

A disturbing feature of much contemporary political science is the chasm separating empirical research from inquiry into the philosophical, historical, and legal foundations of the societies it seeks to understand. It is also too seldom that political scientists specializing in U.S. government and politics are engaged in dialogue with those who study other countries.

The contributors to this volume–many of them scholars of international repute–are colleagues, students, and friends of Henry W. Ehrmann from the United States, France, Germany, and Canada–the four countries in which Ehrmann has lived and worked as a teacher, scholar, and political activist. Integrating comparative constitutional law and political philosophy with comparative sociological and historical research and theory, Ehrmann's approach to teaching and research sets an excellent example for contemporary political science. The essays in this volume reflect the breadth and scope of Ehrmann's own work, as well as its unifying themes. They range from political theory, constitutional law and theory and methodology of comparative politics, through theoretically-oriented studies dealing with such problems as interest group politics, political culture, voting behavior, political parties and representation, and the interrelationships of economic, social, historical, and political developments.

Henry Ehrmann belongs to a generation of social scientists whose work was strongly influenced by the collapse of German democracy, the end of the constitutional order, and the rise of the National Socialist regime. He experienced the cultural splendor and political desperation of the Weimar Republic. He was born in Berlin in 1908, attended the French *Gymnasium* there, and subsequently studied law in Berlin and Freiburg. His doctoral thesis was outside the mainstream of legal studies. It dealt with the relations between the partners and adversaries in collective bargaining, and was based partly on data gathered from trade union files. Upon completion of his studies Ehrmann began training as a law clerk in Berlin. He was dismissed from the administration of justice after Hitler's accession to power in 1933 because of illegal political activity and subsequently arrested by the Gestapo, tortured, and sent to the concentration camp at Oranienburg.

He escaped to France in 1934 and, until 1940, worked as a free-lance journalist in Paris. During this period he was active in the anti-Nazi resistance in France, and was also a research associate of the International Institute for Social History and the Frankfurt Institute for Social Research, which had been taken under the wing of Colombia University.

The fall of the Weimar Republic and the decline of the Third French Republic during Ehrmann's stay in France led to his interests in comparison of the rise of dictatorships in the 19th and 20th centuries, of social movements, both progressive and reactionary, and of the fate of representative institutions in times of economic and social crisis.

After the German invasion of France in 1940, Ehrmann emigrated to the United States where he became an associate of the New School for Social Research. From 1943-1947 he worked for the U.S. Government as an Educational Specialist in the war effort against Germany and the subsequent occupation. In the United States he continued his studies of comparative constitutional law (now including American constitutional law) with emphasis on the roles of bureaucracy and pressure groups. His methodological orientation, earlier that of a social historian, shifted increasingly toward functionalist studies of social movements and toward intensive efforts to find a basis for systematic comparison of different types of Western democracies. He was involved in the efforts of the Social Science Research Council to select suitable topics for such comparisons, and he also served on the Editorial Board of the *American Political Science Review.*

Since his appointment as Professor of Political Science at the University of Colorado in 1947, Ehrmann has been a university teacher. In 1950-1951, he was a member of the Institute of Advanced Study at Princeton University. From 1961-1971, he held a position at Dartmouth College and, from 1971-1973, at McGill University. He has held numerous guest professorships at Berkeley, Bordeaux and Grenoble, Nice, Paris, West Berlin, and Mannheim. Since his formal retirement, he has taught continually at Dartmouth and the University of California at San Diego. The fact that he has hardly missed a semester of teaching since his retirement testifies not only to his commitment to teaching but also to the close connection between his teaching and research interests.

Henry Ehrmann's research and writings have been shaped and guided throughout his career by his philosophical, sociological, and juristic interests, and by his political experiences in Germany, France, and the United States. His first publications, while he was still living in Germany, dealt with collective bargaining. His interest in the workers' movement was international in scope. In 1947 he published a book about the French labor movement, to which he had belonged, *French Labor from Popular Front to Liberation.* This study was followed and complemented by his research into French employers' associations. His book, *Organized Business in France,* analyzes business associations in the context of changing social and political institutions. In its manner of posing questions, its construction, and in the richness of its conclusions, it blazed new pathways in interest group research. It led its author to deal with general problems of representation of organized interests. He organized and directed an international Round Table Conference on interest groups in 1958, resulting in the book, *Interest Groups on Four Continents,* which continues to stimulate comparative research on interest groups.

Ehrmann has dealt with specific aspects of the French and U.S. constitutions in numerous publications. His *Politics in France* is a comprehensive analyis of the political regime. Proceding from the behavior of citizens, political processes and institutions are represented in their reciprocal relationships with cultural, economic, and social structures. It has become the standard work on France in political science and, more than this, it sets an example for the description of a political system. A throroughly reworked fourth edition appeared in 1983.

In many places, Ehrmann's investigations of institutions and systems of institutions suggest comparisons with other countries. In addition to his comparative studies on interest groups, he has explicitly compared legal cultures. In *Comparative Legal Cultures,* he inquires into the ways in which law and justice influence social behavior and social structures. The comparative analysis deals with countries with Roman Law and Common Law systems, as well as communist and non-European countries. It brings together ideas from legal philosophy, sociology of law, and political science in an attempt to open up a new field of social science inquiry. Rich in testable hypotheses, the work stimulates many different kinds of research.

In his theoretical reflections as well as in his empirical research, Ehrmann has held firmly to the norms of scholarly research. Fashionable empty, formalistic theories are foreign to him. Setting a methodological example he has described and illuminated highly complex interrelationships with great clarity of thought and language.

This *Festschrift* has been compiled in honor of Henry Ehrmann's 75th birthday. Its publication could not have been realized without the financial support of several institutions: the University of Guelph Alma Mater Fund, Internationes, Dartmouth College, University of Colorado at Boulder, University of California at San Diego, University of Hartford, and University of Massachusetts at Amherst. The Universities of Guelph and Waterloo also generously provided invaluable support facilities for which I am grateful. I would also like to thank several people for their assistance in the preparation of this volume. Roger Masters, William Safran, and Michael Stein for their helpful editorial advice, Andreas Pickel for his assistance with the index, Susan Sommerauer, who typed most of the manuscript, and Lloyd Spitzig and Corey Burgener, who advised and assisted in the computerized production of the book. Finally, I would like to thank Wolfgang Hirsch-Weber for allowing me to adapt for this preface several passages from his *laudatio,* delivered on the occasion of the awarding of the degree of *Doktor phil. honoris causa* to Henry Ehrmann by the University of Mannheim in 1982.

Fred Eidlin
University of Guelph
Guelph, Ontario, Canada
June 1983

Chapter 1

CONSTITUTIONAL COURTS AND VALUES OF REFERENCE: APROPOS DECISIONS ON ABORTION

Alfred Grosser

Comparison should not be abused. But the evolving functions of the *Conseil Constitutionnel* (CC) can be understood much better if compared with analogous institutions in other countries. And this comparison will be all the more fruitful if it is brought to bear upon a specific problem submitted to several of these courts at about the same time. Perhaps the most interesting problem is that of abortion, to which (as noted by Louis Favoreu and Loic Philip in their remarkable new edition of *Les grandes décisions du Conseil Constitutionnel)* the U.S. Supreme Court, the Constitutional Court of Austria, the Conseil Constitutionnel, the Constitutional Court of Italy, and the German Constitutional Tribunal all addressed themselves between 1973 and 1977 (the latter three, more precisely, on January 15, January 18, and February 25, 1975, respectively). Not only for reasons of space and competence, but also because it seems to me useful to go beyond the one particular case in order to better determine its significance, the following discussion will be limited to the triangle of Washington-Paris-Karlsruhe, stressing especially the French-German aspects of the comparison.

POLITICAL CULTURE AND INSTITUTIONAL MAJESTY

Shouldn't we note differences right away? Some are important but do not touch the essence of the matter–for example, the timing of the intervention. The newness of the activity of the *Conseil Constitutionnel* with respect to French tradition is such that it is considered normal, in France, that a declaration of nonconformity can be made only before the promulgation of a law. Elsewhere, it is considered quite normal to annul unconstitutional provisions even though the law in question has already come into force. One particularly spectacular example was provided by the Karlsruhe Tribunal (BVerfG) in 1977. Regarding conscientious objection, the law of April 1 permitted, as of August 1, a choice between civilian and armed service to be registered simply by postcard; on December 7, the tribunal suspended application of the law, declaring the new system to be unconstitutional; in the meantime, 33,000 young men had without any challenge opted for civilian service.

Another example of differences that do not touch the essence of the matter is the recruitment and the legal and political qualifications of judges. The human, all-too-human, aspect recently portrayed by Woodward and Armstrong in *The Brethren: Inside the Supreme Court* is not very exciting. On the other hand, the fact that half of German judges have previously been judges serving on other federal courts or presiding judges of courts at the Länder level, while the other half have some solid background such as a law professorship or senior civil service, explains in part a sort of common passion for a justice often detached from political or social factors (although a remarkable evolution has taken place at Karlsruhe: twelve of the sixteen sitting judges are officially members of a political party). This difference in comparison to the CC has considerably diminished recently, as there has been a considerable increase since 1959 in the number of councillors who are experts in public law.

The question of the dissenting opinion is a much more important difference. In France, courts are denied what constitutes the essence of legislative transsubstantiation: for months and months, parties and parliamentary groups confront each other over a text; the latter is amended, sometimes under pressure from sordid interests; the text is adopted with a feeble majority. The day following its promulgation, the text has but one author–the legislator–who furthermore is said to have been animated by a "will" upon which law professors and tribunals alike will comment endlessly. A kind of magic operation has given the text a majesty that seems as legitimating as a royal coronation.

Is this the case elsewhere? Not to the same degree, since elsewhere political culture is not so solidly based on sanctification of the majority as an expression of the public will, the source of all political norms. It is also less true in France today than yesterday, because of the intervention of the CC. The intervention is all the more revolutionary within our tradition, as the *Conseil* started only about ten years ago to make decisions (like its counterparts in Washington and Karlsruhe) according to norms that are *axiological rather than juridical.* But the Washington and Karlsruhe courts function in cultural systems that have always (U.S. Supreme Court) or for some time and in spite of great reticence (BVerfG) accepted an analogous process of transsubstantiation for the agency of constitutional control. The publication of voting results and of dissenting opinions leads one to think that truth is often a matter of chance. In the case of abortion a slight shift in the vote would have been enough to have the Washington majority, reasoning essentially as the Karlsruhe minority did, rejecting what it approved, or to have the Karlsruhe minority, close to the Washington majority, modifying and upholding the law instead of declaring its essential dispositions unconstitutional. But is this not, on the contrary, a highly democratic principle? There is no absolute truth; there is a norm defined in a legitimate manner by a majority empowered precisely to confer majesty on the norm to be respected. The certainties and questions of the majority judges are answered by the equally detailed certainties and questions of the minority judges: where is the majesty of judiciary decisions? But what if this majesty does not rest with judges or parliamentarians? What if, thanks to a mechanism of transsubstantiation, it belongs to the institution? Such mechanism does not prevent subsequent challenge, arising not from a refusal to submit, but rather from an attempt to obtain a reversal of jurisprudence.

THE PARTICULAR CASE OF THE 1946 PREAMBLE

The U.S. Supreme Court and the BVerfG have the advantage of possessing a firm framework of reference. Of course, they can change their interpretations. The Supreme Court has not failed to do so in matters of economic freedoms and minority rights. But there is no room for doubt regarding the binding, normative nature of constitutional amendments defining freedoms and rights. The fundamental rights, defined in the first chapter of the German constitution, constitute, according to Article 1, legal and directly applicable arrangements that link the legislative, executive, and judiciary powers. This is not surprising because the Bonn democracy was explicitly based upon rejection, not of institutional techniques, but of a totalitarianism of the past and a neighboring totalitarianism.

In France, the tendency to regard a constitution as a mere mechanism allowing institutional life to function has long permitted an unquestioning attitude toward norms and moral points of reference. It follows that the CC, conforming to the cultural tradition of the nation, at first strove only to determine whether the rules of the game were being respected; later it felt the need for texts to use as references as soon as it wanted to go beyond such determinations to see whether the texts to be controlled also respected values that somehow constituted the morals of the political collective.

The 1946 preamble, declared valid in 1958, is an exciting text, too long neglected, especially by historians, for it is possible to understand the contradictions of French decolonization politics simply by analyzing its last three paragraphs or to understand Franco-Soviet or Franco-German relations simply by reading its first words: "In the aftermath of the victory of the free peoples (including the USSR) over regimes (and not over peoples). . . ."

But how can statements be utilized that aim sometimes to be a declaration of principle and at other times to establish a norm? Everyone has the right to employment: to whom should the unemployed speak in order to obtain satisfaction? With regard to the next sentence (No one may be wronged in his work or employment because of his origins, his opinions, or his beliefs) things are much simpler. Is worker participation in the management of enterprises a right, since it is affirmed by the preamble? The answer is not obvious, and it would be interesting to make an appeal to the CC regarding an upcoming law on enterprise. At most we can say clearly what the text does not contain: thus, the CC in its 1977 decision on free schools pointed out, and rightly so, that the formulation the Christian Democrats had obtained did not imply a monopoly of public education. How then can we not find quite concise the formulation used by the CC in its decision on abortion, according to which the law "does not misconstrue the principle set forth in the 1946 preamble of October 27, 1946, constitution, according to which the nation guarantees the child protection of its health, nor misconstrue any of the other decisions on constitutional values set forth in the same text"?

It is true that the terseness or even the brutality of CC affirmations constitutes in a permanent and general way an element of difference from the Washington and Karlsruhe courts. In the case of abortion, this terseness is particularly significant.

THE ATTITUDE OF THE SUPREME COURT

The Court admits frankly and at great length its embarrassment regarding the problem of abortion:[1]

> We forthwith acknowledge our awareness of the sensitive and emotional nature of the abortion controversy, of the vigorous opposing views, even among physicians, and of the deep and seemingly absolute convictions that the subject inspires. One's philosophy, one's experiences, one's exposure to the raw edges of human existence, one's religious training, one's attitudes toward life and family and their values, and the moral standards one establishes and seeks to observe, are all likely to influence and to color one's thinking and conclusions about abortion. Our task, of course, is to resolve the issue by constitutional measurement free of emotion and of predilection. We seek earnestly to do this, and, because we do, we have inquired into, and in this opinion place some emphasis upon, medical and medical-legal history and what that history reveals about man's attitudes toward the abortive procedure over the centuries. . . .
> We do not have to resolve the difficult question of knowing the moment at which life begins. Since the specialists in medicine, philosophy, and theology are incapable of arriving at any kind of consensus, the judiciary, as matters stand in the human sciences, is in no position to issue hypotheses as to what must be the right answer. . . .

The seven judges writing the decision thus seem very modest. But, in a rather contradictory manner, they finally take sides when confronting a case submitted to them and on which they pass judgment on January 22, 1973:

> Roe alleged that she was unmarried and pregnant; that she wished to terminate her pregnancy by an abortion performed by a competent, licensed physician, under safe, clinical conditions; that she was unable to get a legal abortion in Texas

[1] The U.S. citations have been taken from the original English texts the German translated directly from German into English.

> because her life did not appear to be threatened by the continuation of her pregnancy; and that she could not afford to travel to another jurisdiction in order to secure a legal abortion. She claimed that the Texas statutes were unconstitutionally vague and that they abridged her right of personal privacy, protected by the First, Fourth, Fifth, Ninth, and Fourteenth Amendments.

First of all, they address a question that evidently does not arise in France and that is not evoked in the German debate either, despite the federalism of the German Federal Republic: Can the federal court impose behavior on the states in this matter? Do states have the right to impose different regulations on U.S. citizens? In Germany, federalism plays but a very small role in the definition of a common ethic in face of Nazism. In the United States, where general principles concerning freedom have never been questioned, federalism represents a basic principle at least as important as that of national sovereignty in the jurisprudence of the CC. This explains the vigor of the *dissenting opinion* of Justice White:

> The Court simply fashions and announces a new constitutional right for pregnant mothers and, with scarcely any reason or authority for its action, invests that right with sufficient substance to override most existing state abortion statutes. The upshot is that the people and the legislatures of the 50 States are constitutionally disentitled to weigh the relative importance of the continued existence and development of the fetus on the one hand against a spectrum of possible impacts on the mother on the other hand. I find no constitutional warrant for imposing such an order of priorities on the people and legislatures of the States. This issue, for the most part, should be left with the people and to the political processes the people have devised to govern their affairs.

Beyond the question of federalism, the minority judge almost catches the majority red-handed in the act of contradiction: If the basic problem is juridically truly insoluble because of the controversy surrounding ethical foundations, is the decision then not political, falling within the competence of the majority creating laws in the name of controversial values?

Actually, the Court is in the end quite precise in its answers, striking down especially all the laws that do not respect the principle that "during the period of pregnancy extending to about the end of the first trimester, the decision concerning abortion and its execution must be left to the medical judgment of the doctor caring for the pregnant woman."

THE KARLSRUHE TRIBUNAL AND FUNDAMENTAL PROBLEMS

Since its creation, the Tribunal has tended to justify its judgments at great length. The 91 typewritten pages of the judgment of February 25, 1975 (to which we must of course add the 28 pages containing the opinion of the two dissenting judges), have nothing exceptional about them, the March 1, 1979, judgment on comanagement, although unanimous, numbers 123 pages.

But never, without a doubt, has the BVerfG gone so far in its interventionism, in weakness of *self-restraint,* as it did in concluding its long, legal, historical and ethical analyses. In effect, if Point I of the judgment declares null and void 218a of the Penal Code in the version of the law of June 18, 1974, by reason of its incompatibility with Article 2 of the Fundamental Law (everyone has a right to life and to bodily integrity) and because it decriminalizes the interruption of pregnancy even when there are no grounds that, in the sense of the reasons given in the judgment, could carry any weight within the scale of values established by the Fundamental Law, Point II bluntly decrees transitional legislation:

Until the coming into effect of new regulations by legislative means, it is ordered. . . .

1. 218b and 219 of the Penal Code in the version of the law of June 18 1974 . . . are applicable to interruptions of pregnancy during the first twelve weeks following conception.

Other sections of the opinion stated that abortion is not punishable during this period if the pregnancy is the result of rape, and that if, during this same period, there is a situation of grave distress, the courts may refrain from applying the prescribed sanctions.

The two dissenting judges (including Rupp von Bruneck, the only woman member of the court) sharply attacked the attitude of the six majority judges of the First Senate:

> It is true that, even if only because of the increasing importance of social measures aimed at rendering basic rights effective, one cannot relinquish control over constitutionality in this matter. . . . But the danger exists that the examination will not be limited to examination of the legislator's decision, but will tend to replace the latter by another that the court would deem to be better. This danger is even greater when, as in the present case, the decision taken by the parliamen-

> tary majority, after long debates of a very controversial question, is being attacked before the Court by the defeated minority. Independently of the legitimate right of the plaintiffs to have, doubts of a constitutional nature clarified in this way, the Tribunal finds itself all of a sudden in the position of being treated as an instance of political arbitration having to decide between competing legislative proposals. Now, the idea of an objective decision in the domain of values must not become a vehicle for transfer to the constitutional tribunal of functions characteristic of legislation in order to organize that social order.

To which the majority replies in its opinion:

> The constitutional commandment to protect life in the process of development addresses itself to the legislator in the first instance. But it is incumbent upon the BVerfG, in carrying out the function assigned to it by the Fundamental Law, to ascertain whether the legislator has respected this commandment. . . . The Tribunal must not substitute itself for the legislator, but it has the task of examining whether the legislator has done all that is necessary to stave off dangers to the protected being within the framework of possibilities at his disposal.

And then the Tribunal makes use of an argument with a dual significance. It must take into account a peculiarly German position: that Germans should not compare their problems with those of other liberal countries, since those nations have not had a Hitler in their pasts:

> The Fundamental Law is based on principles that can only be explained through historic experience and opposition to the national-socialist system. . . . In face of the overwhelming power of the totalitarian State . . . for which the respect due to the life of each individual had basically no meaning, the Fundamental Law has established a value-based order that places the person and his/her dignity at the center of all its provisions. . . . It is based on the idea that the life of each human being must be unconditionally respected, even life apparently "without social value." . . . This basic decision of the Constitution governs the elaboration and interpretation of the entire juridical order. Even the legislator is not free with regard to it. . . . Even a change in the views on this matter prevailing among the population–assuming that it could be recognized–would not change anything.

[2] The Tribunal has not always put this doctrine into practice, especially in its verdict of May 22, 1975, on access of extremists to the public service. In this verdict it bases its decision on a continuity of the principles of this service since the eight-

Hitler thus imposes a particular rigor upon the Germans.[2] And the majority cannot do whatever it wishes. Meaning: if the Germans had had to vote on euthanasia or on the elimination of an ethnic group, would a majority have granted legitimacy to morally condemnable actions? But the argument also has much more far-reaching implications: to what extent can a moral norm be set by the majority, especially (and this is what the Tribunal meant by "assuming that it could be recognized") if it is by reference to opinion polls that changes in the norm are supposedly determined?

This is a central problem that occurs in France and in Germany in approximately the same terms–in France, where proponents of the death penalty and proponents of abortion accept or reject in a contradictory manner the determination of norms on the basis of opinion polls. That is, those favoring the death penalty argue that the majority is for the retention of capital punishment, and it must therefore be maintained, but abortion is morally unacceptable regardless of what the polls may say; those favoring abortion hold that abortion must be liberalized according to the will of the majority, but the death penalty is unacceptable, even if the majority–insufficiently enlightened–demands that it be maintained.

Without entering into the debate on the nature of intellectual freedom that this problem area evokes, it can be noted that the Karlsruhe Tribunal is quite aware of the difficulty: moral norms evolve; and not by chance, but as a function of interdependent social and ideological changes. Hence comes a conclusion much contested by the majority: everything must be avoided that can create new convictions opposed to fundamental principles; now, nothing encourages an evil act as much as its decriminalization. To decriminalize is to allow, is to make not only legal but even normal, in the dual sense of habitual and in accordance with the rule. This explains the principal motive behind the censure of the reform introduced by Parliament, namely, decriminalization of abortion during the first twelve weeks.

eenth century–as if the Tribunal had not itself shown, in its great judgment of December 1953, that respect for personal freedom implies pluralism in the public service, a pluralism that had ceased to exist in this sense in 1933. In Germany, we have shown again and again the contradictions between the grounds quoted from the verdict of February 25 and the laxity in the matter of individual rights of the judgment of May 22.

To which the two dissenting judges respond in a detailed manner, saying notably:

> The fact that the constitutional duty to protect life includes the period prior to birth is incontestable. The debates in Parliament and before the Constitutional Tribunal did not deal with the *whether*, but rather with the means of this protection. This decision is the responsibility of the legislator. Under no circumstances can a duty of the state to punish the interruption of pregnancy at all stages be derived from the Constitution. . . . Our strongest reservations address the fact that, for the first time in constitutional jurisprudence, an objective decision on the order of values is being utilized to postulate a *duty* of the legislator *to decree punitive norms,* and thus to apply the strongest of interventions imaginable in the private domain of the citizen. It turns functions of the basic rights into their opposites. . . . There would no longer be grounds to examine only (through the controls of constitutionality) if a prescription does not intervene too much in the juridical private domain of the citizen, but also, in the opposite sense, if the State does not punish too little.

The constitution did not prohibit legislators from forgoing a threat of sanction, which, according to their unrefuted opinion, would be to a large extent ineffective, inadequate, and even harmful. Their attempt to remedy the impotence of the state and of society, apparent in the present circumstances, through social means more adequate to the service than the protection of life, is perhaps imperfect but corresponds better to the spirit of the Fundamental Law than the demand of sanction and reprobation.

This line of argument is very close to the one used, in the course of the French parliamentary debate of November 1974, by such deputies as Hélène Missoffe and Eugène Claudius-Petit: I am against abortion, hence for a law that makes possible the limitation of its spreading and in any case its prejudical effect on women. But the entire French discussion at the institutional level is limited precisely to Parliament. The Conseil Constitutionnel itself refuses to enter into the problem area, where minorities and majorities oppose each other in Washington and in Karlsruhe.

THE ARIDITY OF THE CONSEIL CONSTITUTIONNEL AND ITS SIGNIFICANCE

The CC takes pains to refrain from really entering into the debate. Once it eliminates the grounds based on Article 55 of the Constitution (conformity to international obligations–grounds that would have to be examined separately and that do not come into consideration in the U.S. or the German debates–the Conseil devotes a total of about twenty lines to the grounds for its decision. Two passages at least merit a deeper comparative analysis.

The first consists of three words: None of the impairments foreseen by this law is, *as things stand,* contrary to one of the fundamental principles. Could we not see here what could be called intervention in the domain of future legislation? The most striking example of such intervention has been given by the Karlsruhe Tribunal in its judgment of 1973 on the constitutionality of treaties stemming from the *Ostpolitik,* namely, the treaty with the other German state. The Tribunal practically imposed upon any future government of the German Federal Republic the limits of concessions that it could make in new negotiations, saying, in substance the treaties were acceptable because they did not say this, that, or the other thing. As if in this matter the jurisprudence of 1973 were not already quite different from that of the 1950s, since the national and international political situation had changed–as had political beliefs themselves. The CC adopted a similar attitude in its decision on conformity to the constitution of the treaty on European elections. But, with regard to interruption of pregnancy, it was satisfied to affirm the existence of limits and to refuse to sign a blank check; it did not define these limits at all.

Yet it went rather far in its affirmation of a principle that is rather obscure and merits at least some discussion. The law admits infringement of the principle of respect for any human being as of the beginning of life only in the case of necessity and *according to the conditions and limitations that it defines.* But what is a principle, what is a right or a freedom that can be limited by law? Which are the criteria fixing the latitude given to the legislator for this kind of legislation? In Germany, there has been a true debate on the last sentence of the second paragraph of Article 2: everyone has a right to life and to bodily integrity. Only in the application of a law can these rights be infringed upon. If this sentence were to be taken literally, all rights could, for practical purposes, be abolished.

The Conseil itself will find itself forced to take a position on this matter, more precisely, with regard to the right whose limitation is explicitly foreseen in the preamble: the right to strike is exercised within the framework of the laws that govern it. Would any law regulating this right be constitutional by definition? Not at all, the CC answered on July 25, 1979, in a lengthy opinion that must be quoted because it shows that the CC was compelled to give up a reserve that was particularly noticeable in its decision on abortion:

> The Framers wanted to note that this right to strike is a principle of constitutional value, but that it has limits, and they have empowered the legislator to trace these limits and to achieve the necessary reconciliation between the defense of professional interests, of which the strike is a means, and preservation of the general interest that the nature of strike may tend to infringe upon; that, especially as far as public service is concerned, recognition of the right to strike must not have the effect of obstructing the power of the legislator to set limits to this right that are necessary to ensure the continuity of public service which, just like the right to strike, has the character of a constitutional value; that these limitations may go as far as withdrawing the right to strike from employees whose presence is indispensable for the functioning of elements of service whose interruption would harm the essential needs of the country.

Let us not dwell here upon the contents of this judgment. Let us simply note that by its nature, it is closer to an opinion handed down by Washington or Karlsruhe than to the dry affirmation of the decision of January 15, 1975. It is true that this aridity is considerably accentuated by the peremptory affirmation of December 30, 1976, according to which limitations of sovereignty foreseen by the preamble have nothing to do with a so-called transfer of sovereignty. The judgment is written as if the retrospective unconstitutionality of the 1951 treaty creating the European Coal and Steel Community were a matter of course and did not at least deserve some explanation or justification.

Is it really necessary to be that abrupt and to decide without getting to the bottom of any difficulties that present themselves? For example, on November 23, 1977, the decision on freedom of educaton and freedom of conscience states. "The obligation imposed on instructors to respect the particular character of a teaching establishment, if it imposes a duty of reserve upon them, must not be interpreted to mean an infringement upon their freedom of conscience". How simple it is! The central problem–for which there exists no hard and fast solution–is being denied, thus making superflous, in advance, the passionate debates of 1979 and 1980 concerning Hans Küng's freedom of conscience and the prohibition from teaching imposed on him because of the particular character of a faculty of Catholic theology.

Why does the CC proceed in this manner? It gives the central answer itself in the first judgment of the decision on abortion: "The Constitution does not confer upon the *Conseil Constitutionnel* general power of *appreciation* and of decision identical to that of Parliament."

And, in effect, when we read the parliamentary debates of November 1974 and November 1979 of the Veil law, we notice that all the fundamental questions that were treated more or less thoroughly by the majority and minority judges in Karlsruhe and Washington are raised here: not only the human problems such as the terrible solitude of the woman (raised by the minority in Karlsruhe and by Dr. Paecht in the 1979 debate); not only the scope and limits of demographic policy (It is true that Rupp von Bruneck's formulation is not as nice as that of Joseph Comiti, who stated, in answer to his RPR colleague Michel Debré, that, to put it as crudely as General Bigeard might have, a woman is not a cow that must, under compulsion, reconstitute the livestock; but, indeed, the central conflict between the rights of the woman, denied in the past, and the rights of the developing child, affirmed in a peremptory manner by Henry Baynard: The mother is the hostess of the child, not its owner. The parliamentary debates also show the tension between the necessity of no longer sanctioning in order to avoid numerous disasters and the concern not to go from the lack of sanction to moralizing, to incitement. The manner in which Joel Le Tac explains his change of mind, from approval in 1974 to abstention in 1979, corresponds to parts of the majority's line of argument in Karlsruhe.

One even finds the first suggestions, in the Palais Bourbon debate, of the most difficult problem area, which the Karlsruhe judges had avoided somewhat in 1975 before confronting it in their December 21, 1977, judgment on sexual education in schools, namely, the definition of free choice. What bears on this freedom? What pressures, especially coming from the family? With regard to abortion, do the requirements of an interview and time delay enhance the free character of the woman's decision or do they not? Would the absence of constraining legislation augment the constraint exercised by the father or would it not?

CONSTITUTIONAL COURTS AND ETHICAL FOUNDATIONS OF THE POLITICAL COMMUNITY

The CC is obviously very careful not to substitute itself for the legitimate representatives of popular sovereignty. Probably it finds profoundly repugnant the idea of "government by judges" such as the Karlsruhe tribunal had a tendency to practice during the 1970s. Nevertheless, since the day when the reference to the preamble was added to the narrowly juridical references to articles of the Constitution (previously it was necessary to say only whether the articles had been correctly applied), the *Conseil* has been caught in a bind. It will now have to express itself more and more on the basis of principles whose juridical translation is not evident at all and cannot be examined with the aid of logic alone.

If this is the case, then it could be that dry formulations and apparently neutral statements will meet with more and more criticism, even to the extent that decisions demanded of the *Conseil* will touch upon controversial principles, not juridical but moral. It so happens, contrary to what is often said with regard to a decline of morals, that the evolution of society has been tending to multiply axiological controversies, essentially since the legitimation of values can no longer take place by simple transmission through family or school or by unconscious internalization.

It is not that common values of reference no longer exist. On the contrary, never have freedom, justice, and truth been so unanimously evoked and invoked. But which concrete norms can be derived from these values? One day, undoubtedly, the *Conseil* will have to deal with some law on regionalization and will not be able to ask itself questions of this kind: "Have primary school teachers, "black cavaliers" of the republic, been liberators of they people to whom they brought reason and knowledge or have they been the instrument of colonization that imposed cultural alienation on Corsica and Brittany?"

As long as, despite political divisions, certain norms were so well accepted that they did not appear to be norms, one could hide behind the principle of neutrality, of secularity of a state founded on institutions (eg. the judiciary) whose principles of functioning appeared to be self-evident. The doubts and questions that have been gradually applied to the very foundations of social life, including questions concerning relations between the private and the public, between individual liberties and the molding of the future of society by the legitimate political authority, between freedoms to be preserved and liberations to be obtained–these questions have developed the need to better define the mechanisms or authorities capable of regularizing or at least dedramatizing antagonisms with regard to norms, to give certain laws a legitimacy going beyond mere legitimation by the majority, since the risks of rejection of such legitimation by minorities have multiplied as a function of the multiplication of disputes touching upon what has been experienced as essential by these minorities.

It seems clear that the practice of the German Tribunal and of the U.S. Court have advantages in this respect. The detailed judgments of the majority and of the minority contribute to a dedramatization of confrontation, inasmuch as relativity of the conclusions appears clearly, also inasmuch as the weighing of arguments is substituted for the vehemence of debates. And statements of judges are more likely to concentrate on serious arguments than are the oratory matches of parliamentarians who tend to think more about their reelection than about their conception of moral truth.

But the disadvantages of German and U.S. practice are just as clear. Are constitutional judges really qualified (putting all questions of legitimacy aside) to clarify antagonisms that touch the citizens where they are most sensitive? And does not the existence of ultimate intervention by the Court itself incite the parties present to abandon all restraint in their confrontation? Of course, German

Catholicism and French Catholicism have, in any case, known different evolutions and are situated in different political cultures, even disregarding constitutional courts. But the very fact that the *Conseil Constitutionnel* is not and does not want to be, at least for the moment, a definer of norms has probably helped to give the declarations on abortion of the French episcopate a tenor completely different from the extremist cursing of the German bishops. Reading especially the declaration of the permanent council of the episcopate, approved at Lourdes on October 26, 1979, we can see the extent to which the French bishops would like to respect the rules of democracy based upon the legitimacy of the majority and the majesty of the majority: it is necessary to take part in "debates of opinion which engage everyone's conscience." It is necessary to intervene to have an impact on the reexamination of the law. Once the law has been approved, Catholics are asked not to take advantage of the provisions it grants. But there is no appeal for a questioning of the legitimacy, no condemnation of the people and the parties who constitute the majority giving the law its content.

Comparative reflection on decisions of constitutional courts in the matter of abortion thus allows us to do more than determine better the respective roles each of them plays in the political system. It leads to questions regarding the manner in which, today, pluralistic political societies manage to live with axiological conflicts whose importance does not cease to grow, and to live with them while finding regulations that permit the legitimation of rules based on values that are simultaneously common and shattered.

Chapter 2

THE SUCCESS OF CONSTITUTIONAL REFORM IN CANADA: A COMPARATIVE HISTORICAL ANALYSIS

Michael Stein

In November 1981, after years of intensive but fruitless effort to achieve constitutional reform in Canada, success was finally attained. An agreement was struck between the prime minister and nine of the ten provincial premiers on a method to patriate Canada's constitution from the United Kingdom and provide it with an amendment formula and bill of rights. The Constitution Act, 1982, was proclaimed as law in April 1982 by Canada's head of state, Queen Elizabeth II. One hundred fifteen years after its birth as a nation-state, Canada at last had achieved formal independence from the United Kingdom. It had also managed what few western democratic countries had been able to engineer in recent times: a peaceful, negotiated alteration of its fundamental law protecting the civil liberties and linguistic rights of its citizens.

What makes this achievement even more remarkable is that the quest for patriation and an amendment formula had first been initiated fifty-four years earlier, at the time Canada was negotiating its political independence from the United Kingdom under the Statute of Westminster. During the subsequent years, determined efforts to achieve this result were made on no less than eight different occasions by five of Canada's last seven prime ministers and several of its most distinguished provincial premiers; all had failed.

What was the reason for the success of this latest venture after so many failures? Are there ingredients in the most recent constitutional reform package that were absent from earlier proposals and that may account for the current success? Can one explain the

This paper is a modified version of an article prepared for a forthcoming issue of *Publius, the Journal of Federalism.* I would like to thank the editors of that issue for permission to publish the article in this *Festschrift.*

achievement in terms of the personalities of the political actors involved, the strategy and tactics used by the principal negotiators, or the timing and sites of the negotiations? How important were such factors as political and economic elites, interest groups, and political party allegiances? What role did public opinion play in the final outcome? How important were institutions such as Parliament and the courts?

In an attempt to answer these questions, we shall examine systematically and comparatively the role that these and other factors played in the various efforts at achieving constitutional reform. If some factors are present both in the current phase and in earlier unsuccessful phases, then it seems likely that they are not central to an explanation of the success. On the other hand, if certain important elements are present in the recent phase but were notably absent in earlier attempts, then they may be regarded as likely explanatory variables. The explanatory method we are selecting, then, for this case study, may be described as comparative historical.

A primary reason for adopting this method is that the traditional cross-national comparative method used in most comparative political studies cannot be easily applied to this particular problem. There are very few instances of successful negotiated constitutional reform in contemporary times, and these are generally quite different in substance from the Canadian experience. Even though historical circumstances may vary over time, there is greater similarity between the earlier Canadian efforts at constitutional reform and the current attempt than there is between Canadian and non-Canadian experience.

But if in this narrower methodological sense the Canadian experience is considered as unique, it should still be regarded as broadly relevant to other, particularly Western, democratic systems. Constitutional engineering has long been of interest to students of comparative politics because the central forces in a nation's political life are reflected in struggles over constitutional questions. Moreover, constitutional engineering, however difficult it may be, is still a principal method for achieving major institutional reforms. The case outlined below should highlight these points clearly.

EFFORTS AT CONSTITUTIONAL REFORM IN CANADA PRIOR TO 1980

In the first sixty years of Canada's existence as a nation-state, from 1867 to 1927, there was little explicit interest in constitutional reform.[1] Canada did not yet seek full independence from the United Kingdom. The British North America (BNA) Act, 1867, Canada's founding constitution, did not include a formula detailing specific procedures for the enactment of constitutional amendments. Formal change was left to established practice and convention, and the Imperial Parliament in the United Kingdom served as ultimate guarantor of the federal system.[2]

The British North America Act had clearly established the preeminence of the central government within the federal system, so much so, in fact, that a leading constitutional authority has described Canada as having a "quasi-federal" rather than federal constitution.[3] Among its more sweeping quasi unitary powers, the central government was given the right to disallow or reserve acts of the provincial governments, the right to legislate in matters involving "peace, order and good government," the power to declare "works" within provincial jurisdiction under federal control, and the residual authority in matters not allocated to either level of government. It was also given control over an integrated national economy. The provinces were confined to matters of a local nature or to those in which cultural traditions between French and English had differed under the Union.[4]

[1] Because of space limitations, we cannot provide anything more than the most cursory treatment here of the historical aspects of constitutional reform. The analytical explanation must also be greatly abbreviated. However, the historical record of constitutional reform and the explanation for the success of the 1980-82 package are set out in much greater detail in an unpublished essay by the author. That essay serves as the primary background document for the analysis that follows. See Michael Stein, "Constitutional Reform in Canada, 1927-82: The Trudeau Patriation Package in Historical Perspective," March 1982, typescript, 94 pp.

[2] Paul Gérin-Lajoie, *Constitutional Amendment in Canada* (Toronto: University of Toronto Press, 1950), p. 38.

[3] K.C. Wheare, *Federal Government,* 4th ed. (New York: Oxford University Press, 1964), pp. 18-20.

[4] Donald V. Smiley, *Canada in Question: Federalism in the Eighties,* , 3rd ed. (Toronto: McGraw-Hill Ryerson, 1980), pp. 18-27.

Initially the federal government actually exercised its overwhelmingly predominant power in federal-provincial relations, including its power of disallowance of provincial laws. But beginning in the 1880s some of this preponderant authority was successfully challenged in the courts and in a series of inter-provincial and federal-provincial conferences. By 1907, the provinces had succeeded in wresting from the federal government the concession that they be consulted and their approval be gained in any proposed amendments directly affecting their (provincial) interests. Amendments would also have to have the approval of both houses of the federal Parliament. No clear rule was established concerning the veto rights of individual provinces or the weight to be accorded an opposition provincial bloc.

1927

The first serious attempt to find a suitable amending formula for Canada was initiated by Prime Minister Mackenzie King in conjunction with his effort to win complete political independence for Canada from the United Kingdom. At a federal-provincial conference in 1927 the provinces strongly opposed his plan, and the elite and public opinion showed little interest in the subject. He decided, therefore, to drop the matter.

1935-36

In order to enable the federal government to cope with the economic problems caused by the Depression, Mackenzie King again tried to achieve agreement on an amending formula. Under the proposal, different parts of the constitution would have been subject to different formulas. For some matters bearing directly on the provinces, approval of Parliament and at least two-thirds of the legislatures representing at least 55 percent of the population would have been required. The possibility for a province to opt out was also reserved. On more fundamental sections, unanimity of the federal Parliament and the provincial legislatures was specified.

Some of these ideas were to reemerge in 1980-82.[5] Again, the provinces objected and the matter was dropped.

1950

Prime Minister Louis St. Laurent asserted the federal government's right to amend its own constitution unilaterally but ran into the anticipated provincial opposition. Other portions of the BNA Act would have been amended in a manner similar to that proposed in 1935-36. However, numerous meetings of the attorneys-general failed to bridge the wide gap between Ottawa and the provinces. Again an initiative had failed.

1960-66 (The Fulton-Favreau Formula)

Under the Conservative government of John Diefenbaker and then the Liberal government of Lester B. Pearson, surprising progress was made on a formula involving both entrenchment of certain provincial powers and a flexible delegation procedure, and an agreement was actually attained at one point. Before the plan could be implemented, however, unforeseen opposition emerged in Quebec because of a fear that the newly assertive province would be straitjacketed and prevented from achieving its aspirations. The subsequent reversal of position by the Lesage government killed the proposal.[6]

[5] Gérin-Lajoie, op. cit., pp. 245-246, 249. For parallels in the November, 1981 constitutional accord, see below.

[6] Agar Adamson, "The Fulton-Favreau Formula: A Study of its Development, 1960 to 1966," *Journal of Canadian Studies (JCS)*, v. 6 (1971), p. 54. For a more traditional legal perspective on the Fulton-Favreau formula negotiations, see E.R. Alexander, "A Constitutional Straitjacket for Canada," *Canadian Bar Review*, v. 18 (1965), pp. 262-313.

1968-71 (The Victoria Charter Formula)

The Pearson government moved in new directions in 1968, basing its strategy on the principles of constitutional entrenchment of official language rights, entrenchment of a bill of rights, and formalization of the federal-provincial consensus to reduce regional disparities. These remained the centerpieces of the federal concept of constitutional reform up to and including the patriation package of 1980-82.

Again the Quebec government, now led by Daniel Johnson, was in the vanguard of opposition because of its desire for greater powers in fields such as social security, culture, communications, and even foreign affairs, all designed to foster French-Canadian nationalism. By 1971 there had been some progress, and a host of new actors, including Pierre Elliott Trudeau and Robert Bourassa, had appeared. Then a breakthrough on the amending formula was achieved: approval by the federal Parliament and a majority of the legislatures in each of the four regions of Ontario, Quebec, the West, and the Atlantic provinces. The proposal was brought to the federal-provincial conference at Victoria in 1971, where Quebec was pushing for an amendment to s. 94A of the BNA Act so that it would obtain "paramountcy" in the area of social security, broadly construed.

Although agreement was achieved at Victoria, the proposed constitutional package was rejected by the Quebec cabinet, under severe public pressure, because "it produced no solution to the problems of Quebec, and its ratification would shelve the process of review."[7]

1976-80 (The Search for Renewed Federalism)

After a hiatus of several years (which, however, included a threat by the federal government to patriate the constitution unilaterally, made during a round of federal provincial constitutional consultations in 1975-76), interest in constitutional reform was regenerated in response to the election of the Parti Québécois (PQ) government in 1976. In the interim, the earlier consensus on the Victoria

[7] Claude Morin, "Le cul-de-sac de Victoria," *Action Nationale*, v. 61 (1972), p. 68.

formula dissolved, and the Western provinces became more assertive. The threat to the continued existence of Canada and the federal system stimulated thought and action by the Trudeau government, even though it was fully aware of the limitations to possible agreement imposed by Quebec's separatist tendency.

In 1978 the government tabled comprehensive reform proposals and the Constitutional Amendment Bill (Bill C-60) based on principles such as bilingualism, multiculturalism, fundamental individual rights, democracy, and social justice and economic oportunity. Perhaps the most far-reaching proposal was the House of Federation, a body designed to replace the Senate, with half its members to be appointed by the provinces and half by the federal government. There were also proposals for significant reform of the Supreme Court. Opposition to the initiative came from many quarters and prevented advancement of the legislation.

Meanwhile the Pépin-Robarts commission (officially the Task Force on Canadian Unity) reported its own recommendations early in 1979. These included a redistribution of powers, "quasi-special status" for Quebec, and a Council of the Federation appointed by and responsive to the provinces, which would replace the Senate. Despite some positive initial response, the report was eventually left to gather dust on the shelves, like so many other documents of this nature.

After 1979 the focus shifted to the battle over "sovereignty-association" in Quebec. The P.Q. program represented the threat of constitutional revolution, not reform, and was rejected by the other governments in Canada, as well as by 60 percent of the voters of Quebec, in May 1980. Although not a viable alternative in the quest for constitutional renewal, it did help to set the parameters and shape the course of the most recent phase of the reform process.

THE SUCCESS OF THE TRUDEAU PATRIATION PACKAGE

Prime Minister Trudeau barely allowed a day to pass after the referendum votes were counted before initiating this last phase in the constitutional reform proposal. He promised to negotiate unconditionally, without adherence to previous federal government proposals, and sent Justice Minister Chrétien on a whirlwind tour to the provincial capitals to determine what the premiers wished to see in a new constitution. He also met with the federal opposition leaders in an effort to win their support for a common front of federal parties, but months of effort yielded no significant gains.

In a nationwide television address on October 2, 1980, the prime minister revealed that he had finally selected the course of action that he had been threatening to follow since 1975, namely, unilateral patriation of the constitution and entrenchment of an amendment procedure similar to that negotiated at Victoria. In addition, he had decided to include a Charter of Rights and Freedoms, including linguistic rights, and an equalization formula in what came to be called his patriation package. He promised quick action on this new package in the federal Parliament, to be followed by immediate ratification by the British Parliament, as pledged to him by Prime Minister Thatcher in June. A new constitution would be in force by July 1, 1981.[8]

The Trudeau patriation package consisted of two bills that were to replace or amend various sections of the 1931 Statute of Westminister and the 1867 British North America Act and transfer to Canada authority over all provisions contained in these and other British constitutional statutes relating to Canada. A Charter of Rights and Freedoms was to be binding on all levels of government, and it included fundamental freedoms, democratic rights, legal rights, equality rights, mobility rights, official language rights, and minority language education rights. A more innovative element was the provision for an interim amending formula and a method for adopting a final amendment formula. A third component, an equalization provision, had been present in all earlier federal government constitutional reform proposals since Victoria.[9]

The fundamental freedoms guaranteed by the charter were those traditionally protected in liberal democratic constitutions, such as freedom of conscience and religion, freedom of speech (thought, belief, opinion and expression), and freedom of peaceful assembly and association (Constitution Act, 1980, s. 2). The democratic rights

[8] *The Globe and Mail,* October 3, 1981.

[9] *The Canadian Constitution, 1980: Highlights of a Proposed Resolution Respecting the Constitution of Canada* (Ottawa: Publications Canada, 1980), pp. 2-3. A more detailed discussion of these contents will be found below.

protected under the act were also familiar to Western democracies: the right of every citizen to vote or hold elective office, the requirement that all legislative bodies renew themselves at least once every five years, and the requirement that there be at least one legislative sitting every year (ss. 3-5). The legal rights extended to include the right to life, liberty, and security of the person; the right to security against unlawful searches or seizures and against unlawful detention or imprisonment; the right to know the reasons for one's arrest; the right to counsel; the right to challenge the validity of a detention in the courts; and others (ss. 7-14). After some pressure by civil liberties groups, the textual qualification that these rights could be limited in accordance with procedures established by law was removed. The right to trial by jury in serious criminal matters and the right not to be denied reasonable bail without just cause were also subsequently added.[10] Equality rights[11] provided guarantees of nondiscrimination against citizens in general, and particularly on the basis of race, national or ethnic origin, color, religion, age, or sex (s. 15). Mobility rights involved the rights of Canadians to move freely from one province to another, take up residence and employment there, and to enter, remain in or leave the country at will (s. 16).

Official language rights entrenched in the constitution those guarantees for the use of the English or French language already contained in the BNA Act or provided for in federal language legislation. These included the right to use either of the two official languages in the federal Parliament, in the federal courts, or in receiving services from or in communications with the head offices of the central government, and a similar right concerning the use of English or French in the legislatures, courts, and statutes and records of the provinces of Quebec, Manitoba, and New Brunswick. The province of New Brunswick also accorded the right to receive services and communicate with the head office of their government in either official language. Ontario, however, which has the largest minority French-language population of any province, refused to accede to these official language provisions and was therefore excluded. Minority-language educational rights provided members of an English-speaking or French-speaking minority of a province with the right to educate their children in that language, where

[10] *The Globe and Mail*, January 13, 1981.
[11] Originally referred to as "nondiscrimination rights".

numbers warrant it (s. 23). The federal government, when pressed for a more precise guarantee of acquired language rights, added an amendment that permitted all Canadians whose mother tongue is English or French, or who have been educated in Canada in one of the two official languages, to have their children educated in the same language. This additional guarantee, and for that matter this entire section of the charter, was in direct conflict with the Quebec French Language Charter of 1977 (Law 101), which generally allows only the children of those educated in English in Quebec to receive an English language education. Finally, the section defining undeclared rights and freedoms (s. 24) was broadened under pressure from native peoples' organizations to guarantee the aboriginal, treaty, or other rights and freedoms pertaining to the aboriginal people of Canada or recognized by the Royal Proclamation of 1763.[12]

The amending formula provided under the Constitution Act, 1980, allowed for an interim period of two years in which unanimous consent of the federal Parliament and the provincial legislatures would be required for all formal changes to the constitution. During that interim period, a concerted effort would be made to attain unanimous agreement in an annual First Ministers' Constitutional Conference. If agreement was reached, then that formula would supersede the interim formula. If no agreement were reached then a complex method to resolve the problem was proposed, which embodied the basic principles of the Victoria Charter formula.[13]

Although this patriation package was presented as an important step in the constitutional reform process, it was far from a comprehensive constitutional transformation. The federal government chose to include in this package only two items on which it had failed to achieve an agreement in the federal-provincial negotiations the previous summer, the amendment formula and the charter of rights. Even the amendment formula was only a slight variant of the formula originally accepted by all the provinces at Victoria nine years earlier. Moreover, the Charter of Rights was opposed in prin-

[12] *The Globe and Mail,* January 13, 1981, p. 10.

[13] Three alternative approaches to the resolution of the problem were proposed: a national referendum to choose between a federal government plan and a provincial government plan, a modified version of the Victoria formula, and a national referendum, with special majorities, on a federal proposal.

ciple by seven of the ten provinces.

In fact, apart from real differences over the charter, the patriation package could be understood as a slightly new substantive proposal for a long-standing historical problem in Canada that had defied all previous efforts at solution. What was truly distinctive, however, was the radically new approach used to end the impasse: unilateral action. It appeared that the federal politicians and bureaucrats had finally discovered the one approach to constitutional amendment and reform in Canada that seemed capable of breaking the fifty-three-year-old logjam.

Events in the months that followed seemed to confirm this diagnosis. In the first weeks after the patriation package was announced, it was clear that the prime minister had succeeded in splitting potential opposition, both federal and provincial. At the federal level, the New Democratic party agreed to support the package, provided certain amendments on natural resource ownership were added to the charter. At the provincial level, Premier Davis of Ontario, pleased with the federal concession on linguistic rights, joined Premier Hatfield of New Brunswick in supporting the prime minister. Premier Blakeney of Saskatchewan was initially undecided on his position but later joined the opposing provinces. The federal government also managed to undercut opposition from constitutional and legal experts, who criticized the wording of the bill, and special interest groups, which demanded changes in specific substantive areas by incorporating most of their suggested amendments into a revised package, tabled in January 1981 by Justice Minister Chrétien. The effort by Premier Lévesque in November 1980 to win the support of the Quebec Liberals for a unanimous resolution of the National Assembly opposing the package failed. Two of the three provincial courts, Manitoba and Quebec, that were asked to pronounce on the legality of the prime minister's action, ruled in his favor, while the Newfoundland court ruled unanimously against him. Even public opinion, at first strongly opposed to the unilateral action, seemed to moderate somewhat as time passed. Efforts at parliamentary filibuster by the Conservative opposition in the spring of 1981 finally came to naught. Potential opposition from some British parliamentary backbenchers was effectively countered by diplomatic maneuvers.

The strategy of unilateral action reached an impasse, however, in late September 1981, when the Supreme Court of Canada finally ruled on the appeal brought before it in April of that year. The Court, by a 7-2 margin, accepted the federal government's argument that unilateral action was permissible in strictly legal terms. But it also declared, in a 6-3 division, that such an action violated the accepted constitutional convention that the provinces be consulted on matters affecting their status and powers. Moreover, in answer to a specific question on the point, it indicated that provincial unanimity was unnecessary for a change in provincial powers; "substantial consent" was sufficient.[14]

The ambiguity in this decision was enough to discourage the federal government from proceeding further on its unilateral course. On November 2 the prime minister and the premiers met in Ottawa for a final effort to reach an agreement. On the fourth day of round-the-clock bargaining, after an all-night session that included a crucial "kitchen meeting" of key ministers from Ontario, Saskatchewan, and the federal government,[15] the prime minister and nine of the ten premiers announced that they had signed a compromise agreement, which the Quebec government refused to join. But it seemed clear that the requisite "substantial consent" had been obtained.

The compromise involved several crucial changes in the content of the patriation package. First, the preferred amendment formula of the eight opposition premiers, which would require approval of the federal Parliament and seven of the ten provincial legislatures representing at least 50 percent of the country's population, was adopted in lieu of the federal government's modified Victoria formula. Dissenting provinces were also given the right to opt out of all amendments that affected their status and powers. Second, the federal government and the provinces were given the right to pass laws overriding the charter rights in three major areas: fundamental rights, legal rights, and equality rights. Mobility rights were also declared not binding on all provinces where the unemployment rate is above the national average. Third, all English-speaking provinces guaranteed the rights of francophone minorities to French-language schools where numbers warranted it; the entrenchment of anglo-

[14] *The Globe and Mail,* September 29, 1981, pp. 1-2.
[15] *The Globe and Mail,* November 6, 1981, p. 10.

phone educational rights in the province of Quebec was subject to federal government discretion after it attempted to come to an agreement with that province. In addition, other rights such as provincial ownership of natural resources and equalization were reaffirmed.[16]

The Quebec government angrily rejected the compromise on three grounds: the entrenchment of minority-language educational rights, the inclusion of a mobility clause, and the adoption of the amending formula without the added guarantee of financial compensation for provinces that opt out of programs initiated by constitutional amendments.

Other major opponents of the compromise agreement were women's groups and native peoples, who deplored the absence of adequate protection of their rights through entrenchment without the override provision. After an intensive lobbying effort over several days, they succeeded in persuading the provincial governments to reverse themselves and entrench their rights in the new charter.[17]

The amended agreement was embodied in a new constitutional resolution, which was placed before Parliament in late November and passed without significant opposition.[18] It was forwarded immediately to Westminster, where it was once again subjected to a detailed if rather dull debate in February and March 1982. The Canada Bill passed in late March and was signed into law by the queen. Two weeks later she traveled to Canada, and on April 17, in her capacity as head of state in that country, she proclaimed the Constitution Act, 1982, as the new fundamental law of the land. After 115 years, the British North America Act was finally patriated to its country of origin.

[16] *The Toronto Star,* November 6, 1981, p. 1.

[17] *The Globe and Mail,* November 24, 1981, p. 1. There was continued dissatisfaction, however, among native peoples over the insertion of the term "existing" in the provincial guarantee of existing aboriginal rights. The insertion was intended to assuage Premier Lougheed, who was opposed to the creation of new rights.

[18] *The Globe and Mail,* December 3 and 8, 1981, p. 1. The resolution passed the House of Commons on December 2 by a margin of 246 to 24. It passed the Senate on December 7, 1981.

EXPLANATIONS FOR PAST FAILURES AND CURRENT SUCCESS

There are a number of possible explanations that might be offered to account for the past failures and the recent success in the long quest for constitutional amendment and reform. Among the factors which are worth examining are: (1) the content and approach of the constitutional amendment formula and package, (2) changing public opinion, (3) patterns and strengths of federal-provincial governmental/party alliances, (4) shifts in the balance of power between federal and provincial governments, (5) roles of major economic elites and classes, (6) leadership and personality input, and (7) the sequence of options and choices in federal-provincial bargaining and the role of catalysts. We shall discuss and evaluate each of these possible explanations in turn.

The Content and Approach of the Constitutional Amendment Formulas and Packages

It has been argued that the current constitutional reform package has achieved success where all earlier efforts had failed because its content and approach are more flexible. According to this line of argument, it has taken fifty four years to evolve and refine a constitutional formula that satisfies Canada's peculiar national, regional and linguistic-cultural needs. The 1980-82 package contains the minimum that must be included in a constitutional renewal at this time to make it effective; patriation, an amendment formula, and a charter of rights including linguistic rights. This is only a first stage in the constitutional reform process, but it is one that both in substance and in approach is a distinct improvement over proposals that preceded it. The amendment formula and charter of rights are more supple in content and more flexible in meeting the various regional and group interests than were earlier attempts of a similar nature. The approach adopted in the reform, i.e., devising a procedural formula prior to attempting genuine substantive change, is also the most sensible way of proceeding on the question.

But this explanation does not stand up to careful political historical analysis. The amending formula incorporated into the 1982 Constitution Act was precisely that initiated and supported by the provincial premiers from 1976 on. Its underlying principles were not radically different from those of the Victoria Charter formula of 1971, which in turn related to other proposals dating back forty years. They were the adoption of a uniform rule for all amendments and approval by a double majority: a national majority and a provincial majority.

Nor was the approach to constitutional reform adopted in the 1980-82 package sufficiently innovative to explain the reform's success. The package was essentially a return to the procedural approach to constitutional reform that had characterized every attempt prior to that of the Constitutional Amendment Bill (Bill C-60) of 1978, with the partial exception of the Victoria Charter. The rationale of such an approach is that it is easier to strike an agreement on the voting procedures necessary for the adoption of specific items in a constitutional reform package than it is to achieve a consensus on the substantive items themselves. It therefore is desirable, as a first step in any constitutional renewal, to negotiate an amendment formula. It was precisely this type of thinking that led Prime Minister Trudeau to attempt his 1975 initiative, yet this effort failed. In 1978 he reversed himself and attempted to negotiate an agreement on a large number of substantive items, without confronting the procedural question at all. This initiative also came to naught. The 1980-82 package is a repetition of the procedural approach attempted in 1975, with one significant change: Trudeau acted on his threat to achieve the desired reforms by unilateral action, and this ultimately induced a negotiated settlement.

The only other part of the 1980-82 package that might be viewed as contributing to its success is the amended charter of rights, including linguistic rights, that was ultimately accepted in November 1981. Here again there is very little change in content from earlier reform proposals since 1971. The final amendments to the Charter of Rights and Freedoms, including the override clause, are insufficiently significant or fundamental to serve as a major explanation for the success of the 1980-82 package.[19]

Favorable Public Opinion

An essential ingredient of success in any democracy is the mobilization of public support. This is particularly true of fundamental policies or measures such as constitutional reform. Since the very notion of constitutionality implies broad public approval or consensus, it is imperative that the public participate in and concur in contemplated changes in the constitution.

In Canada, unlike many other democratic countries, there has not been a strong historical tradition of consulting the citizenry or mobilizing its support for particular constitutional changes. The BNA Act itself was never ratified by constitutional convention or referendum. The same was true of other fundamental acts such as the Statute of Westminster, which gave Canada its full independence from Britain. When the first proposals for constitutional patriation and amendment were advanced in 1927, public opinion, both elite and mass, was indifferent. By 1935 a change had occurred in elite opinion, particularly that of journalists and academics, who now strongly favored domiciling the constitution in Canada, together with an appropriate amendment procedure. Since there were no opinion polls conducted on a regular basis during this period, it is impossible to gauge with precision the attitudes of the mass public at this time. But newspaper coverage suggests that there was little mass sentiment calling for such a reform.

Although regular Canadian Institute of Public Opinion (CIPO) opinion polls were initiated after World War II, there were no surveys taken of public opinion toward constitutional amendment reform during the 1949-50 (St. Laurent) period. This may well reflect continued public lack of interest in such esoteric and technical matters. This pattern seems to have continued until the mid-1970s. In a poll conducted in April 1976 (during the prime minister's initiative on patriation), Canadians were asked about their attitude toward patriation. In the population as a whole, 42 percent considered patriation to be very important, 23 percent considered it to be fairly important, and 24 percent considered it to be not

[19] The override clause is unlikely to be used by any province, with the exception of Quebec, since such an action would probably be too costly politically.

important at all. Another 11 percent did not know or were undecided.[20] Thus there seemed to be a greater awareness of and interest in the issue than was the case in the preceding years.[21]

A real upsurge in public awareness and concern about constitutional reform came with the election success of the Parti Québécois. A large number of unity groups sprung up everywhere, calling for constitutional reforms. When the Pépin-Robarts task force commissioned a Centre de Récherche sur l'Opinion Publique (CROP) survey on the subject in 1978, public opinion strongly favored such reforms and was much more crystallized on the direction they should take.[22] Public support for constitutional renewal persisted until well after the Quebec referendum on sovereignty-association. It continued to favor a negotiated agreement between the two levels of government and to oppose unilateral patriation by the federal government.[23]

[20] Canadian Institute of Public Opinion, May 5, 1976.

[21] For example, in a CIPO poll published on October 16, 1971, a few months after the Victoria negotiations had failed but while the Molgat-MacGuigan committee was still active, it was revealed that only 45 percent of the population was aware of the negotiations. Of those who were, 50 percent considered patriation to be very important, 26 percent considered it to be fairly important, and 19 percent considered it to be not important at all.

[22] Centre de Récherche sur l'Opinion Publique, Statistical Table and Methodology for a Study of Public Opinion Regarding National Unity and Proposed Constitutional reforms, August, 1978, pp. 36-37 (from the author's personal files). In answer to the question, Should we create a new constitution, change the BNA Act, or leave it as it is, 15 percent thought that we should create a new constitution, 32 percent felt that we should change the BNA Act, 38 percent replied that we should leave it as it is, and 15 percent didn't know or refused to answer. Concerning the method used to reform the constitution, about the same proportion were very favorable (17 percent) or favorable (50 percent) to a special constituent assembly as were very favorable (18 percent) or favorable (49 percent) to direct negotiations between the federal and provincial levels.

[23] Canadian Institute of Public Opinion *The Toronto Star,* September 20, 1980. The poll asked how constitutional matters should be dealt with. The largest group, 30 percent, felt that it should be decided by a majority of the eleven negotiating parties. A fairly high proportion, 26 percent, nevertheless thought it should be decided by the federal government alone. On December 10, 1980, the CIPO published another survey that asked Canadians if they approved or disapproved of the federal government's acting on its own. 58 percent disapproved and only 27 percent approved. Not surprisingly, the highest proportion of those who approved, 35 percent, came from Ontario. On December 13, 1980, *The Globe and Mail* also revealed that federal polls taken during July and September, and released in December, revealed a high proportion in favor of patriation and a charter of rights but against unilateral federal action on these matters.

In short, over the course of Canadian constitutional history, there does not seem to be a close correlation between highly favorable public attitudes in support of constitutional amendment or broader constitutional renewal and successful negotiations or effective government action on the question. In earlier periods prior to the mid-1970s, when public opinion remained largely indifferent to or uninterested in patriation and amendment reform, several efforts at negotiation, including the 1964 (Fulton-Favreau) and 1971 (Victoria Charter) conferences, came close to achieving an accord. In the recent period, when public interest in and support for constitutional renewal increased dramatically, all federal-provincial efforts at negotiation failed dismally. These include the first ministers' meetings in 1975-76, 1978-79, and September 1980. Moreover, prevailing opinion clearly favored a negotiated federal-provincial agreement or a constitutional convention rather than unilateral federal action, as indicated consistently in opinion polls conducted since the latest phase began after the Quebec referendum. Yet during this period the federal government chose to disregard these polls and proceed unilaterally with its patriation package. Public opinion cannot explain the earlier failures and the ultimate success of the 1980-82 constitutional reform effort. The role that public opinion did perform successfully in 1980-82 was that of a catalyst to successful negotiation after the "split decision" of the Supreme Court. More will be said on this point below.

Patterns and Strengths of Federal-Provincial Governmental/Party Alliances

One of the standard hypotheses in the theoretical literature on federalism is that federal-regional negotiation and agreement can be facilitated by intraparty bargaining at the two levels of government.[24] This hypothesis has been tested against Canadian experience by a number of students of Canadian federalism and found wanting. They have pointed out that the party system is too loosely integrated to have a great impact on federal-provincial relations.[25]

[24] See particularly William Riker, *Federalism: Origin, Operation, Significance* (Boston: Little, Brown, 1964), chapter 5.

[25] See Donald V. Smiley, *Canada in Question: Federalism in the Eighties,* 3rd ed. (Toronto: McGraw-Hill Ryerson, 1980), p. 121, and Garth Stevenson, *Unfulfilled Union*

Many of the major federal-provincial conflicts have occurred between governmental leaders of the same party label, and some of the closest alliances have been struck between leaders of nationally opposing or rival parties. Another related hypothesis is that federal-regional outcomes will be influenced and determined by the relative strengths of the various governmental parties at each level. Thus, weak minority or coalition governments at one level will tend to be at a bargaining disadvantage with strong majority governments at another level, particularly if they represent larger or more powerful units.

These hypotheses may be applied to the problem we are considering here, namely, what accounts for the current success and what explains the recurrent failures in the past in federal-provincial constitutional negotiations in Canada. Thus it might be hypothesized that all previous attempts at federal-provincial constitutional negotiations in Canada between attorneys-general or first ministers failed because the governmental/party alignments were unconducive to overall agreement. For example, a strong majority government at the federal level might take a constitutional initiative and gain support from some provinces, but also face strong opposition from one or more strong majority governments of larger or more powerful provinces such as Quebec, Ontario, British Columbia, or Alberta; the result in this case would likely be a bargaining standoff. Similarly, a weak minority government at the federal level might be reluctant to take a constitutional initiative or to risk compromises in constitutional bargaining situations, for fear of being overpowered or outmaneuvered by an alliance of powerful opponents. Thus no serious constitutional negotiations would be launched during the life of such a government.

These hypotheses do not seem to be validated when applied historically to federal-provincial constitutional conferences in Canada. The first conference that dealt with the question of constitutional amendment was the November 1927 conference in Ottawa, but available information is too skimpy for meaningful analysis in such terms.[26] R.B. Bennett's majority Conservative government

(Toronto: Macmillan of Canada, 1979), p. 188.

[26] According to Gérin-Lajoie, the King government, which had a narrow majority, had "a considerable amount of support" for its proposal that future amendments be made entirely in Canada. But it also faced "very strong opposition . . . by a

replaced that of Mackenzie King in 1930 and remained in office until 1935. Bennett, who had strong provincial support, promised to call a federal-provincial conference to consider the question of a constitutional amendment procedure but never pursued the matter.[27] Despite the conducive governmental/party alignment pattern and the federal government's relative strength, no negotiations or action on the issue occurred; the hypotheses about intra-party bargaining and relative strengths of the different governmental parties are not supported in this case.

Mackenzie King regained power late in 1935 with his majority considerably enhanced. He decided to act on an earlier recommendation of a special committee of the federal Parliament that a federal-provincial conference be convened that year to examine the issue of constitutional amendment procedures. He convened a federal-provincial conference in Ottawa in December 1935 in which this matter was placed on the agenda. There was a consensus on the general principle of an entirely Canadian amendment procedure, but the agreement broke down in the subcommittee of the committee of experts appointed to work on the precise formula for such amendments. Although the reasons for this breakdown in negotiations were not made public, and there is no available report of the proceedings, a leading authority has attributed it to lack of agreement among the provinces.[28] It is clear, however, that governmental/party alignments and relative strengths had little to do with the breakdown of these negotiations. A majority federal Liberal government had aligned itself with six of the strongest provincial governments. They faced a common front of much weaker governments of different party labels from the Maritime provinces. Yet they failed to win these governments over. Even the attempted compromise could not satisfy all the negotiating parties, and the federal government decided not to press the matter. The dominant consideration in the

number of provincial representatives" (p. 229). There were several strong majority Conservative provincial governments then in power, particularly in larger provinces such as Ontario and British Columbia. The Quebec government, also majoritarian, was headed by the Liberal Alexandre Taschereau. Premier Howard Ferguson of Ontario was then a leading proponent of the compact theory of confederation, and he had support from the Quebec premier for his view.

[27] Gérin-Lajoie, op. cit., p. 229. He did, however, allow a select committee of the federal House of Commons to be established in early 1935.

[28] Gérin-Lajoie, op. cit., p. 247.

bargaining alignment appears to have been shared provincial and regional interest. The hypothesis is once again invalidated.

Similar analyses can be made of later federal-provincial constitutional negotiations, such as those of 1950, 1964, and 1971, with comparable results.[29] Yet in 1980, although Trudeau faced determined opposition from every provincial premier except the minority Conservative premier of Ontario, William Davis, and the majority Conservative premier of New Brunswick, Richard Hatfield, he proceeded with his patriation action, and indeed succeeded (in this instance Trudeau had a Liberal majority). It is clear, then, that an adequate explanation for these various failures and temporary or long-term successes cannot be found in the pattern and strengths of governmental/party alliances.[30]

Shifts in the Balance of Power Between Federal and Provincial Governments

A related but nevertheless analytically distinct explanation of federal-provincial bargaining outcomes is the pendulum or balance of power theory of federalism. According to this theory, whenever the pendulum shifts too far in one direction in a federal system, a

[29] In 1950 a newly elected St. Laurent with a strong majority government at first faced a united front of opposition from provincial premiers of various party affiliations and parliamentary strengths, led by Premier Duplessis (Union Nationale) of Quebec, Frost (Conservative) of Ontario, and Manning (Social Credit) of Alberta, all with strong majority governments. This common front did not last long, however, and the final breakdown in negotiations some months later seems to have occurred over other issues. In 1964 the conference of attorneys-general under the chairmanship of Guy Favreau, federal justice minister in a minority Pearson Liberal government, managed to achieve a tentative agreement on a formula that had been initiated in 1961 by Davie Fulton, justice minister in the strong majority government of Conservative John Diefenbaker. Each faced strong provincial majority governments led by Liberal premier Jean Lesage in Quebec, Conservative premier John Robarts on Ontario, Social Credit premier Ernest Manning in Alberta, and Social Credit premier W.A.C. Bennett in British Columbia. At Victoria in 1971 Pierre Trudeau headed a strong majoritarian federal Liberal government. His chief opponent was Quebec Liberal premier Robert Bourassa, who also had a strong majority. The other provincial premiers were prepared to accept the charter. Yet it failed to gain ultimate acceptance.

[30] At least this factor cannot be viewed as a major explanatory variable. It may serve as a supportive or secondary causal factor in certain instances, such as the tentative agreement in 1964 over the Fulton-Favreau formula.

corrective mechanism or balancing force tends to be triggered in the opposite direction. Among the major institutions in a homeostatic-like operation that help maintain the balance in the federal system are the informal bargaining processes within the executives and administrations of the two levels of government. Judicial review by the courts may also play a central role in preserving such a balance. But if the informal executive/administrative or judicial processes are unable to operate effectively so as to maintain the equilibrium over the long run, or if the system becomes unbalanced due to the increasing lack of congruence or disequilibrium between underlying social forces and the formal structures of federalism, it may be necessary to resort to constitutional renewal to recreate this balance.[31]

Such a theory may be quite useful in explaining the impetus or motivation behind the various efforts at constitutional reform in Canada and their relative success or failure. The impetus for such a reform is that the balance of power within the federal system is not being properly maintained or reflected within the formal institutional framework. This balance can be affected formally in one of two principal ways: (1) by formal adjustments and modifications of the distribution of powers in the constitution or (2) by altering or affecting the formal role which one level of government plays within the institutions of the other level. According to such a theory, the various constitutional reform efforts in Canada all had as their principal rationale the desire on the part of one level of government to stabilize or readjust the system so as to consolidate its own gains or reverse the gains made by the other level of government. This could be achieved by formalizing these changes in a new or revised constitution.

When confederation was first established in Canada in 1867, the structure of federalism formalized in the BNA Act was highly centralized. But over the next half century, this imbalance in favor of the federal government was partially readjusted by a series of decisions of the Judicial Committee of the Privy Council that strengthened the status and power of the provinces.[32] Informal

[31] For further elaboration of this theory, see A.W. Johnson, "The Dynamics of Federalism in Canada," *Canadian Journal of Political Science*, v. 1, no. 1 (March 1968), pp. 18-39. See also Claude Morin, *Quebec Versus Ottawa*, op. cit., chapter 15-16, for some trenchant criticisms of the theory.

negotiations in federal-provincial conferences in 1887 and 1906 also enhanced the provinces' role in confederation. Therefore, when the question of a formal amendment procedure arose at the negotiations on dominion status in 1926, it was natural for the provinces to demand an equitable formal role in the process, though the federal government was insufficiently forthcoming. By 1960, the provincial governments had begun to challenge the federal government's dominance partly through the self-assertion of their much expanded civil services. The federal government under Pearson evolved a philosophy of cooperative federalism, in which it sought to manage the growing number of common policy concerns and overlapping jurisdictional claims by the two levels of government by methods of cooperation rather than conflict. In some quarters cooperative federalism under Pearson was viewed as a serious erosion of federal power or at least attenuation of federal dominance.[33]

When Pierre Trudeau succeeded Pearson and captured an overall majority in the 1968 elections, he offered a new concept of federalism. It was considerably more centralist than that of his predecessor, particularly with regard to the distribution of powers; Trudeau attempted to reaffirm this position at Victoria without success. Quebec proved to be a major stumbling block, using social policy as a means of countering the federal government's constitutional reform initiative. By 1975, several other provincial governments, such as Alberta and British Columbia, had come to share Quebec's perspective on many constitutional and federal-provincial matters. Consequently, Trudeau's procedural initiative of 1975-76 was met by broadly based provincial demands for a greater share in national policymaking institutions affecting the provinces and a larger role for the provinces in areas of overlapping or concurrent jurisdiction, all of which were unacceptable to him. Moreover, after November 1976, the Quebec government no longer even accepted the new equilibrium demanded by the decentralist-minded provincial premiers, because its *indépendantiste* orientation allowed for a

[32] See W.R. Lederman (ed.) *The Courts and the Canadian Constitution* (Ottawa: Carleton Library, 1964), Part 2, ss. i. See also Alan C. Cairns, "The Judicial Committee and its Critics," *Canadian Journal of Political Science*, v. 4, no. 3 (September 1971), pp. 301-345.

[33] See Donald V. Smiley, *The Canadian Political Nationality* (Toronto and London: Methuen, 1967), pp. 83-86. See also Audrey D. Dooer, *Erosion of Federal Power*, M.A. thesis, Carleton University, 1968, esp. chapter 7.

confederation at best.

The crushing defeat of the proponents of sovereignty-association in May 1980 and the ensuing disarray that it brought to their forces provided a rare opportunity for the Trudeau government and its centralist supporters. The unilateral initiative embodied in the 1980 patriation package was labeled a constitutional coup d'etat by its opponents; it certainly was an attempted reassertion of federal dominance within the current constitutional framework. It was partially frustrated by the Supreme Court ruling of September 1981 and the concessions made to the provinces in the November negotiations. The 1982 Constitution Act does not in and of itself alter much in the current federal-provincial balance, but its implementation will provide some impetus for precisely such a centralist reaffirmation. Thus the balance theory of federalism goes a considerable distance toward explaining the underlying motivations for the attempted unilateral action in 1980-81 and its culmination in a successful negotiated agreement.

Roles of Major Economic Elites and Classes

Recent writings on Canadian federalism have drawn attention to a neglected dimension of this phenomenon, the role of economic and class factors. This approach has been referred to as the political economy approach. The approach attributes shifts in federal-provincial relations to changing patterns of the economy and resulting pressures exerted on the central or provincial governments by different economic elites or class fractions. It views the federal and regional authorities as the main engines behind a complex web of state-private sector interactions that define the preeminent economic activities or accumulation functions of governments. Federal-provincial conflict, seen from this perspective, is essentially conflict between competing national and regional economic elites or rival fractions of the economically dominant bourgeois class.[34]

[34] See Garth Stevenson, "Federalism and the Political Economy of the Canadian State," in Leo Panitch (ed.), *The Canadian State: Political Economy and Political Power* (Toronto: University of Toronto Press, 1977), chapter 3, and *Unfulfilled Union*, op. cit., chapter 4. For a non-Marxist political economy analysis of Canadian federalism, see J.R. Mallory, *Social Credit and the Federal Power* (Toronto: University of Toronto Press, 1954).

The approach is considered to be particularly applicable to Canada because of the highly differentiated and regionally based nature of the Canadian economy and its impact on a relatively decentralized political federalism. Another related feature is the historically active role that the state has played in Canadian economic development. According to the approach, confederation can be viewed as essentially a pact between economic and political elites that enabled the former, with assistance from the latter, to exploit the potential economic advantages of a large, unified east-west economic market. The federal government was given extraordinary powers to foster economic development, which it succeeded in doing to a large degree in its first seventy-five years through its national policy, linking Canada economically on an east-west basis while maintaining a high degree of centralism.

After World War II there was a further shift to oil and gas energy resources, based largely in Alberta, and to the export of resource and secondary manufacturing products. Foreign investment, ownership, and control, particularly from the United States, increased dramatically in all sectors. The flow of trade also shifted significantly from an east-west to a north-south axis. Canadian federalism became much more decentralized, although the state sector expanded considerably at both levels. By the 1970s, a sharp cleavage had emerged between the national economic elites or national bourgeois fraction identified with the commercial and industrial interests of Ontario and the federal government, and the regional economic elites or petit bourgeois fraction identified with the resource interests of the West. This cleavage was carried over directly into the federal-provincial arena in a range of issues pitting the central government and Ontario against the West.[35]

After the Quebec referendum of 1980 the federal government moved to reassert its power. Its main ally in these efforts was the Conservative government of William Davis, which shared its concern that the economic power of the central government not be further eroded. Both governments depended heavily on the political and financial support of the dominant commercial, financial and indus-

[35] See Larry Pratt, "The State and Province-building: Alberta's Development Strategy," in Leo Panitch (ed.), *The Canadian State, op. cit.*, chapter 5. See also John Richards and Larry Pratt, *Prairie Capitalism: Power and Influence in the New West* (Toronto: McClelland and Stewart, 1979), esp. chapter 11.

trial elites centered in southern Ontario, which were strongly urging this reassertion of central economic and political control in order to protect their own positions.

This explanation obviously serves as a useful supplement to the balance of power discussed above. Unfortunately, much of the argument must be presented in a speculative way, since it is difficult to find direct empirical evidence to support its propositions. It is also impossible to draw precise linkages between economic forces and groups and specific constitutional activities and events. Nevertheless, in the political economy approach we have a deeper understanding of the motivations behind the patriation initiative of 1980-82.

Leadership and Personality Input

Perhaps because journalists often tend to make the question of personality and leadership their central concern in dealing with political matters, social scientists generally neglect this aspect in their explanations of political phenomena.[36]

MacKenzie King was the first prime minister to attempt a constitutional amendment reform in 1927, and again in 1935-36. King was by temperament a temporizer and conciliator who preferred to postpone or pigeonhole difficult decisions, which he did in both his efforts at constitutional reform. St. Laurent was a prestigious lawyer prior to his entry into active politics who had expressed an interest in the question of constitutional amendment reform as early as 1929, when president of the Canadian Bar Association. He was also an exponent of strong central government leadership, particularly in the economic sphere, but was unwilling to press forward constitutionally in the face of concerted opposition in 1950. John Diefenbaker had been a criminal lawyer prior to entering politics, and one with a strong civil libertarian bent. Diefenbaker first pursued his more cherished goal of a bill of rights with considerable success. He then offered lukewarm support to Fulton's initiative on an amendment formula. Fearing future conspiracies by groups of provinces, he soon grew disenchanted with the justice minister's

[36] For a comprehensive discussion of the importance of this variable for political science, see Paul Fox, "Psychology, Politics and Hegetology," *Canadian Journal of Political Science*, v. 13, no. 4 (December 1980), pp. 675-690.

compromises, thereby ensuring the project's failure. Pearson revived the negotiations on this formula a few years later, under the guidance of his able but inexperienced justice minister, Guy Favreau. A former celebrated diplomat, minister of external Affairs, and Nobel Peace Prize winner, Pearson believed strongly in flexible political leadership and negotiation. It is not surprising, therefore, that under his overall tutelage, compromises were accepted and negotiations reached an accord. The subsequent collapse of this agreement can in no way be attributed to Pearson's personality or leadership style.[37]

Pierre Trudeau assumed the leadership in 1968 with a clear vision of what he wished to achieve in federalism and French-English relations, two subjects about which he had previously written as a law professor and journalist. He was a liberal rationalist, a centralist by inclination, whose ideas had been shaped by the economic thinking of the Keynesian school while he was studying at the London School of Economics. He strongly opposed Quebec nationalism and independence and entered federal politics explicitly to combat these trends in his home province. Above all, he was a determined and somewhat autocratic leader who would not hesitate to use his power in pursuit of his ideals or goals, as became apparent during the October Crisis of 1970.[38]

One of Trudeau's major goals when he assumed the prime ministership was to recreate a strong federal government in which French Canadians participated actively. He soon became convinced that one of the best ways to achieve these goals, together with his liberal ideas of fostering individual as opposed to collective rights, was to entrench them in a new constitution. It would contain a Charter of Rights and Freedoms, including linguistic rights, and

[37] For a general sketch of the personality charateristics of Canadian prime ministers, see Bruce Hutchison, *Mr. Prime Minister* (Don Mills: Longmans, Canada, 1966). See also John C. Courtney, "Prime Ministerial Character: An Examination of MacKenzie King's Political Leadership," *Canadian Journal of Political Science,* v. 9 (1976), pp. 77-100; J.E. Esberey, Prime Ministerial Character: An Alternative View," *Canadian Journal of Political Science,* v. 9 (1976), pp. 101-106; Dale C. Thomson, *Louis St. Laurent, Canadian* (Toronto: Macmillan, 1967); Peter C. Newman, *Renegade in Power: The Diefenbaker Years* (Toronto: McClelland and Stewart, 1967); and John R. Beal, *The Pearson Phenomenon* (Toronto: Longmans, Canada, 1964).

[38] On Trudeau's personality traits and leadership style, see George Radwanski, *Trudeau* (Toronto: Macmillan, 1977), and Richard Gwyn, *The Northern Magus* (Toronto: Macmillan of Canada, 1978).

modernized national institutions better reflecting the cleavages in the country. Once committed to these goals, he pursued them relentlessly, albeit with little success, over the next twelve years. Because he had both the tenacity and the leadership skills to keep this objective at the forefront of his political agenda, he eventually wore down his opposition. At the time that he introduced his patriation package, in 1980, most of those opposed to patriation had neither the skills nor the discipline to combat him effectively.

The personality and leadership explanation has an obvious major weakness in the context; it does not explain why it took Trudeau so long to find the successful formula for achieving his goal of constitutional reform. Trudeau's personality and leadership qualities were essentially the same in 1968-71 as they were in 1980-81. The route of unilateral patriation was open to him at this earlier stage and was contemplated and even overtly threatened in 1976. Yet it was not until four years later, after two further attempts at federal-provincial negotiation, that this course was finally adopted. Clearly, in order to account for adoption of the unilateral strategy of 1980 that ultimately led to a successful agreement, a further explanatory variable or factor is required.

The Sequence of Options and Choices in Federal-Provincial Constitutional Negotiations and the Role of Catalysts

The most important factor accounting for the resort to a unilateral strategy in 1980 was undoubtedly the conclusion by the federal government and its close advisers that alternative options had been closed off in the efforts at negotiation over the previous fifty-three years. The only choice left to the federal government, apart from abandoning the entire constitutional reform effort–something it preferred not to contemplate because of Trudeau's personal commitment to the idea and his pledge to Quebec during the referendum campaign–was to attempt the unilateral route. He had been advised that such a strategy could succeed if adopted, although not without a long and bitter fight.[39] The federal government deter-

[39] This advice was contained in the famous Kirby Memorandum. The memorandum, drafted by Federal-Provincial Relations Office (FPRO) head Michael Kirby,

mined that this was the only course left open to it.

The alternative options to unilateralism had gradually disappeared over fifty-three years of intermittent but nevertheless determined effort. Moreover, the sporadic attempts of the earlier years had been followed by much lengthier and more exhaustive efforts in the 1970s, particularly in the period from 1975 to 1980. Yet it was clear from the abortive negotiations at the previous first ministers' conference in February 1979 that unanimous agreement on even the most basic items had been almost impossible to attain. Since the Victoria charter negotiations, the gap had widened rather than narrowed. Many items that had been accepted in 1971 were adamantly opposed in 1980. The chances of concurrence on a compromise package–even a very limited one–were most remote.

The experience over fifty-three years seemed to have exhausted the multilateral options. Thus when Trudeau returned to power in early 1980 with an overall majority, and shortly after helped to defeat the *indépendantistes* in the referendum by promising one more effort at constitutional renewal, there were no longer any alternative options available to him. Procedural formulas and substantive approaches, negotiations on a few items and deliberations on a comprehensive package of reforms, closed talks and open federal-provincial negotiations, cross-country soundings and expert study and research–all these approaches had been tried without success. The chances of agreement in 1980 seemed more remote than ever. There was only one remaining option left to the prime minister, namely, carrying through his earlier threat to reform the constitution unilaterally. By June 1980, immediately after the referendum defeat, Trudeau had decided to take the risk.

What the prime minister and his advisers had not anticipated was that the stick of unilateral action would serve as the crucial prodder and catalyst for a successful negotiation settlement. It enabled the provinces to draw first the lower courts and then the Supreme Court of Canada into the debate. The latter used its authority as final

was submitted to cabinet in June 1980, shortly after the P.Q. referendum defeat. It contained a long analysis of alternative strategies for constitutional reform including the recommendation that a unilateral course be adopted if efforts to negotiate reform failed that summer. The memorandum was leaked to Premier Lévesque and the press in September 1980, but this did not deter the federal government from adopting the unilateral strategy it recommended.

arbiter in the federal system to offer each side a sort of carrot and a clear incentive to find a mutually acceptable accord. It also helped provide a bypass around the roadblock created by Quebec provincial opposition. Public opinion in the country strongly supported such a compromise. There remained merely the problem of defining what that compromise entailed, and this was solved at the November 1981 conference. Unfortunately, it was achieved at the expense of the government, a majority of the opposition, and much of public opinion in Quebec.

CONCLUSIONS

In the previous section we examined seven possible explanatory factors accounting for successful constitutional reform in 1980-82. We found the first three–(1) the content and approach of the amendment formulas and constitutional packages, (2) favorable public opinion, and (3) patterns and relative strengths of governmental/party alliances–to be inadequate as basic explanatory variables. On the other hand, we considered the last four–(4) shifts in the balance of power between federal and provincial governments, (5) roles of major economic elites and classes, (6) leadership and personality and (7) the sequence of options and choices in federal-provincial bargaining and the role of catalysts–to be mutually reinforcing, major contributing factors. The interrelationship of these four explanatory factors needs to be elaborated.

The initial impetus for constitutional reform appears to come from a desire to formalize changes in the balance of federal-provincial power or to promote future changes in this balance. These changes either are supported by or are a reflection and consequence of shifting economic elites and class forces. If adequate leadership and personal commitment are provided by the top political leader or leaders, then there is a strong likelihood that a constitutional initiative will be undertaken. The ultimate determinant of this action, however, is the range and sequence of past options and actions taken on the issue. In issues such as constitutional reform, especially in western liberal democratic and federal systems like Canada, the norms of the system create an inherent bias in favor of consultation among the major actors and jurisdictions involved in the process, until a consensus among them is attained. Thus there will be a tendency to exhaust all alternative methods, approaches, and types of consultative action or negotiated agreement before any nonconsultative, unilateral action is seriously contemplated. This will tend to be the case regardless of the prevailing federal-provincial balance, the alignment of economic elites and classes, and personality, and leadership attributes of the top decisionmakers.

These are the prime factors that appear to have shaped the decision taken by Prime Minister Trudeau in 1980, after fifty-three years of alternative strategies and efforts, to introduce his unilateral patriation strategy. This decision, once taken, triggered a sequence of catalytic actions that led ultimately to a successful negotiation. Precisely what the appropriate sequences and mix were in ensuring success can only be offered in a tentative and hypothetical manner here.[40]

A final question concerning the 1980-82 patriation package has yet to be answered. What is the significance of the prime minister's short-term success in terms of the longer-run possibilities for comprehensive constitutional renewal? Will the 1980-82 initiative prove to be only a Pyrrhic victory, a largely symbolic success that will effectively bring the reform process to a halt? Or will the federal government capitalize on the success of Phase I in their announced program to initiate a much more sweeping package of reforms in Phase II?

This question is a speculative one that cannot be answered here with assurance or with strong supporting evidence. Nevertheless, the comparative historical examination of constitutional amendment and reform that we have conducted does suggest that the demand for

[40] In order to deal more adequately with this question, it would be necessary to examine the events of 1980-82 in considerably more detail than we have done. (Such a detailed case study is beyond the scope of this essay.) What seems to be required, in this case, is a comprehensive analysis and assessment of the major contending groups, their alliance patterns, relative resources and goals, strategies and tactics, and the outcomes of their successive actions. For an excellent model for such a study, see Richard Simeon, *Federal-Provincial Diplomacy* (Toronto: University of Toronto Press, 1972), chapters 6-11.

constitutional reform in Canada would not be removed by a few relatively minor constitutional changes. Much more than just the partiation package of 1980-82 is required to alleviate some of the abiding shortcomings of the Canadian federal system.

Chapter 3

THE EVOLUTION OF THE INSTITUTION OF THE FRENCH PRESIDENCY, 1959-1981

François Goguel

On September 28 1958, General de Gaulle, who had been recalled to power in early June by President René Coty because the leaders of the dominant parties of the Fourth Republic were incapable of handling the rebellion in Algeria, had a new constitution of the republic approved by the French people, with a majority of four-fifths of the votes cast. Few persons, if any, predicted that this new structure of public powers would result in the decisive preeminence of the president of the republic over both the government and parliament.

Undoubtedly, the circumstances under which the general had come back to power (which he had relinquished twelve and a half years earlier because he disapproved of the role that the parties wanted to play) as well the resounding vote of confidence suggested by the results of the referendum indicated that he would be the one who, a few weeks later, would accede to the presidency of the new republic. There was also little doubt that he would play a major role in determining and conducting a new Algerian policy for France.[1] But it was generally felt that presidential supremacy would be exercised fully only in regard to the Algerian problem and that, in terms

[1] It is true that the predictions as to what this new policy would be were very divergent. Some relied on General de Gaulle to defeat the rebellion and definitely attach the three Algerian departments to France through a policy of integration. Others were hoping, quite differently, that, sensitive to the "wind of change" that, after World War II, had transformed the relationship between old imperial powers and their colonial territories, he would follow a policy that would satisfy the aspirations of Algerian Moslems. Had not the creation of the "Community" to which the population of black Africa, except Guinea, had given a resounding yes on September 29, 1958, created a structure into which, at the right time, an Algeria freed of the colonial domination it had known for more than a century could be inserted?

of time, that supremacy would be limited to the presidency of Charles de Gaulle.

According to the new constitution, the president of the Republic was to be appointed by an electoral college composed of about eighty thousand people (whereas there were 26.5 million voters in France): in addition to the members of parliament, the college comprised departmental and municipal councillors whose number was arranged so as to favor, just as for senatorial elections, the least populated departments and communes. In other words, this was an electoral body in no way representative of public opinion. Whatever the role Charles de Gaulle was to play in the affairs of state, it seemed obvious that such a method of electing the president was not meant to confer upon those who would succeed him at the Élysée the same amount of authority. Even if there was to be preeminence of the presidency, it would essentially be a matter of circumstances rather than one of structure.

Moreover, the constitution of the Fifth Republic was supposed to have defined a parliamentary regime. The parts that were different from the constitution of the Fourth Republic seemed merely intended to prevent the return to the so-called *régime d'assemblée:* the new arrangement gave the government–but still a government responsible to parliament–the authority and permanence sufficient to insure that this responsibility did not degenerate into dependence.

As for the president of the republic, he was seen as an arbiter, not in the sense, according to Littré, of being the "absolute master," but rather, still according to Littré, as the one who, "agreed to by the parties, settles a conflict."

In other words, presidential intervention was expected only in cases of disagreements between government and parliament. This was made clear in a speech with which Michel Debré, minister of justice in Charles de Gaulle's government and the most prominent among those who drafted the constitutional text, presented the constitution to the Council of state.[2] "The president of the republic," he said, "must be the keystone *of our parliamentary regime*" (emphasis added). After enumerating the means the head of state would have to play this role–that is, to prevent the return to a *régime d'assemblée*–Michel Debré concluded on this point: ". . . the president

[2] See the text of this speech in Jean Louis Quermonne, *Le gouvernement de la France sous la Ve Republique* (Paris: Dalloz, 1980), pp. 621-622.

of the republic, *as is proper, has no other power than the one to solicit another power:* (emphasis supplied) he solicits parliament [by the nomination of the government, as well as by the possible request for a new reading of a bill before its promulgation, and by the right of addressing a message to parliament, an act which no longer needs to be countersigned]; he solicits the Conseil Constitutionnel [by referring laws to it if there is any doubt about their constitutionality]; he solicits the electorate [when he decides to dissolve the National Assembly or when, upon the suggestion of either the government or the parliament, he calls for a referendum]. But the possibility to solicit in these ways is fundamental" (emphasis added).

We must, however, point out that this description of the role of the president did not take into consideration certain provisions of the new constitution. Partisans of a strictly parliamentary interpretation of the text tended to consider these changes stylistic passages, but Charles de Gaulle attached to them capital importance.

This is true, first of all, of Article 16, which authorizes the president to temporarily assume full powers "when the institutions of the Republic, the independence of the nation, the integrity of its territory or the fulfillment of its international commitments are threatened in an grave and immediate manner and when the regular functioning of the constitutional public authorities is interrupted." To justify the insertion of this article in the constitution, de Gaulle had invoked the events of June 1940, when President Albert Lebrun was said to have been powerless to counteract Philippe Pétain's and Pierre Laval's policy of surrender. Therefore, one would assume that the conditions necessary to apply clause 16 would make its use entirely exceptional.

But the same was not true of Article 5, which states that "the president of the republic shall see that the constitution is respected. He shall insure, by his arbitration, the regular functioning of governmental authorities, as well as the continuity of the state. He shall be the guarantor of national independence, of the integrity of the territory, and of respect for community agreements and treaties." If among those belonging to the political class there was an inclination to underestimate the impact of such formulas, it is obvious that de Gaulle these statements were, on the contrary, essential: to him, they conferred upon the president (in spite of Article 68, which states that the president is accountable only in cases of high treason) an imperative duty; in de Gaulle's estimation, a president who would not assume personally and fully the responsibilities described in Article 5 would thereby have betrayed his duties.

No less significant for the new dimension that the duties of the president acquired (compared with those of the president in the Third and Fourth Republics) are the sections defining his powers on military matters. According to Article 3 of the constitutional law of February 25, 1875, the president merely had the armed forces "at his disposal"; he did not command them. According to Article 33 of the 1946 constitution, the president "took the title" of the Commander of the Armed Forces. But, according to Article 15 of the constitution of 1958, the president of the republic "*is* the Commander of the armed forces" (emphasis added), obviously a considerable difference from the rather ridiculous formula of 1946!

All this leads to the conclusion that the constitution of 1958 left open various possibilities for the effective functioning of the new institution and, in particular, for the role to be played by the president of the republic. His role could have been merely that of a referee, as the word is used in sports: someone who, without getting involved in the game, would limit himself to making sure that the rules were observed and to adding up the score: but this would have meant that the president would ignore Article 5 and consider his title of commander of the armed forces nominal. The latter duties implied that unless he decided otherwise, he would become, maybe not the "absolute master" (for in a democracy, the last word always belongs to the electorate, as long as the people can be consulted), but at least the master of those holding public power and, as long as the people had confidence in him, he would be invested with an undeniable supremacy over all the other powers, government as well as parliament.

THE EVOLUTION OF PRESIDENTIAL POWER

As is well known, the practice of the Fifth Republic has been oriented toward the preponderance of presidential powers. Under what circumstances did this come about?

The first indication of the entirely new role of the president of the republic compared with the tradition of the Third and Fourth Republics and with rules of a classical parliamentary system was the communiqué of January 9, 1959, in which de Gaulle announced the day after he took office the appointment of Michel Debré as prime minister. The latter, the communiqué announced, "has *submitted for General de Gaulle's approval* his conception of the general policy [of the government] and the names of the personalities who would, *if the occasion presents itself,* become his collaborators in the government" (emphasis added). The president's approval of the prime minister's general policy and of the composition of the government corresponded neither to former customs nor to the rules of the parliamentary regime; according to them, the chief of state has neither to approve nor to disapprove of the program of the majority leader whom he appoints to constitute the government. During the first years of the new constitution it was believed that the personal role of de Gaulle would manifest itself mainly in regard to Algeria. He was still president of the Council of Ministers when he set forth his program for development of the Algerian economy in his speech at Constantine on October 3, 1958. He then said that it was completely useless to freeze into words an undertaking that would have to develop gradually. But as president of the republic he announced on September 16, 1959, the policy of self-determination that would recognize, after the end of the fighting, the right of the Algerians to decide themselves the fate of Algeria. A month later, on October 12, the prime minister assumed his government's responsibility before the National Assembly with a declaration of general policy that contained the themes of the presidential speech of September 16. During the debate, the socialist speakers made it clear that their vote of approval expressed their confidence in the president of the republic and not in the prime minister and the government. On the other hand, a right-wing deputy, François Valentin, supporter of both a French Algeria and a strictly parliamentary interpretation of the regime, pretended to ignore the September 16 speech, maintaining that the assembly did not have to take cognizance of the statements made by the president, since the president was not responsible to the assembly; instead, he concentrated his criticism on Michel Debré's declaration. The declaration was approved by 441 votes, which included all of the deputies left of center–i.e., the Socialists and the Radicals–while the 8 communists abstained. Sixty deputies, most of them from Algeria, refused to vote, and only 23, among them François Valentin, voted against. By their vote the opposition on the left not only had approved the policy of self-determination, but also had ratified unanimously de Gaulle's interpretation of his powers.

In February 1960, after the "week of the barricades," which the partisans of a French Algeria had set up in Algeria, the same opposition on the left continued to emphasize its support of the broadest possible interpretation of presidential powers. The government had asked parliament, in accordance with Article 38 of the constitution, to authorize it to take by ordinance certain measures concerning Algeria that would normally belong to the domain of the law. Article 13 of the constitution prescribes that the president of the republic must sign all ordinances. A deputy of the Popular Republican Movement (MRP) proposed nevertheless that all ordinances enacted under this particular enabling act would be signed explicitly by de Gaulle. The entire Left voted for this amendment, which was adopted. Although without legal signifiance, this vote nevertheless had a very clear political significance: the deputies and parties opposed to the government or (as was the case with the MRP) cautious toward it wanted the president of the republic to determine and apply France's Algerian policy.

Space does not permit me to go into further details. But on the whole, throughout the first years of the constitution, the political formations theoretically the most attached to a parliamentary interpretation of the new institutions of the republic gave their approval to the presidential interpretation whenever Algeria was involved. By doing so, they did much to persuade public opinion of the legitimacy of that interpretation. And they acted in this way in spite of their opposition–argued, incidentally, not on constitutional grounds but for substantive reasons–to the defense and European policies pursued by the government in line with the concepts publicly affirmed by the president of the republic.

This attitude can be explained mostly by the conviction shared by nearly all deputies of the old parties of the Fourth Republic–Moderates, MRP, Radicals, and Socialists–that once the parenthesis opened in 1958 because of the necessity to rely on de Gaulle for the solution of the Algerian problem was closed, France would necessarily return to the normal functioning of its institutions–in other words, to the traditions and habits of the Third and Fourth Republics.

This explains why, as soon as the voters had approved the Évian agreements by the referendum of April 8, 1962, the opposition, composed of the old parties from right, center, and left, took courage and assumed a critical view of Charles de Gaulle and his policies. It also explains the reduced majority (far fewer than half of the total number of deputies) for the government of Georges Pompidou (who had replaced Debré at the helm) when that government sought, after the Évian agreements, parliamentary approval for its programs. Furthermore, the attitude explains the resignation of the ministers belonging to the MRP one month after the government had assumed office, because they considered utterances by de Gaulle during a press conference to be anti-European. And finally, it explains a manifesto, read in parliament on June 13 during a debate on foreign policy, signed by 293 deputies, a clear majority of the assembly, and violently hostile to the international policy of de Gaulle.

But out of fear that parliament might be dissolved, the majority of opponents refrained from voting for a motion of censure on that occasion as well as in July, during a vote on the French nuclear deterrent. The opposition hoped to get rid of de Gaulle at the occasion of the parliamentary elections, scheduled for March 1963. But his counteroffensive would thwart this all-too-long-term strategy.

On June 8, 1962, the president had announced that there would be "by way of referendum" an occasion "at the appropriate time to insure that in the future, beyond the men who come and go, the republic could remain strong, well-ordered, and continuous." Obviously this meant that the method of electing the president would have to be changed to insure for future holders of the post the same authority de Gaulle owed to his historical role. In other words, the election by a college of departmental and municipal notables would have to be replaced by universal suffrage.

The emotion caused by the failed attempt on his life at Petit Clamart on August 22, 1962, led Charles de Gaulle to think that the "appropriate time" to which he had referred on June 8 had arrived.

Upon de Gaulle's return from his triumphant trip to the German Federal Republic, the communiqué by the Council of Ministers of September 12 announced a referendum to establish the election of the president by popular vote. The meaning of this decision was clear: it was to give an unshakable base to the preeminence of the head of state over the other holders of public powers.

As soon as parliament reconvened, opposition broke loose. On October 5, the National Assembly censured the government for having proposed the referendum, whose date had already been set for October 28. As expected, de Gaulle pronounced the dissolution of parliament. The referendum would therefore be followed by parliamentary elections three weeks later.

These two votes would spell total defeat for the opposition. On October 28, the "No" vote, supported by all old parties, received only 28.29 percent of the votes of the registered voters (and 37.74 percent of the ballots cast) as opposed to 46.64 percent of the registered voters (and 62.25 percent of the ballots cast) for the "Yes" vote. By deciding to vote themselves for the president, the French people evidently had ratified de Gaulle's interpretation of the role he had exercised since January 8, 1959.

In the November elections, the parties favorable to the president of the republic obtained 269 seats, a clear majority of the 482 members of the National Assembly. As Jacques Chapsal put it, it was "the absolute beginning of the Fifth Republic."[3] The universal suffrage had chosen unequivocally one of the two possible interpretations of the constitution.

THE GROWTH OF PRESIDENTIAL PREEMINENCE

The development that the functioning of the French institutions has undergone from late 1962 to early 1982 has confirmed and increased presidential preeminence by broadening its scope.

However, it would be inaccurate to think, as is sometimes done, that General de Gaulle, while keeping for himself matters concerning defense and foreign policy, left his prime minister and other members of the government full freedom in other fields, espe-

[3] Jacques Chapsal, *La vie politique sous la Ve République* (Paris: Presses Universitaires Françaises, 1980), p. 260.

cially in economic policy. A book by one of his former staff members at Élysée[4] has shown how the plan of stabilization and of controlling the overheating economy in 1963 owed its existence to the president of the republic much more than to the prime minister (Georges Pompidou) and the minister of economy and finances (Valéry Giscard d'Estaing) who were less convinced than was de Gaulle about the disadvantages of inflation. In the fall of 1968 the general talked with me about the stabilization plan that he had "imposed on Giscard and other Pompidous." We also know that in the fall of 1969 de Gaulle had personally decided (on the advice of Jean-Marcel Jeanneney, Raymond Barre, and Roger Goetze) to brush aside the devaluation plan proposed by the finance minister.

As can be seen, de Gaulle did not refrain from intervening personally in all spheres of governmental activity. But, apart from matters of defense and foreign policy, he did so only from time to time when he thought it necessary. "In order not to interfere with the authority and the responsibility of the ministers," wrote Jean-Marcel Jeanneney, who held ministerial office for more than six years, "he never intervened directly in their affairs and would not have tolerated his staff members doing so."[5] Perhaps other ministers, less competent than Jeanneney, would correct this testimony somewhat. Moreover, Jeanneney himself admits that even in matters other than defense or foreign policy, the general from time to time "determined the general orientation."

But it is certain that the first two successors of de Gaulle at the Élysée, Georges Pompidou and Valéry Giscard d'Estaing, took, in both theory and practice, a far broader view of the presidential role than had de Gaulle.

Having been prime miniter at Matignon for more than six years, Pompidou was familiar with all aspects of governmental activity. This helps to explain why, beginning in June 1969, intervention of the president of the republic increased in all areas. Nobody would have imagined, for example, during the days of de Gaulle, that the president would personally take decisions concerning urbanism in the Paris region.

[4] Alain Prate, *Les batailles économiques du Générale de Gaulle* (Paris: Plon, 1978).
[5] Jean-Marcel Jeanneney, *A mes amis gaullistes* (Paris: Presses Pocket, 1973), p. 33.

The differences of temperament between Pompidou and Jacques Chaban-Delmas, named prime minister in June 1969, and the antagonism that rapidly created opposition between some advisers of the president (Pierre Juillet and Marie-France Garaud) and those of the prime minister (Jacques Delors and Simon Nora) contributed to the president's watching the daily action of the government much more closely than had been the case from 1959 to 1969. Jacques Chaban-Delmas wrote, "Georges Pompidou, having been prime minister for a long time, tended to follow the affairs of the state very closely and, on occasion, preceded them."[6] It seems also that the project of a "new society" developed before the National Assembly on September 16, 1969, by Chaban-Delmas was not submitted to the president of the republic in advance, except in a vague manner. Chaban-Delmas has himself admitted[7] that the text of his speech was conveyed to the Élysée at the last minute, and at the request of the president. It is clear that Pompidou's pragmatic and conservative temper made him skeptical and even alarmed about the reform projects of his fiery prime minister; it is not out of the question that some of the difficulties that the latter encountered with his parliamentary majority were due to the fact that the feelings of the president were not unknown at the Bourbon Palace. Jacques Chaban-Delmas nevertheless always recognized presidential supremacy, to the point of once proclaiming that a prime minister who held on to his position against the will of the president would be "a sad specimen."

However that may be, these difference of opinion and a certain incompatibility of temper would lead Pompidou, in the summer of 1972, to ask Chaban-Delmas to resign, which he did immediately. The new prime minister, Pierre Messmer, had been de Gaulle's minister of the army for a long time. Less accustomed to showing initiative than to being a faithful executor of a policy determined by the president of the republic, he never had any problem in recognizing that the power of decision resided always and in every way with Pompidou.

It was during his presidency that the so-called restricted councils and the interministerial committees, which owed their origin to mere practice but were of great importance, became institutionalized,

[6] Jacques Chaban-Delmas, *L'Ardeur* (Paris: Stock, 1975), p. 346.
[7] Ibid., p. 368.

having first appeared under de Gaulle but less frequently and less systematically.

Under the Third and Fourth Republics, ministers met regularly without the president of the republic in a "cabinet council" to prepare the decisions of the Council of Ministers. At the very beginning of the government of Michel Debré, de Gaulle told his prime minister that he did not find it normal for the ministers to meet together except under his chairmanship. Nevertheless, certain decisions of the cabinet pertaining to several ministerial departments had necessarily to be prepared by the ministers concerned. Eventually, this led inevitably to the creation of two different types of working groups whose meetings prepared the meetings of the whole cabinet.

The restricted councils (Conseils Restreints) are held at the Élysée, under the chairmanship of the president of the republic. Up until the presidency of Giscard d'Estaing, the general secretariat of the government was represented. Always present are the prime minister, the ministers involved in the matters under discussion, and a few high civil servants. The interministerial committees meet at Matignon under the chairmanship of the prime minister. Besides the relevant ministers and their staffs, there are always members of the General Secretariat of the president of the Republic present. Thus the Élysée can constantly monitor the orientation of governmental activities and, if necessary, change it in accordance with the intentions of the president of the republic.

Except for the elimination of members of the general secretariat of the government by Giscard d'Estaing–an elimination that caused and probably was meant to increase the preeminence of the president of the republic–the functioning of this mechanism of the restricted councils and the interministerial committees, intended to prepare the work of the Council of Ministers, has not changed since the early 1970s. Whatever differences exist are related to the respective importance of these two types of meetings: since the election of François Mitterrand to the presidency of the republic, it seems–although no statistic can be quoted yet–that the proportion of committees gathered at Matignon has increased considerably in comparison with the councils held at the Élysée. But this does not necessarily mean that the influence of the president on the conduct of public policy has diminished, even though it has become less visible.

During the presidency of Giscard d'Estaing, the interventions of the president into public policy took a new turn. The president took to making public every six months the letters he wrote to the prime minister in which he defined the agenda for governmental work. But the then prime minister, Raymond Barre, once implied to reporters that he played a great role in drafting those "instructions." In other respects, it is certain that Giscard d'Estaing was not as careful as his predecessors had been in avoiding direct contacts with ministers and thereby short-circuiting the prime minister. One source has cited a letter of the president to the secretary of state for culture concerning street names in old sections of cities.[8]

We must also point out that when Jacques Chirac's government was formed, the president, Giscard d'Estaing, imposed the appointment of his adviser and former staff member, Jean-Pierre Fourcade, as minister of economy and finance and that for two years the economic, financial, and fiscal policies (for example, the bill introducing an excess profit tax) seem to have been determined directly between the president and the finance minister without any effective intervention by the prime minister. This explains why, in his letter of resignation (dated July 16, 1976, but published only a month later), Jacques Chirac explained his decision to leave office by the fact that the president did not seem willing to increase unequivocally the authority of the prime minister, an increase that to him seemed indispensable.[9]

From 1976 to 1981, Raymond Barre having become prime minister, the job of determining and conducting the economic and financial policies was left to him to a far greater extent than had been the case for Jacques Chirac. Giscard d'Estaing went even so far as to imply that an unpopular measure (the increase of Social Security contributions) was not his doing and that he had pleaded with the government that it be a temporary measure.

[8] Francis de Baecque, *Qui gouverne la France?* (Paris: Presses Universitaires Françaises, 1976), p. 140.

[9] See the text of this letter in Didier Maus, *La pratique institutionnelle de la Ve République* (Paris: Documentation Française, 1978), p. 80.

On the other hand, the personal intervention of the president of the republic in regard to the nominations of high civil servants or even of mere members of the advisory committees existing in certain ministries became more frequent. I could cite, if I did not feel bound by an obligation to be discreet, a case in which a nomination approved by a minister was blocked by a presidential veto.

It is true that, with regard to an appointment approved by the prime minister, the latter told me that there would be no obstacle, since he would speak personally to the president about it and that difficulties arose only when such a matter was handled by the staffs *(entourages)*.

Judging from the first months of the presidency of François Mitterrand, it does not seem that the election of the socialist candidate to the presidency of the republic will alter the preeminence of the president. "The institutions were not made with me in mind," declared François Mitterrand at the beginning of his term, "but they suit me well."[10] Even before he was elected, the president-to-be had said he would be bound only by his own declarations. He confirmed this in his speech at Montélimar on June 8, 1981: the "commitments which I undertook during the electoral campaign will constitute in all areas the charter of governmental action." Can a clearer statement on the subordination of the government to the president be made? "No one ignores," he also said, "that the president of the republic can, at all times, make his conception of the national interest prevail."[11] And on September 8, 1981, in a conversation with Oliver Todd, on British television, he reiterated that "between a President of the Republic and a prime minister, it is agreed, under the Fifth Republic, the prime minister must leave when it is necessary."

In other words, it is clear that François Mitterrand, whose political orientation is different from that of his predecessor, except in matters of defense and foreign policy, has no intention of giving up the presidential supremacy that Charles de Gaulle legitimized by getting the president elected with universal suffrage and that Georges Pompidou and then Valéry Giscard d'Estaing have anchored deeply in the political culture of the French people.

[10] Interview in *Le Monde*, July 2, 1981.
[11] Ibid.

Chapter 4

FREEDOM OF SPEECH, JUDICIAL REVIEW, AND PUBLIC POLICYMAKING IN THE UNITED STATES

Dean Alfange, Jr.

INTRODUCTION

A fundamental problem of government, in an age in which the preservation of individual liberty has come to be justly prized as an essential element of the common good, is the maintenance of a proper balance between liberty and authority. Where one would locate the balance point in a precise case, of course, depends on the values assigned to the particular liberty that is to be abridged and the social interest to be defended. Yet, in all cases in which social interests are at stake, there must be a point at which the protection of freedom can begin to undermine the capacity of society to promote effectively the well-being of its members. Until recent years, judicial power, notably in the United States, could generally be counted on to be on the side of the persons and groups with ample economic resources who zealously insisted upon the recognition of the widest scope for their economic liberty. This judicial defense of the economic liberty of those capable of assuming a position of dominance in society in the absence of government intervention came under increasingly bitter criticism in the early years of the twentieth century from observers who perceived that such liberty could be maintained only at the expense of government efforts to promote the social welfare.

In the years following the New Deal reaction to the Depression, U.S. judges lost their concern for the protection of property rights and began to develop a constitutional jurisprudence that emphasized the protection of the rights of racial, religious, and political minorities against abridgment by an intolerant majority. The broad favor with which these more recent decisions have been received has emboldened the judges to expand the range and scope of constitutionally protected liberty,–generally with salutary results. Yet every expansion of liberty–even in the area of speech–has to be paid for by a certain loss of governmental capacity to protect the public interest through control of private behavior. Where the liberties to be protected are those of powerless minorities, this diminution of governmental authority may be of little consequence. But expansion of the social and political liberties of those in a position to exercise broad power in the society–like expansion of their economic liberties–entails a much greater risk of disabling critical governmental authority. Examination of trends in the protection of freedom of speech by the U.S. Supreme Court in the past decade seems to suggest that the current willingness of the judiciary to force U.S. society to run that risk may be far greater than is either necessary or desirable.

FREEDOM OF SPEECH AND THE PROTECTION OF ECONOMIC POWER

One of the great milestones in the development of the constitutional law of free speech in the United States was the decision of the Supreme Court in *Gitlow* v. *New York*[1] in 1925, when, in the course of deciding whether the state of New York could constitutionally punish advocacy of revolution (a question it answered affirmatively), the Court held for the first time that the guarantee of free speech in the First Amendment to the federal constitution applied to the states as well as to the federal government.[2] In so doing it specifically repudiated the contrary position it had asserted only three years before in *Prudential Insurance Co.* v. *Cheek,*[3] where it categorically declared that nothing in the federal constitution "imposes upon the states any restrictions about freedom of speech."[4] This shift of posi-

[1] 268 U.S. 652 (1925).
[2] *Id.* at 666.
[3] 259 U.S. 530 (1922).
[4] *Id.* at 543.

tion from *Cheek* to *Gitlow* has generally been looked upon as a liberal move, and so, in fact, it turned out to be–but only after the composition of the Court later changed.

As the outcome of the *Gitlow* case itself clearly demonstrates, the Court majority in 1925 had little interest in providing constitutional protection against the suppression of unpopular ideas. Why then did they abandon the position that had been enunciated in *Cheek?* The probable answer is that the holding in *Gitlow* was intended to have a conservative, not a liberal, thrust. There were three dissenters (without opinion) to the decision in *Cheek:* Chief Justice Taft and Justices VanDevanter and McReynolds–by any measure the most conservative members of the 1922 Court. The issue in that case had been the validity of a Missouri law requiring employers to provide persons leaving their employ with a letter stating the character of their service. The Prudential Insurance Company did not wish to comply with this requirement, presumably because it would lessen the impact of a threat of discharge, and unsuccessfully challenged the law, among other grounds, as an abridgment of its freedom of speech, or, more precisely, its corollary freedom to remain silent when it did not desire to speak. But between *Cheek* and *Gitlow* President Harding had the opportunity to appoint three new Justices (Sutherland, Butler, and Sanford) with powerful conservative leanings. These three joined with the dissenters in *Cheek* to announce in *Gitlow* that freedom of speech was thenceforth to be constitutionally protected against state abridgment.[5] Since this protection was not to extend to those holding dissentient beliefs, it would appear that what the *Gitlow* majority had in mind was the creation of a constitutional weapon that could be used in a proper case to protect businesses or other similar worthy claimants against certain kinds of burdensome state regulations. If, in the future, the Prudential Insurance Company were to decline to provide a statement of the character of service of a former employee, it would be able to call on the judiciary for protection.[6]

[5] By 1925, the dissenters in *Gitlow*–Justices Holmes and Brandeis–were also willing to accept the proposition that freedom of speech was protected by the Constitution against state abridgment, but, in contrast to the majority, these two Justices thought that the Constitution ought also to protect the speech of political radicals. See 268 U.S. at 672-673 (dissenting opinion).

[6] For a clear indication of what the *Gitlow* majority evidently hoped to accomplish through the use of the First Amendment, see *Associated Press* v. *NLRB*, 301 U.S. 103

The *Gitlow* majority had ceased to be a majority before it found an occasion to employ the free-speech guarantee for such a purpose, and, when opportunities to do so arose later, the new majority of the 1930s ignored them.[7] But developments in the constitutional law of free speech in the 1970s seem to suggest a renaissance of the constitutional approach the *Gitlow* majority had evidently sought to establish. As Archibald Cox has recently noted, the "major new departures" in the area of free speech undertaken by the Supreme Court since 1976 have been "the extension of the first amendment to 'commercial speech' and the recognition of a first amendment right of both individuals and corporations to make at least some kinds of political expenditures in connection with referendums or election campaigns."[8] For the most part, these new departures have nothing to do with protecting the right of political, religious, or social dissidents to express attitudes or beliefs repugnant to the public or to particular government officials; they serve rather to enhance the translation of financial resources into political power or economic

(1937), in which the Supreme Court rejected the claim that it was a violation of the First Amendment to restrain the Associated Press, under the National Labor Relations Act of 1935, from discharging editorial employees for union-organizing activity. Justices VanDevanter, McReynolds, Sutherland, and Butler–the four remaining members of the *Gitlow* majority–dissented, although none of them had seen any constitutional problem with the imprisonment of political dissidents in *Gitlow* or in *Whitney* v. *California*, 274 U.S. 357 (1927), or with the imposition of prior restraint on critics of government in *Near* v. *Minnesota*, 283 U.S. 697 (1931). In his opinion for the dissenters in the *Associated Press* case, however, Justice Sutherland wrote passionately of the importance of defending the First Amendment rights of news organizations as employers: "Do the people of this land–in the providence of God, favored, as they sometimes boast, above all others in the plenitude of their liberties–desire to preserve those so carefully protected by the First Amendment . . . ? If so, let them withstand all *beginnings* of encroachment." 301 U.S. at 141 (dissenting opinion) (emphasis in original).

[7] See *Associated Press* v. *NLRB*, supra note 6, at 130-133; *Associated Press* v. *United States*, 326 U.S. 1, 19-20 (1945), where the Court, in an opinion by Justice Black, rejected the claim that the application of the Sherman Anti-Trust Act to enjoin the Associated Press from limiting its membership and prohibiting sales of AP news to nonmembers was a violation of the First Amendment; *Mabee* v. *White Plains Publishing Co.*, 327 U.S. 178, 184 (1946) and *Oklahoma Press Publishing Co.* v. *Walling*, 327 U.S. 186, 192-193 (1946), in which the Court, almost without discussion, dismissed First Amendment challenges to the application to newspaper publishers of the wage and hour provisions of the Fair Labor Standards Act of 1938.

[8] Archibald Cox, *Freedom of Expression*, (Cambridge, Mass.: Harvard University Press, 1981), pp. 86-87.

success. Like the contrast between the issues presented to the Court in *Gitlow* and *Cheek,* the nature of these developments demonstrates that a wide variety of claims can be fitted, however awkwardly, under the umbrella of freedom of speech–a fact that ought not to be without significance in determining the proper role of courts in the review of legislative actions in this area.

THE NEED FOR JUDICIAL PROTECTION OF FREEDOM OF SPEECH

It now seems so much of a commonplace that courts will grant little or no deference to legislative judgments with regard to laws touching on freedom of speech that it is difficult to recall that it remains true, as Earl Latham wrote over thirty years ago, that "the notion that freedom of speech is the care of the judges is relatively recent."[9] Prior to 1919, the Supreme Court treated as essentially frivolous the rare free-speech claim that found its way to its docket.[10] But it was the refusal of the Court to give adequate consideration to the First Amendment claims presented in the free-speech cases of 1919 and the 1920s arising from the enforcement of federal legislation enacted to safeguard the war effort during World War I[11] and of state laws aimed at suppressing the expression of revolutionary radicals[12] that demonstrated starkly that active judicial protection of freedom of speech was essential if that freedom was to have any real meaning for those whose ideas were looked upon by the public as hateful.[13] And this demonstration was subsequently reinforced by judicial acquiescence in the harassment of the radical left undertaken by both the federal and state governments in the

[9] Earl Latham, "The Theory of the Judicial Concept of Freedom of Speech," 12 *Journal of Politics* 637, 638 (1950).

[10] See, e.g., *Patterson* v. *Colorado,* 205 U.S. 454 (1907); *Fox* v. *Washington,* 236 U.S. 273 (1915).

[11] See, e.g., *Schenck* v. *United States,* 249 U.S. 47 (1919); *Abrams* v. *United States,* 250 U.S. 616 (1919).

[12] See, e.g., *Gitlow* v. *New York,* 268 U.S. 652 (1925); *Whitney* v. *California,* 274 U.S. 357 (1927).

[13] For the classic discussion of the First Amendment issues arising in the courts in the years following World War I, see Zechariah Chafee, *Free Speech in the United States,* (Cambridge, Mass.: Harvard University Press, 1941), pp. 36-354.

late 1940s and the 1950s.[14] At the same time, the salutary effects of an activist judiciary in this area were clearly to be seen in the Supreme Court's defense of the right of Jehovah's Witnesses to refuse to participate in a flag-salute ceremony that was contrary to their religious beliefs,[15] of the right of civil-rights advocates to be free from oppression by state and local governments in the south in the 1950s and 1960s,[16] and, beginning about 1963, of the rights of expression and association of left-wing dissidents.[17]

The lesson of this history is that if the freedom of speech of those whose ideas and beliefs are intensely objectionable to the public or the government is not "the care of the judges," that freedom will exist for such persons only at the sufferance of a majority likely to be decidedly disinclined towards tolerance. Because the legislative and executive branches of government can be expected to be responsive to the intolerances and emotions of their constituents, close and skeptical judicial scrutiny of the asserted justification for governmental action aimed at the suppression of unpopular beliefs or the penalization of those who hold them is absolutely essential. In such cases, judges should withhold deference to the judgment asserted by the legislature as to the need for a particular limitation on speech and should undertake to determine for themselves whether the restriction to be imposed is genuinely necessary to meet that need. That is the heart of the wisdom reflected in Justice Stone's *Carolene Products* footnote of 1938, where

[14] See, among many examples, *Dennis* v. *United States,* 341 U.S. 494 (1951); *Scales* v. *United States,* 367 U.S. 203 (1961); *Uphaus* v. *Wyman,* 360 U.S. 72 (1959). See also, generally, C. Herman Pritchett *Civil Liberties and the Vinson Court,* (Chicago: University of Chicago Press, 1954); C. Herman Pritchett, *The Political Offender and the Warren Court* (Boston: Boston University Press, 1958).

[15] Compare *Minersville School District* v. *Gobitis,* 310 U.S. 586 (1940), with *West Virginia State Board of Education* v. *Barnette,* 319 U.S. 624 (1943). For an excellent discussion of the confrontation between the Jehovah's Witnesses and state and local governments in this period, with special attention to the flag-salute controversy, see David Manwaring, *Render Unto Caesar* (Chicago: University of Chicago Press, 1962).

[16] See, *e.g., NAACP* v. *Alabama,* 357 U.S. 449 (1958); *Edwards* v. *South Carolina,* 372 U.S. 229 (1963). See, generally, Harry Kalven, *The Negro and the First Amendment* (Colombus, Ohio: Ohio State University Press, 1965).

[17] See, *e.g., Aptheker* v. *Secretary of State,* 378 U.S. 500 (1964); *United States* v. *Robel,* 389 U.S. 258 (1967); *Keyishian* v. *Board of Regents,* 385 U.S. 589 (1967). As Harry Kalven perceptively observed in 1965, "it would not be a bad summary of the last three decades of First Amendment issues in the Court to say simply: Jehovah Witnesses, Communists, Negroes." Kalven, *op. cit. supra,* note 16, pp. 135-136.

it is suggested that "prejudice against discrete and insular minorities may be a special condition . . . which may call for a correspondingly more searching judicial inquiry" into the need for the challenged legislation than would otherwise be appropriate.[18]

Moreover, one can readily agree with the Supreme Court's pronouncement in 1964 that protection of the right to criticize the policies of government or the conduct of government officials is "the central meaning of the First Amendment."[19] And that "central meaning" can legitimately be described in still broader terms. What ought to be at the core of the amendment is a respect for the inviolability of the right to hold and to express *any* belief, without regard to considerations of how good, bad, or dangerous that belief may be deemed to be.[20] There can be no valid justification for punishing an individual merely for holding certain beliefs or, at least in the absence of a genuine "clear and present danger," for attempting to explain or defend those beliefs or to persuade others of their soundness.

The demonstrable need for judicial activism to protect critics of government or those who hold and express unpopular ideas, however, says nothing about the need for such activism where regulation of speech takes place in a context in which there is no indication that harassment of particular individuals or groups or suppression of their beliefs is the government's aim. That the courts ought not to defer to the judgment of a governmental body that schoolchildren of an unpopular religious faith should be required to express patriotic sentiments that are offensive to the beliefs of that faith does not demonstrate that courts ought not to defer to a legislative judgment that employers must be required to provide a letter for former employees stating the nature and character of their service. In the latter situation, in the absence of special circum-

[18] *United States* v. *Carolene Products Co.*, 304 U.S. 144, 152-153 n.4 (1938).

[19] *New York Times Co.* v. *Sullivan*, 376 U.S. 254, 273 (1964). For a strong endorsement of the view that prohibiting the punishment of seditious libel should be at the heart of the First Amendment's guarantee, see Kalven, "The New York Times Case: A Note on 'the Central Meaning of the First Amendment,'" 1964 *Supreme Court Review* 191, 205.

[20] See Thomas Scanlon, "A Theory of Freedom of Expression," 1 *Philosophy and Public Affairs* 204, 213 (1972). Cf. Laurence Tribe, *American Constitutional Law*, p. 581 (1978); John Hart Ely, *Democracy and Distrust*, (Cambridge: Harvard University Press, 1980), pp. 111-112.

stances that might generate suspicion regarding governmental motivation, why would it be inappropriate to allow the legislature's judgment as to the need for the law to prevail? It is hard to see why Justice Reed was wrong when he wrote for the Court in 1953: "Regulation and suppression [of speech] are not the same, either in purpose or result, and courts of justice can tell the difference."[21]

Failure to make such distinctions among free-speech claims, and insistence in all cases upon rigorous application of strict judicial scrutiny–which, in its purest form, would place essentially insuperable obstacles in the way of sustaining the constitutionality of legislation–could have pernicious effects by frustrating valid governmental efforts to protect important social interests in the name of safeguarding speech against restrictions that pose no realistic threat to the values that the Constitution should be expected to protect. In many respects, the "major new departures" of the Supreme Court in the area of First Amendment adjudication that Archibald Cox has identified would appear to have done just this–to have extended judicial activism beyond the areas where it is undeniably justified in order to strike down laws whose manifest purpose was the protection of important–in some cases, urgent–social interests, whose effect was not to suppress particular ideas or information, and whose burden did not fall most prominently on "discrete and insular minorities" incapable of defending themselves adequately in the political process, but frequently fell on groups notable for their political efficacy.

THE PROHIBITION OF LIMITATIONS ON CAMPAIGN EXPENDITURES

Perhaps the most striking of the "new departure" decisions was *Buckley* v. *Valeo*[22] in 1976, in which the Court invalidated key provisions of the Federal Election Campaign Act Amendments of 1974[23] limiting the permissible expenditures of individuals or groups on behalf of candidates for federal elective office, limiting the amount an individual candidate could spend from personal or family funds

[21] *Poulos* v. *New Hampshire,* 345 U.S. 395, 408 (1953).
[22] 424 U.S. 1 (1976).
[23] 88 Stat. 1263 (1975).

on his or her campaign, and limiting the total amount of money that could be spent by a candidate in a federal election campaign. These amendments were enacted by Congress following the dismaying revelations of Watergate, plainly not for any suspect purpose, but to protect the integrity of the federal electoral process against corruption or the appearance of corruption and against possible domination by wealthy candidates.[24] The Supreme Court had accurately described the interests at stake in this case in a 1957 opionion: "[W]hat is involved here is the integrity of our electoral process, and, not less, the responsibility of the individual citizen for the successful functioning of that process. . . . [These are] issues not less than basic to a democratic society."[25]

Treating campaign expenditures as speech, and, therefore, as not subject to regulation except where such regulation is absolutely indispensable to the protection of a compelling governmental interest, the Supreme Court held, in essence, that independent, uncoordinated expenditures by individuals or groups on behalf of a candidate–even in unlimited amounts–could not be constitutionally regulated because such expenditures, being uncoordinated, pose no real danger of corruption,[26] that limiting a candidate's ability to use personal or family funds to finance his or her campaign was an impermissible restriction on public discussion,[27] and that the ceiling on overall campaign expenditures was unconstitutional because government has no legitimate justification for controlling the amount of money spent for promoting political views.[28]

It is not simply that such assertions are ludicrous on their face–particularly the claim that massive expenditures on behalf of a candidate pose no real danger of corruption if not coordinated in advance with the candidate or the campaign staff. The important point is that they are assertions of policy choices in an area where the Court is not justified in substituting its own views for those of Congress as to whether legislation is needed. The challenged provisions were content-neutral–they applied to all expenditures without regard to the nature of the political message being conveyed. They

[24] A succinct statement of these purposes may be found in H.R. Report 93-1239 (93d Cong., 2d Sess.), p. 3.

[25] *United States* v. *United Automobile Workers,* 352 U.S. 567, 570 (1957).

[26] 424 U.S. at 47.

[27] *Id.* at 52-54.

[28] Id. *at 57.*

suppressed the expression of no ideas, popular or unpopular. Although they could have had the effect of curtailing the quantity of political expression, no claim was made that an effective campaign would have been difficult or impossible to conduct within the limits set by the law or that any ideas would have been denied expression. The claim made, and accepted by the Court, was that *any* limitation on campaign expenditures, however marginal its impact, would be a violation of the First Amendment.

Equally significantly, the Court's substitution of its views for those of Congress as to the desirability of this legislation occurred without any apparent basis for believing that the challenged amendments, although neutral on their face, might, by design or inadvertence, have a disproportionally severe impact on candidates holding unpopular views or opposing entrenched interests. In fact, the Court rejected the evidence for these propositions as speculative and inconclusive.[29] For all that appears in the Court's opinion, the expenditure limitations were struck down because of the impact they might have on the candidates of the Republican and Democratic parties for president, vice president, or member of Congress. Yet, surely, of all the people in the United States, these are the least ineffectual politically and thus are least in need of judicial solicitude. While the judiciary must be prepared to override legislative policy judgments in order to protect the rights of "discrete and insular minorities," the justification for activism must be at its lowest ebb when the persons whose rights are to be defended are those who not only influence but actually control the legislative process. One may be quite confident that if the expenditure limitations had proved in practice to impose undue restrictions on the ability of major-party candidates for federal office to conduct their campaigns, to express their ideas, or to reach their desired audience, they would have been promptly amended.

Finally, it is extremely ironic that the Court, whose opinions in other cases repeatedly stress the importance of First Amendment guarantees to the effective functioning of the democratic political process,[30] should use those guarantees to impose severe restraints on the power of Congress to protect the very integrity of that process.

[29] See *id.* at 30-35.

[30] See, among many examples, *New York Times Co.* v. *Sullivan,* 376 U.S. 254, 269-270 (1964).

To be sure, as Justice White noted in his dissent, it must be recognized that "money talks" in politics,[31] but, in Paul Freund's phrase, "that is the problem, not the answer."[32] Whatever indirect and conjectural impact the expenditure limitations may have had on political expression, these limitations were content-neutral and fell primarily on those most capable of protecting themselves politically. And they were justified by the need to safeguard an interest of overwhelming importance. As the Court of Appeals had concluded, the effort by Congress to promote a social interest of such magnitude ought not to be invalidated because it "might have some incidental, not clearly defined, effect on First Amendment freedoms."[33] In the words of Justice White, although there may have been no intention to rule that "federal candidates have the constitutional right to purchase their election, . . . many will so interpret the Court's conclusion in this case."[34] Regrettably, that is so.

To cite another example, in 1978, the Supreme Court, in *First National Bank of Boston* v. *Bellotti*,[35] by a margin of 5-4, struck down an attempt by the state of Massachusetts to control the influence that corporate expenditures might have in influencing the outcome of political referenda by prohibiting such expenditures in relation to referenda except where the result could have a material effect on the corporation's "property, business or assets." Such a limitation, the majority held, was violative of the First Amendment because speech relating to referendum questions is public discussion and is thus "at the heart of the First Amendment's protection." It ought not, the Court held, to lose "that protection simply because the source is a corporation that cannot prove, to the satisfaction of a court, a material effect on its business or property."[36]

By insisting that the constitutional issue whether speech otherwise protected by the First Amendment should lose that protection because its source is a corporation, the Court managed ingeniously

[31] 424 U.S. at 262 (separate opinion).

[32] See Harold Leventhal, "Courts and Political Thickets," 77 *Columbia Law Review* 345, 359 (1977). Judge Leventhal quoted this remark from a column by Anthony Lewis (*New York Times*, February 5, 1976, p. 33), and then noted that Lewis attributed it to Freund.

[33] *Buckley* v. *Valeo*, 519 F.2d 821, 898 (1975).

[34] 424 U.S. at 266 (separate opinion).

[35] 435 U.S. 765 (1978).

[36] *Id.* at 776.

to beg the real question presented by the case. For the simple fact is that speech was not limited by the Massachusetts law–neither speech advocating the approval nor speech advocating the disapproval of any referendum question was prohibited. What was prohibited was the use of corporate funds for such advocacy. Despite the fact that the Court repeatedly discusses whether a corporation may "communicate to the public *its* views" or whether corporations may "make *their* ideas public,"[37] such statements of the issue are plainly misleading. A corporation, being inanimate, has no views or ideas. The views and ideas whose expression was affected by the Massachusetts law were those of the corporation's managers and directors. Since they, as individuals, remain free to advocate adoption or defeat of any referendum question, to spend money for that purpose, and to organize associations and pool their resources to accomplish that end, when one asks whether a corporation may communicate its views to the public, one is really asking whether its managers and directors, in addition to being able to spend their own money to publicize their own ideas, should be free to use corporate funds *(i.e.*, other people's money) to do so. That they must have such a right is far from clear. Surely it ought not to be shocking that government should retain power to control how corporate directors use the money belonging to others that is entrusted to their care by law, even where the money is to be used for the purpose of political advocacy. As Justice White, dissenting, put it, the issue that should properly have been addressed is whether "institutions which have been permitted to amass wealth as a result of special advantages extended by the State for certain economic purposes [may constitutionally be prevented] from using that wealth to acquire an unfair advantage in the political process."[38]

There is no basis in logic or necessity for uncritically extending to corporations the First Amendment rights of natural persons, and, prior to the *Bellotti* decision, the only corporations recognized as having a constitutional right to freedom of expression were newspaper companies and other media corporations[39] and those, such as the NAACP, established for the purpose of advocating and

[37] *Id.* at 784 (emphasis added).

[38] *Id.* at 809 (dissenting opinion). See also *id.* at 823-827 (dissenting opinion of Rehnquist, J.).

[39] See *Grosjean* v. *U.S. Press Co.*, 297 U.S. 233 (1936).

promoting particular ideas.[40] If, as Thomas Emerson, Laurence Tribe, and others have argued, one of the critical reasons for the constitutional protection of freedom of speech is the preservation of human dignity,[41] that purpose is not at all advanced by granting speech rights to corporations,[42] and, as Arthur Miller has commented: "[T]o suggest that AT&T, for example, is the same as a natural person for purposes of the first amendment is to be wilfully blind."[43]

The Court in *Bellotti* sought to overcome these difficulties by ignoring the distinctions between corporations and natural persons and focusing instead on the speech involved. If, it argued, public discussion is constitutionally protected because it provides the people with greater information on political issues and therefore leads to more enlightened decisions by the electorate on these issues, corporate speech is no less informative than individual speech and therefore should be as fully entitled to the protection of the First Amendment.[44] The problem is that that argument proves too much. Simply because speech may serve to inform the public on important matters does not mean that any and all means of conveying a speaker's message to the public or of financing its conveyance should be constitutionally guaranteed. Presumably, a state may validly prohibit the message from being written on the walls of public buildings or of private buildings without the consent of the owner. Presumably, the federal government may forbid a person from using a broadcast frequency without a license even though that person may desire to do so in order to convey a political message. Presumably, also, the Court would reject a constitutional challenge to a conviction for embezzlement or misappropriation of funds based on the claim that the defendant wished to use the money to inform the public on a matter of vital importance. It has been held by the Court that labor unions may not use money collected through a member's dues to espouse a political cause to which the member objects, even though

[40] See *NAACP* v. *Button,* 371 U.S. 415 (1963).

[41] Thomas Emerson, *Toward a General Theory of the First Amendment,* p. 5 (1966); Laurence Tribe, *op. cit. supra,* note 20, p. 578.

[42] See the dissenting opinion of Justice White in *Bellotti,* 435 U.S. at 804-806.

[43] Arthur Miller, "On Politics, Democracy, and the First Amendment: A Commentary on *First National Bank v. Bellotti,*" 38 *Washington and Lee Law Review* 21, 22 (1981).

[44] 435 U.S. at 777.

respecting this objection limits the union's capacity to present information on political matters to the public.[45] Why, then, should the mere fact that the information to be disseminated would be useful to the public confer a constitutional right on corporate managers to use other people's money to disseminate it?

Although the Court declared in *Bellotti* that its decision in that case applied only to spending in referendum elections and would not necessarily control the question of the constitutionality of limitations on corporate spending in candidate elections where, as is not the case with referenda, there

is a danger that a quid pro quo may be sought from the candidate,[46] it is not clear why, inasmuch as the Court, in *Buckley* v. *Valeo,* dismissed concern for the possibility of corruption as a justification for limiting individual or group expenditures in candidate election campaigns, it could be expected to accept that same concern as a justification for limiting corporate or union expenditures in such elections. But if such limitations are no longer constitutionally justifiable, the effect, like the effect of the decision in *Buckley* v. *Valeo,* is to weaken substantially the capacity of government to protect the political process against a major source of corruptive influence. As Arthur Miller has put it: "Those with money . . . now have constitutional *carte blanche* to try to manipulate the political process."[47] That is a high price to pay even if it were in fact what the First Amendment required, but the amendment, of course, requires nothing of the sort.

THE PROTECTION OF COMMERCIAL SPEECH

The decision in *Bellotti* is clearly of a piece with the Burger Court's other new departure in the constitutional law of free speech–the abandonment of the long-standing rule that "commercial speech" is outside the scope of the First Amendment's protection.[48] Specific rejection of the commercial-speech doctrine occurred in

[45] *Machinists* v. *Street,* 367 U.S. 740 (1961); *Abood* v. *Board of Education,* 431 U.S. 209 (1977). See also the dissenting opinion of Justice White in *Bellotti,* 435 U.S. at 813-819.

[46] 435 U.S. at 788 n.26.

[47] Arthur Miller, op. cit. supra, note 43, p. 23.

[48] The old rule was established in *Valentine* v. *Chrestensen,* 316 U.S. 52 (1942).

1976 in *Virginia State Board of Pharmacy* v. *Virginia Citizens Consumer Council,*[49] where the Court repudiated the proposition that "speech which does 'no more than propose a commercial transaction' . . . is so removed from any 'exposition of ideas' . . . that it lacks all protection."[50] The Court conceded that false, deceptive, or misleading advertising, unlike false, deceptive, or misleading political speech, could be validly regulated because of the "commonsense differences" between them,[51] but it held that government could not "completely suppress the dissemination of concededly truthful information about entirely lawful activity"[52] because of fear that people receiving this information would be induced by it to act in a manner contrary to their best interests–that is, because of "the advantages of their being kept in ignorance."[53]

There is, of course, great attractiveness to the proposition that government not be permitted to keep its citizens ignorant of information that it would prefer them not to possess, and a broad ban on the dissemination of particular information should normally be regarded as sufficiently suspect to warrant the invocation of heightened judicial scrutiny. Moreover, the *Virginia Pharmacy* case, like the 1977 case of *Bates* v. *State Bar of Arizona,*[54] dealt with restrictions that served to safeguard the dominance of established groups within particular professions by protecting them against the threat of effective price competition by outsiders. (*Virginia Pharmacy* struck down a prohibition on the advertising of prescription drug prices by pharmacists; *Bates* struck down a prohibition on media advertising by lawyers.) Under these circumstances, the exercise of judicial activism in these cases was defensible, and the constitutional results were warranted. Yet there are disquieting implications in the new commercial-speech developments. Even such staunch defenders of freedom of speech as Thomas Emerson have expressed concern that the effect of bringing commercial advertising within the protection of the First Amendment and then allowing for its regulation in order to protect consumers against deception or to safeguard other social interests may be to open the door to the acceptance of similar

[49] 425 U.S. 748 (1976).
[50] *Id.* at 762.
[51] *Id.* at 771 n.24.
[52] *Id.* at 773.
[53] *Id.* at 769.
[54] 433 U.S. 350 (1977).

justifications for regulating other forms of speech.[55] In addition, viewing the problem from the other side, there are substantial difficulties in separating commercial speech from other aspects of commercial activity. The regulation of commercial advertising, even though it may limit the public's access to data that would enable it to exercise freedom of choice, is not substantially different from regulation of business activities in a variety of ways that would also prevent the public from exercising an unfettered freedom of choice.[56]

The traditional treatment of commercial speech as unprotected by the First Amendment requires a line to be drawn that would distinguish such speech from that which is constitutionally protected. The Court's new approach does not do away with the need for such a line because there must still be a distinction between the category of speech that is regulatable in order to prevent deception and the category that is not. However, as Edward Barrett has noted, there is now also a need for a second line–"that between commercial activity and commercial speech."[57] The problem in drawing either of these lines is substantial.[58] The need to draw the first line (which exists under the Court's new approach as well as under the old) creates the risk that speech properly entitled to constitutional protection may be treated as open to regulation. The need to draw the second line (which now exists under the Court's new commercial-speech doctrine) creates the risk that commercial activity properly subject to regulation in the public interest will be given constitutional immunity from such regulation. The location of the lines that the Supreme Court has actually drawn in implementing its new approach suggests that its concern for speech rights may needlessly be stripping legitimate regulatory power from government in areas where the legislative prioritization of interests could safely be allowed to prevail.

[55] Thomas Emerson, "First Amendment Doctrine and the Burger Court," 68 *California Law Review* 422, 458-461 (1980). See also C. Edwin Baker, "Commercial Speech: A Problem in the Theory of Freedom," 62 *Iowa Law Review* 1, 53-54 (1976).

[56] See Thomas H. Jackson and John C. Jeffries, "Commercial Speech: Economic Due Process and the First Amendment," 65 *Virginia Law Review* 1, 25-40 (1979).

[57] Edward Barrett, "'The Uncharted Area'–Commercial Speech and the First Amendment," 13 *University of California, Davis, Law Review* 175, 179 (1980).

[58] See *id.*, pp. 180-207.

[59] 431 U.S. 85 (1977).

In *Linmark Associates* v. *Willingboro*[59] in 1977, a unanimous Court (Justice Rehnquist not participating) invalidated a township ordinance prohibiting the use of "For Sale" or "Sold" signs on residential property. The township claimed that it was doing so to maintain its character as a racially integrated community by discouraging "block-busting" on the part of real estate agents seeking to capitalize on the concern of white homeowners over the influx of black families by panicking them into selling their homes "while there was still time." The apparent theory behind the ordinance was that, in the absence of the fear that might be generated by the appearance of such signs, it would not be as easy to panic homeowners into hasty sales. Since this ordinance was clearly not content-neutral–the township desired to deter the dissemination in a particular way of particular pieces of information–it is proper that it raised constitutional suspicions. However, the ordinance did not restrict the expression of beliefs and affected only a single means of communicating certain information. Moreover, it was evidently directed at the attainment of an enormously important social goal, and the legislative history of its passage, as described by the Court, provided no evidence for believing that the asserted purpose was not genuine but was rather a cover for the achievement of some more dubious end.[60] Certainly there was no evidence that the ordinance was intended to protect the economic interests or competitive advantage of one set of realtors or homeowners over others, or to protect the interests of realtors or homeowners as a group, or that it was designed to suppress information potentially embarrassing to the township government or to the township itself.

Nor did the ordinance create an insuperable barrier to the dissemination of information regarding the availability of homes for sale, other means of advertising were not closed off. To be sure, these other means may have been somewhat more costly and may have made it more difficult for a seller to reach persons not actively looking for a house to buy, but these effects would seem relatively insignificant in terms of the values that the First Amendment ought to protect, and would appear tolerable in light of the important role that the ordinance might play in the attainment of a vital social goal. The only real reason offered by the Court for its decision was its claim that interference by the government with the flow of truthful

[60] *Id.* at 87-91.

information on the ground that its recipients might use it to take socially undesirable actions is unacceptably paternalistic.[61] But the protection of individuals or of society in general against ill-advised choices is a major purpose of the regulation of commercial activity, and the control of "blockbusting" through a limitation on the use of certain signs is but a regulation of a particularly unwelcome form of commercial activity. It is not less so because the commercial speech being restricted is not the speech of the individuals whose commercial activity is to be restrained. Thus, denying government power to regulate commercial speech may in some cases–as it did here–undermine its capacity effectively to carry out its essential function of regulating undesirable commercial activity in the public interest. The justification, in terms of constitutional values, for judicial displacement of the legislative choices made here by the township is difficult to understand.

In the 1980 decision in *Central Hudson Gas & Electric Co.* v. *Public Service Commission,*[62] the Court (with only Justice Rehnquist dissenting) struck down an order of the New York State Public Service Commission that, in the interest of energy conservation, prohibited promotional advertising by electric utilities. It is true that one of the cardinal purposes of the First Amendment is to prevent suppression of ideas even where acceptance of these ideas might endanger the achievement of essential social goals.[63] Therefore, regardless of the importance of energy conservation to the public interest, government should be constitutionally powerless to impose a general proscription on the advocacy of energy waste. But the commission in this case did not generally prohibit advocacy of energy use; it merely prohibited a public utility from using funds acquired through the monopoly status granted and guaranteed it by state law to drum up business for itself.[64] Thus, even though the

[61] *Id.* at 96-97. For a trenchant criticism of the Court's paternalism argument, see Daniel Farber, "Commercial Speech and First Amendment Theory," 74 *Northwestern University Law Review* 372, 400-402 (1979). As Daniel Farber points out, if it were true that it is unconstitutional for government to suppress truthful information because its recipients might misuse it, "much of the law of evidence is apparently unconstitutional." *Id.*, p. 402 n.137. For Farber's criticism of the *Willingboro* decision, see *id.*, pp. 404-405.

[62] 447 U.S. 557 (1980).

[63] See text supra notes 19-20.

[64] See the dissenting opinion of Justice Rehnquist, 447 U.S. at 585-588.

utility's advertising expenditures are genuinely related to its business, and, therefore, unlike the situation in *Bellotti,* no objection can be made to the use of shareholders' money for that purpose, why shouldn't the fact that a public utility is involved be sufficient to bring the nature of its promotional advertising within the scope of the regulatory power of government?

On the same day that the *Central Hudson* case was decided, the Court, in *Consolidated Edison Co.* v. *Public Service Commission,*[65] also struck down the New York Public Service Commission's ban on the inclusion by public utilities of statements in their bill mailings relating to public issues not necessarily affecting the utility's business. The Court did so despite the fact that the commission's order appeared to be based in part on the ground that, since the cost of bill mailings is passed on to consumer, the utility is forcing the consumers to subsidize the dissemination of views they may oppose.[66] Moreover, not only did the utility in this case have the ability to send out its directors' messages on public issues in envelopes paid for by the consumer and with postage also paid for by the consumer, it also had the power to exclude from the same envelopes statements of opposing views that other groups might wish to put before the consumer equally cheaply.[67] Although the Court argued that the issue of subsidization was not properly before it in this case because it was not in fact one of the grounds of the commission's order,[68] the presence of such issues points up the fact that the line between commercial speech and commercial activity is necessarily blurred and indistinct. It is not to be doubted that the means by which a public utility carries out its business activities are properly subject to comprehensive regulation. To deny government power to regulate such activities because they touch on speech is to bar limitations having only marginal impact on freedom of speech while substantially curtailing the ability of government to safeguard the public interest against the abuse by utilities of the monopoly status granted them by law.

[65] 447 U.S. 530 (1980).

[66] See the dissenting opinion of Justice Blackmun, *id.* at 551-555.

[67] The commission's order challenged in this case was issued after the utility had refused to include in its billing envelopes a rebuttal to an insert advocating the development of nuclear power that it had sent out in a previous bill mailing. See 447 U.S. at 532.

[68] *Id.* at 543.

CONCLUSION

The political-expenditure and commercial-speech decisions of the current Supreme Court–the Burger Court's "major new departures" in the constitutional law of freedom of speech (to use Cox's category once again)[69] –have finally succeeded in bringing the accepted interpretation of the First Amendment to the location where the *Gitlow* majority in 1925 evidently desired it to be but lacked the time and opportunity to take it. Although the Burger Court does not share the utter insensitivity of the *Gitlow* majority to the need to extend constitutional protection to those who hold unpopular beliefs,[70] it has nevertheless accomplished the goal of the 1925 majority by fashioning the First Amendment into a guarantee that also serves to protect businesses and individuals who control substantial concentrations of wealth from regulations that would restrict their ability to use that wealth in a manner incompatible with the public interest. It has shielded from government regulation not only the politically powerless (the "discrete and insular minorities" of Justice Stone's concern), but individuals and groups either prominent in the political process or fully capable of demanding and receiving a respectful hearing in that process–groups toward whose First Amendment claims the *Gitlow* majority would likely have been entirely solicitous.

This extension of the First Amendment transforms the role of the judiciary in free-speech cases from that of protecting dissidents, minorities, critics of government or of the politically powerful, or those whose expression would be repugnant to the public, to that of final decision maker on all questions of public policy involving any form of regulation of communication or expression, thereby displacing the authority of the legislature to make policy choices among competing social interests, even in contexts in which there is no reason for considering the legislative action to be in any way suspect. The lessons of history teach that injustice and perhaps tragedy may result if courts decline to play an active role in protecting freedom of speech where the government's goal is the suppression of ideas it disfavors or of information it finds embarrassing or is the harassment of unpopular minorities. But those

[69] See text supra note 8.
[70] But see *Kleindienst* v. *Mandel*, 408 U.S. 753 (1972).

lessons do not demonstrate that equally unfortunate results will follow if courts allow the policy choices of the legislature to stand where the restrictions imposed on speech are *not* aimed at suppressing ideas or information or at harassing the unpopular–especially where these restrictions are content-neutral and their adverse impact does not fall disproportionally on the politically powerless. To intrude upon the legislative domain in such circumstances is not to defend the values that the First Amendment should be understood to protect. It is to immunize speech against marginal restraints while simultaneously depriving government of power effectively to safeguard a broad range of social interests–including some of truly urgent importance, such as preserving the integrity of the political process. The exercise of judicial activism in such cases does not promote the triumph of the human spirit but evokes a melancholy recollection of the hazards of judicial activism in the *Gitlow* period, when the Court employed unwarrantedly broad interpretations of constitutional prohibitions to thwart legislative efforts to defend the social welfare against the economically powerful.

Chapter 5

THE DUTIES OF HUMANITY: LEGAL AND MORAL OBLIGATION IN ROUSSEAU'S THOUGHT

Roger D. Masters

Rights–whether defined as "natural," "civil," or "human"–have been central to Western politics since the eighteenth century. In contrast, discussions of ethics often focus on issues of obligation and duty. It is, of course, frequently noted that rights presuppose duties, since one person is obligated to do (or not to do) something by another's rightful claim. But what is the precise status of the duties without which rights cannot be effective? Is the only source of obligation the positive law of a specific political society? Or do humans have duties that derive from their humanity, i.e., moral or ethical obligations independent of political and legal institutions? And perhaps most difficult of all, when do humanitarian or moral grounds make it not only legitimate but imperative for good citizens to disobey the laws of their own country?"

It is particularly fitting to pose such questions when honoring Henry Ehrmann. Civic duty and moral obligation have been central both to Henry's scholarship and to his life: few contemporary scholars have focused so sharply on how specific political and legal institutions contribute to a decent society, and even fewer can claim respect for such continuous devotion to humanitarian principles. Henry Ehrmann's reaction to Nazi Germany should remind us that such difficult but necessary choices reveal the theoretical foundations of legal duty and moral decency.

Posed in abstract terms, however, the relationship between ethics and politics is notoriously perplexing. Perhaps I can contribute to an understanding of these issues by considering the political thought of Jean-Jacques Rousseau. This is all the more appropriate because a shared interest in Rousseau was the occasion of my first meeting with Henry in Paris in 1958.

ROUSSEAU'S CONCEPT OF HUMANITARIANISM

In the *Discourse on the Origins of Inequality* or *Second Discourse* (1755), Rousseau is under no illusions about the way humans typically behave toward each other. "When society is considered with calm and disinterested attention, it seems to show at first only the violence of powerful men and the oppression of the weak" (*Second Discourse,* Preface, ed. Masters, p. 97). Since the most savage and brutal events of our century would probably not have been a total surprise to Rousseau, his analysis cannot be dismissed on the ground of some presumed romantic "softness."

Although aware that power is rarely restrained by selfless virtue, Rousseau sought to go beneath violence and injustice in search of "unshakeable" and respectable "foundations" for rights and duties toward our fellow humans (ibid.) He analyzes these "foundations" in terms of "natural right." Today, of course, one often hears of "civic rights" or "human rights." But civic rights presume an established society or legal system, whereas the question is whether citizens ought to obey such institutions for reasons transcending the accidents of time and place. And if "human rights" exist apart from the prescriptions of one particular culture or legal system, clearly they must be related to our nature. As Rousseau notes, "knowledge of the real foundations of human society" is hidden as long as one is in "ignorance of the nature of man" (ibid., p. 93).

According to the *Second Discourse,* one cannot approach this problem without recognizing the historical changes that have occurred to our species. A century before Darwin's *Origin of Species,* Rousseau sets forth a radically evolutionary approach to human nature, based on the assumption that our earliest ancestors must have been animals subject to what biologists now call natural selection (ibid., Part 1, p. 106). If so, Rousseau insists, human rights and duties cannot originate in a rational discovery or philosophical definition of natural law (ibid., Preface, pp. 94-96).

Since virtue based on reason is attained by only a few humans, even in civilized society, Rousseau insists that social obligations cannot be said to have a natural status unless they have an innate, prerational foundation.

> Meditating on the first and simplest operations of the human soul, I believe I perceive in it two principles anterior to reason, of which one interests us ardently in our well-being and our self-preservation, and the other inspires in us a natural repugnance to see any sensitive being perish or suffer, principally our fellow-men. It is from the conjunction and combination that our mind is able to make of these two principles, without the necessity of introducing that of sociability, that all the rules of natural right appear to me to flow. . . (ibid., pp. 95-96).

Like contemporary biologists, Rousseau treats the existence of social groups as a *problem:* hence natural sociability cannot be *presumed* to limit self-interest in the name of the species' "common good" (Hamilton, 1964; Williams, 1966; Alexander, 1974; Wilson, 1975; Kummer, 1979; Masters, 1978a, 1983).

By focusing on self-preservation and pity, Rousseau claims to have identified two "principles" accessible to all humans as primary "sentiments" or "feelings."

> In this way one is not forced to make man a philosopher before making him a man; his duties toward others are not dictated to him solely by the belated lessons of wisdom; and as long as he does not resist the inner impulse of commiseration, he will never harm another man or even another sensitive being, except in the legitimate case where, his preservation being concerned, he is obliged to give himself preference (*Second Discourse,* Preface, p. 96).

Just as today's biologists analyze "helping" behavior in terms of the natural tendency of all animals to perpetuate their genes (Hamilton, 1964; Alexander, 1974; Wilson, 1975; Barash, 1977; Trivers, 1981), Rousseau sets aside theological or philosophical concepts of obligation in the quest for a universal foundation for human rights and duties.

Some, of course, would be tempted to dismiss Rousseau's approach as mere sentimentality: why proclaim that pity is a natural sentiment when human brutality is so evident? But Rousseau insists we cannot conclude anything about human nature from our contemporary situation (*Second Discourse,* Preface, pp. 91-93). His assessment of human history is a tough-minded condemnation of those changes we usually praise:

> The extreme inequality in our way of life: excess of idleness in some, excess of labor in others; the ease of stimulating and satisfying our appetites and our sensu-

> ality . . . numberless sorrows and afflictions which are felt in all conditions and by which souls are perpetually tormented: these are the fatal proofs that most of our ills are our own work, and that we would have avoided almost all of them by preserving the simple, uniform, and solitary way of life prescribed to us by nature (ibid., Part 1, p. 110).

Reason and civilization cannot be the primary basis of human obligation, if only because the progress of reason has coincided so evidently with social inequality, injustice, human misery, conflict, and degradation. "If nature destined us to be healthy, I almost dare affirm that the state of reflection is a state contrary to nature and that the man who meditates is a depraved animal" (ibid.). The criticism of the development of the sciences and arts in Rousseau's *First Discourse* thus rests on a sober correlation of human vice with the rationality often considered the foundation of humanitarianism.

But if the origins of social rights and duties cannot be traced to some kind of "natural law" based on reason (as in the Stoic or Thomist traditions), what of the opposed criticism? How can Rousseau claim that there is an innate feeling limiting human selfishness? Contemporary studies of other animals indicate that his position is not simply absurd: although organisms tend to behave in ways that preserve themselves, evolutionary biology has demonstrated convincingly the existence of contrary factors sometimes leading animals to help others (Alexander, 1974; Wilson, 1975; Barash, 1977; Trivers, 1981). Granted that self-preservation is stronger than such motives as pity or "altruistic" helping–as, indeed, Rousseau argues–it is impossible to account for the evolution of social behavior without reference to a tension between the principles of competition and cooperation (Campbell, 1972; Masters, 1976a, 1978b, 1981, 1982b). Rousseau's mode of analysis thus deserves careful reconsideration in the light of new scientific research.

Rousseau reduces the natural root of obligation to a characteristic that is primarily animal in nature: "It seems, in effect, that if I am obliged to do no harm to my fellow-man, it is less because he is a reasonable being than because he is a sensitive being, a quality that being common to beast and man, ought at least to give the one the right not to be uselessly mistreated by the other" *(Second Discourse),* Preface, p. 96). If even lower animals have essential rights, obviously all humans have a correlative duty not to "uselessly" mistreat each other.

With this definition, Rousseau presents a doctrine of humanitarianism that is strikingly *negative.* Whereas many moderns have conceived of duty in positive terms, as an injunction to help others in need, Rousseau insists that the natural duty toward others is founded on pity, i.e., on a prerational feeling that leads us to abstain from harming others while satisfying the legitimate and primary need for individual self-preservation.

> Pity is a natural sentiment which, moderating in each individual the activity of love of oneself, contributes to the mutual preservation of the entire species . . . Instead of that sublime maxim of reasoned justice, *Do unto others as you would have them do unto you,* it inspires all men with this other maxim of natural goodness, much less perfect but perhaps more useful than the preceding one: *Do what is good for you with the least possible harm to others (ibid.,* Part 1, pp. 132-133).

In place of the active commandment of the Golden Rule *Matthew* 7: 12), Rousseau thus describes a passive or limited obligation to avoid harm–and makes even this negative obligation subordinate to the natural desire for self-preservation.

At first, it is hard to see how such a feeling of pity, especially when its effects are limited to *not* harming others when one's own self-preservation is assured, could be a foundation for human social obligation. On the one hand, duties typically require positive action, whereas Rousseau's "natural goodness" merely amounts to avoiding unprovoked and unnecessary malice. And, on the other, humanitarianism by definition suggests an obligation to fellow *humans* that is not extended, indiscriminately, to all living beings. On both counts, Rousseau's replacement of reason with pity as the foundation of social obligation seems inconsistent with any meaningful duties. Natural rights so defined seem thoroughly amoral, especially since they so closely approximate the behavior of other animals that are usually not treated as moral beings (ibid., Preface, p. 96; Part 1, pp. 128-132).

Rousseau does not come to this conclusion, however. Instead, he claims that pity is the source of "all the social virtues" (ibid., p. 131). This result does not come from unaided pity, but rather from "pity in support of reason" (ibid). That is, in a being that has evolved the capacity of comparing itself with others, pity can be focused in a conscious way–and if so, according to Rousseau, one can see the linkage between the prerational sentiment of compassion and the duties or obligations of morality. "In fact, what are generosity, clemency, humanity, if not pity applied to the weak, to the guilty, or to the human species in general? Benevolence and even friendship are, rightly understood, the products of a constant pity fixed on a particular object" (ibid., pp. 131-132).

So defined, humanitarianism is indeed an obligation toward all other human beings on the grounds of their humanity. But while natural, this duty is also sharply limited. Not only is it reduced to avoiding unnecessary harm to others, but the primacy of self-preservation provides no guarantee that pity will be effective. To justify harming others, one need merely invoke self-interest based on fear of violence, as Hobbes does (*Leviathan,* ch. 13; ed. Oakshott, pp. 98-101. Whatever the difficulties of establishing theological or philosophical justifications for human obligations, Rousseau's substitute does not seem a match for the terrifying unethical and unjust behavior we have witnessed since the eighteenth century. Was Jean-Jacques simply naive?

Before answering, it is well to reflect further on the fact that appeals to self-restraint and justice based on revealed religion or philosophic tradition are so often ineffective. Pity may only create a very limited duty to our fellows, but for Rousseau this limitation is a source of strength rather than weakness. Because "commiseration [pity] is only a sentiment that puts us in the position of him who suffers," it "will be all the more energetic as the observing animal identifies himself more intimately with the suffering animal" (*Second Discourse,* Part 1, p. 132). If humans can identify with others, therefore, humanitarianism is natural precisely because it rests on a prerational feeling–albeit one easily overcome by theological dogma or rational instruction.

Two questions arise, each of which has practical as well as theoretical significance. First, is it *possible* for all humans–including our ancestors or contemporary "primitives"–to "identify" with others, experiencing "a sentiment that puts us in the position of him who suffers"? And second, even when we experience this identification with one of our fellow-creatures, to what extent does it produce an obligation in any meaningful sense of the word?

THE EVOLUTION OF HUMAN FEELINGS: THE PROBLEM OF PITY

Rousseau's *Second Discourse* forces the thoughtful reader to reflect on the evolutionary origins of rights and duties. If our obligations are at all natural, they must have roots in an earlier period of human prehistory, before the development of language, civilized society, and written law.

According to Rousseau, the most obvious characteristic of this primeval human condition–the "state of nature"–is isolation and solitude. "Let us conclude that wandering in the forests, without industry, without speech, without domicile, without war and without liaisons, with no need of his fellow-men, likewise with no desire to harm them, perhaps never even recognizing anyone individually, savage man [was] subject to few passions and self-sufficient" (ibid., Part 1, p. 137).

This condition of isolation solves the Hobbesian problem: according to Rousseau, early humans were so rarely in contact, and so stupid, that their pursuit of self-preservation gave rise to little mutual hostility (ibid., pp. 128-130). But if our ancestors were isolated animals with "such inactive passions" that they "were not subject to very dangerous quarrels" (ibid., p. 133), how could they have the imagination to identify with their fellows and feel pity (cf. *Emile,* Book IV; ed. Bloom, p. 221)? When discussing pity, Rousseau claims that "savage man . . . is always seen heedlessly yielding to the first sentiment of humanity" *(Second Discourse,* Part 1, p. 132); when discussing sexual desire, Rousseau admits that "imagination"–presumably necessary for putting oneself "in the position of him who suffers" (ibid., p. 135).

Rousseau's treatment of pity thus forces us to question whether it could be an active sentiment in early humans. In the text of the *Second Discourse,* this problem is underscored by his use of contradictory adjectives in asserting that pity is "a sentiment that is obscure and strong in savage man, developed but weak in civilized man" (ibid., p. 132). Elsewhere, Rousseau admits that savage men are cruel (ibid., Part 2, p. 149; *Essay on the Origin of Languages,* ch. 9; ed. Moran, pp. 32-33; *Geneva Manuscript,* I, ii; ed. Masters, p. 162). And like the savage, the human child does not naturally feel pity *(Emile,*

IV, pp. 212-227; Masters, 1968, ch. 1). Hence Rousseau's psychology does not really provide a principle that is fully active as a check on human selfishness either in the state of nature, where pity cannot function, or in civil society, where it is overwhelmed by vanity, pride, and selfishness *(Geneva MS.,* I, ii, pp. 158-159).

In the notes to the *Second Discourse,* often dismissed by superficial readers, Rousseau indicates the precise psychological configuration needed for an effective feeling of "humanity." Distinguishing sharply between love of oneself *(amour de soi)* and vanity *(amour-propre),* he remarks: "Love of oneself is a natural sentiment which inclines every animal to watch over its own preservation, and which, directed in man by reason and modified by pity, produces humanity and virtue" *(Second Discourse,* note c, p. 222). Pity generates a commitment to help others only insofar as it can modify the natural sentiment or desire for self-preservation–and this would seem to presuppose the emergence of reason, itself an unnatural capability that some humans never acquire and most develop only slowly and with difficulty even in civilized society *(Geneva MS,* I, ii, p. 161; *Emile,* IV, p. 222).

Rather than condemn Rousseau, it is well to consider why he sought a foundation for natural obligation in a sentiment that he admitted was "obscure" if not totally absent in the first epochs of human evolution as well as in the civilized child. The alternatives were presumably the two main psychological theories in the Western tradition. The *tabula rasa* view, elaborated by Hobbes *(Leviathan,* ch. 30; p. 249) and Locke *(Essay Concerning Human Understanding,* II,i,2; ed. Fraser, vol. 1 pp. 121-122), implies that all standards of behavior are learned from one's society. If so, there is no duty whatsoever to others in a state of nature or in any situation where humans are not governed under law in a civil society. Such theories tend to limit cooperation to mutual self-interest and deny the existence of moral obligations not enforced by legal institutions (Masters, 1980). The classical alternative, epitomized by the psychology described in Plato's *Republic* (esp. IV.435c-441c; ed. Bloom, pp. 114-121), avoids this conclusion by postulating a natural distinction between the rational faculty and other psychological principles (desire and spiritedness). But while Plato's perspective generates human obligation in the name of virtue, for Rousseau this option was foreclosed by the unnatural status of reason and the social inequalities it would authorize.

One can see well enough why Rousseau sought a prerational foundation for human social obligation: if humans evolved from an animal condition in which even the family may not have existed, how can universally binding duties be primarily founded on reason? We know today that Rousseau's question was well put–but that his answer to our evolutionary origins was incorrect (Masters, 1978a, 1978b). The early hominids were not solitary animals like orangutans, but rather social hunter-gatherers; the best evidence now available indicates that our ancestors formed social groups in which some individuals were dominant over others–and in which a degree of cooperation existed, at least in hunting and in a sexual division of labor (Leakey and Lewin, 1977; Lovejoy, 1981). Like chimpanzees, and indeed most other primates, the early hominids must therefore have had much more ability to compare themselves to each other than Rousseau attributed to savages *(Second Discourse,* note c, Rousseau, 1964, p. 222).

Could it be that Rousseau's evolutionary approach suggests the answer to the shortcomings of his psychological theory? It should not be forgotten that, at the outset of the *Second Discourse,* he warned us of the tentative nature of his empirical hypotheses:

> Let my readers not imagine, therefore, that I dare flatter myself with having seen what appears to me so difficult to see. I began some lines of reasoning, I ventured some conjectures, less in the hope of resolving the question than with the intention of clarifying it and reducing it to its true state. Others will easily be able to go farther on the same road, though it will not be easy for anyone to reach the end of it . . . (ibid., Preface, p. 92).

Let us therefore consider briefly the current evidence in the hope that, by so doing, we can fulfill Rousseau's "intention" that we "go farther on the same road" he outlined.

CONTEMPORARY BIOLOGY AND PLATOS THEORY OF HUMAN NATURE

While ingenious, Rousseau's psychology is neither fully consistent with the evidence he himself presents nor substantiated by more recent scientific research. The last generation of ethological observation has shown that, in many instances, chimpanzees and other primates kill others of their own kind (Itani, 1982). Particularly striking are the observed cases of infants being killed by adult males, since bystanders generally do not intervene or take retaliatory action against the aggressor. In contrast, social comparisons akin to vanity or pride seem implicit in the establishment and maintenance of dominance hierarchies among primates. Thus there is little evidence of pity among our nearest animal relatives, whereas they apparently can make the sort of social comparison *(amour-propre)* Rousseau rejected as unnatural.

It does not follow, however, that Rousseau's entire approach to the problem of human morality and justice is demolished by these findings. Although pity cannot be shown to have the natural status and function Rousseau ascribes to it, his insistence that some prerational feeling must be involved in moral obligation remains an important challenge to the *tabula rasa* psychology of the Hobbesian-Lockean tradition. And, in effect, contemporary research locates such emotions in anger, guilt, and aggression, i.e., sentiments associated with punishment for departures from expected social behavior.

Although Rousseau rejected both the tripartite psychology of the Platonic tradition (desire, spiritedness, and reason as natural components of the human "soul") and the *tabula rasa* approach of the British empiricists, contemporary biology leads one to assess these two perspectives differently. The blank slate model is indeed untenable in the light of ethological research, which shows that at least some behaviors are the consequence of natural selection and have been programmed to some degree in the central nervous system (Lorenz, 1970-1971; Masters, 1976b). Curiously enough, however, the classical alternative finds considerable support in the scientific research of the last century.

Freud, as has sometimes been noted, developed a psychology that is remarkably similar to that of Plato: the id or libido can be compared to desire, the ego-ideal or superego to spiritedness, and the ego to reason. More important, recent work on the structure of the human central nervous system reveals what Paul MacLean calls the "triune brain": a basic structure inherited from our reptilian ancestors (the structures surrounding the midbrain or "R-complex"), a mammalian addition (the limbic system), and the primate heritage (the neocortex, with its particularly human addition of the large frontal lobes of *Homo sapiens).* Made popular by Carl Sagan's *Dragons of Eden* (1977), MacLean's analysis suggests that social feelings are rooted in the limbic system, i.e., the structures readily identifiable as the locus of the passions Plato described as spiritedness.

Unlike earlier philosophic speculations, this view of human psychology can be confirmed by experimental evidence. The behavior of other species can be modified by destroying different parts of the central nervous system and observing the consequences. For instance, many motor coordinations–including those associated with dominance–are typically programmed in the "R-complex" and can be observed in strikingly similar behaviors of reptiles, mammals, and primates. In contrast, emotional bonds between individuals–the animal root of ethical obligation–seem absent in reptiles as well as in mammals whose limbic system has been destroyed or damaged. Whereas the cortex, the brain structure associated with human thought, is not needed for social bonding and helping behavior, the limbic system must function normally if social behavior is not to be disturbed (MacLean, 1982). To take but one well-known example in humans, diseases of this area, such as temporal lobe tumors, are often associated with acts of unprovoked aggression and violence.

Rousseau had noted the precursor of moral behavior in his own dog, in the form of evident signs of aggression and submission *(Emile,* IV, pp. 286-287, note). MacLean's contribution to our understanding of the evolution of the human brain and behavior confirms this insight: in mammals, unlike reptiles, we see the rudimentary signs of what can only be described as fellow-feeling, associated with guilt and anger toward others, but also producing acts of helping and even courageous defense of the group (see Ardrey, 1961, pp. 80-81). Hence there is now good scientific evidence for the existence of prerational sentiments that provide a natural ground for humanitarianism, even if they do not rest as exclusively on pity as Rousseau would lead us to believe.

Had Rousseau accepted the Platonic psychology, it would have been possible for him to use spiritedness *(thymos)* as a foundation for duty. Rousseau does not do so because this passion seems inseparable from a kind of aggressiveness and sociability inconsistent with his image of the state of nature. But now we know that early hominids were not solitary beings but rather lived in groups with social interactions–including social conflict–like those observed in chimpanzees or baboons (cf. *Second Discourse,* Part 2, p. 145, and note j, pp. 204-209). As a result, it is no longer necessary to reject Platonic psychology as inconsistent with the evolutionary development of human passions and mental faculties.

The substitution of something akin to Plato's psychology for that presented in the *Second Discourse* and *Emile* would have surprisingly little effect on Rousseau's conclusions. Guilt, like pity, is prerational or subrational: it is a feeling or emotion without which reason is incapable of checking the desires. Guilt, like pity, avoids the vice of pride by leading the individual to feel his or her current position is not a basis for claiming power or preeminence over others. And guilt, like pity, can be silenced by selfishness masquerading as philosophic rationalization (cf. *Second Discourse,* Part 1, p. 132).

In evolutionary terms, the transformation of feelings of anger and attachment into guilt can be explained as a consequence of the increasing role of reciprocity and cooperation. As Trivers points out (1981), selfish or competitive behavior can be checked by "reciprocal altruism" when animals engage in social actions in which roles may be reversed in the future (cf. *Emile,* IV, p. 224). The early hominid hunting band fits the conditions necessary for such cooperation. Hence, as Trivers argues, mechanisms of "moralistic aggression" can be expected to enforce social responsibility in small groups of related individuals like those presumed to have existed in earlier epochs or found in the surviving preliterate ("primitive") hunter-gatherers (Trivers, 1981; Willhoite, 1981).

In individual development, the infant's display of anger when frustrated or hurt indicates that we are dealing with a primary emotion much less fragile than pity *(Emile,* I, pp. 65-66). Emotions of guilt are obviously related to the emergence of self-control–and therewith to the acceptance of obligation. It is thus at least plausible that the prerational element underlying the sense of duty is something akin to Plato's spiritedness or Freud's ego-ideal, generating anger at signs of selfish or immoral behavior in others, restraint on one's own temptation to violate internalized social norms, and courageous defense of the group.

By extending the scope of pity to the entire species, Rousseau claimed that self-love could be transformed into the feeling of "humanity." Applying his evolutionary approach in the light of contemporary biological findings, one is tempted to replace pity with the principle underlying anger, courage, and guilt. The natural foundation for duty and morality would then be our feeling of anger at others for violating social norms, or guilt for our own transgressions. If the social norms involved relate to our own society, the resulting obligation would typically take the form of legal or moral duty. But when generalized to the entire species, or to other humans as such, one could describe the result as "humanitarianism." Hence one can well ask whether Rousseau's teaching concerning the relationship between legal duty and moral obligation, even if based on inaccurate psychological mechanisms, might not still be relevant today.

"HUMANITY" AND BINDING DUTIES

The distinction between ethics and politics would seem to parallel the difference between the private and the public. More precisely, however, it concerns the distinction between self-imposed moral obligations undertaken by the virtuous or decent individual, and civic duties established by law and enforced by the political community.

Rousseau himself makes this distinction quite explicitly in the first draft of the *Social Contract (Geneva MS,* I, ii, pp. 157-163). Because he does so in a chapter that was deleted from the final version of his most famous political treatise, the discussion is not generally known. Yet, as we will see, it bears directly on the issue in a way that is confirmed by contemporary theories of social behavior in both evolutionary biology and political economy.

Entitled "On the General Society of the Human Race," this chapter considers whether there are any morally binding duties incumbent on humans solely on the basis of their humanity. For

Hobbes, no such duties could exist in the absence of a government capable of enforcing them:

> For the laws of nature, as justice, equity, modesty, mercy, and in sum, doing unto others, as we would be done to, of themselves, without the terror of some power, to cause them to be observed, are contrary to our natural passions, that carry us to partiality, pride, revenge, and the like. And covenants, without the sword, are but words, and of no strength to secure a man at all, (Leviathan, ch. 17, p. 129).

This view is tantamount to denying any externally visible manifestation of humanitarian or moral obligation except where it is consistent with the positive laws of a political community.

Rousseau's friend Diderot had attacked the Hobbesian position in the article on "Natural Right" that appeared in Volume 5 of the *Encyclopédie (1755).* In this article, Diderot claimed that ethical obligations could be derived from the "general will of the human species," which could be discovered by consulting individual "conscience," international law, and *consensus mundi.* Hobbes' principles are dismissed in a dialogue between Diderot and a fictional "violent reasoner" who claims, as does the *Leviathan,* that without a guarantee that others will abide by moral duty, the individual would be foolish to engage in self-restraint for moral reasons. (For citations, see *Geneva MS,* editorial notes 8-13 or Masters, 1968, pp. 261-265).

In reading Rousseau's analysis of the same problem, one is surprised to see him attack Diderot on Hobbesian grounds. Indeed, Rousseau goes so far as to adopt, in his own name, the position that Diderot had criticized as that of a "violent reasoner" *(Geneva MS,* I, ii, pp. 161-162). His reason for rejecting Diderot, moreover, will surprise readers of the *Second Discourse:* pity, the conscience, and reason are all equally unreliable as means of *knowing* just what the demands of "humanity" truly are.

> Thus nature's gentle voice is no longer an infallible guide for us, nor is the independence we have received from her a desirable state. We lost peace and innocence forever before we had appreciated their delights. Unfelt by the stupid men of earliest times, lost to the enlightened men of later times, the happy life of the golden age was always a state foreign to the human race (ibid., pp. 158-159).

Rousseau bases his argument on the absence of any means by which the needs of the entire species can be communicated directly to the individual, insuring that moral behavior will be reciprocated. But he adds that

> what reasoning demonstrates to us in this regard is perfectly confirmed by the facts, and simply by turning back to very ancient times one easily sees that the healthy ideas of natural right and the brotherhood of all men were disseminated rather late and made such slow progress in the world that it was only Christianity that generalized them sufficiently. . . . Hobbes's mistake, therefore, is not that he established the state of war among men who are independent and have become sociable, but that he supposed this state natural to the species and gave it as the cause of the vices of which it is the effect (ibid., p. 162).

Elswhere, I have shown that the implications of this passage are of great importance in Rousseau's thought. He was under no illusions about the primacy of force at the origins of human institutions (Masters, 1968, pp. 275, 302). Nor did he place any reliance on the supposedly natural principle of "pity" as an active foundation for goodness, virtue, or social obedience. Rather, Rousseau seeks–in his famous concept of the "general will"–a logic of social obligation that is directly connected to the political community of which the individual is a free citizen. Like Hobbes, therefore, Rousseau minimizes the effectiveness of moral duty unless it has been specified by legal enactment and will be enforced by political institutions.

In practice, Rousseau's doctrine of the "general will" thus takes a concept that Diderot had used to describe *ethics* and converts it into a powerful foundation of the *political* community. Duties cannot be formally obligatory without some guarantee that others will be equally bound by them–and reason alone is radically insufficient to insure that this will be the case: "There is without doubt a universal justice emanating from reason alone; but to be acknowledged among us, this justice must be reciprocal. . . . therefore there must be conventions and laws to combine rights with duties . . ." (*Social Contract,* II, vi, ed. Masters, p. 66). Ironically, Kant–unaware of the suppressed chapter of the *Geneva Manuscript* (I, ii)–reconverted Rousseau's logic of political right into the ethical doctrine of the Categorical Imperative.

It is not possible here to present a more detailed exegesis of Rousseau's concept of the "general will" (see Masters, 1968, ch. 7). But one striking deduction from this principle deserves emphasis. Accoring to Rousseau, the larger the social group, the weaker the "general will":

> All political societies are composed of other, smaller societies of different types, each of which has its interests and maxims. . . . it is true that since particular societies are always subordinate to those that contain them, one ought to obey the latter in preference to the former; the citizen's duties take precedence over the senator's, and the man's over the citizen's. But unfortunately personal interest is always found in inverse ratio to duty, and it increases in proportion as the association becomes narrower and the engagement less sacred . . . (*Political Economy* ed. Masters, pp. 212-213).

While one can therefore describe the "law of nature" as the "general will" in the "large town of the world" (ibid., p. 212), for practical purposes the political community is the largest social group with a sense of "self" and a possibility of enforcing duty. Rousseau insists on the need to focus the vague feeling of "humanity" into the active love of one's country both in the *Social Contract* (e.g., II, ix, pp. 71-73; III, i-ii, pp. 78-83) and elsewhere in his works (e.g., *Government of Poland, Letter to d'Alembert, Letters Written from the Mountain*). As he puts it in a critical passage in the *Political Economy:*

> It seems that the sentiment of humanity evaporates and weakens as it is extended over the whole world, and that we can't be moved by calamities in Tartary or Japan as we are by those of a European people. Interest and commiseration must in some way be confined and compressed to be activated. Now since this inclination in us can only be useful to those with whom we have to live, it is good that the feeling of humanity, concentrated among fellow citizens, gains fresh force through the habit of seeing one another and through the common interest that unites them. It is certain that the greatest miracles of virtue have been produced by patriotism (*Political Economy*, p. 219).

Throughout Rousseau's major political works, from the *First Discourse* to the *Emile*, one can find a similar emphasis on patriotism as the primary basis of virtue. But this means that, apart from those few who–like Socrates or Jesus–base their virtue on reason or faith, human moral and ethical standards must primarily depend on political enforcement.

This does not mean, of course, that for Rousseau, "Whatever is, is right." The general will provides a standard, in the form of "principles of political right," that can be used as a yardstick to measure and criticize existing governments (*Emile,* V, pp. 458-459; Masters, 1968, ch. 7). But where a regime is illegitimate, Rousseau's principles often justify moral reproach rather than political upheaval. Indeed, as he put it in an important note to the *Second Discourse,* knowledge of the extent of actual political injustices leads men like himself to "obligate themselves" to the practice of virtue, to "obey the laws"–and to "scorn a constitution" that is intrinsically imperfect (*Second Discourse,* note i, pp. 202-203).

Rousseau differs from Hobbes on the extent to which the legitimate community can make demands on the citizen, but not on the primacy of political duty over moral or ethical ideals (*Social Contract,* IV, viii, p. 127). Subordinating both theological teachings of divine law and rationalist theories of natural law to positive law, Rousseau finds in patriotism a sentiment in which the feeling of identity with one's fellow citizens represents the closest feasible approximation to an active humanitarian duty. In practice, of course, we have become accustomed to something like Rousseau's conclusion: with the rise of the nation-state, there is little room for the individual unprotected by a sovereign political community. And despite our proclaimed emphasis on "human rights," there is little one can do to enforce definitions of ethical obligation on a foreign society unless–as with the leadership of Nazi Germany–that country has first been decisively defeated in war. Whatever our judgment of Rousseau's psychology, his stress on political right as more effective than moral duty seems confirmed by practical experience.

PRIVATE INTEREST, COLLECTIVE GOODS, AND VIRTUE

In considering the adequacy of Rousseau's political teaching, one can go beyond the intuitive recognition that–as he taught–"humanitarianism" is generally impotent in the face of power and self-interest. In a number of fields, recent theoretical developments have focused on a cost-benefit analysis of social behavior which confirms the fundamental position set forth by Rousseau. It is thus perhaps useful to mention some of these contemporary approaches in evolutionary biology, political economy, and rational choice theory, if only because in so doing we discover the utility of taking great political thinkers like Rousseau with utmost seriousness.

The logical relationship between private self-interest and the willingness to work for the community has been extensively studied by economists and political scientists over the last generation. Game theorists can show, for example, that in the case known as the Prisoner's Dilemma, rational maximization of immediate self-interest makes it impossible for individuals to cooperate in their mutual benefit (Masters, 1982b). Particularly since Downs (1957), it has been customary to analyze this question in terms of "collective goods," i.e., nondivisible benefits that a selfish individuals are tempted to enjoy without providing a fair share of support as long as one is not punished for being a "free-rider." Originally formulated by the pre-Socratics (Plato, *Republic,* II 358c-361d), this problem is particularly relevant to Rousseau's political thought.

As has been noted, Rousseau argues that "personal interest is always found in inverse ratio to duty, and it increases in proportion as the association becomes narrower and the engagement less sacred" *(Political Economy,* p. 213). Current rational choice theorists have reached the same conclusion: as Olson shows (1965), willingness to contribute to collective goods declines as the size of the community increases–unless the individual gains a "selective" or private benefit for participating.

A similar dialectic can be found in the version of cost-benefit theory developed in evolutionary biology under the name of "inclusive fitness theory" (Masters, 1982a). As in rational choice theory, it can no longer be merely assumed that individual organisms act in order to benefit the "common good": rather, natural selection generally favors behaviors increasing the probability that the individual organism's genes will be transmitted to future generations ("reproductive success"). Just as Rousseau denies that human behavior is determined by the good of the "general society of the human race," most biologists now concede that individual animals do not directly contribute to the good of their *species* (Williams, 1966).

Although it has sometimes been thought that this view commits evolutionary biology to a rigorous individualism reminiscent of laissez faire economics (Caplan, 1978), inclusive fitness theory is not biased in favor of any particular ideological position (Bressler, 1981; Masters, 1982a). Rather, this conceptualization of natural selection suggests a dialectical relationship between the benefits of the organism and those of the local group or breeding population; although most behaviors seem to have evolved in order to maximize the *individual's* inclusive fitness, under some circumstances traits can evolve that are directly in the interest of the *group*, even at a cost to the survival of the individual concerned (Wilson, 1975; Masters, 1982b). In nature, therefore, both individual interest and group benefit coexist (Margolis, 1982). To use Rousseau's formulation, "the agreement of all interests is formed in opposition to the interest of each" (*Social Contract*, II, iii, note, p. 61).

For the biologist, as for the rational choice theorist, individuals are much more likely to contribute to the collective good if others reciprocate (Trivers, 1981; Axelrod and Hamilton, 1981). As a result, the smaller the population and the greater the individual recognition among its members, the more likely it is that animals will sacrifice individual fitness for others in the group. Rousseau's conclusion was exactly correct: "To be acknowledged among us . . . justice must be reciprocal" (*Social Contract*, II, vi, p. 65)–and the narrower the group, the greater the likelihood of what we call, in human terms, virtue or duty (Campbell, 1972; Masters, 1982b).

It would be possible to extend this comparison, showing the extraordinary similarity between the details of Rousseau's analysis in the *Social Contract* and the theoretical developments in rational choice theory, game theory, or inclusive fitness theory. But hopefully the point is by now clear. Although Rousseau's political thought rests on a psychology which has not been confirmed by contemporary scientific research, his overall assessment of the relation between moral duties (humanitarianism) and political obligations (citizenship) is fully consistent with a broad range of current theoretical and empirical research (cf. Masters, 1981, 1982b, 1983).

This conclusion may help to explain the persistent appeal of Rousseau's thought despite its reliance on an outmoded concept of pity. The *Social Contract* presents a yardstick for measuring the legitimacy and justice of political regimes. As citizens, we need some such measure in order to judge whether the legal commands of the state are morally binding; as human beings, we seek to know whether other communities are more–or less–just than our own. Where injustice prevails, we cannot fail to react without developing an insensitivity that can ultimately undermine the virtue of our own lives. But if we equate injustice at the farthest ends of the earth with injustice to our neighbor, we are guilty of the inhumanity Rousseau attributed to "reason" and "philosophy" (*Second Discourse*, Part 1, p. 132).

Unlike his political theory, however, Rousseau's psychology has not stood the test of time. Pity does not seem to be the primary feeling that engages us to act, either as citizens trying to improve our own community or as human beings condemning injustice elsewhere in the world. If pity–mere identification with the victim of injustice–were the active feeling underlying moral and political duty, why would we have a more pressing obligation to our own community than to people elsewhere in the world, as Rousseau rightly shows we must? Instead, as has been suggested, it seems that we are moved to act by anger at injustice, courage in committing ourselves without the assurance of personal safety, and a desire to avoid the guilt of betraying ethical ideals.

Although Henry Ehrmann has not himself written along the lines discussed here, his research reflects the importance of these issues. His studies of organized business and labor in France, as well as his unusually accurate analyses of that country's entire political system, reveal the dynamic tension between private group interests and the collective good in one of the world's most interesting and complex societies. His studies of comparative legal systems focus on different ways that the judicial process gives citizens that sense of justice without which the common good is a mockery. And his response to injustice in his native land and elsewhere has confirmed that the foundation of virtue is not mere pity, but courage and even anger when those in power fail to live up to the highest ideals of humanity.

REFERENCES

Alexander, Richard D. 1974. Evolution of Social Behavior. *Annual Review of Ecology and Systematics*, Vol. 5, pp. 25-83.

Ardrey, Robert. 1961. *African Genesis.* New York: Dell.

Axelrod, Robert, and Hamilton, William D. 1981. The Evolution of Cooperation. *Science*, Vol. 211 (27 Mar.), pp. 1390-96.

Barash, David. 1977. *Sociobiology and Behavior.* New York: Elsevier.

Bressler, Marvin. 1981. Biological Determinism and Ideological Indeterminacy. In Elliott White, ed., *Sociobiology and Human Politics.* Lexington, Mass.: Lexington Books, pp. 181-191.

Campbell, Donald T. 1972. On the Genetics of Altruism and the Counter-hedonic Components in Human Culture. *Journal of Social Issues*, Vol. 28, pp. 21-37.

Caplan, Arthur, ed. 1978. *The Sociobiology Debate.* New York: Harper and Row.

Downs, Anthony. 1957. *An Economic Theory of Democracy.* New York: Harpers.

Hamilton, William. 1964. The Genetical Evolution of Social Behavior. *Journal of Theoretical Biology*, Vol. 7, pp. 1-16. Reprinted in Arthur Caplan, ed., *The Sociobiology Debate.* New York: Harpers, pp. 191-209.

Hobbes, Thomas. 1962. *Leviathan.* Michael Oakeshott, ed. New York: Colliers.

Itani, Junichiro. 1982. Intraspecific Killing among nonhuman primates. In Margaret Gruter and Paul Bohannan, eds., *Law, Biology, and Culture; Journal of Social and Biological Structures*, vol. 5 (October), pp. 361-368.

Kummer, Hans. 1979. On the Value of Social Relationships to Nonhuman Primates: A Heuristic Scheme. In Mario von Cranach et al., eds., *Human Ethology.* Cambridge: Cambridge University Press, pp. 381-395.

Leakey, Richard E., and Lewin, Roger. 1977. *Origins.* New York: E. P. Dutton.

Locke, John. 1959. *Essay Concerning Human Understanding.* Alexander Campbell Fraser, ed. New York: Dover.

Lorenz, Konrad. 1970. *Studies in Animal and Human Behaviour.* Vol. I. Cambridge, Mass.: Harvard University Press.

Lorenz, Konrad. 1971. *Studies in Animal and Human Behavior.* Vol. II. Cambridge, Mass.: Harvard University Press.

Lovejoy, C. Owen. 1981. The Origin of Man. *Science,* Vol. 221 (23 Jan.), pp. 341-350.

MacLean, Paul D. 1982. A triangular brief on the evolution of the brain and law. In Margaret Gruter and Paul Bohannan, eds., *Law, Biology, and Culture; Journal of Social and Biological Structures,* vol. 5 (October), pp. 369-379.

Margolis, Howard. 1981. A New Model of Rational Choice. *Ethics,* Vol. 91 (Jan.), pp. 265-279.

Masters, Roger D. 1968. *The Political Philosophy of Rousseau.* Princeton, N.J.: Princeton University Press.

Masters, Roger D. 1976a. Exit, Voice, and Loyalty in Animal and Human Behavior. *Social Science Information,* Vol. 15 (Dec.), pp. 78-85.

Masters, Roger D. 1976b. The Impact of Ethology on Political Science. In Albert Somit, ed., *Biology and Politics.* The Hague: Mouton, pp. 197-233.

Masters, Roger D. 1978a. Jean-Jacques is Alive and Well: Rousseau and Contemporary Sociobiology. *Daedalus* (Summer), pp. 93-105.

Masters, Roger D. 1978b. Of Marmots and Men: Human Altruism and Animal Behavior. In Lauren Wispe, ed., *Altruism, Sympathy, and Helping.* New York: Academic Press, pp. 59-77.

Masters, Roger D. 1980. Hobbes and Locke. In Ross Fitzgerald, ed., *Comparing Political Thinkers.* Sydney and New York: Pergamon. pp. 116-140.

Masters, Roger D. 1981. The Value–and Limitations–of Sociobiology. In Elliott White, ed., *Sociobiology and Human Politics.* Lexington, Mass.: Lexington Books, pp. 135-65.

Masters, Roger D. 1982a. Is Sociobiology Reactionary? The Political Implications of Inclusive Fitness Theory. *Quarterly Review of Biology,* Vol. 57 (September), pp. 275-92.

Masters, Roger D. 1982b. Evolutionary biology, political theory and the origin of the state. In Margaret Gruter and Paul

Bohannan, eds., *Law, Biology, and Culture; Journal of Social and Biological Structures,* vol. 5 (October), pp. 433-50.

Masters, Roger D. 1983. The Biological Nature of the State. *World Politics,* Vol. 35 (January), pp. 161-93.

Olson, Mancur Jr. 1965. *The Logic of Collective Action.* Cambridge, Mass.: Harvard University Press.

Plato. 1968. *Republic.* Allan Bloom, ed. New York: Basic Books.

Rousseau, Jean-Jacques. 1964. *First and Second Discourses.* Roger D. Masters, ed., New York: St. Martin's Press.

Rousseau, Jean-Jacques. 1966. *Essay on the Origin of Languages.* J. H. Moran, ed., New York: Unger.

Rousseau, Jean-Jacques. 1978. *Social Contract, with Geneva MS and Political Economy.* Roger D. Masters, ed., New York: St. Martin's Press.

Rousseau, Jean-Jacques. 1979. *Emile.* Allen Bloom, ed., New York: Basic Books.

Sagan, Carl. 1977. *The Dragons of Eden.* New York: Ballantine.

Trivers, Robert. 1981. Sociobiology and Politics. In Elliott White, ed., *Sociobiology and Human Politics.* Lexington, Mass.: Lexington Books.

Willhoite, Fred H., Jr. 1981. Rank and Reciprocity: Speculations on Human Emotions and Political Life. In Elliott White, ed., *Sociobiology and Human Politics.* Lexington, Mass.: Lexington Books.

Williams, George C. 1966. *Adaptation and Natural Selection.* Princeton, N.J.: Princeton University Press.

Wilson, Edward O. 1975. *Sociobiology.* Cambridge, Mass.: Harvard University Press.

Chapter 6

THE PROBLEMATIC OF CITIZENSHIP IN LIBERAL DEMOCRACY: AN ESSAY ON POLITICS AND FAITH

Jerome B. King

Religion has not confined itself to enriching human intellect, formed beforehand, with a certain number of ideas; it has contributed to forming the intellect itself. Men owe to it not only a good part of the substance of their knowledge, but also the form in which this knowledge is elaborated.

Émile Durkheim,
The Elementary Forms of Religious Life

Religion is . . . the companion of liberty in all its battles and triumphs; the cradle of its infancy, and the divine source of its claims. The safeguard of morality is religion, and morality is the best security of law, and the surest pledge of freedom.

Alexis de Tocqueville, *Democracy in America*

The ultimate transcendence of the individual over communal and social process can be understood and guarded only in a religious culture which knows of a universe of meaning in which this individual freedom has support and significance.

Reinhold Niebuhr, *The Children of Light and the Children of Darkness*

A true Christian . . . serves the state as he performs all other works of love . . . He . . . serves the state not because he needs it, but because others need it - that they may be protected and that the wicked may not become worse.

Martin Luther, *Secular Authority: To What Extent It Should Be Obeyed*

THE PROBLEM

The duties of citizenship are easily enumerated. They include not only obeying laws and paying taxes–resident aliens are expected to do as much–but also taking an active, intelligent, and even impartial interest in public affairs, informing ourselves conscientiously about them in order that we may form and act upon our own disinterested judgments about what is fair and best for the communities in which we live. Knowledgeable and willing participation is the heart and soul of good citizenship, and it requires of us to give our time, our money, our energy, our thought, and perhaps even our goods and lives for the maintenance of those political practices that give substance to our rights and freedoms.

Yet everywhere among the liberal democracies the duties of citizenship are more lamented than practiced. The most knowledgeable and "willing" actors in their political systems are today, and always have been, major corporate interests, whose concern for the public good is clearly subordinate to pursuit of private gain. Among natural persons, it is a rare one who can bring sufficient good will to political activities to practice them with conscientious regularity. As for people who seek and win public office, are they not only a special case of that lusting of power after power that, Hobbes tells us, ceases only in death? We should certainly doubt an argument claiming that elected officials were better citizens than the rest of us, perhaps for the same reason we respond to "public service" advertisements placed by major corporations with reserve. Mustn't a good citizen engage in political activities not because he wants to further his own interests, whether they be monetary or psychological, but because he wants to promote the right, perhaps even in the very face of his own interests if justice so requires? But if this is the case, what motive, what underlying moral obligation, can be set forth that will enable us to overcome our usual tendency to shape our political judgments and activities from the perspective of our personal interests?

An easy answer is, no doubt, love of country: "Ask not what your country can do for you. Ask rather what you can do for your country". John F. Kennedy's words sounded inspiring when they were uttered. But, as a columnist noted a couple of years later, it ironically seemed that what you could best do for your country was to ask for a personal income tax cut. The insufficiency of patriotism as an inspiration to the accomplishment of civic duty is illustrated in more obvious ways. Patriotism may just as well produce "good Germans," Iranian revolutionaries, Red Guards, or any other kind of collective feeling that could by no stretching be called helpful to the duties of citizenship enumerated above. Love of country too often derives from hatred of foreigners, and too many historical examples show its force abetting the arbitrary, unreflective, and violent in public life, to allow the assumption that it will serve only constitutional regimes and democratic practices.

THE DEFICIENCY OF LIBERAL POLITICAL THEORY

If love of country is put to one side (and I shall come back to it later when touching on civic religions),–then our next move can be to consider liberal political theory in and of itself. Here again, however, the search will hardly be rewarding. The title of a book of essays published some years ago,– *The Poverty of Liberalism*,–suggests the direction commonly taken by contemporary criticism. That apostle of liberalism, John Stuart Mill, pointed out the problems more than a century ago in a number of essays, of which the one on Bentham is perhaps the most telling. Speaking of that reformer in terms that may fairly be said to apply to liberal theorizing in general, Mill wrote:

> Bentham's knowledge of human nature . . . is wholly empirical; and the empiricism of one who has had little experience. . . . He saw accordingly in man little but what the vulgarest eye can see; recognized no diversities of character but what he who runs may read. . . .
>
> The bad part of his writings is his resolute denial of all that he does not see, of all truths but those he recognizes. . . . By that . . . he has put himself at the head of the school which exists always, though it does not always find great men to give it the sanction of philosophy: thrown the mantle of intellect over the natural tendency of men in all ages to deny the existence of spiritual influences of which they have no consciousness themselves.[1]

[1] *Essays on Politics and Culture by John Stuart Mill*, G. Himmelfarb, ed.(Garden City, N.Y.: Doubleday, 1963), pp. 96-97. See also pp. 99-100.)

Mill's criticism finds reflection in recent comment:

> The particular harm that a century of liberalism has accomplished . . . has been to trap much of the human spirit of emancipation within the false imagery of individualistic pursuit of happiness and civil liberties. Liberals have persistently tended to cut the citizen off from the person; and they have placed on their humanistic pedestal a cripple of man, a man without a political or moral nature; a man with plenty of contractual rights and obligations, perhaps, but a man without moorings in any real community; a drifter rather than a being with roots in species solidarity. Liberalism, in short, for all the comparative advantages for the better-off in liberal societies (in contrast to feudal, fascist, or military-ruled or even allegedly socialist societies) has drastically impoverished our appreciation of man's nature and potentialities.[2]

Liberal political theory seems to reflect a kind of Newtonian conception of society, as if a political regime were a machine for the efficient production of goods and services, and as if the primary function of government was to keep all the parts in smooth working order. Since the basic part of society is the individual, appeals to a certain conventionalized and standardized self-interest become the predominant motive for action. Whether such appeals are best ordered by spontaneous forces in the marketplace, according to Adam Smith's Unseen Hand, or by skillful manipulation according to the plans of enlightened despots and technocrats, is of little moment here. For the conception of human motives is throughout the same: What makes Sammy run? And when a political system has discovered what can make Sammy run, for the sake of its own stability it clearly has no interest in educating Sammy to march to a different drummer. Hence it is that once liberal political thought has reduced human nature to a stimulus-response mechanism, all considerations of public morality, or civic virtue, are put aside. The mechanism assures political and economic order without dependence on the good will of any participant. *Homo economicus* takes pride of place over the citizen. Hence it is a constant of liberal political thought to regard appeals to self-interest as the most reliable instrument of social control. As David Hume wrote:

[2] Christian Bay, "From Contract to Community: Thoughts on Liberalism and Post-Industrial Society," in Fred R. Dallmayr, ed., *From Contract to Community: Political Theory at the Crossroads* (New York: M. Dekker, 1978), p. 30.

> A republican and free government would be an obvious absurdity if the particular checks and controls provided by the constitution had really no influence and made it not the interest, even of bad men, to act for the public good.[3]

Thus Bentham's "idea of the world" as

> a collection of persons each pursuing his separate interest or pleasure, and the prevention of whom from jostling one another more than can be helped, must be attempted by hopes and fears . . . derived from legal, religious, and social sanctions . . .[4]

expresses the goal of all liberal political theory, for which the division of all things into "mine" and "thine" constitutes the essence of political sagacity. Mill himself is partially victim to this way of thinking in his attempt to protect "self-regarding" actions from the pressure of public opinion and the tyranny of the majority. But that he also recognized its defects is shown in his judgment on Bentham's theory:

> There is no need to expatiate on the deficiencies of a system of ethics which does not pretend to aid individuals in the formation of their own character; which recognizes no such wish as that of self-culture, we may even say no such power, as existing in human nature.[5]

Through its development in the doctrines of utilitarianism, liberalism not only has created an "atomistic" individual, but has taken giant strides toward destroying sense of the self necessary to individuality. "Doing your own thing" is only a current expression of reduction of moral problems to conventional legal formulas, on the one hand, and "personal preferences," on the other. "Life style" has long since replaced consideration of the good life in the popular imagination, while the apparent variety of such styles masks their essential similarity–to optimize personal pleasurable feelings without reference to, or discussion of, community values, standards, or norms. From utilitarianism's point of view, life-styles are not to be judged by any such standards. They are simply facts subject to quantitative analysis. Because there can be no discussion of moral

[3] David Hume, "That Politics May be Reduced to a Science," in *Hume's Moral and Political Philosophy,* H. D. Aiken (ed.), (New York: Hafner, 1948), p. 296.

[4] Mill, "On Bentham," op. cit., p. 100.

[5] Mill, *op. cit.*

obligation within a philosophical framework that treats the human individual as having no interior culture, and hence no power of moral choice, the "good" is necessarily reduced to abstract matters of number, size, or power. In Hobbes's terms, all things, including persons, are worth what they will bring in the marketplace.[6] Or, as Rousseau claimed in *The Discourse on the Arts and Sciences,*

> Our modern politicians will tell you that in such or such a country a man is worth what he will sell for in Algiers; another, following this calculation, will find countries where a man is worth nothing, and others where he is worth less than nothing. They price men like herds of cattle. According to them, a man is worth no more to the State than the value of his domestic consumption.[7]

We are thus brought back to the notion of social engineering so dear to the hearts of liberals from the eighteenth century on. From the perspective of the social engineer, the only thing of interest is the external behavior of the human subject. The engineer's function is to experiment with various stimuli until the desired behavior results. In the liberal view, personal hopes of wealth and status, on the one hand, and personal fears of poverty and loss of social position, on the other hand, are by so far the two most dependable motivators of human behavior that all other causes may be ignored. The social order of industrialization and consequent economic growth, especially over the last century, have made it possible to provide an enormous range of things available on the marketplace to reflect and channel such hopes and fears. Contemporary liberal regimes have thus been able to replace political ideas with economic symbols. The social and political mores of modern life in the United States are probably better expressed by the Internal Revenue code than by the Constitution of 1789. For the code, by suitable appeals to monetary self-interest, guides fundamental corporate and individual decisions–savings, investment, charitable giving, inheritance, patterns of home building, cultural and artistic endeavors, urban and land development, and often even marriage. Were Rousseau alive today he would surely see little reason to change a view he expressed

[6] *Leviathan,* Part 1, ch. 10: "The *value* or worth of a man is, as of all other things, his price–that is to say, so much as would be given for his power . . . . As in other things, so in men, not the seller but the buyer determines the price."

[7] Jean-Jacques Rousseau, *Rousseau's First and Second Discourses,* Roger D. Masters, ed. (New York: St. Martin's Press, 1964), Part 2, p. 51.

in his first *Discourse:* "[While] ancient politicians spoke ceaselessly of morals and virtue, ours speak only of commerce and money. . . ."[8]

To restate the obvious, then, it would appear that liberal political thought does not contain within it a source capable of giving rise to the obligations of citizenship or, indeed, to any moral obligation at all. Personal calculation of advantage is assumed to be the only general and reliable motive for action. And if Tocqueville found in American culture a disposition to see how one's own advantage was linked to that of others, so that self-interest "rightly considered" could produce collective action for the common good, such action was nevertheless dependent not on a wish for the welfare of the public thing as a good in itself but rather only on the urge to satisfy one's own desires. In Tocqueville's view, democratic citizenship in the age of liberalism could no longer derive from noble sentiments. It must rather depend on informed and prudent judgment by individuals about how their own material interests are bound up with the well-being of the whole.[9] To the extent such a sense is lost, or weakened, as it has been by the unimaginable complexities of an interdependent world, to that degree must a citizenship so based be equally vitiated.

But we do not need to look to the moderns alone to see why liberalism provides a weak moral basis for citizenship. Plato raised the issue long ago when he explained why the social contract, on which liberal political theory is based, precludes moral obligation. The reason is that agreement to the social contract requires a self-conscious agent, knowing the reasons for his consent. Were this not the case, the contract would have no foundation among those nominally approving it. And for what reason is the social contract accepted? It is the desire to escape harm to oneself in a world in which one cannot always be sure of getting the better of others:

> When people do and suffer injustice in dealing with one another . . . those who cannot both escape the one and take the other think it profitable to make an agreement neither to do nor suffer injustice; from this thay make laws and compacts . . . and they name the injunction of the law lawful and just.[10]

[8] Ibid.

[9] Alexis de Tocqueville, *Democracy in America.* H. Reeve, tr. (New York: Schocken, 1961), Part 2, Book 2, chs. 8 and 9.

[10] Plato, The Republic in W. H. D. Rouse, tr., *Great Dialogues of Plato* (New York: Mentor, 1956), p. 156 (358c).

The purpose of political association based on social contract cannot, in short, rise above the self-interested calculation underlying its establishment. It must remain forever wedded to each individual's concern to protect his or her own personal interests, the condition for which is to put aside any wish to enhance shared values through participation in community making, and to accept instead a particular statement of the Golden Rule: *do not do unto others what you would not have them do unto you.*

THE CLASSICAL GREEK TRADITION

These negative reflections on liberal political thinking suggest turning to the classical political philosophy of ancient Greece in the search for an underlying moral motive for citizenship. For it is clear that we owe much of our current thinking about public life and social justice to the tradition of political theory first reflected in Plato and Aristotle. Do not their arguments about the moral importance of the *polis,* and of active participation in the life of the city, provide the very terms for our own ideals of citizenship? As George Armstrong Kelly has recently argued, a renewed theory of citizenship would first seem to require a renewed theory of the state as a moral entity, so that the moral obligation to act deliberately on behalf of the public interest could be grounded on a broader ethic than utilitarian self-interest.[11] If we are to say that a person has a duty to participate in public life, do we not have to find reasons for so doing that go beyond mere external personal advantage? Were we to follow Kelly's thesis, we should likely have to say, with Rousseau, that a renewed theory of the state must produce

> a truly remarkable change in the individual . . . substituting justice for instinct in his behavior, and giv(ing) to his social actions a moral basis which was formerly lacking. Only when the voice of duty replaces physical impulse and the cravings of appetite does the man who, till then, was concerned wholly with himself, realize that he is under compulsion to obey quite different principles, and that he must now consult his reason and not merely the promptings of desire. . . . By dint of being exercised, his faculties develop, his ideas take on wider scope, his sentiments become ennobled, and his whole soul be so elevated, that, but for the fact that

[11] George A. Kelly, "Who Needs a Theory of Citizenship?" 108 *Daedalus* 4 (Fall 1979): 21-36.

> misuse of the new conditions still, at times, degrades him to a point below that from which he has emerged, he would unceasingly bless the day which freed him forever from his ancient state, and turned him from a limited and stupid animal into an intelligent being and a Man.[12]

And if we think for a moment of the other great tradition in modern thought–the Judeo-Christian–with its apparent emphasis on family and personal belief, we may feel all the more driven to consider the Greek inheritance as the only one from which a theory of public life can be derived. Indeed, the fundamental liberal principle of the separation of church and state, of religion and politics, would at first seem to push us in the same direction, toward a theory of autonomous political values from which may be deduced a moral obligation of citizenship.

It is the burden of this essay to show why the temptation to imagine a secular politics based on Greek notions of reason and a natural ethics is deceptive for those of liberal disposition, for whom, as I hope to show, a Judeo-Christian tradition of theology and a revealed ethics must remain a *sine qua non* of their political theory. To do this I shall have to review aspects of both Greek and Hebrew traditions, to show how a Christian attempt to combine the two has to constitute the ground of liberal political thinking even today.

The key to the underlying moral obligation of citizenship in the classical Greek tradition is enlightened self-interest. The good citizen recognizes in the performance of his civic duties his best practicable opportunity for self-fulfillment. But the critical terms of this statement need clarification, lest one suppose the modern liberal's notion of self-interest has simply brought the ancient idea up to date. Nothing, in fact, could be further from the truth. The critical terms concern what enlightenment and the self really are.

As Socrates makes clear during his trial before the Athenian jury, taking part in the institutional offices and functions of the city does not constitute the whole, or even the basis, of civic duty. Indeed, he says that if he had devoted himself to such offices and functions he would have been condemned by Athens long before his seventieth year. The basis of one's true civic duties is, rather, active and disinterested participation in an ongoing moral discourse that, in Socrates' view, constitutes the city to which loyalty is owed. It is the

[12] Jean-Jacques Rousseau, *Social Contract*, Ernest Barker, ed., (Gerard Hopkins, tr. (New York: Oxford, 1962), p. 185, Bk. 1, ch. 8.

nature, or purpose, of this ongoing moral discourse to provide enlightenment for all involved. How can it do so? It does so because it engages those who share in it in examination of the meaning of life, since the "unexamined life is not worth living." Mill would call it a stimulus to self-culture, and hence, we may add, a moral theology. The true self will never come to light unless we are prepared to reflect earnestly and constantly on the place of humanity in the grand scheme of things, so that we may think and act in order to fulfill our parts in that scheme. To pursue these questions is to open up the possibility of becoming truly human, i.e., of discovering one's true self. Becoming truly human is, in the classical Greek tradition of political philosophy, what both the city and the citizen essentially must do, for the ultimate end of both lies beyond time and history in eternity.

Socrates' fundamental argument–repeated in Plato's *Republic* and Aristotle's *Politics*–is that the sophists and ordinary opinion characteristically mistake the real truth of human nature. Their vulgar error is to suppose that self-interests are opposed to those of the community, that if one could only get the better of others one could be really well off. The wily Odysseus is a kind of role model for this vulgar error. Surrounded by seducers, demons, and wild creatures, all willing to destroy him for their own purposes, Odysseus manages, mostly by his own wits, to find the way safely home to Penelope, where he slays his last tormentors and lives happily ever after. Underlying this common error is the feeling that all trouble is external to us, and that therefore the answer to our problems is sufficient wherewithal to defend ourselves from them. "The world is too much with us" because we take for granted that good and evil lie outside of us and that happiness is based on control over agreeable and disagreeable stimuli. So we naturally desire to have those things–money, power, reputation–that we suppose to constitute our safety against the world. But the great tradition of rationalist Greek political thought tells us that such opinion is ignorant error. If we only understood that the truth of all eternal things really lies in our own souls we should be ready to pursue our happiness by rational method.

What is that method? It is the way of the true self. And understanding it opens the path not only to personal happiness but also to social concord, justice, friendship, and community. The true self is, however, not an individualist in the sense modern culture understands the term. It is, rather, part of a spiritual whole or unity, reflected temporally in the city. Conflict within the self and between persons in society can only result from the false notion that our personal destinies are not linked to the community. But no one can fulfill his destiny outside the city, for its culture is the only available temporal expression of ultimate meaning. All our attempts at self-fulfillment and the pursuit of happiness must come back to the moral fact that we cannot think at all except in the terms and according to the structures provided us by our society. Thus when Aristotle says that we are "political animals" he means that we are very creatures of the *polis,* whose own culture of "reasoned speech" gives meaning and substance to our particular lives.

From this point of view, the moral life of the part is inseparable from the moral life of the whole. Those actions by which the city develops its own culture of reasoned speech are essential to the development of each citizen's self-culture. The moral obligation of citizenship rests on two duties that are radically one: a filial duty–witness Socrates' saying that the laws of Athens are his parents–and a duty to oneself. For all that is positive in our own moral development we must, like Socrates, share in our city's universe of discourse, because it is only in that sharing that we can pursue our own fulfillment. In Socrates' metaphor, the morally and intellectually lazy thoroughbred horse, Athens, needs him, the gadfly, to stir her to suitable activity, i.e., philosophical discourse. But he, as gadfly, needs the horse in order to accomplish his destiny, too. He and Athens have a symbiotic relationship. When he tells the jury that his sentence should be free board and lodging at public expense, he is expressing his own sense of moral obligation: to help both himself and his fellow citizens avoid the living death of an unexamined life. The only thing for which Athens might properly censure him, or any other citizen, would be failure to carry on this duty seriously.

Personal virtue is thus a matter of carrying out one's appropriate function in the city according to the needs, material and moral, of both the part and the whole, both the self and the city. Where needs are material–reproduction of the population, production of goods and services vital to its physical survival, things that are summed up under the term "household" and that we today generally include under the term "economics"–those who perform them are subject to suitable training in order to develop the appropriate specialized skills. Where the city's needs are moral and political, on the other hand, they must be provided for by a class of free men, i.e., citizens, who are deliberately raised to promote the universe of moral discourse whose continuity is the city's *raison d'être.* The just city understands and furthers the appropriate division of labor, or function, so that each contributes what nature, or destiny, best fits him to do. Civic virtue and personal virtue are thus two sides of the same coin. Both are summed up in the term *arete*–functional excellence. The just city generates enough public understanding of community goals that the purposes of each of its members are fulfilled by their undertaking those community activities for which they are best prepared by talent and education. Provision of such places and the people to fill them, i.e., the giving to every person of his or her due in the city, is distributive or social justice. Thus does the rationalist Greek perspective on the political nature of man resolve the apparent conflict between the One and the Many.

So long as classical Greek political philosophy controls the idea of citizenship, therefore, performance of its duties remains the only path, short of divine understanding, to self-fulfillment. As Socrates shows in his manner of life and death, the good man and the good citizen are logically one and the same, because the spiritual purpose of the universe of moral discourse they mutually share and uphold identifies them both with freedom and eternal truth.

THE CONFLICT OF CLASSICAL AND LIBERAL THOUGHT

The appeal of this classical Greek tradition of political thought has lasted long after the city-state, its only historical setting, passed from the scene. A vision of communitarian life, in which conflict between the individual and society is resolved to the ultimate benefit of both by discovery of a common ethical purpose through free and open discussion, has attracted thinkers throughout Western history. But for modern culture it must remain a vision of mythical, not to say mystical, character. Aside from the economic and military weaknesses of the city-state, there remain its moral and intellectual drawbacks from the modern point of view. As Rousseau suggested, modern man has already been corrupted by commercial wealth and cosmopolitan tastes. A rigorous sense of one's own self as a moral being, linked through the city to Truth, has long since been lost. It has been replaced by a hypersensitive individualism that, again in Rousseau's words, draws the sentiment of its own existence from seeing its reflection in the eyes of others. We are ill-equipped by history on either material or psychological grounds to be the builders and upholders of city-states–so ill-equipped, indeed, that contemporary admirers of that tradition are sometimes gently mocked, not altogether inappropriately, as "*polis* romantics."

Objections to *polis* romanticism from the liberal point of view are fundamental. The city-state has no conception of individual human rights because its values are rooted in moral and physical functionality.

Political participation thus means what its etymology implies: we participate because we are parts of a greater whole, without which our own individual lives would be not only impoverished but quite without meaning or value. It is for this reason that the classical idea of law as a moral norm, reflecting the ultimate values of the community, must also be rejected. The liberal looks not to the law but to individual conscience for ethical standards, lest place or function in the social order should determine all human value. Rather, the law sets minimal standards of outward behavior, and its mode of operation is coercive rather than educative.

"*Participation*" is indeed the wrong word to apply to the liberal's political activities, for it properly implies sharing in a common moral life, a conception of politics that the liberal must deny, whatever the temptation to think of his community as an entity to which filial respect is owed. In brief, liberals must apparently reject virtually the whole of the Greek rationalist political philosophy in order to save human rights and constitutional checks and balances.

How can they do so? On what grounds do they have the temerity to deprive both themselves and their fellows, as a matter of constitutional principle, from sharing in the kind of political life that could transform humans from "limited and stupid animals" into "intelligent beings and men"?

The liberal undertakes this denial on theological grounds by following a moral theology that is at critical points Hebraic rather than Greek. Since individual things, including individual human beings, are all part of a world deliberately willed into existence by a Creator, the meaning of any one of them does not come from its functional relationship to the rest or to some hidden pattern, but rather from the intention of God himself. People have special meaning not because of their reason or their consciousness, but because they are created *imago dei.* Their particular capacities are made not because there is "nothing superfluous in nature" or, as in the case of Socrates' ugliness, to intimate to metaphysical initiates that true beauty lies behind appearances, but simply because it pleases God to make them as he does. At the same time, of course, evil is not thought of as ignorance or lack of intellectual coherence. On the contrary, it is both specific and immediate, arising from each individual's own will to godlike power. The righteous life is not, as the Greek rationalist must logically think, ends oriented. On the contrary, since the end of all life must remain hidden in the Creator's intentions, the meaning of one's own life arises not from reason but from worship of the Lord of all things. The Fall, however, has rendered impossible this undertaking by humans unaided. Left to our own devices, we are more inclined to curse God for his inexplicable unfairness than to worship him for the beauty of his creation. Only the living Word of God can provide the help necessitated by humanity's own sinful choice.

Hebrew moral theology thus focuses on individual will, on the one hand, and on the ways in which the Word of God may be brought home in order to allow humans to change their ways, on the other. The Word of God is present in Scripture only insofar as it is put there by individual searching and interpretation. Not to find or hear the Word of God is a failure occasioned by a more or less deliberate refusal. So for the Hebrew the motto *"know thyself"* has a very different sense than that given it by Socrates. It means not seeking the truth obscured in the soul by the misleading faces of corporeal existence, but rather becoming aware of those desires and intentions by which every individual continues to participate in Adam's sin.

These traditional differences between Greek and Hebrew culture mean that truth, after which all humanity strives in one way or another, enters into political and social processes in radically different ways. Classical Greek political philosophy makes the city's method of pursuing the truth, through its own universe of discourse, the substance of its constitutional legitimacy. Justice in the city is the very condition of meaning for its members' lives. But in the Hebraic view, the pursuit of truth has a radically individual character, representing every person's own responsibility for the disposition of his heart.

THE THEOLOGY OF LIBERALISM

Historically speaking, the theology of liberal political thought is Augustinian in the earliest major attempts to incorporate elements of the radically different Hebraic and Greek traditions into one doctrine while reflecting and giving meaning to the inherent conflict between the two. Based on the idea of the Fall, this theology posits the existence of two cities that may be called, perhaps without being wholly misleading, the *Hebrew* City of Man and the *Greek* City of God. Both are spiritual cities, and both are characterized by love. But the first is ordered by the worldly love of domination, while the second is ordered by love for God and neighbor.

The City of Man is founded on fratricide: Cain killing Abel or, for pagan understandings, Romulus killing Remus. But this fratricide has its origin in Adam's rejection of or, more explicitly, his attempt to replace God, by eating the fruit. Far from making him free, however, Adam's new knowledge enslaves him to sin and death–a slavery that every generation has since willingly adopted on its own account.

Members of the worldly city thus give it its essential character of faithless will to absolute power. The evils of the city are outward manifestations of the inward disposition of those who constitute it. Like us, the worldly city identifies itself with the rule of the sword, and with symbols of wealth and honor. As a consequence, our lives are filled with

> gnawing cares, disquiet, griefs, fears, wild joys, quarrels, lawsuits, wars, treasons, angers, hatreds, deceit, flattery, fraud, theft, robbery, perfidy, pride, ambition, envy, murders, parricides, cruelty, ferocity, wickedness, luxury, insolence, impudence, shamelessness, fornications, adulteries, incests . . . and innumerable other crimes that do not come easily to mind, but that never absent themselves from the actuality of human existence.[13]

Nor is it as if, through the simple recognition of its sinfulness, humanity could organize its city on mutual forbearance alone, thereby avoiding conflict. On the contrary, the Fall is always an actual reality, politically and socially reflected in all human institutions, including what is perhaps the most fundamental of them all, language. For, as St. Augustine points out, in our fallen state even "the tongue is instrument of domination"; the love of power is ineradicable in fallen human nature, and knowledge is not only no check on it but rather only lust's fig leaf. As Bacon says, knowledge is power.

Not even the visible church could escape Augustine's corrosive analysis. Who should understand the lust for domination better, indeed, than the Bishop of Hippo, who never liked to lose an argument and, if his *Confessions* are testimony, never did? Once his prophetic view of the temporal world informed the Mediterranean world view, no longer could Greek conceptions of justice hold exclusive sway in thinking about worldly values. Since those values are but rationalizations of worldly power, a true moral education must rather distance itself from them. The discourse of God's City can only be undertaken in the language of his truth as revealed in his Word. Far from having us share in the rationalist's notion of the good life, St. Augustine demands of us that we share in the suffering of this world, taking upon ourselves, as Christ took upon himself, the Cross.[14]

The good life is therefore not synonymous with a patient and systematic self-discipline based on what our culture takes to be its best values. Nor is it the pursuit of identity through contemplation

[13] *Augustine, City of God,* XXII, 22. from H. Paolucci, (ed.), *The Political Writings of St. Augustine,* (South Bend: Regnery, 1962), p. 2.

[14] "That all men wish to be happy is a certitude for anyone who can think. But as long as human intelligence remains incapable of deciding which men are happy and how they became so, endless controversies arise in which philosophers waste their time and toil." Ibid., X, 1.

of eternal truths. It springs rather from an immediate and personal recognition of one's own sinfulness, thus opening the way to the subordination of the socially constituted sense of self to God's will. The way of the truth is no longer guided by social idealism, and good will is no longer the educated moral habit of the right-thinking community. For if we tend to think today that religion is "consciousness of our highest social values," as the modern Augustinian Reinhold Niebuhr has put it,

> nothing could be further from the truth. True religion is a profound uneasiness about our highest social values. Its uneasiness springs from the knowledge that the God who it worships transcends the limits of finite man, while this same man is constantly tempted to forget the finiteness of his cultures and civilization and to pretend for them a finality they do not have.[15]

Of course we are all socialized by our cultures and civilization. And there is an illusion of freedom arising from our intellectual ability to see the contradictions they inevitably present us with. But true freedom has a radically different source. It lies in *metanoia*–repentance–turning one's back on the values inculcated by socialization in order to accept the will of God.

The moment realization of the absolute necessity of good will in this sense takes root, one is "twice born." Will is no longer what it was for Greek rationalism, an instrument of self-discipline for leading the good life. It is, rather, a power of the heart to turn away from one's self toward the concrete other, in whom one perceives the Other.

The moral education of the citizen, which Greek rationalist political thought makes the key to social justice, is thus removed by Augustinian theology from political authority altogether. This removal is indeed the very condition of secular politics. Far from meaning indifference to spiritual values, however, the removal shows that the liberal has to ground spiritual values in the conscience of the individual informed by the Word of God, thus protecting them from the institutional exercise of the lust for worldly power. Such protection implies bills of rights, of course. But even more fundamentally it depends on a state of mind that rejects every government's, every society's, and every person's attempt at self-

15 Reinhold Niebuhr, *Beyond Tragedy* (New York: Scribner's Sons, 1937), p. 28.

legitimization through claims to justice and truth.

are summed up in Richard Hooker's words:

> Two foundations there are which bear up all public societies; one is the natural inclination whereby all men desire sociable life and fellowship; the other an order . . . touching the manner of their union in living together. The latter is what we call the law of the commonwealth. . . . Laws politics, ordained for the external order and regiment among men, are never framed as they should be, unless presuming the will of man to be inwardly obstinate, rebellious and averse to all obedience to the sacred laws of his nature; in a word, unless presuming man to be in regard of his depraved mind little better than a wild beast.[16]

The checking of power by power is, in short, what a constitution is all about. Coercion is the political means par excellence precisely because truth is not available to power:

> The business of the laws is not to provide for the truth of opinions, but for the safety and security of the commonwealth, and of every particular man's goods and person. And so it ought to be. For the truth certainly would do well enough if she were once left to shift for herself. She has seldom received, and I fear never will receive, much assistance from the power of great men, to whom she is rarely known and more rarely welcome. . . . [I]f truth makes not her way into the understanding by her own light, she will be but the weaker for any borrowed force violence can add to her.[17]

Liberal political theory, we can now see, arises out of an appreciation of the inherent conflict between the two cities. The only practical expedient for the routine managing of this conflict is to insist on the secular character of the earthly City. But the secular character of the earthly City is dependent absolutely on a living faith in the heavenly City. So liberal political theory necessitates a series of paradoxes, the most fundamental of which is that liberal citizenship depends on a spiritual faith that both that faith and secularism itself forbid being propagated in a legally authoritative way. Liberal political thinking involves us, in short, in two conflicting universes of moral discourse, of different origins and histories. The one reflects

[16] Cited by John Locke, *The Second Treatise of Government,* sec. 135, n. 11. from Richard Hooker, *Of the Laws of Ecclesiastical Politiy,* 8 books. (London: John Windet, 1594-1597), lib. 1, sec. 10.

[17] Locke, *A Letter Concerning Toleration,* 2nd ed. (Indianapolis: Bobbs-Merrill, 1955), pp. 45-46.

civic, or public, values, the other divine. Their combination puts us as citizens in a morally and intellectually disturbing position. It obliges us to take freedom as acting on choices between the two.

Under these circumstances, it is not surprising that liberalism has lent itself to civic religions; for true faith, on which it must logically depend, makes demands that cannot be fulfilled by humanity's own devices. Civic religions remedy this drawback, because, as Machiavelli pointed out, they can be manipulated by worldly powers to avoid a freedom so apparently dangerous to social stability. (The example of Savonarola was fresh in Machiavelli's mind.)

True faith, on the other hand, can be neither indoctrinated nor manipulated. The universe of discourse properly its own requires voluntary entrance on the part of the individual into participation in the Word. Faith grants full freedom within the terms of that willingly assumed responsibility. But this means that each of us is always engaged in a struggle between what Niebuhr has called the "priestly" and the "prophetic," choice between which can never be struck in any final way:

> The imperfect human achievement is a symbol and sacrament of the eternal. The priest does not condemn a man's love for his country, though there is always the possibility that the nation will usurp the place of God and make itself the center and source of all meaning. The priest sees in men's devotion to a cause greater than themselves the possibility of faith and devotion to the God who is greater than the causes which are greater than man.[18]

The prophet, on the other hand, warns us against the temptation of false loves, for they lie at the root of real hatreds. He must ever call the human capacity for loyalty, for faithfulness, back to its true and transcendental source.

So what liberalism has today come to understand as the "private" realm of consciousness is, cries the prophetic voice, just what most needs to be shared. Civic religion recognizes the need by providing pseudoreligious rituals, such as pledging allegiance to the flag, in order to reaffirm what our own love of power causes us to believe anyway, that evil lies outside ourselves and our tribe. Thus may any who do not worship, or even who do not fully share in, our society's values be despised when it serves the interests of power to have them

[18] Niebuhr, *op. cit.*, pp. 63-64.

despised.[19]

This cultivation of hatreds suggests why the motive underlying citizenship cannot find its source in the City of Man but must look instead to the City of God. Political service is required of us ultimately for the same reason that any service to our fellows is an obligation: the command to love our neighbors as ourselves. But because property defines our neighbors by the fences between us and them, we too easily ignore who it is who needs our service, and on what terms.

Yet we need still ask why one should render service as citizens rather than in other ways. Doesn't the common sense of politics as the "art of the possible" advise us to render service where we can be most effective, rather than according to formal distinctions between private and public? Indeed, since our personal interests will give us plenty of reasons for identifying with the satisfactions of the rich and powerful whenever we think we can safely do so, and since moral obligation based on the command to love our neighbors as ourselves is too easily contaminated in the political realm by self-interest, are we not driven to conclude that liberal citizenship is a contradiction in terms? If to love our neighbors means to share in the sufferings and injustices inflicted upon them by chance and the ambitions of the strong, is not the only way through acts of private charity?

To take such a position is to neglect the broad powers of law and government. Though all injustice has a private origin, and its ultimate remedy must be self-recognition and repentance, we can hardly expect these to be realized collectively before the millenium. Prior to that time it is reasonable to bring law and policy to bear against concrete injustices, even though it is clear neither that the reign of justice will be established by so doing nor even that an apparent remedy for one injustice will not sometimes entail another. From the liberal point of view it is therefore vital to distinguish political action against concrete injustices, which may be possible and desirable, from the establishment of social justice, which will ever remain cruel illusion.

[19] What Henry Adams once said of Massachusetts' politics–that it is "the systematic organization of hatred"–is in fact true of all politics. But the capacity to systematize depends on recognition of a moral authority lying outside the system.

Since, on the other hand, the most obvious injustices are often sanctioned by law–as Anatole France once remarked, "In its supreme majesty, the law forbids rich and poor alike to sleep under bridges"–it is equally clear that obedience to governments and laws, or even to the priestly side of our consciences, can never be the touchstone for citizenship. On the contrary, citizenship, like wisdom, must begin in the "fear of the Lord." It is the prophetic factor alone that gives rise to both.

Here, then, is the second paradox in the liberal theory of citizenship. It forces us to put the question of political obligation in a negative way: *When must I be prepared to disobey the law?* When does a concrete injustice sanctioned by law–which may well have been legislated with good intentions–compel me in good faith to witness against it so that my legal punishment may open the eyes of my fellow citizens?[20]

The paradox of secular political life and institutions depending on a faith in a spiritual community of all people requires this second paradox of citizenship's finding its quintessential expression in potential civil disobedience against worldly power. For though the fear of the Lord is only the beginning of citizenship, no obligation to undertake its practices can take force from any other source. So in liberal thinking the good person turns out to be the good citizen after all. But the lines of derivation run the other way than they do in the classical tradition of Greek rationalism. Good citizens in this world are they who mean to act on participation in a City that transcends time, place, and historical circumstance. Good citizens know that all people are citizens of Jerusalem first and forever, but of Babylon only secondarily and for a little while.

[20] In characteristically pungent language St. Augustine assesses the personal risk of legal punishment thus: "This powerful enemy, what [can] he take away? . . . That which a thief or housebreaker could take: in his utmost rage he can but take what a robber can take . . . . I did him too much honor when I said *robber* . . . . He takes from thee what a fever or an adder, or a poisonous mushroom, can take. Here lies the whole power of the rage of men, to do what a mushroom can." *Sermons on Selected Lessons of the New Testament,* 2 vols., R. G. Macmullen, tr. Oxford 1845, from Paolucci, *The Political Writings of St. Augustine, p. 312.* The counterpoint of personal risk is, of course, "Greater love has no man than this, that he lay down his life for his friends." See Mulford Q. Sibley, *The Obligation to Disobey: Conscience and the Law,* (New York: Council on Religion and International Affairs, 1970).

THE PROBLEMATIC

All social and political authority rests on particular relationships with a transcendental realm available only to faith. The commonest reflection of this fact lies in the intimate association, seen in virtually all times and places, of priesthoods and power. The unique and rare contribution of liberal political thinking has been to try to distinguish between the origins of political and social institutions, on the one hand, and spiritual authority, on the other, in order to bring the former under the autonomous judgment of the latter. This contribution itself springs from a unique theology that develops a creative conflict between Hebrew and Greek approaches to moral thought and action. Early cultivated by St. Augustine, this theology bore fruit in Reformation Europe during the breakdown of the medieval synthesis of reason and faith. At that time it nourished a view in which man's rebellion against God was the origin of all secular history, and this view thus enabled thinking about government to turn from considerations of truth to those of practical management of conflict through immediate rewards and punishments. This political theory historically evolved from Pauline theology, which, insisting on the necessity of grace for salvation, at one and the same time opened the door to a politics responsive to temporal needs (since salvation could no longer be its aim), and to a psychology of suffering (rather than of pleasure or positive reinforcement) as the critical mode of individual self-understanding, for repentance. Love of neighbors therefore requires sharing in their suffering–a sharing that means turning against the worldly hopes and expectations underlying the social contract. The possibility for this turning depends on the propagation and understanding of the Word, not by the state or other nominally public entity, but only by individuals aware of their citizenship in the City of God. Within that City, faith effectively renders without meaning all social distinctions: "neither Jew nor Greek, neither slave nor free, neither male nor female . . . "[21] Such transcendentally understood citizenship means that all temporal institutions are necessarily subject to prophetic judgment. None may lay claim to the mantle of self-assumed righteousness, not even–indeed, especially not–the visible church.

[21] (Galatians 3:28.)

Social contract theory is built on this theological perspective. Like all private contracts, the social contract is meant to provide reasonable expectations of determinate performance, not a community of faith, hope, or love. The social contract, far from reforming its members' souls, is but a reflection of their fallen state. At best it provides a civic order based on mutual acceptance of private and human rights and the power of law to enforce breaches of them. Thus do liberals mean to make government as "neutral" as possible among contending interests. For them, Pontius Pilate is the appropriate model of responsible political activity. Skeptical that the truth is available to any human mind, he decides to execute a person with whom he can find no fault and to release a person who has duly been found guilty of a crime, for fear of public disorder. Thus does expediency, not justice, necessarily govern the liberal conception of governmental action. And hence it is that the social contract is not merely an attempt at remedying the worst secular effects of the Fall but also at one and the same time confirmation of the Fall's actuality in everyday political and social life.

And yet the so-called separation between church and state, between moral and political life, between the real security of individuals and mere police protection, can never be absolute. As Locke notes:

> A good life, in which consists not the least of religion and true piety, concerns also the government, and in it lies the safety both of men's souls and the commonwealth. Moral actions belong therefore to the jurisdiction both of the inward and outward court . . . I mean both of the magistrate and the conscience. Here, therefore, lies great danger, lest one of the jurisdictions entrench upon the other and discord arise between the keeper of the public peace and the overseers of souls.[22]

[22] Locke, op. cit., p. 46. This concern of Locke is expressed more profoundly by St. Augustine when he notes that the Greek *political* virtues of prudence, temperance, fortitude, and justice are necessarily transformed when infused by the Christian virtues of faith, hope, and charity. And this transformation leads to a confrontation with classical political values. The medieval synthesis of reason and faith, usually associated with St. Thomas Aquinas, is in fact a hierarchical arrangement of Greek and Christian virtues in which, if I may be permitted the expression, Christian virtues appear as a kind of frosting on the cake of Greek virtues. But then the Thomistic world is constituted of agreeable hierarchies, whereas the Augustinian world is full of radical conflicts.

It is the great danger that freedom may weaken worldly powers by undermining their self-righteousness.

As it is part of the conventional wisdom of our age to say that God is dead, the kind of analysis put forth here will no doubt appear to most readers as quaint or antiquarian, and at any rate quite beside the point of our present moral and intellectual needs. But the gods of nationalism, industrialism, scientism, rationalism, and any other of a dozen or so "isms" are still anything but moribund. If we may know a tree by its fruits, contemporary faith in these false gods has produced not hope but despair, not love but hatreds so consuming that only personal torture, on the one hand, and the technological and organizational possibility of destroying life on this planet, on the other, seem capable of satiating them. We can hardly know whether God exists or not until we stop betraying him. As Isaiah said:

> No, the hand of Yahweh is not too short to save, nor his ear too dull to hear.
> But your iniquities have made a gulf between you and your God.
> Your sins have made him veil his face so as not to hear you, since your hands are stained with blood, your fingers with crime, your lips utter lies, your tongues murmur treachery.[23]

The nuclear age now confirms where theological argument may have failed to convince. Any political system that has come to believe that its security depends on its capacity to carry out the total annihilation of its enemies clearly conflicts with that "good life" over which both civil magistrate and conscience have jurisdiction. And thus we are confronted with a third paradox of liberal citizenship: the love that must motivate civic action will not stop at national frontiers, even though its immediate realm may be so confined; it must embrace one's neighbors everywhere. In the late René Dubos's words, the good citizen today thinks globally and acts locally. Civic action not so grounded is either fatuous or blasphemous, and likely both.

Fatuity and blasphemy are readily apparent everywhere, and not just in the so-called totalitarian nations. Britons and Americans, who have been the greatest beneficiaries and heirs of liberal thinking, now both have governments that plan to use even their own peoples as weapons of deterrence and possible war. Nuclear weaponry has

[23] Isaiah 59:1-3.

brought to a head what was already foreshadowed in earlier twentieth-century wars: that the claim to national sovereignty, combined with modern technological power, must undermine and annihilate all human purposes whatever.

Between the civic culture that pretends to a high moral truth derived from its particular gods and historical outlook, and one that self-consciously takes what Leo Strauss once–mistakenly, in light of nationalism–called the "low but safe road," liberal citizens cannot hesitate. But in so doing they must remember the condition for their modest choice: to know that they and all other human beings are pilgrims, ever faithful to a course of action against which the world has always hardened its heart.

Of course such a faith is problematic. But problematic as it is, it provides liberal political theory with the only ground upon which human power can be contained within a moral frame, committed to life rather than death. Only this problematic faith makes it possible for us to aspire to good citizenship in the City of Man.

Chapter 7

SOCIAL THEORY AND THE BREAK WITH TRADITION

Reinhard Bendix

In a review of my work, Talcott Parsons states that I reject the three basic concepts of sociological theory: system, function, and evolution.[1] It will focus my discussion if I indicate why I regard these terms with some skepticism. Concepts should serve our thinking about society, not dominate it. We adopt them because they fit in with how we look upon the world and because we find them useful. We reject them because they conflict with basic assumptions and because they obstruct our view of what we want to investigate. I shall confine myself to elementary considerations. If simple notions present great difficulties, then one has grounds for skepticism towards a more recondite use of such abstractions.

Following this theoretical review, I shall turn to the prerevolutionary situation in eighteenth-century France, which has been a point of departure for the modernization of countries around the world. At an ideological level, later transformations like the Industrial Revolution, the Bolshevik revolution, and the process of decolonization can be understood with reference to that precedent. But my main concern is to show that the transformation of eighteenth-century France is worth exploring as a prototype of societal transitions from tradition to modernity.

[1] In an untitled review article dealing with Bendix and Guenther Roth's *Scholarship and Partisanship* (Berkeley: University of California Press, 1971), in *Contemporary Sociology*, 1 (1972), pp. 200-203.

SYSTEM AND FUNCTION

At a minimum the term "system" implies a high degree of interdependence. Changes in one part are inevitably followed by changes in other parts. Second, system implies that this interdependence is regulated internally. Specific variables may change only within specifiable limits. Third, systems are marked off by boundaries. The inside is clearly separated from the outside. We are in no doubt when we attribute features or parts to a system. Examples from biology provide some sociologists with their favorite model. Increases in heartbeat when running, the lower and upper limits of body temperature, attributes of the body as distinguished from attributes of the world outside of the body: these illustrate the systemic dimensions I have in mind.

To me the difficulties of the term "system" loom large. The *interdependence* of whole societies varies with their degree of integration. In complex social structures this integration is seldom high. It is easier to think of aspects like the stock market or medical care in systemic terms than of the entire society. The reason is that it is difficult to foresee the repercussions that follow an action in different parts of society. Societies do not have an equilibrium in the way the body has a normal temperature. In all complex societies there is much uncertainty. The actions of individuals fall within a range of tolerance. But the limits of this range are difficult to specify, because people redefine what individuals may or may not do. Émile Durkheim made crime a normal aspect of culture without which the awareness and enforcement of norms would be insufficient; but he did not say how much crime is needed to help maintain the norms of society. Similarly, Talcott Parsons has found it difficult to state what he means by a sufficient degree of motivation and satisfaction. Robert Merton has called the idea of social health (which I take to be a synonym for equilibrium) one of the cloudiest and empirically most debatable concepts of functional theory. Finally, societies do not have *boundaries* in contrast to bodies that are clearly defined organisms or nation-states that are politicialy defined units. Perhaps the idea of boundaries suggests itself because we live in a world of nation-states. Often we use "society" and "nation" interchangeably. Yet generally accepted frontiers around a contiguous territory are a historical phenomenon. Primordial ties like those of race, kinship, language, or religion cut across national boundaries. So do secondary ties like those of intellectual or organizational affiliation. Ideas and techniques cross frontiers with special ease. And the center of cultural activities has shifted frequently. During the last century France was the center of culture for Russia and Latin America. England, France, and Germany were the center for the United States, in about that sequence. The former colonial power continues to be the center for many of the new nations. And the United States itself has moved from the periphery as a cultural dependent to the center of cultural diffusion.

Since I do not accept the assumption of society as a system, I am in trouble with the term "function" also. We would all be functionalists if we meant no more than our common interest in causal relations. The terms "function" and "cause" are easily interchanged, but "function" implies purpose while "cause" does not. When you say that fighting against a common enemy has the function of increasing group solidarity, you are close to a statement of purpose. Conservatives defend war in these terms. You can say just as easily that fighting against a common enemy increases group solidarity–a causal statement. The functional approach fuses fact and purpose; the causal approach separates them. Some sociologists see in the persistence of group structures the main object of their analysis. For them it makes sense to ask what specific social facts contribute to the functioning (or the dysfunctioning) of a social system. No doubt, functionalists would be surprised to learn that they are beholden to a belief in providence; they are secularists who do not hold theological views. But language can betray intellectual influences of which we are not aware. Causal inquiry emancipates us from an earlier world view in which purpose was inherent in nature as part of a providential design. Functional analysis has not cut this umbilical cord.

I have stated an alternative approach in *Embattled Reason.*[2] Group structures persist while individuals come and go, but they do not persist unchanged. Sociological analysis should move back and forth between the social structure and the action and subjective awareness of individuals. My main objection to system and function is that these concepts obstruct the second part of the analysis. As

[2] *Embattled Reason: Essays on Social Knowledge* (New York: Oxford University Press, 1970).

long as our understanding of what people do depends in part on how they see their own world, we should not move to a level of abstraction that makes the individual a mere function of the social structure. Also, sociological theory should focus attention on the boundary-extending as well as the boundary-maintaining activities of individuals. This conceptual strategy is one social scientist's critique of utopian thought, which asks us to search each fact for its intended and unintended, its valued and devalued, consequences. In this perspective the term "function" is too undirectional to be useful.

In addition, I try to keep in mind that the concepts we use are not free inventions. Sociologists are like the people they observe. After all, even scholars interact with others in an effort to make sense of the world and attain some mastery over it. In what historical setting did the view emerge that society is a self-sufficient system in which individuals interact so as to achieve a sufficient degree of pattern maintenance, integration, goal attainment, and adaptation, to employ Parsons's terminology? Of course, his particular formulation is indebted to recent technological developments like cybernetics. But the biological mode of functional differentiation and integration has older intellectual roots, going back to classical antiquity as Robert Nisbet has shown. In modern times, the idea that society is a self-sufficient, functioning system came into its own during the eighteenth century, following two centuries of European expansion overseas. In the U.S. this approach has been revived following the United States' ascendance to the position of a world power. Obviously other factors are at work as well. Newtonian cosmology and biological models have been used as successive analogues appropriate to the study of society. But I believe it would be difficult to view society in these terms if you see the world from India, the USSR, or modern Japan rather than from France, England or the United States.

Thus, there are reasons for skepticism when sociologists use their terms "system" and "function". Apparently societies retain their identity while encompassing many apparent incompatibilities and conflicts of interest. Evidence for this view is on all sides. Consider the primordial ties that divide us along religious, ethnic, racial, and familial lines. Add to these our innumerable secondary affiliations through formal organizations. The people in this country are divided, yet they are all recognizably American in speech, behavior, and ways of thought. Some unity is achieved through the medium of culture. A certain degree of comprehensive decision making is achieved through the political process. But these are proximate and often precarious achievements. Perhaps the most serious objection to the terms "system" and "function" is that they take as given what is problematic, namely, the degree of interdependence and of unity that characterizes societies. And it is at this point that an evolutionary approach to social and political change is especially questionable.

SOCIAL CHANGE AND THE CONCEPT OF "EVOLUTION"

Social change refers to the differences we observe in a society before and after a given interval of time. The later social structure may show point-for-point contrasts with the earlier one; the literature is filled with contrasts of this kind. Since this proliferation of terms is bad, Parsons has provided us with a comprehensive set of categories at a higher level of abstraction. Yet the application of his categories is no simple matter, because neither the earlier nor the later social structure possesses a consistent set of attributes.

To perceive a society as a consistent whole is easiest for a foreign visitor. De Tocqueville said that he did not write a page of his book on America without thinking about France. The things he noted most were those that differed from what he knew of France. Similarly, comparisons between traditional and modern societies tend to bring out the distinctions between them in more or less dichotomous fashion. But these distinctions are the starting point of analysis, not its endproduct. There are no completely modern societies: think of the role kinship and status play in our own experience. There are no completely traditional societies: think of the role contract and religious universalism played in medieval Europe. Only mixed types exist that should be understood in their own right. U.S. society is surely modern. On the whole people in this country are oriented toward achievement. But the achievement of one generation becomes the ascriptive status of the next. And during the last few years many children of well-to-do parents have rejected achievement *and* ascription by opting for a life of affluent poverty. Let me use this most recent and familiar experience to make a more general point. If we knew as much about other societies as we do about the 1960s, we would recognize our experience as quite typical. Complex social structures are never true to type; societies are always in transition from past to future. We should try to develop categories for coping with this phenomenon intellectually.

Since I have published these antievolutionist views elsewhere, I can summarize them here. There is much continuity between traditional and modern societies. It is appropriate to think of a build-up of modernization over many centuries. Even major disruptions like the French Revolution or the Industrial Revolution in England have been traced to much earlier antecedents. But once such revolutions have occurred, they may represent breakthroughs that have repercussions around the world. It is in this sense that democratization or industrialization cannot occur in the same way twice. For such breakthroughs provide an incentive for other countries to do likewise. Social change is always a combination of extrinsic and intrinsic stimuli. This is true of the many societies that have been transformed in conscious adaptation of the changes they have witnessed from afar. But it is just as true of the interaction between England, France, and the United States in the eighteenth century. In this process of adaptation intellectuals and governments have played a major role. With the model of another, pioneering country before them, they see their own country as politically and socially backward, and they seek to overcome this backwardness. By adapting items from the arsenal of foreign ideas and practices they hope to create a better society. (In principle this includes the opposite reaction, namely, a society that uses foreign models to reaffirm its traditional structure, but I exclude this consideration for the present.) I want to explore the prerevolutionary situation in France in order to understand the social structure of transition. I am less concerned with the revolutionary outcome as a unique event than with the preceding period as a prototype of transition from tradition to modernity. My warrant for this exploration is that in eighteenth-century France we can witness the process of modernization that influences us still.

EIGHTEENTH-CENTURY FRANCE AND MODERNIZATION

Reference Societies:

Eighteenth-century France was the major European power, both politically and culturally. Its population increased from 18 to 25 million people. In Europe only Russia was close to the latter figure by the end of the century. In contrast to Germany and Italy, France had been a unified state for a long time. For much of the century the country was prosperous though this economic position grew worse. Politically and militarily the country suffered major setbacks. But these economic and political ups and downs did not jeopardize France's cultural preeminence. French had superseded Latin as the international language. Prussia's Frederick II observed that he who knew French could travel throughout Europe without an interpreter. In fashion, France and specifically the court at Versailles set the tone for the continent.

But while France was the cosmopolis of other countries, in France itself England was the fashion. Following the death of Louis XIV in 1715, the French aristocracy sought to reverse a century of autocratic rule. French aristocrats looked with envy on the political power of the English aristocracy in the provinces and in Parliament. Montesquieu's interpretation of English government (1748) in terms of checks and balances among its three branches enjoyed wide influence. To scientists and men of letters England was the home of Newton and Locke. Voltaire made invidious contrasts between Descartes, who had to leave France to philosophize in liberty, and Newton, who lived his whole life in a free country where he was entirely tranquil, happy, and honored. Leading strata of French society suffered from Anglomania, as it was called derisively. English ideas were encouraged further when Scotch refugees established Masonic lodges in France. Freemasonry provided an organizational setting for the growing communication between discontented aristocrats and men of letters.

The Seven-Year War (1756-1763) ended with the defeat of France, and the idea of England as a model did not survive intact. But meanwhile the idea of America had increased in importance.

Earlier in the century some note had been taken of the British colonies, both favorable and unfavorable. America was a new and primitive land, with the Indians being considered good savages by some and an inferior breed by others. The American climate was believed unfavorable to human life. Attractive only to settlers motivated by avarice, the country was thought incapable of producing any notable cultural achievement. A Dutch writer, publishing in French in 1768, considered the discovery of America the most important and disastrous event in the history of civilization; he believed a second such catastrophe would bring the extinction of mankind. One should add, of course, that he was influenced by his sojourn at the Prussian court, which actively discouraged emigration, and that he opposed the evils of colonialism and the myth of the good savage. The counterarguments went back to the end of the seventeenth century when some French writers noted the accomplishment of the Quakers in Pennsylvania. Another writer remarked that in New Jersey there were neither lawyers, doctors, nor theologians, which to the French of the period seemed a very good thing. These pamphlets were addressed to French Huguenots in order to encourage their immigration. Similar ideas were broadcast by Locke, Montesquieu, Voltaire, and the writers of the *Encyclopédie,* who noted the principles of religious toleration and enlightened government in several colonies. Following the Treaty of Paris in 1763, interest in America gradually increased. A number of American artists and scientists visited France. Prime Minister Choiseul prepared to redress French reverses by exploiting the troubles in England's American colonies. When Benjamin Franklin came on the scene as the American colonists' representative in London (1767). his scientific and political reputation won him ready acclaim, which he proceeded to exploit in a propaganda campaign favorable to the American cause.[3]

I shall return to France presently, but I want to illustrate my theme of reference societies by a brief glance at this side of the Atlantic. Among the cumulative grievances against England the American fear of standing armies loomed large. In the pamphlets of the period that fear was elaborated by telling references to despotic countries overseas. Turkey headed the list because the power of her despotic rulers rested on the swords of the janissaries. Next came the

[3] Cf. Durand Echeverria, *Mirage in the West* (Princeton, N.J.: Princeton University Press, 1957), ch. 1.

French kings who had used force against the liberties of their subjects and reduced to nothing the puny privileges of the parliaments. Poland, Spain, Russia and Egypt were other despotisms mentioned. A still more forceful warning was given by reference to Venice, Sweden, and above all Denmark, countries that had enjoyed liberties at one time but were now the victims of autocratic rule. On the other side were the countries like Switzerland and Holland that had struggled successfully against the abuse of power by the few. Above all, there was England. Her glorious history of constitutional government was cited in evidence against current English abuses of authority in the colonies. Indeed, the colonists built their case for independence by developing a theory of government based on English precedents while English practice was likened to the despotic states of Africa and the notorious cases of European autocracy. Thus, the transition from tradition to modernity involves an intense awareness of positive and negative reference societies in the process of defining new national goals.[4]

Men of Letters

This process depends on a group of men sensitive to the fate of their nation, aware of what goes on elsewhere, and capable of formulating ideas. In eighteenth-century France such men called themselves *gens des lettres.* These were men well versed in many fields rather than specialists in any one field. Voltaire pointed out that their philosophical spirit, their searching and purified reason, had greatly contributed to instructing and refining the nation.[5] That partisan description is peculiar to its country and period; elsewhere other characteristics would be more appropriate, such as the term "intelligentsia" and its connotations in nineteenth-century Russia. It may be futile to search for a uniform terminology when dealing with men of ideas whose sense of identify depends upon *their* definition of the situation. But diverse as they are, such men have a certain family

[4] For a discussion of the American case see Bernard Bailyn, *The Ideological Origins of the American Revolution* (Cambridge, Mass.: Harvard University Press, 1967), pp. 63ff., 79, and passim.

[5] Voltaire, "Men of Letters," in Stephen J. Gendzier, ed., *Denis Diderot's The Encyclopedia* (New York: Harper and Row, Harper Torchbooks, 1967), p. 167.

resemblance.

They depend upon a reading public because they do not want to write only for each other. In France such a public developed with the proportion of literates doubling between 1700 and 1786-1790.[6] They depend as well upon social recognition from the leading strata of society. In 1726 Voltaire was beaten up by hired thugs because he had offended the Chevalier Rohan-Chabot and was sent to the Bastille for daring to seek revenge. By 1778 he returned to Paris in triumph, being treated with adulation at the Academy, the Comédie Française, and in the streets. Related to social recognition is the development of a sense of importance among literati. In 1734 Voltaire had noted how much consideration was accorded to men of letters in England, in pointed contrast to their lowly position in France. By the 1770s an English observer noted that French men of letters had considerable weight on the manners and sentiments of people of rank and of the public in general and consequently were not without effect on the measures of government.[7] As a result the closer relation between men of letters and the leaders of high society became a favorite theme of philosophical writing.

Yet this new sense of importance was never untroubled. At one point Diderot speaks of philosophy as the opium of the passions, suggesting a painful awareness of the discrepancy between theory and practice. Among the contributors to the *Encyclopédie* a certain tension developed between activists and literati over the relative emphasis upon propaganda and style. Because he rejected the neglect of literary quality Voltaire voiced his skepticism to the two editors, Diderot and d'Alembert. He addressed them occasionally as Atlas and Hercules who carry the world on their shoulders, the department for the instruction of mankind.[8] As Robert Darnton has shown,the familiar figures of the Enlightenment were an elite.

[6] This estimate is based on the proportion of men and women who could sign their names on the marriage registers. Cf. John Lough, *An Introduction to Eighteenth Century France* (New York: David McKay Co., 1960), pp. 235-236. The author documents the rising economic position of writers during the eighteenth century.

[7] Quoted in *ibid.*, pp. 266-267. In addition to Lough's chapter, "The Writer and his Public," cf. Fritz Schalk, "Die Entstehung des schriftstellerischen Selbstbewusstseins in Frankreich," in *Einleitung in die Encyclopaedie der Französischen Aufklärung* (Heft VI of Münchner Romanistische Arbeiten; München: Max Hueber Verlag, 1936), pp. 45-65.

[8] Quoted in Schalk, *op cit.*, pp. 61-62.

> In their view taste belonged to a very small number of privileged souls. . . . It is unknown in bourgeois families, where one is constantly occupied with the case of one's fortunes. Yet in the wake of these famous men a host of lesser writers flocked to Paris. Intent on making their fortune they were often condemned for prolonged periods to eke out their existence by hack work. These declasse men of letters were instrumental in turning the main ideas of the Enlightenment into a revolutionary ideology.[9]

It may be a distinguishing characteristic of eighteenth-century France that up to a point the ancien regime allowed the expression of such ideas–owing in part to the considerable number of prominent aristocrats who embraced and protected the philosophy of humanity.

Revolutionary Ideology

It is somewhat daunting to say anything in brief compass about this philosophy. The shortcut I choose depends upon my belief that in breaking away from tradition men of letters coalesce as a class and status group of their own. Dependent upon the new way of life made possible by a growing reading public, they are animated by certain archetypical ideas that give them a new sense of identity. I shall presuppose the existence of a hateful regime that in France had governed the country autocratically since the early seventeenth century. The medieval assembly, the so-called states-general, had last met in 1614. The country had witnessed famines, epidemics, and wars for over a century. Religious persecution was rife. And a centralized police regime had preempted the quasiautonomous, governmental functions of municipalities and the land-owning aristocracy.

> The spectacle of so many wrongful and absurd privileges, of which the weight was felt more and more, and the cause was less and less understood . . . seeing so many irregular and bizarre institutions . . . which no one had attempted to harmonize with each other . . . they readily conceived a loathing for things ancient and for tradition.[10]

[9] Robert Darnton, "The High Enlightenment and the Low-Life of Literature in Pre-revolutionary France," *Past and Present,* no. 51 (May 1971), pp. 81-115. The quoted sentence is taken from Voltaire's article on taste in the *Encyclopédie.*

Faced with this system of iniquity men of letters and their friends wished to rebuild society . . . by the sole light of reason, as de Tocqueville put it. Long before the revolution occurred, the old regime had become unacceptable in many, very influential strata of the population.

The starting point was the attack upon privilege–even among the privileged. The breakup of tradition depends upon some such black-and-white contrast between the hateful present and the ideal future. In eighteenth-century France the old, religious conception of a transcendental order embodying truth and justice was rejected in favor of the sovereign national will as the ultimate source of law. Yet this populist appeal to the intrinsic goodness of human nature was expressed by men of letters proudly conscious of having acquired social recognition for themselves. The Freemasons are an instructive, organizational example of this combination of populism and elitism.

Between 1772 to 1789 the number of Masonic lodges increased from 104 to over 600, with 65 of the most prominent in Paris alone. There was nothing suspicious about an organization engaged in drinking, singing, philanthropy, religion without orthodoxy, vague mysticism, and fake chivalry, all combined with a belief in progress and the value of science. The order made much of its secret rituals. Each member pledged himself to guard them or undergo penalities that would obliterate his memory from the minds of men and Masons. Each member obliged himself to be a religious believer and a peaceable subject–with no further questions asked. Religious and political controversy were excluded from all Masonic meetings. The order as a whole declared time and again that it had no interest in affairs of church or state. It was nondenominational and nonpolitical in its endorsement of religious tolerance and civic probity. But where a humanitarian appeal is combined with a great secret, a new and better and as yet unknown life seems promised. Eventually the initiate can discover that life. Meanwhile he joins all other Masons as equal sharers in a promised revelation. The rest of the world is foreign territory where caution or distrust is indicated and the danger of treason lurks. Toward the outside all masons are equal. But internally the order is divided into a multitude of hierarchic ranks, with each rank harboring an arcanum of its own. At the highest rank a Mason could hope to learn the innermost secret and

[10] Alexis de Tocqueville, *L'Ancien Regime* (Oxford: Basil Blackwell, 1947), p. 149.

thus partake of a final enlighhenment. On the long road to that rank he must give willing obedience to the brothers who are entitled to judge whether he is worthy of promotion. This multiplication of ranks increased the incentives of those below while also increasing the attraction of the order for the nobility.

Separation from organized religion and political activity was indispensable for achieving external acceptance and internal harmony. Free from the bonds of the outside world, the Mason is a man among men, engaged jointly with them in the cultivation of morality. Here is a poetic description of the Masonic spirit:

> The cry of nature, friend, is Liberty;
> This right so dear to man is here respected.
> Equality without anarchy, liberty without license,
> In obedience to our laws lies our freedom.[11]

By separating the order from all narrowly religious or political preoccupations and by their secrets the Masons institutionalized an independent realm of morality. Nonpolitical as they were, the Freemasons vindicated to this realm the capacity of sitting in judgment over the outside world, of being the conscience of humanity. Within the order and guarded by its secrecy the brotherhood of man had been realized. By comparison churches and states appeared as necessary evils.

To be sure, Freemasonry was only one facet of the break with tradition. Its importance for the revolution should not be exaggerated. But the order exemplifies two aspects of the revolutionary ideology that I would like to emphasize. The order was elitist in terms of the social composition of its members and the emphasis on hierarchy. But the order was also populist by resolutely denying religious and social differences among the members, by emphasizing fraternity, and by virtue of its appeal to a philosophy of humanity. Secondly, the well-guarded secret of the order implicitly linked virtue and ideas with power. Where esoteric knowledge is guarded by secrecy, there is an intimation of power. For where secrets are kept, men must have something to hide. The more is made of secrecy, the greater the power that it is designed to hide. In *The Magic Flute* the wisdom and majesty of Sarastro appears indeed

[11] Quoted in Paul Hazard, *European Thought in the Eighteenth Century* (Harmondsworth: Penguin Books, 1965), p. 291.

larger than life, and Mozart based his treatment of that figure upon the master of his own Masonic lodge. Only a few are permitted to learn the secret of the order. When they do they discover that the cultivation of virtue establishes both the brotherhood of man and the moral ability to judge the affairs of the world.

Ambivalence between elitism and populism, tacit assumptions about the relation between virtue and power, between ideas and power: these are archetypical ingredients of an ideology that breaks away from tradition. Men of letters cannot pursue ideas without implying or affirming their own preoccupation with ideas. That preoccupation sets them apart from ordinary folk. But these men of letters also seek a responsive audience in their own society. And as they sense their isolation while seeking a response they realize the backwardness of their country in comparison with others. This situation creates ambivalence enough, but it is compounded further by a sense of impotence. Typically, men of letters do not have access to positions of power, and just as typically they are highly sensitive about the fate of their country. Thus, powerlessness is experienced most acutely just when men of letters develop a group consciousness of their own. They are confronted with the tragic discrepancy between what is and what ought to be, with their political impotence and the significance of ideas in their own lives. In this setting it is a great temptation to implicitly attribute to theory, to principle, and to ideas a potential impact, a power to move men. For men will seek mastery where they can find it, and when ideas are their only weapons they will attribute power to ideas.

POPULAR SOVEREIGNTY, EQUALITY, REPRESENTATION, AND PROPERTY

Now we must turn from the social context to the content of ideas. To do this succinctly I confine myself to the concepts of popular sovereignty, equality, representation, and property. This is an arbitrary selection, but it allows me to focus attention upon problems of government. Once again I am concerned with the archetypical patterns that emerge when the leading state in a society undertakes to break with the continuity of its tradition.

Popular Sovereignty

In the Western tradition appeals to popular sovereignty were associated with the concept of lawful rule. Monarchical government is absolute and yet subject to God's law. However vague and disputed, this limitation meant that when a king's rule became tyrannical the people had a right to resist his unlawful acts. For the people, like the king, owed their first allegiance to God, and unlawful acts were a violation of divine justice. I mention this traditional view in order to note that the eighteenth-century appeal to popular sovereignty became absolute. As the Abbé Sieyes put it: "The nation is prior to everything. It is the source of everything. Its will is always legal; indeed it is the law itself . . . the source of all legality."[12] The law under God was limited in principle by a higher law; the law that a nation gives to itself has no limit. This absolute consisted in the will of the people. A government based on that will would be founded on ethical principles. It is in virtue and the sovereignty of the people that one must search for the guarantee against the vices and the despotism of government, as Robespierre put it.[13] If one comes to this literature afresh one is struck by the degree to which the *philosophes* of the eighteenth century were made comfortable by a proliferation of synonyms. The people and the nation, virtue or ethical principles and the general will, fraternity and equality and freedom of men as citizens and as participants in the sovereign power: these and related terms were used interchangeably.

In practice the matter was more complex. Popular sovereignty became a historical reality when on June 17, 1789, the Third Estate–having been convoked under rules that had been in abeyance for 175 years–rejected these rules and arrogated to itself the title of National Assembly. Until 1614 the three estates had met and voted separately; their charge was to petition the king under an imperative mandate of their respective electorates. Now the National Assembly constituted itself as an extraordinary, collective representative of the nation. When the assembly was joined by the clergy and nobility on orders from the king, it proceeded to formulate a new constitution

[12] Emmanuel Joseph Sieyes, *What is the Third Estate?* (New York: Frederick A. Praeger, 1963), pp. 124, 126.

[13] Quoted in Alfred Cobban, "The Fundamental Ideas of Robespierre," in *Aspects of the French Revolution* (London: Paladin, 1971), p. 139.

of fundamental laws. (The French used philosophical principles in contrast to the Americans who used an idealized version of the English constitution; one result was that the Bill of Rights precedes the French Constitution but was added in amendment to the U.S. one.) The basic problems facing the assembly can be seen in its statement of principles, the famous *Declaration of the Rights of Man and Citizen.* There it is stated that the aim of every political association is the preservation of the natural and inalienable rights of man and that all men are equal in their rights of liberty, property, security and resistance to oppression. All citizens have the right to concur personally or through their representatives in the formation of the law as the expression of the general will. Also, all citizens, being equal before the law, are equally admissible to all public offices, positions, and employments, according to their capacity and without other distinction. These familiar phrases from the 1789 declaration were omitted from, or reformulated in, the subsequent declarations. This suggests that fundamental issues were in dispute. I shall discuss three of these issues.

Equality

The ideal of equality in the declaration referred to natural or moral equality, not to an absolute or literal equality. Time and again the *philosophes* asserted that they were well aware of the necessity of different ranks, honors, and prerogatives, that in all government subordination must prevail. In their gifts and possessions men are unequal, but let the state not add an unjust inequality of rights alongside this actual inequality of means, as the Abbé Sieyes put it.[14] The impulse behind this ideal was generous and humane. Let men value and treat each other as natural equals. Let those who rise above others avoid insults to their inferiors, demand nothing beyond what is required, and be humane in demanding what is their due. Certain universal rights to justice should be enjoyed equally by all or enjoyed in some distributive manner that removes all suspicion of contempt or partiality.[15] The accent upon opposition against privi-

[14] Quoted from a statement of 1789 in G.G. van Deusen, *E.J. Sieyes: his life and his nationalism* (New York: Columbia University Press, 1932), p. 82, n. 27.

[15] This is the interpretation of the Chevalier de Jaucourt in his article on natural

lege is apparent in this interpretation.

The practical realization of equality was something else again. The disputes that followed the *Declaration* of 1789 make clear that no one quarrelled with the idea of a *passive equality* before the law. This meant that the law itself should not be discriminatory, in contrast to the old law, which had protected many special privileges. Under these circumstances little attention was paid to the many privileges of the rich that would survive, even where formal equality was assured. But the *Declaration* also referred to the *active rights* of citizenship, the right of each to concur in the formation of laws and to be considered for public office or employment. This active right was much disputed. As a practical matter the idea of representation and special qualifications for public office won out over the idea of a plebiscitary democracy and equal access to public positions. But both standpoints were aired in debate and mark a recurring issue of democratic rule to this day.

Representation

It is difficult to think of equality and representation as mutually compatible. Logical consistency was clearly on the side of Robespierre and his friends, who argued strongly for equality of participation in the expression of the sovereign will which were to them the same basic idea. Every representative agency would give disproportionate weight to special interests. The defeat of special privilege had been the main purpose of the revolution. The Jacobin wing could not see the logic of reinstituting under a democratic veneer what had finally been eliminated in its aristocratic guise. This logically consistent position did not prevail. Robespierre had no answer to the practical question of how direct democracy was to be implemented without representation and still remain compatible with orderly government.[16]

law in the *Encyclopédie.*

[16] An instructive analysis of Robespierre's changing views as he moved from the opposition into a position of authority is contained in Alfred Cobban, "The Political Ideas of Maximilien Robespierre during the Period of the Convention," in *Aspects of the French Revolution, op. cit.,* pp. 159-191.

Today we know also that the Bolshevik extension of the Jacobin principle led necessarily to a further development of representation. To be sure, the Bolshevik attack on bourgeois capitalism was made again in the name of the people. The argument for the working masses as the true source of sovereignty is very similar to the argument by Sieyes that the 25 million members of the Third Estate represented the nation while the two hundred thousand clergymen and nobles were merely trivial. In the constitutional thought of the French Revolution the rights of the minority were no more protected than in that of the Bolshevik revolution, though the two revolutions differ in other respects. In the end the Bolshevik leaders were as inconsistent as the leaders of the French Revolution. They favored direct democracy as a revolutionary weapon. But once in power they interpreted this to mean the sovereign power of workers and peasants as represented by the Communist party.

Eighteenth-century France witnessed an analogous reinterpretation. For decades the ancien regime had been attacked in the name of popular sovereignty. Diderot's article on political authority opposed authority based on conquest with the ideal of authority based on consent ten years before Rouseau's *Social Contract* (1762). Now, during the first months of the revolution, the Abbé Sieyes distinguished between the great mass of the population who enjoy the passive equality of the law and those members of the Third Estate who have an active right of citizenship. The former make no economic contribution to the state; hence, like women, children, and foreigners, they should be excluded from active influence upon public affairs. On the other hand, there are

> *available* classes in the Third Estate; and like everyone else I call "available" those classes where some sort of affluence enables men to receive a liberal education, to train their minds and to take an interest in public affairs. Such classes have no interest other than that of the rest of the People.[17]

In structure this argument is no different from the contention that the members of the Communist party represent the interests of the people. However, in this case political loyalty and a party career are substituted for education and income as the qualification required for active citizenship. Elsewhere, Sieyes states that all can enjoy the advantages of society; but only those who contribute to the public

[17] Sieyes, in van Deusen, op. cit., p. 78.

establishment are like true shareholders in the great social enterprise. Only they are active citizens, properly speaking, and hence true members of the political association.[18]

In France neither direct nor representative democracy came to prevail, but rather a mixture of the two. The franchise embodies the idea of popular consent–to the fundamental laws by voting for a constitutional assembly and to the policy decisions of representatives by voting in elections that provide a choice of candidates. The principle of representation without imperative mandate embodied the ideal that elected deputies would speak on behalf of national rather than local partisan interests. In practice, democratic institutions can only approximate these ideals. But it is my belief that their viability depends upon conditions and institutions that allow the meaningful coexistence of both the plebiscitary and the representative principle.

Finally, I turn to the question of property.

Property

It is difficult to think of equality and property as mutually compatible. Logical consistency was again on the side of the Jacobin party. They argued strongly for equality and hence against the distinction between a passive enjoyment of rights and active citizenship. Robespierre and his friends opposed a franchise limited by property qualifications. They questioned whether probity, talent, or patriotism depended upon ownership. In their view the rights of active citizenship belonged to all adult males who would constitute the general will. The rich merely represented a special interest. The Jacobins distrusted the rich and had little regard for their property rights. But they also wanted to make sure that everyone had an equal opportunity to aquire property. Clearly, it was difficult to square a policy of redistributing wealth with the theory of a natural right of property that was a basic tenet of the French Revolution. Yet in 1793 Robespierre asked whether the legal safeguards provided for property had not in fact been made for the rich, for monopolists, for speculators, and for tyrants. He wanted the assembly to consider the nature and legitimacy of property. To this

[18] Quoted in Heinz Klay, *Zensuswahlrecht und Gleichheitsprinzip* (Heft 19 of Berner Untersuchungen zur Allgemeinen Geschichte; Aarau: Verlag H.R. Sauerlander, 1956), p. 107.

end he proposed that the right of property cannot prejudice the security or the liberty or the existence or the property of our fellow creatures. Consistent to the last, he also proposed that the state assume the duty of providing work or relief for everyone and that the relief of poverty is a debt, owed by the rich to the poor.[19] But France was a nation of small property owners. They did not feel reassured by an approach that considered their property sacred but not that of the rich.

With the defeat of the Jacobin party the original position was reaffirmed. The declaration of 1795 reiterated that property is the right to enjoy and dispose of one's property, one's income, and the product of one's labor and industry. The inequality of means was not considered. In the words of the Abbé Sieyes:

> Political rights derive from a person's capacity as a citizen. These legal rights are identical for every person, whether his property happens to be great or small. Any citizen who satisfies all the formal requirements for an elector has the right to be represented. . . .[20]

The conditions of the franchise included minimum age, residence, and tax payments equivalent to the earnings of a certain number of working days. It was assumed that such a property qualfication would go together with a certain level of education, interest, and judgment on the part of the qualified voter.

In conclusion, I want to raise a question that will lead me back to the theoretical problems with which I began. How could the men who endorsed a limited franchise still claim that they believed in equality? The answer is, I think, that they did not believe in equality, but in an equality of legal rights. The law does not evaluate. Since all men have the right to develop their capacities, the law must protect the whole range of moral and esthetic values. To ensure that all men possess the same legal rights, the law asks only whether or not this man's acting as he does prevents another from developing to the full his own natural capacities. The law does not even facilitate equality. It only seeks to ensure that each man can do what he will with his person and property without thereby curtailing the freedom

[19] Quoted from Robespierre's speech of April 24, 1793, in Richard Schlatter, *Private Property* (London: George Allen & Unwin, 1951), pp. 229-230.

[20] In van Deusen, op. cit., pp. 79-80.

of another. This highly abstract idea considers men only in their capacity as legal agents and stipulates their equality in this respect. As such legal equality has proved to be an instrument not for combating inequality but for ignoring all the distinctions dividing men except those bearing on their formal legal capacity.

In the eighteenth century these views were formulated on the assumption that the rights of property owners required legal protection. The spokesmen of natural rights were combating a social order in which special privileges enjoyed the protection of the law. Hence the idea that a man's rights to his property are equal to the rights of every other was a revolutionary, not a conservative, doctrine. And in that context it was quite plausible to maintain that property and equality were compatible. Commenting on Rousseau's *Social Contract,* G.H. Mead has stated that "the citizen can give laws only to the extent that his volitions are an expression of the rights which he recognizes in others . . . [and] which the others recognize in him." Mead points out further that such consent upon the terms of interaction presupposed the institution of property. For "the individual wills his control over his property only in so far as he wills the same sort of control for everyone else over property."[21] I see in this approach an early antecedent of the sociologist's analysis of interaction. This analysis is as abstract as the economist's classic definition of the *Homo economicus* interacting with others like himself on a free market. The actual inequalities dividing men do not come into the picture in either case. For when it is said that the social system is made up of the interaction of individuals who are in each case both actors and objects of orientation, the actors concerned are treated implicity as equals in just the way that property owners may treat each other as equals.[22]

To me this assumption seems unwarranted. I see men interacting in society in a manner that combines three aspects. Their actions make sense to themselves, they are oriented towards the reactions of significant others, and through ideas and interactions they seek to attain increments of mastery. This last element is missing from theo-

[21] G.H. Mead, *Movements of Thought in the Nineteenth Century* (Chicago: University of Chicago Press, 1936), pp. 21, 17.

[22] The formulation but not the inference is that of Talcott Parsons, *Societies, Evolutionary and Comparative Perspectives* (Englewood Cliffs, N.J.: Prentice Hall Inc., 1966), p. 8.

ries that seek to explain social structures from interactions among equals. There is no consensus on the terms of interaction between property owners and those without property. There may be a formal agreement, of course, but that presupposes the presence of authority. I see a basic flaw in social theories that seek to account for social structures without focusing attention on the role of authority.

Chapter 8

ENTITLEMENT AND LEGITIMACY: WEBER AND LENIN ON THE PROBLEMS OF LEADERSHIP

Tracy B. Strong

A legal order thought of as sovereign and general, not as the instrument of the struggle of power complexes, but as the means of *preventing* all struggle . . . would be a *principle hostile to life*. . . .

Nietzsche, *Genealogy of Morals*, II, 11

INTRODUCTION

This essay is part of a larger attempt to find structural parallels between thinkers of obviously divergent political persuasions in the early part of this century. The virtue of whatever I conclude is obviously mitigated by the willful overlooking of factors such as these: Lenin was a revolutionary and a man of practical action; Weber was an academic sociologist whose political allegiances are best described as nationalistic and centrist. Lenin gave his name to a school of thought; Weber hoped that none would be identified with his.[1]

All this and more is of importance if my enterprise be justified, it is because I hope to show that common preoccupations govern the most serious thinking of the early period of this century. Weber and Lenin both try to elaborate criteria by which correctly to judge that a given person (or persons) is entitled to make decisions for others. Both men think, I shall argue, that true leaders are revealed in their acts, much in the manner that a work of art is revealed in its execution. And, as with a work of art, in the end the actions of the true

[1] Paul Honigsheim, *On Max Weber*, trans by Joan Rytina (New York: Free Press, 1968).

statesman provide the standards by which he is to be judged. A mode of thought that I might characterize as "esthetic" replaces the moral and the prudential. Politics moves close to art.

For both men, the French Revolution and Hegel were the back projections. The revolution had demonstrated to an astonished Europe that human action acquired full meaning only in a context much larger than the foreseeable. That an apparently minor *jaquerie* over the price of bread should have resulted within twenty-three years in French armies trying to take Moscow and in the total reform of the nature of the legal system in much of Europe demanded a perspective larger than that of intentions and results, larger that that of individual morality. Events had now to be interpreted–if they were to have meaning at all–in terms of history; it was only in terms of process that their importance was retrospectively revealed. Hegel, who understood this first and better than anyone else, wrote in the *Philosophy of History:* "What is involved here is that in world history something else results from the actions of men than what they intend and achieve, something else than they know or want."[2] History was for Hegel, as is well known, a drama of butchery signifying everything.

There were dangers inherent in the Hegelian view, even if Hegel avoided many of them. Most centrally, the Hegelian view of history involved a commitment to the proposition that if something passed away, it deserved to pass away. By 1884, Nietzsche had noted this in the chapter "On Redemption" in *Thus Spoke Zarathustra* in the context of his general discussion of the various attempts made during the nineteenth century to deal with the relation of the past to the present. As Nietzsche realized, if one thought that everything that passed away deserved to, then one had effectively limited the possibility of attributing to human action qualities independent of their place in history. Most centrally, from the historical standpoint, individual judgments about the meaning of an act became pointless indulgence, relying as they must on the intentions of the actor.

By the end of the nineteenth century, the relationship of morality to action was even more problematic. Modern Europeans stood as inheritors without a testament. The contributions of Marx, Kierkegaard, and Nietzsche had made difficult any relationship at all

[2] G.W.F. Hegel, "*The Philosophy of History,*" in C. J. Friedrich, ed., *The Philosophy of Hegel* (New York: Modern Library, 1954), pp. 16-17.

between the sense made of individual action and that made of history. Hannah Arendt has succinctly summarized these three attacks in her essay "Tradition and the Modern Age":

> The greatness of these three thinkers lies in the fact that they perceived their world as one invaded by new problems and perplexities which our tradition of thought was unable to cope with. . . . Kierkegaard, Marx, and Nietzsche are for us like guideposts to a past which had lost its authority. They were the first who dared to think without the guidance of any authority whatsoever.[3]

"Thinking without any authority" means that thinking must be action and can no longer be separate from activity. It means that one can find no independent or transcendent categorical framework by which to judge one's actions. When Nietzsche spoke of the death of God, he meant at least that we no longer live in a world bounded by horizons that insure meaning and that allow us to make confident sense of what we do and what we see. In these circumstances, political activity suffers from much the same problem as does political thought. Political actors find themselves engaged in choices for which there is no given authority and without a framework by which to make clear sense to themselves or their followers and constituents of the justification for their action.

Part of Lenin's argument, for instance, for the notion of the vanguard party in *What Is To Be Done?* derives from his understanding that what is being essayed in Russia is without historical precedent and thus must rely on "the most advanced theory" for proper guidance. Such a theory, he hastens to add, *cannot* be derived from experience.[4] The past is no guide.

Similarly, a central and oft-ignored focus of Weber's sociological writing is on the changes modern social structure produces in individuals. "Most generally, one can only say," writes Weber in *Economy and Society*, "that the bureaucratization of all domination *(Herrschaft)* very strongly furthers the development of rational 'matter of factness' and of 'men of calling and professional expertise' *(Berufs und*

[3] Hannah Arendt, *Between Past and Future* (New York: Viking Press, 1968), pp. 27-28.

[4] V. I. Lenin, "What is to Be Done?", in *Selected Works*, Vol 1, part 1 (Moscow: Foreign Languages Publishing House, 1950), p. 228 and p. 233 (hereafter cited as WD).

Fachmenschentum)."[5] In a world of such beings, all knowledge becomes instrumental and is no longer a standard for judgment. For the *Fachmenschen,* the only good reason to choose one action over another is that it works, or possibly that it is esthetically more attractive. It is with this point in mind that Weber argues that we confront a *crisis* in legitimacy, in the sense that we no longer have (our old) criteria by which to recognize the correctness of a policy choice. The question that confronts all serious thinkers, no matter to what political persuasion they might adhere, has to do with *the kind of justification* that can be advanced for political choices in a context in which the past no longer seems to provide relevant or valid criteria.

In both Weber and Lenin, there is a tendency to fuse the answers to the question "What is to be done?" with the answer to "Who is to do it?" For Weber, as for Lenin, *the* political question of our times is: "What kind of person must one be, if one is to be allowed to set one's hand on the spokes of the wheel of history?"[6]

WEBER AND THE LUTHERAN STAND

The premise of Max Weber's social science is that it must deal with those objects that have meaning for us. Social science deals with "culture," which Weber defines in the "Objectivity" essay as "a finite segment of the meaningless infinity of the world process, given meaning and significance from the standpoint of *human beings.*"[7] In

[5] Max Weber, *Wirtschaft und Gesellschaft. Grundriss der verstehenden Soziologie.* 2 Halbaender. (Tübingen: Mohr-Siebeck, 1956), p. 584 (hereafter cited as WG). Translated in Max Weber's *Economy and Society.* Edited by Guenther Roth and Claus Wittich. Two volumes. (Berkeley and Los Angeles: University of California Press, 1978), (hereafter cited as ES).

[6] Max Weber, "Politik als Beruf," in *Gesammelte Politische Schriften,* herausgegeben von Johannes Winckelman (Tübingen: Mohr-Siebeck, 1971), p. 584 (hereafter cited as GPS). Translation in Hans Gerth and C. W. Mills, *From Max Weber* (New York: Oxford, 1958), p. 115 (hereafter cited as GM).

[7] Max Weber, "Die 'Objektivität' socialwissenschaftlicher und sozialpolitscher Erkenntnis," in *Gesammelte Aufsätze zur Wissenschaftslehre,* Herausgegeben von Johannes Winckelman (Tübingen: Mohr-Siebeck, 1973), p. 180 (hereafter cited as WL). Translation in Edward Shils and Henry A. Finch (eds.), *The Methodology of the Social Sciences (New York: The Free Press, 1949),* p. 81 (hereafter cited as MSS). See the discussion in David Goddard, "Max Weber and the Objectivity of Social Science," *History*

fact, Weber goes on to say, in a conscious echo of Kantian metaphysics, the fact that we are "cultural beings," i.e., beings who can lend significance to the world, is the "transcendental presupposition" of every cultural science. A "transcendental presupposition" is what has to be the case for a given entity in question to have existence at all. In other words, for Weber, the possibility of social science is premised on the existence of a *particular* type of individual, namely, *"historische Individuen,"* whose nature it is to lend meaning and who cannot help doing so, because of being human.

For Weber, objectivity in social science then requires acknowledging the fact that as a scientist, one is a "historical being" and never transcendent to the object of investigation. Since social science is about human beings, it must in its activity reflect the premise of human culture, namely, that meaning has been and is being conferred. It must do so not only prior to the social scientist's activity but also in that activity itself. This is the premise of Weber's understanding of "objectivity" in the social sciences.[8] In principle, this differentiates the social sciences from the natural sciences for Weber, in much the same manner that Hegel had made a differentiation between the mathematical sciences, whose truth lay outside themselves, and philosophy, whose truth was part of its activity.[9] For Weber, like Hegel, the objects of investigation of the natural sciences are built by theory: these objects do not affect us and have no scientific existence independently of our cognition of them. For example, how we understand the tides does not affect what the tides are. The tides have no intentions; they do not and cannot confer meaning. Thus, in the natural sciences, most especially in mathematics and physics perhaps, objectivity is a necessary part of the theoretical construct. One cannot imagine a natural science that is not what one would call objective.[10]

and Theory, Vol. 12, no. 1 (1973), pp. 1-22, esp. 10-17.

[8] See here H.H. Bruun, *Science, Values and Politics in Max Weber's Methodology* (Copenhagen: Munksgaard, 1972), esp. pp. 131ff.

[9] G.W.F. Hegel, *Phenomenology of Spirit* (Oxford and New York: 1979), pp. 23ff.

[10] This appears to be Weber's position, but one can read "Science As A Vocation," WL 610/GM 154, with its implication of a parallelism of Kant's epistemology and Lukacs' aesthetics as implying only a pragmatic judgment. See Goddard, *op. cit.* , p. 3, n. 5.

The "transcendental premise" of social sciences, on the other hand, is that human beings give meaning from a *"particular point of view."* Due to the human condition, some of these meanings are "more meaningful" than are others. Indeed, the basic social sciences seem to be defined by the meaning vantage points that lie at their bottom. Thus, Weber can refer to the question of the "scarcity of means" as the "fundamental social economic problem."[11] However, Weber is quick to assert that no meaning is in any way privileged in the sense of escaping its human origin. Meaning cannot be derived from the "facts themselves" (Weber places the expression in quotation marks) because all social science starts from the concerns of the social scientist as a being in history. It follows from this for Weber that whatever we mean by "objectivity" cannot rest on the "facts" or on being "true to the facts," since the "facts" are always what has been selected from a world that in its multiplicity far exceeds any attempts we can make to exhaust it.[12]

To this Weber adds a number of central claims. Even though to do social science is to pursue "causal explanations," it is not to pursue "general laws." The goal of social science is the explanation of particular events that have meaning to and for the investigator, not the explanation of the world "as a whole." It is important to note that when Weber talks of an "investigator" and the "meanings" that that investigator has, he does not mean meanings to the investigator considered in some sort of subjective, narrow, individual fashion. At the beginning of *The Protestant Ethic,* for instance, Weber gives an example of such interests. He places authors squarely under the compulsion of their own history: "Any product of Western civilization is *bound* to ask himself. . . ."[13] The meanings that are the subject matter of the social scientist are those meanings that he investigates in response to and out of *his own historicity:* one might even say they derive from the social scientist's "thrownness" in

[11] WL 161/MSS 64 I use Shils' translation, which is very free, though it conveys Weber's point. Lawrence Scaff, "Weber Before Weberian Sociology" (unpublished paper, 1982) has a related point in his analysis of "labor relations" in earlier Weber.

[12] See "Science As A Vocation," WL 601f/GM 146f. For parallels in Nietzsche see Alexander Nehamas, "Immanent and Transcendent Perspectivism in Nietzsche," *Neitzschestudien,* volume 12 (Berlin: Walter Gruyter, 1983), pp. 473-490 and my response in ibid., p. 491-495.

[13] Max Weber, *The Protestant Ethic and the Spirit of Capitalism* (New York: Scribners and Sons, 1958), p. 12 (hereafter cited as PESC). Emphasis added.

historical civilization. Like Nietzsche, the social scientist understands the past by what is most powerful in the present. In this anti-Hegelian mode–we know that Weber disliked the influence of Hegel in Germany[14] –Weber writes, still in the "Objectivity" essay, "The number and type of causes which have influenced any given event are always infinite and there is nothing in the things themselves to set some of them apart as alone meriting attention. . . . Order is brought into this chaos only on the condition that in every case only a *part* of concrete reality is interesting and *significant* to us, because only it is related to the *cultural values* with which we approach reality."[15]

What are *now,* , one might ask, the conditions that govern the significance(s) that we can attribute to cultural phenomena? It is clear that for Weber an infinity of meanings can *logically* be attributed.[16] But it is equally clear that this in no way implies to him that we as historical beings will/can give that infinite set. We are not logical beings for Weber, but historical ones. Thus understanding our attribution of meaning to cultural phenomena–social science–results for Weber not so much in the *discovery* of ourselves, but in the practical *acknowledgment* of who we are, i.e., of our position in history. Indeed Weber seems to argue that the choice is between a recognition of self and an insistence on self-ignorance.[17] It is clear that as historical beings we are *certain kinds* of beings and do not have the choice not to be those kinds of beings. Though we can of course *insist* that we are not, that stand will not *make* us different.

So the question one must ask first is "What kind of historical beings are we?" To this the simplest answer from Weber is that we are creatures who live under the conditions of the general rationalization of social relationships, namely, the "bureaucratization of all forms of domination."

[14] Honigsheim, op. cit., p. 12; see W. Schluchter, *The Rise of Western Nationalism: Max Weber's Developmental History* (trans. G. Roth) (Berkeley and Los Angeles: University of California Press, 1981), p. 21.

[15] "Objektivität . . .," WL 177-178/MSS 78.

[16] Ibid., WL 213-214/MSS 111.

[17] Ibid., WL 194-195/MSS 94.

By "bureaucratization of all forms of domination," Weber does not mean simply the system of organization by which large institutions govern their day to day affairs. Rather, he notes,[18] bureaucracy is the typical expression of the form of legitimacy in which obedience is due to and rests on norms rather than persons. It is thus a form of domination *(Herrschaft)* in which commands are linked not to human beings but rather to an abstract and nonpersonal entity. Bureaucracy has nothing to do with the truly political, for, Weber says, "politics means conflict." However, "Bureaucracy failed *completely* whenever it was expected to deal with political problems." The two forms are "inherently alien" to each other.[19]

In part, this seems to be because bureaucracy effaces or disguises the fact that there is ruling going on at all. Officials, even at the highest level, tend to think of themselves merely as the first official of their enterprise. Rule replaces ruling.[20] I suspect here that Weber again attaches himself to Nietzsche and the latter's anxieties about "all herd and no shepherd."[21]

There are, however, political consequences when the procedures of bureaucracy supplant the choices of politics. Weber argues that to the degree that election (through some kind of voting, e.g. plebiscite) does not play a major role in the structuring of an organization, that organization will more easily tend to rationalize its procedures i.e., to make them rule-governed. Over the long term, bureaucratic organization must devalue any power obtained through

[18] ES 954.

[19] "Parliament und Regierung im neugeordneten Deutschland," GPS 329n1, 351/ES 1399, 1417.

[20] ES 958.

[21] See my discussion in *Friedrich Nietzsche and the Politics of Transfiguration* (Berkeley and Los Angeles: University of California Press, 1975), ch. 7. Bureaucracy supplants not only political domination but also, if I read closely between the lines, institutionalized religion, i.e., any link with a transcendental meaning. Weber writes that "the political official–at least in the fully developed modern state–is not considered the personal servant of the ruler. Likewise the bishop, the priest and the preacher are in fact no longer, as in early Christian times, carriers of a purely personal charisma, and have become officials in the service of a functional purpose, a purpose which in the present day 'church' appears at once impersonalized and ideologically sanctified" (ES 959). The form of bureaucratic organization owes something to the Church in its form. In each, loyality was to an office and not to a person. As in Dostoevski's vision, the Grand Inquisitor conforms also to the distinction of secular and sacred and insists on the centrality of the secular.

election, since that tends to lessen the claim to rational competence. However, to the degree that rational competence becomes a basis for social organization, the introduction of anything new to that framework must necessarily come from beyond the organization. In a bureaucracy, the political problem is to find the sources of the new, sources that must come from outside the rationalized structure.[22]

For Weber, over the long term, rationalization of social relationships runs counter to all forms of political and social democracy. At first, it is true that social democratization tends to increase and enhance social rationalization, for it encourages the notion that all individuals are to be judged on the same basis. But political decision-making procedures–e.g., voting–are ultimately nonrational. Hence, Weber argues, there is a tendency to reduce the importance of procedures such as voting in favor of rules. To the degree that this happens, specifically "human" solutions, i.e., policies that must rest on nonrational *choice,* , will increasingly be devalued. They will be seen as nonrational or irrational precisely because they derive from historical and changing human beings, not simply rules with an inherent claim to universality. "It is decisive for the specific nature of modern loyalty to an office that, in the pure type, it does not establish a relation to a *person,* like the vassal's or disciple's faith in feudal or in patrimonial relations of authority. Modern loyalty is devoted to an impersonal *functional (sachlichen)* purpose *(Zweck).*"[23] For Weber, there is a real danger that persons (and thus the nonrational) will be eliminated from the modern world.

In relation to the conduct of political and social life, the entire quality of human relations is affected by the rationalization of society. Weber notes that rationalization tends to promote situations where the business is discharged according to calculable rules and without regard for persons. But this behavior– *sine ira ac studio*–is "also the watchword of the market place and, in general, of all pursuits of naked economic interests." Hence, consistent bureaucratic domination means in fact the political domination by those classes (defined in purely economic terms) who profit from the market, i.e.,

[22] ES 961. See the discussion by Erik Olin Wright, "To Control or to Smash Bureaucracy: Weber and Lenin on Politics, the State and Bureaucracy," *Berkeley Journal of Sociology, Vol. 19* (1974-75), pp. 69-108, esp. pp. 70ff. Wright focuses too much on a liberal-revolutionary dichotomy.

[23] ES 961.

the rich. "If the principle of the free market is not at the same time restricted," Weber continues, "[This] means the universal domination of the 'class situation.'"[24] In other words, *bureaucratization tends to encourage the domination of the market over politics,* or, more precisely, over whatever is left of politics.

A Marxist analysis might have said that the domination of the market over politics encourages bureaucratization. Weber arrived at his diagnosis on a very different path from the one that Marxists undertook, and his conclusions were correspondingly different. In particular, for Weber, class consciousness does not result from the increasingly obvious domination of politics by economics; rather, Weber argues, *no* common consciousness is formed. "Bureaucracy develops the more perfectly, the more it is 'dehumanized,' the more completely it succeeds in eliminating from official business love, hatred, and all purely personal, irrational, and emotional elements which escape calculation. This is appraised as its special virtue by capitalism."[25]

Bureaucracy is thus seen as the front of a great historical process of rationalization that has as its consequence the increasing destruction of affective or status relations between individuals and the progressive domination of the economic over the political.[26] The bureaucrat is the vanguard of the historical process, implicitly a participant in a vast revolutionary process that has totally transformed all relationships. Weber sketches out this development in the last pages of *Economy and Society.* The democratic ethos is tied in with specific substantive questions (on rights, for example,) that are not a necessary part of the rational legal system; but the rational legel system is *instrumentally* oriented. Such instrumentality can make *use* of "rights" and so forth, but clearly rights are merely instruments to its instrumentality. In fact, Weber claims, instrumentality has become the world historical *Zweck* for Western society.[27] When there arises a conflict between the substantive parts of the democratic ethos–treating an individual not only fairly, but with dignity, for instance–there arises also an incompatibility between bureaucratic

[24] ES 975.

[25] ES 975.

[26] See Karl Löwith, "Marx und Weber," in *Gesammelte Abhandlungen. Zur Kritik der geschichtlichen Existenz* (Stuttgart: Kohlhammer Verlag, 1960), pp. 1-3.

[27] Weber states at the beginning of PESC.

procedures and democracy. This incompatibility will most especially be of importance to those in the lower classes, since they are increasingly subject to those who have money, that is, to those classes that will tend to dominate the bureaucracy. "The propertyless masses *especially* are not served by the formal 'equality before the law' and the 'calculable' adjudication and administration demanded by the bourgeois interests." Thus, for Weber, *those who suffer most under bureaucracy from the historical process are the working classes.*[28]

Weber is thus arguing that democratization is a more complex phenomenon than would have the standard argument for "mass society." His is not a position that simply notes with a sad gray regret the decline of aristocracy and the rise of the plebs. He is furthermore reasserting an argument he had originally made against Schmoller and others,[29] that although it is in the *nature* of bureaucracy to be "neutral" and instrumental, it is not and cannot be in the *practice* of bureaucracy to so be. In fact, Weber argues that the practice of bureaucratic domination goes "hand in hand with the concentration of the material means of management in the hand of the master."[30]

This is the central development of modern society. Thus, as Robert Eden has pointed out,[31] to live by the division of labor as a member of the bureaucracy is to partake of the most widespread revolutionary process in the world. Marx had argued in *The Communist Manifesto* that it was the nature and glory of the bourgeoisie to wipe out all structures that threaten to become permanent. "All that is solid melts into thin air," he wrote, signifying by that that the Faustian urge of the bourgeoisie would tolerate nothing to remain in the form that it was in, neither human relations nor commodities.[32] Weber's vision is a cousin to Marx's, but with real family differences. It is quite true for him that bourgeois society, as expressed socially in rationalized structures, tends to eliminate anything that is "solid." But the "solids" that melt–love, friendship,

[28] ES 980.

[29] Ibid.

[30] Ibid.

[31] In a forthcoming paper in *Political Theory.* My thanks to him for making his paper available to me and discussing these issues. Eden's work and Scaff's are among the most subtle in English.

[32] See the discussion of this passage in Marshall Berman, *All That Is Solid Melts Into Air: The Experience of Modernity* (New York: Simon and Schuster, 1982), ch. 1.

passion, hatred, marriage, honor, etc.–are specifically *human* relations, not just those of stages prior to the bourgeois. For Weber, the bureaucracy leaves nothing as it was and transforms previous orders into its own rational vision. To be a bureaucrat is to partake in a world historical transformation of the world, far more extensive than any that particular political parties or groups would happen to be advocating. Bureaucrats are the locomotive of the train of historical rationalism, destroying all other structures of domination.[33]

Rationalization and bureaucratization are ensured both an objective and a subjective basis of perpetuation. As Weber remarks at the end of *The Protestant Ethic,* , we are compelled to live in such a world and have no choice but to think in its categories. Ruling is now impossible without a bureaucracy. Furthermore, Weber tells us, since bureaucracy bears no necessary relation to any given political economic system, the drive towards perpetuity will take place under both socialist and capitalist states.[34]

Weber implies that under no *foreseeable* conditions will humans be able to live in other than in a rationalized society. Thus, the dream of doing away with the division of labor that had attracted Marx as well as the utopian socialists is seen to be a foolish dream. Weber would not have had Lenin's hope for the slow reemergence of "the elementary rules of social life that have been known for centuries. . . . " We live in a steel box outside which there is nothing we can see.[35] Weber does not think, as does Émile Durkheim, that the social division of labor is necessary because society and justice are founded on it. Rather, Weber thinks, as does Marx, that the historical process and not the functional basis is the most important thing to look at in understanding society. Weber thinks that rationalism is the force that animates history and that one has no choice but to acknowledge oneself a subject of that force. Thus, what Marx had seen as the source of our alienation–the socially forced and necessary division of labor–is in fact for Weber the fundamental precondition and characteristics of our life.[36] It is still "alienation,"

[33] ES 1002.

[34] ES 988.

[35] V. I Lenin, "State and Revolution," in *Selected Works,* vol. 1, part 1 (Moscow: Foreign Languages Publishing House, 1950), p. 74 (hereafter cited as SR).

[36] Compare the parallel argument in Steven Lukes, "Alienation and Anomie," in Peter Laslett and W. Runciman, eds., *Politics, Philosophy and Society* Series III (Oxford: Blackwell, 1967), pp. 134-155.

but we can no more live without the division of labor implied by bureaucracy than we can get off the track of history.[37]

There is no way around this problem. The inevitability of the bureaucracy has nothing to do with its power or potential power. Indeed, Weber wrote to his friend and student Michels in November 1906 that "indispensability in the economic process means nothing, absolutely nothing in the power position and power chances of the class."[38] The importance of the bureaucracy derives solely from the fact that it comes to structure all relations in its own image.[39]

Before we ask who can provide an alternative to the progressive demagification of the world, we must ask what it means to understand this world. If the world is in fact inexhaustible chaos, then understanding of the world must be derived from the person who understands it, not from the grasping of "facts" about the world. What capacities must that person have to make "objective" claims about our condition?

The answer is the ability to elaborate what Weber calls "ideal types." Much has been written both for and against this notion, but the role of the ideal type in establishing the *right* to make claims about the world has most generally been overlooked. An ideal type is for Weber an artificial construction–it is not found but is built. Therefore, it is a "utopia," not intended to describe or reflect reality but rather to provide for an "unambiguous means of expression to such a description."[40] Weber seems to mean by this that there has never been in history any set of circumstances that looked just like the "spirit of capitalism." Rather, Weber's elaboration of capitalism derives from his own ability to understand and accept *himself* as a historical being, under the compulsions of his age. The "spirit of capitalism" is the assemblage of all those traits that "in their singularity draw upon and respond to *(entnommen)* their truth from the

[37] "Parliament und Regierung," GPS 321-322/ES 1394. I thus agreed with Scaff, *op.cit.* (and with Jameson, see n. 46, and Bryan Turner, *For Weber,* (London: Routledge and Kegan, 1981), that there is a "structuralism" in Weber, but I see it as much more diachronic.

[38] Cited from Wolfgang Mommsen, *Max Weber und die* deutsche Politik (Tübingen: Mohr, 1959), p. 97. See Lawrence Scaff, "Max Weber and Robert Michels," *American Journal of Sociology,* Vol. 86, no. 6, pp. 1269-1286, esp. 1281-1283.

[39] The ruler, says Weber, is helpless against it, unless "he finds support in parliament," that is, unless he finds support from an outside and nonrational source.

[40] WL 191/MSS 90.

meaningful traits of our culture."[41] It is a thought experiment that makes sense of all the experiences of our own that we are able to acknowledge. At the end of *The Protestant Ethic* , Weber hermeneutically closes the circle of his thought and reaffirms the compulsion with which he had started his book. The Puritan may have had a choice, but "we are compelled to live" in the rationalized world.

From this conclusion, three things seem to follow. First, to the degree that we are aware of the inchoate complexities that make up who we are, our construction of ideal types will be better. Self-knowledge is the prerequisite for good social science. (One remembers here the story Marianne Weber reports that when asked why he learned so much and what his vast knowledge meant, Weber responded: "I want to see how much I can bear.") Second, the ideal type has a "moral" intent integral with its "scientific" role. It compels the acknowledgment of one's own historical stance and thus keeps one from pretending to a transcendence to which one is not entitled. Last, the criterion for a "better" ideal type must be *power*. "There is only one standard: that of success in the recognition *Erkenntnis)* of concrete cultural phenomena in their interdependence, the causal determination *(ursachliches Bedingtheit)* and their *signficance*."[42]

The ideal type is a "clearly thought out" construct and creates a *historical* and *human* realm of transcendent meaning, which compels recognition by its power to make us see ourselves objectively–as we are in history. Such knowledge is objective as an ordering of the world in categories whose power it is to show ourselves to ourselves as meaningful. It is transcendent in that it shows us why it is our necessary human burden to make sense. We do not, as with Kant, make sense because of something that we have; rather, for Weber, the noumenal realm is a historical product and can be grasped only through this kind of historical sociology. Weber writes nearly at the end of the essay "Objectivity," "The *objective* validity of all knowledge of experience *(Erfahrungswissen)* rests on and only on the ordering of given reality according to categories which are subjective in a specific sense, namely as presenting the *presuppositions* of our knowledge and are tied to the presupposition of the value of that truth which the knowledge of experience alone is able to give us."[43] *Our*

[41] WL 192/MSS 91.

[42] WL 193/MSS 92.

[43] WL 213/MSS 110. M. Merleau-Ponty recognizes his affinity to Weber in *Les*

knowledge is knowledge which we have as members of certain cultures.

Weber goes on immediately to make an extraordinary assertion: to anyone by whom "this truth is not valued–and the belief in the value of scientific *(wissenschaftlicher)* truth is a product of a given culture and not given in nature *(Naturgegebenes)* –to him we have nothing to offer of the means *(Mitteln)* of our science."[44] To be able to have accepted truth as a criterion for one's own life means to be a man of science *(Wissenschaft);* however, as Weber informs us in *Science As A Vocation,* that means to have accepted what sociology enforces upon us: the permanence of the division of labor, the necessity of specialization, the demagification of the world, the end of amateurishness. Therefore to *acknowledge oneself as bourgeois is a precondition for being able responsibly to make a claim to (scientific) truth.* Only such a person can face what Weber calls the "fate of the times," which he enjoins us to "bear like men."[45]

But, one should ask, what does the (bourgeois) truth seeker "bear"? It is precisely not the dispassionate image of the social scientist, such as the one that Edward Shils presents in his introduction to the *Methodology.* It is a demand that one take upon oneself the various and now irreconcilable fragments into which the modern world has been shattered. It is as if our world has returned to a state in which it existed before there was coherence. "We live as did the olden world, not yet disenchanted of its gods and demons, but in another sense: just as the Hellene at times sacrificed to Aphrodite and then to Apollo and before all to the gods of his city, so do we still, but disenchanted and disrobed of the mythic but inwardly true plasticity of that stance *(der mythischen, aber innerlich wahren Plastik jenes Verhaltens)* The destiny of our culture is however that we will become again more clearly conscious of these struggles, after our eyes have been for a millenium blinded by the allegedly or presumably exclusive orientation towards the great fervor *(Pathos)* of the Christian ethic."[46] For Weber as for Nietzsche in *Beyond Good and*

aventures de la dialectique (Paris: Gallimard, 1961), ch. 1.

[44] WL 213/MSS 110-111; see "Science As A Vocation" WL 610-611/GM 154. This is a parallel point to Nietzsche's question about the "value of truth" in *Jenseits von Gut und Boese.*

[45] "Science As A Vocation," WL 612/GM 155.

[46] "Science As A Vocation;" WL 604-5/GM 148-9. Gerth and Mills mistranslate this passage in their edition. Frederic Jameson uses their translation in his very inter-

Evil (see paragraph #39), and contrary to a millenium of Christianity, we must *refuse* to make sense of the whole world, and take that meaningless upon us as far *as we can.* The world for Weber ultimately cannot cohere; the danger that confronts us is that we are always going to be tempted to make it cohere.

If we move to the realm of politics, important consequences follow from this position. Weber's analysis of the social and economic conditions of advanced industrial countries sketched above indicated that 1) an increasingly large group of people will suffer under the structural developments of such societies–the working class especially will be oppressed; and 2) as the world becomes demagified, there will develop an increasingly large group of those who suffer from that process and who want to make an integrated sense of their world; they want to find themselves bound together with each other, but can't. Hence, under modern conditions, theodicy is the core of an increasingly dangerous politics.

The last point is at the center of Weber's repeated fear that Germany will be unable to make good use of its war experience, namely, of the fact that Germans had found themselves during that time at last bound truly together in one group.[47] When Weber so famously insisted to Luddendorf that, as commander in chief, Luddendorf should sacrifice himself for the good of the nation, it was out of the sense that this offering would keep the nation together in the coming years.[48]

Weber is thus faced with a political dilemma: the demands of the time require that all people take upon themselves what is properly theirs to do and seek no meaning beyond that. This course, however, does not link people together. As he says at the end of "Science As a Vocation," "It is not accidental that our highest art is intimate and not monumental, nor that today, only in the smallest communities *(Gemeinschaftskreise)* something pulsates from person to person, in pianissimo, which corresponds to that which erstwhile, as prophetic *pneuma* , swept through the great communities in a

esting discussion of this passage in "The Vanishing Mediator: Narrative Structure in Max Weber," *New German Critique* (Winter 1974), pp. 61ff.

[47] Cf. "Politics As A Vocation," GPS 551/GM 120; see especially "Parliament und Regierung," GPS 406. On theodicy, see "The Social Psychology of World Religions," in GM.

[48] See introduction, GM, pp. 41-42.

storming fire and welded them together." The linkage of people into communities–the overcoming of the randomness of bourgeois society–can only be accomplished by the political equivalent of a new prophet.

When Weber concludes that only a new "prophet" can resolve the epistemological nihilism in which humans find themselves, his mode immediately becomes Augustinian. St. Augustine had with great circumspection come to the conclusion in the course of his conflict with Bishop Donatus and his heretic followers that under certain conditions coercion could be used in the name of love. He hastened, however, to express concern that only those who were truly acting from love could be held entitled to use such coercion.[49] Similarly, the central focus of *Politics As A Vocation* is on the personal characteristics that the political leader must have in order to be entitled to act so as to weld people together into a community.

In "Politics as a Vocation," Weber spends much time describing both the bureaucratization of the world and the necessity of accepting it while concomitantly insisting on the *reality* that "we are placed into different life orders, each under differently understood laws."[50] The premises of the political sphere are thus roughly the same as those of the scientific sphere. I see the problem confronting Weber as this: Any action will constitute an attribution of meaning; we know that all claims to general meaning are invalid; yet the world is filled with those who have not the self-discipline to hold unto themselves the world with all its chaos. "Seeing how much I can bear" is the premise of facing the political world as it is.

What do we then do with the range of those who claim they love "the future of socialism" or "international peace" or "fatherland" more than their soul?[51] This formulation gives us, says Weber, the problem as it now stands: what are we to make of those who claim to be able to use violence in the name of a transformation of the chaos of the world? It does no good to say that one shouldn't, since the nature of politics is to admit the *legitimate* use of violence. The question is, What makes that use legitimate?

[49] Augustine, *Letter* 185 in *Letters,* Vol. 3 (New York: Catholic Publishers, 1953); See the discussion in Peter Brown, *Augustine of Hippo* (Berkeley and Los Angeles: University of California Press, 1975), esp. pp. 233-243.

[50] "Politics As A Vocation," GPS 554/GM 123.

[51] "Politics As A Vocation," GPS 558/GM 126.

In the past, Weber seems to say, this was not really a problem. Legitimacy stopped at borders and was recognized as doing so. In the modern age, however, where borders are of less importance and ideologies transcend national boundaries,[52] the question of legitimacy is central. Weber does not, I think, argue, as some commentators claim, that the legitimate is what people accept.[53] Weber's fear, rather, is precisely the fact that there is *nothing that people will find to be legitimate,* and thus they will turn to almost anything. The source of legitimacy must come, in politics as in religion, from "true" prophecy.[54] And Weber turns here to detail a number of characteristics of such a leader, no example of whom does he see around.

Weber's account here is both enticing and frustrating. The true political leader, who is entitled to lead a state, must "become conscious of these ethical paradoxes and of his responsibility for what can become of himself under their pressure."[55] The danger that threatens is that of succumbing to the "diabolic." Indeed, anyone will be "helplessly taken over" *(hilflos preisgegeben)* by the devil unless "he sees him." (It is an old Teutonic belief that the devil will get you unless you see him first.) The ability to see what may become of oneself derives not from age, but from a kind of Aristotelean notion of maturity.[56] This maturity is the "trained relentlessness" *(geschulte Rücksichtlosigkeit)* in looking at the realities of life and the "ability to bear them inwardly as an adult" *(sie zu ertragen and ihnen innerlich gewachsen zu sein).* Anyone who does not is still a "political infant," as are "nine out of ten" of those Weber meets who claim to be "mature." Most of those, like the "politicians of disposition" or "ideologists" *(Gesinnungspolitiker),* who claim that they are going to eradicate the false and the base, are "spiritual lightweights," who become "enraptured with romantic sensations."

[52] Cf. "Politics As A Vocation," GPS 557/GM 125; see the analogous recognition in Arno Mayer, *From Wilson to Lenin: Political Origins of the New Diplomacy, 1917-1918* (New Haven: Yale University Press, 1959), ch. 1.

[53] See John Schaar, "Legitimacy in the Modern State," in P. Green and S. Levinson, eds., *Power and Community* (New York: Pantheon, 1969).

[54] Cf. Jameson, op cit, p. 68.

[55] This and following citations from "Politics As A Vocation," GPS 557ff/GM 125ff.

[56] Cf. Aristotle, *Ethica Nicomachia* (Oxford: Clarendon, 1963), 1095 a, 6-10.

What kind of man is mature? Weber presents the following as his summary.

> However, it is immeasurably moving, when a mature *(reifer)* man–whether old or young in years–who feels truly this responsibility for consequences and acts with a whole soul in terms of the ethic of responsibility, arrives at some point where he says: "I can do no other; here I stand." This is something which is truly human and impressive *(ergreift)*. For this situation truly must be possible at some point for each of us, who is not inwardly dead. Insofar as the ethics of disposition and the ethics of responsibility are not absolute contraries, but complements, which only in combination constitute a genuine person *(echten Menschen)*, one who can have the "calling for politics."[57]

At the last word, morality gives way to esthetics. The final justification of the leader who is entitled to lay hands on "on the spokes of the wheel of history" are Luther's words before the Diet of Worms. It is clear that Weber is himself nervous about this position, for he immediately warns his audience that a test of the justification takes at least ten years of the "polar night of icy darkness and hardness," through which few pass without having succumbed to temptations. Succumbing to those temptations means for Weber "not having measured up to the world as it really is in its everyday routine."[58] Weber argues that for most humans, life is and should be routine; the most dangerous thing people can do is to think that they can do more than what is before them–a modern doctrine of hubris. Since most of us are not such "sober (schlicht) heroes," we should go about "our daily work," i.e., be the rationalized beings that we are and are becoming.

Some actions, however, do escape the everyday *(alltaglich.)* These are the actions of those who truly have the calling *(Beruf)* for politics and are, for Weber, something like works of art–they provide the terms of their own justification. But they do not for Weber justify themselves in terms of anything other than themselves. They are actions of those who may make new sense of the oppression of and chaos for the populace in Germany; the sense they make will be self-referential. All one can say in the face of them–the true leaders–is that one is for them or against them. Puritan divines were

[57] "Politics As A Vocation," GPS 559/GM 127. Gerth and Mills give "ethics of conviction" for *Gesinnungsethik*.

[58] "Politics As A Vocation," GPS 560/GM 128.

fond of exhorting their doctrinally less straight Anglican compatriots to "choose this day which God you will serve," as if the act of choice were a bedrock. Once such choice is made, there is no alternative or turning back.

In the politics of true statesmen, Weber holds out the possibility of a transformation by the intrusion of the purely personal, the not yet rationalized. Those who *truly* have the "vocation for politics" (who stand in complete distinction from bureaucrats) may–they are entitled to–try and recast the categories of the world in their own image. To be entitled to do this is very rare: only occasionally does the fire storm break over the polar night.

What remains difficult about Weber's vision of the world is precisely its Jansenist quality. The alternatives are very stark, but Weber thought that we were in a century of starkness. I do not want to assert that this vision corresponds to some psychological predisposition in Weber. There is perhaps a correspondence between Weber's vision and psychological traits, as Jameson has argued following Mitzman, but this is in no way an explanation. The starkness was in the world that he analyzed, or so he claimed. What Weber's vision does not allow for is action that is based on probable surmise, for human continuity. Sartre once said that probability is a necessary predicate of what comes to be, meaning by this statement that all volitional activity is based upon the proposition that what will be, can be. Weber suggests that first we must change the structures of possibility; how we do it is akin to magic.

The choice is between ice and fire. For most of us, the truly honorable course consists in doing what is ours to do–"one's damned duty"–with the recognition that this and only this can constitute an acceptance of our human condition. Knowing oneself is for Weber as much the imperative as it was in the days of those ancient Greeks whom he appears to have admired. The self was given by external conditions, by history, and one could make no change in it. There was no other sense to be made out of it: one had, in fact, to resist the desire to be more than the division of labor left one to be.

The choice is uncomfortable. There is a real force to the Weberian claim that we should eschew all attempts and temptations to ground our judgment on something outside the human world. Weber does not deny "objective" knowledge of the world but does refuse to recognize in the external world any structures more permanent than those that are historically in us.

This makes it difficult to act in the name of another and most centrally makes it difficult to claim the right to do so. It is to establish the legitimacy of these claims that Lenin elaborates the doctrine of the vanguard party.

LENIN AND THE CALL OF THE PARTY

In *Materialism and Empirio-Criticism* (1908), Lenin writes: "From the standpoint of Marxism, the *limits* of approximation of our knowledge to the objective, absolute truth are historically conditional, but the existence of such truth is *unconditional,* and the fact that we are approaching nearer to it is also unconditional. The contours of the picture are historically conditional, but the fact that this picture depicts an objectively existing model is unconditional. . . . (This is) the boundary between dialectical materialism and relativism."[59]

Truth, then, exists but is hidden from us because of our historical condition. There exists a test by which one may determine the correctness of a particular political line, namely, if it becomes historically objective. This means, of course, that the truth of a policy is attested to by the fact that it becomes the policy of the proletariat. It does not have to arise spontaneously from the proletariat; a considerable portion of *What Is To Be Done?* is focused on a subtle criticism of spontaneism, never rejecting it, but never relying on it. Lenin's motive is the same as Weber's. He does not want the party to hold up its line to the *idea* of a revolution and conclude that since the world does not match up, it is, in Weber's words, "the world that is base," not the party. This would be in politics precisely the kind of idealism masquerading as empiricism that Lenin attacked in Machian epistemology.[60]

[59] V. I. Lenin, *Materialism and Empirio-Criticism* (New York: International Publishers, 1970), p. 134-135 (hereafter cited as MEC).

[60] See M. Merleau-Ponty, op. cit., pp. 170ff. Compare Lenin's comments on the richness of history in "Left-wing Communism: An Infantile Disorder," in *Selected Works,* vol. 3 (Moscow: Progress Publishers, 1977), p. 352 (hereafter cited as LWC) and on Rosa Luxembourg in "The Right of Nations to Self-Determination," in *Selected Works,* vol. 1, part 2 (Moscow: Foreign Languages Publlishing House, 1950), p. 339ff

If both men attack all idealisms, they have different hopes. Let us look carefully at the arguments that Lenin presents in *What Is To Be Done?* in favor of the role of the party. The important first realization is, as Robert Eden has pointed out, that Lenin's original question is really "what is to be done about the trade unions?"[61] "The history of all countries shows that the working class," writes Lenin, "exclusively by its own effort, is able to develop only trade union consciousness, i.e. the conviction that it is necessary to combine in unions, fight the employers and strive to compel the government to pass necessary labor legislation, etc."[62] In other words, the working classes, like the other classes, have no possibility of reaching a consciousness other than one that reflects their dialectical position in society. *By itself,* the working class can do nothing about the (false) consciousness that characterizes its social and historical position. Lenin, oddly enough, shares with Weber the sense that most people can do nothing about the world and also shares the sense that most people insist that they should be able to. Both men see these temptations as signs of and tacit reinforcements of the historical position in which they and others find themselves.[63]

Lenin and Weber share here a common concern with all that openly or covertly partakes of and reinforces the presently dominant society. This is at the root, for instance, of the tendency they both share to attack without mercy and with equal vehemence *all* possible targets, be they obscure social scientists as well as the top political leaders of Germany for Weber, or *Rabocheye Dyelo,* a short-lived journal, and the entire Menshevik movement for Lenin. For both thinkers, all manifestations of what they oppose are imbued with the same structure and are therefore equally subject to onslaught. Rationalized capitalism must be dealt with in *all* its aspects. Neither are liberals who think that one can pick and choose qualities of a society.

Lenin then moves to an attack on "spontaneism." His point here is that nothing (other than the bourgeois) can emerge "spontaneously," i.e., directly, from the conditions in which the working class

(hereafter cited as RN).

61 Eden, op.cit. (n. 31).

62 WD 233-234.

63 In this sense they share a perspective we might call Calvinist. See here Michael Walzer, *The Revolution of the Saints* (Cambridge, Mass.: Harvard University Press, 1966).

finds itself.[64] The conditions in which people exist provide only false hopes for change. The problem with spontaneism is that it constitutes a false belief that there is something deeper than the structure of the situation in which people live and work, which might constitute a springboard for change. For Lenin the moment is not the source of what is *not* to be done.[65]

One *must* get away from the demands and drives of the moment. Weber had written in "Wahlrecht und Demokratie in Deutschland" that "only the ordered *leadership* of the masses by responsible politicians can break the unruly *(regellos)* domination of the streets and the lead of the demogogues of the moment."[66] Now it is true that Weber's ultimate aim is "das Vaterland,"[67] whereas Lenin's is the conditions of socialist revolution. But what is of importance here is that this transformation can only be accomplished by a particular leader who is "responsible," not to the demands of the moment and of the crowds, but to something else. For Weber, as we have seen, the responsibility was ultimately to a particular form of existential Lutheranism, which transformed the question of justification from moral and "objective" criteria to a form of esthetic entitlement. In the context of Lenin's thought, the question that now arises is *To what or whom is the party responsible?* Because of what we have said above, it clearly cannot be responsible to the working classes, insofar as these are living under working-class conditions. Those conditions of themselves lead to trade union consciousness.

Louis Althusser gives us an entry to this problem when he comments on the relation of philosophy to partisanship in Lenin. "We can say that, in (Lenin's) view, philosophy *represents* the class struggle, i.e. politics."[68] For Althusser, philosophy "represents" politics in the domain of science, that is, in the domain of theory. I take Althusser to be arguing something like the point that I argued above in relation to Weber. It is only possible correctly to do philosophy from a *wertfrei* position, that is, from *a position in which the practitioner acknowledges his historicity and does not pretend to transcendence.* I claimed that Weber saw as a precondition for doing *Wissenschaft* the

[64] WD 240-241.

[65] Cf. "Science As A Vocation," WL 601/GM 146; see L. Althusser, *Lenin and Philosophy* (New York and London: Monthly Review Press, 1971), p. 52.

[66] "Wahlrecht und Demokratie in Deutschland," GPS 287/GM 395.

[67] Ibid., GPS 291 (not in GM).

[68] Althusser, op cit., p. 65.

recognition of himself as a product of the general rationalizing tendency of world history, and specifically as a member of a structurally bureaucratized middle class. Lenin holds to the analogous point that the theorist must understand himself as part of a historical process. Recognition of this constitutes the first step towards responsibility.

If there is implicit in Lenin a test of the truth of a policy in the realization of the policy by the proletariat, it is still clearly the role of the party to advance such policies. Earlier, toward the beginning of this chapter, I noted that the theory that guided such policies could not, in Lenin's view, be derived from experience. What then is the nature of the test? A final recognition of validity comes in the concept of revolution. There are times in history when, for a fleeting moment, everything seems to fit together and to flow by itself.[69] But these moments, which do occur in history, are precisely not what the party seeks to bring about. They are only the touchstones by which the correctness of a policy can be seen in retrospect.

Thus, the party and the revolutionary theoretician for Lenin both have an aspect comparable to the great political leader in Weber. He (the female is notably absent from the work of both writers) acts in such a way that his actions have the aspect of coherence for others. The party does not precisely try to "make" the revolution for Lenin; it tries to make for as much coherence as possible. The revolution will then make itself, which is why relying on working-class spontaneity is not possible. One might thus say that for Lenin the proletariat is the vocation, the *Beruf,* , of the party. The working classes are not the means or even the purpose of the party action, any more than a calling is a means or a goal of a life or than serving God was the means or the goal of the life of a Calvinist.[70]

Marxism claims to be a "scientific" judgment of capitalism, not the simple elaboration of a point of view, still less a value judgment. For Lenin, a potential problem with Marxism comes from the fact

[69] See here also Aristides Zolberg, "Moments of Madness," *Politics and Society* vol. 2, no. 2 (Winter, 1972), pp. 183-207.

[70] I am conscious of a generalized debt here to Merleau-Ponty, op. cit. As a parenthesis, it is worth noting that this is precisely the source of the confusion in Trotsky's notion of "permanent revolution," with its implication either that one always knows what is making for the coherence of revolution or that one never knows.

that it is possible to think that the simple objective criticism of capitalism is itself a sufficient preparatory condition for action leading to liberation and development of socialist freedom. I do not think that Marx ever really meant to imply this, but it is well known that the politics of the postcapitalist development were not well worked out in his writings. To counter this tendency, Lenin brings to Marx precisely the recognition that the period after capitalism would itself have its problems, dangers, and tyrannies, petty and large. From this recognition, Lenin's thought and work must constitute a choice against bourgeois capitalism, on the grounds that *anything that is not capitalism is preferable to capitalism,* "no matter," as Merleau-Ponty once remarked, "what that be."[71]

From the *point of view of the proletarian,* therefore, Lenin may be seen in terms precisely like those that have been used for a Weberian leader. Mayakovsky, for instance, in his great poem *Lenin,* describes a man who though apparently human in every detail, was more than ordinary men; indeed, for Mayakovsky, Lenin and the Party were "brother-twins."

The choices that the party makes are to be experienced as grounded in the same form of authority that Weber recognizes in his man of political vocation and to which Mayakovsky draws attention. It seems to be a fact that no revolution ever occurs successfully without a central leader who is able to perform precisely the creative role that Weber and Lenin respectively suggest that the man of true political vocation and the party perform. These figures do not precisely or only *lead* , in the sense of having followers. Rather they make for a kind of coherence and sense in the midst of what appear to all others as disparate and incongruous elements. Lenin pays a great deal of attention during the middle passages of *What Is To Be Done?* to the problem of focusing too narrowly on simply one aspect of the conditions in which people find themselves. "Working class consciousness cannot be genuinely political consciousness unless the workers are trained to respond to *all* cases, without *exception,* of tyranny, oppression, violence and abuse, no matter *what class* is affected."[72]

[71] Merleau-Ponty, op. cit., p. 244.
[72] WD 276. (Emphasis added)

With this, Lenin's original question, "What is to be done about the trade unions?," is now transformed into "What is to be done to bring political knowledge to the workers?"[73] And here Lenin's response specifically avoids thinking of any one factor or another as somehow basic or key. The point is that the party is to react to all situations, most of which are ignored by any given other group, and bring them under the semantic umbrella of the party line. It is the ability to make sense of the *whole* and to ignore no occurrence that distinguishes the responsibility of the party.

Just as Lenin did, so also did Weber worry about the state of political education. From the times of the *Antrittsrede* onwards, and most especially in "Parliament und Regierung," Weber attributes most of the problems of the German polity to the structural lack of political activity induced by the developments during the Bismarckian period. The difference here between Weber and Lenin is that Weber thinks the political immaturity of the German middle and working classes to have been induced by political choices in the historical process of rationalization, whereas Lenin thinks it inherent in the system of capitalism. For Weber, it is *now* inherent in the German capitalist state but has become so as the result of human action.

In this context, Lenin feels obliged to provide criteria by which to recognize such leaders. He advances an argument for responsibility not dissimilar to the one Weber uses. Lenin begins by listing the kinds of *behavior* by which one may recognize true members of the party. The next several pages of *What Is To Be Done?* are filled with behavioral "we musts": "be ahead of everybody," "confront every general democratic problem," "obtain all possible support of every opposition strata," etc. As with Weber, with Lenin the justification of the party is that it will behave along these lines: in its *action,* not its claims, it is recognized.[74] Political actors are known by their fruits, not their intentions.

Thus, specialization and expertise are the only answers. A party that so behaves will not be "amateurish" but rather "professional."[75] Political leadership turns out for both Weber and Lenin to require a particular training and status–it is not something that springs from

[73] WD 287.
[74] WD 299.
[75] WD 323.

the people; it is somewhat more like a job. The party is to consist of "people who make revolutionary activity their profession."[76] For Lenin, there is therefore no structural distinction between being a worker and being a revolutionary. Both are jobs that are given to be done by the historical situation in which we all find ourselves. The important thing is that one do what one does, *as a job.* When Lenin talks of effacing the "distinctions between workers and intellectuals" he does *not* mean that intellectuals should become workers (or vice versa) but rather that the occupations of both should be understood in the same terms, as *professions.* What is important is the integrity of the actor. "A person who is flabby and shaky in questions of theory, who has a narrow outlook, who pleads the spontaneity of the masses as an excuse for his own sluggishness, who resembles a trade union secretary more than a people's tribune, who is unable to conceive of a broad and bold plan that would command the respect even of his opponents, and who is inexperienced and clumsy in his own professional art–the art of combatting the political police–why such a man is not a revolutionary, but a *wretched amateur.*"[77] The disciplining of such individuals, Lenin goes on to say, must be left to "professional standards," not those of "toy democracy."[78] This, he says, is something "more than democracy": it is "responsibility" derived from experience in and of an organization.

Finally, having established the professionalism of his enterprise, Lenin begins his conclusion with the call to "dream" of what such a leadership party can bring about. He then interprets himself humorously and pictures an interrogation by Martinov, his opponent on the editorial board of *Iskra,* , who asks him "sternly": "Permit me to ask you, has an autonomous editorial board the right to dream without first soliciting the opinion of party committees?" Indeed, the question of whether a Marxist is permitted to dream– *at all* –follows closely.

Actions based on "dreams" are the answer to "What is to be done?" They *must* be phrased as a dream, since they cannot derive from past experience. In a manner very close to that of Weber, Lenin describes the unity of the morality of disposition and the morality of responsibility in the party men of true profession.

[76] Ibid.

[77] *WD 328-329 (emphasis added).*

[78] WD 354; see the accusation of "childishness" in LWC 368.

> If a man were completely deprived of the ability to dream . . . if he could not from time to time run ahead and mentally conceive, *in an entire and completed picture,* the product to which his hands are only just beginning to lend shape, then I cannot imagine at all what stimulus there would be to induce man to undertake and complete extensive and strenuous activity. . . . The rift between dreams and reality causes no harm *if only the person dreaming seriously believes in his dream,* if he attentively observes life and compares his observations with his castles in the air and if, generally speaking, he works conscientiously for the achievement of his fantasies. If there is some connection between dreams and life, then all is well.[79]

In the end, the revolutionary's dreams are justified because they are the deepest and most serious commitments of a serious professional, of a man for whom revolution is a *Beruf.* They are the dreams of "adults." Lenin concludes with a revealing set of metaphors. The party is to be compared to a child in its development. The "first period" is birth, indeed "foetal development." During the "second period," it grows without much control, the time of childhood and adolescence. Finally the party reaches a third period "of adolescence (when) a youth's voice breaks."[80] False notes are sounded. We must, Lenin says, "liquidate the third period," that is, *grow up* and be who we are, professionals of one kind or another.

The call in both Lenin and Weber and the final justification of the actions of the political responsible actor is "maturity." The situation requires adults; it tempts toward the self-indulgence of adolescence. For both men, an adult is, I suppose, an individual who recognizes that any action taken is taken under circumstances where the consequences of that action are not apparent. The *acceptance* of this and the avoidance of the plea of good intentions, no matter what the outcome, is what distinguishes a grownup from a child. If mistakes are made, they are the mistakes of insufficient professional skill and commitment. After all, both Lenin and Weber realize, no one ever sets out to do evil on purpose. The danger is that if one sets out to do good and does evil, one may come to think the evil good. "Politics," as Hannah Arendt once remarked, "is not like the nursery." It does no good to say "I didn't mean it."[81]

[79] WD 388; (emphasis added).

[80] WD 396-397.

[81] Hannah Arendt, *Eichmann in Jerusalem: A Report on the Banality of Evil* (New York: Viking, 1974), p. 279.

Chapter 9

RATIONAL CHOICE AND CULTURE: A THICK DESCRIPTION OF ABNER COHEN'S HAUSA MIGRANTS

David Laitin

In the 1950s and 1960s, political scientists became enamored of cultural explanations for political action. The culture of a people–its authority structures in the family or in the Church,[1] its sense of civic competence,[2] or, in broadest terms, its "orientation to action"[3] –could explain the probability of democracy, political stability, or both. These studies, for a variety of methodological reasons, were severely criticized by scholars who examined the arguments carefully.[4] The severest criticism leveled at these studies, in my view, is that their proponents claimed far too much for the explanatory power of culture. Although it may be true, for example, that the Italians have a culture of "mistrust" for authority,[5] much of their

An early formulation of this paper was presented to the Department of Anthropology at the University of California, San Diego in November, 1980. I owe special thanks to F. G. Baily and M. Meeker, one of whom helped to sharpen the lines on my duck, the other to deepen my portrait of the rabbit.

[1] S. Verba, "Germany: The Remaking of Political Culture," in L.W. Pye and S. Verba, *Political Culture and Political Development* (Princeton, N.J.: Princeton University Press, 1965).

[2] G.A. Almond and S. Verba, *The Civic Culture* (Boston: Little Brown, 1963), ch. 6.

[3] This phrase is from Max Weber, *Economy and Society,* G. Roth and C. Wittich eds., (Berkeley: University of California Press, 1968), e.g., p. 245; and it is a sociologically derived probability statement. Talcott Parsons et al. in *Towards a General Theory of Action* (New York: Harper and Row, 1951), use that phrase to comprehend the social and cultural bases of action in any social system.

[4] See Brian Barry, *Sociologists, Economists and Democracy* (London: Collier-Macmillan, 1970), and C. Pateman, "Political Culture, Political Structure and Political Change," *British Journal of Political Science* (July 1971), for the best critiques of the political culture literature.

[5] Joseph LaPalombara, "Italy: Fragmentation, Isolation, and Alienation" in Pye and Verba, op. cit.

behavior can be easily explained by the fact that any Italian citizen who trusted authority would pay a very high cost for doing so. If it is rational to mistrust authority, why must one explain the behavior by cultural orientation?

The most compelling counter theory to that of political culture to explain action has come from those students working under the "rational choice" paradigm, sometimes called the "economists". These students carefully examine structural incentives provided by the economy or polity and assume that citizens will act rationally to maximize utilities given that structure. Peasants who smuggle crops to the marketing boards of neighboring countries are not doing so to subvert their government (exhibiting a negative orientation to the civic realm) but are probably doing so because the marketing boards in the neighboring countries are paying far more for the crop.[6] The economists, through arguments of this type, have provided a far more parsimonious and disconfirmable approach to action than have the culturalists.

The impact of the economists on the field of comparative politics has nonetheless been less than overwhelming. Many sensitive observers of political life–Henry Ehrmann is an exemplary figure here[7] –remain unhappy with the assumption that people act rationally in the pursuit of generalized goals. First, preference functions will look different in different societies, leading to different choices when there is rationality. But the rational choice theorists must assume generalized preference functions to keep their theories parsimonious. Second, culture often provides direction and meaning to action vitiating any need for rational calculation. But the rational choice theorists also assume continued calculation concerning all actions. The realm of culture cannot be barren. Yet a coherent response by those political scientists who are unhappy with economistic explanation, but who nonetheless appreciate the significance of it, has not been made. In an important sense, the argument between culturalists and economists has been a battle of the deaf.

[6] See Robert Bates, *Markets and States* (Berkeley: University of California Press, 1981), for far more sophisticated examples of rational action by peasants that subvert the intentions of government planners.

[7] Henry W. Ehrmann, *Comparative Legal Cultures* (Englewood Cliffs, N.J.: Prentice-Hall, 1976).

The purpose of this chapter is to highlight the controversy as it exists in another discipline–anthropology–where cultural explanations are far more sophisticated than in political science. In the course of my examination of two different approaches to culture in anthropology, I hope to demonstrate that cultural explanations are a necessary counterpart to rational choice theory and that, without a theory of culture, rational choice theory degenerates into tautology. I hope as well that by giving due credit to the power of rational choice theory that I can save cultural explanations for political action from the dustbin of the political science discipline.

RATIONAL CHOICE OR CULTURE

Anthropological description of culture must be "thick," argues Clifford Geertz in his seminal essay introducing his *The Interpretation of Cultures* (hereafter cited as *IC*). But, in an equally formative essay, Abner Cohen proposes that in social anthropology, the good practitioner should not be content with "mere description" *(Two Dimensional Man,* p. 13, hereafter cites as *TDM)* but should seek out causal "probabilities" *(Custom and Politics* p. 213, hereafter cited as *C&P*).[8] These two methodological treatises are both so compelling, both so different, and both so critical of most anthropology (Geertz does not refer to Cohen at all; Cohen writes Geertz off in a paragraph) that this foreigner to the anthropological discipline is impelled to ask, with Geertz, "What manner of men are these?" *(IC,* p. 16).

What I propose to do in the following sections is to compare the anthropological ideal as stated by Geertz in his "Thick Description: Toward an Interpretive Theory of Culture" and by Cohen in his *Two Dimensional Man.* I shall then describe (perhaps too thickly) the arguments by Cohen in his *Custom and Politics in Urban Africa: A Study of Hausa Migrants in Yoruba Towns,* an exemplification of the rational choice method that he later formalized in *Two Dimensional Man.* That done, I will attempt to poke some holes in Cohen's argu-

[8] Clifford Geertz, *Interpretation of Cultures* (New York: Basic Books, 1973); Abner Cohen, *Two Dimensional Man* (Berkeley: University of California Press, 1974); and Abner Cohen, *Custom and Politics in Urban Africa: A Study of Hausa Migrants in Yoruba Towns* (Berkeley: University of California Press, 1969).

ment by using my training as a political scientist (a discipline in which "mere" describers were already professors emeritus when I entered graduate school) and some random observations I made of Hausa-Yoruba relations in the Yoruba city of Ile-Ife while I was doing field work (1979-80) on a related topic. Next, I shall try to point out that at least part of the real merit of Cohen's Hausa study lies in his compelling interpretation of urban Hausa culture–a thick description of no small achievement.[9] Finally, I shall try to make some comments on the relative value of the "thick descriptions" of cultural theory and the causal explanations of rational choice theory in social science research.

GEERTZ AND COHEN ON THE AIMS OF ANTHROPOLOGY

Geertz and Cohen differ in their definition of "culture," in their prescriptions on how to study it, and finally in their views concerning the ultimate goals of their discipline. As for culture, Geertz, relying on Weber, sees it as those "webs of significance" that humans have spun and in which we are all suspended *(IC,* p. 5). What we (or a Balinese cockfighter or a Jewish shopkeeper) mean by power, by authority, by love, or by change is unavoidably ambiguous and is embedded in symbols. These symbols–or, better, the various systems of symbols– constitute, for Geertz, "culture". For Cohen, who has a professional commitment to avoid "mumbo-jumbology" (a concept duly indexed in his *Two Dimensional Man,* a culture group simply has a "special style of life or a special combination of a variety of symbolic formations, that distinguish it from the rest of the society" *(TDM,* p. 91). For Cohen it is the *sharing* by a group of symbolic forms that makes for culture; for Geertz, it is the *meaning* of symbolic forms that constitutes culture.

Not only do they disagree about what constitutes culture, they disagree about its significance. For Geertz, culture is both a constraint and an opportunity, for it not only (remember the web)

[9] Ironically, I could take Geertz's *Peddlers and Princes* (Chicago: University of Chicago Press, 1963) or his *Islam Observed* (Chicago: University of Chicago Press, 1968) and demonstrate how, through the sophisticated use of the comparative method, Geertz was able to isolate variables in a not antipositivist manner; but that effort must be deferred.

locks people into a certain approach to life but also provides answers to the deepest questions about the meaning of life (why, for instance, less rain falls on the unjust, and what that unjust fella is doing with the just's umbrella; *IC*, "Religion as a Cultural System," p. 106). For Cohen, although symbols do provide meaning, or at least a sense of what ought to be done the significance of symbols lies in their ambiguity, and therefore manipulability by groups to enhance their political and economic power. Symbols, then, are resources for groups to help them solve a variety of problems *(TDM*, p. 85).

The methodological implications of these differences for anthropological research seem considerable. Geertz advocated the "interpretation" of cultures, which is sometimes portrayed as similar to the activity involving the interpretation of great literature or art (see *IC*, "Ideology as a Cultural System," p. 213, and the discussion of metaphor), and sometimes portrayed as the scientific method of medical diagnosis involving an inscription (thickly describing situations from an actor orientation) and then specification (diagnosing what the meaning of the observations are for that society and about social life generally). Cohen won't settle for interpretation or even diagnosis but seeks instead "to probe into the nature of politico-symbolic causation" *(TDM*, p. 39). With a statement that most positivists would agree to, Cohen seeks to separate analytically abstract variables–like the "power order" and the "symbolic order"–in order to discern the social conditions under which each of these variables influences the other. Not interpretation but the proposition of causal relationships among abstract variables is the hallmark of Cohen's methodology.

From this, some other methodological differences follow. Whereas Cohen seeks the articulation of abstract categories to make generalization across cultures possible (e.g., the cousinhood, the long-distance trader), Geertz tries to avoid abstraction to achieve generality through delicate distinctions *(IC*, p. 25). Geertz derives methodological delight from distinguishing the variety of themes of violence–"animal savagery, male narcissism, opponent gambling, status rivalry, mass excitement, blood sacrifice" *IC*, p. 449, "Deep Play")–that can be spun together in a single cockfight. For Cohen, each distinction reduces the possibility of verifiable causal laws, for the more the categories, the fewer the cases; for Geertz, causal laws are chimeras *(IC* p. 14), and abstract categories hide rather than elucidate meaning.

And, of course, the issue of verification must be faced. For Cohen, Geertz' anthropology is lacking because its "formulations have often been conjectural, non-verifiable, non-cumulative, 'meanings' attributed to symbols and are mostly arrived at by sheer intuition and individual guesswork" *(TDM,* p. 5). Cohen wants his own formulations to be verifiable in the sense that his propositions must be clear enough that future scholars will know what evidence must be adduced in order to disconfirm his causal statements. It should be clear to any reader of Geertz that although one can ignore, ridicule, savor, or reject his interpretations, one would not know how to disconfirm them. Geertz would certainly agree to this formulation; he prefers the "appraisal" *(IC,* p. 16) of interpretations to their verification, and instead of the cumulative development of theory, he seeks the "refinement of debate. What gets better is the precision with which we [anthropologists] vex each other" *(IC,* p. 29). For Cohen, good theory can be verified or disconfirmed; for Geertz, good theory enables us to write about social life with more penetration.

With the two men's different conceptions of culture and different methodological approaches, one should suspect very different views as to the goals of their discipline. Indeed, that is the case. "The essential vocation of interpretative anthropology," concludes Geertz in his "Thick Description," "is not to answer our deepest questions, but to make available to us answers that others, guarding other sheep in other valleys, have given. . ." *(IC,* p. 30). And why do we want to hear their answers? To enlarge "the universe of human discourse" *(IC,* p. 14). When we think about "pride" in social life, we can no longer avoid the case of the Jewish shopkeeper (Cohen!) in Morocco who demanded his payment for a wrong done to him by a Berber group. He was insured by another Berber group and went with his agents to collect sheep as payment. "The two armed Berber groups then lined up on their horses at opposite ends of the plain," Geertz records, "with the sheep herded between them, and Cohen, in his black gown, pillbox hat, and flapping slippers, went out alone among the sheep, picking out, one by one and at his own good speed, the best ones for his payment" *(IC,*

p. 8). Nor, in thinking about "ideology," can we omit the case of Sukarno, who vainly tried to recreate the image of the *Nagara,* the "capital city" that served as the "exemplary center" of the Javanese state, to serve his purposes in giving direction to contemporary (1964) Indonesia *(IC,* pp. 222-224, "Ideology as a Cultural System"). We have no causal theory about pride or ideology from these cases: it is only (only?) that we now have these cases to enlarge our repertoire as we try to enrich our understanding of "Pride" and "Ideology" and other such important but impenetrable concepts.

Cohen's (now the social anthropologist, but equally true of the trader) purposes are of course very different from Geertz's. "The challenge to social anthropology today," concludes Cohen in his study of Hausa migrants, "is the study of sociocultural change, of the involvement of custom in the change of social relations. . . . We seek to answer the broad question: Under what structural conditions what customs will perform what political functions, within which political unit?" *C&P, p. 212-213)* Cohen asks us to avoid seeing secret Masonic orders in Sierra Leone as a reflection of Creole values about information, but to see them as a Creole response to a difficult dilemma. The Creoles required hierarchical organization to further their political and economic aims but also required maintenance of a low profile, as this economic elite group, which formed a numerical minority in an increasingly democratic political system was in a precarious political situation. Secret Masonic orders were a rational response to this dilemma *(TDM,* pp. 106-110). Similarly, Cohen asks us to see antiwar demonstrations in the 1960s United States and United Kingdom, where seemingly well-educated people chanted "Ho! Ho! Ho Chi Minh," not as childish nonsense but rather as a ritual designed to overcome organizational problems in the antiwar movement *(TDM,* p. 135). Once we see that Sierra Leone Creoles, Hausa migrants in Yoruba towns, and U.S. antiwar demonstrators face similar organizational problems and respond to these problems in similar ways, we can begin to construct a general, and causally informed, theory about the role of symbolic manipulation for the attainment of social, political, and economic ends. This is Cohen's vision.

COHEN'S EXPLANATION OF HAUSA MIGRANT CULTURE

Cohen seeks to answer a series of related questions in his *Custom and Politics in Urban Africa.* As someone who had already studied Moslem villages in the Middle East, Cohen was first struck by how avidly Ibadan Hausas prayed. Both young men and old, in regularly prescribed Islamic prayers and in special prayers for the Tijaniyya order, spent an average of some twelve hours each week in ritual activity. This degree of reverence is not characteristic of Hausas in Hausaland and is relatively recent among those in Yorubaland. How did it come about? Furthermore, why have not the Hausas, as have the Western Ibos in Ibadan, begun to assimilate into the dominant Yoruba culture in Ibadan? In fact, the Hausas, if anything, have become "retribalized." In cosmopolitan Ibadan where they operate "within a contemporary formal political set-up" *(C&P, (C&P,* p. 98), they have become more Hausa than the Hausas. What explains this intense degree of retribalization in an urban context?

The standard explanation in the anthropological literature for the retribalization of any group focuses on the culture of that group. Something about the Hausas, it is suggested, leads them to emphasize their traditions especially when they are abroad. Perhaps they are so very different from the cultural groups with whom they are living (unlike the Western Ibo in Ibadan) or perhaps they have a very conservative culture resistant to assimilation (again as opposed to the Ibos) or perhaps they are more transient than other groups and haven't had time to assimilate. Cohen rejects this sort of explanation; as he assumes that Hausa retribalization is a rational exploitation of resources to further some economic or political ends. So when his Hausa informants regularly told him that "our customs are different," Cohen saw that not as an explanation for their nonassimilation but rather as an ideological interpretation of their culture to further their ends.

The answer to the anomalies of retribalization in a cosmopolitan context and the sudden and rapid adoption of the Tijaniyya brotherhood lies, for Cohen, in the requirements of long-distance trade in a preindustrial society. Problems of credit and communication, among others, without modern banks and widespread literacy, can only be overcome by economic relationships that are governed by "categorical" (i.e., moral) rather than "hypothetical" (i.e., based on contract) imperatives. The Hausas took advantage of certain opportunities in the colonial political structure to monopolize the cattle and kola nut trades and managed these trades efficiently. The ideology of cultural distinctiveness enabled them to separate themselves culturally and economically from the Yoruba and thereby maintain a cohesive moral community (i.e., one based on categorical imperatives).

This system was deeply threatened by the end of colonial rule and political incentives developed for Yorubas to penetrate into the Hausa community. Out of this threat emerged the immediate success of the Tijaniyya order, which, while restructuring authority relationships within the Hausa community, also helped retain the cultural distinctiveness of the Hausa population in Ibadan, thereby perpetuating their trade monopolies. Retribalization and mass initiation into a Sufi brotherhood were both creative responses by a community to develop and maintain economic control over long distance trade.

Custom and Politics fleshes out this brilliant skeletal argument. In Chapter 1, Cohen demonstrates that the Sabo (where the Hausa live in Ibadan) community, although made up of Hausa, is culturally distinct from the Hausa in northern Nigeria, the place from which they come. He needs this argument because retribalization implies cultural adaptation and not merely cultural conservatism. And so he shows that "Hausa" is an acquired status and that non-Hausa can attain such status. He demonstrates the settledness and stability of the Sabo population in order to make clear that the community is not made up of short-term visitors whose hearts are really in Hausaland to the north. And, finally, he shows that the Sabo has its own social security system (through begging), so even failures in the business of formal trade are provided for by community structures. Sabo is therefore not a mere reflection of northern Hausa culture; it is rather an institutionalized response to urban life by a migrant community which has developed its own culture.

Chapters 2 and 3 explicate how the development of Sabo culture has furthered the economic and social ends of its inhabitants. Marriage is carefully regulated so that Hausa men do not marry Yoruba women. If this were to happen, the trust that exists between northern sellers of cattle or buyers of kola and their middlemen in Sabo (both of these markets exclude Yoruba men from entry) might be eroded. So Sabo culture emphasizes the mystical dangers inherent in marrying a Yoruba. But since a pool of eligible women is needed to provide for a stable community of men, Sabo culture gives relatively high status to prostitutes, providing northern women with proper incentives to migrate south. With no stigma attached to prostitution (and a certain degree of freedom associated with it), Hausa men need not rely on Yoruba women for mates. Sabo culture also demands that wives remain secluded and not be seen in public. Although this may be uneconomic, as the men must hire people to do the family laundry, it enables Hausa men to control and to maintain economic supremacy over their wives, and this stabilizes the population (as wives, enriched by their own trade, would have a high incentive to divorce and then to migrate out). Further, since men find that their first sons are not the most reliable agents, the institution of fostering has been cultivated in Sabo culture to ensure widespread and loyal family ties. In family relations, then, Hausa culture in Sabo has adapted, not in any planned or conscious way, but nonetheless in a way consistent with the needs of the successful monopoly of long-distance trade.

Chapter 4 discusses how Hausas related with their hosts, the Yorubas. At first, Yorubas were landlords to the Hausas while they sold their cattle. But with an increasing Hausa presence in rapidly urbanizing Ibadan many "undesirables" (i.e., thieves), most of them Hausas, made life unbearable for the Yorubas. The Hausa traders cleverly argued that only they could control the thieving (only the Hausas can distinguish Hausa traders from thieves), and, if given some autonomy, they would settle things down in Ibadan. At about this same time a new British administrative system called for the reliance on "natural" leaders. This system of "indirect rule" played right into the hands of Hausas seeking a self-governing subcommunity in Ibadan. Both the "thievery" issue and the new administrative system led to the development of the Sabo, the distinct Hausa community in Ibadan. In the northern outskirts of the city (at the time), it was the perfect place to develop monopoly relations with northern traders. Yorubas were quick to grasp the significance of Hausa autonomy, and they fought against it on a number of issues.

The Yorubas successfully monopolized the butchering trade by setting license fees in Ibadan exhorbitantly high and by dispersing markets all over the city. The Hausas were ill-equipped to penetrate every small market in Ibadan. But they won when Yorubas attempted to control the sale of kola nuts from the farms to distribution centers. The Hausas developed subcommunities near all the prime farming lands. The Hausas, through their tight knit community, also were able to maintain a commission system in which the seller paid in kola but the buyer paid in cattle. Yorubas paid Hausa agents the full commission in both trades. But, at least for a while, the Yoruba community was able to coerce the Hausas to dilute their separateness by joining Yoruba Muslims in the Ibadan central mosque for Friday afternoon prayers. They argued about Islamic and Malikite law: but both parties knew they were fighting over economic and political control. In all these battles, the Hausas attempted to exploit their cultural distinctiveness to maintain and enhance their economic power, and Yorubas tried to challenge that power.

Political independence (internally granted in the early 1950s) gave the Yorubas their opportunity. They, rather than the British who tended to protect the minority community, would control Ibadan. In chapters 5 and 6, Cohen analyzes the implications of the emergence of national politics for Sabo. With party politics, Sabo was put in a weakened position. Its leaders had to interact with the Yoruba political leaders and to bargain with them. The parties were able to penetrate the Sabo and develop alliances with discontents. The parties split loyalties, and the cohesiveness of Sabo was severely threatened.

It was almost exactly at that time, not by any clear choice, but "'vehicled' in a series of countless small dramas in the lives of men" (p. 152), that the Tijaniyya Sufi order began to spread. This order was surely not the only plausible response to the threat posed in the 1950s, but it was a reasonable one. With the chief of Sabo's position threatened by the existence of warring political factions, some new authority was required. The Tijaniyya order was able to provide new authorities (mallams, hajjis, the symbol of Allah) and an ideology that while consistent with the previous commitment to Islam, was also (unlike most Sufi orders) consistent with the commercial ethic in Sabo. The ritual groups that were formed created new loyalties and rehomogenized Sabo culture. When Cohen left Ibadan in 1963, Sabo had maintained its distinctiveness and its monopoly positions in long distance trade through the new commitment to a Sufi brotherhood. This commitment explains the extraordinary religiosity among the Hausa that was Cohen's primary dependent variable. Cohen concludes from all this that "the Hausa in Ibadan are more 'retribalized' . . . not because of their conservatism . . . and not because of special elements in their traditional culture . . . but because their ethnicity articulates a Hausa political organization which is used as a weapon in the struggle to keep the Hausa in control of the trade. Ethnicity is thus basically a political and not a cultural phenomenon . . ." (p. 190).

SOME PROBLEMS WITH COHEN'S ARGUMENT

One cannot but be impressed by the cogency of Cohen's argument. Nonetheless, I shall be critical of it not to reduce its significance as a contribution to social science but rather to enhance that significance. My criticisms are based on some observations I have made in Nigeria, on certain social science standards, and on the goals Cohen set for social anthropology in his *Two Dimensional Man.*

From my experience in some Yoruba cities, I was struck by how "one dimensional" the Yorubas appeared in Cohen's study of Ibadan. Certainly it should appear natural that the majority population, a population of people extraordinarily sophisticated for centuries in long-distance trade, would be able to cope more effectively with Hausa monopolization tactics. If Hausas could adapt their culture to fit the requirements of monopolization, why shouldn't the Yorubas do similarly to counter the Hausa gambit? Why, for example, did not some Yoruba Muslims assimilate into Hausa culture? ("We are all Muslims," they could have claimed). Cohen records the Yorubas' pressuring the Hausas to pray at Ibadan's central mosque, but that had more to do with generalized political control of the Hausas than with any desire for mutual identification. I asked many of the most devout Yoruba Muslims in the town of Ile-Ife (a city just east of Ibadan, also with a significant Sabo of long distance Hausa traders) whether they ever shared a meal with any of the Hausas. The men laughed at me uproariously at the thought. Indeed, in the whole Yoruba region, any attempt to shift symbolically Yoruba identification to one of "Muslim" has failed, even when it was to their economic and social benefit.

And again, in Ile-Ife, to make a different point, the Hausas got their own mosque and became Tijannis even though the Yorubas in that town never put any direct pressure on Hausa autonomy. If there was no threat to autonomy and no counterpenetration in Ile-Ife's Sabo in the early elections, why should the same pattern hold as held in Ibadan? It was these two observations that I made in the field that led me to reassess Cohen's methodology.

In doing so, I found two problem areas. First, if Cohen was indeed committed to the isolation of variables to make probability statements, why did he not examine cities (like Ile-Ife) where parties did not penetrate the Sabo community? If he did so (and controlled for other variables) he might have tested his proposition that it was the penetration of parties that was related to the sudden growth of Tijaniyya. Alternatively, he might have searched for other explanatory variables that could better account for Tijaniyya spread. Perhaps the Tijaniyya order was spreading rapidly through the continent in a predictable pattern without considering local nuances? But Cohen did not seek out potential alternate hypotheses to explain his dependent variable. Again, if the requirements of long-distance trade were the explanatory variables accounting for early retribalization among the Hausas, with the Western Ibos juxtaposed as a people who became assimilated into Yoruba culture, why did Cohen ignore Western Ibos in faraway places who managed long-distance trade? Or maybe he could have looked at Western Ibos in Hausaland engaged in short-distance trade. If he found them assimilating with Hausas then his proposition would have more validity. (Ibos in Hausaland did not assimilate.) My point is that Cohen has made no attempt to find critical cases to use the comparative method or a great enough number of cases to use the statistical method and has therefore not provided convincing evidence that the explanatory variables he proposes are valid.

A second problem area concerns the nature of the relationship between explanatory and dependent variables. Although he claims to be interested in causal theory, Cohen–to protect himself and to be honest with his data–resorts often to functional language, to arguments that say the exact nature of the relationship is sociologically unimportant, and to "fudging". Functionalist arguments crop up when Cohen finds "solutions" to problems but no conscious "solvers". The Sabo community needed women for a stable community. Prostitutes appeared. "The significance of this institution," Cohen tells us, "is not that it has supplied migrant men with sexual pleasures . . . but that it has been perhaps the most important channel for mobilizing potential housewives for the pioneering communities?" (p. 62). But did prostitutes come because they were needed or functional? The same argument is used in regard to Hausas' becoming initiated into the Tijaniyya order. We are told that "it is not important for the present to consider what were the motives of individuals in joining the order. . . . What is analytically significant here is what the Tijaniyya has done to Sabo and how it has interacted with the other social institutions . . . " *(C&P*, p. 152). But without knowing the Hausas' motives, how can we know if "retribalization" is a *strategic* use of culture to attain political ends, the phenomenon Cohen sees at the center stage of social anthropology? As for fudging, the already quoted term "vehicled" to describe the adoption of Tijaniyya by the Hausa is a classic example.

My final criticism concerns the question of whether Cohen's methodology in *Custom and Politics in Urban Africa* is a faithful model of the methodology justified in *Two Dimensional Man.* Two differences between the two works appear significant. First, although Cohen often sees cultural change as a result of strategic action, he sometimes sees culture as a constraint, explaining political outcomes. To explain why Hausas feel little pressure to return to the North, he informs us that they are "bilateral and the range of economically, politically, or morally significant kinship relationships among them is very narrow" (p. 42). Now while it is true that Cohen emphasizes that culture and politics are in a dialectical relationship in *Two Dimensional Man,* what he means by the dialectic is not germane to the issue here at hand. He portrays politics affecting culture (in the sense that political changes in wider society ramify throughout local communities) and culture affecting politics (in the sense the cultural groups use their ties of trust to act collectively and successfully in the political arena). But, because culture signifies for Cohen sharing, there is no place in this dialectic for an analysis of cultural meanings (e.g., the relative value of different concentric circles of kinship) to demonstrate how they shape political action. Hausa bilaterality therefore appears as a deus ex machina, helping to explain how population stability developed in Sabo and, more important, why the meaning of the northern homeland had only limited value to the Sabo Hausas, enabling them to remain content as permanent migrants. (The Yorubas, in contrast, go far and wide to acquire wealth in large part to display it in their ancestral communities). Cohen provides us with an analysis of cultural meanings in his study of Ibadan but is skeptical of the worth of studying them in his *Two Dimensional Man.*

Second, throughout *Custom and Politics,* Cohen treats us to a bevy of "delicate distinctions" and "thick descriptions" that have no apparent bearing on his argument but would be savored by anyone suffering from Geertzophilia. Descriptions of the variety of meanings of the commission *(lada)* in each of the trades, of the meaning of "Allah" and "brother" in Sabo religion, of an incident of intra-Hausa thievery, of the distinctions of job categories in the kola trade or in the begging trade, and of the method by which Hausa women accumulate capital are all "thick". Why thick descriptions when Cohen's goal is to reduce the number of variables *(TDM,* p. 21); why delicate distinctions when Cohen's task is to develop variables for which there are a large number of cases? Why the not-so-strategic methodological choices; why the unnecessary concessions to Geertzian anthropology?

COHEN'S THICK DESCRIPTION OF URBAN HAUSA CULTURE

Action theorists in social anthropology (e.g., Bailey) and "political economists" in political science (e.g., Popkin) both assume that individuals are "rational" and will strategically design means to fulfill their political and economic ends.[10] Although Cohen criticizes these

[10] F.G. Bailey's work is a forerunner of the "rational actor" approach in political science. See his *Strategems and Spoils* (New York: Schocken Books, 1969). The most

theorists in his *Two Dimensional Man* (pp. 40-43) for their tendency to ignore sociocultural realities that often raise the costs of apparently strategic maneuvers, he is essentially sympathetic with their general approach. It is just that he feels some of the practitioners do not give an accurate picture of the decision-making environment. Yet, as I have already shown, in his use of functional language, Cohen is not fully comfortable with the assumption of rationality.

Cohen's malaise with the assumption of rationality is never made explicit, as he centers his criticism on the level of analysis (individual versus group) problem in his criticism of the action theorists. Nonetheless, the assumption, however useful for some research purposes, has high costs. Graham Allison (who dubs this school "the rational actor approach") has aptly pointed out that any set of actions can be made to appear rational if the investigator is permitted to define the goal. In the politics of deterrence, which is Allison's field of endeavor, he demonstrates how, by the scholarly redefinition of Soviet goals, it is possible to demonstrate that the Soviets are brilliant maximizers–no matter what they do.[11] I do not think that Allison fully appreciates the power of such reasoning, even if the assumption isn't quite right.

But suppose one wanted to specify the conditions under which different groups were maximizers within a certain range of goals. Or to know under what conditions the countless individual dramas of social life find "vehicle" adaptive solutions to individual and/or group problems and when they do not. Should that be one's scholarly purpose (and I think it is Cohen's), then it is necessary to develop independent indicators of actor goals. For if the scholar derives actor goals from data about actor behavior, the conclusion–that the behavior is rational–is of course tautological. There must be some other source of information concerning actor values. Enter thick description and the interpretation of symbols.

By providing us with a vivid description of Sabo life, Cohen is able to present compelling pictures of the links between explanatory and dependent variables. What appears as a "fudge" from the point of view of causal theory is in actuality a sign of sensitivity to causal links. The level of Machiavellian maximization in Hausa behavior is

self-conscious development of rational choice theory in political science is in S. Popkin, *The Rational Peasant* (Berkeley: University of California Press, 1979), ch. 1.

[11] See his *Essence of Decision* (Boston: Little, Brown, 1971), chs. 1-2.

different for each aspect of Cohen's dependent variable, giving his reader a better appreciation of the limits of rationality in Hausa society.

When he discusses the thievery issue as a source for the creation of an autonomous Sabo, Cohen suggests that Hausa traders did not initiate the thievery as a ploy to be given the responsibility of ending it; rather,they saw the problem and developed a solution consistent with their wider goals. On the issue of the acceptance of prostitutes as wives, a social adaptation functional for Sabo stability, Cohen leaves the reader with the understanding that this was rather an unconscious adaptation, not at all the plan of traders attempting to manipulate values to fulfill economic goals. As for the seclusion of wives, Cohen portrays conscious action by Hausa men, but action that was economically ambiguous in outcome. Although seclusion made the wives medium-term captives to a stable community, it did reduce their potential usefulness to the household. Finally, on the question of why the Hausas in Sabo became Tijannis, Cohen is able to demonstrate a certain degree of rationality. There was a search for a cohesive ideology to stay the inroads Yoruba (and Ibo) politicians were making in Sabo. But there was an unconscious element as well. Tijaniyya teachers were present, were preaching messages not inconsistent with Sabo values, and were winning converts for reasons having nothing to do with Sabo cohesion. Here we have a case of individual action that was only partly seen by the actors as helping to solve a wider community problem.

It seems to me that only if we know the degree of individual rationality involved in cultural adaptation can we learn when culture is manipulated, when it adapts autonomously to changes in the environment, and when it isn't open to change at all. By providing independent data on societal goals and on the politics of attaining those goals, Cohen has done a great service to students of comparative analysis. Macro-sociological theorists assume that social structural change constrains individual action, no matter what individual goals are. Political economists assume rational exploitation of structural change by individuals and groups. Cohen's study gives us a grip on which type of analysis is more useful for what types of situation. This important contribution is only possible–no matter how useful the statistical, comparative, or rational actor approaches are for other purposes–through the examination of individual cases with, to use Geertz's metaphor, diagnostic care.

RELATIVE VALUES OF THICK DESCRIPTION AND CAUSAL EXPLANATION

Abner Cohen, as we have seen, postulates that the source of action lies in strategic choice. For Clifford Geertz, imagination is the key source of action. One apparent implication of this difference is in the research sites both of these anthropologists have chosen. Cohen has worked in humid and congested Ibadan and in desolate Arab villages in the Middle East. In these places, there is an abundance of conflict and a necessity for strategic behavior. Geertz has worked in Java, Bali, and the Atlas Mountains–exotically beautiful sites that seem to trigger his own imagination. Both have found, in their chosen fields, something of what they sought.

What this suggests is that perhaps there is no bridge between the rational-choice theorists and the theorists of culture. The argument between the deaf can go on and on as rational choice theorists seek environments in which calculation is omnipresent and students of political culture seek milieux in which the people have bizarre and non-transitive preference functions. In this case, critical tests between approaches will remain elusive.

But I am more sanguine than that. The opportunity is great. With thick descriptions of culture, rational-choice theorists are not compelled to generalize about preference functions in order to avoid tautology. And with a carefully worked out theory of rational action, theorists of culture can more carefully specify the boundaries of the cultural orientation to action.

Chapter 10

AREA STUDIES AND/OR SOCIAL SCIENCE: CONTEXTUALLY-LIMITED GENERALIZATIONS VERSUS GENERAL LAWS

Fred Eidlin

THE PROBLEM OF AREA STUDIES AND SOCIAL SCIENCE

Is it, or should it be, the aim of political science to discover general laws of politics, or is it the case that each political event and each political regime is so infinitely rich in unique, irreducible detail that such a search for general laws is bound to be futile, if not actually counterproductive? This kind of question reappears perennially in debates about the proper aims and methods of comparative politics.

What, for example, is the proper relationship between history and area studies, on the one hand, and social science, on the other hand? Since World War II, political science–including the subdiscipline of comparative politics–has become concerned with its status as social science. And this concern with social scientific status is usually associated with the view that political science should search for general laws. The concerns of history and area studies with the assumed uniqueness of each country and each event have thus appeared antithetical to the social scientific enterprise.

To be sure, the polarization is no longer as sharp as it used to be. Area specialists in political science have come increasingly to understand and apply social scientific methods and theories, and scientifically minded political scientists more or less acknowledge the importance of the historians' and area specialists' in-depth knowledge

I would like to thank Stanley Barrett, Robert Robbins, William Safran, and Nicholas Tilley for their helpful criticisms and suggestions for improvement of an earlier version of this paper.

of particular countries and particular events. Virtually everything written in recent years about the relationship between area studies and social science acknowledges that each side has something to contribute to the other. And yet no coherent account has as yet, emerged of just how the generalizing spirit of social science can be systematically integrated with the concern for uniqueness of history and area studies.

Even more importantly, the current state of theory in comparative politics is not very satisfying. On the one hand, quantitative cross-cultural studies may be genuinely comparative, but their contribution to theoretical knowledge and understanding is dubious. On the other hand, there are many singlecountry and multicountry studies that are rich in comparative and theoretical insights but that do not lend themselves very well to systematization and testing.

This chapter seeks to contribute to a solution of the problem of synthesizing an interest in generalization with proper concern for the uniqueness of particular countries and events. It does this by giving an account of what will be called "contextually limited generalizations." The search for general laws, it will be argued, far from being the principal task of social science, is of considerably less interest in the social sciences than it is in the natural sciences. Most of what is called "theory," as well as "middle range generalizations," in the social sciences consists of generalized reconstructions of *types* of social situations or settings or events. These reconstructions may be cast at any level of abstraction, from the historian's richly detailed account of a particular event to the organization theorist's highly abstract model of a complex organization. There is continuity across levels of abstraction. Abstract contextually limited generalizations may be used in constructing hypothetical explanations of particular events or situations, and particular events and situations may be generalized. These contextually limited generalizations may be rough, rudimentary, oversimplified, and overschematized, but, like theories in the natural sciences, they are objective, empirically criticizable, and capable of improvement or competitive comparison with alternative models of the same situation or type of situation.

HAUNTED BY THE NATURAL SCIENCES

The social sciences have grown up in the shadow of a vigorous and successful tradition of natural science founded by Galileo and Newton.[1] They have, since their origins, been "haunted by the natural sciences."[2] Social scientists and philosophers who have reflected upon the social sciences differ greatly on the question of how much (if at all) the social sciences should model themselves after the natural sciences. But what goes unexamined throughout most discussions about the nature of the social sciences is a shared image of the natural sciences–the image of Newtonian mechanics. Even those who have argued that, for one reason or another, the social sciences cannot be genuine sciences have tended to assume that "science" meant Newtonian science.

This has been the image of science implicit in the debates about area studies versus social science. Almost everyone, whether sympathetic or opposed to the integration of social science and area studies, assumes that if investigation of the social world is to be scientific, it will be causal and nomothetic in the sense of Newtonian physics. To be sure, many have argued for the legitimacy of approaches that fall short of the ideal of discovering universal laws. The term "idiographic science," for example, is often applied to area studies which do not attempt to generalize their findings.[3] Arend Lijphart's much-cited discussion of "comparative method" clearly allows for studies that fall short of establishing universal generalizations.[4] Chalmers Johnson and Samuel H. Beer have both elaborated valuable frameworks for generalizing approaches to area studies, which do not aim at universal laws and theories.[5] And yet, all these

[1] Ian C. Jarvie, *The Revolution in Anthropology* (London: Routledge and Kegan Paul, 1964), p. xiii.

[2] Jarvie, "The Notion of a Social Science," in H. K. Betz (ed.), *Recent Approaches to the Social Sciences* (Calgary, Alberta: Faculty of Social Sciences, The University of Calgary, 1979), p. 77.

[3] See, for example Nimrod Raphaeli, (ed.), *Readings in Comparative Public Administration* (Boston: Allyn and Bacon, 1967), pp. 69-198; Frederick J. Fleron, Jr., "Soviet Area Studies and the Social Sciences: Some Methodological Problems in Communist Studies," in Fleron, Jr., *Communist Studies and the Social Sciences* (Chicago: Rand McNally, 1969), pp. 6-7; Fred W. Riggs, "Trends in the Comparative Study of Public Administration," *International Review of Administrative Sciences* 28 (1), pp. 9-15.

[4] Lijphart, "Comparative Politics and the Comparative Method," *American Political Science Review* 65 (3), pp. 682-693.

writers see such approaches as compromises falling short of the ideal of a nomothetic science, or they argue that important features of social science make such an ideal unattainable.

The perspective developed in this chapter has much in common with Johnson's "style analysis"[6] and with Beer's "limited generalizations."[7] I will try to show that the belief in a sharp dichotomy between the methods of the social and natural sciences, as well as the belief that any genuine social science must be modeled after Newtonian physics, are both based on faulty understanding of the contemporary natural sciences.

SCIENTIFIC EXPLANATION THAT APPEALS TO STRUCTURE

Science seeks order in the world of experience. It searches for commonalities, patterns, invariances, recurrent features in the infinite universe of facts. And yet, as I will argue in this section, the order science seeks is not always describable in terms of universal laws. Often, the lawlike behavior of certain things is explained in terms of their underlying structure.[8] Even in the contemporary natural sciences there has been a shift away from the Newtonian program of atomistic reductionism toward an increasing concentration on organization–as Ervin Laszlo puts it,

> Not what a thing is *per se,* nor how one thing produces an effect on another thing, but rather how sets of events are structured and how they function in relation to their environment–other sets of things, likewise structured in space and time.[9]

[5] Johnson, "Political Science and East Asian Area Studies," in Lucian W. Pye (ed.), *Political Science and Area Studies: Rivals or Partners* (Bloomington: Indiana University Press, 1975), pp. 78-97; Beer, "Political Science and History," in Melvin Richter (ed.), *Essays in Theory and History* (Cambridge, MA: Harvard University Press, 1970), pp. 41-73 and 260-263.

[6] Johnson, "Political Science and East Asian Area Studies."

[7] Beer, "Political Science and History."

[8] Karl Popper, *Realism and the Aim of Science* (Totowa, N.J.: Rowman and Littlefield, 1983), p. 138.

[9] Laszlo, *The Systems View of the World: The Natural Philosophy of the New Developments in the Sciences* (Oxford: Basil Blackwell, 1972), p. 20.

In other words, instead of the type of question: "Which universal laws (e.g., gravity) account for the phenomenon that is to be explained?", one finds scientific explanations that appeal to structures. Since these structures belong to the initial conditions, it is initial conditions, properly speaking, rather than the universal laws that actually do the "explaining": for example, in genetics, explanation in terms of DNA structure; or in physics, explanation of why light is refracted in a certain way by a crystal in terms of the crystal's molecular structure; or in evolutionary biology, explanation of the survival of an organism with reference to the environment and the characteristics of the organism that allow it to survive in this environment, the law of natural selection playing a trivial role in the explanation. In all these examples, it is structures (or initial conditions) that are the unknowns, and it is the object of scientific research to discover these structures. And once the structures are found, it is they that account for the order in experience, not the many universal laws scientists take for granted in this kind of explanation, such as laws concerning the behavior of light, laws of chemistry and physics which relate DNA structure to the genetic makeup of organisms, and the law of natural selection in evolutionary biology.

Indeed, in many cases, when a lawlike regularity is found, this turns out to be the beginning rather than the end of the search for explanation, since a new problem arises of explaining *why* the regularity obtains. And many regularities in science can be explained by appealing to underlying structures.

Finally, many areas in the natural sciences are concerned exclusively with generalizations that hold only in sharply delimited contexts. For example, many generalizations that are true of dogs do not hold for other mammals, and many generalizations about mammals do not hold for other vertebrates. Science does not always seek the highest degree of universality but is often quite content with contextually limited generalizations.

Part of the reason for the prejudice that the ultimate aim of a mature science is to discover universal laws is that the context described (or constructed) by Newtonian mechanics is so broad as to encompass all of our everyday experience. But broad as this context may be, it is not, as is widely believed, a *universal* context, and thus even Newton's laws are contextually limited. Newton's prime assumption was that space is everywhere flat and infinite as it is in the world of our immediate experience. As Jacob Bronowski points out, this assumption was criticized even in Newton's time by Leibnitz. And it is not even probable in our own experience. "We are used to living locally in a flat space," Bronowski writes, "but as soon as we look in the large at the earth, we know it not to be so overall."

> The earth is spherical; so that the point at the North Pole can be sighted by two observers on the equator who are far apart, yet each of whom says, 'I am looking due North'. Such a state of affairs is inconceivable to an inhabitant of a flat earth, or one who believes that the earth is flat overall as it seems to be near him. Newton was really behaving like a flat-earther on a cosmic scale: sailing out into space with his foot-rule in one hand and his pocket-watch in the other, mapping space as if it were everywhere as it is here. And that is not necessarily so.
>
> . . . [I]n laying out space as an absolute grid, Newton had given an unreal simplicity to our perception of things.[10]

The main point of this section has not been to dismiss the search for broader generalizations–even for universal laws–as one of the legitimate aims of science. Among the many different aims of science is that of unifying and simplifying what is known by discovering more widely applicable generalizations. But what I have tried to stress is that scientific problems always arise within some limited context and are often solved or explained by generalizations that apply only within this limited context.

EXPLAINING ORDER IN SOCIETY

What accounts for the patterns, regularities, and/or invariants in both individual behavior and society? Obviously, some of the determining factors belong to the individual, some to the social environment in which individuals act. Some regularities in the behavior of individuals result from the physical and social settings in which they find themselves. Some are attributable to regularities in such factors as the aims, resources, and dispositions of the individuals themselves.

[10] Bronowski, *The Ascent of Man* (Boston: Little, Brown, 1973), pp. 240-241.

The structure of the social environment is manmade, notes Karl Popper, in the sense that its institutions and traditions are "the results of human actions and decisions. But this does not mean that they are all consciously designed, and explicable in terms of needs, hopes, or motives." Social institutions are rarely the products of conscious design. Most have "just 'grown' as the undesigned results of human actions."[11] And once social institutions come into existence, they take on a life of their own. They become, to some extent, autonomous and independent of the will (and even awareness) of those who created them, as anyone who has attempted to change a social institution (such as a bureaucracy or a language) knows very well.

The task of the explanatory or theoretical social sciences is, in Popper's view, to discover and explain "the less obvious dependencies in the social sphere." It is to discover "the difficulties which stand in the way of social action–the study, as it were, of the unwieldiness or the brittleness of the social stuff, of its resistance to our attempts to mould it and to work with it."[12] Hopes, fears, ambitions, and aspirations explain little because of the wide gap that always exists between human aspirations and achievements. This is so because "social life is not only a trial of strength between opposing groups: it is action within a more or less resilient or brittle framework of institutions and traditions, and it creates–apart from any conscious counteraction–many unforeseen reactions in this framework."[13]

Much of generalizing social science consists not of a search for general laws, strictly speaking, but rather of reconstructions of typical social situations or settings or conditions at varying levels of generality. The theoretical social sciences, Popper contends, usually ask questions about kinds or types of events or phenomena, and they almost always make use of a method that consists of constructing *types* of situations or conditions, that is to say, the method of constructing models. The central idea underlying situational analysis is thus that we can construct models of typical social and political situations and that this is the only means we possess of understanding social events.[14] By situational analysis Popper means a kind of tenta-

[11] Popper, *The Open Society and Its Enemies Vol. II, The High Tide of Prophesy: Hegel and Marx* (Princeton, NJ: Princeton University Press, 1965), p. 93.

[12] Popper, *The Open Society,* p. 94.

[13] Popper, *The Open Society,* p. 95.

tive explanation of some human action that appeals to the situation in which the agent finds himself.

It may seem strange to some readers that, in arguing against the view that the ultimate aim of a mature science is to discover universal laws, I am drawing upon a philosopher of science who is widely believed to advocate the view that the aim of science is to find explanations in terms of such universal laws.[15] In fact, although Popper assigns an important role to universal laws in scientific explanations, he does not suggest that the discovery of such laws is always, or even usually, the aim of scientific inquiry. Popper writes:

> I suggest that it is the aim of science to find *satisfactory explanations,* of whatever strikes us as being in need of explanation. By an *explanation* (or a causal explanation) is meant a set of statements by which one describes the state of affairs to be explained (the *explicandum)* while the others, the explanatory statements, for the 'explanation' in the narrower sense of the word (the *explicans* of the *explicandum).*[16]

And what kind of an explanation may be satisfactory in Popper's view? "[A]n explanation in terms of testable and falsifiable universal laws and initial conditions."[17]

What many people overlook when they read this kind of statement in Popper is that there is no implication whatever that it is the universal laws that are the unknowns. It may just as well be the initial conditions–i.e., some components of the "situation" that situational analysis attempts to reconstruct–which is unknown, while the universal laws that enter into the explanation are trivial and taken for granted. Explanations in both history and the generalizing social sciences take for granted, for example, the laws of physics, chemistry, and biology, as well as many trivial lawlike generalizations of sociological and psychological character. A historian does not waste

[14] Popper, "La rationalité et le statut du principe de rationalité," in Emil M. Claasen, ed., *Les fondements philosophiques des systèmes économiques* (Paris: Payot, 1967), p. 143.

[15] See, for example, Beer, who represents his "limited generalizations" as a more realistic fallback position resulting from his failure to achieve what he understands to be the Popperian ideal of causal explanation. "Political Science and History," pp. 41-43.

[16] Popper, *Objective Knowledge: An Evolutionary Approach* (Oxford: Oxford University Press, 1972), p. 191.

[17] Popper, *Objective Knowledge,* p. 193.

any time while reconstructing a historical event, such as the assassination enumerating of Julius Caesar, on the laws of physics that account for the blood spurting out of Caesar or the laws of biology that account for the death of a human organism. Neither does the generalizing social scientist bother to articulate all the many laws of nature and trivial sociological and psychological generalizations taken for granted in social science theorizing. In the explanation of types or kinds of events, initial conditions can be completely replaced by the construction of a model that incorporates *typical* initial conditions. In other words, a social phenomenon that is puzzling and in need of explanation is explained by showing it to be a special case of a generalized situation (or typical set of initial conditions).

The logic of the situation is at bottom a very simple and intuitive notion. "We assume," writes Ian Jarvie,

> that people have certain aims, that they also have certain means (restricted by their physical nature and by the social set-up of institutions and traditions), and certain knowledge and beliefs about their means and about the social set-up. Armed with all this, they act to achieve their aims within the social situation created by traditions, institutions, and the aims and actions of other people."[18]

"Situational logic is explanation of human behavior as attempts to achieve goals or aims with limited means."[19]

> A man, for the purposes of social science, can be viewed as in pursuit of certain goals or aims, within a framework of natural, social, psychological and ethical circumstances. These circumstances constitute both the means of achieving his aims and constraints on that achievement. A man's conscious or unconscious appraisal of how he can achieve his aims might be called sorting out the *logic* of the situation he is in. . . .[20]

Situational analysis assumes a physical world in which we act. This world contains, for example, physical resources which are at our disposal and about which we know something (often not very much). Beyond this, however, situational logic must also assume a social world, populated by other people, about whose goals we know

[18] Jarvie, "Explanation in Social Science," *British Journal for the Philosophy of Science*, vol. 15, no. 57 (1964), p. 71.

[19] Jarvie, *Concepts and Society* (London: Routledge & Kegan Paul, 1972), p. 5.

[20] Ibid., p. 4.

something (often not very much) and furthermore, social *institutions.* They exist in an objective sense–that is, independently of any individual's subjective understanding of them.[21] They have properties that are "mapable" and at least partly outside the awareness and control of those who participate in them–even of those who supposedly control them. As Jarvie writes:

> Between hard and soft [reality], constraining us, canalizing all we do–the frame of reference, so to speak–is the social world made up of other people, institutions, groups, friendships, relatives, etc. These are neither hard nor soft, but a bit of both. . . . On the one hand, social entities are, like mental states, intangible; like friendliness and good will they may come out of nothing and fade into nothing. On the other hand, they are like physical states, they react strongly to our probes; when, as an exercise, one *acts* as though a brick wall is not there, one may suffer severe consequences, and the same is true of social institutions from table manners to taxes.[22]

In situational analysis every complex social situation, institution, or event is seen as the result of a particular configuration of individuals, their dispositions, beliefs, and environment.[23] We may be

[21] Karl R. Popper, "The Logic of the Social Sciences," in Theodor W. Adorno et al., *The Positivist Dispute in German Sociology,* trans. by Glyn Adey and David Frisby (London: Heinemann, 1976), p. 103.

[22] Jarvie, *Concepts,* p. 159.

[23] Popper's own discussion of the regulative principle of methodological individualism implicit in situational analysis is fairly rudimentary, although it flows naturally from his philosophy. See especially: Popper, *The Poverty of Historicism,* Second Edition (London: Routledge & Kegan Paul, 1960) pp. 136, 142, 149 and 157; also Popper, *Open Society,* Vol. II, p. 324. The principle has been refined, elaborated, and defended by some of Popper's followers. See especially: J. W. N. Watkins, "Ideal Types and Historical Explanation," *The British Journal for the Philosophy of Science,* vol. 3 (1952), in John O'Neill (ed.), *Modes of Individualism and Collectivism* (London: Heinemann, 1976), pp. 143-165; Watkins, "Historical Explanation in the Social Sciences," *The British Journal for the Philosophy of Science,* vol. 8 (1957), in O'Neill, *Modes,* pp. 166-178; Watkins, "Methodological Individualism: A Reply," *Philosophy of Science,* vol. 22 (1955), in O'Neill, pp. 179-184; Joseph Agassi, "Methodological Individualism," *The British Journal of Sociology,* vol. 2 (1960), in O'Neill, *Modes,* pp. 185-212; John Watkins, "Imperfect Rationality," in Robert Borger and Frank Cioffi (eds.), *Explanation in the Behavioral Sciences* (Cambridge: Cambridge University Press, 1970), pp. 167-217; J. O. Wisdom, "Situational Individualism and the Emergent Group-Properties," in Borger & Cioffi, *Explanation,* pp. 271-296); and Jarvie, *Concepts* (ch. 1). Jarvie also provides, in *Concepts,* a brief historical overview of the methodological individualism debate, pp. 173-178.

unable at any point in our investigation to give complete explanations in terms of individuals, but the ideal of eventually doing so remains a regulative principle of research. That is, we continue to attempt to reduce our explanations to statements about the dispositions, beliefs, resources, and interrelationships of individuals. *The individuals may remain anonymous, and only typical dispositions may be attributed to them.*[24]

To this it may be objected that there exist irreducible social wholes–that is, social and political entities and phenomena whose behavior cannot be explained entirely (if it can be explained at all) in terms of individuals. How, for example, can a "tradition" or "culture" or "spirit of the times" or organizational *esprit de corps* possibly be explained in terms of beliefs, dispositions, resources, and interrelations of individuals. Unlike psychologistic individualism Popper's methodological individualism or "situational individualism"[25] is compatible with several aspects of a holistic view. Social "wholes" exist, which are more than the sum of their parts. These "wholes" include social groups as well as social institutions in the widest sense of the word. They cover a wide variety "from customs to constitutions and from neighborhoods to states."[26] Situational analysis assumes that social "wholes" affect the aims of individuals and that "the social set-up influences and constrains the individual's behavior."[27]

What Popper denies is that social wholes have *distinct* aims and interests *of their own.* An institution (or other social whole) may have aims and interests only *when individuals give it aims* or act in accord with *what they consider should be its interest.* A society or institution cannot have aims and interests of its own.[28] Thus, in Popper's view, traditions exist as do cultures, "group spirits," and other social institutions. They are more than the sum of the individuals they

[24] Watkins, "Historical Explanation," pp. 167-68.

[25] For this critical elaboration of Popper's views, see Wisdom, "Situational Individualism." Although defending situational analysis as a powerful method, Wisdom also discusses emergent properties of social wholes, the explanation of which, he holds, cannot be entirely reduced to situational analysis. For the problem of emergence, see also Nicholas Tilley, "Popper, Historicism, and Emergence," *Philosophy of the Social Sciences* 12 (1), pp. 59-67.

[26] Agassi, p. 188.

[27] Ibid., p. 186.

[28] Ibid., p. 188.

contain. They can exist before the individuals who make them up at any given time belong to them and can survive while maintaining continuity or identity and spirit after all the individuals they contained at any given time have left them.[29] But *it is individuals who carry these traditions, spirits, etc.* If, for example, enough individuals in a society abandon or alter their behavior or attitudes with respect to a tradition (whether intentionally or unintentionally), that tradition will obviously change or die.

What about those aspects of social situations that appear to be psychological and therefore subjective, such as wishes, motives, memories, and associations? In situational analysis such concrete psychological experiences are replaced by abstract and typical (objective) elements of the situation such as ends or knowledge.[30] Thus, for example, the man with certain wishes becomes a man whose situation may be characterized by the fact that he pursues certain *aims,* and a man with certain memories and associations becomes a man whose situation can be characterized by the fact that he is equipped objectively with certain theories or with certain information. We then hypothesize that the persons or agents in our analysis will act in a manner that is adequate or appropriate–that is conforming to the situation.[31] In Popper's words:

[29] See, for example, Popper's "Toward a Rational Theory of Tradition," Chapter 4 in his *Conjectures and Refutations: The Growth of Scientific Knowledge* (New York: Harper & Row, 1965).

[30] For a discussions of the similarities and differences between this method and Collingwood's method of subjective reenactment, see Popper, *Objective Knowledge,* pp. 186-90.

[31] It is this notion of the person or agent acting in a manner that is "adequate or appropriate" (the rationality principle) which "animates" the reconstructions or models of situational analysis. This rationality principle, Popper contends, is nearly empty, since everything has been emptied into the initial conditions. To say that the agent is acting in a manner that is "adequate or appropriate" is to assert almost nothing. Nevertheless, argues Popper, the rationality principle is empirical and false. Some actions cannot be accounted for in terms of the rationality principle no matter how richly the situation has been reconstructed. Nevertheless, he recommends, for methodological reasons, the rationality principle should be the last assumption to be given up, since to give it up means abandoning the attempt to explain the action. Popper, "Logic of the Social Sciences," pp. 102-103; Popper, "La rationalité et le statut," p. 145; Popper, *Objective Knowledge,* pp. 162-63.

> This enables us then to understand actions in an objective sense so that we can say: admittedly I have different aims and I hold different theories (from say Charlemagne); but had I been placed in his situation thus analyzed–where the situation includes goals and knowledge–then I, and presumably you too would have acted in a similar way to him.[32]

The theoretical reconstructions of situational analysis will inevitably be rough, rudimentary, oversimplified, and overschematized. Consequently, they will usually be false. However, they can be good approximations to the truth, and the fact that they are objective hypotheses permits us to learn from their falsity. Like scientific theories, situational analyses are rational, empirically criticizable, and capable of improvement or competitive comparison with alternative models of the same situation.[33]

Popper admits that no creative action (like a decision) can ever be fully explained. Nevertheless, we can try to give an idealized reconstruction of the *problem situation* in which the agent found himself. In this way the action may be made "rationally comprehensible" or "understandable"–that is to say, *adequate to his situation as he saw it.*[34]

PERSPECTIVE AND CONTEXT

It is well known that the social sciences make use of models or constructs, or ideal types, in their efforts to organize and make sense of the social world. What remains unclear, however, is the relationship of these models, types, or constructs to the reality they are presumed to represent. Almost everyone would agree that such constructs are abstractions from reality, which reflect the interests of the social scientists who construct and make use of them.

The role of perspective or point of view is most apparent in the writing of history. It is now widely recognized that there is no universal history that has simply to be uncovered or revealed by the historian and that historical facts do not speak for themselves.

[32] Popper, "Logic of the Social Sciences," p. 103.

[33] Popper, "La rationalité et le statut," pp. 144-145; Popper, "Logic of the Social Sciences," p. 103.

[34] Popper, *Objective Knowledge,* p. 179.

Rather, the historian imposes a perspective that determines not only which facts are relevant but, also, what are to be considered as facts. What is often called "the history of mankind" turns out upon closer examination, to be nothing more than "the history of political power."–one of countless histories of mankind that could conceivably be written.[35] Each generation has its own problems, its own interests, its own background assumptions, which is one reason why history continues to be rewritten. Many conflicts among historical interpretations result from differing points of view. The "facts" (by this I mean the infinite number of uninterpreted facts as they are independently of anyone's selection and interpretation) do not change. But facts are never known independently of some statement of them. And every statement of fact presupposes selection and interpretations in the light of some preexisting point of view or perspective.

Perspective also plays a role in the generalizing natural sciences. In the generalizing natural sciences, however, perspective is provided by the prevailing theory or paradigm. But even in the generalizing natural sciences, the perspective or point of view of a theory is determined, to a significant extent, by prevailing cognitive interests. For example, Newton's laws work very well within the world as we experience it. It is only when the cognitive interests of the physicist extend to objects moving at very high speeds that Einstein's new perspective becomes necessary.

What is the difference between perspective and context? While the two terms may sometimes be used synonymously, I am using the word "context" to refer to the objective setting of the phenomena to be explained–to the initial conditions that actually obtain, rather than to any particular description or reconstruction of them. In other words, by "context" I mean the human agent's objective situation, as opposed to any particular description or reconstruction a social scientist might attempt of that objectively existing situation. Any reconstruction of the context will, of course necessarily, single out only those features of the context or setting relevant to the investigator's theoretical framework and the problem under investigation. For example, a historian may be interested in explaining why Hitler ordered a certain military action that at first glance appears irrational or out of character for Hitler. Normally, the features that

[35] Popper, *The Open Society*, p. 270.

would go into an explanation of Hitler's military decision making would have nothing to do with such elements of his personal situation as what he had had for dinner, what he had done for entertainment, etc., even though such elements clearly belong to his total life situation. Yet it may be that this particular military decision can be attributed to indigestion or to a nightmare Hitler had had the night before. It is the historian's stock in trade to provide as rich a reconstruction of the actor's situation or context or setting as is necessary to make his action rationally comprehensible–that is, adequate to the situation as he saw it.

When the historian becomes the social scientist his interest shifts from explanation specific events to generalized explanation. His interest may turn, for example, to Hitler's military decision making style. He abstracts from each particular instance of Hitler's military decision making those contextual features common to all these instances. In making such an abstraction, the social scientist inevitably loses much of the richness of the historian's reconstructions. As a result, his generalized reconstruction of Hitler's military decision making may fail to explain some particular decision, since it will not include the bout of indigestion or the nightmare that was crucial for the explanation of that particular decision.

Such reconstruction of Hitler's military decision making style seeks to model reality as it actually is. But it selects out for description only those aspects of reality deemed relevant to the explanation of a certain type of problem. The fact that it oversimplifies the situation and thus may not provide a "complete" explanation of any particular instance of Hitler's military decisionmaking poses no impediments to the ideal of generalizing social science. It merely reflects what is widely accepted at the level of common sense, namely, that society and human behavior exhibit enough orderlikeness to make social science possible and useful but that they contain enough haphazardness and variation that even a mature social science will have to integrate its organizing theories with this variation and haphazardness.

A generalized reconstruction of Hitler's military decision making would, of course, be useful to the historian interested in explaining any particular instance of it. The historian would simply enrich his reconstruction of Hitler's behavior in that specific instance to explain whatever problem is imposed by his own perspective. On the other hand, another social scientist might be interested more broadly in military decision making by contemporary European heads of state with dictatorial control of their respective regimes. Such situational reconstructions would lose much of the richness that could be provided in reconstruction of Hitler's own peculiar military decision making situation. All the detail about Hitler's personality, knowledge, and theories would be lost. Some similarities relating to typical personality features (if there are any) of contemporary European dictators might remain. The details of German political culture, German military organization, and other features peculiar to Germany under Hitler would be lost. Nevertheless, the similarities of the military decision making situations of European dictators may share enough features to make such a generalized situational reconstruction theoretically interesting. Again, the model or reconstruction would refer to facts in the real world. In other words, it would refer to facts (concrete features of the decision making situations of concrete individuals) that bear upon their behavior. But because of the level of abstraction of the model, it will naturally not account for all the variance in any given instance.

SITUATIONAL ANALYSIS AND THE UNITY AND CONTINUITY OF AREA STUDIES AND SOCIAL SCIENCE

In genetic and historical explanations, the focus of explanatory interest is almost always upon initial conditions; the laws or generalizations are usually trivial and are taken for granted. If, for example, the question to be answered is something like, "What caused the cold war?" or "Why does Germany have an authoritarian political culture?" or "Why does a two-party system prevail in the United States?" or "Why did the Soviet Union invade Czechoslovakia in 1968?", the explanation will take the form of a narrative account. Such an account will consist of some combination of statements of fact plus statements of generalizations from which the previously puzzling (i.e. explained) phenomenon can be validly deduced. Such a genetic or historical account may make use of nontrivial generalizations discovered by social scientists, but need not necessarily do so. For example, generalizations taken from theoretical literatures related to the nature and causes of hostility among states may be brought to bear upon the problem of explaining the cold war. Generalizations and theories derived from the study of political culture may be brought to bear upon explanation of authoritarianism in German political culture. And generalizations derived from the study of party systems may be used to explain the two-party system in the United States. But, for the most part, histórical and genetic explanations take for granted all kinds of lawlike generalizations, many of them being trivial and unstated, and focus on the problem of producing an adequate reconstruction of initial conditions.

Social science theory, as has been shown, reflects an interest in typical settings or initial conditions. Organization theory, role theory, small-group theory, and game theory are only a few examples of such typical initial conditions that are used as explanations in social science. When, for example, small-group theory is used to explain a specific instance of the behavior of a particular small group, the "explanation" amounts to an assertion that the initial conditions in this instance represent an occurrence of typical initial conditions in small-group theory. Such theories, like maps, attempt to model the social world faithfully. And yet, just as different kinds of maps reflect the differing perspectives and purposes of those who make and use them (e.g. road maps, topographical maps, population maps), so do different bodies of social science theory model the social world from different perspectives and for different purposes.

It is important to note that such models of typical initial conditions may be constructed at any level of generality. For example, the setting of one particular small group, such as one congressional committee or the U.S. Supreme Court, may be reconstructed and such a model used to explain specific instances of the group's behavior. This is, as a matter of fact, just what some scholars who study congressional committees and the Supreme Court do. They seek to model (at least roughly) the institutional setting they study, so that specific instances of the institution's behavior can be understood and explained by reference to this model. Such generalized settings resemble genetic or historical explanations in that it is mainly initial conditions that do the explaining. But, as in the case of genetic explanations, explanations in terms of generalized social situations include lawlike statements–trivial as well as non-trivial.

Chapter 11

COMMUNISM AND POLITICAL CULTURE THEORY

Gabriel Almond

A TEST OF POLITICAL CULTURE THEORY

The success or failure of communist regimes in transforming the attitudes and behavior of populations, may constitute a test of the explanatory power of political culture theory.[1] We may view communist regimes as "natural experiments" in attitude change. Such regimes seek and usually succeed in establishing organization and communication media monopolies, as well as penetrative police and internal intelligence systems. Ideological conformity is rewarded; deviation is heavily penalized. Communities and neighborhoods come under the surveillance of party activists. Children of all ages are organized in party-related formations, and school instruction places emphasis on appropriate ideological indoctrination. In addition to this powerful array of institutional and communication controls, the communist movement has a clear-cut, explicit set of attitudes, beliefs, values and feelings which it seeks to inculcate.

Political culture theory imputes some importance to political attitudes, beliefs, values, and emotions in the explanation of political, structural, and behavioral phenomena, national cohesion, patterns of political cleavage, modes of dealing with political conflict, the extent and character of participation in politics, and compliance with authority. Political culture theory has never seriously been advanced as the unidirectional "cause" of political structure and behavior

[1] This is a position argued by a number of British specialists on Communist countries. See Archie Brown and Jack Gray, *Political Culture and Political Change in Communist States,* (N.Y.: Holmes & Meier, 1977); also, Stephen White, *Political Culture And Soviet Politics,* (London, MacMillian, 1979). We have benefitted greatly from these studies, and conclusions.

although it has been represented as taking such a position by some of its critics.[2] The relaxed version of political culture theory–the one presented by most of its advocates–is that the relation between political structure and culture is interactive, that one cannot explain cultural propensities without reference to historical experience and contemporary structural constraints and opportunities, and that, in turn, a prior set of attitudinal patterns will tend to persist in some form and degree and for a significant period of time, despite efforts to transform it. All of these qualifications and claims are parts of political culture theory. The argument would be that however powerful the effort, however repressive the structure, however monopolistic and persuasive the media, however tempting the incentive system, political culture would impose significant constraints on effective behavioral and structural change, because underlying attitudes would tend to persist to a significant degree and for a significant period of time. This is all that we need to demonstrate in order to make a place for political culture theory in the pantheon of explantory variables of politics.

The Communist experience is particularly important as an approach to testing political culture theory since from one point of view it represents a genuine effort to "falsify" it. The attitudes that communist movements encounter in countries where they take power are viewed as false consciousness–whether they be nationalism, religious beliefs, liberal-pluralistic views, ethnic subcultural propensities, or attitudes toward economic interests. These attitudes are viewed as the consequences of pre-existing class structure and the underlying mode of production, as transmitted by associated agents of indoctrination. communist movements either eliminate or seek to undermine the legitimacy of these pre-existing structures and processes and replace them with a quite new and thoroughly penetrative set. If they succeed in some reasonable length of time–let us say a generation–in transforming attitudes in the desired direction, we might conclude that political culture theory has been falsified, that it is a weak variable at best.

[2] See inter al. Brian M. Barry, *Sociologists, Economists, And Democracy,* (London: Collier-MacMillan, 1970); pp. 48ff.; Carole Pateman, "The Civic Culture: A Philosophical Critique" in Almond and Verba (eds.) *The Civic Culture Revisited,* (Boston, Mass.: Little Brown, 1980); and Ronald Rogowski, *A Rational Theory of Legitimacy,* (Princeton, N.J: Princeton University Press, 1976).

Surely Communist take-overs are the best historical experiments we have for these purposes. In addition there are quite a few of them; they have occurred in different cultural–developmental settings; and most of them have been in operation for a generation. The principle problem with this approach to testing theory is that it leaves much to be desired as an experimental test. The "laboratories" are not open to investigators; the data are spotty, and in large part inferential. And finally the scale and intensity of the effort at attitude change varies from one country to the next. The experience of Poland, Hungary, and Czechoslovakia are quite different from the USSR, Cuba, and Yugoslavia.

One further intriguing point about this topic is that it represents a good illustration of a pay-off for theory, derived from area case studies. From this point of view the reader should not expect a contribution to area depth, but rather an exploitation of area findings in efforts to develop theory.

POLITICAL CULTURE THEORY IN MARXISM AND LENINISM

This utilization of Communist experience in an effort to test political culture theory fits quite congenially into the great themes of marxist and leninist ideology. The term itself has come into increasing usage in Soviet and Eastern European social science. Stephen White notes that Lenin employed the term, and that Brezhnev used it more recently.[3] The President of the Soviet Political Science Association, Georgi Shakhnazarov, in an article published in *Pravda* in January 17, 1979, announcing the meeting of the International Political Science Association in Moscow, listed political culture as one of the three major subjects of political science. He defines political culture as follows: "The participation of diverse social opinions in politics, the political culture of the people and political culture training, the regulation of social-political attitudes." He presents this topic as being at the same level of

[3] Archie Brown and Jack Gray, *Political Culture and Political Change in Communist States*, (N.Y.: Holmes and Meier, 1977), p. 58. See also White's book-length treatment of this subject, op. cit.

importance as the study of the state and the political system, and the study of foreign policy and international relations.

Quite aside from this terminological receptivity, political culture phenomena have an important place in Communist theory, though the terms employed by Marx, Lenin, and contemporary Communist scholars are ideology, consciousness, spontaneity, economism, and the like. In the works of Marx and Engels political culture phenomena are important intervening variables; in Lenin political culture and in particular elite political culture, are independent variables. Indeed, an elite with a particular political culture, in the sense of an indoctrinated Communist party, and an "objective revolutionary situation" very broadly defined, are the necessary and sufficient conditions of communist revolution. No one can read Lenin's organizational text *What Is to Be Done?* without becoming aware of how much importance he attached to the proper indoctrination of the Communist party, the unambiguous explication of beliefs, procedures, and appropriate affective modalities.

For Marx changing political consciousness was a consequence of underlying structural alterations–it developed first gradually, changing its cognitive content and affective tone as the means of production and class characteristics and relations changed. At certain points in the historical process the cultural transformation would be more rapid as at the point of extreme proletarian "immisertion." In marxism the concept of political socialization and elite political culture are not well developed though they are present. Capitalist ideology gradually loses its force as its deviation from reality becomes increasingly plain. Men are rational actors, the leaders "catch on" first, the followers soon after. The transformation of political culture occurs in bursts and is congruent with major structural changes–the dictatorship of the proletariat, the introduction of socialism and of communism. The learning process may be slow, but it is sure.

Marxism, thus, is clearly a structural theory. Marx would probably have sided with Brian Barry, Carole Pateman, and Ronald Rogowski on the priority of structure in the causal interaction with attitude, belief, and feeling. Changes in culture follow inevitably from changes in structure; cultural properties have a consequential relation to structure. Attitudinal variables explain *lead* and *lag* in the processes of historical change, and hence may be viewed as intervening rather than independent variables.

The leninist strategy of elite and mass political socialization makes it clear that he understood the interactive character of structure-cultural relationships. He believed in the possibility of indoctrinating a revolutionary elite, in other words transforming its political culture. At the same time he did not believe in the possibility of the revolutionary indoctrination of the masses. The ordinary workers and peasants had to be manipulated into revolution by appealing to their immediate values and interests, in other words by adapting revolutionary tactics to their cultures. Once a revolution had been attained Lenin expected these subcultural tendencies among the workers, peasants, ethnic, and religious groups to persist for some unknown length of time until the communist millennium would be brought about by these fundamental structural changes.

In marxism-leninism as currently explicated in the theoretical and "social science" literature in socialist countries, the full conceptual framework of political culture theory is employed. It is easy to see why the term has been so quickly adopted among socialist social scientists. While the term "sub-culture" has not itself been employed until recently it is assumed that each class under capitalism has its own sub-culture and thereby imposes a constraint on communist strategy and tactics. The peasantry is mobilizable for land reform but not for socialism. Even under socialism residual peasant proprietary attitudes persist and impose limits on policy. The working class is inclined toward "bread and butter" economistic and not socialistic goals; and these attitudes persist under socialism as residual attitudes affecting productivity and public policy. An incentive system inconsistent with the egalitarian values of communism must be continued in order to take these propensities into account. Professionals and technical specialists are seduced by the values and special interests of their professions; and these cultural propensities persist under socialism and explain the constant struggles between the party and the various specialists in the bureaucracy and the society.

Ethnicity as an ineradicable basis of sub-culture manifests itself, according to marxist-leninist doctrine, in secessionist and autonomist tendencies. Under capitalism ethnicity may be mobilized in the form of liberation movements affiliated with or led by indoctrinated communists. Under socialism ethnicity persists, justifying federal governmental arrangements. Ethnic subcultures in the form of linguistic, literary, and cultural identities (cuisine, costume, festivals, and the like) are acknowledged as legitmate and reconciliable with socialist universalism. Religious subcultures are viewed as basically reactionary formations fostering vestigial attitude patterns. Accomodations to religious communities under socialism in contrast to ethnicity, are expediential and entered into only on tactical political grounds.

The theme of political culture change is a powerful one in leninist theory. Certain attitudinal changes are assumed to occur in the transition from feudal forms of political economy to capitalist forms; and from early capitalist forms to later ones. And once a communist revolution takes place certain attitude changes are supposed to accompany the shift from the period of the proletarian dictatorship to the period of socialism. And there is a set of related structural and cultural changes which are assumed to be associated with the shift from socialism to communism.

Marxist-leninist theory has well articulated views on political socialization agents and processes. All the agents of socialization treated in the western socialization literature, are to be found in the socialist literature. Family, church, school, work place, interest group, political party, the media of communication, local government, government output and performance, are all recognized as having some impact on political attitudes and culture. The principle distinction made in leninist theory is between those socialization agents that foster traditional patterns of political culture, and those socialization agents which foster rational and appropriate ones. Families, religious bodies, ethnic communities, professional groups, and face to face communication media outside the Communist party and related organizations, tend to foster residual cultural tendencies; while schools, the Communist party and related organizations, and the mass media of communication are the principle agents of appropriate political socialization.

POLITICAL CULTURE IN COMMUNIST REALITY

If we turn from ideological formulations to the political reality of Eastern Europe, the picture we get of political attitudes and values is a complex and varied one. We may perhaps distinguish three versions of political culture in Communist countries; (1) the official or ideological political culture which is a mix of exhortation and imputation, (2) the operational political culture or what the regime is prepared to tolerate, and believes it has succeeded in attaining, and (3) the real political culture based on evidence such as opinion surveys and other kinds of research, or on inferences drawn from the media or official statements. The distinction between these three versions of political culture needs to be elaborated a bit. All communist regimes have some version of the leninist ideological culture, though in those countries which made their own revolutions (e.g., Yugoslavia, China, and Cuba) these ideal models may deviate from the Soviet Union. The operational political culture is the version of values, attitudes, and feelings which the regime is prepared to tolerate at least in the short run, given the universal shortfall from the ideological model in all Communist countries. This operational model may vary from the extreme of Hungary where Kadar's slogan of the 1960's "He who is not against us is with us," represents a substantial admission of defeat in efforts at positive culture transformation, to the situation in the Soviet Union where the operational expectations are a good deal more positive, and are in part supported by reality.

The difference between what is sometimes called the operational political culture and the real political culture, is defined in a sense by the battleground between the regime's immediate campaigns and efforts at attitudinal and behavioral change, and the beliefs and affective tone in the population and its various parts. From this point of view we can argue that Kadar's slogan (he who is not against us is with us), would be an acknowledgement that the Communist party of Hungary had failed to falsify political culture theory, or similarly that the "Czechoslovak Spring" is dramatic evidence of a similar sort that a score of years of organizational and media monopoly, repression and terror, and powerful incentives had failed to alter in any significant degree the civic propensities among the Czechoslovak population. Insofar as the operational political culture itself acknowledges the resistance it is encountering, and in the degree that it has lowered its sights from some reasonable approximation of a marxist-leninist culture, we may similarly argue that political culture theory survives unfalsified. If in addition there is evidence of a direct sort on attitudes and beliefs among the population suggesting that they fall significantly short of this operational official political culture, then we have even stronger confirmation of the validity of political culture theory.

The ideological political culture in every communist country posits an ideal communist who is both the builder of the new society and a product of its institutions and practices. The fullest elaboration of the qualities of this ideal Communist is to be found in the Programm of the Communist Party of the Soviet Union (CPSU), adopted by the 22nd Congress in 1961, in a section entitled "The Moral Code of the Builder of Communism." Some version of this moral code, or something very similar in the values and qualities stressed, is to be found in a central place in the most important ideological formulations, training manuals, school books, and the like, of all the communist countries.

The qualities stressed include "dedication to the Communist cause, love for the socialist motherland and other socialist countries; conscientious labor for the good of society; a high consciousness of social duty; collectivism and comradely mutual assistance and respect; moral integrity in public and private life; intolerance of injustice, dishonesty or careerism; friendship and brotherhood with the other countries; and firm opposition to the enemies of communism, peace and freedom."[4]

The evidence does not suggest that any of the communist regimes have succeeded in inculcating these values among significant parts of their populations. Even in the Soviet Union where the regime has been in substantial control of the population for two full generations, and where the revolution has been led by an indigenous elite, the extent of success in remodeling man has been relatively modest. Samuel Huntington's claim that the Soviet Union is a dramatically successful case of planned political culture change would seem to be exaggerated.[5] This is not to argue that there have been

[4] Stephen White in Archie Brown and Jack Gray, op. cit., pp. 35-36.
[5] See Stephen White, op. cit., pp. 114ff.

no positive accomplishments in culture change. The Soviet regime has widespread legitimacy; its centralized, penetrative, and relatively unlimited institutions are accepted. A diffuse notion of socialism has widespread validity, and acceptance of the obligation of sociopolitical activism in the sense of participating in campaigns has strong and widespread support. But these limited successes in the very center of the Communist world hardly extend into the countryside, into the blue-collar, relatively uneducated working class, or into the non-European parts of the USSR. Particularly in the Asiatic parts of the USSR traditional religious attitudes and ethnic nationalism display considerable staying power, where it might be argued that the Soviet indoctrinators have had to come to terms with stubborn traditionalism of various kinds.[6] Much of the legitimacy of the Soviet regime, one writer argues, results from the fact that the structure of the Soviet system is very much like the preexisting tsarist one in the sense of centralization, the extensive scope of government, and its arbitrariness. The acceptance of socialism as well as the obligation of sociopolitical activism is the success story of communist political socialization, but these attitudes tend to be concentrated in the European center and among the educated, professional, and white-collar strata of the population.[7] Political activism in this context is not to be confused with civic and political participation, but rather takes the form of mobilized activity and voluntary public service. One writer describes Soviet participation in the following terms:

> The many political and administrative activities in which Soviet citizens participate take place within a dual framework of control. The hierarchical structure of the Soviets, and of the Soviet political system in general, serves to coordinate the agenda and priorities of the participatory organs at any given moment, concentrating them on centrally determined goals, while the supervision of Communist party organs provides control of staffing, leadership selection, and auditing of the quality of activities.[8]

[6] Ibid., p. 95; See also Gregory J. Massell, *The Surrogate Proletariat: Moslem Women and Revolutionary Strategies in Soviet Central Asia; 1919-1929*, (Princeton, N.J.: Princeton University Press, 1974), pp. 322ff.

[7] Stephen White, *Political Culture and Soviet Politics*, op. cit., chaps. 3 and 4. For a detailed analysis of participation in the Soviet Union, see Theodore H. Friedgut, *Political Participation in the USSR* (Princeton, N.J.: Princeton University Press, 1979), chap. 1 and pp. 307ff.

[8] Ibid., p. 49. The Soviet regime has succeeded in inculcating a sense of "participatory-subject competence" particularly among the educated strata of the

This contrast between the ideological and the operational political culture creates a certain tension among communist ideologists, students of public opinion, and the media of communication. With the introduction of public opinion research in the Soviet Union and Eastern Europe in the 1960s the problem of opinion and attitude differences had to be confronted and produced a polemic of modest proportions among "monists" and "pluralists." A. K. Uledov, Soviet interpreter of public opinion presenting a monist point of view, argued that deviations in opinion from the ideological model simply reflect lag between the old and the new, between progressive and backward forces. A pluralist point of view reflected in the writing of Grushin, but to a much greater extent in the work of Polish, Czechoslovak, and Yugoslavian scholars, argues that under socialism nonconforming opinion may contribute to social progress. Thus the pluralists seek to legitimate oppositional and critical tendencies, thereby reducing the tensions among the ideological, the operational, and the real political culture, tending to reduce the ideological model to that of a credo, and adopting an operative normative model more reconcilable with reality. This treatment of pluralism as legitimate, however, is distinctly a minor theme in the more conservative communist regimes and surfaces primarily in such countries as Poland, Czechoslovakia, and Yugoslavia.[9]

In testing political culture theory in Communist countries it is useful to sort the nations into three categories: (1) the Soviet Union itself where the Communist "experiment" began and was carried through by an indigenous Communist elite; (2) other countries like Yugoslavia, China, Cuba; and Vietnam that imported the communist revolution but where it was carried out by an indigenous elite; and (3) countries like Poland, Hungary, Czechoslovakia, Rumania, and East Germany where communist regimes were imposed from the outside. For our purposes in this paper we will briefly examine the experience of (1) the Soviet Union (as above); (2) Yugoslavia and Cuba, and (3) Poland, Hungary, and Czechoslovakia. If political culture theory is to be falsified we would

society. See G. A. Almond and S. Verba, *The Civic Culture,* (Princeton, N.J.: Princeton University Press, 1963), and cited and discussed in Friedgut, op. cit., pp. 319ff.

[9] Walter D. Connor and Zvi Gitelman, *Public Opinion in European Socialist Systems,* (New York: Praeger, 1977), ch. 1.

expect to see major change in political culture in the desired direction in all three categories, but to a large degree in the case of the Soviet Union because its revolution was indigenous and it has been in operation more than sixty years; to a substantial degree in Yugoslavia and Cuba because their revolutions were made by indigenous elites; and to a lesser degree in Poland, Hungary, and Czechoslovakia because their communist regimes have been in existence for only a single generation and were imposed on them from the outside and maintained by the threat or actuality of Soviet military occupation.

POLITICAL CULTURE IN YUGOSLAVIA AND CUBA

In the case of Yugoslavia it may be inappropriate to speak of three versions of political culture. The leninist ideological version is not seriously propagated. The operational version is a relatively loosely formulated set of norms and expectations that on the basis of empirical evidence is not too far from the reality of opinion and attitude. These norms include an acceptance of ethnic identity and of political autonomy of the various ethnic components, an acceptance of private land ownership among the peasantry, and acceptance of religious freedom. The two new elements in Yugoslavian political culture are political activism and participation, and enterprise self-management, which ideologically is supposed to represent the fulfillment of the ideal of participation and the essence of Yugoslavian democratic socialism. Here one can distinguish a difference between the official political culture and the real political culture. The official political culture implies "classlessness" in participatory patterns; but much evidence that has been gathered from studies of political recruitment and opinion surveys demonstrates that political participation in the sense of officeholding and other forms of activism is biased toward the upper social and economic groupings in the population and is dominated by members of the League of Communists. Enterprise self-management appears to be effective and involves all levels of workers in matters having to do with wages, hours, conditions of labor, and similar trade union issues, but not in production and other management decisions.[10]

[10] David Dyker, in Brown and Gray, op. cit., ch. 3; Jan Triska and Paul M. Cocks,

Thus in the case of Yugoslavia the political leadership has settled for a set of operational political cultural norms that accommodates the prerevolutionary ethnic, religious, and economic propensities and the socialization agencies that tend to perpetuate them. The novel elements of participation and decentralized socialism have been accepted in a limited way and particularly among the educated, advantaged, and politically mobilized strata of the population.

In contrast with Yugoslavia, another country that made its own revolution–Cuba–has been subjected to concentrated indoctrination of a new "Cuban Socialist Man" sort. This ideological political culture differs from the leninist one in the absence of emphasis on the "party" and the greater emphasis on heroism, selflessness, *personalismo,* and the propaganda of the deed. It appears to draw upon a Latin American revolutionary tradition as much as on the specifically leninist ideological norms. In the two decades of Cuban communism these ideals have been propagated in connection with major campaigns of mobilization for purposes of defense, literacy, sugar cane harvesting, and revolutionary-military activities abroad. Such evidence as we have from reports and surveys of one kind or another suggests that these campaigns have had moderate success in creating regime legitimacy, the acceptance of the norm of activism in the implementation of goals, and the acceptance of socialism in the diffuse sense of that term. But in recent years there is evidence of growing bureaucratization, less stress on utopian ideals and mass mobilization, and more stress on efficiency and regimentation. A pattern similar to that in the Soviet Union may emerge in which the utopian socialist man culture takes on the proportions of an eschatology and the operational political culture stresses compliance with the regime's policies and programs. Real popular values and attitudes may increasingly take the form of adaptations to constraints and incentives as well as the according of legitimacy to the new institutions.[11]

(eds.), *Political Development in Eastern Europe,* (New York Praeger, 1977), pp. 158ff.

[11] See Richard R. Fagen, *The Transformation of Political Culture in Cuba,* (Stanford, Calif.: Stanford University Press, 1969); Jorge I. Dominguez, *Cuba: Order and Revolution,* (Cambridge, Mass.: The Belknap Press of The Harvard University Press, 1978), Ch. 12; and Francis Lambert, "Cuba: Communist State in Personal Dictatorship" in Brown and Gray, op. cit., ch. 8.

Thus our three cases of indigenous communist revolutions–the Soviet Union, Yugoslavia, and Cuba–fail to falsify political culture theory. The revolutionary aims of creating a "socialist man" have been largely given up in the Soviet Union and Cuba and were never seriously pursued in Yugoslavia. The Soviet Union has settled for popular legitimacy, a general belief in socialism, and a willingness to participate in regime-initiated campaigns. The Yugoslavian political elite has tended to accommodate itself to powerful ethnic commitments, peasant proprietary values, and religious beliefs and has successfully inculcated a sense of legitimacy, an acceptance of decentralized socialism, and an obligation to participate.

In the case of Cuba a personalistic version of leninism seems to be giving way to a more bureaucratic, apathetic relationship between elite and mass, with the positive political culture changes taking the form of regime legitimacy, belief in "socialism", and acceptance in some sense of the obligation to take part in campaigns.

The changes that have taken place under these relatively favorable circumstances are of a limited sort and not of the magnitude and character as to falsify political culture theory and accord validity to a structural one.

THE CASES OF POLAND, HUNGARY, AND CZECHOSLOVAKIA

The Communist experiences in Poland, Hungary, and Czechoslovakia are even stronger supports for political culture theory. Communist parties have been in control in all three countries for over thirty years, and Soviet troop deployments and the Brezhnev Doctrine impose constraints on their policies. Despite these penetrative pressures and external threats and constraints, pre-revolutionary nationalist, religious, economic, and political attitudes have persisted and have resulted in the renunciation of sanguine expectations of fundamental attitude change. Were the Soviet threat neutralized, there is little doubt that liberal regimes would be established, even initiated by the Communist parties themselves, as was the case in Czechoslovakia in 1967-1968. Communist efforts at resocialization may actually have been counterproductive in the sense of having created strong liberal propensities in countries such as Poland and Hungary where these traditions were relatively weak in the prerevolutionary era.

In Poland after thirty years of revolutionary experience something like a legitimate pluralist regime emerged in 1981 with the Solidarity Union, the Catholic church, and the army emerging and engaging in bargaining relations with the Communist party. As of this writing it is unclear what stable arrangements will survive the martial law regime. On the positive side there is evidence of an acceptance of a diffuse egalitarian socialism among a large proportion of the Polish population. But the evidence is overwhelming that the Polish working class continues to be passionately Polish, Catholic, and bread and butter oriented.[12]

In Hungary peasant proprietary attitudes continue strong, as reflected in surveys showing that the private garden plot and household improvements are the focus of most of the agricultural population. Similarly, religious attitudes continue strong even among young people. Hungarian nationalism shows no signs of abating. One writer describes the legitimacy of the communist regime in Hungary in the following terms: "The current standoff in Hungary between elites and potential publics is tenuous, but it appears as if everyone fears the hazards of questioning the situation too closely."[13] Although most Hungarians accept an egalitarian socialism, there is little acceptance of marxism-leninism among the population. In Hungary the reaction to ideological indoctrination takes the form of a thorough-going depoliticization.[14]

Of all the Communist cases, that of Czechoslovakia accords strongest support to political culture theory. As one writer observes of the period after 1948:

> Neither the new economic base nor the new institutional structures succeeded in changing the political cultures of Czechs and Slovaks in the direction which the holders of institutional power desired. If anything, the opposite happened. The old values and beliefs were reinforced. . . . If a Czech new man had been created by 1968, he was, ironically, one more firmly devoted to social democratic and

[12] See Connor and Gitelman, op. cit., ch. 2 and pp. 184ff; Brown and Gray, op. cit., ch. 4; and Triska and Cocks, op. cit., ch. 5.

[13] Zvi Gitelman in Connor and Gitelman, op. cit., p. 161.

[14] See also Brown and Gray, op. cit., ch. 5; and Triska and Cocks, op. cit.

libertarian values than the Czech of 1946. In the interactions between structures and cultures it would appear that the dominant Czech political culture came much closer to changing Czechoslovak communism than Czechoslovak communism came to procuring acceptance of its official political culture.[15]

CONCLUSIONS

What the scholarship of comparative communism has been telling us is that political cultures are not easily transformed. A sophisticated political movement ready to manipulate, penetrate, organize, indoctrinate and coerce and given an opportunity to do so for a generation or longer ends up as much or more transformed than transforming. But we have to be clear about what kind of a case we are making for political culture theory. We are not arguing at all that political structure, historical experience, and deliberate efforts at attitude change can have no effects such as those Alex Inkeles and David Smith and Herbert Hyman demonstrate with the powerful and homogenizing effects of education, the introduction of the mass media, and factory employment in very different cultural contexts.[16] There is a major literature of experimental studies on some of the conditions and possibilities of attitude change. What all this seems to demonstrate is that man is a complex animal, tractable in some respects and intractable in others. Both the successes and the failures of our Communist cases suggest that there is a pattern to this tractability-intractability, that liberty once experienced is not quickly forgotten, and that equity and equality of some kind resonate positively with the human spirit.

[15] Archie Brown and Gordon Wightman, "Czechoslovakia: Revival and Retreat," in Brown and Gray, op. cit., p. 189; see also Connor and Gitelman, op. cit., p. 178.

[16] Alex Inkeles and David H. Smith, *Becoming Modern: Individual Change in Six Developing Countries*, (Cambridge, Mass.: Harvard University Press, 1974); and Herbert Hyman, *The Enduring Effects of Education*, (Chicago: University of Chicago Press, 1975).

Chapter 12

POLITICAL CULTURE IN THE GERMAN CONTEXT: SOME REFLECTIONS ON THE SHORTCOMINGS OF STUDIES IN POLITICAL CULTURE

Kurt Sontheimer

KULTUR AND POLITICAL CULTURE

Within the last ten years the concept of *political culture* has found its way into current political terminology in the Federal Republic of Germany. The term had not been used before in political language, although Germans have always been prone to make ample use of the word *Kultur,* which, however, was largely restricted to mean the sphere of intellectual, spiritual, and artistic life. It betrays, to my mind, a substantial change of that *Kultur* itself that it became possible to combine the traditional understanding of *Kultur* with politics as is the case in the new concept of *politische Kultur.*

Traditionally, the realm of *Kultur* had been interpreted in Germany as an almost irreconcilable opposite to the field of politics. It had been the pride of the representatives of German *Kultur* in the late nineteenth century that it kept aloof from the more ugly sphere of politics, which was associated with power, interests, and other uninspiring aspects of ordinary life. Thomas Mann's "Reflections of a Non-political Man" (1918) is the best-known literary document of this tradition. From that point of view, the term *politische Kultur* can, of course, only be seen as a misleading concept, mingling two aspects of social life that should be kept apart.

The fact that the term political culture has now–in the Federal Republic of Germany–found general acceptance in social science as well as in normal political argument indicates two significant trends within German political culture: (1) that the concept of culture has lost its exclusive "spiritual" meaning, and (2) that politics is no longer considered to be outside of culture.

It follows from this that the concept of political culture, as it is used nowadays in West Germany, is not as clear and unequivocal as social scientists would like it to be, but there is at least general agreement about the underlying assumption that political culture is extremely important in assessing the political quality and stability of a democratic political system and that for this reason it deserves constant observation and cultivation.

The term political culture has surprisingly found its way into our political language through the intermediary of political science. Had not U.S. political science invented the new concept and made it a new and promising field of social research, and had German political scientists not taken up the new approach, it would certainly not be in political use. In German political science the fields of interest that are now being covered under the label of "studies in political culture" formerly had been treated under headings like "political style" or "political traditions" or simply "empirical research on beliefs and attitudes with regard to politics," but the new term has undoubtedly given this field of investigation and research a much higher ranking and significance because it is generally assumed that findings about the political culture of a nation are crucial for the assessment of its stability and of greater importance than traditional knowledge about the life of political institutions. I would rather question this, looking at what has been found out in scientific research on Germany's political culture in the last decade, but there is no doubt that the invention of the new term has helped to raise general interest in the new field.[1]

There is, however, a markedly different reading of the new term when it is used by politicians and journalists than when it is used by empirical political scientists. A typical statement by a German politician runs as follows: "We must pay attention to the state of our political culture and–like other democracies–do everything to cultivate and develop it" (Minister of State Hildegard Hamm-Bruecher in *Rheinischer Merkur,* 25 September 1981). Politicians use the new term, as a rule, in a twofold way: They talk about political culture as

[1] For a critical appraisal of work in the new field see: Max Kaase, "Sinn oder Unsinn des Konzepts politische Kultur, in Kaase/Klingemann, *Wahlen und politische Kultur* (Opladen: Westdeutscher Verlag, 1982).

an ensemble of *empirical* factors, which they then *evaluate* within their individual normative framework. To them political culture is never only what it is or seems to be; it is at the same time something that should be influenced, corrected, and changed so that it exerts a positive effect on the democratic quality and stability of the political system as a whole.

This is quite normal for a democratic politician, for, if political culture is of great importance to the viability of a democratic system, then it is indeed the duty of politicians–and even of every citizen–to do their best for the positive development of a political culture that does not seem to be in full accordance with the normative requirements of a democracy. Almond and Verba's distinction between political culture in general and the *civic culture* rests likewise on the assumption that there are particular conditions, beliefs, and attitudes that make for a *democratic* political culture.

POLITICAL CULTURE AND GERMAN DEMOCRACY

The intrusion of the new concept into German political science and German politics has shed new light and brought a new focus upon a debate that has accompanied German politics since the beginning of the new experiment in democracy after World War II. It centered around the question of whether the newly established democracy of Bonn was–with regard to its institutions–efficient and stable enough to maintain itself and whether–with regard to political culture– the German people really had espoused democratic values and could be relied upon in their respective attitudes and behavior. There can be little doubt that Germany's second attempt to establish a liberal democracy was much more successful than the first one during the 1920s, which ended in fascist totalitarianism. It can likewise be demonstrated that on the level of institutions, including the party and pressure-group system, the Federal Republic of Germany has achieved a comparatively high level of efficiency and stability, but German and foreign observers have always been somewhat distrustful about the democratic reliability of the German people, that is, about Germany's political culture. They continue to remain skeptical about the civic quality of Germany's political culture and refuse to believe in the democratic strength of its political culture before the system has really come under heavy stress, be it through a deep economic depression or through other external challenges. It is in this context that studies dealing with the political beliefs and attitudes of Germans have always attracted public interest within and outside of Germany, because they were supposed to give substantial information about the German people's democratic potential in times of crisis.

Yet, despite a number of different studies undertaken in the new field of political culture, despite continuous observation of political opinions and attitudes through surveys, it is still difficult to give a reliable answer to the intriguing question of whether the German people have learned the lessons of democracy for good.

Political culture is viewed here as a kind of democratic *reserve potential* that can be drawn upon if the political system runs into serious difficulties. One would like to know whether the great majority of Germans can be trusted to back up their democratic institutions even if these no longer provide a satisfactory output for the citizens.

It is my own experience with the existing empirical studies on political culture in West Germany that they are largely unable to fulfill the expectations raised in this particular context. This is so for two main reasons: (1) The students of political culture have, in most cases, no adequate theory about the relation of the subsystem of political culture to the overall political system–they do not know how important political culture really is: and (2) most students of political culture have no consensus about the values and attitudes considered to be democratic and are therefore unable to make reliable statements about the civic, democratic quality of a political culture.

It is, indeed, difficult to establish a convincing theoretical framework that relates political culture to political institutions and to the political system as a whole. Although it is quite evident that the life and functioning of the institutions are in some way nourished and influenced by the ensemble of things that we define as political culture, it is nevertheless nearly impossible to indicate precisely how much political-cultural underpinning, as it were, and what kind of it the institutions need in order to function adequately, let alone to come to realistic assumptions about this crucial relationship that can be tested in empirical research. The pioneers of the new branch of political science that focuses on values, attitudes, beliefs, and opinions of citizens in a democracy have, for obvious reasons, tended to view *participation* as a clue to the democratic quality of a political culture, but they have not been able to qualify the *kind* of participation that is most propitious for a democracy. If one determines the stability and quality of a democratic system preferably on the basis of participation, one cannot derive from such findings any reliable conclusions about the real strength and stability of the democratic system. Electoral participation during the Weimar Republic, for example, was highest right before its collapse.

The example of contemporary West Germany is another case in point. The numerous polls about the political culture of the West Germans have indeed shown that there has been, over the last twenty years, a growing amount of participation and an increasing awareness of democratic rights by the citizens, but while in terms of democratic political culture a substantial improvement could thus be registered because, to use Almond's terms, German political culture was progressively losing traits of a "subject political culture" and gaining the characteristics of a "participant political culture," the very same political culture has undergone since 1968, for the first time since World War II, a significant partial change in the purposes for which participation was engaged in. It was a change in favor of participating in actions *against* the dominating patterns of politics in post-war Germany. However, participation in movements that fight for the rigid implementation of ecological principles in politics or for peace through unilateral disarmament or for a kind of basic democracy that runs counter to the conventional principles of representative and parliamentary democracy can hardly be viewed as a support to a political system based primarily on representative institutions or as a strengthening of liberal attitudes. In other words, participation, irrespective of its contents, cannot be taken as an indicator of the maturity of a democratic political culture.

It is precisely this development that in the last ten to fifteen years has made Germany's political culture *look* more democratic while, at the same time, the system as a whole has been, more than ever before in its history, openly challenged by minorities. No one who has observed the inner life of German democracy during the last decade can deny that the events that disturbed and upset it most and gave rise to extremely divergent interpretations concerning its democratic justification, namely, the antiauthoritarian revolt of the students, the acts of terrorism by small minorities on the extreme left and the extreme right of the political spectrum, and, quite generally, the intrusion of violence as a means of politics into the German political sphere, were of capital importance to the political culture of the Federal Republic. But while these things occurred and continued to intrigue public opinion and the political institutions, the political culture studies reported a notable increase in democratic attitudes and behavior patterns within German democracy. Apparently, the polls and empirical surveys, as they are normally undertaken in order to assess the democratic quality of German political culture, place too much stress on the factor of participation as the crucial one for a democratic political culture to render an adequate picture of what really goes on in the political culture of a particular political system.

POLITICAL CULTURE AND THE FUNCTIONING OF THE POLITICAL SYSTEM

This is why not all political scientists who engage in research on political culture content themselves with the findings produced by empirical studies. I, myself, have tried to sort out some of the historical traditions, mostly developed during the nineteenth century and later, that still pervade and, in part, determine our German orientation towards politics, such as for example, the state-tradition (etatism), the idealistic tradition, the formalistic tradition, the apolitical tradition, and the tradition of conflict avoidance.[2] These traditions are all more or less *illiberal,* to use Fritz Stern's term, and they explain some of the peculiarities of German political culture, although they are in reality often superposed by more democratic traditions in the sense of grass-roots democracy, individualism, and liberalism. Although it seems to be true that our political culture has, on the whole, moved away from some of the more traditional

[2] See my introduction to the German political system, *Grundzüge des politischen Systems der Bundesrepublik Deutschland,* , 8th ed. (München: Piper, 1980), pp. 77-90.

traits of our historical "subject-culture," it cannot be argued that there is at present a greater congruence between the constitutional institutions and the political culture than the empirical findings suggest.

This is why I tend to regard some of the surveys on German political culture as partly irrelevant to the real problem of our political culture, which I see mainly in the adequate relationship between values, attitudes, and opinions about politics, on the one hand, and the life of the institutions according to our constitution, on the other. There is within our present political culture a widening gap between some values and attitudes that are considered to be democratic and the democratic institutions that this political culture should serve and support.

Such a gap can be explained in two different ways. One can say that our political culture is in substance more democratic than the working of our institutions and that therefore the institutions should be adapted to a higher level of democracy. This is the position taken by many critics of the German political system who thus interpret the rebellion of a minority of the population that is engaged in protest movements as a fight for more democracy. Professor Greiffenhagen, in his rather popular book on West Germany's political culture,[3] ventured the thesis that the German political establishment, especially the parties and the administration, have fouled, so to speak, some of the positive developments in Germany's political culture by such negative policies and actions as, for example, the "persecution" of individuals whose loyalty to the constitution was doubted by the authorities. Greiffenhagen found West Germany's political culture ambivalent and partly nondemocratic despite the surveys with their rather positive findings. The people, he found, manifested more democracy than the institutions–a rather dubious statement, to my mind. The other explanation, which I find more pertinent, lies in the better adjustment of political culture to the existing institutions of representative democracy.

This shows, at any rate, that statements about the state of a political culture that are exclusively based on empirical evidence from surveys are insufficient to cover the whole range of the problem, but it is extremely difficult to collect all the necessary

[3] *Ein schwieriges Vaterland: Studien zur politischen Kultur der Bundesrepublik,* München: 1979).

information about the whole of a political culture because the various elements that compose it, beyond the empirically observable phenomena in a population sample, are not clearly identified and cannot be found through the same scientific approach. Therefore, scientific attempts to describe and analyze a political culture will have to be manifold and should be based on a variety of approaches.

More attention should certainly be given to the problem of the function of political culture within the whole system. We do not know how important the quality of a political culture really is for the functioning of the system. We have to explain why, at least in the German case, the usual survey techniques do not yield significant insights into the real cleavages within the political system so that the kind and amplitude of existing patterns of defiance to the established political order and its institutions cannot be identified by them.

POLITICAL CULTURE AND THE QUALITY OF DEMOCRACY

I propose, therefore, to focus in our research more on the problem of *consensus* with the established democratic institutions than on the problem of participation, for participation can clearly have rather conflicting aims. It is this particular problem that, for some time now, has intrigued German political culture and eroded the relatively broad consensus that has existed in German politics about the basic principles of social and political democracy far into the 1960s. Since then there has been a remarkable change in the interpretation of standard democratic values like liberty, equality, and the idea of democracy itself. Liberty, for example, has come to be interpreted more in an anarchistic understanding of total freedom, with "law and order" as its real enemies, than in the traditional understanding of freedom connected with obligation. Likewise, the understanding of democracy was shifting more and more from an Anglo-Saxon interpretation in the tradition of Locke and Montesquieu to a Rousseauean interpretation with a focus on direct participation in all public affairs at all levels as well as on plebiscitarian models. Such changes of understanding with regard to the key values of a democracy do, of course, change a political culture, and this, along with more recent hot issues like ecology, atomic energy and the peace problem, is one of the main reasons for the apparent cleavages in our political culture that are scarcely detectable with the means of public opinion polls, however sophisticated they may be.

It is not sufficient to conduct surveys on the political culture of a particular democracy if we continue to put our main emphasis on the cognitive and participatory aspects of it and do not, at the same time, try to find out how political knowledge and political action are related to the institutions and whether the institutional and the cultural aspects of politics are more or less in accord with each other. The political culture approach was originally developed to overcome the onesidedness of the institutional approach to politics. It is now in danger of becoming divorced from the life of the institutions. It should be kept in mind that both political culture and political institutions are essential for the working of a political system. If one looks at political culture apart from the institutions, one misses the very problem for which the new approach was developed, namely, the intricate interplay between the attitudes, beliefs, values, and opinions in a society and the institutions and procedures through which these factors find their way into politics and the political process.

It is, after all, not surprising that those German politicians who have, in recent years, come to adopt the new concept of political culture for their own purposes use it in a normative way. To them political culture in a democracy comprises everything that is necessary and helpful for the positive development of a democratic system, the democratic quality of the institutions as much as the democratic beliefs and attitudes of politicians and citizens. Political culture is, in their view, something to be developed and cultivated in order to achieve, as nearly as possible, a kind of harmony between both spheres of politics (political institutions and political culture).

Political scientists would rather refrain from such a normative use of the concept, in which there is again an undertone of the positive associations that the term *Kultur* still evokes in the German context; but they can at least learn this from the triumphant inroads of the new concept into current political lingo: that our scientific interest in political culture can, in the final analysis, only be legitimized by our interest in the stability and, even more, in the quality of a democratic system. Questions of quality do imply value judgments. We should not shun them if they are necessary.

This is particularly true in the German case. Germany has, between 1919 and 1933, undergone the fatal experience of a democracy that turned into a brutal dictatorship. This experience was, to a great extent, possible because of a political culture that was not enough in tune with democratic values, attitudes, and institutions. This is why I have come to the conviction that a political culture should not only be studied through empirical research but also be cultivated with the help of political science. political science should not forget that it has a dual responsibility in this matter for the facts and for the values.

Chapter 13

TWO-PARTY CONTEST AND "INNER-PARTY DEMOCRACY": ROOTS AND REMEDIES OF A FUNCTIONAL CONFLICT

Richard Löwenthal

The theme of this essay is the conflict found in modern, representative mass democracies (particuarly in those with actual or approximate two-party systems) between a party's chances of winning a democratic electoral majority and the strength of the internal democratic pressures of its activist members. Broadly, a party's chances of electoral victory improve, at least in normal times, the closer its policy platform and general image come to occupying the "middle ground." Yet it is a fairly general experience that the active members of a mass party tend to exert a pull toward the fringes of the political spectrum, the more so the more "ideological" the party's concept of itself: they tend to drag a left-wing party more to the Left and a right-wing party more to the Right. The pressure of the party activists is thus normally exerted in the direction opposite to what would attract the uncommitted and potentially decisive section of the electorate. Hence the stronger the internal democratic pressures on one of the leading parties at a given time, the more its chances of democratic victory at the polls are likely to be impaired.

This statement appears paradoxical from the viewpoint of the traditional Western democratic belief that a democratic electoral system and inner-party democracy naturally belong together. That was the belief underlying the great democratic party reforms imposed by the legislation of a number of U.S. states around the turn of the century; it is also embodied in an article of the constitution of the Federal Republic of Germany that makes a democratic internal structure compulsory for all recognized political parties. Yet the facts of the conflict stated above are obvious - though the subject seems hardly to have been discussed in general terms in political science.

That the major parties in an actual or approximate two-party system must try to occupy the "middle ground" in order to win an election is a commonplace. That inner-party democracy tends to pull many of them away from that desirable position on frequent occasions, due to the ideological zeal of their active members, has often been observed–particularly, but by no means only, for parties of the Left with their stronger explicit ideological background. The most striking recent example is the apparent conquest of the British Labour party by left-wingers now dominating both most of its constituent organizations and at least a number of its most important affiliated trade unions. The extremist platform adopted under the influence of these left-wingers by the party executive and the attempt to impose it on a parliamentary group still moderate in its majority have greatly reduced the party's prospects of an early electoral comeback even in the face of the massive unpopularity of Margaret Thatcher's Conservative government and have recently led to the breakaway of a number of leading moderates and their formation of a new Social Democratic party amid widespread popular acclaim.

The German Social Democratic leaders, who controlled the federal Government in coalition with the Liberals for thirteen years, had to fight repeated waves of a left-wing inner-party opposition standing for policies that would break up the coalition and put the party back in the wilderness. A first wave, largely inspired by neo-Marxist ideas in the wake of the student revolt but utterly unrepresentative of broader strata of the electorate, was eventually defeated. Against the present wave, inspired mainly by pacifist and ecological demands and linked with a much broader movement outside the party ranks, the leadership is still fighting an uphill struggle. It is typical that in both Britain and West Germany the leftists are in a minority–in Germany a small minority–in the parliamentary group but strong within the party organization.

In the United States, where the two great parties used to boast of their nonideological character, both Democrats and Republicans have acquired increasingly visible ideological hues since the profound changes worked in the country's social and political system by Franklin Roosevelt's administrations. In the Democratic party, another major change occurred under the impact of the Vietnam War, when after their loss of power at the end of the Johnson administration a large part of the active membership turned to the Left and at the same time put through a "democratizing" party reform decisively weakening the party machine and the traditional leading elites. The first result was the disastrous McGovern candidacy of 1972 on a platform far left of the middle the second a general loss of cohesion manifesting itself in the unusual difficulties of candidate selection in 1976 and 1980. The loss of cohesion appears to have far outlasted the leftward turn.

Nor have the conservative parties remained free of the drawbacks of ideological zeal. One of the outstanding cases of a party's suffering defeat by moving obviously too far to the Right for its own good was Senator Barry Goldwater's presidential candidacy in 1964. A more recent case is the defeat of the West German Christian Democrats under the leadership of Franz Josef Strauss.

It would, of course, be wrong to conclude from those examples that cautious and colorless moderation is a safe prescription for electoral success in all situations. There are times when, under the impact of serious crises and a felt need for great decisions, the "middle ground" itself shifts to one side or the other, and the party that seizes the opportunity to call for a major change may be rewarded by a political landslide. The first two elections of Franklin Roosevelt, the British Labour victory of 1945, Willy Brandt's reelection at the critical moment of *Ostpolitik* in 1972, and the recent victory of François Mitterrand are examples of such major turns to the Left, as Margaret Thatcher's and Ronald Reagan's recent triumphs are of big shifts to the Right. But in the absence of such dramatic occasions, the permanent fervor of the party activists is *not* representative of the electorate. Hence in those humdrum, normal periods, the "inner-party democracy" of those activists does not make for good prospects of an electoral victory.

IDEOLOGICAL IDENTITY VERSUS WINNING A MAJORITY

The problem we have raised appears akin to the old dispute between the advocates of "representative" and "plebiscitary" democracy, and the left-wing party militants generally tend to present it in that light. Indeed, the more radical among those militants question the right of the elected members of parliament to follow their own conscience, which is an essential feature of representative democracy, and wish to subject them to an "imperative mandate" and the threat of "recall." But as the situation in present-day Britain shows, those ideological militants are much further removed from the bulk of the electorate than are the elected parliamentarians: they could never obtain their recall by popular vote, only by decision of an inner-party caucus.

When Edmund Burke first fought the imperative mandate in order to assure the scope for parliamentary compromise between different interests, without which parliamentary government is not possible, the vote belonged in many English constituencies to small cliques grouped around a single interest; fighting the "plebiscitary" concept of the deputies' dependence on the instructions of their voters amounted to fighting the veto power of those small cliques over parliamentary decisions. Today, the electorate comprises all adult citizens, but the "imperative mandate" is still demanded in the name of small cliques or factions. For within our modern mass parties, the managing of "inner-party democracy" has in many places fallen into the hands of small factions of young ideological activists who not only concert their views before any public discussion or vote but have developed techniques for getting rid of the "ordinary" party members, who are older and tire earlier, by endless highfaluting talk and by dragging out the vote until they can be sure of a majority. The result evidently, is not plebiscitary democracy, but "democracy" for a small elite of ideological activists. That procedure is not only potentially harmful to their own party, it is, like every form of "imperative mandate," harmful to the necessary parliamentary process of democratic government by compromise and hence by consent.

However, although our problem is only apparently related to the old dispute over representative versus plebiscitary democracy, it has an equally old origin in the different historical roots of the modern political party–broadly speaking, the British and the French roots. The older, British concept of the party, which evolved from Bolingbroke to Burke in the age of the oligarchic and at times highly corrupt parliaments of the eighteenth century, was that of a union of members of parliament for the purpose of forming a majority strong and disciplined enough to sustain a government and resist corrupting royal "influence." The creation of party organizations outside parliament came much later and was clearly intended to support the parliamentary group, not to direct it–though such organizations did, of course, influence the nomination and election of its members. The parliamentary party itself arose as an alliance of admittedly diverse interests, united by a compromise in order to win governmental power; the modern political science term of "interest aggregation" fits those early parties perfectly. This is not to deny that they also had common ideas, or rather a broad common outlook, that made possible agreement on a common government policy; but there was neither need nor scope in such a party for quarreling about ideological shadings.

Conversely, ideology stood at the cradle of the French parties arising in the course of the French Revolution. At a time of a total reshaping of political institutions and of a corresponding ferment of ideas, the parties were formed around the evolving concepts of the new order, both in the clubs outside the assemblies and inside them. Where the British parties were formed around Westminster's face-to-face confrontation of goverment and opposition, the French parties created the hemicycle in the image of their own ideological tendencies. In course of time, they would have to become concerned with interest aggregation as well–but they still saw themselves primarily as *familles spirituelles* or parts of such, with internal discussion and external mission as two of their principal activities.

It may be said that our consciousness of a party's primary need for winning and preserving a majority, and hence for occupying the middle ground, is our heritage from the British party tradition. Our consciousness that a mass party needs a core following based on common principles, and that those principles must guide it to an extent that will always limit its capacity for compromise, is our heritage from the very different type of party created by the French Revolution. A modern mass party needs both a capacity for winning a majority and a core of ideological identity a capacity to govern democratically and a democratic responsibility to its followers. But as we have seen, the two requirements are liable to get into conflict with each other once the core of identity and the responsibility to the followers are represented by comparatively narrow groups of ideological activists dominating the party membership. Is there an alternative solution?

THE PRIMARY ELECTION AS AN ALTERNATIVE SOLUTION

It is interesting to compare our present discussions about inner-party democracy and the imperative mandate with the seemingly parallel reform movement, around the turn of the century, against the rule of party machines and corrupt bosses in the United States, which culminated not only in the introduction of the referendum but above all that of the primary system in a number of states. Of course, the introduction of both innovations was a step away from representative toward plebiscitary democracy, and in the case of the referendum that movement was obvious. But the primaries, in breaking the power of the bosses, did not hand it to the rank and file activists of the parties but to all voters willing to engage in the very minimum of activity in addition to going to vote–that of registering for the party of their basic preference and thus obtaining the right of taking part in the preliminary selection of its candidates for president and, in some states, for governor or senator. The result has been not an "ideological" democratization of the U.S. parties "from within" (that only happened many years later to the Democratic party after the Vietnam crisis), but a nonideological but very effective democratization of those parties "from without."

It is true that lately there have been many complaints about the U.S. primary system, but they chiefly concern accidental details such as the large interval between the beginning and the end of the presidential primaries in the different states, which leads to an extension of the preelectoral campaign over many months. There are also the irregularities due to differences of state legislation, with "crossing over" of registered members of one party to vote in the other's primaries being permitted in a few states but not in the majority, and with still other states leaving their candidate selection to inner-party caucuses rather than primaries. But the general usefulness and democratic character of the primary system is hardly contested after three-quarters of a century: it is widely regarded as a useful element of plebiscitary salt in the U.S. representative system. In particular, there seems to be little complaint that the need for preregistration with the party of one's basic preference impairs the secrecy of the vote: after all, people do not *need* to register with a party unless they want to participate in its primary, and they do not need to vote in the actual election for the party with which they registered for the primary–indeed, voters often may not if their preferred candidates were eliminated at the primary stage.

Under these circumstances, I should like to raise the question of whether some form of the primary system could not be devised for Western European countries too, and possibly on an even broader basis–such as a preliminary vote of a party's registered potential voters for the selection of parliamentary candidates in the constituencies. (No similar system seems practicable in countries where a strict system of proportional representation confines candidates to national or regional lists, or in countries with mixed systems, like West Germany, for that party of the candidates presented on such lists.) The purpose would be to eliminate the conflict between electoral appeal and inner-party democracy not by *eliminating* party democracy but by *broadening* it beyond the ranks of the inscribed party activists to the much larger circle of all those who are willing to register a basic preference for one of the parties without committing their ultimate vote. Such a right of the voters to indicate whom they would like to see as a parliamentary candidate of the party with which they generally sympathize would make parties not less but more democratic, because more responsive to the will of the electorate; and it would at the same time, for that very reason, eliminate the conflict between party democracy and electoral prospects.

At first glance, the idea of introducing such a system of "constituency primaries" appears contrary to all European political usage. But so was the idea of presidential, or gubernatorial and senatorial, primaries when it was first introduced in the United States. The present abuse of inner-party democracy is in some countries no less dangerous for the working of the democratic system than was the abuse of the party machines by the U.S. bosses in its time, and I believe it calls for an equally innovative remedy. The introduction of the primary system in the United States required state legislation to impose it on the party machines. A general introduction of "constituency primaries" in any European country would, of course, also require legislation; but depending on the state of the electoral and party laws in some country, one party or another might first introduce it of its own free will and thus secure a popular advantage. Certainly, the introduction of so radical an innovation would also have profound repercussions on the internal organization of European mass parties, which is in many respects out of date. But it is in the interest both of the working of our democratic system and of the great, competing parties themselves to open them to a kind of "basis democracy" that transcends the relatively narrow circles of their membership.

Chapter 14

DEATH AND TRANSFIGURATION OF THE MICHIGAN PARADIGM: REFLECTIONS ON SOME RECENT RESULTS CONCERNING THE SOCIOLOGY OF POLITICAL BEHAVIOR IN THE UNITED STATES

Daniel Gaxie

The American "voter" has changed. This is the principal conclusion of recent studies devoted to the sociology of political behavior in the United States.[1]

These studies are impressive because of both the fullness of the material presented and the sophistication of the techniques used. The French researcher remains somewhat spellbound by the substantial resources and quality of the scientific debate. For it

This article was first published in vol. 32, No. 2, April 1982, of the *Revue Française de Science Politique.* I would like to thank Georges Lavau and Louis Bodin, the editors of the *Revue,* for their permission to publish the article in English translation in this volume.

[1] Here I will analyze mainly the work of Norman H. Nie, Sidney Verba, and John R. Petrocik, *The Changing American Voter,* (Cambridge, Mass.: Harvard University Press, 1979), 2nd ed. Without attempting to present an exhaustive list of recent works, one might nonetheless mention the following: Gerald Pomper, *Voter's Choice: Varieties of American Electoral Behavior,* (New York: Dodd, Mead and Company, 1975), 259 p.; Harold Mendelsohn, and Garret J. O'Keefe, *The People Choose a President. Influences on Voter Decision Making,* (New York: Praeger, 1976), 253 p.; Walter Dean Burnham, *Critical Elections and the Mainsprings of American Politics,* (New York: Norton, 1970). On this last point, refer to the controversy around the works of Walter Dean Burnham in the September 1974 issue of *American Political Science Review.* These works or, more often, their previous versions which shall not be mentioned here have provoked many debates. Since this article is not intended to paint a complete picture of the controversy, we will limit ourselves to citing two comprehensive studies: Philip E. Converse, *Public Opinion and Voting Behavior,* in Fred I. Greenstein and Nelson W. Polsby, *Handbook of Political Science,* vol. 4, *Nongovernmental Politics,* (Reading, Mass.: Addison-Wesley, 1975), p. 75-169; Warren E. Miller, Teresa Levetin, *Leadership and Change. Presidential Elections from 1952 to 1976,* (Cambridge: Winthrop Publishers, 1976), 303 p.

certainly is a debate. The objective is to refute the conclusions of a group of researchers from the University of Michigan. These conclusions are, among others, exposed in their classic *The American Voter.*[2]

According to Walter Dean Burnham,[3] the Michigan group's work established the dominant paradigm for American political science in the field of political behaviorism. Researchers therefore appeared on the periphery to try to discover its inadequacies and to refute it.[4]

The recently obtained results of the studies examined in this chapter deal with fundamental problems relating to politicization, mechanisms of electoral behavior, and the formation of opinions, and hence to the workings of democracy.

For Nie, Verba, and Petrocik, the conclusions of *The American Voter* are outdated. The Michigan researchers have not described the factors governing the behavior of the American voter, as their title suggests, but rather the behavior of the American voter in a particular situation: that of the 1950s. Hence, Chapter 2 is devoted to the "American public in the 1950s"[5] and serves as a prelude to the work, summarizing the certainties of the American specialists gathered under the banner of the Michigan empire.

[2] Angus Campbell, Philip E. Converse, Warren Miller, Donald E. Stokes, *The American Voter,* (New York: John Wiley and Sons, 1960), 1st ed.

[3] Walter Dean Burnham, "Theory and Voting Research: Some Reflections on Converse's Change in the American Electorate", *The American Political Science Review,* 68 (3), September 1974, pp. 1002-1023.

[4] In addition to this explanation by the logic of scientific competition, it can be assumed that it is also the contents of the Michigan group's work that is being questioned. The findings from the empirical works of the 1950s and 1960s–those of the group from Michigan but also those of the group from Columbia–in fact give a description of the behavior of citizens that is hardly compatible with the expectations of the democratic theory. Despite certain attempts to reformulate this theory [for example, see the last chapter of Bernard R. Berelson, Paul F. Lazarsfeld, and William N. McPhee, *Voting,* (Chicago: University of Chicago Press, 1954), or Talcott Parsons, "'Voting' and the Equilibrium of the American Political System," in Arthur J. Brodbeck and Eugene Burdick, eds., *American Voting Behavior,* (Glencoe, Ill.: Free Press, 1959), pp. 80-120], the recent works come closer to meeting the "prerequisites" of the democratic theory.

[5] Note that Nie, Verba, and Petrocik's analysis is undifferentiated. As their title suggests, the object of their research is the American "voter," not the American voters in all their diversity. The scope of their criticism of the Michigan group is similarily reduced.

THE AMERICAN PUBLIC IN THE 1950S

The characteristics of this public can be summed up in five points:

1. The lack of interest in politics and lack of any psychological investment in political affairs (political involvement) except during election campaigns.
2. The existence of unsophisticated views concerning political issues and the inability to express opinions about questions deriving from abstract, ideological categories.
3. The existence of contradictory and politically inconsistent opinions regarding a great number of issues. Here, the authors are referring specifically to the work of Philip E. Converse, which shows the poor ideological consistency and instability of the responses of mass publics"[6] to questions calling for an opinion. These "opinions" are discontinuous and superficial. In some cases they are randomly stated.
4. The existence of a strong and firm attachment to one of the two major political parties acting as a guide to the political behavior of Americans.
5. The apparent satisfaction of the citizens with their political system and their feeling that they have control over it (a feeling of political effectiveness).

CHANGES IN POLITICAL BEHAVIOR

For Nie, Verba, and Petrocik, the "voter" of the 1970s is quite different from that of the 1950s. Very important changes have taken place in six areas:

1. First of all, Nie, Verba, and Petrocik show that there has been an increase in the average level of ideological conceptualization of the American voter in the sense given to this notion in *The American Voter*.
2. The authors draw attention to an increase in ideological consistency of opinions (based on correlation coefficients between responses provided to various questions of opinion) since the beginning of the 1960s. From this they deduce the existence of more clearly formulated political attitudes (attitude consistency).
3. Changes in manner of voting can also be noted with the emergence of issue voting. Analyzing the criteria by which the voters make up their minds, Nie, Verba, and Petrocik note that the importance of positions taken by candidates, with regard to political issues, tends to increase at the expense of the party "label," even if the personal attributes of the candidates remain the element of predominant reference.
4. This new awareness of controversies over issues has brought about an ideological

[6] Philip E. Converse, "The Nature of Belief Systems in Mass Publics," in David E. Apter ed., *Ideology and Discontent*, (New York: Free Press of Glencoe, 1964), pp. 206-261.

polarization. Sharply defined leftist and rightist opinions are more widespread within the two parties, which are thus more divided than they were in the 1950s. The same kind of evolution can be noted within all social, ethnic, and religious groups.

5. This polarization might explain, although the authors do not explicitly use it to do so, the decline of political parties. In fact, there is, first of all, a decline in the party system that might lead to a realignment of the party divisions. The traditionally Democratic groups (with the exception of blacks) or the Republicans are much less firmly aligned, as if the internal ideological polarization of the parties prevented the traditional exchange relations between the parties and the groups. Even more astounding is the decline of party identification. Nie, Verba, and Petrocik here confirm well-established results (of Gerald Pomper, among others). Their originality lies more in their multiplication of convergent indicators (noncongruency of party identification and of voting, split tickets, decline in the labeling of candidates in party terms, decline in identification with a party and an increase in independent voters, a more negative evaluation of the parties). This decline in party identification takes place according to the same mechanisms that prevailed in the 1930s when the preferences that still structure the U.S. party system were formulated. When age is controlled for, party identification hardly varies at all between 1950 and 1976. At the same time, the percentage of independents increases greatly while their age decreases. Therefore, it is the new voters who are most strongly detached from parties. This lends force to the thesis of the demise of the party system, born of the crisis of 1929 and of the emergence of a new realignment.
6. The new hostility in the United States, towards the parties is accompanied by an attitude of defiance towards to the government and a sense of "political alienation."[7]

The results of Nie, Verba, and Petrocik have evoked a broad, essentially methodological, controversy which indicates that although there may be an attempt to impose a new paradigm, the old one is still struggling to hold its own. The criticisms of *The Changing American Voter* deal mainly with the thesis of an alleged increase in the ideological consistency of opinions.[8] Some authors have pointed out that the measures implemented resulted in artifacts. The work of Nie, Verba, and Petrocik is based on a secondary analysis of surveys from the Survey Research Center. This organization has, on several occasions, modified the wording of its questions. And when

[7] Nie, Verba, and Petrocik find here a theme made popular by Samuel P. Huntington in the *Report on the Governability of Democracies to the Trilateral Commission*, (New York: New York University Press, 1975), pp. 79 ff.

[8] This thesis has not been contested by the members of the Michigan group. Philip E. Converse, as well as Warren E. Miller and Teresa E. Levitin, admits the increase in the ideological consistency of opinions measured by paired correlation coefficients. It is mainly ulterior works that raised various objections.

we compare the evolution of the correlation coefficients of answers, keeping questions with identical wording, it can no longer be established that there was significant change between the 1950s and the 1970s.[9]

Another line of criticism raises questions of coding conventions, on the one hand, and the technique of calculating correlation coefficients by pairs, on the other hand.[10] Regarding this first point, Hugh LeBlanc and Mary Beth Merrin suggest that one can be more or less rigorous regarding the criterion of consistency by accepting only strong opinions of the left or right (entirely consistent opinion) or else by tolerating less firm opinions classed as being of the centre, or even one contradictory opinion among a series of clearly marked responses of the left or right (nearly consistent opinion).

On the second point, LeBlanc and Merrin note that consistency of opinions can be tested by two given responses, that is to say, in using the correlation by pairs technique of Nie, Verba, and Petrocik, or else by a greater number of items, themselves producing calculations of up to five items. Their results suggest that the consistency of opinions will vary sharply according to the number of questions used to measure it. Hence, in 1972, 55 percent of the people questioned showed consistency in their responses if this consistency is measured by their answers to two questions. If, however, consistency is required in the responses to three questions, the result falls to 19 percent. The data suggest that it is only with respect to the two responses and especially the nearly consistent responses that any evolution appears to have taken place between 1956 and 1972. In other words, stricter coding conventions and operationalization of the consistency of opinions make the transformations that Nie, Verba, and Petrocik believe to have taken place disappear.

In the second edition of their work, published in 1979, Nie, Verba, and Petrocik admit that explanation of their results by the artifact of the measure is plausible, albeit insufficiently established to convince them to give up their thesis."[11]

[9] George F. Bishop, Robert W. Oldendick, Alfred J. Tuchfarber, and Stephen E. Bennet, "The Changing Structure of Mass Belief Systems: Fact or Artifact?," *The Journal of Politics*, 40 (3), August 1978, pp. 781-787.

[10] Hugh L. Leblanc and Mary Beth Merrin, "Mass Belief Systems Revisited," *The Journal of Politics*, 39 (4), November 1977, pp. 1082-1087.

[11] See Nie, Verba, and Petrocik, op. cit., p. 370.

But they also note that their thesis concerning the transformations of political behavior in the United States is based on other factors that, to our knowledge, have not been called into question.

The first concerns the increase in the level of ideological conceptualization. By modifying the coding conventions of the Michigan group, Nie, Verba, and Petrocik estimate the number of "ideologues" and "quasiideologues"[12] at 20 percent in 1956, as opposed to 51 percent in 1972.

Obviously it is difficult to judge the merits of the coding criteria used in *The American Voter* and in *The Changing American Voter* to estimate the level of ideological conceptualization of the people surveyed. It can, nevertheless, be pointed out that one U.S. citizen out of two in 1972 (and even more in 1976 since the data show a decrease in level of conceptualization from 1972 to 1976) is unable to master the "ideological" categories and that this fact is not taken into consideration in Nie, Verba, and Petrocik's analysis. Why is it the case then, if, as their analyses state, the political framework of U.S. society encourages politicization, that at least one out of two U.S. citizens seems to have missed out this process? However, in addition to their own coding conventions, Nie, Verba, and Petrocik have also taken the traditional measurement methods of the Survey Research Center. Using these methods, the percentage of ideologues and quasiideologues would rise from 13 percent, in 1956, to 23 percent.

The rise in level of ideological conceptualization would thus be weaker than the comprehensive analysis of *The Changing American Voter* suggests, but nonetheless real. The recent increase in level of political competence of U.S. citizens seems an established fact which cannot be dismissed, and which the partisans of the "Michigan paradigm" would be mistaken to ignore.[13] More especially, Nie, Verba,

[12] Let us recall that in the vocabulary of *The American Voter,* the ideologues and quasiideologues designate surveyed persons who were able to judge the candidates during a presidential election or the political parties on the basis of ideological categories (liberal or conservative), regardless of the degree of mastery over these categories.

[13] The Michigan group researchers do not question the reality of these changes. They themselves even present data that go in this direction. They simply note that (1) despite the changes, half the voters cannot evaluate the U.S. parties in terms that could, in other respects, allow them to express preference with respect to the main competing political options Miller and Levitin); and (2) it is the agents who are

and Petrocik also show evidence, uncontested to our knowledge, of changes in voting criteria.

The percentage of people questioned who had decided on the candidate of their choice in the presidential election on the basis of the candidates' position on the main issues of the day rose from 49 percent in 1952 to 67 percent in 1972, reaching a peak at 77 percent in 1964.

At the same time, party identification, as a criterion for selecting a candidate, has continued to decline, falling from 46 percent to 24 percent. Party identification as total dedication to the party, as dependence without control, has declined markedly. In 1976, 30 percent of U.S. citizens questioned made their choice exclusively on the basis of the party membership of the candidates (pure partisan voters) as opposed to 42 percent in 1960. And inversely, 17 percent in 1976 (26 percent in 1972) based their decision exclusively on the positions of the candidates (pure issue voters) as opposed to 13 percent in 1956. For 26 percent of the voters, the party criteria and the positions of the individual candidates are both taken into consideration (27 percent in 1956 and 37 percent in 1964).

In recent years, voting has been more often the expression of an opinion regarding particular issues and the positions on these issues than it was in the late 1950s.[14] Of course, this phenomenon is limited: it affects a maximum of 54 percent of the people surveyed in 1964 and 53 percent in 1972. Also, it diminishes from 1972 to 1976 (43 percent of the voters based their choice exclusively or partially on the positions of the candidates) for reasons to be examined shortly. But a progression can be observed since 1956 (40 percent of the people surveyed) even if a decline in the partisan criterion, in addition to that of position taking, is more evident than the progression.[15]

already relatively politicized who have increased their level of conceptualization. Those who were ranked lowest in this hierarchy did not make any significant advance in their ability to manipulate the ideological categories in use in the United States (P. E. Converse).

[14] Here again, these findings are not contested by the members of the Michigan group although they attempt to downplay them. If we were to give an analysis of the controversy over this point, we would be forced to cover topics not related to this article. See, therefore, Philip E. Converse, "Public Opinion and Voting Behavior," op. cit., p. 125ff and Warren E. Miller, Teresa E. Levitin, *Leadership and Change . . .*, op. cit., pp. 49 and 49ff.

Of course voters who have no precise political criteria upon which to base their decision must also be taken into consideration. They made up 22 percent of the electorate in 1956; 15 percent in 1964. This tendency has been on the rise, however, making up 24 percent of those surveyed in 1968 and 27 percent in 1976. attempting to prove that the voter has indeed changed, our authors have ignored this piece of information–perhaps not entirely by accident–in their analysis. Similarly, decisions based on the individual candidate remain the most frequent and one can scarcely detect any significant change here, since 75 percent of those surveyed in 1952 had said that this was a partial or decisive factor[16] in their decision on a candidate, 84 percent in 1964 and 72 percent in 1972. The personalized criteria, often weak and unstable, expression for the most part of a retranslation of the purely political logic of political rivalry based on appreciation schemes taken from daily life, remain predominant. Once again we see a poorly integrated element in the analyses of Nie, Verba, and Petrocik. It is not acceptable to sift through evidence, using some as proof and throwing other bits away. All the data must be integrated into the work, not merely those that strengthen the authors' thesis.

Despite these important reservations, three new elements appear in *The Changing American Voter.* The level of ideological conceptualization has risen, voting more usually expresses an opinion on specific issues, and opinions are more clearly formulated, that is, notably more defined as left or right than they were in the past. Although it is quite legitimate to inquire into the extent to which these developments are real or, rather, produced by the conditions of the survey, it would be wrong and hardly fruitful to brush them aside under the pretext of defending an earlier state of research.

[15] See Nie, Verba, and Petrocik, op. cit., p. 377.

[16] The total number of the frequencies of appearance of the various criteria is higher than 100 percent because a considerable number of the people questioned gave several responses.

QUESTIONING THE MICHIGAN PARADIGM

But, after the facts have been established, what is the explanation? Which interpretation do Nie, Verba, and Petrocik give to the change suggested by their data?

First of all, their interpretation is negative, and would represent a departure from earlier works.

The interpretation of the Michigan researchers may hold for the 1950s but it has become outdated due to recent changes in U.S. society. For Nie, Verba, and Petrocik the conclusions of *The American Voter* are based essentially on data collected in 1956. The book is concerned with a particular year. Rather than giving a description of the voters, this work gives a description of the voters during the Eisenhower era.

It is therefore not possible to generalize the results obtained by the Michigan group and to draw broader theoretical conclusions. A similar line of reasoning reasoning is also expressed by Walter Dean Burnham. Studying changes in voter participation, he shows that it reached a peak in 1896, decreased sharply until 1920, slowly climbed from 1920 to 1960, and has been declining ever since (which incidentally raises another problem for the thesis of Nie, Verba, and Petrocik). He concludes that there was a kind of golden age of electoral participation in the United States. According to Burnham, at the end of the nineteenth century the proportion of voters who were concerned with the political issues and who were politically active was greater than contemporary surveys indicate. There again the conclusions of *The American Voter* and even of the "empirical sociology" of the years between 1950 and 1960 are valid only for the period when the surveys on which they are based were conducted. They could not be generalized to other historical situations. They gave birth to a paradigm that became dominant, but this paradigm should be revised; it has become obsolete.[17] It has become essential

[17] I will not discuss here the analyses of Walter Dean Burnham. The decisive criticisms, from my point of view, were addressed to him by Philip E. Converse and Jerrold G. Rusk (in particular, see the September 1974 issue of the *American Political Science Review*). These criticisms tend to show: (1) that it is unnecessary to have recourse to the unproven hypothesis of the existence, at the end of the nineteenth century, of a strongly politicized electorate, an hypothesis that remains inconsistent with what is known about the factors relevant to politicization; (2) that the strong electoral participation at the end of the nineteenth century is more probably due to

to find a system offering a different explanation. The main idea is that the way people vote and conceptualize political reality is not merely a function of their social and psychological characteristics but also of the political framework, notably the orientations of the candidates and the nature of the issues.

EXPLANATION BY THE POLITICAL FRAMEWORK

Once an increase in level of politicization has been established, one might feel that it is the social characteristics of the American voters that have changed, notably their cultural level, which is known to be a determining factor in the process of politicization. Thus from 1952 to 1972 the percentage of Americans not reaching secondary school dropped from 61 percent to 38 percent while the percentage of those going on to post secondary studies rose from 15 percent to 29 percent.

But Nie, Verba, and Petrocik show that the increase in level of political competence remains constant when level of education is controlled for. Certainly, on one hand, in 1956 as in 1972, the percentage of ideologues increases when one goes from a primary to a more advanced level of education. This is a classic result that remains true despite the recent transformations and that Nie, Verba, and Petrocik do not integrate into their explanation. On the other hand, from 1956 to 1972, the percentage of ideologues has been growing at all levels of instruction, passing (according to the coding conventions of the authors) from 7 percent to 24 percent at the primary level, from 10 percent to 30 percent at the secondary level, and from 26 percent to 48 percent at the advanced level.

If the lengthening of schooling is indeed a factor explaining the recent politicization of voters, it cannot be held as the only factor nor as the determining factor in the recent evolution even if it maintains its character of key variable in the process of politicization.[18] Once it has been shown that changes in sociodemographic

the conditions of voting rights and the organization of polls, the characteristics of the party system of that era, and the organization of the electorate within the political machinery; and (3) that these hypotheses are compatible with the findings made in the early 1960s notably those of Campbell, Converse, Miller, and Stokes.

[18] Philip E. Converse accepts this conclusion and furthermore defends the thesis

characteristics do not sufficiently explain the recent changes in political behavior,[19] two additional elements of explanation may be introduced.

The first relates to changes in the political issues. A secondary analysis of responses to the question, regularly asked in Gallup polls since 1949, as to what "the most important problems [are] facing Americans today," reveals significant changes. The main problems noted during the Eisenhower era were relatively abstract and distant problems of foreign policy relating to communism, the cold war, and the atomic bomb.

During the 1960s, problems of foreign policy were not ranked as important in the hierarchy of concerns, with the notable exception of the Vietnam problem, which first emerged during the Johnson administration. But this issue affected Americans more directly and concretely in their daily lives than most foreign policy issues do. In addition to Vietnam, given top ranking between 1965 and 1969, problems in the areas of civil rights and racial integration seem to have been the most important between 1963 and 1965, along with economic problems (unemployment, taxes, inflation, strikes) from 1970 to 1972. Around 1968 new concerns such as lawlessness, juvenile delinquency, street riots, drugs, and the problems of youth[20] began to emerge. They are still present although they have never been ranked first. It can be noted that from 1950 to 1970, when questioned about their hopes and fears for the future, Americans referred less and less frequently to individual problems and more

that the progression of the political consistency of opinions was more perceptible than that of the ideological conceptualization levels. He explains this difference by pointing out that the consistency of opinions would be somewhat more a function of the length of schooling. The first factor could therefore vary more on a short-term basis whereas the second would progressively increase with the level of education of the subjects. The findings of Nie, Verba, and Petrocik, showing that the progression in level of conceptualization is verified if the level of education is controlled for, weaken, at least with respect to this last point, the hypothesis of Converse.

[19] The authors also establish that the effects of politicization are to be found among all age groups.

[20] An identical thesis is defended by Richard M. Scammon and Ben J. Wattenberg, *The Real Majority: An Extraordinary Examination of the American Electorate,* (New York: Coward McCann, 1970). For them, a new era appears around the 1960s, that is characterized by the emergence of a social issue defined as "a series of public attitudes concerning the extremely disturbing aspects of ravaging social change" (crime, student unrest, terrorism, drugs, pornography, urban riots).

and more to collective issues.

The second element, influencing the level of politicization in recent years, concerns the orientations of political personalities. Nie, Verba, and Petrocik show that until 1960 it was the "moderate" candidates who were selected by the two major parties. Beginning in 1964 there was a increase in presidential candidates more clearly identified as liberal or conservative. This was the case with Goldwater in 1964, Wallace (if not Nixon) in 1968, McGovern in 1972, and, we could add, Reagan in 1980. The election of 1976 was an exception and was closer to the electoral confrontations of the 50s since it was marked by the opposition of two moderate candidates, according to the criteria prevailing in the United States. The 1976 election was accompanied, significantly according to our authors, by a decline in all the indicators of political competence brought out in their work.[21]

On the whole, the manner in which the people surveyed react to political events is not only related to their social characteristics (age, sex, socioprofessional category, level of education or unionization) and individual political competence. It also reflects "the stimuli which the political world offers to them: the nature of issues, the salience [or even better, pertinence] of these issues and the way in which they are presented." "Issues have become more salient for citizens and are presented to citizens as meaningful bundles of issues." In other words, political competition, in recent years, seems to bear somewhat more of an affinity with the daily and personal concerns of people and at the same time be more real. As Philip Converse notes,

[21] The influence of the two political factors (the transformation of issues and the polarization of positions) is recognized by the members of the Michigan group. Warren Miller and Teresa Levitin propose, for example, an analysis of the evolution of the political rifts in the United States, that does not differ much from the one put forward by Nie, Verba, and Petrocik. At best, they accentuate the role of the political personalites. According to them, political leaders brought about a rebirth of the American tradition of public debate over the issues of the day. They brought out the connections between diverse problems. In doing so, they encouraged a better understanding of the issues. They were directly at the source of the more sustained interest given by the "American public" to debates and public politics during the 1960s. The role of the political leaders is, according to Miller and Levitin, the key factor in explaining the growth of the formation of structured opinions.

> When the issue referents are remote, the attentiveness [given to politics] is worth the candle only at the higher levels [of the hierarchy of "benefits" directly removed from all political activity]. When they are doorstep issues for large sectors of the population, such as whether one's child or grandchild will be obliged to ride a bus to a distant school perceived as being less physically safe than the neighborhood one, then a vastly greater proportion of the population rises above the tilt point where attentiveness is galvanized.[22]

Under these conditions, social and political opposition movements, polarized around the more dramatic issues (civil rights movement, black movement, Vietnam War, antiwar movement, urban riots), would be mutually radicalized. At the same time the emergence of more deeply entrenched positions on these new issues and on the others, and stress placed on the interdependence of problems through the confrontation of more systematically differentiated global options, encouraged (1) sharper perception of the political issues; 2) closer attention to the public debate as well as a greater concern for political problems; (3) greater aptitude at discerning ideological oppositions and at using distinctively political categories of evaluation, which also encouraged 4) expressions of opinion that were more politically formulated and consistent.

If we can agree with Nie, Verba, and Petrocik in this area, there is some doubt as to whether their explanation is inconsistent with earlier findings. Although their work is significant in that it emphasizes certain previously neglected variables, it is also true that these variables do not rule out other factors whose influence has already been evidenced.

At the same time, it isn't enough simply to make note of the influence of political factors termed significantly by Philip Converse as "external"(?).[23] To speak of external political factors is to maintain implicitly an explanation that gives precedence to the individual characteristics of social agents by claiming that elements external to the model have interfered.

Rather than substituting one paradigm for another or acquiescing to a more or less peaceful coexistence of concurrent explanation schemes, we must try to integrate the new results with the old within a new framework of analysis that is neither eclectic nor conciliatory.

22 Converse, "Public Opinion," op. cit., p. 98.
23 Ibid., p. 92.

FROM THE RIVALRY OF PARADIGMS TO THE INTEGRATION OF FINDINGS

In some ways, the analyses of Nie, Verba, and Petrocik refer to other well known and established studies. We know, in fact, that the percentage of "unanswereds" to the questions asking for an opinion can be seen as an approximate indicator of the familiarity with the political issues and that this percentage diminishes when the level of politicization, political competence and education, or social status increases.

But it has also been established that the percentage of "unanswereds" also depends on the nature of the question asked. There is a somewhat lower response to questions dealing with abstract, ideological issues. On the other hand, there is a higher response to surveys that deal with people's daily concerns (e.g., unemployment, prices, length of work day).

For these kinds of questions, the percentage of "unanswereds," still very slight, scarcely varies with age, sex, social status or level of education. Even if the people surveyed do not answer the questions on the basis of purely political criteria, they nevertheless feel capable and entitled to answer the questions.

We also know that although the percentage of "unanswereds" tends to increase when the people surveyed occupy a lower position in the social hierarchy, farmers in France are characterized by a very low rate of "unanswereds" for questions relating to the agricultural policies of the EEC; and the same can be said of workers in questions relating to strikes or the role of the unions.[24]

Converse, for his part, has shown that the correlation coefficents between answers given to questions of opinion which measure the degree of ideological consistency of the "opinions" are higher for issues relating to national politics than they are for problems of external politics.

[24] On these problems see Daniel Gaxie, *Le Cens Caché,* (Paris: Editions du Seuil, 1978).

Similarily, the correlation coefficients intended to measure the degree of stability of answers obtained by using the technique of panels are highest for questions relating to desegregation in the schools or racial discrimination at work.[25] In contrast, these coefficients are particularly low for questions on foreign military or economic aid, and especially for the problem (highly ideologically formulated) of the comparative merits of private initiative and federal government intervention in the area of construction.[26]

We can therefore see that the capacity to express opinions and, more generally, the interest shown towards political problems depends on the degree of reality of the political issues. The level of politicization will therefore vary with the degree to which the problems raised as political issues by the political parties and professionals are seen as being pertinent to the daily concerns of the subjects.

At the same time the ability to express oneself politically on political issues–that is, in most cases, the ability to repeat to a certain extent the ideas of professional politicians–will depend on the polarization of the positions. Political issues will remain (relatively) indistinct if the positions regarding these issues are indistinct because they are poorly differentiated.

To take the analyses of Nie, Verba, and Petrocik, one could therefore explain that the Eisenhower era, characterized by the predominance of issues related to foreign policy and by the moderation of political opposition, was not very conducive to politicization of the subjects. In this sense, the degree of alienation voters feel with respect to the debates that structure the political domain depends not only on the social characteristics of the voters. It is also a function of: (1) the degree to which political issues relate to the real and concrete problems that the voters encounter in their daily life; and (2) the degree to which the positions regarding these issues are clearly differentiated.

The political competence of the voters depends not only on technical mastery of political language and of the authority they ascribe to themselves and which others ascribe to them with respect to political issues; it also depends on the functioning of the political

[25] The maximum coefficient is obtained by the question dealing with the problem of party identification, but, properly speaking, it is not an opinion question.

[26] Converse, "The Nature of Belief Systems," in *Mass Publics*, op. cit., pp. 228-229 and 240.

system, that is, on the nature of the problems designated by professional politicians as being political issues, and on the acuteness of the oppositions that separate the political enterprises. The system of political competence components, which we have attempted to construct,[27] must therefore be modified to integrate the whole range of influencing factors, as indicated in figure 1

But although the political alienation of the voters can be attenuated when professional politicians adopt the voters' real concerns or in certain situations when more intense political opposition is manifest, such as during crises, this alienation can nonetheless never disappear completely due to the existing gap built into the social division of labor, between actors in the political field and other social actors.

The work of Nie, Verba, and Petrocik shows that during the crisis period of 1960-1970 in the United States the level of political competence, as well as the ability of many Americans to express consistent political opinions, increased. It does not necessarily follow that in each case there is a cause and effect relation between these two phenomena or even that the politically consistent opinions are always politically formulated.

In other words, opinions showing real ideological unity may very well be produced without any intention of being consistent, and it is even possible that the speaker will be unable to point out the consistency, due to a lack mastery of the schemes of political evaluation that are the basis of the unity.

The speeches given by speakers representative of reference groups–notably the parties–can, according to Converse, promote the formation of "ideological patterns," (just as a dressmaker who works from a pattern) guiding the political attitudes and behaviors of the social actors without necessarily being accompanied by much explicit understanding of the abstract and architectonic reasons why these patterns go together in the conventional ideological sense.[28]

When the social actors are capable of taking up a significant number of their spokesmen's positions, such as, for example, in situations where political speeches are highly differentiated and the political issues directly related to the daily concerns of the majority, then a group of politically impeccable opinions can be expressed

[27] Gaxie, op. cit., pp. 85, 159, 161, and 243.
[28] Converse, "Public Opinion," op. cit., p. 106.

Table 1
Summary of Factors Relevant to Politicization

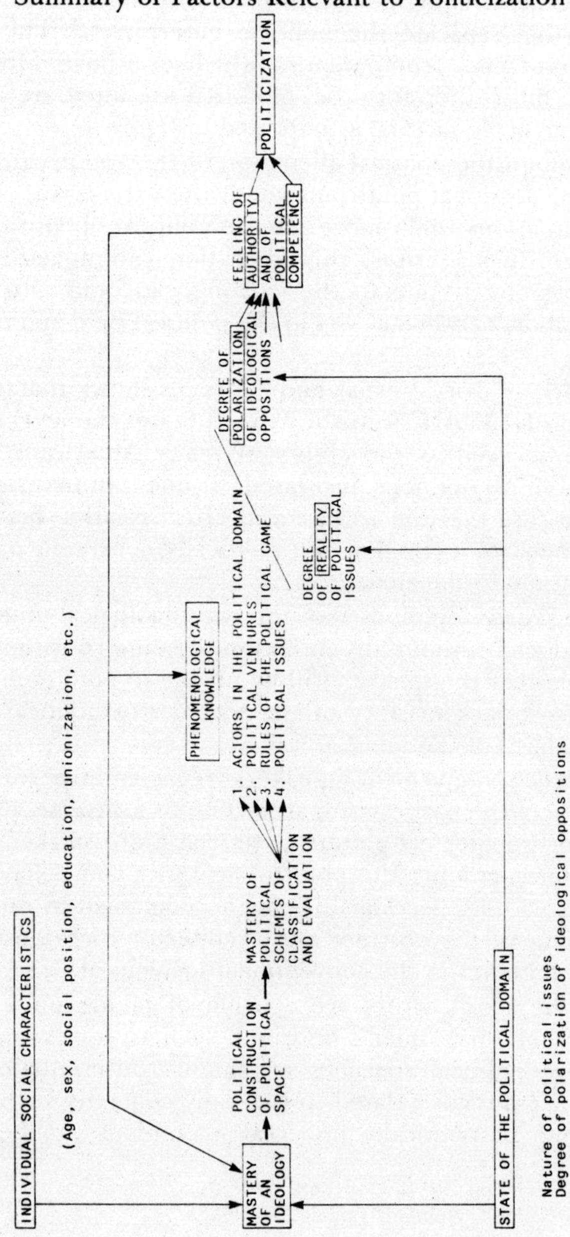

even if their producers have not mastered the schemes of evaluation that form their opinions and that spokesmen use to express explicitly and intentionally consistent positions.

If ideology influences the political behavior of Americans more than it has in the past, it is undoubtedly, in many cases, an ideology by proxy, which reflects, more than it negates, the division of labor between professional politicians or political language manipulators and laymen.

We can therefore see the conditions that allow a crisis to have its full politicizing effect.

As Moses Finley has forcefully demonstrated, the immediate experience of government and high degree of familiarity with public affairs of large numbers of Athenian citizens in the days of Pericles is inseparable from the absence of a differentiated political arena.[29] In this type of polity, when the citizens make a political decision they determine their future in an immediate and concrete way. The Athenian example thereby shows that it is only when the separation between political and social issues vanishes–that is, when social problems become problems immediately taken on by the polity and political problems are concrete problems affecting the daily existence of the social actors–that political alienation disappears.

It is therefore with an undifferentiated polity that the politicization of daily life, never fully removed, can be carried to its fullest in times of crisis.

As Thucydides notes, relating the debates of the Athenian assembly in the winter of 415 BC, concerning the organization of a military expedition to Sicily:

> Everyone was excited about the venture. The old people hoped that we would conquer this land which we were to attack, or at least that a force as large [as the expeditionary Athenian corps] would be protected from accidents. As for the men old enough to fight, they hoped to travel around and to get to know this far-off country from which they also expected to return safe and sound. Most of the other people called to serve thought of the money they were about to earn and future conquests which would enable them to become steady employees of the State. The enthusiasm expressed by the majority was such that those who were

[29] Moses I. Finley, *Démocratie antique et démocratie moderne,* (Paris: Payot, 1976). By "political field" I mean the network of competitive relations for the conquest and exercise of political power. For further details, see my *Le cens caché,* op. cit.

against the undertaking, in their fears of being taken for bad patriots if they voted against it, did not show up.[30]

At dawn on the day set for the departure, almost the entire population of the city, both citizens and foreigners, went with them down to the port. The local people all had someone they were seeing off, a friend, a relative or a son. . . . At that moment . . . they weighed the risks of the venture better than they did at the time of the vote.[31]

And when news of the disaster reached Athens . . . the city and every one of its citizens were heavily affected. . . . what is more, it was evident that there were no more ships in the dockyard, not enough money in the treasury, not enough sailors to form crews. . . . they decided nonetheless . . . that they could not give up. They resolved to build a fleet . . . to introduce . . . certain reforms aimed at reducing public expenditures. . . . Once these resolutions were drawn up, they were carried out. . . . having procured some wood, they (the Athenians) began to build a fleet. . . . Still elsewhere, wherever they felt they were bearing unnecessary costs, they reduced their expenses to lighten the burden of the State.[32]

[30] Thucydides, *Histoire de la guerre entre les Péloponnésiens et les Athéniens,* (Paris: Gallimard), p. 1125, translation by Denis Roussel.

[31] Ibid., p. 1128.

[32] Ibid., pp. 1253-1256.

Chapter 15

THE AUTONOMY OF POLITICS: A LONGITUDINAL STUDY OF SELECTED PARLIAMENTARY CONSTITUENCIES IN GREAT BRITAIN, FRANCE, AND WEST GERMANY

William G. Andrews

One of the great preoccupations of political science is the exploration of relationships between politics and government and major aspects of their environment. Geography, occupational class, type of society, and ethnicity are among the factors that are studied as independent variables for the dependent variable of political behavior. Elections are obvious places to look for clues to those relationships. During democratic election campaigns and the voting that follows, those who govern and those who aspire to replace them communicate with the governed more fully, intensely, and concretely than at any other time in normal political life. That arena is scoured frenetically with survey research and close analysis of electoral demography to discover non political influences on political behavior. Also, much recent attention has been given by psephologists to the impact of the spread of television set ownership on election campaigning and voting.

This chapter offers a contribution to that continuing discussion. It reports on a series of longitudinal studies of election constituencies in three major European democracies that seem to have shown surprising resistance to non political influences on campaign and voter behavior. They suggest that politics may have greater autonomy than is often supposed. The principal field research was conducted on the parliamentary elections of 1964 and February 1974 in Basingstoke, England; of 1962 and 1973 in Evreux, France; and of 1965 and 1976 in Osnabrück, West Germany. Less extensive field research was conducted for parliamentary elections in Basingstoke in 1966 and Evreux in 1968, for referenda in Basinstoke in 1975 and Evreux in 1962, and for presidential elections in Evreux in 1965, 1969, and 1974.[1]

Each longitudinal study tests, in effect, one notable independent variable. The one for Basingstoke examines the impact of social change on electoral life. Between 1964 and 1974, that traditional Tory seat was virtually inundated by working class immigrants from London. The Evreux research scrutinizes the effects of relevant and major constitutional reform. Between 1962 and 1973, direct election of the national chief executive became part of the political system. The Osnabrück elections bracketed a reversal of national partisan coalitions with clear implications for the significance of the religious factor in political behavior. Finally, the number of television sets increased rapidly in all three districts during the period of study, providing a basis for assessing their impact on politics. Thus, social class, the nature of the regime, national coalition politics, and television ownership all were tested for electoral salience in this series of studies, and all were found wanting as explanations for political behavior.

THE DISTRICTS

The validity of those tests depends, of course, on a number of factors. High on that list is the representativeness of the districts. Whether these studies have much to say about politics in general

[1] Some of the results of that research were reported in my studies "Basingstoke," in David E. Butler and Anthony King, *The British General Elections of 1964,* Macmillan, London, 1965, pp. 254-265; "Social Changes and Electoral Politics in Britain: A Case Study of Basingstoke: 1964 and 1974," *Political Studies,* September 1974, pp. 334-346; "Evreux 1962: the Referendum and Election in a Norman Constituency," *Political Studies,* October 1963, pp. 308-326; "The West German Election Campaign in Osnabrück," in *European Political Institutions,* 2nd ed., Van Nostrand Co., New York, 1966, pp. 303-313. The 1962 study was supported by a Fulbright research fellowship; those of Basingstoke 1964 and 1966 and Evreux and Osnabrück 1965 by Tufts University; those of Evreux 1968, 1969, and 1973 by the State University College at Brockport; that of Basingstoke 1975 by the SUNY Research Foundation; those of Basingstoke and Evreux 1974 by the National Endowment for the Humanities; and that of Osnabrück 1976 by the German Academic Exchange Program. William Harper assisted me in Basingstoke 1964 and Franz D. Scholz in Osnabrück 1965. I am grateful for so much help.

results largely from whether these districts' many fellows can be expected to behave much as they did.

Like all constituency studies, this set has the strengths and weaknesses of the case approach. It sacrifice breadth for depth. In this instance, the cases are very small percentages of the whole. Basingstoke was one of 630 districts in 1964, one of 635 in 1974 (0.16 percent). Evreux was one of 490 (0.2 percent), and Osnabrück was one of 248 (0.4 percent). Nor are the studies claimed to be perfectly typical, any more than are any other example. Nevertheless, a good case can be made to show that they were as typical as any.

This was especially true of Evreux and Osnabrück. Evreux is the administrative capital and principal city of the Norman *département* of Eure, which one of its prefects described as a microcosm of the nation politically, economically, demographically, and socially. The evolution of its politics, economy, and demography have paralleled closely that of France as a whole. Osnabrück's status in West Germany was similar to that of Evreux in France it has been described by a sociological study as the most characteristic middle-sized West German city, and the middle-sized city was the most characteristic place of habitation in West Germany. Furthermore, like Evreux, it had enough small-town and rural population included in its constituency to give it that additional dimension of typicality. Like Evreux too, its political, economic, demographic, and religious history has flowed resolutely down the mainstream of its country's life.

The case for Basingstoke is not so clear. Given Britain's highly urbanized character and the dominance of London, the market center that was Basingstoke in 1964 could hardly be called typical. Moreover, its steadfast Conservatism denied it any claim to being a political barometer. However, like 81.1 percent of British constituencies in 1964 and 81.3 percent in 1974, Basingstoke was English. Also, its location in the southeast placed it in much the most populous region of the country. Even in population density it had become, by 1974, reasonably close to that of the country as a whole, outside Greater London, with 446.7 inhabitants per square mile. Thus, if Basingstoke was not so remarkably typical as Evreux and Osnabrück, it certainly lay well within the broad mainstream of British society.

Indeed, Basingstoke was less weathervane than harbinger. Through central planning, Basingstoke had become an overspill town, designed to accommodate part of London's excess population on Hampshire's hospitable slopes within commuting distance of the metropolis. Thus, Basingstoke was, in a sense, the planners' model of the typical constituency of the future.

THE QUESTIONS

Basingstoke and the Electoral Salience of Occupational Status

Basingstoke offered an especially attractive opportunity for a microcosmic study of the influence of occupational status on politics with the overspill program getting underway in 1964.[2] Through that, it received aid from the national government and the London local authorities for public housing and infrastructural facilities to attract workers and employers from rundown, overcrowded London. Also, the 1972 revisions of parliamentary constituency boundaries had a major effect on Basingstoke.

Basingstoke's new population differed significantly from the old in occupational characteristics. Factory employment increased as a result of the overspill program, bringing fifty manufacturing plants to the town. Also, the parts of the Hartley-Wintney Rural District that had been added to the constituency in 1972 were less agricultural than the Andover Borough and Rural District that had been severed. Industrial employment increased from one-third to one-half of the labor force, and the agricultural work force fell correspondingly. Also, office jobs became a major occupation in Basingstoke for the first time, and commuters to London increased from 600 to 2,500. No significant unemployment existed in either 1964 or 1974.

The anticipation of those changes led most political observers in 1964, in Basingstoke and outside, to expect the political character of the district to change substantially in a few years. It had a virtually unsullied Conservative record. Only once, fleetingly back

[2] I am grateful to David E. Butler of Nuffield College, Oxford, for having suggested Basingstoke to me.

in 1923, had it flirted with the Liberals. Since World War II, the Conservatives had averaged 55 percent of the vote in parliamentary elections. Moreover, that strength had shown remarkable stability. In the four elections, 1959-1970, Tory support had slipped only from 52.2 percent to 51.0 percent. The Conservative margin had averaged 14.6 percentage points since 1959 but was expected to be buried under the deluge of London workers.

Evreux and the Electoral Salience of Constitutional Change

The Evreux studies offer an interesting opportunity to observe the effects of major changes in the national governmental structure on parliamentary electoral politics. This is especially so because of the character of the constitutional reform that the French made in 1962. The French republic had been parliamentary since at least 1877. Even the 1958 constitution remained firmly parliamentary, despite the ways in which it had reduced the dependence of the executive on the legislative. This had been obscured somewhat by the changes that had been made, the rhetoric of the day, and de Gaulle's domineering presence in the presidency.[3]

Any doubts of the initial parliamentary character of the regime should have been removed by the overthrow of the Pompidou government in October 1962, the only successful motion of censure in the history of republican France. However, that was the dramatic stroke of a permanently crippled constitutional principle. It had been precipitated by the announced intention of the government to submit to popular referendum a proposed constitutional amendment to introduce direct election of the president.

Passage of that proposal ensured that the parliamentary elections would be overlaid and, perhaps, buried by presidential elections. Except in 1848, members of the legislature had been the only national public officers chosen by popular vote. Now, they were to share that noble distinction with the chief executive. In fact, it seemed unlikely that parliamentary elections could retain their viability in face of the crushing dominance of presi-

[3] For an elaboration of this point, see my *Presidential Government in Gaullist France*, SUNY Press, 1982, especially chapter 1.

dential elections. De Gaulle had carried all before him. He had transformed four successive referenda into plebiscites by threatening to resign if his will were defied. He had seemed to do the same with the parliamentary elections of 1958 and 1962, making them, in effect, votes of confidence in him. He had done all that without direct popular election and the power and legitimacy it seems to confer. Could not he and his successors now subvert parliamentary elections completely to presidential politics?

In Evreux of 1962, that outcome seemed highly likely. The 1962 parliamentary elections manifested some very presidentialist symptoms. The two principal candidates had been leading figures in presidential politics, one of de Gaulle's most conspicuous[4] ministers (Jean de Broglie) and his most prominent national opponent (Pierre Mendès-France). De Gaulle, his performance, and his policies had been the principal issues of the campaign. De Broglie had adopted as his main campaign slogan that the voters should be logical (consistent) with their votes in the referendum of the previous month. This implied clearly that the parliamentary elections should be aligned with the presidentialist referendum.

Both major candidates in Evreux 1962 had eschewed party labels. This seemed to be another portent of presidentialism. Conventional parties had dominated politics in the parliamentarist Fourth Republic but were seen as largely irrelevant to the presidential politics that were emerging in the Fifth Republic. The alacrity with which Evreux's major candidates shed their partisan images was an indication of the certainty with which they viewed the demise of traditional parliamentary politics as the regime shifted toward presidentialism. Both de Broglie and Mendès-France had been party candidates in recent parliamentary elections in Eure. De Broglie had drawn 18.9 percent of the vote when he had headed the Gaullist RPF ticket for all of Eure in 1951 and would have been elected except for an electoral law provision that discriminated against Gaullist and Communist candidates. His 38 percent won the Evreux seat in 1958 as the candidate of the conservative National Center of Independents (CNI, *Centre national des indépendants).* In between, he had given negative proof of the need for a party label by drawing only 9.1 percent of the vote in 1956 as an unaffiliated candidate. He

[4] As the head of the team that negotiated Algerian independence.

remained loyal to the CNI until it opposed de Gaulle on the constitutional reform issue.

Mendès France had been a Radical Socialist deputy from Eure 1932-1940 and 1946-1958 and one of its unsuccessful candidates in 1958. He had been a Radical Socialist prime minister in 1954-1955 and president of the national party, 1955-1957. Although he had been expelled by the Radical Socialists in 1959, he had joined the Unified Socialist Party (PSU, *Parti socialiste unifié)* soon thereafter. Despite their long commitment to partisanship, neither man used any party label or had any partisan nomination for the 1962 elections. This left the Communist, Roland Plaisance, as the only candidate to fly party colors.

The disaffection from parties in Evreux of 1962 weakened the parties' organizations, also. Although official membership figures were not disclosed, their aggregate total seems to have been no more than 400 in an electorate of 61,488, less than 0.7 percent. The Communists claimed 250, the PSU, 25, the SFIO *(Section française de l'international ouvrier,* the Socialists) 40 or 50, and the MRP *(Mouvement républicain populaire)* fewer than 30. The other major parties of the Fourth Republic (and of the national elections of 1958)–the Radical Socialists, the CNI, and even the Gaullists–were moribund in Evreux of 1962.

The principal issues discussed during the 1962 election campaign also reflected the intrusion of presidentialism. The main preoccupation of the candidates was to deal with the fear (which they seemed to believe was shared by most voters) that de Gaulle would resign from the presidency if the new parliament were not controlled by his supporters. The Gaullist de Broglie warned of that consequence. Mendès-France and Plaisance endeavored to allay those fears. De Gaulle himself spoke to this issue with a national radio-television address in which he threatened to resign if confronted by a hostile Assembly.

Beyond that specific presidentialist connection, the campaign rhetoric focused on a less palpable manifestation of presidentialism. In a situation unlike the conventional parliamentarism of the third and fourth republics, one person (the president) was perceived as having been responsible for the governance of the country since the previous parliamentary elections. Thus, the campaign turned largely on the pros and cons of the president's policies, much as in a presidential election.

All of the factors described above contributed to the impression in Evreux in 1962 that French politics were entering a new era. The decentralized parliamentarism of the Third and Fourth Republics seemed in the process of being obliterated by presidential politics with a central focus. Whether this was a temporary deviation or a permanent change could not, of course, be known at that time. Answers to that question were more evident by the 1973 elections, as will be seen below.

Osnabrück and the Electoral Salience of Coalition Politics

The Osnabrück studies shed some light on the relationship between coalition politics at the national level and voting and campaign behavior in the parliamentary constituencies. Moreover, because of the special character of coalition politics in postwar West Germany, they contribute to an understanding of the significance of religious identity for politics. The national governmental coalition before the 1965 elections always had been headed by the Christian Democratic Union (CDU). The opposition always had been led by the Social Democratic party (SPD). That was never the case between then and the 1976 elections. From 1966 until 1969, the CDU and SPD governed together in a Grand Coalition headed by the CDU. After 1969, the SPD headed the government coalition and the CDU the opposition.

Because of the significance of religious identity in German politics, that reversal of alliances had much more than nominal importance. During the Empire (1871-1918) and the Weimar Republic (1919-1933) the SPD was marxist, at least rhetorically. As late as 1948, the party expressed a lingering attachment to the old ideology by celebrating the centennial of the Communist Manifesto. The marxist program it had adopted in 1925 remained its official long-term policy statement until 1959. In contrast, the Christian democratic Center party of the Empire and Weimar was the quasi-official political arm of the Catholic church. Catholics voted for the atheistic and anti clerical SPD at the risk of excommunication. Not until 1961 did all the priests in the Osnabrück constituency abandon the practice of delivering political sermons on election Sunday and leading the faithful to the polls.

Both parties began to retreat from their antagonistic ideologies early in the Bonn republic. The 1952 death of Kurt Schumacher, the SPD's early postwar leader, released the party from his iron anti clerical grip, and the Bad Godesberg Program of 1959 scuttled its marxism, even its socialism. Meanwhile, the CDU had been founded as an ecumenical Christian party and had included Protestants in its leadership from the beginning. The break from Weimar was underlined by the insistence of some Center partisans on resurrecting that Catholic-bound organization. Its presence in Osnabrück was enough to cost the CDU its normal plurality in the 1951 state and 1952 local elections.

Religious conflict had a long tradition of political consequence in Osnabrück. The district straddles one of the historical boundaries between Catholic and Protestant Germany. The city itself was one of the two locations for the signature of the Treaty of Westphalia that ended the religious wars of the seventeenth century, and neighboring Munster was the other.

That legacy had continued to mark Osnabrück politics in the 1965 parliamentary elections. The CDU and SPD had abandoned their quarrel over the church, but the Free Democratic Party (FDP) had made its anti clericalism the main point in its campaign pitch. Moreover, religious identity had been the single best explanation for voting behavior. Comparison of first and second ballot results at the polling-station level showed clearly the tacit alliances of the traditional anti clericals (SPD, FDP, and the quasi Communist German Peace Union or DFU) against the similarly allied clericals (CDU and three minor parties).[5] More strikingly, a perfect correlation appeared between sectarian dominance at the commune level and partisan success. All of the forty-four communes with Catholic majorities gave pluralities to the CDU list, and all but two gave it majorities. All of the thirty-five communes with Protestant majorities gave majorties to the secular

[5] In the German electoral system, each voter may cast one ballot for a single-member district candidate and one for a list of a state party. Although most voters are consistent in their choices, enough of them vote for a hopeless district candidate and vote usefully for a state list to suggest affinities.

parties' lists.

This was not a by product of occupational status, for no such correlation emerged on that basis. The communes with majorities of the labor force in manufacturing split, thirty-four to twenty-nine, for the CDU and those with agricultural majorities did so, ten to five. The only commune with a majority of its labor force in the services voted by a majority for the secular parties.

Nor did religion fall out neatly geographically. Both Catholic and Protestant communes were found in all quadrants of the district. Finally, commune size was not the explanation. Communes over 2,000 population were CDU twelve to seven. Those under 2,000 were CDU thirty-two to twenty-eight. In short, religion was unquestionably the clearest indicator of voting behavior in Osnabrück 1965.

The big question for 1976, then, was whether the secularization of the national parties that had begun with the first stirrings of political revival in 1945 and had been consummated by the Grand Coalition in 1966 had affected campaigning and voting in parliamentary elections. Had the acceptance by the national CDU of the SPD as a respectable coalition partner undermined the obvious unwillingness of Osnabrück Catholics to vote for the SPD? Similarly, had the secularization of the CDU made it more attractive to significant numbers of non-Catholic voters? Was national coalition politics, cause and symptom of the decline of religious identity, a factor in campaign and voting behavior at the local level?

The Impact of Television on Parliamentary Election Campaigning

The intervals between the elections included in this study were periods of rapid growth in television ownership in all three countries. Observers expected that development to have a significant effect on campaign techniques and issues. The increased reliance by voters on television for electoral information and appeals was seen as likely to reduce their interest in traditional means of campaign communication.

The possession of television receivers increased most dramatically in France. It had only 73 sets per 1,000 population in 1962. By 1973, this proportion had zoomed to 238, a 226 percent increase. The corresponding figures for West Germany were 193 in 1965 and 311 in 1976, a 61 percent growth, and for the United Kingdom 243 in 1964 and 315 in 1974, a 30 percent increase. In France, 1962 was the first election in which television figured prominently. The same was true of West Germany in 1961 and Britain in 1955.

In all three countries, the first of the election campaigns under study here already reflected some effects from the wide use of television. Political leaders readily assumed that further changes would be substantial. In particular, they believed that television had reduced the significance of local campaigning in general and the use of local meetings especially. They expected that trend to continue and accelerate. Also, they thought that television had shifted emphasis in campaign rhetoric from local to national issues, as television was organized mainly on a nationwide basis with very little local or, except for Germany, regional programming. That trend, too, was projected forward. Comparison of the campaigns included in this study should indicate the extent to which those expectations were sound.

THE ANSWERS

On the Effects of Changes in Occupational Status

Despite the dramatic changes in the constituency, Basingstoke in February 1974 remained safely Conservative. The hopes and fears of 1964 had not been realized. Neither overspill nor the boundary commission had moved Basingstoke into Labour's camp. (Incidentally, this was still true in the 1979 elections.) Basingstoke of February 1974 re-elected for the third time the Tory, David Mitchell, whom it had sent to the House of Commons for the first time in 1964. His margin was 10.9 percentage points, down from 14.9 in 1964 and 13.7 in 1970, but up from 6.4 in 1966. So modest and inconsistent a change was hardly what had been expected in 1964.

Moreover, even that slight erosion could not be attributed to the change in occupational composition within the original constituency. It came partly from the nationwide resurgence of the Liberals as reflected in Basingstoke. Their Basingstoke vote was 8.3 percentage points higher than in 1964. If half of that amount had come from the Conservatives, it deprived them of a 47.3 percent result. The other main cause of the Conservative decline seems to have been the boundary changes. This shift from Andover to Hartley Wintney seems to have accounted for another 2.3 percentage points. The restoration of that amount would have raised the Tory share to 49.6 percent, 0.3 percentage points above 1964. Thus, overspill had not had any perceptible effect on voting behavior in Basingstoke.[6]

Several factors may help to explain Basingstoke's intractability. First, the 1964 expectations may have been based on unrealistic perceptions of the prospective overspill immigrants. Because they would be coming from Labour-dominated London and would be employed mainly in manufacturing, a Labour-dominated industry, they were expected to be heavily Labour in their politics. However, the immigrants may have been atypical of London workers. For one thing, they were employed in modern, light industry, where Labour is much less powerful than in older, heavy manufacturing. Secondly, they were volunteers leaving London for better housing, better schools, and a better environment in general. In short, they were upwardly mobile and that attitude might have taken political form in Conservative voting. Third, there may have been a certain chameleon effect, some of the immigrants adapting to their environment by changing from Labour red to Tory blue on the Hampshire landscape. Finally, some of the apparent loss of Labour supporters may have had more specific causes. Labour's opposition to the sale of public housing units to their tenants was especially unpopular among the overspillers. Also, David Mitchell's long incumbency and assiduous attention to constituent errands may have helped him among the uprooted Londoners.

6 Details of these calculations appeared in my "Social Changes and Electoral Politics in Britain," op. cit.

Whatever the explanation or explanations, the Basingstoke experience suggests that social class composition may be too crude a concept to explain voting behavior satisfactorily and that it may not be able to override more specific and more political factors. Certainly, it had little predictive value in Basingstoke of 1964.

The Effects of Constitutional Change

Like Basingstoke, Evreux's parliamentary electoral politics changed remarkably little in the period under review. Indeed, some of the most apparent changes were the reverse of those that had been expected to result from the introduction of direct election of the president of the republic. Constitutional reform - even as drastic as a shift from parliamentarism to presidentialism–had had very little effect on the way campaigners and voters behaved in a parliamentary constituency such as Evreux.

Perhaps the most striking and unexpected change was the dramatic resurgence of the political party organizations. The traditional parties that had dominated politics during the third and Fourth Republics bounced back vigorously from their near-eclipse in the 1958 and 1962 elections. The number of major candidates bearing national party labels rose from one of three to all four. Non partisan Mendès-France was replaced by a Socialist. A centrist entered the lists under the banner of the Democratic Center. Even de Broglie had abandoned his haughty independence for the endorsement of Valéry Giscard d'Estaing's Independent Republicans, of which he was one of three national vice presidents. Of course, the Communist still flaunted his partisanship.

The Socialist, Independent Republican, and centrist parties were better organized than in 1962, though the Radicals and Communists had slipped a bit. None of the new political organisms that had been spawned by the drastic constitutional changes of 1958 and 1962 seemed to be making perceptible inroads on the turf of the partisan artifacts of parliamentarism. The aggregate membership of political parties had more than doubled to between eight and nine hundred, not counting several hundred members of the Perspectives and Réalités Club that de Broglie had organized after 1962. This was not large for an electorate of 72,000 but it represented a significant advance over 1962 in a direction opposite from the one that had been expected.

Other signs of the renewed vitality of parliamentary partisan politics in Evreux in 1973 were the greater number of nominations and the increased vigor with which they were contested. The fall in the number of candidates from eight in 1958 to three in 1962 had been seen as presaging the demise of the Fourth Republic style of parliamentary electoral politics. The rise, then, from three to five in 1967 and 1968 and to eight in 1973 must be interpreted as having the opposite significance. The 1962 nominations all had been uncontested. In 1973, the Socialist and centrist nominations were contested, de Broglie's claim to be the sole Gaullist candidate was challenged, and the Communists avoided a fight only through a last-minute maneuver. In any case, the increase in the amount and intensity of the rivalries indicated clearly that the rise of presidentialism was not suppressing life in the parliamentary electoral arena.

The 1973 campaign provided further evidence that parliamentary electoral politics were continuing to flourish. For one thing, the 1973 elections were preceded by a much longer pre campaign than those of 1962, about nine months rather than one. Furthermore, the 1973 activities were significantly more intense than those of 1962. The public candidates' meetings that had seemed to be dying out from 1958 to 1969 revived. More than twice as many were held in 1973, 666 compared to 288 in 1962. Attendance was similar in size, except that the two largest meetings of 1962 could not be replicated in 1973 because the only large hall in the district had burned in the interim. Some new campaign devices were introduced after 1962 (factory gate and market visits, press conference luncheons, campaign movies), and none of the old had disappeared. Furthermore, such traditional devices as brochures, posters, and campaign newspapers were used to about the same extent as in 1962.

Presidentialism produced little change in campaign rhetoric. The most widely discussed issue in 1973 was the Common Program that the Communists and Socialists had signed the previous year. Otherwise, the campaign topics were hardly distinguishable from the bread-and-butter, parish-pump politics of the

Third and Fourth Republics. Scarcely a word was said about foreign affairs, defense policies, or constitutional issues. President Pompidou was mentioned only once inconspicuously, in print and de Gaulle was completely absent. No national leaders campaigned in the district. The only intrusions of national campaigning were the formula broadcasts on the state radio-television network, which drew only cursory notice, and two issues of national party posters. The denationalization was dramatic since 1962, when the campaigns of all three candidates had turned mainly on national issues.

The 1973 election results in Evreux underlined the renascence of traditional parliamentary electoral politics. All of the political movements that were legacies of the Fourth Republic gained at the expense of all of the Fifth Republic newcomers. De Broglie and the candidates of the New Left declined. The centrists, Socialists, and Communists gained. Presidentialism had little apparent impact on voting behavior.

The Evreux experience confirmed that of Basingstoke. Major constitutional change had had no more impact on parliamentary electoral politics than had had major occupational change. The dramatic events of 1958-1962 had not destroyed the politics of the Fourth Republic. They had merely submerged it, and it had reemerged in the circumstances of the early 1970s when political life was more routine than during the Algerian crisis but when, also, presidentalism had become more securely anchored in the political system.

The Effects of Coalition Change

The autonomy of electoral politics and behavior that seemed so evident in Basingstoke and Evreux appeared in Osnabrück also. The reversal of national governmental coalitions did not have the expected effect of reducing significantly the electoral salience of religious identification. The correlations between Catholicism and the CDU and between Protestantism and the secular parties remained virtually as high as before the respectability of the SPD had been enhanced through membership in the Grand Coalition, 1966-1969, and possession of the chancellorship, 1969-1976.

Those correlations survived despite the reinforcement of the effects of national coalition politics by the SPD's rejection of anti clericalism, Vatican II, and a decline in church attendance in the constituency.

One manifestation of those correlations was the survival in 1976 of campaign issues of religious significance, though they were more muted than in 1965. The FDP published an anti clerical tract in 1976 but did not make that position the central argument of its campaign, as it had in 1965. Other leading issues in 1976 had religious implications, though these were rarely made explicit. They included legalization of abortions, liberalization of divorce legislation, and allegations that the national government was encouraging school teachers to indoctrinate children in atheistic marxism. A staff vote to forbid abortions in an Osnabrück hospital gave that issue specific local salience. That action was condemned by the secular parties and applauded by the CDU. An SPD round-table discussion on what is Christian in socialism and what is socialist in Christianity seemed designed to reduce religious barriers in politics; also, the SPD campaigned more in solidly Catholic villages. However, no party raised any issue specifically intended to broaden its appeal in the religious stronghold of its rivals.

Other evidence of religious influence came from voting patterns. Revision of communal boundaries after 1965 prevents direct comparison across the board. However, the new communes were nearly as likely as their predecessors to cleave along religious lines. Of the forty-one Catholic communes in 1976, all but one gave majorities to the CDU on the second ballot. The exception had been the most marginal CDU commune in 1965. Of the thirty Protestant communes, twenty-seven cast majorities of their second ballots for the secular parties. Looking at pluralities, the perfect correlation of 1965 had been eroded, but it remained 94.4 percent pure. Looking at majorities, the percentages fell from 97.5 to 94.4. Certainly, that softening was much less than had been expected in 1965, even before the formation of the Grand Coalition had been ensured.

A more notable effect of the change in national coalition politics was observable in the local party organizations. The fall from power by the national CDU because of the switch by the FDP shocked it deeply. Emulating the British Conservative party after its 1945 defeat, the CDU turned from the high affairs of state to the low affairs of party. It set about with determination to strengthen its organization.

The results of that effort were especially evident in Osnabrück. Perhaps the determination to rebuild had extra bite in Osnabrück because in 1972 the CDU had lost the seat to the SPD for the first time. In any case, its renewal began in 1969 and accelerated with the appointment of a bright young man as party agent in 1972. Under his direction, the party acquired new, larger quarters and clubrooms for its youth and women's auxiliaries. It tripled the number of its regular and campaign employees from five to fifteen. Finally, it set up an ultramodern printing plant. Those efforts had produced gratifying results. Its membership tripled (to 3,700) and it formed auxiliaries with another 1,880 members.

The Osnabrück SPD followed a somewhat similar course after 1969. It determined to hold the seat it had won in 1972 and strengthened its organization. By 1976, it, too, had larger quarters, better equipment, a larger staff, and more members than in 1965. However, it fell well short of the CDU organizationally.

On the other hand, the Osnabrück FDP suffered greatly from the coalition switch. It split in two between those who favored the old alliance with the CDU and those who preferred the new SPD partners. As a result, it had lost half its members and was barely functioning as an organization by 1976.

On the Effects of Television

The growth of ownership of television sets had nowhere near the dampening effect on local campaigning in parliamentary elections that had been expected in all three constituencies in the first half of the 1960s. The only decline occurred in Basingstoke. Both in Evreux and in Osnabrück, the amount of campaign activity increased during the period under study.

In fact, Basingstoke's decline had occurred already in 1966. Between 1966 and February 1974, the amount of campaign activity actually increased, although it remained below that of 1964. The coverage of canvassing fell from an average of about 40 percent per party to about 35 percent. The number of public meetings by all parties fell dramatically to less than one third of the 1964 figure (from 156 to 43), and attendance at them dropped by one third (3,775 to 2,512). Similar amounts of printed material were used in the two campaigns, although a total of about 1,400 pounds was spent on them in 1964 and 2,900 pounds in 1974.

Some evidence suggests that, in the case of Basingstoke, the decrease in amount of campaign activity was not connected to the spread of televison. For one thing, the difference may have resulted from the timing of the elections. Those of 1964 came at the latest possible moment in the term of the parliament. The parties, candidates, and voters had expected them for many months and were all prepared for them. Meetings could be organized with a minimum of additional effort and voters were well conditioned to turn out for them. Also, among the three countries, Britain had the least change in the saturation of television coverage between elections. The rate of increase there was one-seventh that in France and one-half that in West Germany.

Surely, then, if the spread of television viewing should drive out local campaign activities, Evreux and Osnabrück would have been struck more deeply than Basingstoke. In fact, the contrary was true. The case of Evreux was discussed above in showing the tenacity of traditional parliamentary electoral politics and increase in volume of campaign activities. The change was even greater in Osnabrück. Every sort of activity of 1965 reappeared in 1976 with more intensity and extensiveness, and new types appeared. Twice as many public meetings were held (from 83 to 211), although total attendance declined slightly (from 31,550 to 30,000). The number of posters increased from 14,300 to 18,700 and brochures and handbills from 450,000 to 1,776,000. The total expenditures of the major parties were 77,000-95,000 DM in 1965 and 130,000 DM in 1976. On the other hand, local newspaper coverage was much less in 1976 than in 1965.

In any case, the least that can be said is that television did not wipe out local campaigning–or even come close to doing so–in the twelve years under review. Local campaigning slipped a bit in Basingstoke after 1964, but not after 1966. In Evreux and Osnabrück, campaigning actually became more active and vigorous through the rise of television.

CONCLUSIONS

Comparison of the longitudinal studies of Evreux, Basingstoke, and Osnabrück suggests a phenomenon that might be called the autonomy of politics. Campaign politics and voting behavior seem to change relatively little in response to non political change. They seem more responsive to direct political stimuli. Furthermore, the more directly the connection is organizational, the more substantial is the response.

There seems to be a sort of cake mixer effect. The closer the batter is to the beater, the faster it moves. The closer the campaigners or the voters are to the organizational stimulant, the faster they change. Furthermore, the greater the mass, the slower it gets moving. Campaign organizations change much faster than constituencies.

The greatest change observed in these studies occurred in the campaign organizations in Osnabrück. The CDU organization in Osnabrück changed in response to instructions from the national party. Those instructions were prompted by the fall from office of the national party. The SPD and FDP in Osnabrück responded both to the Osnabrück CDU and to their own national parties. All of this turned within the closed circle of partisan politics. It had nothing to do with changes in society, in religious observance, in constitutions, or even in voting behavior. On the other hand, the religious patchwork quilt continued to blanket Osnabrück voting patterns, despite social and political changes that had seemed likely to erode the religious connection to politics. The religious cleavage in Osnabrück politics remained nearly 95 percent complete at the village level.

The least change occurred in the campaigning or partisan voting behavior in Basingstoke. Yet Basingstoke had undergone the greatest amount of social change. Contrary to expectations, with a sort of chameleon effect, the thousands of workers from Labour's London seemed to produce as high a percentage of conservative votes as did the natives.

Little change, also, occurred in the campaigning or voting behavior in Evreux, despite fundamental constitutional changes. Campaigning and voting in 1973 was remarkably similar to that of 1962. Presidential politics became simply an overlay without penetrating the parliamentary electoral layer effectively.

Technological change had relatively limited impact. Television became an important medium for national campaigns. Yet, it simply overlay more traditional activities. Their vitiation–which had been so widely anticipated in the early 1960s–failed to occur. Local campaigns were at least as active in 1973-1976 as in 1962-1965, despite the spread of television, which was unavailable to them.

These studies suggest new difficulties in predicting political change. The correlations discovered so often between political behavior and certain environmental characteristics are not so easily translated into explanations of change. Furthermore, the changes seem to have the greatest effect within the closed circle of politics. Perhaps because political science is such a crossroads discipline, this is not always perceived. Political scientists who take sociological, geographic, legal, economic, or psychological approaches look for corresponding explanations. Perhaps it may be in order occasionally to remind ourselves that politics may also be explained politically.

Chapter 16

LABOR UNIONS IN THEIR SOCIAL AND POLITICAL ENVIRONMENTS: BRITAIN, WEST GERMANY, AND THE UNITED STATES

Wolfgang Hirsch-Weber

This chapter compares trade unions in the United Kingdom, the Federal Republic of Germany, and the United States in order to show how and why they differ and and what they have in common, to better explain each of the three labor movements. Space being limited, the inquiry focuses on why workers join or do not join a union, how they structure their organizations, and why they strike. It concentrates on the influence social and political environments have on union membership and structure and looks into the relationship between membership, structure, and strike behavior. The economic motives of union activities are not investigated, and the union's political activities are examined only in passing. Their history, however, will have to be examined, as present patterns can be understood only if past events are taken into account. Because comparative research on labor unions is a new field, many of the statements that follow should be regarded as hypotheses in dire need of empirical corroboration.[1]

[1] For a comparison of British and U.S. unions see Andreas Villiger, *Aufbau und Verfassung der Britischen und Amerikanischen Gewerkschaften: Wachstum und Strukturentwicklung der Gewerkschaftsbewegung, Probleme der Innerverbandlichen Demokratie,* (Berlin: Duncke und Humboldt, 1966). Klaus von Beyme analyses union structures in Western countries in *Gewerkschaften und Arbeitsbeziehungen in Kapitalistischen Landern,* (München and Zürich: Piper Verlag, 1977), English translation (London and Beverly Hills: Sage, 1980). Eric Owen-Smith has edited a comparative volume on unions in Australia, France, Japan, Sweden, the United Kingdom, the United States, and the Federal Republic: *Trade Unions in the Developed Economies,* (London: Croom Helm, 1981). I have compared German and U.S. unions in "Trade Unions and Gewerkschaften," in *Public Seminar Course in Comparative Government,* (Berlin: Colloquium Verlag, 1965). Wilfred Brown and I have discussed differences between the British and German labor movements in: *Bismarck to Bullock. Conversations about*

MEMBERS

In 1979, the British unions had 13,498,000 members, composing 51 percent of the total working population and 55 percent of the employed labor force.[2] Their number had risen dramatically since 1968, when no more than 10 million persons, or 38.9 percent, of the working population were organized. Before that the degree of organization had stagnated for over two decades: in 1946 it had already reached 39.6 percent.[3]

The German unions, in 1979, reached a strength of 9,411,602 equivalent to 34.6 percent of the working population and 42.1 percent of the employed.[4] They too went through a period of growth after almost two decades of stagnation, but it was not as spectacular as was the case in the United Kingdom. In 1968, their membership stood at 7,621,000, or 28.5 percent of the working population–exactly the same proportion as in 1952.

The trend in the United States was quite different. Since the mid-fifties, unionism has been exhibiting a steady decline. To be sure, the number of members has grown from 17,749,000 in 1955 and 20,752,000 in 1970 to 21,784,000 in 1978, but union density decreased from 24.4 percent to 22.6 percent and then to 19.7 percent of the total labor force.[5] The U.S. economy has a significant rural sector. Therefore, union membership as a percentage

institutions in politics and industry in Britain and Germany, (London: Anglo-German Foundation, 1983).

[2] Central Statistical Office, *Annual Abstract of Statistics: 1982 Edition* (no. 118), (London: HM Stationery Office, 1982), pp. 150 and 185. Later British data than for 1979 were not available at the time of writing. The latest official U.S. statistics were those for 1978.

[3] All figures for Britain and Germany for years earlier than 1970 were supplied to the author by Winfried Pfenning of Zentralarchiv fur Empirische Sozialforschung, Universität Köln.

[4] Statistisches Bundesamt, *Statistisches Jahrbuch 1980 fur die Bundesrepublik Deutschland,* (Stuttgart and Mainz: Kohlhammer, 1980), p. 93. Institut der Deutschen Wirtschaft, *Zahlen zur Wirtschaftlichen Entwicklung der Bundesrepublik Deutschland Ausgabe 1980,* (Köln: Deutscher Institutsverlag, 1980), table 84. The British and German categories of "working population," "employed labor force," "*Erwerbspersonen,*" and "*Abhängige Erwerbstatige*" do not correspond exactly to one another or to the U.S. "total labor force." However, rough comparison of the figures is possible.

[5] U.S. Department of Commerce, *Statistical Abstract of the United States: 1980,* (Washington, D.C., Government Printing Office, 1980), p. 429.

of nonagricultural employees should also be considered. In the years under consideration, these figures were 33.2 percent, 27.5 percent, and 23.6 percent, respectively.

According to an old maxim, unions grow in times of prosperity, rising real wages, and full employment, but decline in periods of economic recession. Whether or not short business cycles did in fact affect union membership during the period under consideration cannot be investigated here.[6] Long economic cycles apparently had no discernible effects. It would also require further investigation to determine whether or not labor's share of the national income was related to rate of union participation in one way or another. In Britain income from employment amounted to 73 percent of the national income in 1960, 77 percent in 1970, and 82 percent in 1980. In Germany the corresponding figures were 60 percent, 68 percent, and 72 percent, and in the United States 71 percent, 76 percent, and 75 percent.[7] These figures do not, of course, correspond directly to trends in the relative size of real wages and profits. Furthermore, methods of calculating them differ so greatly from country to country that it is left to the reader to speculate as to a possible relationship between changes in income distribution and rate of union participation.

The "economic miracle" of the fifties and the early sixties brought German workers an unprecedented rise in living standards, but their propensity to organize increased only when the sailing got rougher, in the late sixties and in the seventies. Real wages continued to improve, it is true. Between 1970 and 1979 the index of hourly wages in industry rose from 63 to 126.9 (1975 = 100), consumer prices only from 74.2 to 115.6.[8] Employment

[6] The considerable rise in the membership of British unions in 1969 and 1970, for instance, is attributed to a "wages explosion." Hugh Armstrong Clegg, *The Changing System of Industrial Relations in Great Britain*, (Oxford: Blackwell, 1980), p. 177. The United States, in the second half of the sixties, saw a fall in the unemployment rate and a slight rise in union strength. U.S. Department of Commerce, op. cit., p. 429, and Institut der Deutschen Wirtschaft, op. cit., 1981, table 77. Before the welfare state brought unemployment insurance, etc., the impact of short cycles on membership was probably greater than it is now.

[7] Calculated from data in Central Statistical Office, op. cit., 1971 and 1982, p. 283 and pp. 345f.; Statistisches Bundesamt, op. cit., 1981, p. 528; and U.S. Department of Commerce, op. cit., 1981, pp. 424f.

[8] Sachverstandigenrat zur Begutachtung der gesamtwirtschaftlichen Entwicklung,

declined, however. During the sixties, in most years unemployment had remained well below 1 percent, while during the second half of the seventies rates of 4 percent and more were registered.[9]

The gains of British unions in the seventies were even more surprising, taking place while real wages stagnated and many workers lost their jobs. Between 1970 and 1979, the index of hourly wages in industry rose from 47 to 168.4, that of consumer prices from 54.2 to 165.8. Unemployment increased from 2.5 percent to 3.8 percent in 1975 and to over 5.2 percent thereafter.

It was not an economic boom but rather a change in the composition of membership that accompanied growth in the United Kingdom. For decades, the proportion of white-collar workers in the work force had been rising. The tendency of white-collar workers to organize, however, had been low. In the seventies it rose steeply. The same phenomenon can be observed in the Federal Republic. Its cause may be that with their numbers growing, non-manual workers lost status. In the United States, rate of union participation among white-collar workers has increased slightly in the private and significantly in the public sector (above all, among teachers). Since the criteria that define blue- and white-collar workers and civil servants differ in the three countries, it is difficult to compare density according to occupation. Nonetheless, it can be stated that in Britain and Germany the rate increased in all occupations but most of all among white-collar workers, while in the United States the rise among private employees and public servants was accompanied by a decline among manual workers. In all three countries, females too, became less reluctant to join a union.

How to explain the differences among the three countries? Scope and intensity of industrial disputes, union structure, labor legislation, and the social and political environment should all be taken into account.

One would assume that the broader the scope of collective agreements and the greater the intensity of industrial disputes, the stronger the motivation to join a union would be. No Western state has regularized and institutionalized industrial relations to a

Investieren fur Mehr Beschäftigung: Jahresgutachten 1981/82, (Stuttgart and Mainz: Kohlhammer, 1981), pp. 244f.

[9] Institut der Deutschen Wirtschaft, op. cit., 1979 and 1981, tables 76 and 77.

higher degree than the Federal Republic. In that nation, many matters that in Britain and the United States are objects of collective bargaining are governed by statute, must be discussed between management and works councils (which do not represent a union), and might ultimately be settled in labor courts. Also, the number and duration of strikes are much lower than in the United Kingdom and the United States. It is thus to be expected that rate of union participation, too, would be the lowest. In fact it is lower than in Britain. But why is it so much higher than in the United States?

Closed and union shop provisions help to draw members into British and U.S. unions. But to say that "the union shop, and other forms of compulsion, are very important to the strength and stability of labor unions"[10] would be to exaggerate. In Britain, in 1964 it was estimated that "about two trade union members out of five had no choice but to belong to a trade union if they wanted to keep their jobs."[11] Less than two-thirds of the organized U.S. workers have signed union shop contracts (the closed shop is outlawed by the Taft-Hartley Act). There is no compulsory membership in the Federal Republic. Closed and union shops are considered to violate the constitutional provision for freedom of association. Thus, Olson's statement "that large, national labor unions with the strength and durability of those that now exist in [the United States] could [not] exist without some kind of compulsory membership, is worse than parochial.[12] It misconstrues even the U.S. data. The real question is why in the United States, the union shop notwithstanding, the unions are so much weaker and density so much lower than in European countries with or without compulsory membership.

Are U.S. unions inefficient in serving the interests of their members? They have been less successful than British and German unions in obtaining desired social policies and legislation. But a person seldom joins a union for its lobbying activities. They are quite proficient in their dealings with employers. They

[10] Mancur Olson Jr., *The Logic of Collective Action: Public Goods and the Theory of Groups*, (Cambridge, Mass.: Harvard University Press, 1971), p. 87.

[11] Clegg, op. cit., p. 25.

[12] Olson, op. cit. See also p. 137: "...compulsion is essential to a stable labor movement of any size." Olson's statements on unions are meant to support his widely acclaimed general theory of groups.

bargain hard and skillfully for higher wages, job security, and better working conditions. Several unions have secured privileges for their members that put them far above the workers in unorganized branches of industry. Wages have in some instances risen so greatly that industries have been priced out of international competition. (This has, of course, happened in Germany, too.) Thus, it is not lack of bargaining prowess that explains the relative weakness of U.S. unionism.

One answer to our question might be found in social structures, mores, and creeds. Even before World War I, U.S. unions had lagged far behind those in Britain and Germany. In 1910, their membership amounted to 8.4 percent of nonagricultural employment.[13] In Britain as far back as 1892, and in Germany in 1906, more than 10 percent of the total working population (figures for nonagricultural employment alone are not available) had joined a union. Immediately after the war, in 1920, rate of union participation reached 43.4 percent in the United Kingdom, 40.3 percent in the Reich, and only 16.3 percent in the United States. During the twenties, unions everywhere lost many members, but nowhere as many as in the United States. In Britain, up to 1930, rate of participation declined to 23.2 percent, and in Germany to 27.8 percent of total working population, but in the United States it fell to to 8.8 percent of nonagricultural employees.

The British and German labor movements emerged at a time when "feudal" traditions were still strong. Ranking was determined more by birth than by wealth or occupation. Social distances appeared immense; mobility was quite limited. Workers' material condition was miserable; their and the peasants' status were lowest. Since social rank implied moral evaluation, workers' human dignity suffered. By the 1830s "class" was already a widely used term at all levels of British society, and many workers were conscious of being involved in a class struggle. They believed in the rights of free born Englishmen, and they organized. For more than a century and a half, their unions–and their political organizations–fought for better wages, humane working conditions, and a decent place in society. They were highly successful,

[13] See detailed statistics for the United States in Andrew W. J. Thomson, "The United States of America," in: Owen-Smith, op. cit., p. 163.

but British society has not ceased to be deeply divided by interest, class, and status. Even to the present day, for many workers joining a union goes beyond self-interest; it is the thing for members of their class to do. And recently, among white-collar workers as well, an awareness of group if not of class interests seems to lead to association.

Until World War I, the "inherent" social inferiority of the German worker was aggravated by his being a second-class citizens in a semiabsolutist state. From the 1860s socialist unions emerged side by side with the Socialist party. Although it is true that the unions worked for gradual reforms adapted to the existing society, many of their members, including members of some "neutral" unions, professed the party's belief that real emancipation of the working class would come only with the Revolution. For them, belonging to a union meant striving not only for higher wages, but also for a new society. The much smaller Christian (i.e., Catholic) unions did not speak of class struggle; nevertheless, they fought and struck in industrial conflicts.

The fall of the Kaiser and of aristocracy, two lost wars, two periods of inflation, far-reaching social legislation, and, ironically, Nazi imposed *Volksgemeinschaft* have leveled German society to no small degree. Today, social distances are not as great, class antagonisms not as deeply felt as in British mines, docks, and industries. Does this perhaps explain in part why, after 1945, union membership in Germany never again quite reached the British level?

U.S. society has never been "feudal", it has always been inimical to status Germany has never been more egalitarian, more "capitalist" than European societies. The United States' enormous differences in wealth and income did not lead to correspondingly greater social distances. Occupation was hardly a criterion of status. Birth was, but birth into an ethnic group as much as birth into a class. Where race beyond class determines life chances, one should not expect to find a broad class-conscious labor movement. Certainly, well into the twentieth century white workers, like others, received miserable wages, had to work sixty to eighty-four hours a week, were constantly exposed to unemployment, did not enjoy social security, and were denied basic human rights. And even then, socialist unions could not establish themselves permanently. They ran against the grain of the U.S. ideology that theirs was a land of equal opportunities for all and a classless society in which every worker could rise by his own efforts. The U.S. creed of laissez faire and rugged individualism inspired employers to fight unions with no holds barred. And that creed was readily embraced by workers who had emigrated from the class- and status-ridden Old World or whose ancestors had. The unions that survived, those in the American Federation of Labor, glorified self-interest. They believed in the solidarity of the U.S. workers, even of the "workers of the world," and they often acted on this principle. But they were an interest group rather than part of a social movement.[14] With the emergence of the Congress of Industrial Organizations, common-interest orientation became stronger, but those in the unions who wanted to change the structures of society fundamentally remained few.

Opportunities have become fewer and class structures more visible since the turn of the century, but mobility still is considerable, and living standards are now high. Thus, the U.S. ideology has not waned, an ideology that scarcely inspires a person to join a union, even one organized around a particular interest.

Social structures and beliefs may explain century-long trends, but they do not give the whole story. Changes in political climate, in law, and in the courts and government brought with them great changes in rate of union participation. The influence of statutes, and their interpretation by judges, can be studied in the United Kingdom from the combination acts of 1799-1800 (forbidding organization) and their repeal in 1824 over the Trade Union Act of 1871 (conferring legal status) to the Taff-Vale decision (on financial liability for strikes) and the subsequent 1906 Trades Disputes Act (freeing the unions from such liability). The impact of war permitted union membership to double between 1914 and 1920. The government, wishing to win over labor for the war effort, collaborated with the unions and encouraged affiliation. The political temper of the people as well as the militancy of the

[14] Wolfgang Hirsch-Weber, "Die Gewerkschaften: Interessengruppe oder Soziale Bewegung?" in *Gewerkschaft-Wirtschaft-Gesellschaft: Beitrage zu wirtschaftlichen und sozialen Gegenwartsfragen,* Herausgegeben und bearbeitet von Kurt Nemitz und Richard Becker, (Köln: Bundverlag, 1963).

unions rose, and socialist and syndicalist tendencies gained ground. When the political mood changed, when a general strike failed and the Trades Disputes Act of 1927 curtailed union power, almost all members won were subsequently lost. It took circumstances similar to those of World War I for the unions to recover. Since the late forties, however, changing legislation and government policies pertaining to unions and collective bargaining seem not to have had a significant impact on the rate of participation.[15]

The first German unions were founded during the revolution of 1848-1849, only to be prohibited after the victory of the reactionary forces. When the ban was lifted in the 1860s, new unions came to life. With the passage of Bismarck's antisocialist laws, unions close to the party were ostracized. From 1890 onward, they could act freely. This freedom had its limits, of course. Employers fought the unions–all of them–and blacklisted organizers. Government was on the employers' side. If necessary, the police and army were used in support of strike-breakers. For all that, in 1913 the unions counted 4.5 million members (15 percent of the working population). As elsewhere, the war made the government come to terms with the unions. The revolutionary mood of the postwar period brought membership up to 13.3 million. It fell to 8.3 million after the inflation had ended and the worst political tensions had temporarily abated. Rate of participation now remained at almost twice its prewar level, until the Nazis put an end to the unions. Partly in reaction to Nazi persecution, the Fundamental Law of the Federal Republic grants almost absolute freedom of association.

Repression of workers' associations was more vicious in the United States than in Imperial Germany. By the use of blacklists, yellow dog contracts, labor espionage, and company police, many incipient unions were destroyed. Strikes were crushed. Often, they resulted in violence and bloodshed. State and federal governments assisted the employers with troops; the judiciary assisted them with injunctions. A certain respite came under President Wilson, during whose term some social legislation was

[15] For a detailed description of recent changes in state intervention see Clegg, op. cit., pp. 289 f., and Eric Owen-Smith, "The United Kingdom," in: Owen-Smith, op. cit., pp. 125 f.

passed. When the United States entered World War I, the unions' collaboration was welcome. Affiliation was supported in industries controlled by the government. On the other hand, socialist and anarchist groups who opposed the war were mercilessly crushed. Soon, the red scare also helped finish off some trade unions. Nevertheless, total union membership almost doubled between 1916 and 1920. In the ensuing era of "big business," employers, government, and courts united afresh in fighting strikers in particular and unions in general. Membership dropped sharply.

It took the Great Depression to shake the belief in the U.S. creed and the New Deal to bring about an upsurge in affiliation. Between 1933 and 1939 the number of union members grew from 2.9 to 9 million. This spectacular progress probably had something to do with economic recovery. But mainly it was due to a new social and political atmosphere and specific legislation. Already in 1932, the Norris-La Guardia Act had outlawed the yellow dog contract. Under Roosevelt, the National Industrial Recovery Act, the Wagner Act, and the creation of the National Labor Relations Board protected unions and promoted collective bargaining. Further advances were made during the war, when both the government and the employers collaborated with labor in an effort to raise production. In 1945, union membership reached 14.8 million, with rate of participation in nonagricultural employment 35.8 percent, the highest ever in the United States.

The stagnation that followed, and later the decline, can be attributed to various causes.[16] As industries moved from the Northeast to the South, from urban to rural areas, and as the share of women and white-collar workers increased, it became more difficult to recruit members. However, the tendency to organize began to improve among white-collar workers and women, while it declined among blue-collar workers in manufacturing. (In Britain and Germany it rose in all sectors.) So other factors must be sought. Employers once again strove to hinder their personnel from joining a union, not in the old rude ways but sometimes by questionable methods (unthinkable nowadays in the United Kingdom and the Federal Republic). Since the abolition of the closed shop by the Taft-Hartley Act, in 1947, many states

[16] For a discussion of some see Thomson, op. cit., pp. 161f.

have passed "right-to-work" laws that did away with the union shop as well.[17] No postwar government, no majority in Congress has been as friendly towards labor as those of the New Deal had been. The unions have lost public support, partly in conjunction with a general trend toward conservatism and partly because several unions have been shown to be corrupt. Racketeering and even murder in some cases have severely damaged the unions' image.

STRUCTURES

The variety of British craft, industrial, and general unions is remarkable. In 1979, there was a total of 454 unions. Seventy-three of them, mostly craft unions, had fewer than 100 members; 124 had fewer than 500 members. On the other hand, the 11 largest unions had more than 250,000 members each. The bulk of organized workers, 8,424,000 persons, were concentrated in them.[18]

Eleven years earlier, this diversity had been greater still. The total number of unions was 586, 114 of which were of the smallest size. The 9 largest organizations accounted for 5,494,000 members.[19] That is, in 1968 the organizations with more than a quarter of a million members contained just over one-half, but in 1978 about two-thirds, of the total union membership. This decrease in the number of unions had begun shortly after World War II. Caused by amalgamations, it did not mirror a strengthening of industrial unionism. The organizations that absorbed old craft unions were mainly conglomerates.

Multiunionism is an inefficient form of organization. It obstructs bargaining processes and contributes to interunion rivalry. Nevertheless, its persistence is easily explained. Craft unions were founded in the course of the Industrial Revolution to

[17] Until 1978 there were twenty–some of them are preferred territory for new industries. See the list in Eugene C. Hagburg and Marvin J. Levine, *Labor Relations: An Integrated Perspective,* (St. Paul, New York, Los Angeles, San Francisco, 1978), p. 201.

[18] Central Statistical Office, op. cit., 1982, p. 185.

[19] Central Statistical Office, op. cit., 1981, p. 186.

make rules for the protection of their members and to assist them in time of need. They limited their membership to qualified workers. From privileged trades they spread to unprivileged ones, but for a long time it proved almost impossible to organize unskilled labor. The first general union of the world, the Grand National Consolidated Trades Union of 1834, collapsed immediately under onslaught from employers and government. It took another fifty years before large unions with unskilled members could aspire to stability. With economic change, some craft unions extended their range of recruitment and expanded. Others merged, while still others just went on as they were, following the natural tendency of any organization to stay alive. By 1868, craft unions had come together in a federation, the Trades Union Congress, to advance the common interest of the working class. This did not mean that they would stop defending the special interests of their members or insisting on wage differentials. Even to the present day, the process of amalgamation notwithstanding, highly qualified workers, whether manual or not, strive to maintain their own separate organizations. And rivalries between blue-collar unions as well as between blue- and white-collar organizations are frequent. The TUC, as the central representative body of British labor, now embraces craft, industrial, and general unions. Its 112 affiliated organizations include all the major associations and more than 90 percent of union members.[20]

None of the many small unions founded in the United States toward the end of the eighteenth and the first half of the nineteenth century proved capable of surviving economic recessions and employer hostility. Stable unions date from the era of rapid industrialization after the Civil War, in a few cases from the 1850s. They were craft unions, job-conscious and pragmatic. Social reform or uplift organizations could not survive. Neither could a general union like the Knights of Labor, which was successful for a short time. In 1886, the craft unions united in the American Federation of Labor. Their organizational principles were not seriously challenged until a conflict broke out in 1935 that led to the forming of the Congress of Industrial Organizations. At that time, about 30 percent of AFL affiliates

[20] For details see Owen-Smith, op. cit., pp. 136f.

were, in fact, industrial unions. When the CIO was founded, industrial unionism was one of the most important issues separating its leaders from those of the AFL's old guard, even after the merger. Another issue, of course, was political involvement, the CIO being inclined to push for broad social reform. The social and political atmosphere of the New Deal labor legislation and the backing of government allowed the industrial unions to flourish. The dramatic growth in total membership at that time mirrored their success in the large industries.

Subsequently, many craft unions turned into conglomerates. General unions organized new sectors in industry as well as in the public sector. Since the mid-fifties, mergers have reduced the number of unions. In 1955, the year the AFL and the CIO re-united, there were 199 associations. In 1978 their number was 174.[21] Simultaneously, the AFL-CIO's share of total union membership decreased. In 1955 it was 90 percent (16 million members); in 1978 it amounted to only 78 percent (17 million members). This loss was due to the expulsion of the Teamsters and some minor organizations and to the split with the United Automobile Workers. The Teamsters numbered 1.9 million members in 1978, the UAW 1.5 million.

Early German unions were inspired by the British example. (The German Christian organizations, in turn, became models for Latin countries.) Soon, industrial unions evolved alongside craft associations. Because the process of industrialization was shorter, the organizations never diversified as broadly as was the case in the United Kingdom. The 1920s saw amalgamations, and there was a strong trend towards industrial unions representing all occupations and skills. Interunion rivalries existed mainly between the socialist, Christian, and liberal unions. Shortly before their unions were destroyed by the Nazis, the leaders of the three movements attempted to unify the associations.

After World War II, old labor activists who had survived persecution organized new unions with local differences, but always based on the principle of a movement not divided along ideological lines. Hans Böckler, who became the first chairman of the Deutsche Gewerkschaftsbund (DGB), advocated a single national union organized both on a regional basis and by branches

[21] U.S. Department of Commerce, op. cit., 1980, p. 429.

of industry (like Robert Owen's idea of a national union). The occupation authorities would not allow this, and several German labor leaders also opposed the idea. Instead, ideologically unified industrial unions were organized on the principle of one plant, one union. In 1949, they were federated into the DGB. This central organization today consists of seventeen so-called industrial unions, some of which are, in fact, conglomerates.

The unions in the DGB seek to organize blue- as well as white-collar workers and civil servants. In this, they are only partially successful. Among their 7,843,565 members in 1979, 5,387,356 were blue-collar workers, 1,609,960 white-collar were workers, and 846,249 were civil servants *(Beamten).* At the same time, of separate unions for white-collar workers, the Deutsche Angestelltengewerkschaft (DAG) had 487,743 and the Deutsche Beamtenbund (DBB) 824,412 members, respectively.[22] Thus, only about 83 percent of organized labor belongs to the DGB.

In the United States most unions of private, government, and municipal employees belong to the AFL-CIO, and in the United Kingdom even the union of senior civil servants is affiliated with the TUC. Does it follow that they are less status conscious than their German colleagues? Not necessarily. When the DGB was founded on a national basis, the DAG already existed. It was willing to join the DGB but was refused entry on the principle that all workers in an industry should belong to the same union regardless of skill and occupation. To be sure, the DBB has never considered federation, and it places emphasis on the special duties and privileges of the *Beamten* (this, happily, does not prevent it from claiming pay increases on the same scale as those obtained by manual laborers in the public sector). In any case, over the last twenty years the trend has favored the industrial and conglomerate unions. Since 1959, the number of white-collar workers in the DGB has more than doubled and that of *Beamten* increased by 70 percent. The DAG has stagnated, and the DBB has gained by 26 percent.

The TUC, the DGB, and the AFL-CIO are the spokesmen of their members in matters of general policy and represent them to the public and to the state. They do not bargain for wages but

[22] Statistisches Bundesamt, op. cit., 1980, p. 549. There exist several other, very small associations not considered here.

can influence income policies. It is difficult to assess the relative weights of the three central bodies within their respective federations. Yet it is probably safe to say that in Germany and Great Britain (even since the TUC's recent gain in authority) the most significant power lies not with the federations' highest officials but with the leaders of the large industrial or conglomerate unions. The same seems to be true for the United States, notwithstanding the remarkable role men like Samuel Gompers, George Meany, John Lewis, and Walter Reuther played in the AFL and CIO.

There are no empirical studies that answer satisfactorily the old questions regarding union democracy. A few remarks might, nevertheless, be hazarded. High membership dues permit the DGB to maintain a much broader network of service institutions–from schools for activists to building cooperatives and to the country's fourth largest private bank–and to pay a staff that is larger and that performs many more functions than the TUC and AFL-CIO can afford. But the number of bureaucrats alone is not an adequate indicator of a group's democratic character or lack of it.

In the United Kingdom the paramount importance of the plant in bargaining processes led to a shift of power towards the shop stewards. They had come to the fore during World War I as unofficial workers' representatives and were presently integrated into the unions. After World War II, they began to defy their unions, and now they are increasingly in control of them. They are in day-to-day contact with the rank and file, and their gain in authority represents a corresponding loss to that of union oligarchies. Nevertheless, they may often express the opinion of a militant minority rather than the wishes of the majority of the men and women whose interests they profess to represent. In the Federal Republic, due to the role of works councils, union representatives at plant level are of minor importance. Although members of the councils may, and as a rule do, belong to a union, they have no institutional role in it. Informally, though, their opinions often weigh heavily in a union's decision, and thus they too lessen somewhat the leadership's grip on the organization.

There is less conflict over politics within the DGB (and the DAG) than there is within the TUC. Unions on the Left, the center, and the Right of the labor movement belong to both federations, but in Britain factional struggles have been more frequent and bitter, and the Left has gained far more ground. The coexistence of Social Democrats and Christian Democrats in the DGB naturally leads to difficulties. These have been satisfactorily dealt with so far, with the exception of one case in which a group of Christian Democrats opted for a separate Christian union after the DGB had too blatantly supported the SPD election campaign in 1953. To have Communists in the organization did not, for a long time, raise serious problems because their numbers were too small. Recently however, ultra left-wing groups of various persuasions, sometimes in coalitions, have made inroads into several DGB unions, not so much among manual laborers as among their natural leaders: teachers, booksellers, and journalists. They have also made gains in union youth groups. Whether gains by communists and other activists of the far Left, whose democratic beliefs, mores, and goals are not above suspicion, are evidence of increased union democracy is open to question.

In the United States, the hold of officials on their unions is not challenged by the shop stewards, whose tasks are more narrow than in the United Kingdom. It is mediated somewhat by the power of the locals, the basic organizational units. They vary greatly in shape and size and may consist of all the organized workers of a particular craft in a certain area or of all or some of the workers of a particular plant or company. In the nineteenth and early twentieth centuries the size of the United States made it extremely difficult to build national associations. This was one of the reasons for the low rate of union participation. With the automobile and the airplane, organization has become easier. Nevertheless, wide distances and decentralized political structures still strengthen the locals. As a rule, bargaining is the task of the locals. This in turn contributes to employer hostility towards unions, because collective agreements limited to single firms or towns can put the signer at a disadvantage in a competitive market.

Although actual bargaining is mainly in the hands of the locals, national headquarters guide them in many cases. Generally they have the authority to acknowledge or disavow collective contracts and to sanction strikes. Also, in financial and other matters the control of the national unions over their locals has grown over the years.

Some U.S. unions have undergone more ruthless internal struggles than any non-Communist European union ever has, but usually these have been fought less for beliefs than for power and sinecures. (Salaries, of top officials, in a number of cases, are extremely high. In Germany, where they are low, the institution of codetermination permits deserving labor leaders to adjust their personal incomes to the spirit of a capitalist society.) The ideological controversies of the nineteenth century and even those of Walter Reuther's time belong to a distant past.

As in the Federal Repubic, most union conventions are stagemanaged. Once elected, a union leader retains office unless elected into a higher one. There is also little turnover in the paid, nonelected staff, who usually receive quite modest salaries (workers are seldom generous employers). German mores provide that union officials resign at the age of 65; in Britain and in the United States they may stay for life.

Longevity has been a factor in the decline of rate of union participation in the United States. Long terms of office convinced the leaders of the AFL-CIO that they knew best what was good for the worker, the nation, and the world. They became ever more stubborn and inflexible in face of the challenge of organizing new sectors of labor. Their philosophy permitted the most astonishing political liaisons. Efforts at social reform were almost completely abandoned. Thus, the unions of the AFL-CIO did little to attract prospective members. The federation could not even hold the United Automobile Workers in its fold.

STRIKES

Union history is a history of strikes and of measures, private and public, to thwart or to regularize them. Strikes are not the workers' sole weapon in industrial conflicts. Labor also puts pressure on employers by bans on overtime, working to rule, slowdowns, and boycotts (a U.S. specialty). Such actions are not recorded, however, and can therefore not be considered in the present analysis. Of course, many small work stoppages also remain unrecorded.

British workers struck 2,471 times in 1978, 2,080 times in 1979, and 1,330 times the next year. The corresponding figures for the United States were 4,230, 4,827 and 3,873.[23] For Germany, the number of strikes cannot be found in the official statistics since 1969. In the preceding twenty years, the lowest number was 19, the highest 99. At first sight, the differences among these countries are amazing. They become less so when the systems of bargaining are considered.

In the United Kingdom the most important level of bargaining is the plant. The company follows, and industry comes in third. As already noted, in the United States nearly all collective agreements are signed by locals. The 108 unions affiliated with the AFL-CIO in 1978 had over 60,000 locals. In 1973 more than half of the 1,339 agreements covering over more than a thousand workers were concluded with only one employer.[24] In the Federal Republic wages and working conditions are negotiated between industrial (or conglomerate) unions and employers' associations or the government. In private industry they are signed on a regional basis (a region being, as a rule, a Bundesland), but once agreement has been reached in one region the others tend to follow without much ado. If both parties to a contract desire it, the minister of labor may declare it legally binding for the whole industry. An individual firm may negotiate special benefits with its works council but the council is not allowed to call a strike for a company agreement. In the public sector one contract is concluded for the entire country, encompassing federal, state, and municipal blue- and white-collar workers. Thus, when inquiring about relative propensity to strike, what matters most is not the number of strikes but the number of strikers, as well as the duration of stoppages. The number of working days lost in conflicts in relation to the total labor force becomes the relevant measure. These data are given in table 2.

[23] International Labor Office, *Yearbook of Labor Statistics, 1981,* (Geneva, 1981, pp. 608 and 611).

[24] Hagburg and Levine, op. cit., pp. 44f.

Year	Federal Republic		United States		United Kingdom	
	days lost 1000	days lost per 1000 employed	days lost 1000	days lost per 1000 employed	days lost 1000	days lost per 1000 employed
average p.a. 1950-59	985	59	34,240	668	3,252	152
average p.a. 1960-69	316	15	27,570	450	3,555	153
average p.a. 1970-75	1,054	49	41,374	557	12,733	566
1976	534	26	37,859	477	3,284	146
1977	24	1	35,821	414	10,143	448
1978	4,281	199	36,922	395	9,405	414
1979	483	22	35,467	360	29,474	1,288
1980	128	6	30,164	321	11,910	514

Source: Institut der deutschen Wirtschaft, op. cit., 1982, table 83.

The figures in the table refer to strikes and lockouts. The latter have become extremely rare in Britain and the United States. German employers resort to them frequently in response to the unions' strategy of striking only selected factories in an industry. Thus, in the sixties, the seventies, and again in 1978 almost half of days lost were lost through lockouts.

Evidently, in the Federal Republic not only the number of strikes but also their total duration is far less than those in the two other countries. Britain, after twenty years of relatively low frequency, matched the United States in the first and barely exceeded it in the second quinquennium of the seventies. For a quarter-century British workers had struck less frequently than French workers as well, and not even during the seventies did they approach their Italian colleagues, who in most years lost two to three times as many working days.[25] This record refutes popular beliefs regarding the magnitude of British strikes. This false image might be attributable to the fact that the number of stoppages is high while their duration usually is short. It may also be due to the many strikes whose causes seem small in relation to their intensity or whose economic impact far transcends the often tiny group of workers directly involved. Nastiness can also make them appear to involve a greater number of workers than they really do. Yet this chapter is not concerned with the economic or media impact of strikes or with perceptions of social and political phenomena but rather with relative propensities to strike.

Workers strike for higher wages, for better working conditions, for redress of grievances, for control over the access to and the supply of jobs, and also for political reasons. In comparing tendencies to strike, several factors should be considered, including economic matters (which here can only be touched on in passing), the system of bargaining, management-labor relations, plant constitutions, and the social and political environment.

By all accounts, one would expect industrial conflicts to be frequent in Britain. For decades now, inflation has been exerting pressure on workers to strive for wages that keep abreast of prices–and to defend their status in the rank order of occupations. The workplace atmosphere frequently is poor if not tense. Institutionalization of grievance procedures remains rudimentary.

[25] Ibid.

As in politics, one muddles through. Higher management remains almost completely out of touch with the "men" and does not inform, much less consult them. Workers are inclined to view their interests, both as individuals and as members of their class, as opposed to those of their employers. Established associations for the advancement of their interests form a system that, on its own, contains causes for strikes. Multiunionism complicates bargaining, allows strikes for overstaffing and for wage differentials, and may lead to demarcation stoppages. A union wishing to call a strike encounters almost no barrier except for the workers' will and ability to stick it through. The union itself has little to worry about because strike pay is low.[26] Collective agreements are not legally binding (and are often rescinded under inflationary pressure). To strike is socially a widely accepted action. Although judges have at times made unions liable for damages caused by strikes, Parliament has reversed the decisions, declaring unions to be financially immune. Income policies of successive governments and efforts to control strikes legally have broken down, leading in some instances to political strikes. (Whether the laws passed under Margaret Thatcher will survive remains to be seen.) Where union leaders themselves have shown restraint, shop stewards, some of them Communists, have launched unofficial strikes that the unions have subsequently made official so as not to lose members. (Not infrequently, militant shop stewards have obtained favorable votes by avoiding secret ballots.) In addition to this, growth in membership in the seventies may have raised the unions' ability and willingness to strike (but it could also be the other way round, namely, that their militance attracted new members).

Paradoxically, it may be a consequence of the strong position of several British unions that, despite all the "incentives" to strike, the per capita number of working days lost was, for a long time, much lower in the United Kingdom than in the United States. Some unions needed to strike only briefly, if at all, in order to be able to practically dictate wages.

U.S. workers share with their British counterparts grounds for industrial dispute. Inflation rates are lower, but high enough to pressure constantly for wage adjustments. Structural changes in the economy give occasion and multiunionism offers the means to

[26] Cf. Clegg, op. cit., pp. 281 ff., also on indirect benefits to strikers.

defend disappearing jobs as well as wage differentials. Working conditions leave much to be desired. Grievance procedures are not legally formalized but are subject to collective bargaining.

Nevertheless, one might expect U.S. unions to be more reluctant to call stoppages. The strike pay they have to disburse is far from negligible. They seldom are pushed on by shop stewards. Three out of four agreements are negotiated for two years or longer.[27] Although contracts may contain provisions for renegotiation, they also have binding no-strike clauses. Almost all agreements include provisions for voluntary arbitration (but recently in Britain too, arbitration and mediation have become quite widespread). If a conflict might result in a national emergency, the president is authorized to request a "cooling-off" period of eighty days and may even, if Congress agrees, legally prohibit a strike, as in the 1982 case of the locomotive engineers. Public-sector unions find their right to strike severely curtailed by a variety of federal and state laws. Employees of the federal government may not engage in either a strike or a slowdown. The power of the president over public servants and the frailty of the unions became evident when Ronald Reagan crushed the strike of the air controllers, destroyed their union, and dismissed the strikers. Neither in the United Kingdom, nor in any other non-Communist country in Europe does the head of the government have equivalent legal authority or would public opinion tolerate such measures.

Above all, one would expect workers to strike less in the United States than in Britain because union density is so very much lower and labor has to organize in order to strike. What then are the reasons for the opposite being the case? Why are many more working days lost per union member in the United States? Only empirical research into the behavior and attitudes of participants in industrial disputes can yield a satisfactory answer to this question. Nonetheless, it might be suggested that the United States witnesses (the ideology of a classless society notwithstanding) a deep conflict of interests between capital and labor; the organized workers are disposed to fight hard for their immediate concerns; and the employers are ready to face any challenge. Rugged individualism means rugged individualism for all. Where

[27] Hagburg and Levine, op. cit., p. 56. The data refer to 1973.

employers are little constrained in fixing prices and salaries, in competing and combining, and in hiring and firing, unions will have few qualms in calling a strike. Could it be that the U.S. creed masks a society as antagonistic as any in Western Europe?

Why do German workers strike so infrequently? The answer that they love work, order, and discipline is somewhat off the mark, considering that in the first three decades of the century, when they seemed to be even more inclined toward these virtues, both the number of strikes and the days lost per employed person were consistently higher in Germany than in most other European countries. Thus, the argument that the environment is more hostile to strikes than elsewhere also does not go far, as public opinion probably condemned them more severely in times past.[28] Are union leaders more "responsible"? In Britain a good many officials are moderate too, and the fact that U.S. unions can act wisely has been demonstrated recently in the automobile industry.

More to the point is the observation that in the Federal Republic, on the one hand, inflation rates have been low, and, on the other hand, productivity has risen steadily, so that employers could afford to grant ever higher real wages. Furthermore, grievance procedures and other working conditions have been legally institutionalized, whereas in the United Kingdom and even more so in the United States, rules in the workplace are established by collective agreement.

Not only the establishment but also the administration of workplace institutions has been removed from the realm of collective bargaining. Shop grievances and many other matters of concern to the worker are settled between management and works councils, the most important institution of codetermination. The councils may not call strikes; their disputes must be resolved by mediation or by a labor court. Collective bargaining itself is governed by statute and union constitutions. Contracts are legally binding. Generally, they are signed for one year, and for their duration both parties must "keep the peace." In order to call a strike, most unions need the consent, by secret ballot, of 75 percent of their members. Strike pay is high. Jurisdictional

[28] According to polls cited by von Beyme, in 1963-1964 strikes were a measure approved by 53 percent and disapproved by 30 percent of the population. In 1973, 57 percent approved and only 26 percent disapproved Op. cit., p. 166.

strikes or conflicts over wage differentials are not allowed. As already mentioned, agreements apply on a regional basis to whole industries. Thus, occasions for strikes are few. However, because their potential magnitude is great, their cost is to be feared by both sides to a conflict. Political strikes were an issue during the struggle for "industrial democracy", but such stoppages were extremely rare and short.[29]

CONCLUDING REMARKS

In this essay political strikes have not been taken into account. The unions have been regarded as actors on the labor market, but it has been postulated that their behavior could not be understood solely by recourse to economic theory. It has been shown that the willingness of the workers to join a union, their tendency to strike, and the forms they give their organizations are interrelated. The German labor camp has been represented as being dominated by a federation of large industrial and conglomerate unions, in sharp contrast to the great variety of craft and industrial organizations of different sizes and shapes encountered elsewhere. Great Britain exhibits a higher rate of union participation than the Federal Republic. In both countries it has increased greatly in the seventies, while in the United States union participation has declined steadily since the mid-fifties. American workers have always been much more reluctant to organize than their British and German colleagues. When it comes to striking, however, they turn out to be in the forefront. In the U.S., many more days are lost per union member than in Great Britain. By comparison, the propensity of German workers to strike is almost negligible. These and other differences among the three countries have been explained in terms of differences in social structures, mores, and creeds, as well as by labor legislation and history, by political events and governmental policies.

[29] Cf. Wolfgang Hirsch-Weber, *Gewerkschaften in der Politik: Von der Massenstreidebatte zum Kampf um das Mitbestimmungsrecht,* (Köln und Opladen: Westdeutscher Verlag, 1959).

However, unions are not mere products of their social and political environments. They participate in the shaping of social values and structures. They lobby for labor legislation and try to influence governmental actions in all matters concerning the interests of workers. In some countries, close collaboration with social democratic parties gives them leverage on decisions that extends far beyond the field of labor relations.

The political behavior of labor unions has caused concern where they have become so strong that they may impose their will on the legislature or the executive and on the voter. This clearly is the case in the United Kingdom, where organizations affiliated to the TUC dominate the Labour party and compel it to disregard interests or persuasions other than their own. How heavily the trade unions weigh in the political system has been shown three times since World War II, when attempts to enforce incomes policies disapproved by the unions were a decisive factor in bringing down the government.[30]

In the Federal Republic, where no party is organizationally tied to unions, their power is most linked. To be sure, some of their officials tend to believe that they are called to represent all temporal interests of all workers, white or blue collar, and demand to be heard on any matter, from foreign policy to the reform of higher learning and the management of art museums, but their claims meet, as yet, with some doubts as to their legitimacy. In matters in which the unions are considered to have a mandate, however, the SPD is inclined to be led by them, and the CDU listens attentively to their voice. Without the unions' weight in the councils of the two parties, social legislation would certainly not be as broad and far-reaching as it is.

It is remarkable that in the country where the term "to lobby" was invented, the unions have never had much leverage on Congress or the president and that whatever political influence they possessed has been nearly lost. What are the reasons that permit the present administration to treat them almost with disdain? Sometimes it is thought that U.S. unions are politically weak because a social democratic party is lacking in the U.S. This may be true. The question then would be why such a party did not flourish, and the answer might be similar to the one given to

[30] Shirley Williams, *Politics is for People,* (Harmondsworth, Penguin, 1981), p. 137.

account for the low rate of union participation.

The participation of unions in political processes has not been dealt with in this chapter. It would, of course, be a major issue in any attempt at a comprehensive comparison of labor associations in the three countries.

Chapter 17

INTEREST GROUPS IN THREE INDUSTRIAL DEMOCRACIES: FRANCE, WEST GERMANY, AND THE UNITED STATES

William Safran

The purpose of this essay is to compare the interest-group politics of France and Germany with that of the United States; to deal with the heavily institutionalized nature of the relationship between groups and governments in these two European countries; and to discuss the implications of such a relationship for democracy and public policy. It will be argued that the term "corporatism," used in recent years with increasing frequency to describe that relationship, is unfortunate in that it creates, explicitly or implicitly, a false dichotomy between institutionalization and democratic pluralism. In short, this paper will show that Western European patterns, despite their deviations from the American ideal-type, are entirely consistent with pluralism.

GROUPS AND THE STATE: VARIETIES OF RELATIONSHIPS

A survey of the place of interest groups in the United States, France, and West Germany suggests that these countries are roughly comparable with respect to the following: the existence of a wide diversity of socioeconomic associations reflecting an advanced phase of industrialization and a complex and pluralistic social system; nationally structured, hierarchical, and professionalized umbrella organizations; a common interest in developing access to public authorities; the existence of more or less regular linkages, or access points, to decision-making institutions; and open acknowledgment, by politicians and scholars, that the policymaking process is, or ought to be, fundamentally a partnership between public authorities and the private sector. Moreover, there is a "taxonomic" basis of comparison: in all three countries, the three basic types of interest groups, as once posited by Gabriel Almond, may be found: institutional, associational, and anomic.[1]

Nevertheless, such general characterizations obscure the important differences among the three countries with regard to the nature of the access points, the degree of official legitimation of groups and institutionalization of their relationship to the government, and the relative power of, and the equilibrium between, contending groups. Scholars discussing U.S. interest-group politics concentrate on voluntary associations (e.g., labor and farmers' associations) that promote their interests in the first place in a free-market environment by negotiating, autonomously and with relatively little government intervention, with their equally voluntary counterparts (e.g., manufacturers). In addition, these voluntary associations attempt to promote their policy goals by means of lobbying–primarily with legislators, and secondarily with high officials in executive departments and administrative agencies. Such activities are for the most part informal, irregular, unpredictable, and covert, and at no point do they endanger the autonomy and freedom of the interest group.[2] In contrast, in the typical European industrial democracy, such activities, although they do exist, constitute only a part of a continuum of relationships between interest groups and the public authorities. Such a continuum would include the following:

1. Absence of constitutional reference–and hence apparent constitutional indifference–to interest groups (e.g., the French Third Republic).
2. Constitutional-legal acknowledgment of the right of people freely to establish associations (all European democracies).
3. Official acceptance of the notion that interest groups should be consulted by the government and/or the legislators when they determine public policy choices (all Western European countries).
4. Legitimation of groups by the public authorities, on a selective basis, for purposes

[1] Gabriel A. Almond, "Research Note: A Comparative Study of Interest Groups and the Political Process," *American Political Science Review*, Vol. 52, 1 (March 1958). See also G.A. Almond and G.B. Powell, Jr., *Comparative Politics: A Developmental Approach* (Boston: Little, Brown, 1966), pp. 72-79.

[2] For a typical treatment, see "Interest Groups: Who They are and How They Influence" (Special), *National Journal Reprints 1975-76* and *1977-78*, selected by Robert H. Salisbury.

of functional representation, delegation of administrative tasks, invitations to legislative committee hearings, and/or policy bargaining sessions with representatives of the government (most European democracies).

5. Distinctions made, by law or administrative regulation, between "professional" and mere "interest" associations (France, Germany, and Italy).
6. Informal or formal linkage of an interest group to a political party (e.g., West Germany, France, Britain, Sweden), or the encapsulation of a group into the structure of a party (Austria and the Netherlands).
7. Institutionalized, and often legally sanctioned, incorporation of interest-group leaders into the public policymaking structure (e.g., by means of national wage, price or planning councils), such that an "elite management" system is developed.
8. Institutionalization, by legal or practical means, of multipartite central bargaining.
9. Restriction of the parameters of autonomous group actions, e.g., limitation of the scope of "sectoral" collective bargains or the control or banning of strikes.
10. Legal controls over internal group organization.
11. Compulsory memberships and the mandatory setting up of "umbrella" organizations ("cameralization").

This list is not complete, but it does convey the idea that interest group-government relations in Western Europe may be much more regulated, complex, and institutionalized than they are in the United States. To the extent that in many Western European democracies most of the patterns listed above can be found, they appear to conform to a polity model that is said to depart dramatically from the U.S. system–that is, they are "corporatist" rather than "pluralist."[3]

CORPORATISM VERSUS PLURALISM

According to Leo Panitch, corporatism is "a political structure within advanced capitalism which integrates organized socioeconomic producer groups through a system of representation and cooperative mutual interaction at the leadership level and of mobilization and social control at the mass level."[4] For Philippe Schmitter, it is "a system of interest intermediation in which the constitutent units are

[3] Martin O. Heisler and Robert B. Kvavik, " Patterns of European Politics: The 'European Polity' Model," in Heisler, ed., *Politics in Europe: Structures and Processes in Some Postindustrial Democracies* (New York: McKay, 1974), Chapter 2, and especially pp. 38-43.

[4] Leo Panitch, "The Development of Corporatism in Liberal Democracies," *Comparative Political Studies*, Vol. 10, no. 1 (April 1977), p. 66.

organized into a limited number of singular, compulsory, non-competitive, hierarchically ordered, and functionally differentiated categories, recognized or licensed [if not created] by the state and granted a deliberate representational monopoly within their respective categories in exchange for observing certain controls on their selection of leaders and articulation of demands and supports."[5]

These definitions remind one of fascist regimes. In those regimes, interest groups in the proper sense, that is, autonomously functioning agents, were not permitted; instead, the organizations that spoke for professional or economic sectors were sanctioned by the state; their leaders were approved by the state; membership in organizations was in many cases compulsory; autonomous activities, such as intergroup negotiations, strikes, or demonstrations, were forbidden; and the organizations, rather than being capable of freely advancing claims upon society or pressuring the authorities for policy changes, were little more than handmaidens or ancillary units of the government, engaged in the performance of public mobilization and other tasks assigned to them, and nothing more.[6]

Needless to say, this context is a far cry from the interest-group environment in the ideal typical industrial democracy. In the United States, which, in the eyes of many political scientists (particularly those influenced by certain adherents of the structural-functional school of analysis), embodies this ideal type better than other coun-

[5] Philippe C. Schmitter, "Modes of Interest Intermediation and Models of Societal Change in Western Europe," ibid., p. 9. For Schmitter, the "corporatist" mode of interest articulation clearly contrasts with the "pluralist" and "syndicalist" modes. See also Schmitter's earlier "Still the Century of Corporatism?," *Review of Politics*, vol. 36 (January 1974), pp. 91-98, which contains the same juxtaposition.

[6] In the article on fascism in the *Encyclopedia of the Social Sciences* (1931, Vol. 6, pp. 133-38), it is asserted that "in contrast to the pluralistic conception of the state . . ." fascism denotes a situation where "groups are strictly subordinated to serving the interests of the state . . ." and (again) "the corporative, or guild, state is the visible expression of the supremacy of the state over the economic and social groups of the nation." In an article under the same heading in the new edition of the *International Encyclopedia of the Social Sciences* (1968, vol. 3, pp. 334-41), fascism, which represents "a third way between Marxism and liberalism," comprehends certain key notions, among them (1) that "the community alone was to have the right to determine what the national interest required; therefore [(2) that] the conflicting interests of owners, workers, technicians, and the state were to be brought together in a single unit, the corporation, operating under public control; [(3) that] strikes and lockouts were forbidden; and [(4) that] the doctrine of the primacy of the politician over the expert was to be abandoned."

tries, interest groups and the state are (and ought to be) quite distinct in terms of organization and purpose. Groups are based largely on self-motivated construction and are engaged, as free agents, either in autonomous bargaining with another group or in providing an input into the policymaking machinery by means of lobbying. To the extent that states depart from this model, they deviate from the modern pluralistic system: systemic and functional boundaries (e.g., the dividing lines between polity and economy, and between articulative and other input functions) are obscured. This approach to regime types (or "interest articulation structures") is ethnocentric and–irrespective of its possible heuristic value–is increasingly viewed as a caricature of reality. But its vestigial importance become apparent when one examines the terminologies used by Americans (and a small number of European scholars influenced by Americans) for whom the Western European nonconformance to the U.S. ideal (or what is perceived as such) is sufficiently disturbing that they must use nondemocratic labels to describe it.

The application of the term "corporatism" to Western European democracies is misleading, even when the term is qualified or cleaned up with such adjectives as "societal" (Schmitter) or "liberal" (Gerhard Lehmbruch).[7] "Liberal corporatism" is a contradiction in terms, having approximately the same meaning as "liberal fascism"; and "societal corporatism", used (again by Schmitter) in juxtaposition with "state corporatism," implies acceptance of the U.S. classic liberal myth of the separation between economy and polity.[8] Even though Schmitter is careful to distinguish between Western democracies in which there is a high degree of institutionalization of interest group activity and nondemocratic systems, the odor of fascism is not quite

[7] See Gerhard Lehmbruch, "Liberal Corporatism and Party Government," in *Comparative Political Studies,* Vol. 10, No. 1, pp. 91-124; and Schmitter, "Modes of Interest Intermediation," p. 11. Lehmbruch overgeneralizes from the experiences of Austria, whose weak democratic traditions predisposed it to the "chamber state"; while Schmitter was probably excessively influenced by the experiences of certain Latin American countries, with their authoritarian traditions and the corporatist *gremios.*

[8] The notion of a separation (or the existence of "boundaries") between society and economy, and between one political function and another, is essentially a restatement, in functionalist terms, of the eighteenth-century classic liberal ideal of the separation of powers. Cf. Almond and Powell, *Comparative Politics,* pp. 19-20 et passim, and David Easton, *Systems Analysis of Political Life* (New York: Wiley, 1965), especially pp. 256-58. While for Easton the notion of (systemic and functional) boundaries is basically heuristic, for Almond it tends to be used as descriptive of empirical reality.

eliminated from his portrayal of the Western European situation–a situation in which authoritarian patterns are modified, but apparently not enough to transform them into pluralistic ones.[9] Thus he is led to assert that "the resistance to corporatization comes from existing interest associations that prize their organizational autonomy and defend their traditionally pluralistic way of operating" and that "efforts in imposing a solution from above were accompanied [presumably in Western Europe] by the severe repression of such associations, especially those representing the working class, and the establishment of a wide range of other authoritarian practices. . . ."[10] To some readers, such statements may imply (1) that in democracies, traditional pluralism and "corporatization" are incompatible, and that the development of *any* authoritative norms of group behavior is tantamount to, or results in, repression–despite "highly layered subcultures," party systems, and other manifestations of pluralism (2) that may be found within the *"gestälter"* (sic) of these systems.[11] To others, the pluralistic element in corporatism frequently remains hidden because Schmitter and others do not always bother to use "liberal" or "societal" (as opposed to "state") when applying the term "corporatism" to Western Europe.[12] The problem is that "corporatism" (as opposed to "pluralism") has come to be used as a shorthand term for virtually any kind of institutionalized relationship between interest groups and the state[13] in which the latter functions as something more than a mere registration or facilitation agent of private group decisions. Such a juxtaposition of

[9] On this point, see James M. Malloy, ed., *Authoritarianism and Corporatism in Latin America* (Pittsburgh: Pittsburgh University Press, 1977), p. 4.

[10] Schmitter, "Interest Intermediation and Regime Governability," in Suzanne Berger, ed., *Organizing Interests in Western Europe* (Boston: Cambridge University Press, 1981), p. 313. In his study, Schmitter attempts to correlate the degree of "societal corporatism" (as opposed to pluralism) with "stableness" and "ruliness," but the correlations, although suggestive, are neither clear nor convincing.

[11] Schmitter, "Modes of Interest Intermediation," pp. 9-10.

[12] See Suzanne Berger, "Interest Groups and the Governability of European Society," *Items* (Social Science Research Council), vol. 35, no. 4 (December 1981), pp. 63-68, and G. Lehmbruch and P. Schmitter, eds., *Patterns of Corporatist Policy-Making*, Sage Modern Politics Series, vol. 7 (Beverly Hills, Calif.: Sage 1982), where "corporatism" tends to be used without qualifiers.

[13] For a recent example, see the (otherwise excellent) paper by J.T.S. Keeler, "Corporatist Decentralization and Commercial Modernization in France: The Royer Law's Impact on Shopkeepers, Supermarkets, and the State," paper presented at the 1982 annual meeting of the American Political Science Association, Denver.

pluralism and "corporatism" (and the overinterpretation of the meaning of institutionalization) introduces an isomorphic fallacy in that it derives functional conclusions from (partial) structural realities.

TYPOLOGIES OF GROUPS: IMPLICATIONS OF INSTITUTIONALIZATION

One reason for such overinterpretation of the consequences of institutionalization is the ready acceptance of Almond's threefold classification of groups, according to which any organized group other than associational or voluntary ones must be institutional–and this latter category clearly implies governmentalization.[14] In fact, in most Western European countries, the range of legitimation extends from outlawed groups (e.g., certain autonomist associations such as the Corsican Liberation Front in France, and revolutionary or anarchist groups committed to violence, such as the Baader-Meinhof group in West Germany) to "bodies of public law" whose establishment has been encouraged or mandated by the government, whose membership is compulsory, and which have been given public-administrative responsibilities (see Table 1).

It should be kept in mind that interest groups cannot always be pigeonholed under a particular rubric. Thus trade unions, although voluntarily organized and pursuing sectional economic aims, are functionally "corporatized" in the sense that public tasks are delegated to them (such as the administration of social insurance programs), without this activity weakening their autonomy. The "professional orders" that exist in France and Germany were created by governments for specific public purposes, including the enforcement of recruitment and work standards *(Ordnung des Berufsstandes).* In France, the *ordres professionnels,* having been initiated during the ancien régime (and constituting the only permitted type of group organization under the Vichy regime; and hence predemocratic or

[14] "Institutional interest groups are found within such organizations as political parties, legislatures, armies, bureaucracies and churches [and they have] designated political or social functions *other than* interest articulation." Almond and Powell, *Comparative Politics,* p. 77 (emphasis added).

Table 1
Groups and Their Positions on the Private-Public Continuum

Nature of Group	Examples		
	France	West Germany	United States
1. Private groups (associational) "pure lobbyists"	Most trade unions, employers' groups, farmers' associations, and promotional groups		All groups
2. Authorized voluntary group			
a. Bargaining partners of the government	Major trade union confederations	Confederation of German Trade Unions (DGB)	None
b. Performers of selected administrative tasks	Major trade unions, employers' associations, and agricultural organizations		Local bar associations, American Medical Association
c. Legitimated for purposes of functional representation	Major trade unions and employers' associations for representation in (the Social and Economic Council)	DGB, Federation of Employers' Assns (BDA) for (representation on labor courts)	None
3.Statutory groups groups (compulsory membership)	*Ordre des médecins*	Federal Assn. of Health Insurance Physicians (KBV)	None
4. Institutional interest groups (arising in consequence of public policies, and concerned with public adminstration	National Association of Social Security	Federal Association of Local Health Insurance Agencies	None
5. Organic groups preexisting the state, based on ascription e.g., birth, faith):			
a. purely private	Most Religions	Most smaller sects	Religious and ethnic groups
b. Specially legitimated	Catholic church	Three "established" religions	None

Based on, and expanded from, William Safran, *Veto-Group Politics* (San Francisco: Chandler Publishing Co., 1967).

nondemocratic in origin), are the "corporatist" organizations par excellence. However, even the professional orders (which now exist for doctors, lawyers, pharmacists, architects, etc.) are not absolutely "corporatized." They are under the laws of the state but not under the daily control of the government. Moreover, the laws regulating their professional behavior have been made with the participation, and often the initiative, of the orders themselves. Finally, the orders may behave like voluntary groups *(syndicats)* in promoting the economic interests of their members, e.g., by making alliances with other groups and sharing members with them, by lobbying with parliament, threatening strikes, and so on (we shall return to this point below). The same origins and the same duality of roles apply to the chambers of commerce and agriculture.[15]

A special complication for the taxonomist is presented by the religious interest. In both France and Germany, the churches (more specifically, *the* Church in France and the Roman Catholic and Lutheran churches in Germany) historically represented "corporations" that antedated the state and later (in the case of the Catholic church) competed with it in the struggle for sovereignty. These churches were organic or "mystical" rather than functional in origin. In the contemporary period, the question of sovereignty is settled, and the relationship between church and state has been arranged on the basis of each country's particular needs. In West Germany, the two (or three)[16] major religious communities enjoy public-law status; they are supported by taxes; and citizens "blaspheming" them are liable to prosecution under the penal code.[17] In France, the churches were of course "disestablished" in 1905, and legally they are considered mere private cults. Yet even in that country the churches (or at least the Catholic church) enjoy a privileged functional relationship with the state, in the sense that (via parochial schools) they provide contractually established public education to

[15] See Bernard Chenot, *Organisation économique de l'état* (Paris: Dalloz, 1965), Chapter 4, "Les institutions corporatives de l'organisation professionnelle et sociale," pp. 247-71.

[16] The special political legitimation of the Catholic and Lutheran churches of course goes back to the Peace of Augsburg of 1555 ("cuius regio, eius religio"). As for the tiny Jewish *Religionsgemeinschaft,* its special status (sometimes labeled *"Denkmalsschutz")* must be attributed to symbolic rather than practical politics.

[17] Herbert Schneider, *Die Interessenverbände* (Munich and Vienna: Guenter Olzog Verlag, 1965), pp. 71-72.

many pupils.

Thus neither in France nor in Germany are churches considered associational groups like the trade unions; but they are not in a "corporatist" relation to the state either. French citizens are free to join any of the numerous cults or to refuse to do so, and these cults are (except in Alsace) self-supporting. In West Germany, citizens may "contract out" of the payment of church taxes. And in both countries, church leaders may "lobby" (either directly or via parties) for or against certain public policies (e.g., childrens's subsidies, birth control).

The high degree of institutionalization of interest group-government relations does not suggest an etatist-authoritarian arrangement that produces policy decisions to which interest groups tamely submit. It does not suggest that interest groups have been pressured, against their will, into this relationship or that groups, having failed to achieve their policy objectives within the context of unmediated bargaining with the government (or by means of an "intrasystemic" input), no longer have any other means of action at their disposal.

There is no evidence that the "interpenetration" of the (private) group sector and the (public) government sector in postwar Western European democracies has transformed the interest groups into agencies of social mobilization or control on behalf of the government, as happened, for instance, in the case of the "Labor Front" in Nazi Germany. Big business is difficult to coopt as long as capitalism is maintained (and firms are left with substantial freedom to make investment decisions), and labor is difficult to coopt as long as there are reasonably frequent and free elections involving competition among parties. If labor is more or less unified and the degree of unionization is high, as in West Germany, it is difficult to coopt because its monolithic nature renders it electorally powerful. If labor is fragmented, as in France, the interunion competition for members has a radicalizing effect: the Confédération Générale du Travail (CGT) and Confédération Française *Démocratique de Travail (CFDT) by turns try to outbid one another with* antigovernment rhetoric.

THE LIMITS OF "ELITE MANAGEMENT"

There is no evidence that the institutionalized contacts between government and interest-group leaders have resulted either in an irreversible interpenetration or in a form of elite management in which the various members of this elite have interchangeable values.[18] It is true that in the context of "postindustrial society," where intelligent public policy decisions depend heavily on expert knowledge, parliaments and political parties have been functionally demoted, and decisions are increasingly made by a multiplicity of professional elite figures: professors, bank directors, technocrats, and leaders of business, labor, and farmers' associations. In several Western European countries, these leaders meet so frequently and in such a highly structured fashion–e.g., in economic development councils, price-wage boards, and a variety of advisory bodies whose meetings may also be attended by cabinet ministers or high government officials–that (so it is argued) all these participants come to share values, with the result that unmediated central bargains no longer reflect the aspirations of the rank-and-file members of an association. But such a portrayal is misleading. In most European democracies, the leaders of business, government, labor, and agriculture agree largely on *procedural* values: the need to resolve conflicts peacefully in the context of the existing pluralistic political system, and the desirability of basing decision on "objective" (i.e., mutually acceptable) aggregate data rather than ideology. But there remain

[18] Heisler and Kvavik (in "The European Polity Model," pp. 38-43) repeatedly refers to a "cartel of elites," "a faceless group of leaders," and similar descriptive terms; insist that "elites are usually of one mind in terms of goals [such that] a replacement of one man by another has the effect of replacing one technique by another"; and assert that "a consensus regarding goals" has been developing not only among the leadership but in the electorate as well. In this they follow the writings of Dahrendorf, Lehmbruch, and others and their generalization from the experiences of Western European countries (e.g., Norway, West Germany, and Austria) in which, during a period of growth and affluence, there had developed a considerable convergence on policy goals. Illustrative of this is Robert B. Kvavik, "Interest Groups in a 'Cooptive' Political System: The Case of Norway," in Heisler, *Politics in Europe,* pp. 93-116. Those who look at Reagan's policies (as compared to those of his predecessors) or Mitterrand's (as compared to Giscard's) may not agree. And as for Norway, late in 1981, the new Conservative government in that country was preparing legislation to undo the seminationalization of the banks that had been undertaken by the preceding Labor governments.

conflicting *substantive* values–regarding the ideal social order, principles of justice, merit, equality, efficiency, and so on. There are, in short, the same disagreements that prevail among interest group-leaders in countries where institutionalized relationships between groups and government are relatively underdeveloped.

It is true that in France most of organized business shares with most of organized labor a general ideological commitment to one or another form of interventionism, just as in the United States the two sectors share a commitment to the principle of unfettered collective bargaining in the context of a free-enterprise economy, and the two sectors in West Germany have accepted the principle of a "social-market economy." But beyond that there are disagreements on values that are imposed upon economic interest leaders by the nature of the sector they represent, disagreements that the institutionalization of elite management patterns has not succeeded in overcoming despite widely shared commitments to *concertation* or *konzertierte Aktion.* Thus while business leaders (of the Conseil National du Patronat Français [CNPF] and the Deutsche(r) Industrie- und Handelstag [DIHT]) are interested in growth, productivity, and competitiveness, the leaders of the unions in both countries are interested in redistributive policies and high wages. The prospect of management by a homogeneous elite is even further undermined in those European countries where, as a consequence of lagging modernization, value conflicts among elites *within* sectors are exacerbated. Thus in France (as in Italy and Belgium), while big business clamors for price liberalization and free trade, small business wants protection and subsidization.

During the Giscard presidency, contacts between the leaders of the CNPF and members of the government were so frequent, and the dependence of big business on the government (for favorable tax and credit policies) was so significant, that business could be said to have been "incorporated" into the public authority structure. Yet big business was able to prevent both the reform of the tax system and the extension of industrial democracy, in part by mobilizing the support of right-of-center parliamentarians. In Germany and in Mitterrand's France, leaders of organized labor meet frequently with leaders of government; in both countries trade union officials have been coopted by appointment to official positions, and there has been a considerable convergence of policy views between government and organized labor. Yet neither the German government's efforts at maintaining the welfare state, nor the French government's pro-labor moves (including an increase in the minimum wage, tax reforms, and a promised restoration and democratization of economic planning) has sapped the independence of organized labor. In West Germany, DGB leaders in 1981 organized mass rallies to protest against the government's (relatively mild) austerity policies, and in France in the same year both the CGT and the CFDT (despite the cooptation of leaders of the Communist party, the CGT's "patron," into the cabinet, and despite the linkages of CFDT officials to the government team) threatened strikes in protest against inadequate wage rises. Conversely, the new collaboration between government and labor in France, which has implied a partial exclusion of business leaders from the inner circle, has not reduced organized business to powerlessness. But it did introduce a degree of indecision on the part of the CNPF about what tactic to follow: selective collaboration; apathy (and waiting it out until the government discredits itself); a policy of "sabotaging" the government's fiscal policies by irresponsible pricing actions; or a resort to the Conseil Constitutionnel in order to challenge the legality of the government's nationalization program.[19]

THE STATE, GROUPS, AND POLITICAL PARTIES: PATTERNS OF INTERDEPENDENCE

The coexistence of formalized patterns of interaction between interest groups and the various branches of the executive with a system of linkages to political parties and of autonomous bargaining (and other forms of subsystem action) with unmediated bargaining at national levels–that is, the coexistence of *structured,* or *bureaucratized,* with *loose,* or *anarcholiberal* (or "libertarian"), pluralism–creates a *pluralism of opportunities* for interest groups in Western European countries that is absent in the United States. In France, Italy, and elsewhere, the disadvantages of fragmented or weak interests in autonomous bargaining are often compensated for by unmediated

[19] See *Le Point,* July 6, 1981, p. 41, and December 21, 1981, pp. 50-51.

contacts between interest group leaders and high government officials; conversely, central accords resulting from unmediated dealings between group leaders and the government may be elaborated by negotiations within the subsystem or may be nullified by strikes (e.g., the wildcat strikes in Sweden in the early 1970s).

In all Western European countries (including the Scandinavian and low countries and Austria), all the alternatives of group action that exist in pluralistic societies such as the US, Canada, and Britain are equally available, although they may not be resorted to with equal frequency and may be kept in reserve. The progressive institutionalization of direct relationships between interest group and government has not prevented groups from pursuing supplementary parliamentary inputs, on the one hand by lobbying and on the other by political parties. The linkages between parties and groups have not destroyed the independence of the latter. In West Germany, the Confederation of German Trade Unions (DGB) has always kept the door open to the Christian Democratic Union (CDU) (and its "labor wing"), so that the Social Democratic Party (SPD) does not take union support for granted. In France, both the Communist and Socialist parties have vied for the support of the CGT membership (thereby rendering the CGT a somewhat unreliable "transmission belt" of the Communist party); and both the Gaullists and the Giscardists (and, to a lesser extent, the Socialists) have sought the votes of farmers and small shopkeepers. In both France and West Germany, ecologist movements have lobbied for proenvironment legislation and pressured political parties by alternating between promising electoral support and running separate environmentalist candidates in parliamentary elections. (Some observers have been suggesting that the ecologists in France have already been incorporated by the Socialist party, or at least that they have come to constitute one of the various *courants* of the Left; however, the available evidence indicates that at least a third of the ecologists voted for a right-of-center candidate on the second ballot of the presidential and parliamentary elections of 1981.)[20]

[20] *Les élections législatives de juin 1981* (Le Monde: Dossiers et Documents, June 1981), esp. pp. 12-13. Early in April 1981, even the relatively "nonpolitical" Confédération générale des cadres in France was toying (or pretending to toy) with the idea of presenting its own candidate for the presidency. *Le Monde,* April 7, 1981.

Just as a highly structured relationship to the public authorities does not by itself destroy the autonomy of an interest group, so the utilization of methods of action parallel, and even in opposition, to such a relationship does not normally harm a group's image or threaten its position as a recognized interlocutor of the government. It should be noted that where patterns of legitimation exist, a government is not always free to play games of favoritism or punishment, that is, either to grant unwarranted legitimacy to groups that it likes or to withhold legitimation from groups that, for reasons of (antisystem) ideology or obstreperous behavior, it does not like. In the Netherlands, the government could not expel the trade union confederations from the Foundation of Labor in the 1970s, despite their refusal to accept the government's economic policy recommendations and despite the strikes that followed that refusal. In France, the Gaullist-conservative governments did not like the CGT and MODEF, the Communist-supported agricultural association, but could neither withhold the label of "representativeness" from them nor refuse to accord them places in advisory or economic planning councils. In West Germany, the government, in the early 1960s, was unable to delegitimate the Association of Health Insurance Physicians (KBV) as a bargaining partner with respect to medical care policies, despite the fact that this association (apparently ignoring its "public-law" status) lobbied with legislators, organized mass demonstrations, and even threatened strikes.[21] In France (and Sweden, for that matter) no union of public service employees has ever been "decertified" for striking illegally. (Paradoxically, it is in the liberal-pluralist United States that a trade union, the Professional Air Traffic Controllers' Organization [Patco], was decertified for so striking, despite the fact that in the US civil aviation is largely in the private domain.)

Regardless of the degree of irresponsibility of the behavior of important groups, no matter how highly "incorporated," delegitimating them would be counterproductive for the government, either because the state cannot substitute itself for the expertise of a group or because a sector's active collaboration is required for legitimating a policy or else because the state has limited powers of control over a sector's resources. This would apply, for instance, to the medical

[21] See my *Veto-Group Politics: The Case of Health-Insurance Reform in West Germany* (San Francisco: Chandler, 1967), pp. 182-84.

profession, because the characteristics of medical practice are so complex that the government can neither tell physicians exactly how to treat patients nor treat them itself.[22] It would apply to the trade unions, because (apart from their electoral potential) strikes, slowdowns or industrial sabotage can easily undermine a national economic policy. Finally, it would apply to business, whose investment and marketing decisions cannot be completely appropriated by the state, as long as business remains committed to the values of *political* liberalism.

THE BURDENS OF HISTORY

Highly institutionalized relationships between governments and interest groups have been common in Western European countries for at least three reasons: (1) the prevailing cultural traditions, themselves shaped by physical-geographical forces and conditions of economic and political development; (2) a widespread commitment to one or another approach to multiannual, "holistic" national socioeconomic policymaking; and (3) the perception among the leaders of most interest groups of the positive policy-utilitarian effects of such relationships.

Countries in which there is a high degree of classic liberal interest-group pluralism–the United States, Canada, and Australia–are often those whose wide open spaces and vast natural resources encouraged a tending to economic optimism–the belief in constant growth–such that whatever agreements interest groups, bargaining autonomously, arrived at would not be detrimental to the public interest. (Indeed, the very term "public interest" was considered mythical, and therefore suspect, by many U.S. political scientists.) This geographical-physical situation never applied to Britain or Switzerland, which could also be included, *grosso modo,* in the liberal pluralist mold. But Switzerland could escape from the economy-constricting pressures to which small countries are often subject by its avoidance of war. As for Britain (at least until the mid-1960s), the economic advantages accruing to it from its central position in a large empire, and hence its possession of a captive market, insulated

[22] See Deborah A. Stone, *The Limits of Professional Power* (Chicago: University of Chicago Press, 1980), esp. pp. 56ff.

it from these pressures. It is no accident that in the early 1960s, after the traditional optimism about growth had begun to evaporate, a Conservative government became interested in "planning," and, a few years later, a Labour government proposed various measures aimed at a progressive "governmentalization" of industrial relations (including mandatory conciliation and the banning of illegal strikes) as well as a prices and incomes board.[23]

Conversely, countries in which there has been a high degree of institutionalization–such as Austria and the Netherlands–have been those in which, owing to limited resources, a Malthusian spirit has prevailed that has conditioned society to the acceptance of policies of a careful husbanding of these resources. In some of these countries, political parties have been ineffective for screening and aggregating conflicting group demands: in Austria, because of the deadlock that long prevailed between two more or less evenly matched parties; and in the Netherlands, because of such parties' fragmentation and lack of power.

France and West Germany fall into a middle position: they represent a mixture of pluralist and dirigiste patterns that is attributable to conflicting traditions and experiences. In both countries, etatism, legalism, and formalism have created a mindset in favor of a high degree of institutionalization of groups. In Germany, the Hegelian notion that social groups, although natural and necessary, are less rational than (and therefore inferior to) the state predisposed politicians and intellectuals to accept groups only if they were sanctioned and regulated by law. In France, the Rousseauean distaste for intermediaries of all kinds was reflected in the outlawing of associations for nearly a century after the Revolution. But after World War II, Germany and France accounted for the fascist corporatist experience of the Hitler regime and the Vichy state, respectively: the constitutions of both the Fourth Republic and the Bonn republic, and the laws flowing from them, affirm the right of citizens to form associations, to demonstrate, to bargain collectively, to strike, and to participate in the formulation of policies.

In the United States, a distinction is made between the interest group, which exists in private and autonomous fashion in society, and the political party, which, seeking and achieving political power,

[23] Royal Commission on trade Unions and Employers' Associations (The Donovan Report), Cmnd. 3623.

becomes part of the public authority structure. Such a distinction cannot be made with much assurance in France and West Germany. In France, parties, clubs, "movements," *groupuscules,* and interest groups may be arranged under the same rubric, viz., as *forces politiques,* while in West Germany, both interest groups and parties are recognized, constitutionally and in public law, as more or less equal agents of sociopolitical *Willensbildung.* Parties and interest groups cannot be easily distinguished from one another in terms of origins, public legitimation, and political functions. Thus in both France and Germany the trade union movement preceded, and was instrumental in establishing, socialist parties; for many years unions and parties shared Marxist or rival (e.g., Catholic) ideologies. In both countries, interest groups have often competed with political parties in running candidates for elective office (thus in effect becoming parties): in Germany, the Association of Refugees and Expellees (the BHE) or the Greens, and in France, the Poujadists and Ecologists; leaders have moved, laterally, from responsible positions in parties to equally responsible positions in interest groups or vice versa or have combined these positions. In both countries, *various* interest groups, and not just the business community, have colonized both the legislature and parts of the executive. In France under Giscard, the former president of a large farmers' confederation (the FNSEA) was appointed to the cabinet (in 1979); and under Mitterrand, the leader of the National Federation of Teachers (FEN) received such an appointment (in 1981). In West Germany, several high officials of the DGB have been cabinet ministers–and Helmut Schmidt, as chancellor, continued to belong to the DGB (via membership in one of the constituent unions).[24] This trend has been supplemented by parliamentary lobbying in the proper sense. In West Germany, representatives of interest groups thought to be concerned with a pending policy matter are invited as a matter of course to legislative committee hearings–and the impact of this lobbying on the legislative outcome is not negligible. Even in the Fifth Republic, where parliament is relatively weak and its procedures are highly streamlined, old-fashioned lobbying goes on. One observer reports that in the 1960s he overheard a representative of the wine and liquor

[24] *Bulletin* (German Federal Press and Information Office), no. 44 (May 14, 1981), p. 381 (in German). The constituent union is the Union of Civil Service and Transport Workers (ÖTV).

interest "literally dictate the conditions [for a vote on a pending bill] to a deputy who was a member of a legislative standing committee."[25] In addition, in both countries interest groups have been instrumental in the shaping of party ideologies and programs. Thus in West Germany, the DGB played a major role in getting the SPD's endorsement of codetermination, of improvements in statutory medical insurance, and of anti-Nazi legislation, to mention but a few issues. In France, the CFDT helped to foist the idea of *autogestion* (worker self-management in factories) upon the Socialist party and even acted as a midwife of the political Left when it helped to bring various clubs and factions into an enlarged Socialist party.

In all industrial democracies, organized labor is at a disadvantage vis-à-vis organized business because of the programmatic affinities that often exist between business and government (in the sense that both share a commitment to productivity and to the existing political system) and because of a commonality of backgrounds between higher civil servants and business leaders. Organized labor has compensated for this by its mass membership, its electoral power, and its linkage to socialist parties. To the extent that these parties have been successful (and have achieved power), they have ceased to be the automatic vehicles for the transmission of labor demands, and the unions have had to compensate for this by developing more direct relations with the government. It is interesting to note that in France, West Germany, and certain other Western European countries the institutionalization of trade union-government relations increased the in the 1960s and 1970s in proportion to the divergence of the orientations and concerns of Socialist parties from those of the unions.[26]

An unmediated bargaining setup in which unions, management and (occasionally) government officials would resolve conflicts was sometimes encouraged by the Socialists themselves (especially when they were participating in the government) so that the economic struggle could be depoliticized as much as possible and the Socialists could be left free to "maintain the republic." But the substitution and

[25] Jean Saint-Geours, *La politique économique des principaux pays industriels de l'occident* (Paris: Sirey, 1969), p. 22.

[26] On this point, see Rainer Deppe et al., "Zum Verhältnis von sozialdemokratischer Partei und Gewerkschaften in der Klassenbewegung," in Joachim Bergmann, ed., *Beiträge zur Soziologie der Gewerkschaften,* (Frankfurt: Suhrkamp, 1979), pp. 189ff.

compensation pattern–an essential element of unmediated bargaining–should not be exaggerated, for the separation of interest groups and parties has had its limits and is likely to remain incomplete in the foreseeable future, at least in France and West Germany. In both countries, Socialists will continue to need the electoral support unions can marshal, and the unions will need the Socialist parties as a reserve weapon in case of failure to achieve their ends through autonomous bargaining *or* negotiations with the government. This mutual recognition of interdependence makes for periodic liaison experiments. In West Germany, there was established in the early 1970s a working group for problems of employees (Arbeitsgemeinschaft für Arbeitnehmerfragen), composed primarily of union officials and members of factory councils, whose purpose was to pressure the SPD in the direction of a more consistent prolabor policy in Parliament. And in France, the CFDT, as a quid pro quo for the inclusion of prolabor planks in the platform of the Socialist party, campaigned actively for Socialist candidates in the presidential and parliamentary elections of 1974, 1978, and 1981.

At the same time, the lack of precision in the historic and current role distinctions between parties and interest groups made it possible for the interest groups to become infected with the "expressive" virus of the parties: often interest groups (especially trade unions) still behave as if they were concerned less with bread-and-butter policies than with the articulation of ideologies. As a prominent Giscardist politician remarked, "L'esprit de parti tue la vie associative."[27] In Germany, the contempt in which bureaucrats, jurists, and academics held the political parties (before and during the Weimar Republic) for their allegedly selfish wheeling and dealing *(Kuhhandel)* came also to be applied to interest groups.[28] This explains in part why many intellectuals in France and Germany could more easily tolerate the involvement of organized socioeconomic interests in the political process if these appeared, if at all possible, with their private/particularistic labels removed or hidden, that is, in the guise of an *établissement du droit public* or a *Verein des öffentlichen*

[27] Bernard Stasi, *Vie associative et démocratie nouvelle* (Paris: Presses Universitaires de France, 1979), p. 109.

[28] For example, Theodor Eschenburg, *Herrschaft der Verbände?* (Stuttgart: Deutsche Verlagsanstalt, 1955), and Günter Triesch, *Die Macht der Funktionäre* (Düsseldorf: Karl Rauch, 1956).

Rechts. Until two decades ago, there was neither a French nor a German equivalent of "interest group"; and there is still no equivalent of "lobby" in these languages (a fact that may be variously attributed to the lack of independence of deputies belonging to mass parties, to the weakness of parliament, or to a lingering contempt for that institution in some quarters). Among some higher civil servants in West Germany, there is still the pretense that the representatives of socioeconomic sectors or professions furnish their advice to the government not as spokesmen for selfish interests but as experts *(Sachverständige)*.

THE SELECTIVE "AMERICANIZATION" OF THE FRENCH AND GERMAN INTEREST-GROUP CONTEXT AND ITS LIMITS

Today, the U.S. terminology for interest groups and even pressure groups *(groupe d'intérêt, Interessengruppe,* etc.)[29] has become widespread, and there are few serious complaints about the "privatization" or dismantling of the state. In both countries, the major interest groups are known as "social partners"–a term that implies not only a modicum of equality between labor and capital in collective bargaining but also a policymaking collaboration with the government that is more reflective of a pluralistic than a corporatist orientation.

The historically conditioned legal distinction between professional orders or bodies of public law, on the one hand, and ordinary interest groups or voluntary associations, on the other, is losing much of its functional significance. In France, although all physicians must belong to the Ordre national des médecins (which was created by ordinance in 1945 and charged with assuring the internal discipline of the profession), the government normally bargains with the voluntary Confédération des syndicats médicaux français (established in 1930 and embracing about two-thirds of the physicians) on matters of medical fees. In West Germany, the Federal Association

[29] See Jean Meynaud, *Nouvelles études sur les groupes de pression en France* (Paris: Armand Colin, 1962), and Rupert Breitling, *Die Verbände in der Bundesrepublik* (Meisenheim am Glahn: Anton Hain, 1955) for influential discussions.

of Local Health Insurance Funds (Bundesverband der Ortskrankenkassen) is an organization of quasipublic officials that was established in consequence of the creation of a statutory medical coverage system, but (like its French counterpart, the Fédération Nationale des Organismes de Sécurité Sociale) it behaves much like a voluntary group in its attempts at influencing decision makers.

There are other aspects of "Americanization" in the contexts and patterns of French and German interest-group politics. There is a growing acceptance of the state on the part of organized labor and, as a consequence, a replacement of the anarchosyndicalist orientation by "business unionism." This development is much further advanced in West Germany than in France; yet even in that country, pragmatic collaboration among unions with regard to certain concrete issues (such as wages) coexists with ideological conflict on the verbal level. Conversely, there is an acceptance by business of the place of collective bargaining. Furthermore, there has been a grudging acceptance by both public officials and intellectuals of the idea that "lobbying" is a normal activity in democratic regimes and that economic associations are not necessarily subverting the state when they try to promote narrower interests. As one French scholar has put it, "the discredit that once attached itself to the private sector, which was considered unclean, has been attenuated; far from being prohibited or condemned, contacts with [socioeconomic] groups have become an essential element of legitimation of administrative action."[30]

In a sense, the West German federal system has been a better environment for promoting such pluralistic attitudes than highly centralized France. But in that country, too, the current interest in "regionalization" reflects a growing belief in the virtues of "subsystem autonomy."

At the same time, political-cultural and other factors prevent these two countries from Americanizing their interest-group politics entirely. It is difficult to imagine equivalents, in terms of size of membership, wealth, prestige, or political power, of the National Rifle Association in France or Germany, because the Wild West vigi-

[30] Jacques Chevallier, "L'idéologie des fonctionnaires: permanence et changement," in J. Chevallier ed., for the Centre universitaire des recherches administratives et politiques de Picardie, *Discours et idéologie* (Paris: Presses Universitaires de France, 1980), p. 48.

lantism and the individualistic challenge it implies to the role of the state as the guardian of law and order are alien to the traditions of these countries. In West Germany, there does not (yet) exist an equivalent of such promotional groups as the American Civil Liberties Union, for the simple reason that the acceptance of the idea of ordinary citizens challenging the actions of public authorities is still impeded by vestiges of *Obrigkeitsgefühl.* In France, ethnic groups traditionally were feebly if at all organized; they would have been considered less than fully legitimate– if not subversive–given the Jacobin orientations that have nurtured most of the elite. This is, however, in process of change: currently a number of intellectuals have come to admit that France is a "pluralistic" society, not merely in terms of classes, institutions, and ideologies, but also in terms of "*appartenance ethno-culturelle.*"[31] As the perception of this new legitimation spreads, organizations based on such ethnic membership will doubtlessly grow.

In both France and Germany, professors and their associations have enjoyed a much more receptive ear among official decision-makers than they have had in the United States; rather than being considered *wirklichkeitsfremde* "eggheads," intellectuals are respected by the public and perceived as reflecting the interests of the state (as an entity with a rational purpose) better than businessmen. (And *within* the community of intellectuals, the humanists have had better access to the public authorities than have scientists or technologists–almost the reverse of the situation in the United States, with its ahistoricist cultural bias.) Conversely, the medical profession in France and Germany has enjoyed neither the degree of autonomy nor the privileged access to policymakers that have characterized their counterparts in the United States. This has been due not only to the organizational fragmentation of the profession in these two European countries, but also to the fact that neither the entrepreneurialism of medicine nor the myth of the doctor-patient relationship has been as widespread there as in the United States. In both France and West Germany, the unity of the employed has been impeded by the existence of separate white-collar organizations. The distinction that has existed in most European countries between

[31] See Pierre Birnbaum, *Le peuple et le gros* (Paris: Grasset, 1979), p. 208. See also the favorable treatment of ethnic groups in the *Projet socialiste pour la France pour les années 80* (Paris: Parti Socialiste, 1980).

white- and blue-collar sectors has been due not only to the status consciousness that has been one of the relics of feudalism, but also to the fact that it has been buttressed by public policies that differentiate between the two sectors.[32]

The notion of "social partnership" exists both in Western Europe and in the United States. In France and Germany, national indicative planning (whether in the form of *planification* or of *Finanzplanung)* and the welfare state legislation related to such planning depend for their success on the willing participation of both labor and capital. Hence the representation of labor in institutions that prepare economic policy inputs and that help to implement the welfare state is automatic and often substantial (e.g., in France, the Social and Economic Council, the National Commission on Collective Contracts, and the planning committees on various levels), and representation sometimes is based on the principle of parity with business (e.g., in ministerial advisory councils, social security agencies, and labor relations and other tribunals in both France and Germany). In the United States, by contrast, "social partnership" remains largely a functionally irrelevant slogan. To the extent that national arenas for unmediated conflict resolution exist, they are incompletely institutionalized, provisional, and unequal in composition. Thus the Price-Wage Board, set up by President Nixon in 1975 (and abolished later by President Carter) contained seven trade union representatives and eight spokesmen of business; it was set up *after* the president had decided on a wage freeze (but not a price freeze), and its advisory role was without any ascertainable policymaking consequence. The federal Independent Regulatory Commissions occasionally contain representatives of labor unions, but these are always in the minority. The administration of Medicare and Medicaid reflects, in a certain measure, the cooptation of the private sector for the fulfillment of publicadministrative tasks. But the Blue Cross and Blue Shield societies, the chosen intermediaries, represent in essence the physicians' and hospitals' associations (which compromise their mutual claims) but not the beneficiaries of medical care.

[32] For instance, in France, in the existence, for many years, of a better system of payment *(mensualisation)* and more advantageous separation policies for white-collar employees; and in Germany, in the maintenance of separate social security agencies for that sector.

U.S.-STYLE INTEREST-GROUP PLURALISM AND ITS IMPLICATIONS

In the United States, interest groups have not been "incorporated" into the official authority structure or the political parties and hence have retained their autonomy vis-à-vis both. Such autonomy has contributed to the maintenance of a functional distinction between the "articulation structure" on the one hand and the aggregation and central decision-making structures on the other and, in so doing, has also contributed to keeping the U.S. political system close to a once popular model of modernity and democracy.[33] But how well has this autonomy served the interests of labor? It would seem that the labor movement, if shortchanged in the autonomous bargaining process, has little effective political recourse, as compared with the (big) business sector.

Occasionally, spokesmen of big business are given places in the cabinet, but spokesmen of labor are not–unlike the situation in Germany and France, where organized labor has developed squatters' rights to certain ministries, even under conservative administrations.[34] Organized labor cannot use political parties effectively: under conditions of geographical and institutional fragmentation, there is no national party with which organized labor has a dependable connection. (The Liberal party is the exception that proves the rule: its appeal is confined to the New York area and although for years it was the plaything of one union,[35] it never pretended to be the spokesman for organized labor.) Labor cannot always raise its own issues of concern directly with the government (especially with an unsympathetic one), for there are no consultative arenas where it

[33] According to Almond and Powell (*Comparative Politics*, pp. 105-107), "the heavy load of raw, unstructured demands may bring policymaking to a halt . . ." and therefore, "aggregation structures must be differentiated from the central decision-making structures . . . and also from the major articulation structures." Cf. Easton (*Systems Analysis*, pp. 256-258), for whom, in democratic systems, "The party remains the major mechanism for regulating cleavages," and who insists that it is only in non democratic systems that "representative organs . . . become converted into administrative organizations."

[34] During the Eisenhower administration, the cabinet consisted of "nine millionaires and a plumber"; but the latter (Martin Durkin, of the plumbers' union) lasted only a few months in his job.

[35] The International Ladies' Garment Workers' Union (ILGWU).

is legally, reliably, and equitably represented, whose setting is formalized, and whose work (in the form of agreements) is so authoritative as to be embodied in public policy. There is, in short, no institutional substitute for the failure of the leaders of labor (or certain other groups) to be received by the president on tthe chief executive golf course and to be informed about any covert understandings he might have with the leaders of business. For a variety of historic reasons, anarchosyndicalist or other revolutionary ideologies are underdeveloped within the unions and within most of the working class in the United States; hence threats of general strikes are not credible.

Ironically, although the U.S. working class and organized labor have accepted the existing capitalist system perhaps too uncritically, they have not been adequately rewarded for such acceptance, and they are likely to be rewarded even less adequately in an economy that has ceased to grow. Because of the capitalist orientation of organized labor and because of the absence of a convincing threat of nationalization,[36] U.S. organized business has accepted the welfare state much more grudgingly than have its counterparts in Western European countries and has not accepted industrial democracy (a form of unmediated bargaining) at all.

The petroleum crisis has had a debilitating impact on organized labor, family agriculture, small business, and other "traditional" sectors in Western Europe as well as the United States. The need to pay for increasingly costly fuel imports has led to a new emphasis on productivity by means of industrial consolidation, the reduction of per-unit costs, and the development of global markets. One of the consequences of this emphasis is the growth of multinational businesses; however, these businesses cannot be easily coopted or "incorporated" because (almost by definition) they are beyond the jurisdictional grasp of this or that national government. Moreover, both multinational and national firms are tempted to use foreign "workers

[36] The utility of nationalized industry as a weapon for reducing the economic power of private business is evident, but the impact of nationalization on the unions is less clear. On the one hand, nationalized industry can be used by the government as a pacesetter for higher wages and fringe benefits and for industrial democracy; on the other hand, the unions are (albeit indirectly) faced with government rather than the private sector as bargaining opponent, and therefore labor-management confrontations could be interpreted as the unions' fight against "the public interest" rather than against profit-motivated and greedy private firms.

(as scabs)", whose presence has reduced the bargaining power of unions.

In the United States, the bargaining power of some trade unions (e.g., the needleworkers) had begun to be undermined in the 1960s by the influx of cheap foreign goods; other unions (e.g., the once powerful United Auto Workers) were enfeebled at the end of the 1970s and were gradually reduced to negotiating wage reductions. To be sure, the recognition of economic stringency has led to an attitude among Western European unions that has been described as "neo-realism"[37] –reflected in part in union modesty in demanding reductions in the work week. At the same time, unions in both France and West Germany have been periodically organizing mass demonstrations and protest strikes (even illegal ones) to warn the government against projected reductions in welfare state spending.[38]

There is another important reason why the weakness of organized labor in particular Western European countries may not have the same negative substantive consequences as in the United States: their connection with the European Economic Community has resulted in the *transnationalization* (and hence the partial depoliticization on the national level) of certain socioeconomic conflicts and the institutionalization of certain policies such that a hostile combination of government and business forces cannot easily unravel them. Under the Treaty of Rome, national governments have changed domestic laws to "harmonize" them with minimal supranational standards regarding the payment and retraining of redundant workers, the participation of workers in industrial management, social security protections, the maintenance of farmers' incomes, and so on. The effect of such harmonization has been to transform members of weak unions and unorganized or poorly organized interests (e.g., pensioners, small farmers, small businessmen) into "free riders." (Unfortunately, the implications of supranationalism for the power of interest groups have not been adequately studied.)

[37] Jean-Pierre Dumont, in *Le Monde,* July 11, 1980. Cf. "Gewerkschaften finden Verständnis für Beschäftigungsprogramm," *Deutschland-Nachrichten,* no. 40, November 11, 1981.

[38] *The Week in Germany* (German Information Center, New York), December 11, 1981.

There appear to be important policy consequences for the absence of compensatory articulation and bargaining structures in the United States, such as are found in Western European countries. Unlike France and Germany (and most other Western European countries), the United States does not have comprehensive medical coverage, universalized paid vacations, schemes for factory democracy, minimum wages and pension payments that are almost automatically adjusted to keep pace with inflation, or even laws (like the Royer Law passed in France in 1973) protecting the small businessman against threats from big business. In fact, a cross-national comparison of social protection expenditures reveals that the top countries are those in which there are highly formalized relationships between interest groups and the government–i.e., Scandinavia, the Netherlands, France, West Germany, and Austria–and that the bottom countries–the United States, Canada, and Switzerland–are among those where such relationships are least institutionalized (see table 2).

The policy failures in the United States, especially in matters of redistribution, have not led to serious demands for a change in the structures of articulation and bargaining in the direction of equitable and institutionalized interest-group representation. The reasons for this reluctance to change are complex. They may perhaps be sought in a general unwillingness to transform institutions, which may in turn be attributed to a number of myths:

1. The myth of antiquity: the fact that U.S. political institutions (beginning with the constitution) have remained essentially unchanged is transformed into a virtue, that is, into a proof of the adequacy, if not superiority, of these institutions;
2. The myth of countervailing powers (which had especially wide currency during the affluent 1960s): the belief that autonomous bargaining between labor and capital, or producers and consumers, represents a pattern of equitable bilateral relationships and renders a resort to the political authorities largely unnecessary;
3. The general belief that interest groups are in practice afforded equal lobbying opportunities in Congress and elsewhere–if only they do their homework and deserve a hearing;
4. The myth of the efficacy of various autonomous subsystems as instruments of grass-roots participation that at once maintain social freedom and achieve equitable policy results: the belief that justice is served by a jury of peers, that local draft boards make fair selections because they are composed of "your friends and neighbors," that local parent-teacher associations make momentous decisions, and that–if all else fails–local referenda will be held that will reflect the public will–in short, that federalism (i.e., geographical subsystem autonomy) provides a meaningful (and more democratic) alternative to functional representation (this belief

Table 2
Social Protection Expenditure as a Percentage of Gross Domestic Product at Market Prices

Country	*1973*	*1975*	*1977*	*1979*
West Germany	23.1	27.8	27.6	26.6
Sweden	21.5	26.2	30.5	
France	19.8	22.9	24.0	25.2
Netherlands	23.7	28.1	29.2	31.2
Belgium	20.4	24.5	26.2	27.1
Denmark	21.1	25.6	25.1	26.9
Norway	18.1	18.5	19.6	
Austria	18.0	20.2	21.1	
Britain	17.1	19.5	19.7	19.9
Switzerland	12.9	15.1	16.1	
United States	12.3	13.2	13.7	
Canada	13.9	14.7	14.5	
Japan	6.3	7.6	9.7	

Sources: *Basic Statistics of the Community, (Bruxelles: Statistical Office of the European Community, 1981)*, p. 168, and *Eurostat Review 1971-80* (Bruxelles: Statistical Office of the European Community, 1982), p. 134.

has apparently not been affected by the abysmally low turnouts at local elections);

5. The conviction that, as capitalism is not seriously challenged and the class struggle does not exist, there is no need to institutionalize the behavior of the major interest groups in order to make them coexist peacefully.

Such myths have sometimes been translated by political scientists, consciously or not, into analytic components of the ideal type pluralistic system and, by derivation, into ethnocentric models of interest-group politics. A sharper awareness of this translation would constitute a first step toward recognizing that interest-group *pluralism* can be defined in Western European as well as U.S. terms.

Chapter 18

CORPORATISM IN FRANCE: THE GAULLIST CONTRIBUTION

Kay Lawson

INTRODUCTION

France, as everyone knows, is a deeply divided nation. Corporatism is recommended by its advocates as a means of reconciling divisions, particularly those political divisions that stem from conflicting economic interests. It is not surprising, then, that the French have been drawn, time and again, to the corporatist mode. Indeed, France has, from time to time, adopted corporatist institutions and practices. It has never yet, however, become a true corporatist state. Corporatism is resisted with a fervor and dedication at least equal to that of those who recommend its adoption. Sometimes the corporatists gain the ascendancy; sometimes the anticorporatists are dominant. Neither side ever wins a complete or permanent victory. France, as everyone knows, is a deeply divided nation.

Coming full circle–full and ironic if not vicious circle–is a common experience for those who study the politics of France. It is a game French intellectuals delight in playing: no matter what the subject, any suggestion that change is really taking place, that this time a corner is being turned rather than an arc described, is likely to be greeted with amused tolerance if not outright contempt for the ignorance displayed with respect to historical patterns and immutable social laws (plus ça change. . .).

Fred Eidlin, Elijah Kaminsky, William Safran, and Frank Wilson have all read and commented on this chapter. I profited greatly from their suggestions for its improvement and very much appreciate their efforts. In those few instances where I have not agreed with them I hope it is nevertheless clear to them that I have been usefully stimulated to improve the strength and clarity of my arguments.

Nevertheless, the objective observer must occasionally pose the question: Is change taking place? Sometimes the circle does become a spiral, and changes in degree become, finally, changes in direction. Is this the case with corporatism? Have the appeals of this mode of interest representation won over sufficient adherents on both political left and right to mean that France will become progessively more corporatist regardless of which side is in power?

My purpose is not to offer a complete answer to that question but to present evidence that should be useful in moving toward an answer. In France the open advocacy of corporatist practices has been more characteristic of the political right than of the political left, and this chapter will discuss the right-wing approach to corporatism, with particular emphasis on the recent role of the Gaullists in building support for corporatist ideals. Although brief mention will be made of the policies of the current Socialist government in this regard, the full answer to the question of whether or not "France will become progressively more corporatist" would require at least another chapter on left-wing approaches to corporatism. Given the fact that prior to the 1981 presidential and legislative elections the left was out of power for twenty-three years, that chapter probably should not be written until the observation of a few years of contemporary leftist practice can be added to an analysis of leftist doctrine and theory on the question.

It is, however, an excellent time to assess the recent Gaullist contribution to the French corporatist tradition. To understand that contribution we must begin with a brief consideration of the meanings of corporatism, in general and in France. We will explore the former by referring to contemporary scholarly literature on the subject, the latter by examining the history of corporatist practice in France prior to the Gaullist takeover in 1958. The second half of the chapter will be devoted to a study of Gaullist corporatist policy under presidents Charles de Gaulle, Georges Pompidou, and Valéry Giscard d'Estaing and Gaullist corporatist politics under the party leadership of former Prime Minister Jacques Chirac. Inasmuch as Giscard and his party (the Union for French Democracy) are only tangentially "Gaullist," and some of the most active work on behalf of the corporatist ideal during Giscard's tenure in office was carried on by his rival Jacques Chirac through the Rally for the Republic

(RPF) (the current name for the "true" Gaullist party, founded in 1958 as the Union for the New Republic, later renamed the Union for the Defense of the Republic), the emphasis in discussion of the period 1974-1981 will be on the contributions of the RPR. Data gathered in the course of interviewing RPR leaders and militants and attending RPR meetings in 1977-1978 will be incorporated in this section of the chapter.

THE MEANINGS OF CORPORATISM

Contemporary Definitions

The concept "corporatism" is in almost as much trouble as "charisma" or "totalitarianism" (for the latter, see Eidlin, 1981). An amazingly wide variety of systems and practices are currently labelled "corporatist" or "neocorporatist." When a formerly fixed concept is stretched to cover multiple and sometimes conflicting meanings, it is usually a sign of radical change in the nature of the phenomenon (or phenomena) denoted by and made comprehensible by the concept. Such changes usually do not continue indefinitely. As matters settle down, so does our conceptual vocabulary. Sometimes we decide to live with multiple meanings for a once simple and single-dimensional concept (e.g., "participation"). Sometimes we find the concept stretched right out of usefulness or sense and we abandon it altogether, substituting several new terms to denote several old and new realities (does anyone remember "social conditioning"?). Once in a while we recognize that a pulled and twisted old concept would serve us best by being restored to its former meaning, and we develop a new vocabulary just for the new conditions (a kindness extended to "balance of power" once we invented "deterrence" and "détente," for example).

It is not yet clear which of these fates is in store for "corporatism." However, it is very clear that at present the concept has quite different meanings for different scholars and furthermore that at the moment no one is willing to give an inch. "My corporatism is the real corporatism" seems to be the common battle cry.

In this essay an attempt will be made to be a little more accommodating than that. I will simply say what I mean by corporatism, say what I do not mean, and try to show that the meaning I give the term is at least reasonably well connected to some of the meanings it has more commonly been given.

Philippe Schmitter defines corporatism as "a system of interest representation in which the constituent units are organized into a limited number of singular, compulsory, noncompetitive, hierarchically ordered and functionally differentiated categories, recognized or licensed (if not created) by the state and granted a deliberate representational monopoly within their respective categories in exchange for observing certain controls on their selections of leaders and articulation of demands and supports" (Schmitter, 1974, pp. 93-94).

This is almost satisfactory for my purposes, but I would prefer to begin with a slightly more rigorous definition, one that insists further that all the units that are given "representational monopoly within their respective categories" exercise that right while working together in at least one official organ of the government itself (such as the Italian *corporazione* or the Spanish *Cortes* or Vichy's planned but never implemented "professional family"). I would therefore change Schmitter's definition as follows: corporatism is "a system of interest representation in which the constituent units are organized into a limited number of singular, compulsory, noncompetitive, hierarchically ordered and functionally differentiated categories, recognized or licensed (if not created) by the state and granted a deliberate representational monopoly within their respective categories, *which they exercise by meeting together in one or more official organs of government,* in exchange for observing certain controls on their selections of leaders and articulation of demands and supports."

So far, so good. But Schmitter then goes on to identify two sub-types of corporatism: state corporatism and societal corporatism. State corporatism is the corporatism imposed by an authoritarian state; it "tends to be associated with political systems in which territorial subunits are tightly subordinated to central bureaucratic power; elections are nonexistent or plebiscitary, party systems are dominated or monopolized by a weak single party; executive authorities are ideologically exclusive and . . . narrowly recruited and . . .

political subcultures based on class, ethnicity, language, or regionalism are repressed" (Schmitter, 1974, p. 105). It is the kind of corporatism likely to be imposed in an incipiently pluralistic system in response to what is felt as a compelling need to enforce "social peace."

Societal corporatism, on the other hand (according to Schmitter), emerges "naturally," "spontaneously," out of conditions of advanced pluralism and expanding bureaucratic power. Under societal corporatism, the state "structures" group representation. It legitimizes one set of functional organizations by giving them official recognition and by appointing only their members to appropriate government boards and agencies. Sometimes it even offers subsidies to foster their growth. This kind of corporatism (if it is corporatism) "is found imbedded in political systems with relatively autonomous, multilayered territorial units; open, competitive electoral processes and party systems; ideologically varied, coalitionally based executive authorities–even with a wide variety of political subcultures" (Schmitter, 1974, p. 105).

What is happening here? What Schmitter calls societal corporatism and other authors call neocorporatism is not corporatism at all, by the terms of my modified version of Schmitter's definition. It is simply an effort to impose elements of corporatism on a pluralist system. A state cannot be both corporatist and pluralist; the terms are (given the definition of corporatism used here and the most familiar definitions of pluralism) mutually exclusive. However, there is no doubt that there really is something corporatist about these new tendencies in pluralist states. When we look more closely, we can find several reminders of "real" corporatism in this evolving relationship between the pluralist state and its productive forces. To enumerate:

1. The creation of state agencies on which representatives of management and labor serve with government officials (although such service is not, in pluralist states, compulsory).
2. The extension of compulsory bargaining and arbitration throughout public and sometimes into private units of production.
3. The common assumption in official pronouncements that there exists a "profound unity" among all those working in a modern economy.
4. The creation of worker-management committees within industry and the adoption of various schemes of profit-sharing.
5. The cooptation of workers' leaders, often at the cost of their isolation from those they lead.

6. The widespread conviction that any measure that strengthens the national economy will produce long-term rewards for all sufficient to justify short-term deprivation for the less advantaged.
7. A general proclivity on the part of the state to underwrite the continued supremacy, political and economic, of the managerial class.[1]

Even when all are present, these beliefs and practices do not make a system corporatist, not as corporatism has been defined here. Some of them (see especially number 4) are found as well in systems very different from the corporatist state. But together they do strongly suggest a movement in the direction of a new form of government, a pluralism strongly constrained by corporatist ideals, corporatist practices.

Furthermore, this phenomenon–the superimposition of corporatist characteristics on pluralist systems–is on the rise. We live in an era when noncorporatist systems are experimenting more and more frequently with corporatist ideas and practices–and we do need some language for saying so. Perhaps we will eventually agree to call such systems neocorporatist. To my mind, however, that term is a step away from conceptual clarity: it obscures the essence of true corporatism, it obscures the essence of true pluralism. The solution I prefer, especially during this period of transition when we are not sure exactly what this new hybrid will become or what name it should be given, is simply to hold to a firm definition, such as the modified one I have drawn from Schmitter, when labeling whole systems corporatist, and in all other cases to make unambiguously clear that we are merely noticing that certain ideas and practices of particular pluralist systems are ideas and practices that are typically characteristic of corporatist systems. They are corporatist ideas, corporatist practices, manifested in a noncorporatist state.

This paper will endeavor to hold to that rule: let it be said at the outset that France is not a corporatist state. Not since the days of the ancient guilds has France organized units of interest representation corporatively. But pluralist France is a system that has from time to time adopted many corporatist ideas and practices, that has produced a remarkable roster of corporatist philosophers, and

[1] For several of these points I am indebted to the references to corporatism in the works of Audoin (1962), Duclos (1963), and Ehrmann (1957). Ehrmann, by the way, was one of the first to point out that the politics of postwar France were marked by corporatist practices and thought, even when those concerned were "not fully aware of the corporatist strands in their thinking" (Ehrmann, 1957, p. 487).

that has even gone so far as to make heads of state out of committed devotees of the corporatist mode of interest representation.

The Historical Meanings of Corporatism in France: 1150 to 1958

From the Guilds to the Revolution

To understand the fascination of corporatism for the French, we must go back long before the emergence of so-called neocorporatism. The corporatist ideal has a seven-hundred-year history in France. The French take history, especially their own, very seriously, and their response to contemporary corporatist thought is thus strongly conditioned by that history. Anyone interested in understanding the status of corporatism in France today must make some effort, however cursory, to review the past.

Corporatism in France had its origins in the twelfth century, when the first artisanal guilds were organized. Although the guilds never became part of a full-fledged corporatist state, they were sanctioned by French monarchs and did maintain monopolistic control of trade in their products. The early guilds included masters, journeymen, and apprentices in a hierarchical but mutually supportive closed "corporation." Although important sectors of the medieval French economy, such as agriculture and banking, remained outside their scope, their powers were extensive: they set prices, regulated quality, fixed wages and hours, and provided welfare services to their members (Audoin, 1962, p. 40; Elbow, 1953, pp. 14-15).

The heyday of the guilds lasted little more than two hundred years. Beginning in the fourteenth century the expanding power of an ever more centralized monarchy began encroaching on their domain as on all others, and in the succeeding two centuries their rigid structure made them incapable of successful adjustment to the economic and technological changes that accompanied the age of discovery and exploration (Audoin, 1962, pp.38 and 46-47). By the time they were abolished in the course of the French Revolution (by a law passed March 2, 1791) they had been greatly weakened by the competition of unorganized artisans operating under the direct protection of the state.

Nineteenth-Century French Corporatism

Despite this less than distinguished beginning, the corporatist ideal had taken hold and has never since lacked for more or less impassioned advocates in France. The nineteenth century saw the idea resurrected time and again in theory and, in limited fashion, in practice. In 1806 Napoleon set up the conseils de prud'hommes, industrial committees of workers and employers authorized to settle industrial disputes and help carry out the laws regulating labor, and permitted the butchers' and bakers' guilds to reorganize. Utopian socialists Henri de Saint Simon and Charles Fourier urged, respectively, a corporatist legislative body and worker ownership of stocks. Social reformers Simonde de Sismondi, Vicomte Albon de Villeneuve-Bargemont, Félix de la Farelle, Philippe Buchez, and Eugène Buret all argued that some form of a revived guild system was necessary to permit the working class to climb out of the dire poverty into which it had been forced by the exploitative power of the Industrial Revolution. Royalists like Joseph de Maistre and the Comte de Chambord (the latter himself the legitimist pretender to the French throne from 1836 to 1884) wrote in favor of reviving the guilds. Social Catholics Frédéric le Play, Charles Perin, and Émile Keller were less enthusiastic about the guilds but wanted to see some form of fraternal brotherhood established for workers in the industrial age (Elbow, 1953, pp. 18-52).

Meanwhile, however, the second Napoleon suppressed the butchers' and bakers' guiids his uncle had revived, and the words of these early quasicorporatist theorists made little impression on a populace busily carrying out the tenets of economic liberalism, a doctrine with which the corporatists themselves partially sympathized. It was not until the beginning of the Third Republic (1870) and the founding by La Tour du Pin of the Oeuvre des Cercles Catholiques d'Ouvriers, a network of Catholic clubs designed to unite workers "in Christian corporations with employers and to place them under the guidance of directive committees from the upper classes," that corporatism once again began to be taken seriously in France. In some senses an early precursor of societal corporatism, La Tour du Pin believed the grassroots growth of such associations would be the best way to institutionalize corporatism. He argued, however, that eventually the new corporations should take over many of the functions of the state, exercising legislative, judicial, and executive powers in the governance of their members as well as maintaining a mutual aid fund and certifying professional capacity. He saw the corporations as states within the state, capable of preventing excessive centralization and control. His ideas found some support; his friend and associate Albert de Mun carried the corporatist battle into the French parliament but fought in vain for the resurrection of the guild (in the mode designed by La Tour du Pin) and against the rise of separate trade unions and employer associations (Elbow, 1953, pp. 53-80).

1900 to 1940: The Growing Appeal of Corporatist Thought

The arguments of La Tour du Pin and de Mun were pursued in the twentieth century by other Social Catholics, with minor variations, and by independent writers, often with major variations. Émile Durkheim saw corporatism as a solution to the problem of anomie and argued that society should be composed of "a vast system of national corporations" (Durkheim, 1926, ch. 31,, cited in Elbow, 1953, p. 114). Georges Sorel stressed syndicalism; Léon Duguit, pluralism; and Charles Maurras, the founder of Action Française, anti-semitism and jingoistic nationalism, but all three inveighed against individualism and egalitarianism in terms very similar to those used by the corporatists.

After World War I the idea of corporatism became steadily more attractive to the French. Europe's severe social and economic problems in that era provoked not only the rise of socialism but the concomitant quest for an alternative other than the discredited free play of economic liberalism. Portugal, Spain, Italy, and Austria found that alternative in corporatism, and by 1931, when the depression struck with full force, the French were ready to adopt at least some of the corporatist remedies. As a consequence, the 1930s were a period of increased government regulation of the economy, compulsory bargaining and arbitration between employer and employee unions, and even some "spontaneous" corporatist organization (e.g., when the French leather industry faced devastating Czech competition, employers and workers formed mixed committees to determine what import quotas to recommend).

Accompanying this revival of corporatist practice was an entire spectrum of new corporatist theory, ranging from the openly fascist recommendations of Jacques Doriot and François de la Rocque to the socialist *étatisme* urged by Charles Spinasse, minister of the national economy and minister of the budget in the 1936-1937 and 1938 cabinets of Léon Blum. In between these two ideological extremes the renewed enthusiasm of royalists (Jacques Valdour, George Viance), Social Catholics (Eugène Duthoit, Paul Chanson), industrialists (Eugène Mathon, Pierre Lucius, and the members of the Comité Central de l'Organization Professionnelle and Jeune Patron), and intellectuals (the members of the Institute for Corporative and Social Studies, who published a monthly review entitled *Le Corporatisme)* were evidence of the wide range of Frenchmen to whom corporatism now seemed a last, best hope (Ehrmann, 1957, pp. 49-53; Elbow, 1953, pp. 97-137).

Vichy: The Rise and Fall of Corporatist Hopes

Out of the ashes of the Third Republic, the corporatist dream rose undiminished. Indeed, the bitter defeat of 1940 seemed at first to give the corporatists the opportunity to put their ideas to the test as never before. In October 1940 Marshall Philippe Pétain proclaimed that "occupations will be organized, and their organization will be imposed on everyone. The professional organizations will deal with everything that concerns occupations. . . . they will have charge of the drafting and execution of labor agreements . . . . they will prevent conflicts by the total prohibition of lock-outs and strikes, and by compulsory arbitration through labor courts" (Tissier, 1942, p. 234).

In practice, however, corporative organization was introduced only in agriculture and, to a lesser extent, in the seafishing industry. Every other branch of production or trade was placed under an organizing committee, composed only of major employers, appointed by the government. Its powers were extensive, but the government retained a right of veto over all decisions. Separate trade associations and unions continued to exist, under the supervision of these committees, but the leaders of the committees often held important posts in the trade associations as well, which resulted in "an almost complete fusion between Committees and trade associations" (Ehrmann, 1957, p. 80).

Although large business interests were satisfied with this arrangement, corporatists were not, and efforts were made to move more determinedly in the corporatist direction with the promulgation of the Labor Charter in October 1941. The charter called for the gradual establishment of twenty-five "professional families" to be composed of five categories (employers, workers, clerks, agents of management, and engineers and technicians), all working together to set production goals, prices, and wages and to resolve disputes (Elbow, 1953, pp. 182-183). A rudimentary first step was the establishment within factories of "social committees," which were assigned responsibility for such matters as factory canteens, cooperative stores, and health care. Businessmen accepted the social committees, especially as the workers' delegates on these committees were usually selected by the employers, but successfully resisted efforts to take any further steps in the corporatist direction during the Vichy years: "A full-fledged corporatism would have led to the dissolution of employers' organizations and trade unions alike. This, in the opinion of most business leaders, was too high a price to pay at the moment when the trade associations acquired unprecedented strength through their connections with the [organizing committee], and when nothing was to be feared from the labor movement" (Ehrmann, 1957, p. 93).

1945-1958: Corporatism in Retreat

An idea that has not been fully tested cannot be considered fully discredited, however strongly opinion may turn against the would-be testers. Although there was enough talk about corporatism during the Vichy era to mean that the word itself now reminds the French of an era and a national behavior they would prefer not to dwell on, the corporatist ideal was not abandoned in postwar France (Ehrmann, 1957, p. 478). New words had to be found and new structures proposed, but the corporatist cause was still being served by powerful and determined men.

The thinking of Charles de Gaulle typified that of many of the French on this question–as on so many others–in the immediate postwar period. A leading opponent of the Pétain regime and a consummate politician (the latter label one he would of course have scorned), de Gaulle did not use the word "corporatism," perhaps not even to himself. But his pronouncements and his proposals demonstrated a profound affinity for that system of government and that mode of industrial-state relationship.

To begin with, de Gaulle had little or no use for independent associations. His plebiscitarian style made him an ardent foe of intermediary organizations of all types, which he characterized as self-seeking and obstructionist. Political parties were, to his mind, the worst offenders, but other groups were almost equally suspect (Ehrmann, 1976, p. 205; Ambler, 1971, p. 187.) He was sufficiently committed to democratic ideals to resist the temptation to plan for their absolute elimination, but he was determined to find the means to control them and limit the damage they could do. Parties could be controlled by manipulation of the electoral system and the build-up of an all-encompassing national movement, the Rassemblement du Peuple Français (RPF), which would be "above party." Although certainly more liberal and egalitarian ideologically, and entirely devoid of paramilitary accoutrements, the RPF had certain unmistakable similarities in purpose and composition to the national movements typical of corporatist states, such as the Spanish Falange.

However, the Gaullist remedy for the selfish obstructionism of interest groups was much more openly corporatist in nature (although again it must be pointed out that de Gaulle never identified it as such) and much more drastic. When he addressed the question of relations with labor, de Gaulle spoke frequently of "concertation" and urged that workers and employers work together, in associations, to ensure the economic recovery of France. Such composite associations would be an improvement over the wrangling of separate trade unions and managerial groups, but their formation was merely the first step. Far more important, de Gaulle strongly recommended that the new postwar constitution should establish a second legislative body composed only of representatives of these new associations. This second house, which would take the place of the old French Senate, should furthermore be coequal with the National Assembly (Elbow, 1953, p. 202; Safran, 1977, pp. 55 and 127). With this recommendation, de Gaulle was going far beyond the mere espousal of quasicorporatist, quasi-Catholic-socialist hopes and dreams. He was getting ready to put in place an official organ of government–and an extremely powerful one at that–in which specified interests would be able to exercise a representational monopoly. He was, in short, eager to institutionalize the one corporatist practice most likely to transform France into a true corporatist state.

As leader of the Free French and of the provisional government established in Algiers in 1943, de Gaulle led the French through the transition to the Fourth Republic. But although the provisional government remained in power for more than a year and de Gaulle was allowed to initiate several important reforms by decree, he was unable to persuade others of the wisdom of adopting any of his schemes for controlling the intermediary groups he so mistrusted and disliked (Trotignon, 1968, p. 254). Even the RPF. rapidly degenerated into a party very much like any other. Frustrated in these ambitions and generally exasperated by the political "games" as well as the policies of the postwar coalition of Christian democrats, socialists, and communists, de Gaulle resigned from the government in January 1946 and from politics altogether in 1953 (de Gaulle, 1959, pp. 940-977; Williams, 1954, p. 17; Safran, 1977, p. 55). He would, of course, be heard from again, but not during the lifetime of the Fourth Republic.

However, the condition of the French economy, and the place of that economy in the world market, were such as to stimulate continued deliberation regarding the wisdom of corporatist remedies, with or without de Gaulle's support. This is not to say that the economy was in poor shape; on the contrary, France shared in the general postwar economic boom.[2] But corporatism appeals in good times as well as bad. Better control of the work force and production goals can mean an improved ability to take advantage of investment opportunities, at home and abroad, in prosperous times. It can also offer, in the case of a nation like France, a means of uniting the "progressive forces" in a coalition capable of reducing "the continuing weight of peasants, small shopkeepers, and small businessmen . . . politically significant but economically marginal groups" that constitute an almost unendurable drag on productivity at a time when efficient competition in world markets might bring undreamed-of profit (Zysman, 1977, p. 7).

The evidence of unambiguously corporatist practice in the immediate postwar years is, however, relatively limited. The new government was heavily dirigiste, with a strong emphasis on planning, social welfare, government regulation of production and

[2] In the late 1950s, 1960s, and early 1970s France experienced "the highest rate of growth (5.8 percent per year) in the world except for Japan and the Soviet Union" (Warnecke and Suleiman, 1975, p. 25).

commerce, and financial interventionism, but these are not in and of themselves signs the state is incorporating organized interests in its own domain (Trotignon, 1968, p. 329). The new constitution did call for an Economic Council composed of representatives of all sectors of the economy to advise the government on matters of economic policy, but such a body was a far cry from the corporatist second chamber envisioned by de Gaulle (and the French Senate was formed and functioned under the Fourth Republic very much as it had under the Third). Slightly more significant was the 1945 law requiring any business with fifty or more employees to establish an elected workers' committee (comité d'entreprise), whose members would have a "consultative role" regarding work conditions and the management of the enterprise, the right to carry on "social tasks," and the right to elect two members to serve on an advisory Administrative Council (Conseil d'Administration) otherwise composed of management representatives (Blondel, 1974, p. 71). However, only the trade unions had the right to present candidates for these committees in the first round of elections, a concession to the syndicalist perspective that went directly contrary to corporatist doctrine.

THE GAULLIST ERA OF FRENCH CORPORATISM

Corporatist Policy: 1958-1976

When de Gaulle came back to power in 1958 he did so in response to a crisis in foreign affairs, and it was foreign affairs that were to receive most of his attention throughout his eleven years in the newly powerful office of the presidency. Nevertheless, when he did turn his attention to domestic matters, and particularly to economic affairs, it was clear that he was still an ardent corporatist at heart. Although he moved only cautiously in that direction during his first years in office, he was to become more and more persuaded of the need for a corporatist system of interest representation, so much so that eventually he staked all his accumulated power on a corporatist gamble–and lost.

The one condition de Gaulle posed when asked to resume the leadership of France during the Algerian crisis of 1958 was the right to oversee the writing of a new constitution. His purpose in doing so was to create a stronger presidency and a new framework for relations with France's overseas empire. France was on the edge of civil war over the Algerian question; it was no time to institute the major changes in internal socioeconomic relationships that moving to full-fledged corporatism would have required. The new constitution did include an Economic and Social Council, but at first glance the new body seemed even weaker than its Fourth Republic predecessor, the Economic Council, which had been able to study and report on any matters it wished and could be consulted by the assembly as well as by the government. The new council was restricted to matters on which it was consulted by the cabinet and could report only to the cabinet (Pickles, 1960, p. 38).

However, in this domain as in all others, it was soon to become clear to the French and other interested observers that for de Gaulle a constitution provided only the loosest of guides to political practice. Over the years of his tenure in office France was to become far more corporatist in practice than even the most imaginative reading of the constitution could ever have suggested.

To begin with, in addition to maintaining France's very large sector of nationalized business, the new government worked to strengthen the ties between the state and private business, especially big private business. The Gaullists made it clear that to their minds big business was better for France than small business. Following "a determined policy of encouraging mergers," they did what they could to foster the development of firms that would be "large enough and efficient enough to resist the American challenge and . . . able to compete with American firms beyond French borders" (Warnecke and Suleiman, 1975, pp. 26-31; see also Servan-Schreiber, 1967).

Second, and very much related to the first point, the new government carried on the time-honored tradition of *pantouflage*, i.e., moving cadres from government to business posts, and in fact made it standard operating procedure. The grandes écoles had long been the route to high government position; now it became understood that "academic success in the grandes écoles leads forthwith to the attainment of high posts in the public sector, which in turn leads to high managerial posts in the private sector" (Warnecke and Suleiman, 1975, p. 38).

Third, the new Economic and Social Council was given far greater life and significance than had at first seemed likely. The organic law setting its composition called for 205 members, chosen for five years "by appropriate professional organizations or by the Government" to represent workers (45 members), industrial and commercial enterprises (41 members), agriculture (40 members), overseas territories and interests (40 members), and various other economic, social, and cultural interests (39 members) (Pickles, 1960, p. 38, n. 2.).[3] This membership was divided into technical sections, each of which was urged to coopt outside specialists and was put to work devising recommendations for government policy on topic after topic.

Well satisfied with this beginning, the Gaullists proceeded to set up a vast array of other advisory bodies, some attached to particular ministries, some to regional "modernization commissions," some to departmental prefectures. Agricultural chambers, boards of nationalized industries, social security boards, and labor courts (a new version of the old conseils de prud'hommes, designed to settle disputes arising with respect to labor legislation) provided further opportunities to involve representatives of trade unions, employers' associations, and other interested associations. By the end of the Gaullist tenure in office there were more than a hundred such bodies attached to each ministry, and a total of over four thousand advisory groups (Safran, 1977, pp. 131 and 136).

In most cases, access to advisory bodies was determined by the government, and it soon became clear that the government had very definite preferences regarding what types of group it invited to participate and what forms that participation should take. One author's description of how the system worked at the height of Gaullist control is worth quoting at length in order to bring out the clear corporatist overtones:

[3] The exact proportions have changed slightly over the years. There was some indignation in trade union circles that the low membership Force Ouvrière was granted as large a representation as the far larger socialist and communist trade union movements (Duclos, 1963, p. 136).

> The government prefers to consult professional orders (ordres professionnels) where possible, rather than pure interest groups (syndicats). These "orders" have many tasks: the maintenance of intraprofessional standards and discipline, the control of access to the profession, the supervision of training, and finally, "consultative administration."...The fragmentation of, and competition among, interest groups strengthens the government's power to determine which association should be considered the "true" spokesman for a particular socioeconomic sector . . . this legitimation is frequently accorded on a selective basis. . . . When the government has a choice, it selects as spokesmen of organized labor representatives of more tractable and less syndicalist trade unions . . . groups that are underrepresented or whose demands are ignored can do little but articulate their frustrations, or else boycott the advisory councils, a policy occasionally adopted by trade unions and agricultural associations . . . .interest groups that refuse to be coopted or "corporatized" become even more powerless, since, with the relative deparliamentarization of decision making, there are few alternative access routes . . . locally oriented group activities are often of doubtful value . . . owing to the cities' great financial dependence upon the national government" (Safran, 1977, pp. 132-140; on these points see also Warnecke and Suleiman, 1975).

"Corporatist overtones," yes, but "corporatism," no. Not if we hold, with Schmitter, that true corporatism means there will be only "a limited number of singular, compulsive, noncompetitive" functional organizations. The Gaullists made no move to limit the number of organizations; they simply limited the number to which they paid very much attention. Furthermore, important decrees and legislation affecting the interests of various groups–for example, the *loi d'orientation agricole,* the profit-sharing programs, and reforms to the social security system–could still be passed with little or no consultation with the affected groups.

This willingness to work pragmatically, slowly building familiarity with and acceptance of the corporatist mode in a society still formally pluralist, was found in other aspects of Gaullist policymaking as well. The militant trade unions, often functioning in tandem with the opposition political parties, were a source of continuing difficulty in the present and posed a constant threat of political defeat for the future. The communist-dominated trade union, the Confédération Générale du Travail, and, to a lesser extent, the also powerful confederation Française Démocratique du Travail, have both operated on the principle that the class struggle requires a politics of confrontation vis-à-vis management and state. Workers who accept this view of reality are not good candidates for "corporatization," as the Gaullists were well aware. But the Gaullist corporatists were not interested in setting up counter unions; to their minds the trade union movement was itself a mistake. How then could the workers be won away from the traditional unions?

The Gaullist answer was "participation," a program designed to persuade workers that both management and state were interested in workers' advancement as well as their own, that the state could be an effective partner in labor's negotiations with management, and that when a firm prospered, so would its employees. The 1945 law establishing workers' committees had been a step in that direction (see above), but yet more significant was the passage, in January 1959, of a decree that authorized employers to set up profit-sharing programs with workers' organizations, such programs to be approved by departmental commissions (for which read, "the benevolent state") established for that purpose (*Journal Officiel,* 1959). This decree was followed in 1967 by laws that went considerably further, making some form of profit-sharing agreement obligatory for all enterprises having more than 100 employees and placing the benefits thus generated in a special fund that would not be distributed to workers for five years but that could in the meantime be invested in the enterprise itself or in the exterior economy (*Journal Officiel,* August 1967 and December 1967).

However impressed they may have been by these advances, French workers somehow could not resist the recidivist pull of the 1968 student strike. So many joined, including members of professional occupations, that for a while it seemed Sorel was wrong to assert that the idea of a general strike capable of destroying a government was just a useful myth. (See Brown, 1974, for an account of the events of 1968). This is not the place to recount the complex history of that dramatic confrontation, but it should be pointed out that de Gaulle's first response, once he could be persuaded to take the situation at all seriously, was to call for a referendum. The referendum had by then become his favorite means of renewing his bonapartistic relationship with the mass of French voters; whatever the ostensible subject, he habitually made his own leadership the real issue of each plebiscite, promising to resign if the vote went against him. By 1968 it was second nature for him to call upon this method to resolve a crisis. What is significant for our purposes here is (1) that the subject of this referendum was to be "participation" and (2) that de Gaulle's advisers were able to persuade him that such a referendum would not resolve the crisis and could well bring him to defeat.

Reluctantly, de Gaulle authorized his prime minister, Georges Pompidou, to negotiate a settlement to the strike that gave the workers immediate wage increases and promises of elaborate future reforms and then to hold new legislative elections. Pompidou carried out both missions brillantly, but for de Gaulle the overwhelming victory in the June elections meant that Pompidou, not he, had been wrong. The French people were on their side; it would have been possible to use the crisis to achieve true corporatism. Pompidou was forthwith removed from office, and in 1969 de Gaulle went ahead with his cherished referendum.

It was customary for each referendum to ask the French voters to give a simple yes or no to a complex question, but de Gaulle outdid himself in 1969. The April referendum had two distinct parts but called for only a single vote. The first part referred to a program of regional decentralization that had long been pending and was widely endorsed; the second asked the French voters to approve a constitutional amendment transforming the French senate into a quasicorporatist assembly. Under these provisions half the senators would continue to be chosen by regional and local politicians but the other half would be chosen by organized socioeconomic groups. Thus reconstituted, the upper house would be permitted to act only on carefully delimited social, economic, and cultural matters (Safran, 1977, p. 187; Williams and Harrison, 1971, pp. 398-402).[4]

As usual, de Gaulle staked his political fortune on the outcome. But that gesture had begun to pall, the beloved general was not so young and vigorous as he once had been (a fact clearly visible in his handling of the 1968 crisis), and, above all, the French respected their Senate and were far from persuaded that the joys of corporatism would outweigh the disadvantages of weakening that perhaps

[4] For a strong (and angry) argument that the Gaullist emphasis on "participation" beginning in 1968 is simply another name for corporatism, see Cohen (1977, pp. 254-255): "Vertical assemblies and councils will be formed . . . . Their purpose will be to give workers the illusion of participating in the common endeavor (which will remain economic expansion) and to convince them of the paramount importance of that task and of the necessity of preserving the present distribution of economic power . . . it is still best described by the word corporatism."

old-fashioned but still trustworthy bastion of individual liberty. They voted no, and de Gaulle retired again to Colombey, this time for good.

Thus once again it proved impossible to turn France into a true corporatist state. But it was also the case that once again the idea of corporatism proved impossible to extirpate. The Gaullists stayed in office under President Pompidou five more years, and several new laws were added to increase the opportunities for "participation" in the factory. In 1969, the workers of Renault, the nationalized automobile firm, were given stockholding privileges (including tax exemption benefits); in 1972 the same rights were extended to workers in public insurance and financial institutions and in 1973 to workers in private firms. By this time the body of legislation was sufficiently large and complicated to require a further law, also in 1973, to "harmonize" the decree of 1959 with the law of 1967 and its many amendments (Rally for the Republics, "Rassemblement actualité," no. 7, 1977, pp. 22-23).

After Pompidou's death in 1974 and the election of Valéry Giscard d'Estaing as President, the Union for the Defense of the Republic (UDR) remained the largest party in parliament and Giscard chose one of its leaders, Jacques Chirac, as his Prime Minister. The legislative impetus behind the program, however, could not be maintained without presidential leadership, and this Giscard proved unwilling or unable to provide, despite his claims that he and his movement were also inspired by the Gaullist tradition. Laws proposed to expand the program of profit-sharing and stockholding provoked extended legislative debate but no decisive action. Giscard's own pronouncements tended to dwell more on arguments in favor of giving workers full information about the circumstances of the company while firmly resisting the notion that they should also have some part in making management-level decisions (Giscard d'Estaing, 1976, pp. 83-90).

By 1976 the disagreements (on a wide range of topics) between the two leading partners in "la majorité" had become so serious that Chirac resigned the prime ministership, reorganized the UDR as the Rally for the Republic (Rassemblement pour la République, RPR), and set about transforming the party into a mass movement that would, he hoped, be capable of winning the 1978 legislative elections for the party and the 1981 presidential contest for himself (Lawson, 1981). It soon became clear Chirac endorsed the corporatist tradition of Gaullism far more ardently than Giscard, as participation became a major theme in his campaign for electoral success.

Corporatist Politics: 1976-1981

The Two Meanings of "participation" for the RPR.

The concept of participation has taken on new life under the RPR, and a great deal of the party's literature in the past five years has been devoted to explanations of the concept. In this new program, "participation" is used in two ways, both strongly suggestive of corporatist ideology. The first usage attempts to build a general psychology of support for belief in the commonality of citizenship, for the idea that fundamentally the overriding interests of the French are the same regardless of occupation or status and that those interests can best be served by cooperative interaction. In this usage the term is used very broadly and vaguely, often in association with an even vaguer term, *democratie du quotidien* (everyday democracy). When party general secretary Bernard Pons said, "For Frenchmen and women, participation in the town, in the department, in the region, in the nation, that is, in the daily or exceptional exchanges between the citizen and the different levels of government, between the citizen and the state, ought to lead to a widening of individual responsibility, to an enrichment of national solidarity," he was using a rhetoric typical of this usage of the term (Rally for the Republic, "La Lettre de la Nation, Supplément au No. 1133," p. 10). Participation in this sense means changing "our behavior, our habits, our ambitions," and learning to work together for "the grandeur of France and the happiness of the French" (Rally for the Republic, "Rassemblement actualité," no. 4).

The second usage of the term by the RPR is more in keeping with the sense it was given in pre-RPR days, i.e., as a program for developing corporatist practices in the factory or the commercial firm. Here we are back on familiar ground, and we find participation being carefully explained as having "three prongs": participation in profits, participation in stocks, and participation in responsibilities. But here, too, there are what might be called Chiraquian nuances added. For one thing, there is much more emphasis now on the third prong, sharing responsibilities. Thus during the last year's of Giscard's presidency, the RPR often publicized the legislation it had proposed to ensure greater worker involvement in management decisions and did what it could to make political capital out of the failure of its partners in the government to support its work. Rally for the Republic, *(Inter A.O.P.*, no. 8, 1978).

A second difference is that party propaganda about this aspect of participation is now very clearly directed to all workers, including those who may already belong to or be tempted by left-wing parties or trade unions. The authors of the literature intended for this purpose are consequently very careful not to offend such potential supporters by attacking ideas they may have found attractive. Participation is explained as a means of "disalienating" or "decolonizing" the workers, freeing them from both "brutal capitalism" and "collectivism," and the latter is acknowledged to have "been able to obtain results in other places" although it is "not adapted to the French reality" (Rally for the Republic, "Rassemblement actualite," no. 7, 1977).

Finally, and perhaps most significant of all, the party has given new life to an auxiliary organization designed, in a manner reminiscent of La Tour du Pin's nineteenth century "cercles," to build corporatism from the base: the Action Ouvrière et Professionnelle (AOP).

The AOP: Grassroots Corporatism in Todays RPR

The AOP is designed to bring the workers and management cadres of a firm together in an organization exterior to the firm and to involve them in the work of explaining to all employees the benefits to be gained by supporting the RPR. It is a party auxiliary, not a trade union. When it functions well, it simultaneously builds commitment to the corporatist mode of industrial interaction and to the political fortunes of the RPR, while weakening syndicalist trade unionism. A description of the process typically followed in forming a new unit of the AOP will help make clear how this organization works.[5]

[5] The information presented in this section is based on attendance at AOP meetings and interviews with AOP and RPR militants and leaders (including party leader

In order to create a new section of the AOP, the party's departmental secretary and/or the AOP delegate (the party official in charge of AOP organizations in the department) finds out who among the party's members are employees of the target firm. (Another Chiraquian innovation has been to place membership data in a computer, making this kind of information readily available.) These members are contacted and asked to consider the feasibility of forming a section. If their report is positive, the party decides who will form the "provisional bureau" of the section (secretary, treasurer, and someone in charge of information and propaganda), and an organizing meeting is announced. This meeting is attended by the department secretary, the departmental AOP delegate, and, if possible, a representative from the Paris AOP headquarters, as well as by the workers and cadres who are to be the new members (the goal is to begin with at least twenty persons). At the beginning of the meeting the departmental delegate announces who the leaders will be (but softens this imposition of party control by assuring those present that the bureau is provisional and elections will be held in a few months' time) and explains that meetings will be held once a week. (For a description of RPR tactics for maintaining leadership control, see Lawson, 1980). Then the national AOP representative makes a speech, welcoming them to the movement, explaining how the organization works, and stressing the need to recruit all the RPR members in the firm and to carry out positive actions (preparing tracts, holding public meetings, putting up posters).

The AOP delegate for the department speaks next, describing what other AOP sections within the department are doing and expanding on the exhortations of the national representative. The new members must, he says, inform themselves about the RPR issue stances and be able to explain them to others. They should form study sections devoted to such problems as the older worker, reduced employment opportunities in declining trades, and retraining for automation. They are expected to develop analyses of immediate issues in the firm that will be useful, interesting, and attractive. They should be ready, when necessary, to support the

Jacques Chirac and AOP leaders Philippe Dechartres and Georges Repecxky) in the spring of 1978, as well as on the literature cited. Dechartres has since moved on to join the personal team of Chirac and has been replaced by Jean Charbonnel as head of the AOP.

action of AOP militants in neighboring sections. Above all, their work is to recruit more members, for the section and for the party.

Finally, the departmental party secretary takes the floor. His emphasis is on the party: how strong or weak it is in the department, what can be done to make it stronger, how the AOP has helped in past elections and can help in the future by being permanently mobilized "sur le terrain." He reminds the militants that as RPR members they are also expected to attend all the local and regional meetings organized by the party.

Once established, the section is assisted in its work by the party apparatus, in particular the publication *Inter AOP*, a national newsletter published once a month. This sixteen-page document regularly includes the text of a recent speech by an RPR leader on a subject presumed to be of interest to workers, news of successful actions undertaken by various AOP sections, a calendar of future events, an essay on some feature of the RPR platform (e.g., "La emploi des jeunes," "Pour une vraie politique du defense"), a "historical note" reminding readers of some past accomplishment of Gaullism on behalf of workers, perhaps an essay attacking opposition parties or unions, and, particularly helpful to would-be militants, a "tract of the month." The AOP puts great emphasis on the tract, a one-page leaflet that should, according to headquarters, "contain a single message, using simple words, short phrases, and a succession of slogans," make a direct appeal to the reader's "sentiments, habits, joys and problems," refer to a "precise, local situation," and always manifest the AOP insignia clearly and include a membership coupon (Rally for the Republic, *Inter AOP*, no. 1, 1977, p. 14).

Whenever the leadership finds it useful to do so, a departmental meeting may be called. Representatives of all the sections in the department attend, and once again the national office sends a representative. Every section makes a report, and there is an atmosphere of good-natured rivalry among representatives from different firms. Examples of hard-working militance are applauded ("we have 150 members, we have distributed 21 different tracts, including 15,000 at the train station, and we have pasted up posters three times"). Accounts of battles (often physical) with communist trade union militants are openly relished by the workers present and tolerated by the representatives of management and of the movement's leadership. Problems are brought up, and if solutions cannot be decided upon, sympathy is at least expressed. A common complaint is the failure of nonpolitical bosses to understand what the AOP is all about; mistaking it for a trade union, they attempt to halt its activities, even when these are carefully kept outside the factory gates (only authorized unions are permitted in French factories). However, any generalized worker complaints against management are speedily silenced at such meetings: the AOP is an organization dedicated to the corporatist principle that there are no fundamental differences between the interests of worker and boss.

How successful is the AOP? Conceived by de Gaulle in 1947, thirty years later it had succeeded in establishing only 25 sections in 14 of France's ninety-five departments. However, in the course of 1977, stimulated by the work of the reorganized party and the threat of a left-wing victory in the forthcoming legislative elections (in which communists would, it was presumed, be well represented) the AOP grew to over 700 sections with 45,000 members, organized in all but three of the departments (Rally for the Republic, *Inter AOP.*, no. 4, December 1977, p. 10).

This rate of growth is impressive, but could not, of course, be maintained once the immediate fear of communist takeover was eliminated by the victory of the right in 1978, the continued "distancing" of the two leftist parties from each other, the growing strength of the socialists and the concomitant weakening of the Communist party.[6] Furthermore, there are some indications that the fortunes of the AOP have been dimmed not only by the change in the political balance on the left but also by open resistance within its own party. Local party secretaries often resent the competition the AOP sections represent to their own recruiting efforts, and the loss of membership dues thereby entailed. RPR members are not always pleased to be asked to "show their colors" in the workplace, a reluctance as characteristic of white-collar cadres as of laborers. Some of the old-guard Gaullists find the movement more than a touch déclassé if not outright dangerous. Party militants have not grasped

[6] The 1981 presidential and legislative election victories of the socialists seem to corroborate the common view that the poor showing of the party in 1978 was owing far more to its association with the Communist party than to voters' evaluation of its own program or candidates. However, more detailed analyses of the 1981 electoral results are needed before making any positive statements regarding the impact of "distancing" on Socialist fortunes.

the meaning of *démocratie du quotidien* and many of them hold strong reservations about allowing workers to participate in management decisions, making such comments as, "It is good to let the workers know what is going on, but anything further is dangerous" and "It is one thing I cannot accept: I do not see how it could work" (Lawson, 1980, p. 16).

CONCLUSION: WHAT FUTURE FOR CORPORATISM IN FRANCE?

In any case, the RPR has succeeded in providing an arena within which management cadres and workers meet and function together. How significant this will prove to the future of French corporatism depends in large part on the policies to be followed by the new Socialist government, as well as on the response of Chirac and his lieutenants to the interesting new opportunities their electoral defeat has given them.

Corporatism under Socialism

The questions regarding the present government's policies are numerous and largely unanswerable at this point. It can be predicted that if the socialists fail to produce the promised improvement in the worker's lot within a reasonable period of time there will be a natural renewed interest in alternative proposals, but no one can say with certainty whether or not they will fail, nor what the French workers will decide is "a reasonable period of time."[7]

The question of how corporatist the policies of the new government are is also difficult to answer. Although in France it has usually been the political right that has endeavored to institutionalize corporatist practices, the left has had its own corporatist tradition to

[7] In this regard it is interesting to note that the first public address of the new prime minister, Pierre Mauroy, stressed that "la tache est rude" and that "en ces temps difficiles, rien ne nous sera donne sans efforts. Rien ne se fera sans la durée" *Le Monde Hebdomadaire*, week ending May 27, 1981, p. 5).

draw upon beginning with the revolution and carried forward in the more moderate efforts of twentieth century leftist governments. Former Prime Minister Pierre Mendès-France (well to the left of de Gaulle if not always unambiguously "leftist") claimed that "corporatism is only dangerous if one gives the professional organizations the right to make, on their own authority, decisions concerning everything which relates to them or if institutional structures prove incapable of changing when the economic reality is itself changing." The far-left socialist splinter groups the Parti Socialiste Unifié (PSU) has included the recommendation that there be a corporatist assembly, composed of representatives of the different economic sectors proportionate to their number, in its program (Duclos, 1963, pp. 145-146, 153). In general, socialists share with corporatists the conviction that the class struggle can be ended only by permitting both workers and government to become active participants in directing industrial development, although, also like corporatists, socialists do not always agree among themselves on exactly how this is to be done.

The new Socialist government can be expected to draw upon this dual tradition of flirting with corporatism and disagreeing about the means to employ in its implementation. The movement put together by François Mitterrand and now so confidently labeled "the Socialist party" is in fact a coalition of numerous factions sharply divided on questions of economic organization and "worker democracy"–and one of the factions formerly most hostile to Mitterrand was once led by his new minister of planning, Michel Rocard.[8]

The decision-making tasks of the new government are further complicated by the perhaps conflicting campaign promises Mitterrand made (1) to respect the institutions of the Fifth Republic; (2) to extend the range of the public sector by nationalizing all credit institutions, the aircraft industry, metallurgy, and several other major industrial groups; and (3) to move away from the etatism of the Gaullists by strengthening local government bodies. The first of these implies that the Economic and Social Council will continue its work. The second, nationalization of industry, is of course a key aspect of corporatism (although also a feature of noncorporatist states.) But how will strengthening local

[8] Rocard also offered himself to the party as candidate for the presidency in 1981 but speedily withdrew when Mitterrand made clear his intention to run a third time.

government affect France's drift toward corporatism?

proposals for implementing the third promise, decentralization, were not designed to be overly hostile to the corporatist approach and that under the guise of strengthening departmental government the socialists actually plan to increase the power of the central government to carry out its policies at the base. The socialists have transformed the prefect into a mere commissaire d'administration and have strengthened the hitherto largely powerless regional assemblies, the conseils généraux. However, it seems likely the government expected the new conseils to be dominated by the representatives of the major towns, large numbers of which were already under communist or socialist control. Had this proved possible, the new *socialisme de quotidien* would have been a clever way of substituting the strength of grass-roots leftism for the powers of an unambiguous–and therefore often resented and resisted–servant of the state, the prefect. The fact that after the surprise right-wing victories in the cantonal elections of 1982 the socialists appear to have shelved more or less indefinitely their plans to turn significant power over to the conseils strengthens this interpretation. In any case, there is nothing in the actual practice of the government in this or other domains of policy to suggest that the socialists will seriously undercut the moderately corporatist initiatives undertaken by the Gaullists. The similarities between Gaullism and French socialism are often stressed both by the Gaullists (seeking to attract Socialist voters) and by outside observers (see, for example, Bauchard, 1967, p. 265). A sensitivity to the appeals of corporatism may be a further point in common between France's leading popular movements.

Gaullist Corporatism in the 1980s

Meanwhile, what about the Gaullists? Will they continue to seek working-class support via the tactics of the AOP? Will they continue to offer selective support to proposals made by the new government to expand worker involvement in industrial decision making? Perhaps they will do both, but it seems clear that the thoughts of their leader are elsewhere.

To begin with, Chirac was widely blamed for Mitterrand's victory, owing to his less than lukewarm endorsement of Giscard at the time of the runoff election (*Le Monde Hebdomadaire,* week ending May 13, 1981, p. 1; June 10, 1981, p. 7).[9] The fact that the leftist victory in the succeeding legislative elections was clearly owing more to right-wing abstentions than to the left's own improved status in the affections of the electorate lent credibility to this interpretation: the combined vote of leftist candidates actually declined from 13,878,573 in 1978 to 13,832,576 in 1981, whereas the abstention rate climbed from 17.22 percent to 29.64 percent (*Le Monde Hebdomadaire,* week ending July 22, 1981, p. 7).

However, one ironic effect of this "treason," if that is what it was, has been to leave loyal giscardistes with no one to turn to except Chirac. "Whatever may be the good will, talents and fidelity of the current leaders of the U.D.F., it has to be admitted that [that party] lacks men capable of competing with M. Chirac . . ." (*Le Monde Hebdomadaire,* week ending June 10, 1981, p. 7). The chief of the Gaullists has not been shy about taking up this opportunity. He has begun holding a series of meetings in the capital's city hall (he is mayor of Paris) with those interested in planning the future and has called for a multipartisan "study club" to prepare the appropriate position papers for presentation during the 1983 municipal elections, the 1986 legislative elections, and, surely not least in his personal calculations, the 1988 presidential elections.

The benignly elitist giscardistes whom Chirac hopes to attract with such strategies have never shown much enthusiasm for the more populist aspects of Gaullist corporatist politics (such as the AOP), and it will not be surprising if this element of RPR strategy receives less emphasis in the immediate future. Furthermore, given Chirac's propensity to mold and remold the RPR to fit his personal ambitions, it is also not surprising that he has announced a "lightening" of the apparatus of the RPR, a process that presumably makes it easier for him to guide that party into a yet larger *rassemblement* under his leadership (*Le Monde Hebdomadaire,* week ending July 22, 1981; Lawson, 1981). Indeed, the first outlines of the new movement may have already been seen in the broad electoral coali-

[9] The role of spoiler in presidential elections is a familiar one for Chirac; in 1974 he was credited with Giscard's victory because of his refusal to support his own party's candidate, Jacques Chaban-Delmas–and received the prime ministership as his reward.

tion Chirac established during the 1981 legislative elections, the Union for a New Majority.

However, if there are two forces in France that have proved their capacity to rebound from defeat, they are right-wing support for corporatism and the Gaullist political party, by whatever name each may assume. To imagine that either could be destroyed by the political maneuvers of a single opportunistic politician, should he decide on that course of action, would be naive indeed. On the basis of past experience, the most reasonable prognosis would seem to be that the French fascination with corporatist practices will continue under socialism in the immediate future and receive the renewed enthusiastic support of Gaullism in the more distant future, but that France, determinedly if not cooperatively pluralist, will never carry this fascination to the point of becoming a fully corporatist state.

REFERENCES

Ambler, John (1971). The Government and Politics of France. Boston: Houghton Mifflin.

Audoin, Raoul (1962). Le Corporatisme, pseudo-remède contre l'étatisme. Paris: Éditions SEDIF.

Bauchard, Philippe (1967). L'Économie au service du Pouvoir. Paris: Calmann Levy.

Blondel, Jean (1974, fourth edition). The Government of France. New York: Thomas Crowell.

Brown, Berard E. (1974) Protest in Paris: Anatomy of a Revolt. Morristown, N. J.: General Learning Press.

Chirac, Jacques (1977). "La Participation est la dernière chance de la liberté," *Paradoxes* 24 (Octobre-Novembre): 75-79.

Cohen, Stephen S. (1977). Modern Capitalist Planning: The French Model. Berkeley: University of California Press.

Collier, Ruth Berins, and David Collier (1979). "Inducements versus Constraints Disaggregating 'Corporatism,'" *American Political Science Review* 73 (December): 967-986.

De Gaulle, Charles (1959). The Complete War Memoirs. New York: Simon and Schuster.

Duclos, Jacques (1963). Gaullisme, Technocratie, Corporatisme. Paris: Éditions Sociales.

Durkheim, Émile (1926). De la division du travail social. Paris: Félix Alcan.

Eidlin, Fred H. (1981). "Totalitarian Aspirations and Institutional Constraints." A paper presented at the Annual Meeting of the American Political Science Association, September 3-6, 1981.

Ehrmann, Henry W. (1957). Organized Business in France. Princeton, N.J.: Princeton University Press.

(1977) Politics in France. Boston: Little, Brown.

Elbow, Matthew H. (1953). French Corporative Theory, 1789-1948. New York: Columbia University Press.

Giscard d'Estaing, Valéry (1976). Démocratie Française. Paris: Librairie Arthème Fayard.

Journal Officiel de la République Française (1959). Lois et Décrets 7 (Janvier): 641-642.

(1966). Lois et Décrets 171 (Juillet): 6402-6413.

(1967). Lois et Décrets 191 (Août): 8288-8292.

(1967). Lois et Décrets 296 (Décembre): 12436-12439.

(1968). Lois et Décrets 306 (Décembre): 12347.

(1973). Lois et Décrets 302 (Décembre): 13905.

(1973). Lois et Décrets 304 (Décembre): 14151.

Lawson, Kay (1980). "Elite and Non-Elite Attitudes Toward Intra-Party Democracy: The RPR of France," paper presented at the 1980 Annual Meeting of the American Political Science Association.

(1981). "The Impact of Party Reform on Party Systems: The Case of The RPR of France," *Comparative Politics* 13 (July): 401-419.

Le Monde Hebdomadaire (1981). Weeks ending May 6 through July 29.

Mussolini, Benito (1935). The Corporate State. Rome: Laboremus.

Palmieri, Mario (1936). The Philosophy of Fascism, excerpts in COHEN, Carl (ed.) (1962). Communism, Fascism and Democracy. New York: Random House.

Pickles, Dorothy (1960). The Fifth French Republic. New York: Praeger.

Rally for the Republic (1977-1980). Party documents consulted include "L'enjeu"; "Inter AOP" nos. 1-8, 20, and 23; "La lettre de la Nation, Supplément au No. 1133"; "Propositions pour la France"; and "Rassemblement actualité," nos. 4, 7, 16, 21, and 27.

Safran, William (1977). The French Polity. New York: Longman.

Schmitter, Philippe (1974). "Still the Century of Corporatism?", 85-131 in Frédérick B. Pike and Thomas Stritch (eds.) The New Corporatism. Notre Dame: University of Notre Dame Press.

Schmitter, Philippe, and Gerhard Lehmbruch (eds.) (1979). Trends Toward Corporatist Intermediation. Beverly Hills: Sage.

Servan-Schreiber, Jean-Jacques (1967). The American Challenge. New York: Avon.

Tissier, Pierre (1942). The Government of Vichy. London: Harrap.

Trotignon, Yves (1968). La France au XXe siècle. Paris: Bordas-Mouton.

Warnecke, Steven, and Ezra Suleiman (eds.) (1975). Industrial Policies in Western Europe. New York: Praeger.

Wilensky, Harold L. (1976). The "New Corporatism," Centralization, and the Welfare State. London: Sage.

Williams, Philip (1954). Politics in Post-War France. London: Longmans, Green and Co.

Williams, Philip, and Martin Harrison (1971). Politics and Society in de Gaulle's republic. New York: Doubleday.

Zysman, John (1975). "French Electronics Policy: The Costs of Technological Independence," in Steven J. Warnecke and Ezra N. Suleiman (eds.) Industrial Policies in Western Europe. New York: Praeger.

(1977). Political Strategies for Industrial Order: State, Market and Industry in France. Berkeley: University of California Press.

Chapter 19

NEW FORMS OF INTEREST REPRESENTATION IN THE U.S. CONGRESS

Roger H. Davidson

A generation has passed since the "group approach to politics" swept the political science profession and for a moment seemed fated to form its central core of research and analysis. Three decades of scattered studies were codified by David B. Truman in his celebrated volume, *The Governmental Process.*[1] Numerous scholars seized the challenge of describing interest groups' behavior, internal dynamics, and access to governmental decisionmakers.[2] Henry W. Ehrmann rightly observed that "almost everywhere the relationships between groups and parties and between groups, the legislatures and the executive branch must be investigated in order to arrive at a realistic appraisal of the political process."[3]

Despite the enthusiasm it engendered in the post-World War II years, interest-group research failed to live up to its promise. New methodologies and data sources lured political scientists far afield–into voting behavior, for example, and observations of institutional behavior. Competing with these topics, interest-group research lost its comparative conceptual advantage. Interest-group investigations were dominated of necessity by case studies of individual groups or policy decisions. Yet individual case studies fell out of favor; and after Truman's landmark achievement, little effort was made to integrate case studies into a holistic interpretation of political action that combined conceptual clarity with theoretical power.

[1] New York: Alfred A. Knopf, 1951.

[2] See, for example, Bertram Gross, *The Legislative Struggle* (New York: McGraw-Hill Book Co., 1953).

[3] Henry W. Ehrmann, ed., *Interest Groups on Four Continents* (Pittsburgh: University of Pittsburgh Press, 1958), p. 3.

At the empirical level, moreover, analysts began to question the degree and pervasiveness of group influence. Michael Hayes dates this development from the publication of *American Business and Public Policy* (1963), a long-term study of business lobbying on foreign trade issues by Raymond A. Bauer, Ithiel de Sola Pool, and Lewis Anthony Dexter.[4] Examining the history of the Trade Expansion Act of 1962, these authors propounded a revisionist interpretation quite at variance with the older "pressure-group" model of policy making. Although interest-groups spent large sums of money in the aggregate, individual lobbies seemed poorly organized and underfinanced. Lobbyists seemed not so much bold as self-effacing–approaching legislators who agreed with them already and relying on these friends to spread their word. Thus lobbies served primarily as "service bureaus," providing ammunition for allies rather than persuading those on the fence. The 1963 study, as Hayes persuasively argues, propounded these findings as a kind of new conventional wisdom that pushed interest groups into a subordinate role.[5] My own study of area redevelopment legislation, completed at the same time, yielded similar findings.[6]

More recent developments, however, suggest that political scientists too quickly strayed from their study of interest groups. One need not subscribe to a pressure-group thesis to recognize that the study of groups–their characteristics, techniques, and linkages to governmental entities–lies near the center of political research and analysis. Today, the number and range of politically relevant groups must surely be at an all-time peak. No doubt this stems from the capacious reach of contemporary governmental activity and the politicization of a host of issues formerly relegated to the private sector–health, equality, welfare, environmental quality, and consumer rights, for example.

At the same time that groups have burgeoned, political parties have displayed long-term attrition, leaving in their wake an organizational gap in terms of political mobilization, issue development,

[4] Chicago: Atherton Press, 1963.

[5] Michael T. Hayes, "The Semi-Sovereign Pressure Groups: A Critique of Current Theory and an Alternative Typology," *Journal of Politics* 40 (February 1978), pp. 134-161.

[6] Roger H. Davidson, "The Depressed Areas Controversy: A Study in the Politics of American Business" (unpublished Ph.D dissertation, Columbia University: New York, 1963).

and financing. Indeed, the new types of interest groups have at their command all of the tools formerly monopolized by the political parties, thanks to the technologies of advertising, direct mailing, and other techniques of mobilizing grass-roots members. By the same token, new campaign finance laws have enabled interest groups through their political action committees (PACs) to gain a foothold in recruiting candidates and contesting elections. In the 1979-1980 campaign season, political action committees took in approximately $138 million, compared with the $130 million received by political party committees.[7] In 1978 (the latest year for which figures are available), candidates for the U.S. House of Representatives received nearly a quarter of their campaign dollars from PACs but only 7 percent from political party sources.[8] At the very least, the time is ripe for political analysts to recapture the notion that political parties and interest groups are closely interlocked and must be studied together–a view manifested in the textbooks of the late V. O. Key, Jr.[9]

Interest groups also blur the lines between the public and private sectors. A leading phenomenon is the rise of so-called subgovernments–three-way alliances among the congressional committees that shape programs, the executive agencies that implement them, and the clientele groups that benefit from them. Other names for these alliances include "policy whirlpools," "triple alliances," "cozy little triangles," or "iron triangles."[10] The influence of such alliances varies with the nature of the issue, its public visibility, the level of conflict among alliance partners, and the presence or absence of competing subgovernments. If the principal actors are in agreement, they have a good chance of dictating policy outcomes that affect them. If these actors are able to conduct their business outside the glare of publicity, their chances for domination are even better.

[7] Joseph E. Cantor, "Political Action Committees: Their Evolution and Growth and their Implications for the Political System," CRS Report 81-246 (Washington, DC: Congressional Research Service, 1981), p. 67.

[8] Ibid., p. 77.

[9] V. O. Key, Jr., *Politics, Parties and Pressure Groups,* 5th edition (New York: Thomas Y. Crowell, 1964).

[10] The term "subgovernments" was coined by Douglass Cater, in *Power in Washington* (New York: Random House, 1964). See also J. Leiper Freeman, *The Political Process: Executive Bureau-Legislative Committee Relations,* revised edition (New York: Random House, 1965).

Some scholars question whether subgovernments are as tight, stable, or autonomous as is sometimes implied. Hugh Heclo, for example, argues that the term "issue networks" better captures the instability and fluidity of current policy alliances.[11] Whichever view one favors, it can hardly be contested that: (1) such alliances do in fact exist; (2) they often exert decisive influence; (3) their structure and operations vary widely among issues; and (4) concerted research is needed to describe such arrangements and develop generalizations and theories about them.

Another form of interest group that transcends the lines between public and private is the informal caucus–an issue or voting bloc group composed of members of the Senate or House of Representatives. Although informal alliances of legislators are not a new phenomenon, today's caucus groups are noteworthy in several respects. They are now more numerous than ever (more than seventy in 1981). They are diverse–some are partisan and others bipartisan, some span only a single chamber and some are bicameral. Many are institutionalized, boasting staff, office space, dues-paying members, publications, elected officers, and bylaws. Such groups mirror both the balkanization of contemporary politics and the decentralization of legislative bodies. They are, in short, frontline combatants in "the legislative struggle" and are beginning to receive systematic attention from political scientists. The purpose of this chapter is to describe some of the characteristics of such groups and indicate their roles in the process of interest articulation and aggregation.

HISTORICAL HARBINGERS OF INFORMAL CAUCUSES

Informal, special interest caucuses predate formal party and committee structures on Capitol Hill. Indeed, when political parties were still inchoate and committees mainly ad hoc drafting bodies, members were already grouping themselves around regional or factional issues. Early nineteenth-century members, who lived in the nation's capital only part-time, clustered in boardinghouses with

[11] Hugh Heclo, "Issue Networks and the Executive Establishment," in Anthony King (ed.), *The New American Political System* (Washington, DC: American Enterprise Institute, 1978), p. 102.

colleagues from the same states or regions or with the same interests.[12] It is not hard to imagine these members discussing issues and strategems over dinner and libations each evening Congress was in session. Indeed, congressional directories in those days listed members by boardinghouse group rather than alphabetically or by state.

With the rise of disciplined parties later in the nineteenth century, these regional or factional caucuses apparently faded into the background. Yet informal groups of legislators by no means disappeared. One recalls, for instance, Sam Rayburn's "board of education," a group of allies and cronies who met daily in a Capitol anteroom to exhange political information and strategies, accompanied by bourbon and branch water. In the Senate, there was Senator Richard Russell (D-Ga.) and his phalanx of southern "bulls" who dominated the Senate through a system of informal norms and alliances with conservative Republicans.

When the outpouring of "modern" congressional research began in the 1960s, informal groups of legislators were few in number and thus were accorded relatively little attention. A few such groups were, however, noted by observers. Most conspicuous were the state delegations, partisan or bipartisan, that met to trade information on issues impinging upon their states and muster support for favorable committee assignments.[13] In a more partisan vein, there were "class clubs" composed of newcomers to a given Congress. Among Republicans, too, there were several social clubs that brought members together periodically to share information and sociability–groups with colorful names like the Acorns, SOS, and the Chowder and Marching Society.[14]

[12] James Sterling Young, *The Washington Community 1800-1828* (New York: Columbia University Press, 1966), pp. 94-100.

[13] Information on state delegations is found in: John H. Kessel, "The Washington Congressional Delegation," *Midwest Journal of Political Science* 8 (February 1964), pp. 1-21; Barbara Deckard, "State Party Delegations in the U.S. House of Representatives: A Comparative Study of Group Cohesion," *Journal of Politics* 34 (February 1972), pp. 199-222; and Alan Fiellin, "The Group Life of a State Delegation in the House of Representatives," *Western Political Quarterly* 23 (June 1970), pp. 305-320.

[14] Norman C. Miller, "Chowder and Marching Society Does More than Eat and Strut," *Wall Street Journal* (March 4, 1971), p. 1.

By all odds, the most visible and influential caucus prior to the 1970s was the Democratic Study Group (DSG). DSG began in 1956, when a young representative named Eugene J. McCarthy (D-Minn.) circulated among a group of his friends a statement of aims that became known as the Liberal Manifesto.[15] By January 7, 1957, the document had twenty-eight signers; when Representative Frank J. Thompson (D-N.J.) inserted the program in the *Congressional Record* three weeks later the list of signers had grown to eighty. These liberal Democrats, a minority in their own party, expressed their own ideas on the kinds of measures they thought Congress should consider. A rudimentary, informal whip system was soon established to implement these goals, and later the group–McCarthy's Mavericks, it was called–acquired a staff assistant. Bolstered by an influx of young liberals known as the Class of 1958, the group was formally launched in 1959 with Lee Metcalf (D-Mont.) as chairman (McCarthy had moved on to the Senate).

House Democratic leaders initially feared that the new group might turn into an unfriendly rival. Nevertheless, as one student remarked, "the attitudes of the House leadership toward the group which became the DSG might best be described . . . as benevolent neutrality that grew into tacit approval."[16] By the late 1960s the organization was fully institutionalized, boasting several staff aides, a full-fledged whip system, and a fund-raising and publicity program to help liberal candidates campaign more effectively.

DSG's influence in the House naturally fluctuated with the electoral fortunes of the liberal Democrats. After the 1964 Democratic landslide, its membership swelled to about 175 and it pressed a series of internal reform proposals, most of which were accepted. By the end of the decade the group was hurt by rifts in the liberal ranks caused by the Vietnam War and environmental issues. In the early 1970s, DSG again assumed the lead in advocating structural changes in congressional committees and Democratic caucus organization. Through its leadership, committee power was dispersed, the Democratic caucus strengthened, and the seniority system watered

[15] Arthur G. Stevens, Jr., Arthur H. Miller, and Thomas E. Mann, "Mobilization of Liberal Strength in the House, 1955-1970: The Democratic Study Group," *American Political Science Review* 68 (June 1974), 667-681.

[16] Kenneth Kofmehl, "The Institutionalization of a Voting Bloc," *Western Political Quarterly* 17 (June 1964), p. 272.

down.

Even when its ranks were divided, DSG exerted influence through its informative, unbiased issue briefs and weekly summaries of pending business on the House floor. (At the time, party whips provided little such information.) Even non-DSG members and Republicans surreptitiously relied on DSG publications. DSG's prestige as a source of information was reflected in a 1977 survey of members and staff conducted by the House Commission on Administrative Review. Seven out of ten members who were interviewed cited DSG as a source of information on bills considered on the floor but not coming from their committees. More than half of the legislative assistants (LAs) interviewed at the same time stated that DSG was a "very helpful" or "fairly helpful" source of information.[17]

Another early caucus was the Members of Congress for Peace through Law (MCPL), the first such group that was both bipartisan and bicameral. It started in 1959 as an informal breakfast discussion group of members favoring arms control and international cooperation. During the 1960s MCPL became a coordinator for legislators opposed to the Vietnam War. Indeed, it was MCPL's strenuous efforts to get representatives to vote publicly on the war that led to the 1970 innovation of recorded teller votes in the House.[18] By 1980, MCPL had five full-time staff aides and raised some $200,000 in dues, clerk-hire donations from legislators, and private donations to its affiliated tax-exempt educational fund.[19]

The Wednesday Group was, at least initially, the Republican counterpart of the Democratic Study Group. That is, it consisted of members who found themselves in the minority in their own party. Unlike those of the DSG, however, Wednesday Group members were fated to remain a tiny minority within their party, which was dominated by its conservative wing. Thus the group continues to be modest in size, limited in program and staffing, and low in profile.

[17] U.S. House of Representatives, Commission on Administrative Review, *Final Report,* H Doc. 95-272 (95th Congress, 1st session, December 31, 1977), II, pp. 966, 1095.

[18] John F. Bibby and Roger Davidson, *On Capitol Hill,* 2nd edition (Hinsdale, Ill.: Dryden Press, 1972), pp. 266-267.

[19] J. Terrence Brunner and Peter M. Manikas, *Informal Legislative Groups in the House of Representatives: Financing and Organization* (Washington, DC: Better Government Association, 1981), p. 54.

During the 1970s the informal caucuses became a veritable growth industry on Capitol Hill. Prior to 1970, there were only a handful of such groups–DSG, MCPL, Wednesday Group, and a few informal partisan social groups. By 1974 ten additional groups had appeared, including the Congressional Black Caucus, the New England Congressional Caucus, and several partisan groups. The real outpouring of such groups occurred after 1974; more than seventy groups were catalogued by students in 1981–although the number changes almost daily.[20] The Northeast-Midwest Economic Advancement Coalition, known as the "Frostbelt Caucus" and claiming two hundred members from eighteen states, looks after regional interests in such matters as tax burdens and fuel allocations. The one hundred forty-member Textile Caucus is a largely southern group dedicated to protecting the industry against regulation and foreign competition. Other groups bear such names as the Rural Caucus, the High Altitude Coalition, the Senate Steel Caucus, the Forum on Regulation, the Mushroom Caucus, and the Congressional Roller and Ball Bearing Coalition.

A majority of today's caucuses are limited to members of a single chamber, but some embrace both chambers. A few are partisan, but the overwhelming majority are bipartisan. Although such groups are unrecognized by House or Senate rules, many (though not all) boast such resources as separate staffs or offices, newsletters or reports that are circulated, regularized funding, established subunits, regularly scheduled meetings, and whip systems.

Caucus membership is quite widespread, at least in the House of Representatives. Reliable membership lists are hard to come by, not only because some groups are secretive but because memberships are often casual and shifting. According to one study, all but thirteen House members paid dues to at least one caucus during the first quarter of 1981.[21] The average member paid dues to three such groups. This is unquestionably a conservative measure of caucus memberships. After all, only twenty-two of the fifty-seven House caucuses charged dues at the time of the survey. Some of the dues, moreover, ranged as high as $2,000 or $2,500 per year. Thus it is

[20] Daniel P. Mulhollan, Susan Webb Hammond, and Arthur G. Stevens, Jr., "Informal Groups and Agenda Setting," Paper delivered at the annual meeting of the Midwest Political Science Association (Cincinnati, Ohio, April 16-18, 1981).

[21] Brunner and Manikas, *Informal Legislative Groups,* 24.

reasonable to assume that nearly every House member during the Ninety-seventh Congress belonged to at least one informal caucus, and most had joined several of them. One representative, Beryl Anthony (D-Ark.), was reputed to belong to fourteen caucuses; at least ten members belonged to ten or more caucuses each.[22]

The caucuses receive extensive financial and staff support from their members, congressional funds, and outside contributions. As of mid-1981, twenty-six caucuses had registered with the clerk of the House as "legislative service organizations" (LSOs), employing about one hundred full-time and fifteen part-time staff members.[23] They took in almost $2.9 million during the previous year, with the sources of funding indicated in table 5 As will be seen, half of the funds were donated by representatives from their clerk-hire funds. Members simply certify their portion of a shared employee's salary, and the paychecks are issued directly by the clerk of the House. A third of the groups' funds came from outside donations–from corporations, industry associations, lobby groups, or individuals. Another source is members' own dues or subscriptions–which can be paid out of members' official allowances. All told, some 60 percent of the caucuses' expenses are covered by congressional funds; about 40 percent comes from outside sources.

SOURCES OF CAUCUS STRENGTH

Informal caucuses, then, are numerous and institutionalized on Capitol Hill. They have grown and prospered because they perform functions that individual members find useful–in particular, assistance with legislative, political, and electoral goals. For outside groups, they provide a novel and seemingly effective linkage with allies in the House and Senate. Finally, these groups provide an antidote for the fragment committee and partisan leadership in the two chambers.

[22] Ibid., 25.
[23] Ibid., 31.

Table 5
SOURCES OF CAUCUS FUNDING, 1980

Source	Number of Caucuses Using	Percentage of Funds
Clerk-hire	21	50
Outside contributions	7	33
Members' dues, subscriptions	18	10
Outside subscriptions	5	5
Interest and miscellaneous	11	2
TOTALS	26	$2,870,487

SOURCE: J. Terrence Brunner and Peter M. Manikas, *Informal Legislative Groups in the House of Representatives; Financing and Organization,* Washington, DC: Better Government Association, November 1981), p. 31.

INTEREST GROUP LINKAGES

Legislators and their outside allies desire recognition and leverage in Congress. The black, women's, and Hispanic caucuses serve these objectives for their national constituencies. The Congressional Hispanic Caucus, created in 1976, announced that "the fact that we have joined together is a sign of the growing power of our community, and we are looking forward to strenthening the Federal Commitment to Hispanic citizens."[24] The Congressional Black Caucus maintains close ties with various black organizations, sponsoring an annual "legislative weekend" each fall and raising more than half a million dollars in 1980.

Many legislative caucuses represent interests that feel threatened by political developments or that lack other key points of access in the nation's capital. This is dramatically illustrated by those caucuses brought together to voice the interests of declining or threatened regions and industries–for example, the Northeast-Midwest Economic Advancement Coalition and the Steel Caucus. Members

[24] *New York Times* (December 8, 1976), p. 32. See also Marguerite Ross Barnett, "The Congressional Black Caucus," in Harvey C. Mansfield, Sr. (ed.), *Congress against the President* (New York: Praeger Publishers, 1975), 34-50; and Robert C. Smith, "The Black Congressional Delegation," *Western Political Quarterly* 34 (June 1981), pp. 203-221.

from "frostbelt" states, for example, want to retain their share of energy supplies and federal aid. As one such member, Donald Mitchell (R-N.Y.), remarked, the South's economic development "has been financed on a basis of northern tax dollars."[25]

Often, actions taken to protect a region's or industry's interests prompt countermoves on the part of rival interests. The Sun Belt Caucus, one southern Representative explained, was established in 1979 "in large part to counter lobbying and information-disseminating activities of the Northeast-Midwest Coalition."[26]

Sometimes, interest groups themselves are instrumental in forming legislative caucuses. The idea of the Mushroom Caucus–created to protect mushroom growers from foreign imports–originated at a May 1977 luncheon sponsored for House members by the American Mushroom Institute.[27] The Ancient Order of Hibernians, an Irish-Catholic organization of about 1.5 million members, wrote a representative of Italian descent, Mario Biaggi (D-N.Y.), and asked him to form and chair an Irish caucus. He was asked to do this, said Biaggi, because the Hibernians "recognized that I had been concerned for the 10 years I have been in Congress with the troubles in Northern Ireland."[28] It is fair to say that the caucus has generally taken a pro-Catholic, anti-British stance. Differences within the American-Irish community led to formation of a second group, Friends of Ireland, that favored a more conciliatory approach toward the Irish question.[29]

In other instances, regional or industry groups are satisfied to reap the benefits of closer contact with Hill allies. Not surprisingly, the Steel Caucus maintains links with the embattled steel industry and the Textile Caucus with textile manufacturers. (The automobile industry was slow to gain representation through a congressional caucus, but in 1981 an Auto Task Force was formed.) Although not launched by the industry itself, the Congressional Travel and

[25] Neal R. Peirce and Jerry Hagstrom, "Regional Groups Talk About Cooperation, But they Continue to Feud," *National Journal* 10 (May 27, 1978), p. 844.

[26] *Congressional Record* 125 (96th Congress, 1st session, April 3, 1979), HH1904 (daily edition).

[27] *Washington Star* (May 22, 1978), p. A1.

[28] *Congressional Record* 124 (95th Congress, 2nd session, February 23, 1978), p. H1471 (daily edition).

[29] *Congressional Record* 127 (97th Congress, 1st session March 17, 1981), p. S2266 (daily edition).

Tourism Caucus quickly grew to be one of the largest (more than 250 members) and best financed ($550,000 in outside contributions in 1980) of all the caucuses. The travel industry was, at least initially, "delighted [to] finally gain access to Congress," calling the caucus "tourism's radar in the House."[30] When the caucus launched a vigorous fund-raising drive, the industry–composed of a wide range of transportation, travel, hotel, restaurant, and promotional groups–responded generously. Yet, the caucus's continued emphasis on fund raising soon generated criticism and suspicion among industry spokespeople as well as Hill members.

STRUCTURAL GAPS IN CONGRESS

Another springboard for the rise of caucuses is undoubtedly the breakdown of traditional mechanisms for intrahouse leadership and mobilization through party or committee systems.[31] Since the post-Civil War period, congressional parties have exerted powerful leadership in decision making, especially in less controversial issues and those for which party consensus was high. Party cues were disseminated through leaders and enforced by whip systems. Partisan leadership was supplemented by an informal network of cue-giving and cue-taking based on legislative expertise–that is, members relied upon colleagues who served on the relevant committees and thus could be expected to be knowledgeable about the issues handled by their panels. These forms of leadership and information exchange–partisan and committees–seem to explain much of the dynamics of congressional voting up to the last few years.[32]

This kind of information exchange, it can be argued, is impaired by recent developments. Increasingly complex issues throw generalized information networks into confusion. Committee jurisdictions

[30] Cited in Brunner and Manikas, *Informal Legislative Groups,* 46-47.

[31] This argument is persuasively made by Daniel P. Mulhollan and Arthur G. Stevens, Jr., in "Congressional Liaison and the Rise of Informal Groups in Congress," Paper delivered at the annual meeting of the Western Political Science Association (1977).

[32] For a summary of these changes in congressional organization, see Roger H. Davidson, "Subcommittee Government: New Channels for Policy Making," in Thomas E. Mann and Norman K. Ornstein(eds.), *The New Congress* (Washington, DC: American Enterprise Institute, 1981), p. 99-133.

are narrow and overlapping, which is especially confusing in such broad-gauged issues as energy, health, environment, or international economics. In both chambers, bills are often referred multiply to two or more committees. Increasingly, votes are taken on single-purpose amendments of the type that used to be contained within the committees or, in the House, disposed of in unrecorded teller votes in the committee of the whole. Party leaders tend to be geographically and even ideologically diverse; and, in any event, the party loyalty bonds simply do not extend to the diverse issues now being aired on the floor of the two chambers. Thus many informal caucuses form around a single issue or set of issues affecting a given clientele; and of the newer groups, the overwhelming majority are bipartisan rather than party-based.

Thus the contemporary House and Senate have few devices to integrate legislation considered by their many committees and to disseminate information of interest to specific groups of members. Ad hoc groups can provide this leadership, coordination, and informational role. "One joins these caucuses," observed Thomas Daschle (D-S.D.), "because the committees don't go far enough in bringing together people with the same interests or experience on the issue. I believe [the] gasohol caucus has done that. When I came here, over 100 members had different gasohol bills, but they had no communication or coordination among themselves. The caucus gives us a way to find a consensus."[33] In a 1977 survey, the House Commission on Administrative Review discovered that 43 percent of the legislative assistants interviewed regarded informal House groups as "very helpful" or "fairly helpful" as sources of information.[34]

A goal for some ad hoc caucuses is to help legislators anticipate issues and provide analytical support. The House's Environmental and Energy Study Conference, for example, acts as a clearinghouse for information in these fields. There is even a Clearinghouse on the Future to promote forecasting of trends.

The direct link between dispersed party leadership and the rise of informal caucuses is seen in the new members' caucuses–which formed in both parties in the last several congresses. Most notable was the Democrats' new member, caucus of the Ninety-fourth

[33] *Washington Post* (October 7, 1979), p. C2.

[34] U.S. House of Representatives, Commission on Administrative Review, *Final Report,* H. Doc. 95-272 (95th Congress, 1st session, December 31, 1977), II, p. 1096.

Congress. Shortly after the new members were elected, they quickly organized, procured staff assistance, and invited committee chairmen to appear at "interviews" prior to the party caucus that would select them–an unheard-of event. The group was instrumental in eventually removing three committee chairmen at the outset of that congress, in 1975. In that case, the new members' caucus worked in tandem with the established DSG–which had fought for the precedents used in selecting committee chairmen. Yet that new members' caucus, like others, retained its cohesion and refused to dissolve into alliances with more senior members.

Party leaders often complain about the proliferation of informal caucuses. Speaker Thomas P. O'Neill, Jr. (D-Mass.), for instance, remarked that the "house has over-caucused itself."[35] Other party leaders have expressed similar views. Republican leader Robert Michel (R-Ill.), for example, declared that

> . . . the recent spectacular growth of the caucuses, groups, ad-hoc and semi-legislative entities that have sprouted up throughout the House [is] diffusing, denigrating and even in some cases destroying the legitimate constitutional functions of the House, its leadership and its committees.[36]

However, many party leaders belong to such caucuses. And in the Ninety-Sixth Congress the House Democratic Caucus began to mimic the caucus networks by establishing "task forces" on certain bills to supplement the regular whip system. In the following congress, Representative Richard Gephardt (D-Mo.) was named director of task forces–a new post in the Democratic leadership structure. Whether or not this innovation becomes a permanent part of party organization, it is nonetheless a response by party leaders to the trend.

[35] Quoted in *U.S. News & World Report* (February 4, 1980), p. 59.

[36] Statement before Ad Hoc Subcommittee on Legislative Service Organizations, House Administration Committee, U.S. House of Representatives (October 1, 1981), p. 1.

ELECTORAL INCENTIVES

The electoral decline of the traditional political parties has been universally commented upon. If voters no longer consistently ally themselves with the two umbrella-type parties, they seemingly respond to appeals from a host of specialized groups, including the so-called single-interest groups. Such groups have their counterparts on Capitol Hill in the form of the informal caucuses.

Caucus memberships can prove an electoral aid: they are cited to prove members' fealty to certain causes, and they frequently channel campaign assistance in the form of advice, money, or literature. Many groups model themselves after the Democratic Study Group, which prepares weekly guides to upcoming floor decisions that are widely consulted. The DSG has also given campaign assistance to liberal candidates.

Thus it is not surprising that members form and join informal caucuses in order to nurture political strength back home in their states and districts. The House Coal Caucus, for example, was the brainchild of Representative Nick J. Rahall (D-W.Va.). "By providing a congressional forum for the major industry in his district," wrote two observers, the "Coal Group offered Mr. Rahall significant political benefits."[37]

Membership in an informal caucus can be an asset on the campaign trail. Representative Daschle stresses his support of gasohol to voters because the grain alcohol to be mixed with gasoline can be made from the corn, rye, wheat, and potatoes grown by South Dakota's farmers.

> "You and I are in the driver's seat," [Daschle] told a Farmer's Union picnic July 1. He talked about efforts to create a gasohol caucus in the House and how the caucus now has 85 members. The audience gave him a standing ovation.
> Later that day, stopping in Clark, S.D., he conferred with a local farmer who is seeking federal help for a million-dollar plant that would make gasohol from potatoes.[38]

[37] Daniel P. Mulhollan and Arthur G. Stevens, Jr., "Special Interests and the Growth of Information Groups in Congress," Paper presented at the Midwest Political Science Convention, 1980, 15.

[38] *Washington Star* (July 9, 1979), p. A9.

Beyond the symbolic value of these caucuses, some of them also provide campaign and fund raising assistance for their members. Some of them prepare packets of issue information and speech-making material relating to issues covered by the caucus. Even more important, some caucuses promise contacts with private PACs and other funding sources for campaigns.

LEGISLATIVE IMPACT OF CAUCUSES

The impact of informal caucuses is not entirely clear. Some legislators denigrate them. Representative John Erlenborn (R-Ill.) opposes the spread of caucuses because they "lead to nothing but increased expenses, increased staff, decreased available working space, and a further growth of purely provincial points of view."[39] Others believe caucuses undermine party unity and underscore the balkanizaton of Congress.

Although their overall achievements are hard to assess, caucuses have influenced the passage or defeat of specific bills. "We made the phone calls to alert [the House Textile Caucus] Members that the [1978] trade bill was coming up at the 11th hour," commented caucus member Margaret Heckler (R-Mass,). "We also were able to keep together a nucleus of people who could make speeches and carry the vote."[40]

Informal caucuses serve as contact points for executive branch liaison officers. The caucuses provide executive and White House officials with a focal point for information exchange, strategy coordination, and coalition building. "[A]t least a caucus is an organized group you can make a presentation to," declared Frank Moore, Carter's legislative liaison chief.[41]

Finally, informal caucuses permit members to discuss common issues and join with other groups to pass or defeat legislation. Paradoxically, these groups foster both decentralizing and integrative tendencies in Congress.

[39] John Erlenborn, "Rep. Erlenborn on the Caucus Delicti," *Roll Call* (April 27, 1978), p. 4.

[40] *U.S. News & World Report* (February 4, 1980), p. 59.

[41] Ibid.

REGULATING INFORMAL CAUCUSES

Informal caucuses have burgeoned without formal recognition in House or Senate rules, or direct monetary support from public funds. Indeed, one definition of such groups is "voluntary associations of members of Congress, without recognition in chamber rules or line-item appropriations, which seek to have a role in the policy process."[42] As we have seen, however, these caucuses benefit materially from such public aid as members' contributions (which may be paid from official expense allowances), and in many cases space in House office buildings. No such arrangements exist in the Senate.

The House began in 1979 to regulate the caucuses. In an order issued July 18 of that year, the House Administration Committee outlined regulations governing so-called legislative service organizations (LSOs). In order to qualify as LSOs in the House, groups must meet certain standards. They must consist at least in part of House members and be organized primarily to provide legislative services and assistance to members.[43] Of the sixty or so House caucuses in 1981, twenty-six were certified as LSOs.[44]

Working from LSO reports filed with the clerk of the House, a Chicago-based group called the Better Government Association issued a report in 1981 calling for stricter standards for informal caucuses. Because approximately half of all caucuses certified as LSOs also received funds from outside sources, the Better Government Association argued that outside interests were gaining undue influence over groups that were recipients of governmental support.[45] At least one measure was introduced in the Ninety-seventh Congress that would have terminated all House funding and logistical support for LSOs.[46]

[42] Arthur G. Stevens, Jr., Daniel Mulhollan, and Paul Rundquist, "U.S. Congressional Structure and Representation: The Role of Informal Groups," *Legislative Studies Quarterly* 6 (August 1981), p. 415.

[43] Order of the Committee on House Administration (July 18, 1979).

[44] Brunner and Manikas, *Informal Legislative Groups*, 21.

[45] Ibid.

[46] H. Res. 248, 97th Congress. Introduced by Representative Ed Bethune (D-Ark.) (October 20, 1981).

Responding to this criticism, the Committee on House Administration in September 1981 created an ad hoc subcommittee to study the issue and draft new regulations. After considering and amending the subcommittee proposal, the committee on October 21 adopted a new order regulating LSOs. Because the committee has complete authority to issue regulations on housekeeping matters, full House approval was not required.

While reaffirming the notion of LSO certification and support, the new order forced caucuses to choose between House support or outside support. Caucuses certified as LSOs, and therefore eligible for House support, may not accept outside support of any kind. Conversely, groups that accept outside funds cannot be certified–meaning they cannot receive clerk-hire donations, dues from member allowances, or House office space. New caucuses applying for LSO status must be sponsored by either a minimum of 30 representatives or two-thirds of its membership, whichever was less.[47] Every two years the membership must attest that the organization provides "bona fide legislative services or assistance which supports them in the performance of their official duties."[48] Quarterly reports are required, summarizing receipts, disbursements, and staff salaries and listing all prepared reports and materials issued during that quarter.

These regulations will force a degree of specialization among various types of caucuses. Those qualifying as LSOs will have renounced direct outside contributions. However, there is nothing to prevent such groups from forging alliances with outside groups, perhaps even with counterpart "educational foundations" run with private funds. Other caucuses, heavily dependent on outside funding, will remain outside the aegis of the House and will operate outside congressional office buildings. Finally, many caucuses–perhaps the majority of them–will continue to work out of individual members' offices with a minimum of staff or funding assistance.

[47] Brunner and Minikas, *Informal Legislative Groups,* 68.
[48] Ibid., 69.

CONCLUSIONS

Informal caucuses constitute a new sort of multiparty system on Capitol Hill. To be sure, some are little more than paper organizations whose main purpose seems to be to help members claim credit for promoting particular causes. Yet many of these groups perform partylike functions: they provide a label that members find useful, and they focus attention on particular issues or interests. Most significantly for policymaking, such groups provide alternative channels of information and mobilization on issues–channels that usually work independently of party or committee-based groupings.

These Capitol Hill caucuses, needless to say, mirror the present state of interest articulation and aggregation in the political system at large. That is to say, policy concerns are effectively articulated by a multitude of groups, but little aggregation takes place. Few developments, in fact, have been more repeatedly announced than the long-term decline of traditional political parties and the expansion of interest groups. To the traditional producer-oriented federations–labor, professional, business, and agricultural–has been added a plethora of groups, some with quite specific concerns (the famous single-interest groups), some with an ideological cast. Lobbyists represent such diverse interests as individual business firms, cities, counties, states, beneficiaries of hundreds of government programs, antiabortionists, born-again Christians, nuclear power advocates and opponents, and all manner of consumer and environmental interests. It is not the narrowness of these groups that is novel, but rather their number and range and their unwillingness to accept brokerage by political parties.

Facing such a profusion of voices, it is little wonder that legislators seek not one party label but many, shaping their images in terms of factional allegiances. In turn, these groups provide multiple access to information and voting cues, permitting members to participate, however superficially, in floor decisions that once would have been controlled by party leaders or committee experts.

Because of its permeability, congressional policymaking today defies easy description. For more than a generation, students have described policymaking arrangements with such metaphors as "iron triangles"–more or less closed networks of communications among congressional subcommittees, executive agencies, and outside clientele groups. The concept symbolized a great variety of subsystem arrangements, many of which were neither ironclad nor triangular. Today, these relationships are so complex and fluid that the metaphor may be altogether obsolete; Heclo, as we have noted, prefers the vaguer term "issue networks."

The present open system may perhaps be a transitory result of the coming of age of a new set of interests–especially environmental, consumer, ideological, and "public-interest" groups. More likely, it is a long-range shift in our politics, rooted in demographic and institutional changes. Whatever its ultimate meaning, the essential characteristics of the present system of caucuses are openness and complexity.

Chapter 20

THE POLITICAL ECONOMY OF THE POPULAR FRONT IN COMPARATIVE PERSPECTIVE

Peter Alexis Gourevitch

Ni déflation, ni dévaluation!

Electoral slogan, Popular Front, 1936[1]

Si Léon Blum s'est résigné si aisément à abandonner un pouvoir qu'il aurait pu, sans beaucoup de difficulté, conserver, c'est pour n'avoir pas trouvé devant lui une bourgeoisie capable de comprendre et d'accepter ce qu'il lui offrait, une transformation, sans révolution, des structures économiques et sociales de la France de 1937.

Georges Dupeux, 1963[2]

The electoral slogan above expresses a crucial aspect of the economic platform of the Popular Front coalition that came to power in June 1936: what that government tried to avoid in order to innovate new economic policy. Instead of deflation and devaluation, the government tried demand stimulus through wage increases. Why did it try that policy for dealing with the Depression, rather than others? And why did it fail? Georges Dupeux's comment offers what may be called a powerful hint. What was tried and not tried, what succeeded and what failed, depended in large measure on what various economic actors in French society demanded or opposed and on the behavior of political parties in fusing or splintering those preferences.

[1] See reference to this slogan in François Goguel, *La politique des partis sous la III'e République* (Paris: Le Seuil, 1946), vol. 2, p. 42.

[2] Georges Dupeux, "L'échec du premier gouvernement Léon Blum," *Revue d'histoire moderne et contemporaine* 10 (Jan-March, 1963).

Henry Ehrmann saw all this at the time it was happening. Already in the late 1930s, he began gathering materials on interest groups for the books that made him famous: *French Labor from Popular Front to Liberation, Organized Business in France,* and, later, *Interest Groups on Four Continents* and *Politics in France.*[3] Ehrmann provides very valuable insights into the policy outlook of major interest-group actors in the Popular Front drama. It seems appropriate, therefore, to honor him by making use of his work.

This chapter does so by placing the Popular Front experience in a comparative context. The 1930s provides a particularly fascinating opportunity to the comparativist–a universal stimulus (the collapsing world economy) to which there were divergent responses (different economic policies and different political outcomes). The political divergences are well known: the collapse of constitutional government in Germany and the victory of fascism there, the survival of constitutional government in Britain and Scandinavia, and the resistance to fascism in France, followed by internal collapse. Less well known are the divergences in economic policy response: Who pursued deflationary orthodoxy, and for how long? Who turned to tariff protectionism, and when? Who experimented with demand stimulus, and how successfully? Also less well known are the relationships between politics and policy: What were the political correlates of different economic policies?

In exploring these problems for the French case, I will draw on a larger project comparing the politics of economic policy choice in several countries over several time periods. In my earlier work on the economic crisis of the nineteenth century, the situation of interest groups in the international economy seemed particularly important in accounting for divergent economic policy choices (in that case, tariffs).[4] In Germany, for example, the Junkers had been

[3] Henry Ehrmann, *Organized Business in France* (Princeton: Princeton University Press, 1957); *French Labor from Popular Front to Liberation* (New York: Oxford University Press, 1947); *Interest Groups on Four Continents* (Pittsburgh: University of Pittsburgh Press, 1958); *Politics in France* (Boston: Little, Brown, 4th ed., 1982).

[4] Peter A. Gourevitch, "Breaking with Orthodoxy: The Politics of Economic Policy in the Great Depression of 1929, forthcoming in special issue of *International Organization,* "Industrial Sectors and Political Outcomes," James Kurth and Peter Gourevitch, eds., 1983. On the late nineteenth century, see Peter A. Gourevitch, "International Trade, Domestic Coalitions and Liberty: Comparative Responses to the Crisis of 1873-96," *Journal of Interdisciplinary History,* 8, no. 2 (Autumn 1977), pp.

free traders for hundreds of years. Within six years after the collapse of grain prices in 1873, they switched sides to join with the heavy industry producers in development, as well as foreign economic policy, to install a protectionist policy on both industrial and agricultural products. In his study of the famous iron-rye coalition, *Bread and Democracy*, Alexander Gerschenkron notes the formation of "progressive" and "reactionary" alliances among domestic groups (though Gerschenkron does not use these labels).[5] The progressive alliances linked together export industry, labor, and high-quality foodstuff agriculture around a program of free trade, autonomy to labor unions, high wages and welfare payments, autonomy to trade unions, and democratization of the political system. The conservative alliance linked heavy industry, grain growers, and portions of the middle and working classes around a program of tariff protection, restraint on wage levels, some social welfare, and authoritarian control of labor and politics. For the late nineteenth century, we can find parallels to the German case in other countries.

The German experience suggests a pattern: high-technology, export oriented industries, where labor represents a smaller share of value added, were more likely to work out overt accommodations with labor than were middle or low-technology industries, faced with severe problems of foreign competition, in which labor represented a high share of value added.[6] Other European cases fit this pattern: in the United Kingdom, Sweden, and France, we can find parallels. The U.S. experience, though, shows a different pattern: there labor participated in protectionist coalitions with its heavy industry employees, despite the latter's hostility to unions and welfare systems. The difference has much to do with food costs: given the efficiency of U.S. agriculture, U.S. labor could get cheap food along with high industrial tariffs; European labor could only keep food

281-313.

[5] Alexander Gerschenkron, *Bread and Democracy* (New York: Fertig, 1966).

[6] Tom Ferguson, "Normalcy to New Deal: Industrial Structure, Party Competition, and American Public Policy in the Great Depression," forthcoming in a special issue of *International Organization.* See also Ferguson's forthcoming book *Critical Realignments: The Fall of the House of Morgan and the Origins of the New Deal* (New York: Oxford University Press, forthcoming). For a brilliant exporation of the political implications of the product cycle in historical development, see James Kurth, "The Political Consequences of the Product Cycle: Industrial History and Political Outcomes," *International Organization* 33 (Winter 1979), pp. 1-34.

prices down by fighting all tariffs.

The patterns of the late nineteenth century suggests that for the period of the 1930s, it would be useful to examine the situation of different economic actors in the international economy and the alliances that formed among groups around different policy responses. This chapter applies this mode of reasoning to the evolution of French policy in the 1930s. The first part sets out the various policy options available to different countries in responding to the downturn of 1929 and notes the divergent *policy sequences.* The second part examines in detail the preferences of various French interest groups and political parties for these policies and explores the alliances that formed and crumbled.

THE POLICY OPTIONS

In the industrialized, capitalist countries, the arguments over how to deal with the Great Depression were remarkably similar. What differed was the political strength of the holders of various positions. At the beginning of the Depression, the policy debate revolved around two orthodoxies, those of the Right and the Left. *Option 1 was deflation:.* cutting costs through lower wages, lower taxes, and a balanced budget; defending currency. *Option 2 was socialization of investment:* public ownership of the means of production and distribution, nonmarket controlled investment and planning.

Pited against each other, these alternatives had a zero-sum quality in that each required major sacrifices from the "other" side. The deflation school insisted that high wages and high taxes for unemployment compensation and other transfer payments threatened profitability. To induce investment, labor had to yield higher profits to capitalists. For the socialization school, the market forces worked to bear the costs of adjustment; private owners must therefore be eliminated.

This conceptualization of the alternatives had important political implications. Each alternative polarized politics on class lines. Each contained the implication that fulfillment of the economic theory's prescriptions might require destruction of the constitutional system in order to push aside the dissenting class's opposition.

By 1931, two other policy packages entered the debate and began to be tried. These were both mixed games in the sense of blurring the costs and benefits across class lines. *Option 3 was neoorthodoxy:* devaluation of the currency, tariffs, and corporatism, or government-sanctioned cartels. *Option 4 was demand stimulus:* to be achieved through deficit-financed public works or transfer payments.

These alternatives implied a different political struggle because they made it possible to attract support across the boundary lines defined by the two more orthodox schools.

Analytically, these options were all possible alternatives at any moment. Historically, they came in sequence. Everyone started with deflation. When that proved ineffective, countries turned to one of the other alternatives, and, when it proved ineffective or undesirable to certain groups, to yet another. None of the countries in Western Europe or North America tried a full-fledged socialization, though several did engage in some direct public investment and planning.

In comparing the five countries of my study–France, Germany, Sweden, the United States–we may note two patterns of policy sequence. The first may be called the "regular path" in that it entailed a linear departure from orthodoxy toward progressively more unfamiliar and controversial theories of political economy. The second path may be called "irregular" in that the policy jumped from orthodoxy to innovation without intermediate steps. The "orthodox" break with orthodoxy goes as follows: Step 1: orthodox deflation is tried. Step 2: when step 1 fails, the country tries some aspects of neoorthodoxy, such as devaluation, tariffs, and some degree of corporatism. Step 3: when neoorthodoxy proves inadequate, some effort is made to try demand stimulus.

This sequence describes the policies of the United States and Sweden. Sweden started with deflation under a conservative coalition, devalued the currency in 1931 after the British devalued the pound sterling, and began considering demand-stimulus schemes, public works, and higher welfare transfer payments after 1932, when a new political coalition of the Social Democrats and Agrarians came to power. The Swedish recovery was rather good. Some have attributed that success to the innovative fiscal policy of demand stimulus. Current research among economic historians attributes it to the pull of foreign markets brought about by the Swedish devaluation and the revival of the British and German economies. Although the latter interpretation seems plausible, it leaves out the interesting question of why the Swedish Social Democrats were willing to try new political coalitions around new policy analyses when the British Labour party tried neither.

The United States pattern resembles, loosely, the Swedish sequence. There was deflation under Hoover, but also revival of protectionism with the Smoot-Hawley bill of 1931. Roosevelt devalued in 1933, launched a wide range of corporatist measures, helped unions organize, stimulated demand with a variety of transfer payments (social security) and public works, and tried a deliberate demand-stimulus deficit budgeted in 1937-1938. The U.S. economy did do better, and again there is debate as to why and whether it could have done even better with more demand stimulus.

The United Kingdom's case is a foreshortened version of the first path. Deflation began early, when the pound was pegged high in 1924. When the run on the pound proved irresistible in 1931, even after the famous concesssions accepted by MacDonald and Snowden, causing a split within the Labour party, the banks gave up and told MacDonald to devalue. What the British did not do is the third step, experimentation with demand stimulus. That had been urged by the Liberals under Lloyd George, advised by Keynes; it was endorsed by Bevin and the trade unions but rejected by MacDonald and Snowden. As a result, the Lib-Lab coalition needed to put it through never came about. The national government, dominated by the Conservatives, rested with neoorthodoxy. It adopted the first comprehensive tariff in a hundred years. The devalued pound stimulated exports, and low interest rates helped touch off a building boom and investment in new industries. There was thus a real revival under the neoorthodox path, and debate continues as to whether it would have been stronger had the United Kingdom gone to Step 3.[7]

The other two countries, France and Germany, followed what may be called the irregular sequence toward irregularity or the unconventional path to breaking with orthodoxy: Step 1: orthodoxy deflation is tried, as with the regular sequence. Step 2: instead of neoorthodoxy (devaluation, tariffs, and cartels), the countries imme-

[7] For detailed references to the Swedish, U.S. and British cases see Peter A. Gourevitch, "Breaking with Orthodoxy."

diately try some kind of demand stimulus. Step 3: Some sort of backtracking begins to take up various aspects of neoorthodoxy in addition to demand stimulus (Germany) or in place of it (France).

Like everyone else, Germany began with orthodox deflation. Like those of Sweden, Britain, and the United States, the German government resisted devaluation, but unlike those countries, it never gave up (at least not officially–exchange controls had similar effects). The coalition that ended the deflation policy, led by Hitler, moved immediately to demand stimulus via deficit spending for public works and, by the end of 1934, by armaments. The Weimar coalition rejected demand stimulus; the Social Democratic party (SPD) unions supported it, but the SPD leadership, in particular the great finance expert, Hilferding, rejected it. The Nazi government used it, along with very severe exchange controls, tariffs, bilateral trade negotiations, and some measure of direct government investment in specific industries. The economic revival in Germany was stronger, faster, and more thorough than anywhere else.[8]

The French moves through the "irregular path" were a bit different. There, too, the first step was orthodox deflation, though the timing was different. The Depression hit France later than elsewhere, largely because the Poincaré% franc had been undervalued, giving France an advantage that drew gold and stimulated exports. When the other countries devalued in 1931, France lost its edge, and the franc became overvalued. The center-right governments of 1932-1936 applied deflation ever more severely.

What the Popular Front government tried to do in 1936 was use demand stimulus without devaluation and cartelization, and a particular form of demand stimulus not tried elsewhere, that of higher wages rather than deficit budgets. For reasons we shall explore below, the Popular Front government sought to avoid the two alternatives taken by other countries: like the Germans, it resisted devaluation; unlike the Germans, it did not impose exchange controls. One or the other was necessary, as soon proved to be the case, when the run on the franc forced devaluation at the end of September 1936. At the same time, the demand-stimulus techniques were different in France. The ideas of Keynes, Kalecki, Woytinski, and

[8] On the German case see the references in Ibid. and the excellent book by David Abraham, *The Collapse of the Weimar Republic* (Princeton: Princeton University Press, 1981).

Wigfors focused on government deficits. In the face of too much saving and not enough spending, the answer was to infuse *new* quantities of demand into the economy through government deficits. That new demand would increase the sales of products, which would mean expanded production, more profits, more hiring of workers, rising wages, and more investment, all stimulating the cycle ever higher through the multiplier.

In France the Popular Front government stressed higher worker wages rather than deficit spending, though it tried the latter course as well. And it stressed sharing the work. This approach was less strong in producing *new* demand. It reallocated the source of demand from one group to another, from the employers to the workers. To the extent that workers saved less than employers, there would be new demand; and workers certainly saved less. Still, the effects of this were not likely to be as powerful as direct deficit spending, and, as we shall see, the political implications were quite different, as deficit spending suggested a mixed game while rising worker wages suggested a zero-sum one.

As happened elsewhere, the Popular Front government did break with orthodoxy in its willingness to try various forms of market intervention. In addition to the famous pieces of legislation concerning industrial labor markets (the forty-hour week, paid vacations, and higher wages), the government tried to go far beyond the deflationist cabinets in agriculture. The Office du Blé is the most obvious example; it sought to guarantee a minimum price.

To sum up the French policy sequence, we may observe the following: France is the only country that tried demand stimulus as a policy alternative to deflation *before* devaluing the currency. Germany pumped up the economy but *never* devalued, using exchange controls and other regulations instead. Sweden and the United States made tentative experiments at countercyclical policies *after* devaluing; and the British devalued *early* but never tried demand stimulus. And the French were the only ones to try their particular version of demand stimulus, which was direct increase in wages, rather than government deficits.

We have briefly posed the outcome of the French case in comparative terms. There remains the problem of explanation. How can we account for what happened in France, in particular the difference between what happened there and what happened elsewhere? What do we learn by asking who wanted what? What policies did various groups prefer?

INTEREST GROUP PREFERENCES: WHICH POLICY OPTIONS IN THE 1930S?

Group Preferences

Who supported which policy option in the 1930s? By comparing the policy coalitions in the 1930s we may detect several patterns. The deflation option polarized society roughly along class lines, that is, the owners of property, from tiny to large, urban and rural, industrial and artisanal, supported deflation as the correct way of handling a crisis. Labor, of various kinds, resisted it, or at least that aspect of deflation that called for a reduction in wages and welfare benefits. Labor's position on the policy choices were more confusing in those countries where labor or social democratic parties sustained governing majorities (Britain and Germany); there the parties kept alive governments pursuing the overall deflationary strategy while objecting strenuously to one of its principal requirements, wage reduction.

When deflation appeared not to work, the desire for experimentation with new policies emerged. Among what social groups was the interest in experimentation strongest? From where came the support for the break with traditional economic orthodoxy? Clearly very few people understood the economic debates in theoretical terms between the liberal market theorists, the regular socialist theoreticians (Hilferding), and the "new wave" (Kalecki, Keynes, Woytinski).

But everyone supported one side or another of the policy alternatives (higher or lower taxes, tariffs or free trade, higher or lower wages, public works or none, devaluation or currency defense, etc.). Some groups felt desperate about existing policies and were willing to try new things. Which ones?

To simplify drastically, we may say that all across Europe and North America, the core of a break-with-orthodoxy constituency leading to demand stimulus was labor and agriculture, but with some business support or at least acquiescence. The distress in agriculture was extremely intense. Prices had been falling already before the industrial crash of 1929, so that all who made their living from agriculture (farmers, peasants, laborers, agricultural equipment manufacturers, etc.) were already in dire straits. When the industrial contraction then rapidly squeezed urban markets and shut off urban employment alternatives, farmers became desperate. They became willing to try anything, however deviant from official orthodoxy. Price supports, marketing boards, subsidies of inputs like fertilizers, mortgage indebtedness assistance, assistance to urban markets, erosion of the monetary debt–farmers were willing to try any or all of these.

The intellectual break with orthodoxy for farmers was doubtless aided by another tradition, the antagonism of agriculture and the countryside toward industry and cities. Under the intense stress of economic conditions in the early 1930s farmers everywhere pressed for action. Their dissatisfaction with deflation came early. They were thus available for coalitions supporting other options. This happened everywhere; what differed from country to country was the specific character of the coalition into which agriculture was drawn–social democratic (Sweden and the United States) or fascist (Germany) or mixtures of both (Spain and France).

The second group interested in deviating from deflationary orthodoxy was labor. As with agriculture, labor's interest in a new policy mixed the impact of economic suffering with the legacy of alternative intellectual traditions. The suffering imposed on employees during the Depression is certainly well known. Lacking the cushion of savings or even the possibility of growing their own food, the unemployed did indeed go through bad times. They too turned in desperation against deflation. And, like farmers, they too could draw upon other experiences and viewpoints to provide legitimacy in turning away from the orthodox approach. Labor movements of all kinds, Marxian and otherwise, had plenty of complaints against the capitalist market economy and arguments such as the underconsumption theory able to support a range of views and policies.

Nearly everywhere labor movements pressed for action. The interesting split was between unions and party. Trade unions everywhere supported some break with orthodoxy, wanting to gain higher wages either directly or indirectly through deficit spending. In some places labor associated parties accepted the new ideas; in others they resisted them. The Swedish Social Democrats, the U.S. Democrats, and the French Socialists took them up; the German Social Democrats and the British Social Democrats rejected them.

The difference had great consequences: in the United Kingdom, it helped fragment the Labour party, bring the Conservatives to power, and prevent experimentation with new economic policies; in Germany, it helped prevent the prorepublic coalition from defending the regime through new economic policies and left Hitler in a position to coopt the credit of experimentation. I shall return to this matter of union-party relations later in the chapter, after the discussion of interest groups.

Labor and agriculture, then, provided the core of all demand-stimulus coalitions in the 1930s (the first time since the Industrial Revolution that labor and agriculture succeeded in cooperating on economic policy). There were some important exceptions to this generalization, particularly that of Nazism. The unionized labor force in Germany was among the least likely of any German groups to vote Nazi. "We never got the 'real workers,' said one Nazi leader. At the same time, many nonunionized workers did vote Nazi. The Nazis did have some mass urban support, including employees, the sellers of labor. Although the unions ardently defended the republic, were among the chief victims of Nazi repression, and opposed most of what the Nazis did, the fascist government did undertake some economic measures that the unions had wanted constitutional governments to try–public works, demand stimulus, employment boosting. The Nazis drew upon the same elements as other demand stimulus coalitions but put them together in a different political form and with a somewhat different mix of the strength of the various components.

So far, the pattern we have found in other countries applies as well to the French case. The sharpest critics of the deflation policy pursued from 1932 through 1936 were labor and agriculture. Trade unions and political parties drawing labor votes (PCF, SFIO,

Radicals) all attacked deflation. Among farmers the complaints were also quite intense, and the search for alternatives was strong. Some went toward Dogueres and various forms of the new Right; others toward the marxist parties, either Socialist SFIO or PCF. Like those of Germany, Spain, and other countries, French farmers polarized when center-right bourgeois governments refused to take energetic action for market support. Like those everywhere in Europe and North America, indeed, around the world, farmers turned against the market mechanism, even those farmers who owned property and normally defended the market acutely.

Can we make any generalizations about what sorts of farmers moved one way or another? To learn what role parties played it would be interested to know something about the political sociology and political economy of who moved in which direction. Perhaps religious farmers went to the Right, and anticlerical farmers moved further Left. Or it might have been market situations that shaped behavior: farmers who managed to get help from the pre-1936 government may have remained loyal to the governing parties; those who had got little or not enough may have shifted. Thus, wine growers and sugar beet growers seem to be in the first category; they got some kinds of support before 1936 that seem to have done some good. Wheat growers, however, got little. The government passed a price support measure that did not provide for any compulsory market intervention and was widely subverted. It may be that those farmers who felt the most abandoned economically moved furthest politically, the direction being shaped by religion and previous partisan commitments. More careful investigation would help clarify the causal mechanisms.

We do know that the rural vote for the Left did rise, that farmers' discontent with the deflationary policy was intense, and that agriculture was willing to support a wide range of market interventions from import quotas to marketing boards to price support boards to a broad demand-stimulating policy. As in other countries, the support for new economic policies depended considerably on the willingness of farmers to overcome their long-standing dislike of unions and the city to form some sort of de facto coalition.

What of business? Here we return to Dupeux's point cited at the beginning of the chapter. His emphasis on the lack of an understanding bourgeoisie is strongly reinforced by comparison of the French bourgeoisie with those of other countries. In addition to the support of large blocs of labor and agriculture, the third ingredient in experimenting coalitions willing to break with orthodoxy was the support of some segments of capital–owners and managers. Capital is not, and was not, necessarily homogeneous or unified. Some issues push property owners together in the face of common antagonism toward other groups on certain issues–labor costs, agricultural demands. On other questions, the owners of capital diverge. Their positions differ, pulling their interests in quite different directions. Sometimes these conflicts are managed, at other times not. In the latter case, business segments may split apart, some forming alliances with other groups, such as labor and agriculture.

In all the countries studied here, most of the business community supported the orthodoxy of deflation–at least initially. In some countries where protectionist impulses were strong, there were early moves to raise tariffs (the United States is the clearest example) but not to abandon the use of the market to correct the market's deficiencies. As the Depression worsened, dissatisfaction with this course of action spread among business as it had among labor and agriculture. Sentiment grew to take up some of the alternative options. Some business people moved toward neoorthodoxy: tariffs, where these did not already exist (as in the United Kingdom); devaluation; and corporatism in one form or another to regulate market shares (the NRA in the United States, for example). These can be seen as normal breaks with orthodoxy among businessmen. They are moves long regarded as acceptable measures for dealing with emergencies. Each country had experience with them in earlier periods of economic depression or during war.

The demand-stimulus policy option was newer and more controversial. It entailed a degree of government intervention and activism beyond the range of previous experience, or at least experience understood in orthodox terms. Nonetheless, hostility to these ideas was not uniform. Some segments of business in some countries showed increasing interest in government support for demand, particularly for their products, and/or showed some willingness to enter political coalitions making trade-offs with other groups in which demand stimulus was one element of the trade. Where such coalitions came to power and tried some of these new policies, the support of these business elements proved important both in bringing the coalition to power and in influencing the evolution of policy afterward. Where business support was lacking, the coalitions had more difficulty either coming to power or working out their policy preferences.

In Germany, for example, interest in government spending to fight the Depression grew among the heavy industry sector, or the iron part of the famous iron-rye coalition. Government-led stimulus of this sector was not, indeed, a new phenomenon. Naval building in the late nineteenth century helped, as W. W. Rostow noted, keep the steel, iron, and coal industries going when the railroad building boom slowed down.[9] Defense contracts, high tariffs, and antilabor legislation helped construct the iron-rye alliance. Its opponents were labor and industrial interests concerned with cheap food and exports in a thriving open international economy. These included electrical equipment and chemicals, industries in which German technology helped lead the world. The two types of industries conflicted repeatedly. In the 1920s, the latter export group overcame the heavy group for the first time through an alliance with labor. With the Depression, the fight reemerged. The heavy group wanted protection and government stimulated demand through defense contracts and civilian public works.

The policy preferences and political behavior of German businesses suggest the existence within industry as a whole of several "paths" to breaking with economic orthodoxy: the "progressive industrial," "regressive industrial," and "petty proprietor" paths. The first two involve large scale industries fully involved in a profit-maximizing market economy. The difference between the two lies in their attitude toward labor and parliamentary government. The regressive industrial segment sought to control labor and feared parliamentary democracy as giving too much power to labor via the ballot box and independent trade unions. The progressive industrialists, although certainly concerned about their wage bill, were more sympathetic to both free unions and parliamentary government: a higher wage bill would deepen the market for their products and an alliance with labor would provide the political support for a shift in

[9] W.W. Rostow, *British Economy in the 19th Century* (Cambridge: Cambridge University Press, 1948).

national economic policies in favor of exports and international trade. The progressive industrialists tended to come from high-technology export manufacturing (electrical equipment, chemicals in the late nineteenth century and mid-1920s), and the regressive industrialists came from heavy industry, which had once been high technology when they first emerged but had sunk to an intermediate level as the world economy evolved. In Germany these were the intertwined iron, steel, and coal industries.

These splits among various industrial sectors, and their implications for political alliances, are clearer, or at least better documented, in the German case than in those of other countries. Nonetheless, some similarities do appear in the United States, Sweden, and the United Kingdom. Industries weak in the international economy proved the most eager to support market interventions of many kinds, from domestic autarchy through tariffs and other import controls, through stimulus of demand for their products, via government contracts and deficit spending.

What about France? There are some signs that the same tendencies were at work there, but they operated at a lower amplitude. Few industrialists appeared willing to support a major break with orthodox economics, and few were willing to experiment with labor alliances. From a situational interpretation, this caution corresponds nicely with the stress economic historians of France have placed on the disposition of French capitalists to be risk-averse. French business has been characterized as having preferred earning a high margin on a low volume of sales to shallow elite markets to generating profits through a low margin on a high volume of mass markets at home and abroad.[10] In Germany, both the high-technology-export-oriented industrialists and the heavy goods manufacturers wanted the possibility of rapid growth. They were therefore willing to abandon more rapidly a failing orthodoxy. In France, industry appears to have been less growth oriented, less dynamic, less concerned to make colossal gains, more willing to wait, more willing to take the long haul to recovery implied by orthodoxy. Less ambitious, French business may have been less vulnerable, hence more conformist.

[10] David Landes, "French Business and the Businessman in Social and Cultural Analysis," in E. M. Earle, ed., *Modern France* (Princeton, N.J.: Princeton University Press, 1951).

Those French industrialists who were willing to break with orthodoxy resemble their more adventurous foreign counterparts. In the 1920s and 1930s, there did exist in France some "progressive" industrialists–people critical of existing practices in French industrial relations and interested in a dynamic expanding economy. These industrialists were indeed located in the "advanced" sectors. Important examples are Auguste Detoeuf and Ernest Mercier, who were both in the electrical industry. Mercier founded the Redressement Français, seeking collaboration among "business, academia, the high civil service and the military in formulating comprehensive proposals for the renewal of economic, social and political institutions. The America model, a responsible business elite, and a pragmatic reforming temper were the heart of Merciers inspiration."[11] Detoeuf wrote the report on industrial reorganization (in 1927). It called for concentration of industry in order to permit rationalization–economics of scale, research and development, mechanization of work. At this point, in the relatively prosperous 1920s, Detoeuf sought to curtail government; in France the state activism meant preservation of the status quo rather than promotion of change. He asked primarily that the government reverse its harmful policies and attitudes–the protection of situations acquises, the greater esteem accorded to agriculture, the treatment of industrialists as "a crowd of unscrupulous types from whom one must always be wresting their more or less ill-gotten gains."[12] He wanted the state to remove those impediments. In this respect, Detoeuf and others in the Redressement Français resembled the German progressive industry branch. They fought state protectionism of the economically weak, such as declining industrial and agricultural branches. Note that this line of reasoning does not readily lead to demand stimulus policies. It was in the French context quite unorthodox in the sense that it called for a drastic restructuring of French business, from small, fragmented, and stagnant to large-scale, concentrated, and dynamic. But it would use the market to carry this out: the planning of rationally managed enterprises would occur because the inefficient would be absorbed by the strong. Detoeuf spoke of, and used, professional associations of sector owners. Still,

[11] Richard F. Kuisel, "Auguste Detoeuf, Conscience of French Industry," *International Review of Social History* 20 (1975, Part 1), p. 155.

[12] Kuisel, "Detoeuf," p. 154.

while there was some corporatism in his views, he differed from most French corporatists who were decidedly Malthusian. "Where the technocrats identified themselves with economic growth, spurred by technology, foreign trade, and state initiative, the corporatists were Malthusians and decentralizers who relied on semi-autonomous corporations to reduce the state's economic responsibilities."[13]

When the Depression intensified, Detoeuf became more sympathetic to state activism: it could be used as means of defense in desperate times, and it could be used for broader social goals. "Liberalism is dead; it was killed not by human design or by willful governments, but through an irresistible internal evolution."[14] While Detoeuf did not actively support the Popular Front, he was sympathetic to it.

There were, then, at least a few French businessmen on the "progressive path" to breaking with orthodoxy. Were there any on the "regressive path," parallel to the heavy industrialists in Germany, who, while not particularly pro-Hitler, were certainly in favor of an activist government policy to control labor costs and boost demand for products through government purchasing? I have not found any. One place to look would be at François de Wendel and the steel barons. These appear to have been more conservative-corporatist than expansionist-activist-militaristic. Their right-wing drift seems to have given them some interest in curbing parliamentary government and labor unions, but not in right-wing mass mobilization. The difference is between Vichy and fascism, the former seeking to preserve elites and return to a glorified past, the latter seeking some sort of social transformation.

Another interesting place to look would be the armaments industry. These businesses did indeed depend upon government purchasing to sell their products. In Germany, such pressures had sustained the demand for a new economic strategy. Did it produce any outlook of that kind in France or did it produce a rather narrow lobbying for specific orders, cut off from any larger view of managing the economy as a whole? To find the answer one would have to disaggregate: the airplane manufacturers quite probably differed from cement and steel producers, making guns or forts. The

[13] Richard F. Kuisel, "Technocrats and Public Economic Policy: From the Third to the Fourth Republics," *Journal of European Economic History* 2, no. 1 (1973), p. 172.

[14] Kuisel, "Detoeuf," p. 157.

former were creating a new industry from nothing, the latter sought fresh demand to prop up existing sunk investment. Neither seems to have thought in broad terms of a shift in strategy for the economy as a whole, from deflation to something else.

There are other possible cleavage lines among business that could be explored, the banking sector, for example. Jean-Noel Jeanneney pays considerable attention to this in his biography of François de Wendel.[15] He sees rival clusters of banks conflicting the 1920s and 1930s over various decisions of political economy, e.g., tariffs and franc rates. Neither cluster, though, appears to have broken with deflationary orthodoxy in the 1930s. And it would be interesting to look at Andre Citroën, though he died before the Popular Front came to office.

One tiny group of businessmen did make a sort of break from the progressive path away from orthodoxy: the four signatories of the Matignon Agreements, which sought to end the sit-in strikes of May-June 1936. The wage increases of these agreements embodied the core of the version of demand stimulus the French pursued. Under pressure of the strikes, businessmen were willing to sign them, and some business elements in the Chamber of Deputies and Senate were willing to turn them into law. We may call these "acquiescing elements" of business in opposition to the "resisting elements" who were antagonistic to the settlement. The resisting elements were so furious that after the agreements were signed and legislated, the acquiescing elements chased them out of the Confédération Générale de la Production Française and switched from "production" to "patronnat" in their name.

Who were the "acquiescing elements"? Henry Ehrmann notes that

> with the exception of M. Lambert-Ribot, the pressure group official, the members of the delegation headed large scale enterprises and corporations located in Paris. All four were connected with industries, such as steel, metal, railroads, chemicals, and electricity, which belonged to the protected sector of the economy engaged in a multitude of public contracts and sheltered to a considerable extent from the inclemencies of the economic depression.

[15] Jean-Noel Jeanneney, *François de Wendel en République* (Paris: Le Seuil, 1981); and see review of this book by Serge Bernstein, "L'argent et le pouvoir: à propos de François de Wendel," *Revue d'histoire moderne et contemporaine* 25 (July-Sept. 1978), pp. 487-499.

> The enterprises for which M. Duchemin and his colleagues were responsible did not pay the "exceptionally low wages" which set in motion the general wage increase. Although their factories, like others, were occupied by striking workers, those negotiating the agreement were too far removed from the paces of work to resent the occupation of the premises with the same sharpness as did most of the patrimonial employers.[16]

In addition to Lambert-Ribot, the president of the CGPF, the signatorious were the president of the great chemical combine Establissements Kuhlmann, who was also regent of the Bank of France and director of a variety of companies; the president of the Association of Metal Engineering Industries; and the president of the Chamber of Commerce. Duchemin's predecessor at Kuhlmann, Darcy, had come from mining. This is a mix of industries whose major characteristic is size. The most conspicuous absence among large businesses is that of the "dynamic" newer products and companies: no René Citroën and autos, no Detoeuf and Mercier and electrical firms, no airplanes and Dassault. The CGPF's leaders defended both the free market (against state intervention) and cartelization of industry.

What sorts of business people rose up in fury against these signatories? Those who owned or ran small businesses. Ehrmann notes:

> Since the leadership of the employers' movement was identified with big business, the distrust with which most employers regarded their organizations was reinforced by a sometimes anachronistic hostility toward bigness.
>
> The "trusts," the "two hundred families" controlling them, and a dozen "grand commis" running the CGPF in their name were, in the eyes of many owners of small industrial or commercial firms, just as evil as the propaganda of the Popular Front pictured them. However such partial identity of views did not induce the small businessmen to espouse the cause of a political movement that had the backing of the labor unions.[17]

[16] Henry Ehrmann, *Organized Business in France* (Princeton: Princeton University Press, 1957), p. 8. See also Ehrmann's *French Labor from Popular Front to Liberation* (New York: Oxford University Press, 1947), which contains some very interesting passages on the dissatisfaction of agriculture to the deflationary policies. And see Henry Ehrmann, "The Blum Experiment and the Fall of France," *Foreign Affairs* 20 (Oct. 1941), pp. 152-164, for which there exists a longer, more detailed version in typescript, graciously sent me by the author.

[17] Ehrmann, *Organized Business*, pp. 27-28.

After Duchemin had been replaced by Gignoux, not an industrialist but a lawyer-journalist,

> Very strenuous efforts were made to give to the small and medium-sized firms a prominent place at all levels of the employers' movement. From that milieu had come the most violent complaints about the Matignon agreement. Fearful of the consequences of the new social legislation, small businessmen felt sold short and often continued to believe in the existence of a "plot between the 200 families and the marxist government."[18]

Small business in opposition to the Matignon accords, hostile to both big business and labor: a familiar theme in looking at the social bases of fascist support.

Why were the petty proprietors so hostile toward large-scale capital? Because of the interaction of two factors. First, the petty proprietor had a variety of grievances against large capital, and, second, the petty proprietor had a harder time riding out the Depression than had established wealth. The clash between *les gros* and *les petits* is a familiar theme in French politics. From the novels of Balzac to the followers of Gambetta to the writings of Alain, through the Poujadists of the Fourth Republic and the followers of Royer in the Fifth, we have plenty of incidents showing the antagonism the small owners have toward the big. In politics, these small enterpreneurs, like peasant proprietors, are swing groups.[19] In antagonism to radical workers, they can become conservative; in hostility to *les gros,* they can become radical.

In the 1930s, many of the Left's arguments had considerable resonance among the small holders: the *mur d'argent,* , the big capitalists like Citroën, or Mercier-Detoeuf, the bankers, large merchants–these elements of dynamic capitalism were disliked not only by workers but by small holders. When the Depression got worse, the small holders sought help. Devoted in principal to private enterprise and individual initiative, mistrustful of marxism, they were, under the gun of the Depression, nonetheless desperate for help and willing to tamper with the liberal economy to get it. They had little trouble identifying big capitalism as the enemy.

[18] Ehrmann, *Organized Business,* p. 35.

[19] On the ability of small companies to use political leverage in shaping economic policies that help them, see Suzanne Berger's chapter in Suzanne Berger and Michael Piore (eds.), *Dualism and Discontinuity in Industiral Societies,* (Cambridge: Cambridge University Press, 1980).

While many small proprietors were intensely anti-Left, others, as Ehrmann notes, proved willing to make some sort of alliance with labor and agriculture. Small business composed part of the Radical constituency that supported, at least for a time, the Popular Front. What sort of petty bourgeois supported the Radicals, what sort opposed them? The usual argument points to differences in religion, region, and tradition. The Radical bourgeoisie was likely to be anticlerical, from leftist regions like the Midi, and connected with organizations that sustained a prorepublic culture (teachers, associations, and the like). The conservative bourgeoisie was likely to be Catholic, from more conservative regions such as Brittany and the east, and involved in conservatively oriented organizations. Did the bourgeoisie attracted by the quasifascist leagues come from the latter or from both? I don't know.

Are there any economic differences between these groups? Again, I don't know. One can speculate. One source of prorepublican tradition among the bourgeoisie had been hostility to the conservative, monarchical orientations of "big capital." Gambetta, for example, drew on provincial elements seeking assistance from Paris for a variety of policies to help them against the business elite.[20] A similar situation may have occured in the 1930s. Some elements of the bourgeoisie had experience in alliances with leftist social elements for certain policy as well as political purposes–worker, peasant, and small business coalitions had come into being on earlier occasions. The Popular Front could draw on this earlier experience.

To the extent the Popular Front did have bourgeois allies as well as bourgeois enemies, we still have a problem of interpretation. Does the divergence reflect "situation"? That is, did the "acquiescing" bourgeoisie relate to the economy differently than the "resisting" one? Or was the divergence a matter of culture and history, the legacy of past political quarrels and linkages, related perhaps to earlier situational struggles, but struggles that no longer predominated? It would take more careful scrutiny of micro-situations than I have found in the literature to answer these questions.

Although explanations of divergence are hard to test, the fact of divergence seems clear. Owners, large and small, fragmented the way many other social groups in France did. Some went to the

[20] Sanford Elwitt, *The Making of the Third Republic* (Baton Rouge: Louisiana University Press, 1975).

activism of the far Right; others stayed with the Radical party but pressed it into breaking its support for deflation. Through the Radical party, then, the Popular Front was able to mobilize some support among nonagricultural property owners for new economic policies. This support helped elect the Popular Front and keep it going for a time. It also was the major break on reform: the caution of the Radical electorate's rebellion toward the *mur d'argent* limited its demands, which in turn limited what the Communists asked for, which in turn isolated the Socialists from doing more. We have seen this progression in the discussion of devaluation and nationalization. The Socialist leaders were deterred from both policies by the combined opposition of Socialists and Radicals.

We may conclude these musings about business behavior with the following: large-scale industry and banks linked to it did not develop strong demands for a shift in economic strategy. Although some elements of each worried about structural problems with French economy, none pushed hard at a new macro-economic position during the Depression. Only some scattered elements of small industry were interested in linking up to the farmer-labor alliance.

This lack of interest in experimentation with economic policy may have something to do with the sluggishness of French economic growth–the latter being a cause of the former as well as a consequence. Just why there were so few Merciers in French history remains, as noted above, a major subject of controversy. Was this cultural, as the Landes-Sawyer school would suggest? Or was it "structural," as a more Gerschenkronian interpretation would imply?[21] That is, did they not thrust after the Faustian goals of industrialization because of a set of values oriented toward other things, or did they not do so because the French economy was structured via ownership and political control in ways that discouraged such a thrust? Was the problem a cultural barrier against the creation of Citroëns, or was the problem that the incentive system opposed the creation of Citroëns?

I am inclined toward the latter view, largely because the former is so well known. The crucial point for our purposes here is that whatever the reasons for the weakness and regressive quality of the French bourgeois impulse, this quality contributed in the 1930s to

[21] See Landes-Gerschenkron debate, refered to in Landes, *Unbound Prometheus* (Cambridge: Cambridge University Press, 1969).

the difficulty of breaking with economic orthodoxy.

PARTIES AND POLICY OPTIONS

In seeking to explain the evolution of French policy toward the Great Depression, we have so far focused on the behavior of various economic actors or groups. Although workers opposed deflation from the beginning, most other social groups appear to have supported it or at least accepted it. As the Depression worsened, and deflation seemed to have failed to improve matters, more and more social groups changed their policy preferences. Increasingly, farmers and some capital-owning elements abandoned traditional economic outlooks to experiment with new policies. In the elections of 1936, they managed to devise a majority sustaining a government willing to experiment.

The big shift between 1932 and 1936 was not more voters accepting in 1936 a position they rejected in 1932: as many have noted, the vote shift was small. Nor was it solely that the electoral alliance increased the seats won with the same number of votes, though that did happen. Rather it was that the same voters, and groups to whom they belonged, switched positions between 1932 and 1936. In the first year, few persons anywhere in France spoke of demand stimulus, public works, or even devaluation, marketing boards, and the like. By 1936, many did. People shifted in light of the Depression, of existing policy, of examples elsewhere.

The preferences of groups are certainly important, but we must look as well at what political parties and political leaders did with those preferences. Did they accept them, as the U.S. Democratic party did in relation to a variety of reforms developed by pressure groups, or reject them, as the British Labour party and the German Social Democratic party did to their trade unions' demand-stimulus plans; or did they in fact help shape the union position, as the Swedish Social Democrats did with their trade union, the LO? French labor was deeply split. What did the different political parties think about economic policy?

The PCF's policy preferences varied not as a function of what its labor constituency articulated through autonomous labor organizations, but as a function of the PCF's political strategy. The critical watershed was, of course, 1934. Prior to 1934, the party pursued a class-against-class line, attacking the Socialists and all efforts to defend the bourgeois parliamentary order; the PCF's economic policy was resistance plus sweeping socialization for the economy. After 1934, the PCF sought to preserve the republic and a pro-Soviet, anti-Nazi foreign policy. It sought coalitions with other social and political formations and was willing to accept moderate economic policies as a necessary price for those alliances. Indeed, as we shall see, the PCF was more moderate in its economic policy position than were the Socialists.

The PCF derived the crisis from the nature of capitalism. The switch of 1934 certainly did not entail a purge of that aspect of marxism that saw capitalism in a permanent condition of instability. To the PCF, the current situation was the latest of the cycles of ever greater amplitude inherent in the conflict between worker and capitalist over surplus value. The new aspect of the 1934 line was the emphasis on a slice of the capitalist elite as the prime mover. People were suffering because of a tiny group of plutocrats and speculators had vast control over the entire economy. What had to be done was extend public, democratic control over the positions that elite occupied. The PCF thus narrowed its analysis: not *all* private property was attacked, nor even the market mechanism itself, but certain owners of capital able to do certain things in a particular market situation.[22]

The stress on an identifiable band of profiteers enabled the PCF to propose changes without abolishing capitalism and the market altogether. Reforms could weaken or destroy these profiteers without touching the position of smaller property owners. The actual reforms suggested were those of the program of the Popular Front itself. Indeed, the PCF's program was closer to that of the Popular Front than was that of the Socialists. Actually, in their proposals, all parties of the accord converged. The difference came in the way the reforms were situated, in the type of language, and in the type of analysis from which the proposals were derived.

[22] Georges Dupeux, *Le front populaire et les élections de 1936,* Cahiers de la Fondation Nationale des Sciences Politiques, no. 99 (Paris: Armand Colin, 1959), pp. 102-103.

The Socialists constructed a much more conventionally marxist framework. Dupeux calls their text "calme, plus froid, (qui) tend à faire appel à la raison plus qu'au sentiment . . . on dirait un cours d'économie politique." "Le coupable est donc saisi et confondu, c'est le régime capitaliste."[23] All the measures tried by the bourgeois parties had failed. The Socialists implied far more strongly than did the PCF that the only solution was to abolish the capitalist regime. In actual policy suggestion, the Socialists in fact proposed a much broader program of nationalization, that of all major industries of monopoly characteristics, not only those producing war material: they mentioned mines, metallurgy, chemicals, electricity, transport, gas and oil, sugar, insurance, credit, and banking. Some currents in the Socialist Party spoke of the need for planning, but Blum and the dominant Socialist groups rejected it; it could not work in a capitalist system, and it threatened liberty.[24]

The program of the Radical party was both more moderate than that of the Socialists and more cautious in language than that of the Communists. It mixed traditional positions (those it had supported when they were practiced by the governments to which it belonged between 1932 and 1936) with the new ones: the former included la stabilité monétaire, condition de la securité indispensable à l'initiative comme à l'esprit d'entreprise and the latter was "réaliser l'augmentation du pouvoir d'achat des masses . . . lutter contre la sous-consommation,"[25] Whereas the Socialists stressed the link between agriculture's problems and the crisis as a whole, the Radicals, and most parties of the Center and Right, separated the two. "Répétons-le: le parti agraire, cest nous.",[26] The Radicals stressed tariffs and empire purchases and sales.

Within France, the distinguishing features of the economic program of the Popular Front were stress on purchasing power and public works, willingness to try market regulation to help farmers, and some effort to extend public control over banking and military production. What made the Radicals similar to other parties of the Center and Right was its refusal to support currency devaluation. The moderate and conservative formations tied currency protection

[23] Ibid., p. 104.
[24] Kuisel, "Technocrats," pp. 72-73.
[25] Dupeux, *Le front populaire*, p. 107.
[26] Ibid.

to continued deflation, but the center-left alliance broke with the latter policy, but not with the former.

The refusal to devalue was very important. Analysts of the British and Swedish cases think those countries' revivals were strongly aided by devaluation, which stimulated exports. Why, then, did the French refuse so staunchly to devalue? They had, after all, five years of the Swedish and British experience to learn from.

One can easily find a variety of reasons. First, France had a rather traumatic experience in the 1920s with the falling franc. The loss of four-fifths of the prewar value of the franc upset all sorts of savers, small and large. It is revealing that the other of the five countries I have studied that avoided devaluation was the one that also underwent a deterioration of its currency in the 1920s, indeed, a worse deterioration–Germany. The Nazis, who broke with many orthodoxies, never attacked the one concerning the currency, and kept the mark at a constant level.

Another reason may have to do with the size of France's gold reserve. In Britain and Sweden, and to a lesser extent the United States, the devaluation happened when the currency faced a tremendous run against it. With a gigantic gold reserve, the French could imagine that no drive against the franc could ever be strong enough to succeed.

Much of the literature on France speaks of the incredible ignorance of the French regarding economic matters. They were doubtless ignorant in light of contemporary economic ideas, but were they more ignorant than other peoples? I doubt it. Perhaps they were not more ignorant but less economically dynamic.

Whatever the reasons, devaluation was a political impossibility in 1936. The only politician to propose it, Paul Raynaud, was sharply criticized for doing so. In 1934 Léon Blum had written of its necessity, but in 1936 he opposed it. Because the Radicals were against it, the Communists were; with both the Radicals and Communists against it, the Socialists could not afford to be for it even if they had wanted to–and, in any event, they didn't.

If deflation is no good because the conservative governments have tried it to no avail, and if devaluation is no good because it is politically unacceptable, and if the socialization of investment is no good because it too is politically unacceptable, what remains as an alternative economic policy for dealing with the Depression? Some sort of demand stimulus. The next important question is, Which kind: the government spending, state deficits kind or the wage push kind?

As noted before, the Popular Front chose the second. Why? It may have done so partly out of the intellectual preferences of its leaders. To the extent Blum and his advisers understood the demand stimulus argument, they did so by linking it to marxist underconsumption traditions rather than the newer versions of these arguments espoused by Keynes, Kalecki, et al. It was higher wages that made sense to them, not deficits.

Second, and perhaps more relevant, events forced the government's hand. We cannot guess what the government might have done concerning wages and/or deficits, or even devaluation, because the timing of its policy was shaped by the strikes of May-June. These began after the election of 1936 but before the convocation of the new assembly and therefore before the new government formally took office.

The strikers appear to have been both inspired and frightened by the Popular Front victory. Electoral success offered the hope of challenging the sort of relationships inside the factory described by Chaplin in *City Lights* and the fear that conservative forces would manage to sterilize the parliamentary majority, as had happened many tims before. Immediate action on wages, vacations, and the forty-hour week was the only way the Blum government could respond to mass pressure in order to restore authority to the regular governmental process. As a result, the government began its term in office with a large increase in wages; this had been among its priorities. It is conceivable that some ministers might have preferred more caution, more flexibility in the application of wage increases to avoid bottlenecks in key industries and to allow some kind of public works project to stimulate demand at the same time. The strikes foreclosed that possibility.

The government was constrained in its choice of policy by the strikes. It was also affected by a variety of other constraints. First, it was influenced by more events, particularly in international relations: the Spanish Civil War, the German occupation of the Rhineland and growing militarism, Germany's alliance with Russia, Italy, and Ethiopia, and so on.

Second, there were institutional barriers. The most important of these was the Senate. With members selected indirectly and in staggered terms, the Senate was far more conservative than the chamber elected in 1936. In the summer of that year, the Radical senators acquiesced before the pressure of the strikes and popular mandate to vote in the new laws. As such pressures receded, the antagonism of conservative sentiment flowed back. Radicals in the chamber could vote one way, knowing their colleagues could defeat measures by voting another. This helped bring down the government.

Third, there were the barriers imposed on policy by the leverage of various pressure groups directly on critical social functions. The sit-in strikes already discussed are one example of the leverage of labor. The forty-hour week is another. Despite the loss of production that stemmed from preventing skilled workers' taking longer weeks, the government felt unable to revise that legislation. A "capital strike" showed the leverage of other groups. The holders of funds could undermine government policy by fleeing the franc or by refusing to invest. This is the sort of behavior Dupeux had in mind, as did Detoeuf and others who complained that French businessmen were being individually rational and collectively destructive by their behavior.

CONCLUSIONS

The Popular Front coalition resembled other demand-stimulus alliances in linking together farmers and workers who were willing to abandon orthodox deflationary policies and to attempt some form of government intervention other than nationalization. Like other demand-stimulus alliances, it attracted some business support, in the French case that of small businessmen among the Radical electorate. Unlike other experimenting coalitions, however, it was unable to win over any significant support among the large-scale industrial or financial bourgeoisie. Such elements refused to help either politically (by votes in elections or in the Senate and chamber) or economically (by cooperating with government policy).

The strikes show the tremendous difficulty facing the Left in those days: without the strikes, the pressure on the Senate and organized business would have been weaker, and the government may have failed to get much legislation through parliament. With the strikes, it could get specific pieces through in the short run but provoked antagonism over the long.

Between interest groups and policy lay political parties, "transmission belts" in Stanley Hoffman's apt term, which run in both directions, receiving cues and giving instructions. The PCF's willingness to support the Popular Front, at least to some degree, certainly contributed to reform. Had the French Communists pursued the confrontational line employed by their German counterparts, the Popular Front coalition would have had far more difficulty, as it had in Germany. One cannot, though, infer the magnitude of that difficulty from the PCF's figures at the 1936 election. The PCF's rise derived in part from the switch to cooperation; without that change many voters would not have voted for it, and, of course, without the electoral alliance there would have been many fewer than seventy-two deputies. The PCF was much weaker than the German Communist party. An intransigent line would have had less effect. But it would have had some by exacerbation.

The negative effects of PCF participation in the Popular Front are also hard to evaluate. I would speculate that the major negative effect was not through electoral behaviors but via direct economic actions and lobbying by hostile groups and individuals. Few voters who went with the anti-Popular Front parties would have changed their minds if the Communists had not signed up. (Indeed few voters shifted in any direction: the new majority came from effects of desistments, not gaining votes.) What caused the government problems was the hatred of its opponents and their control over levers that were to affect the sequence of events. Here the participation of the Communists doubtless played some role.

If so, it was not because the PCF didn't try to placate the opposition. Its policy line was, as noted above, more moderate than that of the Socialists. The rhetoric aimed at the *mur d'argent* did not differentiate the PCF from the Radicals or even from many anticapitalist antimarket conservatives. But the PCF's past could not so easily be erased; many surely remembered its recent line and remained unconvinced. Finally, I find it hard to evaluate just how frightening the PCF was to various groups of all political persuasions: the political events we seek to interpret preceded the range of events (the purges and collectivisation of the 1930s, the Molotov Pact, the fall of Eastern Europe, the Hungarian uprising, the Prague Spring, Afganistan) that make the PCF of today the object of much suspicion.

Finally, in ending this rather lengthy disquisition on a variety of subjects, I wish to make two observations comparing the PCF in two periods of alliance behavior, the 1930s and the 1970s. In the 1930s, the PCF was moderate on economic policy and it was the Socialists who wanted more; in the 1970s, the positions were reversed. In both cases, nationalizations were a key matter of dispute. The Communists accepted the Radicals' opposition to them for the 1930s, but in the 1970s the PCF used nationalization as a disciplining leash pulling against the potentially meandering Socialists.

The second point concerns the PCF's calculations about the political consequences of alliance strategy. In both cases, the party misjudged the size of the Socialists' increase in seats and votes. For the earlier period, the Communists expected to join a majority dominated by the Radicals. The Radicals had had about one hundred and fifty seats in the previous chamber and had always led center-left cabinets. The PCF sought a broad coalition, particularly one with strength among a section of the French brougeoisie. For that purpose, they assumed, probably correctly, that a Radical premier, such as Herriot, would be best even if he did less in economic reforms. What the PCF never expected was a shift in seats between Radicals and Socialists so great as to make the latter the largest party and the legitimate claimants of the premier's office.

Similarly, when the PCF began discussions with the Socialists in the early 1970s, the latter were very weak, in both votes and organization, compared to the former. The PCF had in mind the Italian situation: a strong Communist party dominating the Left, a weaker Socialist party, and weaker centrist parties. Alliance and PCF moderation would strengthen the Left as a whole, and particularly the Communists. In Italy, the Communists went from one-quarter to one-third of the vote. Instead, to the intense annoyance of the PCF, the Socialists were in France the great gainers of the coalition. They rapidly built back to their earlier 20 percent, matching the Communist score, and then ballooned upward, approaching at times

30 percent in opinion polls. The Communist reaction to this in the 1970s in well known. In the 1930s, they were more moderate. The Popular Front disintegrated because the Radicals defected, not the Communists.

The importance of the Radicals brings us back to Dupeux's comments about the need for bourgeois allies. Then as now, the Socialists had to forge alliances if they were to govern through constitutional means in a mixed economy. Many variables shaped political preferences and alliance behavior–international politics, institutions, individuals, and circumstances. What I have stressed here is the importance of substantive issues, often left out of these discussions: the matter of policy, in particular economic policy, both internal and foreign. How to relate to shifts in the international economy? That problem plagued interest groups all over France, as elsewhere. It affected evaluations of alternative policy options and affected strategies and choices of political allies and alliances. Politicians had to manage coalitions whose members fought bitterly over economic policy, as well as other issues. The Popular Front came into being for multiple purposes–to save the republic, to contain Germany, to promote equality, and to reform the economy. To some degree these pieces interconnected. Coalitions able to mobilize the support for doing the first two also had capabilities for doing the second pair. At the same time, pressures from different social groups put severe constraints on the Popular Front's capacity to experiment and to innovate.

Chapter 21

ON PURPOSES OF MILITARY OCCUPATION

Peter K. Breit

OCCUPATION AND PEACE

Military occupation is a step victors may take toward order and peace. Effective, prospectively directed occupation, whose purpose is peace, requires an agreement of minds and hearts, that is, concord, in St. Augustine's term, between occupants and natives.[1] Concord under occupation includes arrangements to which the defeated rationally acquiesces in the face of the occupant's superior force, and those to which the defeated agrees out of a desire for a reestablished tranquility.

Occupation is an aspect of political technology.[2] An artifact like government itself, it responds to human needs in a humanly produced situation. As part of this political technology, occupation is employed to procure order and peace. These ends, at once political and technological problems, include satisfaction of political, economic, sustentative, intellectual, and moral demands, and therefore they mean more than what St. Augustine called the tranquility of order.

Occupation strives for order in enforced tranquility. Following a lost war, order must be restored by someone. Order in an occupation is created through law and government, a technological condition, administered by the occupant.

[1] Augustine, *The City of God*, quoted in Mortimer J. Adler, *How to Think About War and Peace* (New York: Simon and Schuster, 1944), p. 49.

[2] Cf. Karl R. Popper, *The Poverty of Historicism* (New York: Harper Torchbooks, 1961), pp. 46, 58-63.

Technology, meaning skill, art, or craft, transcends the sense of machinery. Military occupation involves technical competence; it involves practical considerations and organization with an end in mind.

Peace may follow an occupation if the defeated are enabled to rise from their legal and practical inequality so that the tranquility imposed by the occupant shifts gradually to cooperation and collaboration for the good of the occupant and the occupied. In the final analysis, occupation will lead to peace if the occupants and occupied, in a peaceable milieu, begin to develop and share common goals and eventually collaborate for one another's and a communal good.

Occupation and the peaceable milieu associated with it may, in terms proposed by James MacGregor Burns, be *transactional* and limited to the particular situation or *transformational*, elevating both occupant and occupied and involving the concord between them.[3] Transformational occupation strives to transcend its own environment to raise the international system's consciousness and conscience.

Here, the occupied power must not be so defeated as to make it incapable of playing the role assigned to it. Of course, some defeated powers are so thoroughly evil that the system will be transformed only if they are completely eliminated. Still, it may be a transformational peace if the victors distinguish significantly between defeated rulers and their subjects, *and* if the victors seek to engage the moral and rational awareness of other members of the international system in the defeated polity's re-entry into the system.

We may relate peace to Locke's famous dictum about life, liberty, and property. Life means existence as a nation; liberty means sovereignty; and property means territorial integrity. Occupation, however, is a relationship in which one state may legally perform a range of actions that infringe on another state's life, liberty, and property. This right is won as a concomitant to a successful war or battle.[4] Hence, we speak of occupation as an occasion to take the first step toward peace by linking defeat with a peaceable milieu.

[3] James MacGregor Burns, *Leadership* (New York: Harper and Row, 1978), pp. 4 et passim.

[4] See Karl Jaspers, *The Question of German Guilt*, E. B. Ashton, trans. (New York: Capricorn Books, 1959), for variations of this theme.

Peace is a relationship in which one state vis-à-vis other states may, with impunity, perform a range of actions that are in themselves not punishable and that do not infringe on similar rights of the other states to their life, liberty, or property.[5]

Peace is a condition between states in which each heeds and defers to the national existence, sovereignty, and territorial integrity of the other in its impunible actions involving that other state.

Military occupation means a pattern of policy formulation and administration wherein a victorious state temporarily exercises power over another by placing its authorities in the defeated territory. It is a political relationship, emanating from and won as a concomitant of war, in which one state may, legally and with relative impunity, perform a range of actions that infringe upon another's national existence, sovereignty, and territorial integrity. The right to destroy a defeated state permanently is legally denied an occupant, although occupations have succeeded in such deracination.

PURPOSES OF OCCUPATION

Occupation serves several political purposes: allocation of resources (including economic); assurance of victory (ability to make an adversary do one's "bidding)"[6] in arranging a postwar world favorable to oneself; and, finally, establishing peace. This means that the occupant's behavior changes, and it may no longer with impunity infringe upon the attributes of the erstwhile enemy. Once fighting has ended, nations are confronted with concerns different from those that involved the safety of an invading army. The treatment given recalcitrant civilians differs under an occupation during combat from that accorded them after combat has ended.

We focus on occupation after hostilities have ceased. War may continue around the occupier and the occupied; in fact, either may still be at war with others. But in the occupied territory the occupier

[5] We add "in themselves not punishable" to distinguish between acts for which one is not punished because other states are too weak to carry out the punishment and acts that, by custom, morality, or law are not wrong *per se*. Acts in the former class would not qualify as peaceful, whereas acts in the latter class, not giving rise to considerations of punishment, are impunible and hence peaceful.

[6] Anatol Rapoport, ed., *Clausewitz on War* (Baltimore: Penguin Books, 1968), pp. 122-124.

formulates and administers policy to establish a peaceable milieu, a condition that the weaker is not able or inclined to challenge. The three prerequisites for a state are affected: territory, government, and people. The occupier strives for a peaceable milieu in which the conditions precedent for peace, including an end to hostilities and an intent gradually to terminate the occupation, may be laid out. This function, relating to duty, obligates the victors to provide the peaceable milieu. It is they who are able to do so; the losers have only the ethical and practical opportunity to surrender at a point where they can no longer fight. Occupations, when they attempt to deflect into constructive behavior moods that might otherwise lead to further conflict, have been a means of dealing with the consequences of defeat. Duty flows from capacity, be it the duty to cease fighting after one is no longer able or required to fight or the duty to convert one's military success into a peaceable milieu.

Not all occupations integrate the defeated power into the system, as happened in 1815. The balance of power is more frequently reestablished through the loser's exclusion from it. Germany after the two world wars points in this direction. In the post-Napoleonic use of occupation, the erstwhile and potential opponent was woven into the lace fabric of the balance; in the use of occupation after the world wars, the iron fabric was woven around the defeated state. The former establishes a heterogeneous equilibrium that includes the interests of the occupied state as items in the balance and consequently in occupation. The latter establishes a homogeneous equilibrium that excludes, at least initially, the interests of the occupied polity.

Occupations will also obstruct and evade the obligations assigned by duty. As in Germany and Korea after 1945, considerations other than duty may be served by prolonged occupation.

A victor may avoid specific and restrictive policies that may eventually work against it. In this instance occupation may become a means of escaping contradictions between general and pious principles to govern postwar relations and the Realpolitik for which one mobilized one's state.

Occupation is part of a process of transforming the defeated power's politics into behavior compatible with the victor's interests. These interests may extend beyond the immediate actors to include relations between the occupant and others in the international system. An occupant may attempt, as Germany did in the Bohemian-Moravian Protectorate, to demand "unreserved recognition as the price for allowing third powers any official activities in the occupied territory."[7] The occupant thus attempts to alter the behavior of third parties. Yet another occupation, with one's own military stationed near a potential adversary, may illustrate rationalized denial: one occupies to deny another its occupation but explains the occupation in terms involving international duties, the interests of the occupied, the competitor's worrisome behavior, or other, more sublime motives. U.S. occupation of West Germany and Soviet occupation of East Germany after 1945 are examples. In each case occupation was to become the environment into which a complete repoliticization and eventual German rearmament were implanted, even if that was not originally intended.

The consequences of a rationalized denial are striking. As an occupied territory becomes more important, the occupant will increasingly invest its resources there. Eventually a way will be found to integrate the territory into larger political and economic unities. When several parties are joint occupants, the occupation may serve an integrative purpose by harmonizing their objectives and ultimately incorporating the defeated polity.

Occupation may be a nominal means of guaranteeing adherence to the terms of a peace treaty. The Treaty of Versailles provided (articles 428-432) for the military occupation of the Rhineland to assure a political situation in which Germany would be unable to revise the treaty's terms,[8] a practice already employed in antiquity, as Livy relates in a discussion of assuring Celtiberian adherence to treaty obligations. The military after 1919 was clearly used as a political instrument, not only from the international but also from the French domestic perspective, which included avenging German occupation in 1871.

[7] Robert Langer, *Seizure of Territory: The Stimson Doctrine and Related Principles in Legal Theory and Dimplomatic Practice* (Princeton: Princeton University Press, 1947), p. 103.

[8] Cf. Ferdinand Foch, *The Memoirs of Marshal Foch*, T. Bentley Mott, trans. (Garden City, N.Y.: Doubleday, Doran and Company, 1931), p. 480.

The nature of the surrender with which a conflict ends affects an occupation. Occupation following an unconditional surrender differs from that following a limited, traditional capitulation. Perspectives will differ. The defeated will look introspectively toward existence or extinction; the one negates the other. The victorious occupants have at least three directions in which to look: inward to the occupied territory; inward to their own territory; and outward to the complex of relations among themselves and with the defeated. Of course, the defeated may also look outward to the relations with and among the occupants, but there is little it can do about these relations, except to manipulate one occupant against another member of international society.

If war's purpose is to achieve a redistribution of power and resources in ways more favorable to oneself, this purpose will affect the occupation. Occupation is a converter through which pass the occupier's political values and by which the loser's political character is changed. An occupation transforms the defeated power's politics. Thus it contains the forcible elements of war and the harmonizing elements of the peace it is to bring about. Politically in *status mixtus,* the belligerent elements dominate, with persistent reference to a retrospective belligerent or prospective peaceful political order.

Occupation may be used among coalition allies to restrict dismantling and exportation of capital equipment by any one of them. It may also be used to "assure that no country takes equipment without serious intentions of using it"[9] –a problem that arose in connection with the dismantling of plants and equipment in Germany. Occupational policy may also guarantee that the defeated polity's standard of living will not rise above that of adjacent states, as was a French intention upon Germany's surrender in 1945. Many among the occupant's and the occupied's polities will worry about the economic consequences of an occupation's termination. Occupation is a means of determining the speed with which an occupied territory becomes a purchaser or seller on the international market. Some occupants may wish to curtail the competition otherwise provided by the occupied power by restricting its rights and opportunities to engage in foreign trade.

[9] Edwin M. Martin, *The Allied Occupation of Japan* (Westport, Ct.: Greenwood Press, 1948), p. 31.

Whether territory is occupied is both a legal and a military consideration:

> It is considered occupied when it is actually placed under the authority of the hostile army [and] when the enemy government has been rendered incapable of exercising its authority in a given area. The invader [occupier] then substitutes his own authority for that of the legitimate sovereign.[10]

In an occupation it may be permissible to take hostages: even the United States has not shied from the punishment of third parties when those responsible for the acts complained of cannot be found. "The ideal type of military government is one which integrates the local laws, institutions, customs, psychology and economics of the occupied area and a superimposed military control with a minimum of change in the former and a maximum of control by the latter."[11]

Tacitus found that occupation might be used to "root out the causes of war,"[12] but only if it was not accompanied by oppression. As occupation will often be accompanied by oppression, whether objectively intended by the occupant or merely subjectively felt by the defeated, some occupations are as detested as war itself.

German occupation policies in the Soviet Union differed from those of the Japanese, whose occupying authorities sought cooperation with the occupied peoples.[13] Racial similarity rather than alleged disparity distinguished at least a part of the Japanese occupation from the German. German propaganda stressed the parochial interests of the Aryan Germans, whereas the Japanese claimed to fight for "all Asiatic peoples."[14] The demands placed on the occupied populations were, therefore, different.

[10] In *American Insurance Company* v. *Peters,* 1828, 1 Peters 542, quoted in Gerhard von Glahn, *Law Among Nations,* 3rd ed. (New York: MacMillan Publishing Company, 1976), pp. 665-666.

[11] Harry L. Coles and Albert K. Weinberg, *Civil Affairs: Soldiers Become Governors* (Washington: Office of the Chief of Military History, DOA, 1964), p. 10.

[12] Tacitus, *Complete Works,* trans. by Moses Hadad (New York: Modern Library, 1942), pp. 685, 689.

[13] F. C. Jones et al., *Survey of International Affairs: The Far East, 1942-1946* (London: Oxford University Press, 1955), pp. 85-87, 88.

[14] Ibid., p. 86.

States will use pretexts to conceal patently political purposes. When France occupied the Ruhr, it was "enforcing the policy of reparations which had figured so largely in (its) policy of security."[15] From the French side, the occupation served the political objective of creating a *couverture* in the event of another military encounter. Foch argued that "the master of the Rhine is the master of the surrounding country."[16]

One objective of military occupation is *stability,* in which the shock of defeat is borne with relative equanimity; here victory will be enforced with limited additional harm to the defeated. As not all occupations seek such concord, some will compel stability.

Although some occupations, striving for stability, have done so with minimal intentional contradiction of the war's political objectives, this need not be a salutary condition; for some military objectives are clearly antithetical to a peace of reconciliation. Some, indeed, have been meant to enforce the defeated enemy's complete subjugation.

Occupation strives for internal stability. One means of obtaining this is to permit what may be called the stability of a domestic heterogeneous equilibrium on the basis of "local self-government [one of whose attributes] is freedom of association [wherein] local authorities may voluntarily unite [to promote] their mutual interests and the defense of their rights against the encroachment of the state."[17] "Encroachment," however, is an occupational device, and the occupier may find that stability is better obtained by denying such rights of association.

Since antiquity, occupations have been both restorative and destructive. Justinian's goals in the Western Empire, as carried out in Belisarius's occupation, were the "restoration of the Western Empire . . . and the suppression of the Arian heresy."[18]

[15] Ibid., p. 61.

[16] Stefan T. Possony and Etienne Mantoux, "Du Picq and Foch: The French School," quoted in Edward Meade Earle, ed., *Makers of Modern Strategy* (Princeton: Princeton University Press, 1943), pp. 232-233.

[17] Roger H. Wells, "The Revival of German Unions of Local Authorities after World War II," *American Political Science Review,* December 1947, p. 1182.

[18] J. F. C. Fuller, *A Military History of the Western World* (New York: Minerva Press, 1954), vol. 1, p. 307.

A military commander may eschew using his position or authority for personal political purposes in the occupied territory, but the contrasting examples of Eisenhower and MacArthur suggest a further dimension to the question of occupation and national policy.

Since Julius Caesar, occupation has been seen as a means to public office. Even the manner and policies of that commander's Gallic occupation involved partisan political concerns, such as the fear that the Senate might think him weak or irresolute.[19] Caesar engaged in political manuevering among the major factions in occupied Gaul, for those who had welcomed him lacked popular support, while the stronger and more popular opposed him.

In modern nondemocratic occupations the occupant's successor crises may confuse occupation policies and also encourage occupied territories, as occurred in East Germany after Stalin's death, to anticipate an end to occupation.

When the nations of an alliance, as in the Warsaw Pact's experience, invade another's territory, the purpose is not only to enforce policy; it is also to warn the invading allies that their frontiers are pregnable. Occupation becomes didactic.

Occupation, which may lead to territorial reorganization, may involve loss of territory to an occupying power, as occurred with the Kurile Islands and southern Sakalin, which Japan lost to the Soviet Union. Or it may involve changes in traditional administrative arrangements, such as the abolition of Prussia in 1947.

Roman occupation served much the same purpose as is often found in more recent occupations: "to implant law and civilization" or "to conserve; to save from anarchy and ruin. . . ."[20] In the modern world, an occupier will occasionally believe itself called upon to do both, to create and to preserve. This, indeed, was a political motivation of the Allied occupation of France in 1815 and of the Western Allies in Germany in 1945.

In antiquity occupation often served as a sociopolitical integrator.[21] The Roman Empire was integrated by the interest a

[19] Guglielmo Ferrero, *The Greatness and Decline of Rome*, H. J. Chaytor, trans. (New York: G. P. Putnam's Sons, 1909), vol. 2, pp. 41, 61.

[20] W. G. De Burgh, *The Legacy of the Ancient World* (Baltimore: Penguin Books, 1923), p. 252.

[21] Ibid., p. 292.

soldier from one part of the Empire acquired through domicile in another. Citizens were integrated by being encouraged to feel as content in Western Europe as in Turkey or Syria. Regions were intergrated into the Empire by creating a sense of interchange-ability among them. A modification of this exists today, although acquisition of land by citizens of governing states is not frequently a policy encouraged by their governments. And yet, Germany and Japan prior to and during World War II encouraged such activities. Germany sought, for instance, to encourage the Germans to appeal, as *Volksdeutsche,* to Hitler to bring them *heim ins Reich.* In this case one might speak of settlement prior to occupation.

Tacitus raised another instrumental significance of occupation. Having conquered a region, Rome might then grant it to allied peoples in order to assure themselves of their steadfastness in what might be called commutational occupation.[22] Henry VI used his conquest and occupation of Le Maine as a means of securing his subjects' fidelity. Such occupation may be regarded as binding the ruler's interests to those of subjects who occupy the defeated territory. The subjects have an interest in maintaining the occupation because it provides them with subsistence.[23] Even this has not been entirely discarded, as examples from World War II will illustrate, especially in Japanese relations involving certain conquered territories and allies.

Occupation, as of Germany and Japan, may be used to restructure the system of education.[24] In Japan the occupation also had among its benignant objectives placing political powers and functions under popular control, liberalization of family relations, and establishing equality of the sexes.[25] Labor relations may be a major aspect of occupation, as again for example in Japan where labor was strengthened as a counterweight to the power of the *Zaibatsu.* The assumption was that the links between the *Zaibatsu*–or family trusts–and the military had been largely responsible for the decision to embark on expansion.[26] Another goal of occupation may be to

[22] Tacitus, op. cit., p. 685.

[23] C. T. Allmand, *Society at War: The Experience of England and France During the Hundred Years War* (New York: Barnes and Noble, 1973), p. 175.

[24] Martin, op. cit., p. 59; and U.S. Department of State, *Occupation of Germany: Policy and Progress* (Washington: U.S. Government Printing Office, 1947), p. 62.

[25] Martin, loc. cit.

[26] Ibid., p. 89.

modernize and rationalize the agronomy without creating major economic problems.[27]

We find economic and political motives in an occupation whose purpose is to deal with otherwise unassignable soldiers. Two types of soldiers are involved here: professionals for whom war is a livelihood, and recruits for whom no peacetime profession is to be found. The occupation becomes an occupation.[28]

The question of populations too large for the provender natively available is often a critical question of policy. Plato's remedy, colonization, still serves as an inducement to military occupation, whether it was the original cause of the war that resulted in the occupation or not.

Another national purpose of occupation is, in contemporary terms, to serve as a tripwire. After 1815, the allies committed themselves to provide 60,000 men each, if France challenged the occupation. From this provision also came "the distinction between Great Powers and Small Powers . . . according to their ability to guarantee 60,000 troops in the field against a new French aggression."[29]

France's occupation, a device for the balance of power, internationally and domestically, succeeded in diminishing her power to make war without encouraging revisionist impulses.[30] Not all occupations are as moderate and as limited as was the Allied occupation of France; even that one, however, was not so charitably regarded by all Frenchmen.

PROBLEMS OF OCCUPATION

Serious tensions exist between planning for occupation and occupation in fact. Disagreements between the military and civilians as to who will determine the nature, scope, domain, direction, and duration of the occupation may run deep. Not only may the relations of the military to the civilian leadership be challenged: at

[27] Ibid.

[28] Allmand, op. cit., p. 172 and especially p. 174.

[29] Robert L. Rothstein, *Alliances and Small Powers* (New York: Columbia University Press, 1968), pp. 195-196.

[30] Ibid.

times the civilian role, as in the U.S. Civil War, the Philippine insurrection, and the occupation of the Rhineland, will be deemed harmful to the political purposes behind the war. Planning for an occupation guided primarily by military considerations often extends the duration of the military phase and only grudgingly concedes authority to the civilians. A schism may occur in the civilian sector. Civilians may attempt to limit the military phase, while others will worry about the "germs of imperialism" in a "corps of 1000 (civilian) specialists for occupation."[31] Others, as refugees, may, in addition to their expert knowledge of the defeated polity, suffuse their recommendations with the trauma of their native rejection and immigration. Still others will simply be uninformed.

Although the paucity of qualified candidates for soldier-governorship is a hazard to any occupation, not all polities are concerned with the extent to which governing soldiers are qualified for occupational tasks.[32] For example, after 1945, the Soviet Union was more concerned with ideological dependability than with expertise, reflecting traditional Soviet tension between loyalty and competence.

Administrative questions will often determine an occupation's course. Occupational administration is a technological question, akin to Moltke's view of strategy.[33]

Military and civilian occupiers are technologists who administer policy that, as a political act, is formulated and enunciated by others than themselves. But, because it is with administrators and not with formulators that occupied populations interact, the administrators' effects will even influence the occupying government's policy.

In Poland after 1939, the Germans introduced parallel occupational structures in which reliable Nazis, the primary functionaries with direct ties to the Reich Ministry of the Interior, accompanied the military. Relations between military and civilian authorities followed the traditional contentious pattern. Present also was the paramilitary SS, whose tendency to brutality was especially impor-

[31] Coles and Weinberg, op. cit., p. 23.

[32] Ibid., p. 16.

[33] Moltke said strategy is "a system of *ad hoc* expedients; it is more than knowledge, it is the application of knowledge to practical life, the development of an original idea in accordance with continually changing circumstances. It is the art of action under the pressure of the most difficult conditions." Hajo Holborn, "Moltke and Schlieffen: The Prussian-German School," quoted in Earle, op. cit., p. 180.

tant. German occupational policies were clear and included the political objective of removing the area from military authority and transferring it to quasicivilian control, with well-known results for Poles and Jews.[34] In no way did the "rivalry"[35] between the political and paramilitary authorities accrue to the safety of those caught between the claws of the former and the talons of the latter. Where such competition between authorities exists, harshness, not indulgence, becomes the rule, for neither will wish to appear irresolute.

Because they direct the fighting, military spokesmen frequently blame civilian leaders for losing the last peace and seek a major role in the postwar world. Acrimony increases when military authorities ignore distinctions between military government, usually deemed to be in the military's purview, and the political purposes for which it is exercised, which are usually associated with civilians. The military can obstruct, reshape, and contradict civilian policy. It can also ignore the problems civilian policymakers have in laying out objectives that balance the militarily necessary and the administratively possible. An army that is called upon to administer creates and exploits political opportunities. In addition, civilians often bow to military expertise and accept military judgments and requirements; for even if political policy is a civilian matter, it is not purely a question for civilian leaders.

The extent to which the victor wishes and is able to exercise its victory by administering the defeated polity influences occupational policy. War's purpose, whether to defeat a troublemaker or to change basic power relations, likewise influences policy.

Movement toward creative occupation increases as the interests of the occupant and the occupied populations merge and blend. The likelihood of a creative occupation is affected by a number of factors.

Among these factors is that of *memory:* How has the occupier previously behaved in conditions of occupation? How has the defeated behaved in its occupations? Another factor is that of *intent:* Is the occupation's purpose one of military necessity, the extirpation of a loathsome regime, or merely the rehabilitation of an errant one? Is the purpose to avenge one's earlier defeat? The anticipated *dura-*

[34] Cf. Martin Broszat, *Nationalsozialistische Polenpolitik* (Frankfurt A.M.: Fischer Bücherei, 1965).

[35] Isiah Trunk, *Judenrat* (New York: Stein and Day, 1972), p. 6.

tion of the occupation is yet another factor. Occupants' own populations are less likely to balk at the prospect of brief and decisive occupations than at that of termless and vacillating ones. Still another factor is that of *projection:* What does the occupier wish to project to others not bound in the occupation? Does it wish to appear flexible or tough to others? The occupant's sense of the *future* influences the creativity of an occupation: Does the occupant contemplate a special relationship with the occupied area after the occupation has ended?

Whether an occupation has been creative will be a matter of judgment, independent of the occupants' intentions when they began it. Occupation is not intrinsically antithetical to intelligent and liberal policy and does not cease to be an occupation when it strives to benefit the victor and the vanquished.

As indicated by the Rhenish experience after World War I, where the occupation provided the stable framework within which elections took place, occupation is not per se inimical to freedom. One need but consider the differences between elections in the occupied Rhineland and the political turmoil in unoccupied Bavaria. It has been argued, however, that occupation after World War I, rather than serving Germany's political maturation, retarded it by permitting the status quo to prevail over revolution.[36] The links between occupation forces and the German government in quelling revolutionary uprisings account for some of Weimar's conservatism.[37]

Like that of Germany in Poland, harsh occupations may create paradoxic reactions. Among these paradoxic reactions is that of viewing the occupant, whatever its stated goals, as simply a new oppressor. In order to avoid this reaction the Japanese, for example, stopped short of punishing Filipinos who had fought with Americans. In the Ukraine, where the Germans were initially often welcomed as liberators, the population was soon turned into hostile partisans once German racial policies were put into effect.

[36] Harold J. Gordon, *The Reichswehr and the German Republic: 1919-1926* (Princeton: Princeton University Press, 1957), pp. 349-350.

[37] Ernst Fraenkel, *Military Occupation and the Rule of Law* (New York: Oxford University Press, 1944), p. 4.

An unintended paradoxic effect of occupation also occurs when an occupied people develops a national consciousness, thus taking the first step toward founding a modern state, as occurred in Korea under Japan.

Conceptual uncertainty and administrative equivocation, that is, technological ambiguity, will be translated into occupational instability. The divergent denazification policies simultaneously pursued in the Allied occupation of Germany are examples. A German might move to a more lenient zone to escape harsh procedures. Ambiguity approaching idiocy was found in George S. Patton's repeated comparison of Nazis and anti-Nazis to Republicans and Democrats.

The territory of the occupied power provides a locus for experimentation. When allies introduce divergent policies in their respective spheres, they may create a microcosm of broader international dealings with one another; they thereby contribute to instability.

Contradictions will be found in any occupation. One contradiction involves the manner in which the occupation is intended and understood by the occupant compared with its perception by the occupied populace. Even benign occupations will not achieve an identity between the perceptions of the occupants and the occupied. The latter will be resentful, even if they have no tradition of self-governance. If the political objective of an occupation is a peaceable milieu, this objective will have to appear in the occupation itself. Reprisal, repression, and reparations contradict a transformational occupation. They bespeak and intend the institutionalization of a distinct hierarchy between winners and losers. As long as a superior power can alternate between reprisal and reprieve, the occupation will confute the notion of a mutually advantageous relationship.

The decision to institute a benign occupation hinges on several factors, including the extent to which the occupied population is prepared to cooperate in the occupation and the extent to which the occupied population can appeal across the occupied territories to kinsfolks, coreligionists, conationals, or others who might be inclined to challenge the occupation *from without.* If no one is impelled to question it, the occupation will probably go unmolested and may, in fact, become milder over time. If, however, external forces challenge it, a new situation will arise.

If the challenge transcends being verbal and becomes increasingly political, the occupation may become meaner, less because it is felt that the occupied population aids and abets the external opponents, than because the occupier, now frustrated, may be unable to respond directly to the external challengers.

If the occupying power's own government changes, its ability (and much of its authority) to determine policy in the occupied territory may be affected. New regimes even in victorious polities take time to learn the ropes and to steer clear courses. Policies pursued by victorious democratic occupants are bound, despite claims of bipartisanship, to be competitive. Occupied populations become involved in that competition, whether at their own instigation or because of claims and promises of the elective competitors in the occupier's polity.

Occupation will also determine the political expression to be permitted under it, perhaps according to the degree of heterogeneity permitted in the occupant's own society. If an occupation strives to restrict political expression, that political expression may find an outlet in religion. If, as in the Japanese occupation of Korea, religion is suppressed, the effect will be to politicize religion.[38] When both channels are blocked, as in periods of the Soviet occupation of Eastern Europe, and when a resulting drift into dissent becomes the means of expressing values, the occupation will become harsher.

An occupation that excludes the interests of the occupied natives from consideration because it intends to be demonstrative and punitive, and to act as a deterrent against a revision of the eventual peace, will in itself probably be unable to produce either a peaceable milieu or an enduring change in the natives' attitudes. An occupation, on the other hand, that takes cognizance of the legitimate interests of the defeated polity's citizens, while able to produce changes in attitudes, may also have to decide which of several indigenous factions to support and which to risk alienating. Of course, some occupants will not concern themselves with this question. Others may encourage a continuous jockeying among the divided factions for favor with the occupants or may risk a constant search for coalitions among them. Other native factions will find

[38] Woo-Keun Han, *The History of Korea* (Honolulu: University of Honolulu Press, 1970), p. 458.

occupation a rare and temporary expedient to which it may be best not to become too closely or constrictingly tied. Some powers will find their ability to maintain and enforce an occupation too limited to provide more than the framework within which natives act as the occupiers' agents. The occupation policy then must be one of quite different objectives than when the victorious polity is able to administer the occupation on its own. Here substance is affected by form, and the nature and extent of the occupation are determined by the ability to carry it out. A power cannot engage in an extensive occupation if it lacks the means of enforcing it. The recent case of France in Germany, as well as in France's colonial remnants, illustrates the disparity between an occupation's purposes and its ability to meet them.

Even after World War II was clearly lost, Japan still sought a way to coordinate its place in the postwar world with the occupied areas. Its unconditional surrender ended hopes that the occupied territories, bound neither to the United States nor to Japan, would establish a preferred relationship with Japan.[39]

Political considerations that surround rather than require an occupation will influence subsidiary questions. For example, quite different logistical problems arose once occupation forces were shifted from carrying out wartime objectives in Germany to countering possible Soviet (or U.S.) threats.[40] To the occupants, Germany's defense was now as critical as its earlier defeat had been. This defense, including assuring supplies and communications, required assumptions, assessments, and arrangements quite different from those that underpinned the initial occupation.

A different problem arose in the occupation after Germany's defeat in 1945. The Morgenthau Plan and Joint Chiefs of Staff directives 1067 and 1779 proceeded from the clear policy of rooting out vestiges of Nazism, including, in contravention of the Hague Regulations of 1907, its nonpolitical institutions, so far as any existed.[41] JCS Directive 1067 was a document to guide the occupa-

[39] F. C. Jones et. al., *Survey of International Affairs: The Far East, 1942-1946* (London: Oxford University Press, 1955), p. 96.

[40] James A. Huston, *The Sinews of War: Army Logistics; 1775-1953* (Washington: Department of the Army, 1966), pp. 591-599.

[41] Cf. A. C. Davidonis, "Some Problems of Military Governments," *American Political Science Review,* June 1944, pp. 462. et seq.

tion not as liberators but as victors, underscoring the reality that institutions associated with detested social, economic, or political systems will be changed, despite the Hague Regulations.

Whether the occupier becomes the "legitimate successor of the last national government,"[42] as was the basis of Allied occupation of Germany after 1945, or whether a state may be sovereign without an independent national government, are questions that relate to occupation. If an occupier wished, for political reasons, to pretend that sovereignty was being "represented," it would be possible for it to do so. The defeated power would be too weak to claim otherwise.

Legally, occupation without annexation seems not to bestow sovereignty, whereas annexation requires the enemy to be sufficiently beaten and disarmed to reduce virtually to zero the likelihood of its armed resistance. When the Germans and Austrians in November 1916 occupied Polish land seized from Russia and proposed to arm Polish citizens, with the object of defeating the Russians, Russia had not yet been militarily defeated.[43] The political objective of the occupation was enrollment of Poles in the armies of the Central Powers. This was not legally possible because occupation "does not change the juridical status of the territory thus occupied and occupation by enemy armies provides no legal basis for establishing a new juridical status within such territory."[44]

Occupations will generally maintain the distinction between civilians, on the one hand, and the government and military, on the other. But occupations in and after civil wars will be among the harshest because of the contest between orthodoxy and apostasy; for whichever side wins, victory will vindicate its beliefs, and occupation will treat the defeated civilians as severely as the government and the military because all are seen as traitors. Occupation, except in cases of unconditional surrender, often partakes of some compromise. This compromise is practically ruled out in a civil war, as the Reconstruction shows.

[42] Hans Kelsen, "Is a Peace Treaty with Germany Legally Possible and Politically Desirable?," *American Political Science Review*, December 1947, p. 1188.

[43] Robert Langer, *Seizure of Territory: The Stimson Doctrine and Related Principles in Legal Theory and Diplomatic Practice* (Princeton: Princeton University Press, 1947), p. 18.

[44] Yugoslavian minister to U.S. Department of State, 12 May 1941, 4 *Department of State Bulletin*, quoted in ibid., p. 117.

Occupation policies, often shaped in an atmosphere of unhurried abstraction miles from the territory to be occupied, will only later be affected by the realities of the theater of occupation. The enormity of war's destruction will either be underestimated or, as the *Strategic Bombing Surveys* indicated, overestimated. It will make a difference to the occupants if an enemy who is assumed to have been exhausted and beaten has in fact been driven to fanatic resistance. Conversely, it will make a difference of another sort if any enemy is expected to resist despite defeat and if the occupant, girding itself for it, thereby blinds itself to the realities of a situation in which the defeated populace seeks immediate reconciliation.

Germany's occupation in 1945 involved another problem, one perhaps not seen in such enormity since the Thirty Years' War. This was the problem of masses of refugees, often from Allied countries, as well as the freed millions from concentration and extermination camps. How, occupation forces had to decide, could these be as severely treated as were their captors and dispersers, in whose open midst they now found themselves? And yet, how long could the occupants, even under conditions most propitious to a rigorous occupation, continue to distinguish between them and the masses of Germans, especially German children, without sowing seeds of a future problem? In Germany, too, British occupation policy was perhaps most clearly characterized by political considerations elsewhere. British authorities halted the movement of Jews to their zone on the grounds that Jews wandering westward were in fact en route to Palestine, then still a mandated territory. What, additionally, was one to do with defectors and deserters from an Allied Red Army if these were found in one's zone of occupation?

As long as frontiers are penetrable, there will be refugees, or at least some shift in population. This adds enormously to the problem of stability within an occupied territory (one need only consider such ancillary technological questions as provisions for food, shelter, clothing, heat, hygiene, medicine, and education, and the effects of an influx or decrease in populations requiring them).

Occupations are shaped by the political ends they are designed to serve. For instance, the German occupation of parts of Alsace after 1871 was "to facilitate ultimate annexation."[45] An occupation may

[45] Doris A. Graeber, *The Development of the Law of Belligerent Occupation, 1863-1914* (New York: Columbia University Press, 1949), p. 264.

be an indirect means of arms limitation, as when the size of the German army in Alsace-Lorraine was to be proportionate to that of the French forces. To permit an increase in the French army through recruitment in the occupied areas meant an increased German military burden.[46]

Occupation may be affected by an occupied territory's state of development and by the degree to which it has political, social, and economic cohesion. While these may be objective data, occupiers will be moved by their estimates of the degree of modernization and coherence as well as by ideological and demographic factors.

Not all concerns of military necessity will be idle, as the Israeli occupation has indicated. Here the function of the occupation has been essentially two-fold: to provide a modicum of security, which is to say, inaccessibility; and to reclaim biblical areas (Judea, Samaria, and Jerusalem). The question of whether a polity chooses "to close political options in . . . future negotiations" will be critical.[47] This Israel appears to have done by converting its occupation of the Golan Heights into an annexation.

Events and behavior may decrease one's options even if policy is not intended to do so. Occupation may become a thing unto itself, no longer related to any political purpose other than to appear stalwart and consistent.

CONCLUSIONS

Military occupation, known since antiquity as an issue of political technology, remains, in the nuclear age, a multidimensional means of conducting national policy. Related to peace, it often contradicts what peace means because it is so closely related to war. Striving for order in enforced tranquility, occupation often succeeds, but also often results in paradoxic effects, including laying the bases for a future war and political, economic, and social retardation. Occupants often lose sight of an occupation's initial purposes, which may in themselves have been confused; the occupation may become prolonged for purposes other than dealing with a defeated power.

[46] Ibid., p. 261.

[47] Yehuda Zvi Blum, *The Juridical Status of Jerusalem* (Jerusalem: Hebrew University Press, 1974), p. 21.

Occupations also highlight ambiguities within the victor's polity, create tensions between elements of the occupied territory, and encourage or reflect disagreements within occupational alliances.

Ethical and ideal obligations in occupation, to the extent that they exist, frequently run afoul of occupation in fact. The obligation, as we have proposed here, to establish a peaceable milieu is fundamental to all politics. And yet in occupation this obligation, in both its duty-related and practical dimensions, is often not met, because it seeks to transform more than simply the defeated polity. If an occupation does not provide a peaceable milieu, that is to say, a setting in which the conditions precedent to peace can be arranged and can mature, this may be due to the occupant's goals, the defeated polity's successful resistance, the international system, or a combination of these. Five factors affect the establishment of a creative or transformational occupation and determine whether a peaceable milieu will emerge. They must be seen from the perspectives of the victorious occupant and the defeated polity. The extent to which they may be said to be in focus serves to explain the success or failure of particular occupations. These five factors are *memory, intent, duration, projection,* and *future.* The more these converge toward desire for a peaceable milieu, the more likely are they to represent occupation as a step toward peace, which we have defined as a condition in which states heed and defer to one another's national existence, sovereignty, and territorial integrity in their impunible actions with one another.

The five critical factors are refracted through the prism of *ability:* the success of an occupation is often a matter of being able to engage in or to resist an occupation. If the victor is unable to embark upon and enforce an occupation, the other factors become irrelevant. If the defeated polity is able to contest another's occupation, this becomes a vital element in all phases of an occupation.

Occupations succeed or fail in their efforts to procure the political objectives for which they have been engaged in terms of the five factors refracted through the ability of either side to have its way. And this, when all is said and done, is the heart of politics.

We have spoken of occupation as political technology, which states employ with unequal technical competence. At the basis of occupation is also the basis of politics: the quest for order and peace. This means a distribution of resources to meet the political, economic, sustentative, intellectual, and moral demands of the victor at one level, of the loser at another, and finally of politically organized humans generally.

Occupations are appraised in terms of how well they meet each level of demands. One level stresses belligerence, a second the peaceable milieu, and a third peace. Occupations have hovered somewhere between the first and second levels. The requirements of peace are rarely met in an unalloyed fashion. There is little likelihood that occupation following a nuclear war, if occupation is still possible, will be better able to move from belligerency to peace than after a conventional war. It would be foolish to lay the blame for this at the feet of occupation, for that is simply an artifact created by the same human who also seizes upon war as a means of responding to other humanly produced situations. Occupation itself is not inimical to peace, creativity, intelligence, or freedom. Nor is it more productive of these than is the intelligence of the parties to it.

If occupation fails to establish even a peaceable milieu, and ultimately peace, the reasons for this lie in the incapacity of the victorious occupant and the defeated to bring the five factors into focus. Even in this, however, occupation may serve the purposes of national policy.

Chapter 22

DETERMINANTS OF FRENCH FOREIGN POLICY AFTER 1932: ON THE RELATIONSHIP OF NATIONAL AND FOREIGN POLICY AND INTERNATIONAL POLITICS AND ECONOMICS

Gilbert Ziebura

THE PROBLEM

The logic of the peace settlements implemented in Europe after World War I by the Allies should have led to the assumption that the new status quo power par excellence, France, would prove to be the determined opponent to every effort, particularly ones staged by Germany, to change, let alone destroy, this newly found order. The assumption should have been even more obvious from the fact that the "Versailles system" was both subjectively and objectively identical to the national security of France. This argument has to be taken even one step further. The survival of the French social system *(Gesellschaftsformation)*[1] was intricately linked with its ability not only to maintain the security system that protected it against external attacks but also to develop it most efficiently.

What really occurred was the exact opposite: the first signs of it were already visible in the 1920s, clearly evident in the 1930s. From the moment in 1931 when France, supported by Great Britain, Italy, and the Little Entente, succeeded once more in toppling the plan for a German-Austrian tariff union that would indeed have been menacing to the French security system, no further clash with Germany occurred even though the goal of German policy became more and more explicitly the destruction of the Versailles system. Attempts to explain this paradox were made by many contempo-

[1] For this term see G. Ziebura, *Frankreich 1789–1870, Entstehung einer bürgerlichen Gesellschaftsformation* (Frankfurt and New York, 1979), introduction.

raries and are now increasingly being adopted by historians,[2] who point to the general condition of French society during the 1930s, which they label with terms like "crisis," "resignation," or even "decadence."

This self-criticism, which reached its peak after the military defeat of France, did not exclude any social classes; it is significant that it affected the society as a whole. Marc Bloch, the renowned social historian who was murdered by the SS, searched for the main cause of the defeat not in the military leadership but in society, which he perceived to be petit bourgeois, selfish, and self-centered.[3] Almost simultaneously Léon Blum argued along the same lines in his essay "A l"échelle humane' (completed in December 1941), where he denounced the "decline," the "decay," the "obsolescence" that, affecting the leading social class, eventually had to drag society as a whole after it into destruction. Like Marc Bloch, Blum (a socialist) accused the bourgeoisie, society's dominating class, of not having led the way into a modern, developed, capitalist France, which consequently may explain why socialism could not come up with an alternative.[4]

Reflections of this kind can be found by the dozen in the writings of the Resistance. Those who choose to use this kind of argument will find that they have the answers to a lot of questions down pat. How could a society constructed in such a way hope to meet the challenge of National Socialism (Nazism)? One of National

[2] From the extensive contemporary literature see R. Aron and A. Dandieu, *Décadence de la nation française* (Paris, 1931); the first edition of the magazine *L'ordre nouveau* (May 1933), edited by the same authors, was devoted to the topic "Mission ou la démission de la France." It was not coincidental that terms such as "abdication" or "decadence" were part of the ideological vocabulary of a new, authoritarian-oriented Right. Compare also J. Joll (ed.), *The Decline of the Third Republic,* St. Antony's papers 5 (Oxford, 1959); J. Chastenet, *The Decline of the Third Republic,* St. Antony's Papers 5 (Oxford, 1959); J. Chastenet, *Histoire de la Troisième République,* vol. 6, *Déclin de la Troisième 1931-1938* (Paris, 1962); W.L. Shirer's very controversial *Der Zusammenbruch Frankreichs. Aufstieg und Fall der Dritten Republik* (München, 1970); G. Kiersch and R.A. Höhne, " Innerer und äusserer Machtverfall einer bürgerlichen Démokratie," in: E. Forndran,F. Golczewski, and D. Riesenberger (eds.), *Innen- und AuBenpolitik unter nationalsozialistischer Bedrohung* (Opladen, 1977), pp. 32-57; and particularly H. Dubief, *Le déclin de la IIIe République 1929-1938* (Paris, 1976), and J.-B. Duroselle, *La décadence 1932-1939* (Paris, 1979).

[3] M. Bloch, *L'étrange défaite* (written in 1940) (Paris, 1957), especially pp. 205ff.

[4] *L'Oeuvre de Léon Blum 1940-1945* (Paris, 1955), pp. 408-495, especially pp. 437ff., 468.

Socialism's most prominent features was its very ability to mobilize social forces to an unprecedented extent. This was true because, in contrast to every parliamentary democracy, National Socialism did not have to take into account the social costs of the enterprise. Therefore, does not the clash of two social systems, whose reproduction is based on extremely opposite principles, already answer the question of a possible margin for decisions in foreign policy? Without doubt, the most important reason has just been touched on, and yet we are left with the task of defining more closely the facts of the case that proved to be so crucial for the 1930s. The foreign policy of all nation-states during those years can only be comprehended if it is placed at the intersection of three circles that are themselves closely entwined: the crisis of world economics (i.e., of the capitalist mode of production on a worldwide scale), the crisis within society as it manifested itself in individual countries, and the crisis of the Versailles system. This attempt already raises difficult methodological problems. Furthermore, it would be inappropriate to distinguish between "politics" and "economics." The permeation of the worldwide economic crisis with the national social crisis plus the related disintegration of the world's economic and political order led then, as it does today, to both a *politicization of the economy* (in domestic policy through the increasing intervention of the state, in foreign policy through the closure of the markets) and an *economization of politics* inasmuch as the policies adopted to overcome the crisis were of an almost existential importance to the social systems of individual nations. The degree of intensity with which this phenomenon became evident in the 1930s is virtually unparalleled.

It is, therefore, not surprising if foreign policy under these conditions serves chiefly to safeguard the policies adopted to overcome the crisis, to make sure they are not endangered by foreign influences, or, as is common with expansionist regimes, to strengthen the regime externally. However, this is not meant to support the thesis of the preeminence of internal policy; quite the contrary. This thesis would presuppose far too sharp a distinction between internal issues and international issues; this distinction is particularly untenable in the 1930s. Consequently the aim of a sociological analysis of foreign policy must be to clarify the correlation peculiar to each and every form of society, that is, the correlation between (1) the internal "constitution" (in the broadest sense of the word), (2) its position within the international economic system of the division of labor in respect to dominance and dependence, as well as (3) its margin to act in foreign policy.

It was, however, symptomatic of the 1930s that none of the acting parties was able to handle the crisis, despite certain partial successes. The crisis, therefore, developed into a state of continual crisis that could only intensify the crisis of world economics and of the Versailles system. The revisionist powers, led by Germany, unscrupulously took advantage of this destabilization, for it opened up to them the possibility of heading off the mounting internal difficulties (e.g., the imposition of wartime economy) by adopting a policy that seized the bull by the horns, that is, by expansion.[5] To the extent that "success" on the domestic front became more and more short-winded, success in external affairs offered itself as compensation–a veritable escalation that finally had to result in the destruction of world order. The more it became apparent that the Western democracies, headed by France, were not able on their part to cope with the crisis and restore at least partially the world's economic and monetary system through increased cooperation, the more these democracies came under pressure to direct all their strength to the conservation of their own societies. Thus, foreign policy was rendered instrumental and subordinate, making it of course impossible to rescue the pitiful remnants of the Versailles system.

Finally, I would like to draw attention to one aspect that has been particularly neglected by historians so far: the fact that the crisis did not happen concurrently in the *individual* countries and that consequently the effects that the policies adopted to overcome the crisis in each country were different. Whereas most of the countries had given up deflationist policies between 1932 and 1934 and had turned to a more or less distinctive form of Keynesianism (of a leftist or rightist order), France reached the peak of its deflationist policy only in 1935-1936. The question now is whether a causal connection should not be established between the fact just mentioned (and, as we shall see later, the aggravation of the

[5] Appropriate, in spite of all the criticism, T.W. Mason, "Zur Funktion des Angriffskrieges 1939," in: G. Ziebura, ed., *Grundfragen der deutschen Aussenpolitik seit 1871* (Darmstadt, 1975), pp. 376-413.

economic and social crisis resulting from it) and the fact that France lost its position as the most important status quo power of the Versailles system precisely in this period. Claude Fohlen is right in pointing out that three decisive battles were lost in these years: the overcoming of the economic crisis (at least to the extent that other countries at least temporarily managed to do so), the renewal of the political regime, and the chance to adequately tackle the challenge of National Socialism. However, Fohlen, too, only sets those phenomena side by side, listing them without going into the question of their interrelationship.[6]

It is, however, the intention of this chapter to do just that, at least in rough form. Historical research is still dominated by a sometimes meticulous examination of individual factors, based on a conception of history that focuses mainly on events.[7] But by now, the amount of information gathered makes it possible for us to search for explanations that make a more structuralist approach necessary. Only in this way is it possible to prevent the fashionable but mechanical transfer of the experience of the 1930s to the problems of contemporary international politics.[8]

THE DECLINE OF THE ECONOMY: INTERNAL AND EXTERNAL FACTORS

It is a widely accepted fact that the decline of the world economy, originating in the U.S. economic crisis, had a decisive influence on the intensification of international tensions after 1931,

[6] Compare C. Fohlen, *La France de l'entre-deux-guerres 1917-1939* (Paris, 1966), p. 120.

[7] This refers to most contributors to the otherwise very informative anthologies edited by the Centre national de la recherche scientifique: *Les relations franco-allemandes 1933-39* (Paris, 1976) and *La France et l'Allemagne 1932-1936* (Paris, 1980), as well as to older studies, including E.H. Carr's classic *The Twenty Years' Crisis, 1919-1939* (London, 1948).

[8] For instance, the attempt to compare the policy of appeasement applied to Germany during the 1930s to the current policy of the West toward the Soviet Union and to use the comparison as a deterrent. See F.U. Fack, "Frieden schaffen ohne Waffen?," *Frankfurter Allgemeine Zeitung* (June 15, 1981); see also the critical reply, G. Ziebura, "Sumpfblüten der Geschichte: Die Afghanistan-Krise und die falschen historischen Vergleiche," *Vorwärts* (March 27, 1980).

even though this relationship has not yet been systematically examined. The main reason must be seen in the tendency among countries to become increasingly self-centered, self-sufficient, and self-reliant, leading to something akin to seclusion as far as foreign trade is concerned, and certainly intensifying already existing antagonistic tendencies in the relationship between countries. The vicious circle thus evolving has been described many times:[9] the collapse of the world economy provokes a nationalistic trade and monetary policy that may be unusual in the tools used (protectionism, trade agreement policy, clearing agreement, foreign exchange control, devaluation, etc.) and in their mixture and intensity but that ultimately results not only in solidifying the process of decay but in giving it yet another boost. Consequently monetary blocks and large-area economies striving for self-sufficiency arise under the predominance of imperial and imperialistic powers[10] that are bound to intensify politicostrategic antagonisms even further. No wonder that a real regeneration of the world economy did not happen before World War II broke out, despite temporary recuperation in (1935-1937).[11] This regeneration, however, was an absolutely essential prerequisite for the restabilization of international relationships, i.e., for a repression of revisionist powers without war.

The most prominent victim of this development was France, in three respects. On the one hand, the Depression impaired the "camp" of Western democracies as opposed to the revisionist powers inasmuch as economic competition among them, especially between the United States and Great Britain,[12] increased considerably. On the other hand, the Depression prevented the absolutely vital modernization of the French economy; on top of that, the Depression contributed to the solidification of those structures that had emerged from the last third of the nineteenth century and had caused the relative backwardness of France's level of industrialization. Thus the gap between the claim to leadership in foreign policy

[9] Of the extensive literature see the still significant study by A. Sturmthal, *Die grosse Krise* (Zurich, 1937); J. Néré, *La crise de 1929* (Paris, 1968); and C.P. Kindleberger, *Die Weltwirtschaftskrise* (München, 1973).

[10] See S. Helander, *Das Autarkieproblem in der Weltwirtschaft* (Berlin, 1955).

[11] Even alert contemporaries could sense that. For instance, see the numerous publications of the League of Nations.

[12] See, for example, G. Schmidt, *England in der Krise* (Opladen, 1981), pp. 164ff., and the literature quoted there.

and its economic foundation widened at a moment when German capatialism under the Nazi regime reached a new stage of its development with both concentration and monopolization increasing. Finally, the Depression shook the foundations of the Versailles system, which, admittedly, had been rather weak right from the start. Eastern and southeastern Europe in particular proved that. Their economies, already suffering from the blows of the Depression, had to open up more and more to German intrusion.

Despite the intensive research done[13] and the knowledge gained, the reasons for the decline of the French economy have not yet been worked out convincingly. This much is certain: the Depression hit France comparatively late (after the summer of 1931), but its ramifications were all the more devastating in every trade and line of business. There were short, interim economic booms, as in other countries, but they were by no means capable of concealing a kind of structural stagnation. The high level of industrial production of 1929-1930, the best years of the period between the wars, were not reached again until World War II. Table 6 indicates the formidable speed at which the gap between French and German industrial production widened after 1935 (if 1925-1929 equals 100, then already after 1934), a phenomenon that was widely known among contemporaries, thanks mainly to the publications of the League of Nations.[14]

Indeed, the most important effect of the Depression was that it curbed the breakthrough of those high-technology industries of the "Second Industrial Revolution," i.e., the modern sectors of the economy (oil, petrochemistry, electrical industries, automobiles) that had only begun to emerge during World War I and then again during the prosperity of the 1920s, because those industries were at the same time largely export-oriented. The traditional sector was not any better off: the decline of the textile industry could not be halted despite the efforts made to develop its potential, and productivity was decreasing in heavy industry although it had been least hit by

[13] See, for example, C.J. Gignoux, *L'économie française entre les deux guerres 1919-1939* (Paris, 1942); ch. Bettelheim, *Bilan de l'économie française 1919-1946* (Paris, 1947): J.M. Jeanneney, *Tableaux statistiques relatifs a l'économie française et l'économie mondiale* (Paris, 1957); A. Sauvy, *Histoire économique de la France entre les deux guerres*, vol.1, *1918-1931* (Paris, 1965); vol. 2, *1931-1939* (Paris, 1967); best of all, T. Kemp, *The French Economy 1913-1938. The History of a Decline* (London, 1972).

[14] This extremely prolific material has only been used sporadically so far.

Table 6
Index of Industrial Production

	Germany	France
	1913 = 100	
1920	59.0	70.4
1921-1925	77.7	95.3
1926-1929	112.2	130.6
1930	101.6	139.9
1931-1935	90.6	113.7
1936-1938	138.3	118.2
1931	85.1	122.6
1932	70.2	105.4
1933	79.4	119.8
1934	101.8	111.4
1935	116.7	109.1
1936	127.5	116.3
1937	138.1	123.8
1938	149.3	114.6
	1925-1929 = 100	
1931	78.3	96.2
1932	64.6	82.7
1933	73.0	94.0
1934	93.7	87.4
1935	107.4	85.6
1936	130.4	91.3
1937	140.0	97.2
1938	128.8	90.0

Source: League of Nations, Departement économique, financier et du transit, *Industrialisation et commerce exterieur* (Geneva, 1945), pp. 156, 160, and 166.

the Depression. However, a small number of large companies that had already benefited handsomely from World War I in terms of profits were thus able to secure their position unchallenged.

Concurrently, and to a certain extent as a counterreaction, the importance of small business enterprises in trade, industry and agriculture was increasing.[15] On top of that, new methods of rationalization ("Taylorism"), already implemented in the United States (and to a lesser extent in Germany), were unanimously rejected in France by both the Right and the majority of the Left as a new form of economic growth model based on mass consumption, as a dangerous byproduct of overindustrialization with a tendency towards overproduction.[16] While the number of people employed in industry was actually decreasing (in 1931 it was 8.5 million in 1936 7.4 million), it was increasing in the trade sector, and this had the effect, as Alfred Sauvy appropriately remarked,[17] of more tradesmen selling fewer products. During all those years the investment made in the field of consumer goods was considerably higher than that in capital goods. The traditional Malthusian character of society became visible: nobody wanted to accept a cut in a living standard that he had gotten used to; the present was more important than the future.[18] No wonder that a defeatist mood prevailed in the years between 1932 and 1935; there was a feeling that the French economy would never recuperate. During that time about six hundred credit institutes closed down.[19] Deflationist policies under Laval, which reached their peak at the same time, also played a part. But most important, the deflationist policy prevented the revitalization of economic activities, a revitalization that was taking place at that time in the United States and in Germany.

The armament industry is a high-profile example of the archaic state French industrial production was in.[20] It was characterized by extreme fragmentation, disorganization, and obsolescence of the

[15] The number of farms that did not employ workers other than family had already increased from 1.2 million to 1.35 million between 1921 and 1931; see C. Fohlen, *La France,* p. 178. Between 1906 and 1936 the number of companies in the industrial sector with a total of 500-1,000 employees only increased from 421 to 615, and the number of companies with over 1,000 employees decreased from 215 to 196; see P. Sorlin, *La société française,* vol. 2, *1914-1968* (Paris, 1971), p. 88.

[16] A. Sauvy, *Histoire économique,* vol. 2, pp. 22f.

[17] Ibid., pp. 115f.

[18] Ibid., pp. 118, 120.

[19] P. Sorlin, *La société,* p. 81.

[20] A satisfactory investigation of the French arms industry in the interwar period does not exist. See, besides references in A. Sauvy, *Histoire économique,* and T. Kemp, *French Economy,* also J. Minart, *Le drame du désarmement français (1918-1939)* (Paris, 1959), pp. 198-210; L. Mysyrowicz, *Autopsie d'une défaite: Origines de l'effondrement militaire français de 1940* (Lausanne, 1973).

means of production as well as by an artisanlike production process. While, for instance, the aircraft industries in the United States, Great Britain, and later in Germany were in the hands of only a few large companies that had long since changed to mass production and standardization of components, there were at least 40 companies in France that produced more than 332 (!) prototypes between 1919 and 1929.[21] In the Ministry of War's order of 115 aircraft in 1930 there were 37 different models. Only after the Popular Front government had partially nationalized the armament industry (Law of August 11, 1936) did a move towards concentration and production planning set in. A thorough modernization of the production process aiming at mass production did not come about until after the Treaty of Munich, that is, at a time when the German lead was already too substantial to be overtaken. No cooperation with the U.S. armament industry materialized.

DETERIORATION OF FRANCE'S POSITION IN THE INTERNATIONAL DIVISION OF LABOR

The stagnation or even regression of the national economy due to internal and external factors, reciprocally influencing each other negatively, ultimately led to the weakening of France's position in foreign trade and payments, in both the monetary and the trade sector, particularly in respect to capital as the traditional tool to support one's authority in foreign affairs.[22] The comparatively late stabilization of the currency (de facto in October 1926, de jure in 1928) had already resulted in a devaluation of 1:4.5 compared to parity before the war. The devaluation of the British pound (September 1931) as well as the devaluation of the dollar following Roosevelt's accession to office shook the international monetary system and hit France particularly hard, considering that foreign capital had flowed out after the stabilization of the franc and that German reparation payments had been stopped. The most drastic

[21] L. Mysyrowicz, *Autopsie*, pp. 191-196.

[22] See on this point in general R. Girault, "Économie et politique internationale: diplomatie et banques pendant l'entre-deux-guerres," *Relations internationales* (Spring 1980), pp. 7-22; the poor state of research in this respect is also lamented by J.-B. Duroselle, *La décadence*, pp. 222 and 224.

repercussions were that the price for French goods was from now on considerably higher than that for British exports, thus resulting in a dramatic deterioration of France's competitive situation on the world market–a situation that was even further exacerbated by a conservative government that dogmatically declined to devaluate the franc and maintained an orthodox policy with the priorities set on the stability of the currency, and gold cover, thus meeting halfway the bourgeoisie, anxious for its security, and the entrepreneurs in particular.[23]

In foreign trade the precise counterpart of this monetary policy was the attempt made by France after the failure of the London economic conference to form a "gold bloc" (including Belgium, the Netherlands, Luxembourg, Italy, Switzerland, and Poland). In view of the chaotic state of the international monetary system, France cherished the illusion that a remnant of the international stability zone could still be constituted, thus keeping the parity of the franc.[24] However, France was then faced with a new dilemma. In order for it to continue to compete with those countries that had devalued their currencies, the price level within the goldbloc countries had to remain as low as possible. But that was only possible with the aid of a vigorous deflationist policy, which inevitably aggravated the Depression still further. It so happened that the gold bloc countries did not participate in the revitalization of the world economy in the years 1933-1934; on the contrary, recessive tendencies were still on the increase. No wonder that these countries were now trying their luck outside the gold bloc (Italy quit in 1934, Belgium in 1935, Poland in 1936). Consequently trade among these countries as well as trade among themselves declined drastically. Certainly, as Duroselle remarks,[25] there was no direct relationship between foreign policy and this attempt to make France the leading power of a monetary and economic bloc. And yet he admits that an effective foreign policy was impossible as long as France remained economically a prisoner of the Depression. The gold bloc policy, however, ensured precisely that situation. Moreover, it revealed the isolation

[23] Details in J.-M. Jeannenay, *Essai sur les mouvements des prix en France depuis la stabilisation monétaire 1927-1935* (Paris, 1936), and the preface by G. Pirou; J.-B. Duroselle, *La décadence*, p. 214ff.

[24] See for the following J. Néré, *La crise*, pp. 179-182, and 189-196.

[25] J.-B. Duroselle, *La décadence*, p. 220.

of France, especially from Anglo-Saxon countries, in terms of international trade, and hence the fragmentation of the "democratic camp" vis-à-vis the revisionist powers. Caught between Germany's policy of autarky and the inflationist economics of Great Britain and the United States, the gold bloc hampered France's activities[26] and perpetuated self-made domestic constraints.

Today it is undisputed that the devaluation of 1936 came too late. The impetus designed to overcome the economic crisis proved to be insufficiently strong. Moreover, if one considers the flight of capital that began in the early 1930s and picked up after 1935-1936,[27] one can now assess the extent to which France's monetary and economic difficulties increased. The fact that owners of capital were growing more and more distrustful when faced with the continuing economic crisis and with the possible success of a leftist coalition, as well as the unbalanced, discordant federal credit policy, made the money and capital market tumble from one crisis to another. The situation did not improve until Daladier linked the franc to the British pound thus restoring stability to a certain extent and causing some of the capital to return.[28] However, France had to pay a high price for it: further subjection to England's foreign policy.

The decline of France's position in the international division of labor can be demonstrated best by its foreign trade. France's foreign trade balance was, admittedly, traditionally deficiatary; also, the French were less dependent than the Germans on foreign trade surpluses because their level of industrialization was lower. Moreover, before 1914 those deficits could be compensated for by a massive export of capital. Still, foreign trade surpluses did accrue between 1924 and 1927, not least as a consequence of the undervaluation of the franc. Significantly enough, industrial finished goods

[26] H. Dubief, *Le déclin*, p. 29.

[27] It is difficult to assess the extent of this flight of capital. Therefore, figures differ: *Le Temps* talks about 16.5 billion francs' worth of gold leaving the country in 1935; V. Auriol, the finance minister of the Popular Front government, claimed that in 1936 25 billion francs flowed out of the country; see A. Günther, *Frankreich und sein Überseereich in der Weltwirtschaft* (Stuttgart, 1936), p. 247; A. Sauvy, *Histoire économique*, vol. 2, pp. 171, 200, gives us the figure of 30 billion francs for the time between the beginning of 1934 and June 1936 (victory of the Popular Front).

[28] H. Schmidt, *Die Struktur der französischen Bankwirtschaft* (Jena, 1940) (Probleme der Weltwirtschaft, 66), p. 173.

had an increasing share of overall exports in these years. This fact undoubtedly reflects the importance of the modern, export-oriented sector of the economy.

As Table 7 shows, this situation changed dramatically during the 1930s. Although the amount of industrial products imported by France had always been higher than in Germany and continued to be so during the 1930s, its share of the overall export decreased continually as opposed to that of Germany, which was increasing. In 1936-1938 it did not reach even half the amount of 1913. Between 1934 and 1935 alone, the export of finished goods decreased from 10.1 to 8.7 billion francs.[29] At the same time foreign trade regularly showed a fairly considerable deficit: in 1935 5.3 billion francs; in 1936 10.0 billion; in 1937 19.5 billion (exports 24.5 billion, imports 43.9 billion); in 1938 15.1 billion (imports 46.4 billion, exports 31.2 billion). This deficit was coupled with a deficit in the balance of payment (except for the years 1935 and 1938).[30] This is an indication that the stagnation of France's national economy corresponded with France's decline in the hierarchy of the international division of labor, in favor notably of Germany but also of the United States and Great Britain.

It became a decisive factor for France's politicostrategic position in Europe that it was not only pushed back from the world market by the United States, Great Britain, and, most of all, Germany[31] but that it also lost more and more ground in eastern and southeastern Europe, which was the pillar of its system of alliances.[32] In the 1920s France had still been able to increase its influence in this region, partially, of course, as a compensation for the influence over Russia that it had lost. One of the means employed was the export of capital in the form of government loans to those countries, allies as well as nonallies, that were highly in debt. Heavy industry had given more support to this policy of economic infiltration than it had before 1914, expanding its holding of production plants. The best-

29 A. Gunther, *Frankreich* p. 47.

30 Figures taken from A. Sauvy, *Histoire économique,* vol. 2, pp. 562, 563, 572ff.

31 For details see League of Nations, *Aperçu de commerce mondial 1938* (Geneva, 1939), tables IV and V.

32 Compare for the following the relevant articles in M. Lévy-Leboyer, ed., *La position internationale de la France. Aspects économiques et financières XIX-XX siècles* (Paris, 1977); E. Kohlruss, *Die französischen Kapitalanlagen in Südosteuropa im Rahmen der gesamten Auslandsverschuldung der südosteuropäischen Lander* (Leipzig, 1934).

Table 7
Imports and Exports of Finished Industrial Goods

Year	Germany	France	United States	Great Britain (and Ireland)
		1913 Prices Annual Averages in Millions of Dollars		
		Imports		
1930	293	337	530	716
1931-1935	205	245	372	499
1936-1938	a) 168	179	444	552
		Exports		
1930	1,475	765	1,115	1,384
1931-1935	1,159	574	685	1,030
1936-1938	a) 1,357	409	1,116	1,277
		Volume (1913 = 100):		
		Imports		
1930	86.7	98.0	111.6	118.7
1931-1935	60.7	71.2	78.3	82.8
1936-1938	a) 49.7	52.0	93.5	91.5
		Exports		
1930	91.3	87.4	160.2	68.2
1931-1935	71.8	65.6	95.0	50.8
1936-1938	a) 84.0	46.7	154.8	62.9

Source: League of Nations, *Industrialisation*, pp. 191, 193.
a) Average in 1936-1937.

known, but certainly not the only example is the increasing influence of the powerful Schneider–Le Cruzot company over the Skoda factory. It gained an almost strategic position, since Skoda came close to monopolizing arms supplies to the countries of the Little Entente and was working on the standardization of the caliber of ammunition and of other equipment.[33]

[33] For detailes see W. Hummelberger, "Die Rüstungsindustrie der Tschechoslowakei 1933 bis 1939," in: F. Forstmeier and H.-E. Volkmann (eds.), *Wirtschaft und Rüstung am Vorabend des Zweiten Weltkrieges* (Düsseldorf, 1975), especially pp. 313-318.

The fundamental inconsistencies and weaknesses of the French position were revealed by the Depression. If France had to yield to German expansion it was because it could not sell its expensive export goods on a market characterized by a rapidly declining purchasing power. Secondly, France was quite incapable of absorbing the supplies of agricultural products from southeastern Europe as its own agriculture was itself suffering from inflation and overproduction, seeking refuge behind substantial customs duties. This, by the way, demonstrates a basic dilemma: the lack of flexibility of the French economy on the world market; the interests of world economics were always subordinated to agriculture. Germany, however, presented itself as a potential customer of agricultural products, even paying prices that were above world level. Exchanging industrial goods (often of inferior quality) and credits for agricultural products, Germany implemented a type of unequal, imperialistic division of labor[34] that France was unable to counter.

Because France occupied a strong position in public borrowing due to massive stabilization and supporting loans and had in addition neglected private industry in favor of state-controlled companies, the export of capital could not be used, as had been the case before 1914,[35] to intensify trade relations.[36] Moreover, economic competition that sometimes bordered on open trade war escalated not only among the major powers but also among the Balkan countries. All attempts to provide, with British assistance, a solid economic foundation for the French system of alliance failed because of resistance in London. But worst of all, dependence on French loans was felt to be more and more burdensome as the economic crisis hit the Eastern

[34] Compare the well-known studies by B.J. Wendt, H.-J. Schröder, and M.Broszat and also W. Schumann (ed.), *Griff nach Südosteuropa* (East Berlin, 1973); R.Schönfeld, "Die Balkanländer in der Wirtschaftskrise," *Vierteljahresschrift für Sozial- und Wirtschaftsgeschichte* 62 (1975): 179-213; P. Marguerat, *Le III Reich et le pétrole roumain 1938-1940* (Geneva, 1977).

[35] See G. Ziebura, "Interne Faktoren des französischen Hochimperialismus 1871-1914," in: G. Ziebura and H.G. Haupt (eds.), *Wirtschaft und Gesellschaft in Frankreich seit 1789*, NWB 76 (Gütersloh, 1975).

[36] In Yugoslavia, for instance, France was the most important shareholder (17 percent), but only counted for 2.5 percent of the imports as compared to Germany's 26.7 percent; in the same year Bulgaria obtained as much as 61 percent of its imports from Germany and delivered 47.6 percent of its exports there, while France held 11.4 percent of the capital shares. See the article by A.S. Milward in: M. Lévy-Leboyer (ed.), *La position*, pp. 299-311.

and southeastern European countries, as these loans by no means provided a remedy to overcome the crisis.[37] In other words, the most important instrument of economic penetration proved to be deficient. Therefore, after 1934 a general withdrawal of French capital began from the countries of this region, a process that was accelerated after the Munich agreement.[38] The attempt to promote Franco-Russian relations as a counterforce to Germany's growing influence in Eastern and southeastern Europe by concluding a trade agreement failed as well; not even the signing of the nonaggression treaty could alter that.[39] A report from the French ambassador in Prague, dated December 28, 1938, to the Quai d'Orsay demonstrates that contemporaries distinctly perceived the development. It reads: "The collapse of the French system was not brought about by the events of last September alone. The causes can be found in the fact that France has neglected the economic side of the struggle for influence far too much."[40]

These unsuccessful attempts to gain status in the field of informal imperialism[41] constituted one among the many reasons why France had tried its luck within its own colonial empire since the early 1930s in the face of growing economic and political difficulties. But this policy also boomeranged. The attempt linked to such a policy, namely, to build up a large area economy, proved to be far off target: rather than offsetting internal and external economic difficulties, it aggravated them. Trade relations did intensify, though: the share of imports from the colonies increased from 12 percent in 1929 to 28.5 percent in 1936 and the portion of exports to the colonies from 18.8 percent to 33 percent. Yet, in terms of the actual value of the goods exchanged, the level of 1929 could not be reached again.[42] Export of capital certainly underwent a boom: it

[37] E. Kohlruss, *Kapitalanlagen,* p. 89.

[38] See A. Teichova, *An Economic Background to Munich* (Cambridge, 1974); the same in: M. Lévy-Leboyer, *La position,* pp. 331-338; J.-B. Duroselle, *La décadence,* pp. 172-381. In December 1938 the Schneider group had to sell their Skoda shares, thus allowing Germany to step in.

[39] For details see, R. Girault, "Les relations franco-soviétiques devant la crise économique de 1929," *Revue d'Histoire moderne et contemporaine* (April-June 1980), pp. 237-257.

[40] Quoted in J.-B. Duroselle, *La décadence,* p. 224.

[41] Cf. G. Soutou, "L'impérialisme du pauvre," *Relations internationales,* vol. 20, no.7 (1976): 219-239.

[42] H. Dubief, *Le déclin,* p. 41.

rose from 4.1 billion francs in 1914 (approximately 9 percent of the overall capital export) to 19.3 billion francs (or 17.5 billion gold francs) in 1940–an estimate that may be rather too high[43] but that nevertheless reflects the considerable French efforts. Many people perceived the colonial empire to be *la plus grande France*, a kind of life buoy for both French capitalism and the French position of strength in the world.

In reality it was a sad act of calculated optimism, a kind of self-deception, to be more precise. Not only did the "disclosure," let alone development, of the colonies make no headway whatsoever,[44] turning to the colonies was not even sufficient to compensate for the low profitability of the capital invested in metropolitan France. Hence, since this was a preferential area of trade, the Malthusian traits of both economy and society were reinforced. The combined orientation toward the interests of agriculture and toward privileged relations with the colonial empire seemed to render the modernization of the means of production unnecessary, thus inevitably undermining the French position in international trade and politics.

THE INTERNAL CRISIS OF SOCIETY

A final explanation for the development as described so far, however, requires a look at the transformation of the balance of power within French society. The second half of the 1920s seemed to suggest that the bourgeoisie was heading for a new heyday on the basis of Poincaré's policy of stabilization and under the impulse given by the modern groups of industrial capitalists. Whatever hopes may have been linked to that were thoroughly destroyed by the Depression of 1931. Now the bourgeoisie not only was on the defensive but had to experience a process of decay that affected the structure of society as a whole. Although the studies undertaken so far do not make that clear enough,[45] it is true as far as the aggra-

[43] The figures concerning the extent of the export of capital to the colonies differ; see, in particular, "L'investissement français dans l'Empire colonial: l'enquête du gouvernement de Vichy (1943)," in *Revue historique* (Oct.-Dec. 1974): 409-432; the same author in: M. Lévy-Leboyer, *La position*, pp. 388-396; J.-B. Duroselle, *La décadence*, pp. 225ff; and A. Teichova, *Economic Background*.

[44] The metropolitan capital was used mainly in the interest of the mother country to improve the infrastructure in order to facilitate transport to the coast.

vation of the traditional antagonism between capital and labor after 1934 is concerned, as well as the crisis of social and political consciousness within all classes and particularly within the different sections of the bourgeoisie. On the one hand, the propertied classes developed closer ties when confronted with the threat of the Popular Front; on the other hand, they were impelled by the constant fear of revolutionary change to invest their income in gold and real estate or to transfer it to foreign countries, which further shook the economic foundations already weakened by the loss of capital since World War I.[46]

This situation, which I have only roughly outlined, had two effects, which also proved to be decisive for the functioning of the political system. First, the traditional coalition cut between the middle and lower bourgeoisie and the farmers, who, of all the social classes, had suffered most from the Depression[47] and who were now opening up to influences from both the Right (antiparliamentarianism) and the Left (broadening of the *electoral basis* of the Socialist party and even of the Communists in the country). And second, the bourgeoisie itself impaired its power basis by continual internal division. These partisan groups, represented by the Radical Socialist party, were pushed into the leftist camp by the deflationist party of the authoritarian and reactionary rightist cabinets (Tardien, Laval), which constituted the final bourgeois attempt at overcoming the crisis on the back of the workers, employees, civil servants, pensioners, shopkeepers, craftsmen, and small entrepreneurs and paved the way for the victory of the Popular Front in May 1936. Sections of the more open-minded, urban bourgeoisie as well as a number of large capitalists sympathized more or less openly with ultrarightist, fascist organizations (Croix-de-feu), which could not, however, constitute a real danger to parliamentary democracy. In fact, parliamentary democracy in this case even seemed to prove

[45] Besides the treatises by C. Fohlen and H. Dubief see *Histoire de la Bourgeoisie française*, vol. 2 (Paris, 1962); G. Dupeux, *La société française 1789-1960* (Paris, 1964); Comité international des sciences historiques (ed.), *Mouvement ouvriers et dépressions économiques de 1929 a 1939* (Assen, 1966).

[46] P. Sorlin, *La société*, pp. 69-81.

[47] The income of the farmers fell from 43 billion francs in 1928 to 18.5 in 1935; P. Sorlin, *La société*, p. 93; see also D. Halévy, *Visites aux paysans du Centre 1907-1934* (Paris, 1934).

itself capable of integration.[48] The main reason for this phenomenon lies in the fact that the lower and middle bourgeoisie had suffered less from the Depression than it had in Germany; it was split in terms of ideology but was not economically declassed.

Admittedly, the impression forces itself upon us that the continuation of the parliamentary regime, more by chance than by design, is due much more to the exhaustion of the two socioideological camps, which manifested itself in their inability to cope with the Depression. The crisis was intensified by the rule of the conservatives, and, although the Popular Front did satisfy the backlog of needed social reforms, it could not, in spite of some initial success, overcome the economic crisis either.[49] After the failure of the Popular Front the French went back almost as a matter of course to the most banal parliamentary combination the Third Republic had to offer: Right plus Center plus Radical Socialist party. And it was this of all coalitions that in 1939 made France rise for the last time by increasing its armament efforts, achieving a certain emancipation from the "English governess," and entering a confrontation with Germany.[50]

It was too late now, and obviously the domestic political situation also remained fragile. It has been said time and again that the Left as well as the Right was deeply split when it came to facing the challenge of the Nazis. In both camps pacifists, anti-communists, and antifascists (the "hawks") were fighting fierce ideological trench wars.

[48] Industrial magnates from heavy industry and the modern sector (Wendel, Renault, Michelin, Mercier, Coty) as well as some banks supported the Croix-de-feu movement, which was able to increase the number of members from 35,000 in 1934 to some 450,000 in 1936; the movement's importance, however, was overrated by contemporaries. Compare H. Dubief, *Le déclin*, pp. 57-60, 169; P. Machefer, *Ligues et fascismes en France 1919-1939* (Paris, 1974); K.-J. Müller, "Die französische Rechte und der Faschismus in Frankreich 1924-1932," in: D. Stegmann, J.B. Wendt, and P. Witt (eds.), *Industrielle Gesellschaft und politisches System: Festschrift für Fritz Fischer* (Bonn, 1978), pp. 413-430; and particularly D. Irvine, *French Conservatives in Crisis: The Republican Federation of France in the 1930s* (Baton Rouge, La., 1979).

[49] For the causes see the articles by J.-M. Jeanneney and P. Mendès France, in: *Léon Blum: Chef du gouvernement 1936-1937* (Paris, 1967).

[50] Compare J.-P. Azéma, "Die französische Politik am Vorabend des Krieges," in: W. Benz, H. Graml (eds.), *Sommer 1939: Die Grossmächte und der europäische Krieg* (Stuttgart, 1979), pp. 280-313, as well as the articles by R. Girault and F. Bédarida, in: See R. Rémond and J. Bourdin (eds.), *Edouard Daladier. Chef de gouvernement, avril 1938–septembre 1939* (Paris, 1977).

Within these groups there were anglophiles and anglophobes, which made the confusion complete. Associations with a high degree of organization[51] and influence in society, such as the union of the public school teachers, the Comite de vigilance des Intellectuels antifascistes, or the war veterans were bulwarks of a kind of pacifism that had grown deep roots, particularly in the minds of many peasants because they had paid the heaviest toll of lives during World War I.[52] Within certain parties of the Right, a virulent anticommunism pushed back any hostility towards Italy and towards Germany as well[53] here, the cadres of the future Vichy regime were formed on the basis of a national defeatism.[54]

As in all late phases of social reproduction, a host of complete contradictions can be found in the France of the 1930s, shedding a light on a process of decay, which (and this is the first inconsistency) only few people notice and assimilate intellectually. In addition, there was the mistaken appraisal of the economic, political, and military-strategic position of the country–the kind of blindness that afflicts an essentially self-centered and selfish society whose ultimate fear is a change of traditional habits, even where these habits have become the source of grave economic disparities.[55] That paved the way to a paralysis of the social hierarchy, a lack of mobility, and demographic stagnation.[56]

On the other hand, the intellectuals, and especially those of the younger generation, were up in arms against this bourgeois status quo, questioned the bourgeois system of values, and constantly used the phrase "civilization crisis." All revolutionary ideologies were echoed sympathetically, albeit faintly, by members of the intelli-

[51] See M. Cointet-Labrousse, "Le Syndicat National des Instituteurs, le pacifisme et l'Allemagne," in: Centre nationale de la recherche scientifique, *Les relations franco-allemandes*, pp. 137-150.

[52] The novels by Jean Giono give a lively impression of that; see his manifesto "Lettre aux paysans sur la pauvreté et la paix" (1938).

[53] See R. Rémond, *La droite en France* (Paris, 1968), vol. 1, pp. 229ff.; R.H. Höhne, *Faktoren des aussenpolitischen Meinungs-und Willensbildungsprozesses innerhalb der gemässigten Rechten Frankreichs in den Jahren 1934-1936*, Diss. Free University of Berlin (1968).

[54] F. Bédarida, *Daladier*, pp. 240.

[55] C. Fohlen, *La France*, pp. 179.

[56] There was no excess of births after 1935. The number of high school graduates serves as a good indicator for that: it only increased from 8,000 in 1913 to 15,000 in 1935. Quoted in J.-B. Duroselle, *La décdence*, pp. 19.

gentsia. Some began to glorify violence, propagated insurgency, or lapsed into cynicism. Others screamed out their desperation or fell into resignation. All this activity remained superficial and without a goal. Significantly, though, there were quite a few who went through the whole ideological spectrum from the far Left to the far Right (or vice versa). Only after the attempted storming of the house of representatives by radical rightist groups on February 6, 1934, did the political constellations become somewhat more disentangled.[57] Still, these intellectuals expressed a feeling of uneasiness that could be detected behind all their self-righteousness. Could one possibly conceive of a society that was as much the antithesis of fascism as the French of those years?

But the widening gap between the requirements of a status quo power and the means available to it was not caused by the "decadence" of a society that was unable to close the gap; on the contrary, the French society of the 1930s portrayed the logical development of those structural features that had evolved in the last third of the nineteenth century and had become increasingly established. Neither World War I nor the prosperity to the 1920s had decisively altered this process. On the contrary, the social, economic, and international crisis of the 1930s strenghthened the reflexes of self-assertion (even against French fascist forces)–admittedly on the basis of defending the status quo, both internally and externally. Compared to communism or fascism, this seemed to be a far more liveable arrangement, in spite of its deficiencies and limitations. It was the tragedy of this society that it had to face a regime with an excessive drive to power, prepared to dare everything, including self-destruction (according to Hitler). Even if war and defeat were thus programmed, this society, which made so pitiful an impression in comparison to others, was able to develop in the long run more power of survival and renewal than a regime that disappeared from history after its brief and powerful strong-man act.

[57] See H. Dubief, *Le déclin,* pp. 60-66; J.-L. Loubet del Bayle, *Les Non-conformistes des années 30* (Paris, 1969); J. Touchard, in: *Tendances politiques dans la vie française depuis 1789* (Paris, 1960); Detaille, in: Centre de recherche scientifique, *Les relations franco-allemandes,* pp. 77-86.

Chapter 23

TRANSITION FROM AUTHORITARIAN REGIMES: THE CONTRASTING CASES OF BRAZIL AND PORTUGAL

Thomas Bruneau

CONTRASTING CASES IN COMPARATIVE PERSPECTIVE

The mid-1970s saw at least three distinct patterns of regime changes in Southern Europe and parts of the Third World. In the more developed Latin American countries of Argentina, Chile, and Uruguay military coups led to repressive regimes, and there was a generalized concern with the "crisis of democracy" in the highly industrialized world. Revolutions occurred in Ethiopia, Iran, and Nicaragua, and much of Southern Africa became independent also under generally hegemonic one-party systems. In Greece, Portugal, and Spain as well as Brazil, the Dominican Republic, Ecuador, and Peru transitions from authoritarian regimes were initiated and in most cases completed. In this chapter I will describe and analyze the cases of transition in Brazil and Portugal as illustrative of the more general processes of change. These are very different countries, having in common mainly the language and differing with regard to location and size, nature of the authoritarian regime, and sequence and degree of transition. These two cases are not "typical," as indeed no single case is, but they do seem to include most of the elements found in the other Southern European and South American cases of transition. In Portugal the regime that was replaced, the Estado Novo, was similar to Franco's regime in Spain, and the speed of the transition was similar to the collapse of the Greek military regime. But unlike the other cases of transition, Portugal underwent a revolution that in fact gave way to constitutional democracy but as easily could have resulted in another authoritarian regime of the Left or the Right under either civil or military control. In Brazil the transition continues; the process of negotiation and withdrawal of the military from direct control has so far taken eight years, which is longer than in either Ecuador or Peru, and has been even more complex than the transition in Spain, not to mention that in Greece, where the military regime called back civilian politicians less than a week after the debacle in Cyprus.

There is no general theory yet concerning transitions, and the work so far available cannot encompass the present cases from Southern Europe and South America, let alone the shift in Nigeria and the return from the emergency in India. It remains to be seen how the promised transitions in Argentina and Uruguay can be included in a general approach, when one is formulated.[1] What are crucial here are the origins rather than the maintenance of constitutional democracy, although the processes involved in the former cannot be unrelated to the latter. The relatively abundant literature on the maintenance of democracy is not particularly relevant for analyzing its origins, with the exception of the instances where democracy failed.[2] The two cases dealt with here are offered as suggestive of a more general process of transition. Although differing from each other, they each bear similarities to other cases. In order to compare the two cases I will provide material according to the following categories: speed of transition, sequence of events, actors involved, and outcomes, including recent electoral results. The analysis will be based on this material, and a question will be raised as to the possible cyclical nature of regime changes.

[1] The most elaborate efforts to formulate a general theory, or even an approach, can be found in the papers presented in the series "Prospects for Democracy: Transitions from Authoritarian Rule in Latin America and Southern Europe," Latin American Program, Woodrow Wilson International Center for Scholars, Washington, D.C., 1979-1981. For a summary see Kevin J. Middlebrook, "Prospects for Democracy: Regime Transformation and Transitions from Authoritarian Rule," Working Paper 62, the Wilson Center.

[2] I have in mind here the stimulating essay by Juan J. Linz, *The Breakdown of Democratic Regimes: Crisis, Breakdown, and Reequilibration* (Baltimore: Johns Hopkins University Press, 1978). On the distinction between genesis and maintenance see Dankwart A. Rustow, "Transitions to Democracy," *Comparative Politics,* April 1970, Vol. 21, pp. 337-363.

SPEED OF TRANSITION

The speed of the transitions is suggested by the terms used to describe them in each country. In Portugal the term is "revolution," which captures both the rapidity of the regime change and the extent of structural transformation of society. In Brazil the terms are "decompression" and "opening," which imply the controlled and prolonged nature of the regime change. To discuss the speed of transition we must first at least briefly consider the regime that is being replaced or opened.

In Portugal a military coup in 1926 brought an end to the extremely unstable republic and opened the way for economist and Catholic activist Antonio de Oliveira Salazar in 1928. The regime that Salazar fashioned in the early 1930s was to remain virtually intact until his illness in 1968 and for another six years under Premier Marcello Caetano. This was a conservative, authoritarian regime under personal rulership that was avowedly corporatist.[3] It was conservative in that Salazar formulated and used the regime to guarantee the predominantly pre-twentieth-century society and the remains of its colonial empire. The legitimation he used included elements of Portugal's past as one of the oldest nation-states, its colonial and "civilizing" mission, and Catholic teaching regarding authority and nonconflictual interest representation. It was authoritarian in that conflict was not structured into the system and all policy decisions were made without significant representation from all but a minute portion of individuals and groups in the society. Political parties were prohibited, the regime utilized a movement (first the Uniao Nacional and then the Accao Nacional Popular [ANP]) in the infrequent campaigns, and what passed as campaigning and political discussion were allowed only immediately before the elections for the National Assembly–which was in any case not a policymaking body. Voting in these elections was circumscribed by requirements of age, sex, and position, and the size of the electorate was virtually stagnant. The Corporative Chamber was not a policy-

[3] For a characterization of the regime see my "Portugal in the 1970's: From Regime to Regime," *Ibero-Amerikanisches Archiv,* December 1981, pp. 389-429, and the material cited there and, in particular, in the first five essays in Lawrence Graham and Harry Makler (eds.), *Contemporary Portugal: Revolution and its Antecendents* (Austin: The University of Texas Press, 1979).

making body either and in fact was established only in the mid-1950s, some twenty years after the regime was consolidated. The president, elected indirectly since 1959, played a small role in policymaking, and the decisions were in fact made in the Council of Ministers, or Cabinet, and mainly by Salazar.[4] After Salazar's illness and subsequent death in 1970, Marcello Caetano found it difficult to bring this regime under his control. Caetano did seek to innovate in the structure of the regime, its processes, and in particular with regard to the policy of retaining the African colonies at all costs. Due to the regime's intransigence in refusing the colonies independence even after some thirteen years of guerrilla wars, a group within the military, the Armed Forces Movement (MFA), overthrew this longest-lived rightist authoritarian regime on 25 April 1974. The coup not only demolished the government of Marcello Caetano, but, by outlawing the ANP, abolishing the structures of repression, and dismantling the groups and movements which were appendages of the government, it led to the complete breakdown of this archaic regime. The transition from the Estado Novo took approximately one week in that by 1 May there was a new government, the Junta of National Salvation, political parties were forming, and the population was becoming rapidly mobilized into political activities through parties, unions, and myriad local and sectoral groups.

In Brazil the military came to power on 1 April 1964 when it acted as an institution in overthrowing what it considered to be the dangerous government of the populistic president, Joao Goulart. The coup ended what has been called Brazil's "experiment with democracy," which had begun in 1945 when the military overthrew the dictatorship, also an Estado Novo, of President Getulio Vargas.[5] The intervening nineteen years had seen substantial social and economic change in Brazil, but not the institutionalization of a regime beyond the charismatic and contingent legacy of Vargas, who had in fact returned as president in 1950-1954. During these two decades politics was frequently unstable, political parties were extremely personalistic, and the political structures, such as the

[4] On this centralization of power see in particular Lawrence Graham, "Portugal: The Decline and Collapse of an Authoritarian Order," *Sage Professional Papers in Comparative Politics*, Vol. 5, No. 53, 1975.

[5] Thomas Skidmore, *Politics in Brazil, 1930-1964: An Experiment in Democracy* (New York: Oxford University Press, 1967).

congress and the presidency, were poorly articulated with society. Thus an individual, such as Joao Goulart, could effectively threaten the system by his personal actions, particularly in the context of rapid political mobilization in the early 1960s following the Cuban revolution of 1959. The military, pursuant to its "moderating role," intervened in 1964 in order to rid the country of subversion, disorganization, inflation, and corruption, which threatened to radically transform economy and society.[6] This action was intended to be more broad-based than previous short-term interventions since the founding of the republic in 1891, but presumably its duration and long-range effects had not been foreseen. The military, unlike their counterparts in Argentina, Chile, and Uruguay, for example, maintained a normal schedule for elections, and the congress generally remained open. They did, however, ultimately create what has come to be termed a "bureaucratic-authoritarian regime" that by the early 1970s was extremely nondemocratic, centralized, and repressive. This occurred due to factors relevant to the military as institution, the political opposition, and the economic situation.

Between 1964 and 1974 each succeeding military president promised a return to democracy by the end of his strictly defined tenure in office. However, beginning with the first Institutional Act immediately after the coup, the military legitimated their rule according to their own terms and increasingly drew upon the doctrine of national security for their justification to govern.[7] This justification places much emphasis on enemies, internal and external, and the military deemed the political opposition, both the traditional politicians and their parties and then the rural and urban guerrillas, sufficiently dangerous to consolidate their authoritarian rule and institutionalize severe repression. The military also found a convenient further justification, and at times *the* justification for external purposes, in the "economic miracle" of 1968-1974 during which the economy grew at 10 percent per year with substantial deepening of industrialization that aided Brazil in its pretensions to great power status.

[6] See in particular Alfred Stepan, *The Military in Politics: Changing Patterns in Brazil* (Princeton: Princeton University Press, 1971).

[7] For a discussion of the doctrine see Jose Comblin, *The Ideology of National Security: Military Power in Latin America* (Maryknoll, N.Y.: Orbis Books, 1979).

The political processes during this period left an increasingly restricted area in which civilian politicians and pressure groups could operate. In October 1965 gubernatorial elections were held in eleven states, and opponents to the military won in two important states. President Castelo Branco, against hard line opposition within the military, ensured the results but was forced to decree the second Institutional Act, which abolished the already established political parties, created a progovernment party ARENA (National Renovating Alliance) and the loyal opposition MDB (Brazilian Democratic Movement), and ensured that elections to the governorships and the presidency would become indirect. The next plateau would be with the fifth Institutional Act of 13 December 1968 following on a wave of opposition, criticism, and intransigence in the government-dominated congress. The fifth Institutional Act was decreed by President Costa e Silva and included as key measures: temporary closing of congress; increased removal of political rights from individuals; and empowerment of the president to remove the right of habeas corpus and to decree the death penalty in cases of subversion. The Brazilian authoritarian regime with this act was clearly absolutist and with the arbitrary removal of rights allowed for the elaboration of a system of repression that made Brazil infamous for human rights violations. The theme during this period was development and security, and there is no doubt that the country developed economically under military auspices in which the state played a key role. It was in any case a dictatorship.[8]

The military since 1964 has governed as an institution with the periodic transfer of power from one general to another. The military has remained remarkably unified, but this is not to say that there are not different orientations within the institution. The transition began in 1974 when General Ernesto Geisel took office in March as president. General Geisel was a member of the Castellista (from President Castelo Branco) group, which gave more emphasis to a legalist and democratically oriented tradition in the military. Geisel himself was conservative and authoritarian, so the transition represents more than a fluke of his personality.[9] In 1974 he initiated

[8] For this period see in particular Peter Flynn, *Brazil: A Political Analysis* (Boulder, Colo.: Westview Press, 1978). For the behavior of the Church in the most dictatorial period see my *The Political Transformation of the Brazilian Catholic Church* (Cambridge: Cambridge University Press, 1974).

a process of decompression that he stated would be slow, gradual, and sure. Whether it is sure remains to be seen, but at the minimum he ensured that his successor, General Joao Batista Figueiredo, would maintain the same orientation and continue the decompression or opening. The transition has been so far eight years in the making, and the next planned stage will be in 1984 with the indirect election for President Figueiredo's successor.

The speed of transition is very different in these two cases. This is due to the fact that in Portugal the conservative authoritarian regime collapsed in a coup whereas in Brazil the transition takes place within the regime, under its supervision, and generally on its terms. The sequence, then, differs in that in Portugal the coup led to a revolution that then led to constitutional democracy, whereas in Brazil the coup overthrew the unstable democracy that evolved into a repressive military regime that is now undergoing a transition, possibly to a constitutional democracy. This inverted sequence distinguishes Portugal from all the other cases of transition where the processes and timetable of transition has been more heavily influenced by the previous regime, although in Greece, and to a lesser extent in Ecuador and Peru, this influence was much diminished. In the twentieth century, revolution evolving into constitutional democracy is most unusual, and the sequence of events in Portugal must be analyzed with this in mind.

SEQUENCE OF EVENTS

The Portuguese military coup of 25 April 1974 turned into a revolution for three main reasons:

1. The Estado Novo, by the 1970s, found its justification in its intransigence and lack of links with society. With time (and in this case it was almost fifty years) the regime became archaic and Marcello Caetano, despite his best intentions, was unable to innovate. He could not innovate in domestic political processes and structures, nor could he innovate with regard to Africa.[10] The latter situation led to the coup, and with the coup the regime and the system it guaranteed simply disintegrated, leaving few structures or institutions on which to build

[9] For insights into Geisel's government see Walder de Goes, *O Brasil do General Geisel* (Rio de Janeiro: Nova Fronteira, 1978).

[10] This is probably the clearest point in Marcello Caetano's *Depoimento* (Rio de Janeiro: Record, 1974).

another regime.

2. The MFA was effective at military matters of fighting guerrilla wars in far-flung colonies and making the coup, but being composed of middle-level career officers (captains, a few majors, and one brigadier general) with little civilian experience in a regime where politics was prohibited, it was politically naive. From the first day of the coup the officers were upstaged: first by General Spinola, who, although not involved in the coup, became head of the Junta of National Salvation and then president, and then by the rapidly forming political parties, which were not even provided for in the MFA program of 25 April. Elements within the MFA would be increasingly influenced by the Portuguese Communist party (PCP), which provided for the MFA both an organizational apparatus and, more importantly, an interpretation of the MFA's role as a liberation movement in revolutionizing society. From the summer of 1974 until the spring of 1975 politics revolved around the conflict between General Spinola, and the individuals and groups around him, and the MFA with the influence of the PCP and groups to its Left. As General Spinola occupied the Center and Right, the MFA moved further to the Left. In their competition for power in this little-structured environment left by the collapse of the Estado Novo, a dynamic was established whereby political mobilization was promoted and socioeconomic structures changed in line with a variety of inconsistent and competing radical programs for the transformation of Portugal.[11]
3. No single group, party, or institution monopolized power. The PCP had as good a claim as any party but was opposed from its right by the Socialist party (PS), the Popular Democratic party (PPD, later called the PSD), and others, and from its left by a myriad of antirevisionist, Maoist, and even anarchist parties and movements. The MFA should have been supreme but was upstaged, influenced by others, and finally split into at least three main currents: the PCP-related group, which included the premier between July 1974 and September 1975, Vasco Conçalves; the far left group which was led by General Otelo Saraiva de Carvalho who headed the main security force - COPCON - between July 1974 and November 1975; and a moderate group, not closely related to any political party, which was symbolized by Major Melo Antunes. As these individuals, groups, and parties competed for power, such as it was, the state was further dismantled but a regime was not created. The result was that one group stymied another and there was no nexus or center of power. Indeed, in mid- and late 1975 there was a generalized and well-founded fear of civil war as the military was divided and arms had been passed on to civilians.

A constitutional democracy began to emerge only in late 1975 when the moderates in the MFA, in putting down an attempted coup by the Left in the military, began to reestablish discipline in the military, brought the PCP under control, and ensured space for the participation of parties to its Right, including the PS, PPD, and

[11] Of particular utility in understanding this period is Insight Team of the Sunday *London Times, Insight on Portugal: The Year of the Captains* (London: Andre Deutsch, 1975).

Social Democratic Center (CDS). This process, led to a great extent by a member of the MFA moderates and military head of the successful defense against the leftist coup, General Ramalho Eanes, eliminated both the leftist option of the PCP and fringe groups and a rightist option to reestablish a dictatorship. He, others in the MFA, and ultimately the political parties elaborated a pact that ensured the transition to a constitutional democracy by providing for elections to the Assembly of the Republic in April 1976, presidential elections in June, and implementation of a constitution earlier in the spring. The delegates to the constituent assembly had been elected on 25 April 1975, but during the process of radicalization it did not appear that the constitution would ever be implemented. The document that did emerge was long, strongly influenced by the PS and the PCP, and extremely progressive in committing Portugal to a socializing path that would be supervised by the legacy of the MFA, which was a Revolutionary Council (CR) made up of the MFA moderates. What is more, this legacy was also continued in the person of president elect Ramalho Eanes, who was supported by the PS, PPD, and CDS in a four-way race in which he won 62 percent of the popular vote. As the regime that was defined in the constitution of 1976 was semipresidential or bipolar, it seemed clear that the president would also supervise the transition in terms of both the regime and the socioeconomic system that was disarticulated.

In the Assembly elections of April 1976 no party won a majority, but the PS with 35 percent of the votes and 107 seats (of 263) won a plurality. Politics between August 1976, when the first constitutional government was sworn in, and December 1979, when interim elections were held, centered on the difficulty of a government's staying in power and taking the necessary but difficult measures to consolidate the regime and reintegrate the socioeconomic system without entering into coalitions. Only the PCP predated the coup as an organized party, and the PS, in attempting to build itself as a viable organization, was unwilling, and Mario Soares, its general secretary, thought it unnecessary, to enter into coalitions. Consequently there were five governments in this three-year period, and the president drew upon his formal powers in taking an increasingly active part in dismissing and forming governments, vetoing legislation, taking the initiative in regional and foreign policy, and, as commander in chief with the support of the CR, supervising the military.[12]

In the interim elections to the Assembly of the Republic in December 1979 the Democratic Alliance (AD), a coalition of the PSD, CDS, and small PPM (Popular Monarchist Party), won 43 percent of the vote (compared with 27 percent for the PS and 19 percent for the PCP) and received a majority of 128 seats in the 250-seat Assembly. These results were in general terms duplicated in the regular elections in October 1980 when the AD increased its share of the vote to 45 percent. As the socioeconomic system has been sorted out since 1976 it became clear to the members of the AD that they were not in sympathy with the collectivist and socializing measures of the constitution of 1976, which in any case are probably unworkable in a country as peripheral as Portugal in the current economic climate.[13] The AD also lacked sympathy with President Ramalho Eanes, and not only because of his full use of powers in the semipresidential system. Politics between December 1979 and the fall of 1982 were a struggle between the AD government and the president, and at times the CR, over policies and jurisdiction.[14] The solution envisioned by the president of the PSD and prime minister until his accidental death in November 1980, Sa Carneiro, was the election of a president who would support the AD and put the constitution to a referendum. However, the untimely deaths of Sa Carneiro and Amaro da Costa, an influential member of the CDS and minister of defense, were followed by the defeat of the AD candidate when General Soares Carneiro (no relationship to either Mario Soares of the PS or Sa Carneiro) came in a poor second to the incumbent's 56 percent of the vote in the December 1980 elections.

[12] A very useful discussion of the political system in this period is Pedro Santana Lopes and Jose Durao Barroso, *Sistema de Governo e Sistema Partidario* (Lisbon: Livraria Bertrand, 1980).

[13] On the lack of implementation of these measures see, for example, Marcelo Rebelo de Sousa, *Direito Constitucional* (Braga: Livraria Cruz, 1979).

[14] On the battles between the AD and the president over the question of jurisdiction see my "Politics in Portugal, 1976-81, and Revision of the Constitution," paper presented to the SSRC Conference on Contemporary Change in Southern Europe, Madrid, November 1981.

The solution finally implemented was to revise the constitution, which was carried out between mid-1981 and late 1982 in negotiations with the PS. The constitution could be revised in this second legislature with a simple majority without allowance for a presidential veto. That the PS of Mario Soares, which had been instrumental in formulating the constitution between 1975 and 1976, could agree to the revision indicates the political flexibility of Soares and suggests the ongoing tentative nature of the political institutions in Portugal. The revision removed the more socializing aspects of the constitution, and, more importantly, the system became less semipresidential and more parliamentary in nature. The CR was abolished, the role of the president in forming and dismissing governments was diminished, and his veto was circumscribed as was his role in military affairs. His role as defined in this constitution is more that of a figurehead, with the basis of power to be found in the Assembly and the government, and consequently in the political parties. However, although Portugal is indeed a constitutional democracy, it is, in my view, still tentative in that the political parties (except for the PCP) are new and still very personal. With constitutional revision the regime has reached a plateau, but the transition is not fully consolidated.[15]

In Brazil the sequence of events in the opening is in some respects a mirror image of the process of closing a decade earlier.[16] But the present process is more under the control of the regime, or at least one group in it, there is a timetable, and it is planned: the opening is more intentional, calculated, and carefully negotiated than was the closing. The context by the time President Ernesto Geisel took office in March 1974 was very different from that confronted by his three military president predecessors. The economic miracle was in the process of disappearing, and the rapid increase in the price of oil (80 percent of which is imported in Brazil) would make the economic situation particularily difficult for this semideveloped country. By 1974 it was also clear that the benefits from the miracle were distributed very unequally, with an increasing concentration of

[15] The politics of constitutional revision and the policy implications arising from the changes will be the topic of a research project I will be working on in Portugal in late 1983.

[16] The mirror image is noted by Bolivar Lamounier in his "Notes on the Study of Re-Democratization," Working Paper 58, the Wilson Center.

income. And in this society of some 120 million people there was a great deal of activity and dynamism that preceded the economic miracle but gained momentum during it and became manifested in the formation of groups and movements that made demands on the government. In short, civil society became further defined and articulated, and the authoritarian regime (unlike a totalitarian regime) could not rely exclusively on repression as the legitimacy from the economic miracle disappeared.[17] There were pressures from society, and Geisel's strategy would be to respond to them in a negotiated transition in order to broaden the base of legitimacy of the regime.

The first indication of the need to broaden this legitimacy and engage in discussions or negotiations with a political opposition were the regularly scheduled congressional elections in November 1974. Since the MDB was founded nine years earlier, there was question as to its viability as the loyal opposition, and the regime had to encourage politicians to join it. The MDB's situation in Brazil, where it had 28 percent of the seats in the Assembly and but 11 percent in the Senate, was analogous to the role of the political opposition(s) in Mexico where the PRI is hegemonic.[18] In November 1974, however, in the context noted above and with reasonably free access to the media, the results of the elections surprised not only the regime but even the MDB. The MDB won 16 of the 22 Senate seats being contested, its representation went from 87 to 160 (or 44 percent) in the Assembly, and it won in six state assemblies. As had happened almost ten years before under President Castelo Branco, President Geisel allowed the election results to stand but was obliged to make concessions in that he utilized the fifth Institutional Act to remove the political rights of some politicians, tolerated a certain amount of security force repression during the fear of subversion generated by events in Portugal at the height of radicalization, and worked to consolidate his personal control in directing the nature and schedule of the decompression that was clearly desired. A plateau in this consolidation occurred in 1976 when President Geisel

[17] For analyses of context see the chapters by Faucher and Sanders in Thomas Bruneau and Philippe Faucher (eds.), *Authoritarian Capitalism: Brazil's Contemporary Economic and Political* Development (Boulder, Colo.: Westview Press, 1981).

[18] For this point and an analysis of the opening see the very insightful paper by David V. Fleischer, "Da 'Distensao' a 'Abertura': A Evolucao Socio-Politica do Brasil na Decade de 80," 1982, unpublished.

dismissed the commander of the Second Army in Sao Paulo, where severe repression was taking place, and the president, as commander in chief, received the support of the other commanders. He was thus in a position to continue to implement his plan for decompression.

The next critical event was the congressional elections in 1978 when both federal and state deputies would be elected, as well as one-third of the Senate. Elections in the municipalities in 1976 confirmed the trends from the 1974 elections, which showed the MDB gaining in the urban areas, and principally the center south, and ARENA retaining its support in the rural areas, particularly in the less-developed north, northeast, and center west. It was anticipated that the MDB would win forty-four Senate seats, resulting in a simple majority in the Assembly and a two-thirds majority in the Senate, and gain control of more state assemblies. With these results the regime would lose control of the timetable and momentum of the opening; although congress and the state assemblies are not particularly important for policy formation, they do elect the governors and the president. In Geisel's plan it was essential that he maintain control of the momentum, in particular to ensure support within the military for the opening and to determine his successor as well as his successor's power vis-à-vis congress. President Geisel created an opportunity in early 1977 that justified his utilization of the power of the fifth Institutional Act, closed congress for two weeks in April, and modified the constitution. In this series of measures, which was called the April Package, the president determined the following: the one-third of the Senate to be elected in 1978 would be elected indirectly by the state and municipal representatives; the governors, to be elected directly in 1978, would be elected indirectly and the electoral colleges for these were to include aldermen from all municipalities, where ARENA held a majority; the electoral lists for the federal deputies were to be based on population size rather than number of registered voters; constitutional amendments could be passed by a simple majority in congress; the Lei Falcao from 1976 severely restricting political propaganda on radio and television became permanent; and the presidential term after Geisel was extended to six years. The president also utilized the fifth Institutional Act to remove political rights. In the elections

ARENA won twenty of the twenty-one governorships and maintained majorities in both houses of congress. The regime's control was thus guaranteed for the next eight years, and the president could then make concessions on a number of other features of a decompression.

These features have allowed a fuller expression and representation of civil society and have been implemented in a lopsided process of negotiation with the opposition. They have, however, resulted in a much less repressive regime today than was the case in the early 1970s. The most important of these features are the following: in 1978 prior censorship on the printed media was lifted; in January 1979 the fifth Institutional Act was abolished, although the regime can still rely on the Law of National Security and declare states of emergency and of siege; in late 1979 a general amnesty for political crimes was decreed and most political figures who had gone into exile returned; and in November 1979 a party reform was passed whereby elections for the governorships would be direct in 1982 and the two-party system expanded to include a greater, although still limited, number of parties.[19] The regime maintained the initiative in all of these reforms and did an effective job of coopting the opposition and, through the party reform, splitting it, thereby ensuring for the regime substantial room to maneuver. The most recent package for ensuring a continuing opening while retaining control was announced in November 1981 in preparation for the elections in November 1982. By now a term has been coined for these measures, *casuismo* which means an arbitrary and individualized measure to protect the government party: a rule for each case. In this November Package, which was decreed by Geisel's successor, President Joao Batista Figueiredo, the main intention was to ensure the predominance of the government party, the PDS, in the indirect presidential elections in 1984. One features is that the voter must vote for only one party for all the offices from governor, senator, federal deputy, and state deputy to mayor (where elected) and alderman. There is no ticket splitting. This provision favors the PDS as it is the best organized party in the municipalities in the

[19] For fuller details on the party reform see Thomas G. Sanders in Bruneau and Faucher (eds.), *Authoritarian Capitalism,* p. 204. On the elections in the decade see Bolivar Lamounier (ed.), *Voto de Desconfianca: Eleicoes e Mudanca Politica no Brasil, 1970-1979* (Petropolis: Vozes, 1980).

interior. Thus the PDS has a bit more than one half of the 420 federal deputies, but it has 3,000 of the 4,000 city councils and some 26,000 of 30,000 aldermen. Another feature is that alliances or coalitions between parties are not permitted. Thus each party must present a complete list of candidates, and again the PDS benefits as it has the biggest and most elaborate implantation at all levels.[20] The opening continues but is strictly constrained by the rules and measures defined by the regime.

ACTORS INVOLVED

The sequence of events suggests the different patterns of actors and their interactions. In Portugal the crucial fact was the lack of a shift in what might be termed a ruling block in the Estado Novo even after the illness and death of its founder, Oliveira Salazar. Marcello Caetano attempted to broaden the regime, liberalize a bit, and reorient the country to Europe, but he failed.[21] The only solution was a military coup in which civilians played virtually no role. The coup itself was made by the MFA, which included approximately two hundred middle-level officers; this was most definitely not the institutional military making the coup. Only after the coup did civil society play a role in the transition, and a large role at that. As the Estado Novo collapsed myriad political parties (up to sixty in 1975), movements, workers' groups, neighborhood groups, and so on emerged that became active in all sectors and levels of society. The most important actors during this period were the MFA, General Spinola, and the PCP. Their interaction encouraged the further mobilization of these groups and movements. From 1976 the key actors became increasingly circumscribed and were basically those dealt with in the constitution. They included the president, the CR, and the political parties as represented in the Assembly. Other actors such as the armed forces, unions, and owners' groups are active but not predominant. Elections have been critical not only in determining which individuals and governing parties will rule but through constitutional revision in determining the relationship among the actors. Thus the fall 1980 elections put the AD in power

[20] *Veja*, 2 December 1981.
[21] Graham, *Portugal*, pp. 53-54.

but also ensured that the president could be reelected to oppose certain orientations to the AD. The solution for the AD, with the support of Mario Soares, was to change the institutional structure through constitutional revision, thereby giving more power to the Assembly and government. One result of this revision may be to repoliticize the military through political party involvement in naming the commanders. If this is the case then the military, which is now professionalized in nonpolitical modes, will once again become central in politics.

In Portugal a key actor, or, better, series of actors, in the transition were foreign political parties, unions, institutions, and states. These include the Socialist International, International Confederation of Free Trade Unions, the European Economic Community, NATO, International Monetary Fund, the USSR, the United States, and the Federal Republic of Germany–a suggestive list.[22] The USSR and friendly states assisted the PCP. During the height of radicalization Western entities became heavily involved in Portugal in assisting unions and parties, developing links with the military, providing funds for balance of payments support and development programs, etc. In my view the transition in Portugal was very heavily influenced by these foreign actors–countries and international institutions–which of course were not all of one piece or oriented in the same direction. This influence continues today in more delimited economic terms, and the key now is undoubtedly the proposed accession to the European Economic Community.

In Brazil, unlike Portugal, there was both a shift within the ruling block and pressures from civil society before the transition began. The Brazilian military regime, unlike the Estado Novo and military regimes in Argentina and Chile, has provided for periodic replacement of the president. Although the new president has been another general each time, the replacement has still acted to promote a certain circulation of elites and diminish somewhat the struggle over succession. There are different factions within the Brazilian military, and Geisel's coming to power in 1974 was a return to the Castellista orientation of 1964-1967.[23] This orienta-

[22] I have dealt with this little-studied international involvement in my *Politics and Nationhood: Post-Revolutionary Portugal (New York: Praeger, 1984, forthcoming).*

[23] For the various orientations see in particular Ronald Schneider, *The Political System of Brazil* (New York: Columbia University Press, 1971).

tion, in contrast to a *linha dura,* or hard-line, has favored an opening as a way to build support while maintaining the essential features of the regime. Geisel had to consolidate his power in 1975 and 1976 to bring about the opening and in 1977 had to further tighten up in order to provide for a successor who would continue the opening. This involved a complex and potentially dangerous strategy of dismissing in October 1977 the minister of the Army, General Frota, who aspired to be the next president. This could have triggered a coup but was handled very effectively by Geisel, who had the support of General Hugo Abreu, his military liaison, probably because he himself expected to succeed Geisel. On discovering that Figueiredo was to be the candidate Abreu resigned and sought support from the commanders for his candidacy, seeing that he did not receive the support of the MDB.[24] What this brief sketch attempts to show is that there are indeed different factions within the military. And, although there has been a good deal of unity and periodic change of personnel in the presidency, tendencies still exist for a struggle over succession. There are, in short, pressures on unity that have made it difficult to ensure a peaceful succession, and this fact supports a strategy of opening thereby removing the military from direct and obvious control of the government.

The pressures on unity are greatly increased by what can be termed the development and articulation of civil society. During the height of the repression no group or institution except the Catholic church enjoyed sufficient autonomy to oppose the regime. By 1974 groups and movements began to emerge that criticized and made demands; civil society has become more complex. Today these groups include not only the Basic Christian Communities from the Church but neighborhood associations, cultural associations, and unions.[25] They, in conjunction with the MDB and now with the other parties, have put pressure on the government over a wide variety of issues as they seek to have interests increasingly represented in politics. Their expression, however, like the opening in general, has followed something of a pendulum course in that, for

[24] For the details of this process see Andre Gustavo Stumpf and Merval Pereira Filho, *A Segunda Guerra: Sucessao de Geisel* (Sao Paulo: Brasiliense, 1979).

[25] See the description of these groups in the article by Thomas G. Sanders in Bruneau and Faucher (eds.), *Authoritarian Capitalism.* For the Church's role in this more complex civil society see my *The Church in Brazil: The Politics of Religion* (Austin: University of Texas Press, 1982).

example, strikes that were illegal were permitted in 1978 and 1979 and then suppressed in 1980 and 1981 and the leaders of the unions prosecuted under the Law of National Security. Thus the opening has seen a broadening of the range of groups and movements that matter, but within limits and according to the terms of the regime.

It is worth contrasting the role of foreign actors in Brazil to their very important role in the Portuguese transition. In Brazil their role has been slight, and President Carter's human rights campaign, which encouraged opposition elements in pushing for the opening, in fact gave the regime more support in adopting a nationalist stance against the United States, which was attempting to tell Brazil how to behave. Foreign parties, unions, church organizations, and similar groups are involved in Brazil, but their role is not determining and is if anything gradual in results. This is due to the controlled character of the transition, the more complicated nature of Brazil than Portugal as a country, and the fact that Brazil is not located in such a well-defined security (NATO) and economic (EEC) zone as Portugal.[26]

It should be noted that despite very serious economic crises in Portugal and Brazil the transitions continue. Brazil and Portugal both have onerous foreign debts, and the balance-of-payment problems related to these have brought them to the IMF. Inflation is high in Portugal and extremely high in Brazil, unemployment is a serious problem in both countries, and the economic problems are not likely to disappear, given their respective development aspirations. These problems, despite awesome warnings by domestic and international leaders, have not halted the transitions, probably because authoritarian regimes have no better solutions than democratic ones for dealing with the generalized crisis. At least in democratic regimes where broad groups have a link with government all can take the blame for the state of the economy. Democracy is precisely a system in which more can have a say and also can assume responsibility for the resulting situation. In the case of Brazil the civilians have had very little say but through their current involvement will trade participation for some responsibility.

[26] On Brazil and Latin American security see Margaret Daly Hayes, "Security to the South: US Interests in Latin America," *International Security*, Summer 1980, pp. 130-151.

OUTCOMES

In both countries the outcomes remain tentative. Portugal has seen the transition to a democratic regime, but on the basis of the election results in 1980 the AD was able to revise the constitution substantially. This would not matter except that the political parties remain poorly organized and unstable in orientation. They do not, therefore, provide the basis for a stable government, and the rules of the game are not clearly defined, let alone agreed upon. In the municipal elections in December 1982 the AD lost ground to opposition parties, and this was sufficient for the AD government of Prime Minister Balsemao to fall. In Portugal the transition has reached a plateau but remains incomplete.

In Brazil, general elections (except for the presidency) were held in November 1982. The results, which are tentative at this writing, are as follows: the government's PDS party elected 12 governors (generally in the less developed areas), the PDMB elected 9, and the PDT 1.[27] These ten were from states with 59 percent of the area and population and where 73 percent of the sales tax was collected). In the Assembly the PDS elected 234 and in the Senate 46, with a total for the electoral college of 358. In the Assembly the combined opposition elected 245 and in the Senate 47, with a total of 328 for the electoral college. Although the PMDB received the lion's share of these seats, it must still cooperate with the other parties on most issues, and this will be difficult as will its maintaining unity in the face of the government's measures to ensure power for the PDS. The results would seem to indicate a success for the government as in these elections, constrained as they were by *casuismos,* they were clearly not rejected, enjoy ample room for maneuvering in congress, and will control the electoral college for selecting the next president in 1984. The rules of the game remain tentative in that the government through its *casuismos* takes the initiative in defining the rules, and they have been tacitly agreed to by the opposition(s), which wants to at least participate in the game. The larger rules, like

[27] The political parties in the 1982 elections were: PDS–Social Democratic party, largely a continuation of ARENA; PMDB–party of the Brazilian Democratic Movement, largely a continuation of MDB; PTB–Brazilian Labor party, continuation of Vargas's party with new leader; PDT–Democratic Workers party, formed by Lionel Brizola on losing control of PTB; PT–Workers party, the only new grass-roots party from union organizers and Church militants.

the outcome itself, remain contingent, however, as the game becomes more serious now that there are ten opposition governors, and the opposition parties will want more powers for the congress than it currently holds. It is only when the electoral system in fact determines real power that the rules and the outcome will no longer remain contingent. It should be noted that the opposition is keenly aware of the present limits on the opening, and immediately after the elections the opposition governors in the most important states indicated that they would not form a united opposition against the government.

CONCLUSIONS

On the basis of the above material, what can be said about the transitions in Portugal and Brazil and possibly more generally? Portugal is the exception, and at the same time probably the causal case, in that the coup and subsequent revolution occurred due to the inability of the old regime to change, to open. A constitutional democracy has resulted from the complex process briefly described above, but it remains tentative. In Brazil President Geisel and his group, continued now by President Figueiredo, realized that a shift in the processes and legitimation of the regime was necessary as the economy slowed down, civil society became more dynamic, and old enemies were eliminated or showed themselves to be cooptable. The interaction has been more protracted than in Spain where a controlled transition evolved into a full-fledged move into constitutional democracy. It is similar to that in Ecuador and Peru in the sense that the military began to withdraw when it became clear that it could not resolve the problems it thought it could resolve and that civilians had been unable to deal with adequately. By initiating the transition and controlling the form and timetable it has in fact broadened its support while still retaining control. This differs from all the other cases of transitions, for although the military may be ready to take power in Ecuador, or even Spain, at the present it is out of direct control. In Brazil this will begin to become clear in 1985 and probably only be true in 1990 when general direct elections are scheduled for all levels–including the presidency. Neither Portugal nor Brazil seems cyclical, barring a much more serious world economic crisis. Portugal is likely to remain unstable, but a return to a conservative authoritarian regime is unlikely with the current acceptance of democratic legitimation and extensive international ties. Brazil is still in the process of transition, and a reversal would be likely only if a more conservative group could show that it had better solutions to the economic as well as social crisis. Judging from experiences in Argentina, Chile, and Uruguay such a group does not, and in any case even in the terms of this transition the military will retain a dominant role in key areas of policymaking. The transition in Brazil has had much less impact on society, but the elections in Greece in 1981 with PASOK coming to power and the elections in Spain in 1982 with the PSOE show that once electoral systems are used for indicating who can claim power, even the unexpected can happen.

BIBLIOGRAPHY OF HENRY W. EHRMANN

BOOKS AND ARTICLES

Translation from the French of René Benjamin, *Balzac: Sein Wunderbares Leben* (Freiburg i.B.: Urban Verlag, 1927), 425 pp.

"Konkurrenz eines allgemeinverbindlichen mit einem gewöhnlichen Tarifvertrag," *Arbeitsrecht,* 18 (1931), pp. 6-14.

"Auslegungsstreitigkeiten über den Inhalt eines mehrgliedrigen Tarifvertrags," Ibid., 19 (1932), pp. 100-6.

"Recht auf Abwehrkampf bei Verletzung eines mehrgliedrigen Tarifvertrags," Ibid., pp. 400-18.

Der Mehrgliedrige Tarifvertrag (Mannheim: Bensheimer, 1932), 77 pp.

"Der Kampf einer Republik–Die Dreyfus Affaire," *Zeitschrift für Sozialismus,* Karlsbad, 14 (November 1934), pp. 458-62.

"Der de Man Plan," Ibid., 15 (December 1934), pp. 484 ff.

"Faschismus an der Macht," Ibid., 20/21 (May-June 1935), pp. 657-62.

"Die Jakobiner Legende," Ibid., 29 (February 1936), pp. 932-38.

"Strafferett i det tredje rike [Criminal Law in the Third Reich]," *Fritt Ord,* Oslo (1936), pp. 257 ff.

"Napoleon und Hitler: Bonapartismus und Faschismus," *Zeitschrift für den Sozialismus,* 31 (April 1936), pp. 989-94.

"Der Einigungskongress der Französischen Gewerkschaftsbewegung," Ibid., pp. 1004-8.

"Volksfrontwahlen in Frankreich," Ibid., 32 (May 1936), p. 1021 ff.

"Die Volksfront in Frankreich," Ibid., 34/35 (July-August 1936), pp. 1089-99.

Articles published between 1934 and 1940 appeared under a variety of pseudonyms. The listing for this period is incomplete.

"Die Französische Streikbewegung," *Rote Revue,* Zürich (1936), pp. 415 ff.

"Devaluation und Wirtschaftslage im Volksfront Frankreich," Ibid., (1937), pp. 85 ff and pp. 397 ff.

"Krig og Fred: Fransk forfatters on Munich politikken" [French Writers on Post-Munich Policy], *Samtiden* Oslo (1939), pp. 377 ff.

"Le Mouvement Ouvrier en France pendant les années 1852-1864," *International Review for Social History,* 3 (1939), pp. 231-80.

"Ein französisches Kriegstagebuch," *Der Sozialistische Kampf,* Paris (May 4, 1940), pp. 185-87.

"The Blum Experiment and the Fall of France," *Foreign Affairs,* 20 (1941), pp. 152-64.

"No Peace with German Generals," *Current History,* 3, no. 16 (December 1942), pp. 273-79.

"Washington's Plan for Germany," *New Republic* (May 3, 1943), pp. 585-87.

"The Duty of Disclosure in Parliamentary Investigations: A Comparative Study," *University of Chicago Law Review,* 11 (1944), pp. 1-25, 117-53.

"The Trade Union Movement in the Framework of the French War Economy," *Journal of Politics,* 6 (1944), pp. 263-93.

Kleiner Führer durch Amerika (Washington, D.C.: Office of the Provost Marshal, 1945), 55 pp.

"France Builds her Future," *New Republic* (December 10, 1945), pp. 786-88.

French Labor from Popular Front to Liberation (New York: Oxford University Press, 1947), 329 pp.

"French Labor Goes Left," *Foreign Affairs,* 25 (1947), pp. 465-76.

"An Experiment in Political Education, The Prisoner-of-War Schools in the U.S.," *Social Research,* 14 (1947), pp. 304-20.

"Political Forces in Present-Day France," Ibid., 15 (1948), pp. 146-69.

"France and the United Nations," NBC Radio Discussion, *University of Chicago Roundtable,* 552 (October 17, 1948), pp. 1-12.

"France between East and West," *Western Political Quarterly,* 2 (1949), pp. 74-88.

"French Views on Communism," *World Politics,* 3 (October 1950), pp. 141-51.

"The Decline of the Socialist Party," in E. Earle, ed., *Modern France: Problems of the Third and Fourth Republics* (Princeton, N.J.: Princeton University Press, 1951), pp. 181-99.

"The Zeitgeist and the Supreme Court," *The Antioch Review,* 11 (1951), pp. 424-36.

"The French Peasant and Communism," *American Political Science Review,* 46 (1952), pp. 19-34.

"The French Trade Associations and the Ratification of the Schuman Plan," *World Politics,* 11 (1954), pp. 453-81.

(Editor and coAuthor), *The Teaching of the Social Sciences in the United States* (Paris: UNESCO, 1954), 151 pp.

Organized Business in France (Princeton, N.J.: Princeton University Press, 1957), 514 pp.

"Pressures in a Divided France," *World Politics,* 11 (1958), pp. 144-51.

"Pressure Groups in France," *Annals of the American Academy of Politics and Social Science,* 319 (1958), pp. 141-48.

(Editor and coauthor) *Interest Groups on Four Continents* (Pittsburgh: Pittsburgh University Press, 1958), 316 pp.

La Politique du Patronat Français (Paris: A. Collin, 1959), 416 pp. French translation, revised by the author, of *Organized Business in France.*

"The Reign of de Gaulle II," *The Colorado Quarterly,* 7 (1959), pp. 333-49.

"Les Partis Américains et la Politique Étrangère," in Centre de Sciences Politiques de l'Institut d'Études Juridiques de Nice, *Les Affaires Étrangères* (Paris: Presses Universitaires de France, 1959), pp. 405-16.

"Administration et groupes de pression," *Économie et Humanisme,* 14, no. 123 (January-February 1960), pp. 20-30.

"Constitutional Developments in the French Fifth Republic," in Milorad M. Drachkovitch, ed., *French Fifth Republic* (Berkeley, Calif.: Department of Political Science, University of California, 1961), pp. 15-20.

"French Bureaucracy and Organized Interests," *Administrative Science Quarterly,* 5 (1961), pp. 534-55.

"On French Democracy," *Colorado Quarterly,* 9 (1961), pp. 5-27.

"Les Groupes d'Intérêt et la Bureaucratie dans les Démocraties Occidentales," *Revue Française de Science Politique,* 11 (1961), pp. 541-68.

"Die Verfassungsentwicklung im Frankreich der Fünften Republik," *Jahrbuch des öffentlichen Rechts der Gegenwart,* 10 (1962), pp. 353-96.

"Bureaucracy and Interest Groups in the Decision-Making Process of the Fifth Republic," in Gerhard A. Ritter and Gilbert Ziebura, eds., *Festschrift für Ernst Fraenkel* (Berlin: DeGruyter, 1963), pp. 273-93.

"Direct Democracy in France," *American Political Science Review* 57, no. 3 (1963), pp. 883-901.

"Funktionswandel der demoratischen Institutionen in den USA," in Richard Löwenthal, ed., *Die Demokratie im Wandel der Gesellschaft* (Berlin: Colloquium Verlag, 1963), pp. 29-55.

"Les États-Unis d'Amérique," in *Encyclopédie Française.* Vol. L'État (Paris: Larousse, 1964), pp. 257-63.

United Europe, the General and the Bomb," *Dartmouth Alumni Magazine* (May 1964), pp. 22-26.

"Influence" and "Pressure Group," in *A Dictionary of the Social Sciences* (New York: Free Press, 1964), pp. 332-33, 530-31.

(Editor and coAuthor), *Democracy in a Changing Society* (New York, Praeger, 1964), 210 pp.

"European Views of the Atlantic Alliance," in G. Lyons, ed., *European Views of America* (Hanover: Dartmouth College Public Affairs Center, 1965), pp. 16-32.

Politische Bildung, Beobachtungen und Vorschläge (Weinheim: Beltz, 1966), 133 pp.

Los Cambios Sociales y la Democracia (Spanish edition of *Democracy in a Changing Society),* (Mexico City: Ed. Roble, 1967), 312 pp.

"Interest Groups," in *International Encyclopedia of the Social Sciences* (New York: Free Press, 1968), pp. 486-92.

Politics in France (Boston: Little Brown, 1968; revised editions 1971, 1976, 1983), 368 pp.

"Private Man and Political Society," in *20th Century Reflections* Dartmouth Alumni College Lectures, 1968 (Hanover, N.H.: Dartmouth College, 1969), pp. 69-130.

"Politische Erziehung–wofür?" in Gerhard Fischer, ed., *Alpdruck Schule* (List Verlag, München: 1969), pp. 35-43.

"Unterschiedliche Regierungsformen in systemtheoretischer Analyse," in Ruprecht Kurzrock, ed., *Systemtheorie* (Berlin: Colloquium Verlag, 1972), pp. 230-50.

"Les incidences constitutionnelles de Watergate," *Universalia*, Paris (1974), pp. 496-502.

"Politics in France," in G. A. Almond and G. B. Powell, eds., *Comparative Politics Today: A World View* (Boston: Little Brown, 1974; revised editions 1980, 1983), pp. 211-260.

"Les pouvoirs présidentiels après Watergate," *Universalia*, Paris (1975), pp. 224-228.

Comparative Legal Cultures (Englewood Cliffs, N.J.: Prentice Hall, 1976), 172 pp.

Das Politische System Frankreichs (German edition of *Politics in France)* (München: Piper Verlag, 1976), 247 pp.

"Die Entwicklung der Verfassungsgerichtsbarkeit im Frankreich der Fünften Republik," *Der Staat*, 20 (1981), pp. 373-92.

"Die Grenzen der Justiz im Wohlfahrtsstaat–eine amerikanische Debatte" *Mannheimer Berichte aus Forschung und Lehre*, (forthcoming, summer 1983). To be published by the University of Mannheim.

BOOK REVIEWS

"Vorkriegsimperialismus," by Wolfgang Hallgarten. *Zeitschrift für den Sozialismus*, 29 (February 1936), pp. 939-40.

"The Reconstruction of Europe: Talleyrand and the Congress of Vienna 1814-1815," by Guglielmo Ferrero. *Social Research, 9, no. 2 (May 1942), pp. 267-69.*

"Labor in Our Times," by Adolf Sturmthal. *New Republic* (June 7, 1943), pp. 772-73.

"Napoleon III: An Interpretation," by Albert Guerard. Ibid., (September 13, 1943), pp. 368-69; and *American Historical Review*, 49, no. 2 (January 1944), pp. 282-83.

"The Idea of Nationalism," by Hans Kohn. *New Republic* (May 8, 1944), pp. 741-42.

"Germany and Europe: A spiritual dimension," by Benedetto Croce. Ibid., (September 4, 1944), pp. 285.

"The French Revolution," by J. M. Thompson. Ibid., (April 16, 1945), pp. 254-56.

"Europe Free and United," by Albert Guerard. *To-Morrow* (June 1945), pp. 76-77.

"The German Record: A political Portrait," by William Ebenstein. "Hitler and Beyond: A German Testament," by Erich Koch-Weser. "Germany: Economic and Labor Conditions under Fascism," by Juergen Kuczynski. "The Moral Conquest of Germany," by Emil Ludwig. "The Junker Menace," by Frederick Martin. "A Short History of Germany," by S. H. Steinberg. *New Republic* (August 13, 1945), pp. 194-96.

"The German People," by Veit Valentin. Ibid., (September 30, 1946), pp. 418-19.

"Histoire du movement ouvrier en France des origines à nos jours," by Jean Montreuil. "Histoire du syndicalisme français," by Robert Bothereau. *Journal of Modern History*, 19 (1947), pp. 355-56.

"Our Vichy Gamble," by William Langer. *American Journal of International Law*, 42 (1948), pp. 250-51.

"The Foreign Affairs Reader." (ed. by Hamilton Fish Armstrong). *American Journal of International Law*, 12 (1948), pp. 539-40.

"Geschichte der Weimarer Verfassung," by Willibalt Apelt. *American Political Science Review*, 42 (1948), pp. 226-27.

"Germany: Bridge or Battleground," by James P. Warburg. *Journal of Central European Affairs*, 8 (1948), pp. 226-27.

"Staat, Bürger, Mensch," by Herbert A. Strauss. Ibid., 8 (1948), pp. 211-12.

"Austria from Hapsburg to Hitler," by Charles A. Gullick, 2 vols. *Western Political Quarterly*, 1 (1948), pp. 324-26.

"Recognition in International Law," by Hersh Lauterpacht. *Rocky Mountain Law Review*, 21 (1948), pp. 119-21.

"The Reshaping of French Democracy," by Gordon Wright. "The Case for de Gaulle," by André Malraux and James Burnham. *Western Political Quarterly*, 1 (1948), pp. 468-69.

"Die Kommunistische Partei Deutschlands in der Weimarer Republik," by Ossip Flechtheim. *American Political Science, Review,* 43 (1949), pp. 374-75.

"Stalin and German Communism," by Ruth Fischer *Journal of Central European Affairs* 9 (1949), pp. 111-13.

"The Only Way: How Can Germany Be Cured?," by Karl Barth. "Germany, What Now?," by Joachim Joesten. Ibid., 9 (1949), pp. 251-52.

"La vie ouvrière en France sous le Second Empire," by Georges Duveau. *Journal of Modern History,* 21 (1949), pp. 350-52.

"Europe in Our Time, 1914 to the Present," by Robert Ergang. *Western Political Quarterly,* 2 (1949), pp. 638-39.

"A Communist Party in Action," by A. Rossi. *Air University Quarterly Review,* 4. (Summer 1949), pp. 95-98.

"Ivan the Terrible," by Hans von Eckardt. "Stalin: A Political Biography," by Isaac Deutscher. *Western Political Quarterly,* 3 (1950), pp. 472-73.

"Progress and Power," by Carl Becker, *Western Political Quarterly,* 3 (1950), pp. 130-31.

"Germany and the Future of Europe," ed. by Hans Morgenthau. Ibid., 4 (1951), pp. 663-65.

"Der SS. Staat: Das System der deutschen Konzentrationslager," by E. Kogon. "The Origins of Totalitarianism," by H. Arendt. *Journal of Central European Affairs,* 12 (1952), pp. 84-86.

"The Politburo," by G. G. Schueller, Ibid., 12 (1952), pp. 204-5.

"Prelude to War: The International Repercussions of the Spanish Civil War," by P. A. M. Van der Ersch. *Western Political Quarterly,* 5 (1952), pp. 665.

"Communism in Western Europe," by M. Einaudi et al. *Political Science Quarterly,* 67 (1952), pp. 300-302.

"Compulsory Labor Arbitration in France, 19,36-1939" by J. Colton. *Annals of the American Academy of Political Science,* 280 (1952), pp. 230-31.

"Histoire des Cheminots et de leur Syndicat," by G. Chaumel. *Journal of Modern History,* 24 (1952), pp. 85-86.

"Sociologie Électorale: Esquisse d'un Bilan; Guide des Recherches," by F. Goguel and G. Dupeux. "Géographie des Élections

Françaises de 1870 à 1951," by F. Goguel. *American Political Science Review,* 46 (1952), pp. 882-83.

"Negotiating with the Russians," by R. Dennett and J. Johnson *Journal of Central European Affairs,* 13 (1953), pp. 279-80.

"French Corporative Theory," by Matthew H. Elbow. *Journal of Economic History,* 14 (1954), pp. 87-89.

"Unity and Diversity in European Labor," by Adolf Sturmthal. Ibid., 14 (1954), pp. 296-298.

"In the Twilight of Socialism: A History of the Revolutionary Socialists of Austria," by Joseph Buttinger. *Sociological Research,* 21 (1954), pp. 234-37.

"French Politics: The First Years of the Fourth Republic," by Dorothy Pickles. *Western Political Quarterly* 7 (1954), pp. 276-77.

"Germany, Key to Peace," by James P. Warburg. "The Return of Germany," by Norbert Muhlen. *id.,* 7 (1954), pp. 510-11.

"Der Weg nach Jalta. President Roosevelt's Verantwortung," by Max Walter Clauss. *Journal of Central European Affairs,* 14 (1954), pp. 193-94.

"Socialismes Français et Allemands et le problème de la guerre, 1870-1914," by Milorad M. Drachkovitch. *id.,* 14 (1954), pp. 284-85.

"Introduction to French Local Government," by Brian Chapman. *American Political Science Review,* 48 (1954), pp. 862-64.

"Politics in Post War France," by Philip Williams. "Nouvelles Études de Sociologie Électorale," by François Goguel. *Western Political Quarterly,* 8 (1955), pp. 648-50.

Europäische Arbeiterbewegung," by Ludwig Reichhold. *Journal of Central European* Affairs, 14 (1955), pp. 403-4.

"Die Stunde Deutschlands–Möglichkeiten einer Politik der Wiedervereinigung," by Wilhelm W. Schuetz. *id.,* 15 (1955), pp. 101-2.

"Geschichte der Weimarer Republik," by Erick Eyck. *id.,* 15 (1955), pp. 297-98.

"Nationalization in France and Italy," by M. Einaudi, M. bye, and E. Rossi. *American Political Science Review,* 50 (1956), pp. 519-20.

"De Karl Marx à Léon Blum: la crise de la social-démocratie," by M. M. Drachkovitch. *Journal of Modern History,* 28 (1956), p. 197.

"German Social-Democracy 1905-1917: The Development of the Great Schism," by Carl E. Schorske. *Journal of Central European Affairs,* 41 (1956), pp. 299-300.

"France against Herself," by Herbert Luethy. *Western Political Quarterly,* 9 (1956), pp. 498-499.

"The Paris Commune in French Politics, 1871-1880: The History of the 'Amnesty of 1880,' by Jean T. Joughin. *Columbia Law Review,* 17 (1957), pp. 909-14.

"Die Deutsche Sozialdemokratie und der nationale Staat, 1870-1920," by Hermann Heidegger. "Ein Gang durch die Geschichte der Berliner Sozialdemokratie," by Walter Olschewski. *Journal of Central European Affairs,* 17 (1957), pp. 193-94.

"Marxism and French Labor," by Leon A. Dale *American Sociological Review* (1957), p. 488.

"The German Policy of Revolutionary France," by A. Biro. *American Political Science Review,* 52 (1958), p. 584.

"L'Opinion Publique," by Gaston Berger and others. *Western Political Quarterly,* 9 (1958), pp. 729-30.

"As France Goes," by David Schoenbrunn. *id.,* (1959), pp. 222-23.

"The French Nation: From Napoleon to Pétain," by David Brogan. "French Electoral Systems and Elections: 1789-1957," by Peter Campbell. "The French Political System," by Maurice Duverger. "French Socialism in the Crisis Years: 1933-1936," by John T. Marcus. "Les groupes de pression en France," by Jean Meynaud. "Sociologie électorale de la Nièvre au XXme Siècle (1902-1951), pp." by Jean Pataut. *American Political Science Review,* 53 (1959), pp. 524-29.

"Ernst Reuter: ein Leben für die Freiheit," by Willy Brandt and Richard Loewenthal. *Journal of Central European Affairs,* 19 (1959), pp. 330.

"Les Paysans et la Politique," by J. Fauvet and H. Mendras. *Revue Française de Science Politique,* 9 (1959), pp. 1057-60.

"Die Wendung zum Führerstaat," by Jürgen Fijalkowski. *Journal of Central European Affairs,* 20 (1960), pp. 325-27.

"France, Steadfast and Changing: The Fourth to the Fifth Republic," by Raymond Aron. "De Gaulle's Republic," by Phillip M. Williams and Martin Harrison. *Yale Review,* 50 (1961), pp. 298-302.

"Organizing Peace in the Nuclear Age," by the Commission to Study the Organization of Peace. *Western Political Quarterly,* 14 (1961), pp. 261-63.

"Der sowjetische Neutralitätsbegriff in Theorie und Praxis," by Heinz Fiedler. *Journal of Central European Affairs,* 21 (1961), pp. 237-38.

"The Defense of Berlin," by Jean Smith. *Dartmouth Alumni Magazine* (July 1964), p. 4.

"Forces Religieuses et Attitudes Politiques dans la France Contemporaine," ed. by Réné Remond. *American Political Science Review,* 60 (June 1966), pp. 435-36.

"Teachers and Politics in France: A Pressure Group Study," by James M. Clark. *Political Science Quarterly,* 83, no. 4 (December 1968), pp. 670-71.

"The Agony of the American Left," by Christopher Lash. "An Essay on Liberation," by Herbert Marcuse. "Obsolete Communism," by Daniel and Gabriel Cohn-Bendit. "American Power and the New Mandarins," by Noam Chomsky. "Le Mouvement de Mai ou Le Communisme Utopique," by Alain Touraine. *Polity,* 2, no. 3 (1970), pp. 380-91.

"Politik als Interessenkonflikt," by Wolfgang Hirsch-Weber. *American Political Science Review,* 64, no. 3 (1970), pp. 625-26.

"L'Ouvrier Français en 1970," by G. Adam, F. Bon, J. Capedevielle, and R. Mourioux. *Id.* 67, no. 1 (March 1973), pp. 237-38.

"Société et Politique: La Vie des Groupes." Vol. 1: "fondements de la Société Libérale." Vol. 2 "Dynamique de la Société Libérale." by Léon Dion. "Pluralismus: Konzeptionen und Kontroversen," ed. by Franz Muscheler and Winfried Steffani. "Pluralismus zwischen Liberalismus und Sozialismus," by Rainer Eisfeld. Ibid., 58, no. 4 (December 1974), pp. 1733-35.

"Vichy France: Old Guard and New Order, 1940-1944," by Robert Paxton. Ibid., 69, no. 1 (March 1975), pp. 338-39.

"Le P.C.," by Jean Elleinstein. "Lettre Ouverte aux Français sur la République du Programme Commun," by Jean Elleinstein.

"Sur la Dictature du Prolétariat," by Étienne Balibar. "L'Alternative," by Roger Garaudy. "Les Socialistes, les communistes et les autres," by Jean-Pierre Chevènement. "Le Discours Communiste," by Dominique Labbé. "Stratégie de la grève," by Bertrand Badie. "The French Communist Party versus the Students," by Richard Johnson. "Teoria e Movimento nel Partito Communista Francese, 1959-1963: Antologia Critica," by Marcello Montanari. *Problems of Communism,* 27 (May-June 1978), pp. 58-64.

"Elites in French Society: The Politics of Survival," by Ezra Suleiman, *Political Science Quarterly,* 94, no. 3 (Fall 1979), pp. 560-62.

"Socialism in Provence, 1871-1914: A Study in the Origins of the French Left," by Tony Judd. "British Socialists: The Journey from Fantasy to Politics," by Stanley Pierson. *American Political Science Review* 75, no. 1 (March 1981), pp. 240-42.

"Organizing Interests in Western Europe," ed. by Suzanne Berger. *Political Science Quarterly,* 97, no. 2 (Summer 1982), pp. 363-64.

Index of Subjects

Index of Names